T0003344

"Engaging. . . . Brands is a skilled biographer. . . . [He] deftly fills in the contours of Franklin's extraordinary life."
—*The Star-Ledger* (Newark, New Jersey)

"A fluid, clear, and nicely paced book. . . . Enjoyable to read."
—*The Weekly Standard*

"Stunning. . . . Brands, with admirable insight and arresting narrative, constructs a portrait of a complex and influential man . . . in a highly charged world. . . . [He] does an excellent job of capturing Franklin's exuberant versatility as a writer who adopted countless personae . . . that not only predestined his prominence as a man of letters but also as an agile man of politics."
—*Publishers Weekly* (starred review)

"Stirring and eloquent."
—*The News & Observer* (Raleigh, North Carolina)

"Worthwhile reading on an American worth remembering."
—*BookPage*

"A humanizing biography that enhances . . . the founding fathers' greatness."
—*Sun-Sentinel* (Fort Lauderdale)

"Eminently readable. . . . [Brands] create[s] an absorbing portrait of the 18th-century world that was the backdrop—and the stage—for America's multidimensional journalist, inventor, diplomat, propagandist, moralist, humorist, and revolutionary."
—*Library Journal* (starred review)

H. W. BRANDS

The First American

H. W. Brands is Distinguished Professor and Melbern G. Glasscock Chair of History at Texas A&M University. He is the author of many books, among them *T.R.: The Last Romantic*, the critically acclaimed biography of Theodore Roosevelt; *The Reckless Decade: America in the 1890s*; and *The Strange Death of American Liberalism*. He lives in Austin, Texas.

The First American

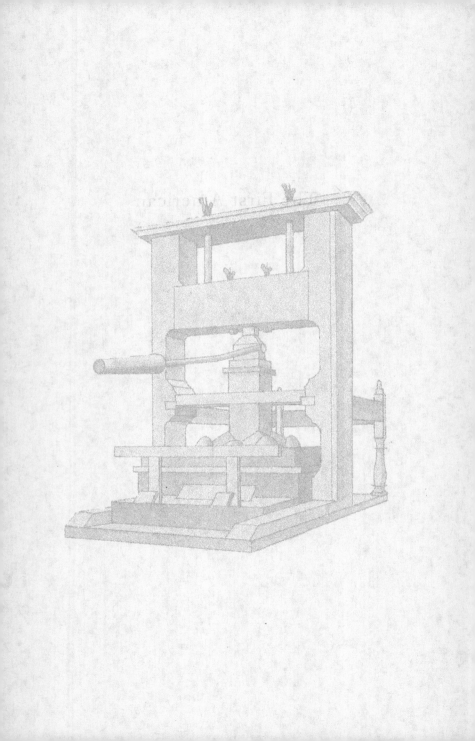

H. W. BRANDS

The First American

The Life and Times of

~ BENJAMIN FRANKLIN ~

Anchor Books

A Division of Random House, Inc.

New York

FIRST ANCHOR BOOKS EDITION, MARCH 2002

Copyright © 2000 by H. W. Brands

All rights reserved under International and Pan-American Copyright
Conventions. Published in the United States by Anchor Books, a division
of Random House, Inc., New York, and simultaneously in Canada by
Random House of Canada Limited, Toronto. Originally published in
hardcover in the United States by Doubleday, a division of Random House, Inc.,
New York, in 2000.

The Library of Congress has cataloged the Doubleday edition as follows:
Brands, H. W.
The first American: the life and times of Benjamin Franklin /
H. W. Brands.—1st ed.
p.   cm.
Includes bibliographical references (p. 717) and index.
ISBN 0-385-49328-2
1. Franklin, Benjamin, 1706–1790. 2. Statesman—United States—Biography.
3. United States—Politics and government—To 1775. 4. United States—Politics
and government—1775–1783. 5. Printers—United States—Biography.
6. Scientists—United States—Biography. I. Title.
E302.6.F8 B83   2000
973.3'092—dc21
[B]
00-027930
CIP

Anchor ISBN: 0-385-49540-4

Book design by Terry Karydes
Illustration by David Cain

www.anchorbooks.com

Printed in the United States of America
28 30 29

Contents

The First American

Prologue

January 29, 1774

~ A lesser man would have been humiliated.

~ Humiliation was the purpose of the proceeding.

It was the outcome eagerly anticipated by the lords of
the Privy Council who constituted the official audience, by
the members of the House of Commons and other
fashionable Londoners who packed the room and hung on
the rails of the balcony, by the London press that lived on
scandal and milled outside to see how this scandal would
unfold, by the throngs that bought the papers, savored the
scandals, rioted in favor of their heroes and against their
villains, and made politics in the British imperial capital often
unpredictable, frequently disreputable, always entertaining.

The proceeding today would probably be disreputable. It
would certainly be entertaining.

The venue was fitting: the Cockpit. In the reign of Henry VIII, that most sporting of monarchs in a land that loved its bloody games, the building on this site had housed an actual cockpit, where Henry and his friends brought their prize birds and wagered which would tear the others to shreds. The present building had replaced the real cockpit, but this room retained the old name and atmosphere. The victim today was expected to depart with his reputation in tatters, his fortune possibly forfeit, his life conceivably at peril.

Nor was that the extent of the stakes. Two days earlier the December packet ship from Boston had arrived with an alarming report from the royal governor of Massachusetts, Thomas Hutchinson. The governor described an organized assault on three British vessels carrying tea of the East India Company. The assailants, townsmen loosely disguised as Indians, had boarded the ships, hauled hundreds of tea casks to deck, smashed them open, and dumped their contents into the harbor—forty-five tons of tea, enough to litter the beaches for miles and depress the company's profits for years. This rampage was the latest in a series of violent outbursts against the authority of Crown and Parliament; the audience in the Cockpit, and in London beyond, demanded to know what Crown and Parliament intended to do about it.

Alexander Wedderburn was going to tell them. The solicitor general possessed great rhetorical gifts and greater ambition. The former had made him the most feared advocate in the realm; the latter lifted him to his present post when he abandoned his allies in the opposition and embraced the ministry of Lord North. Wedderburn was known to consider the Boston tea riot treason, and if the law courts upheld his interpretation, those behind the riot would be liable to the most severe sanctions, potentially including death. Wedderburn was expected to argue that the man in the Cockpit today was the prime mover behind the outburst in Boston. The crowd quivered with anticipation.

They all knew the man in the pit; indeed, the whole world knew Benjamin Franklin. His work as political agent for several of the American colonies had earned him recognition around London, but his fame far transcended that. He was, quite simply, one of the most illustrious scientists and thinkers on earth. His experiments with electricity, culminating in his capture of lightning from the heavens, had won him universal praise as the modern Prometheus. His mapping of the Gulf Stream saved the time and lives of countless sailors. His ingenious fireplace conserved fuel and warmed homes on both sides of the Atlantic. His contributions to economics, meteorology, music, and psychology expanded the reach of human knowledge and the grip of human power. For his accomplishments the British Royal Society had awarded him its highest prize; foreign societies had done the same. Universities queued to grant him degrees. The ablest minds of the age consulted him on matters large and small. Kings and emperors summoned him to court, where they admired his brilliance and basked in its reflected glory.

Genius is prone to producing envy. Yet it was part of Franklin's genius that he had produced far less than his share, due to an unusual ability to disarm those disposed to envy. In youth he discovered that he was quicker of mind and more facile of pen than almost everyone he met; he also discovered that a boy of humble birth, no matter how gifted, would block his own way by letting on that he knew how smart he was. He learned to deflect credit for some of his most important innovations. He avoided arguments wherever possible; when important public issues hinged on others' being convinced of their errors, he often argued anonymously, adopting assumed names, or Socratically, employing the gentle questioning of the Greek master. He became almost as famous for his sense of humor as for his science; laughing, his opponents listened and were persuaded.

Franklin's self-effacing style succeeded remarkably; at sixty-eight he had almost no personal enemies and comparatively few political enemies for a man of public affairs. But those few included powerful figures. George Grenville, the prime minister responsible for the Stamp Act, the tax bill that triggered all the American troubles, never forgave him for single-handedly demolishing the rationale for the act in a memorable session before the House of Commons. Grenville and his allies lay in wait to exact their revenge on Franklin. Yet he never made a false step.

Until now. A mysterious person had delivered into his hands confidential letters from Governor Hutchinson and other royal officials in Massachusetts addressed to an undersecretary of state in London. These letters cast grave doubt on the bona fides of Hutchinson, for years the bête noire of the Massachusetts assembly. As Massachusetts's agent, Franklin had forwarded the letters to friends in Boston. Hutchinson's enemies there got hold of the letters and published them.

The publication provoked an instant uproar. In America the letters were interpreted as part of a British plot to enslave the colonies; the letters fueled the anger that inspired the violence that produced the Boston tea riot. In England the letters provoked charges and countercharges as to who could have been so dishonorable as to steal and publish private correspondence. A duel at swords left one party wounded and both parties aching for further satisfaction; only at this point—to prevent more bloodshed—did Franklin reveal his role in transmitting the letters.

His foes seized the chance to destroy him. Since that session in Commons eight years before, he had become the symbol and spokesman in London of American resistance to the sovereignty of Parliament; on his head would be visited all the wrath and resentment that had been building in that proud institution from the time of the Stamp Act to the tea riot. Alexander Wedderburn sharpened his tongue and moved in for the kill.

None present at the Cockpit on January 29, 1774, could afterward recall the like of the hearing that day. The solicitor general outdid himself. For an hour he hurled invective at Franklin, branding him a liar, a thief, the instigator of the insurrection in Massachusetts, an outcast from the company of all honest men, an ingrate whose attack on Hutchinson betrayed nothing less than a desire to seize the governor's office for himself. So slanderous was Wedderburn's diatribe that no London paper would print it. But the audience reveled in it, hooting and applauding each sally, each bilious bon mot. Not even the lords of the Privy Council attempted to disguise their delight at Wedderburn's astonishing attack. Almost to a man and a woman, the spectators that day concluded that Franklin's reputation would never recover. Ignominy, if not prison or worse, was his future now.

∾ Franklin stood silent throughout his ordeal. Even at his advanced age he was a large man, taller than most people would have guessed. His shoulders had lost some of their youthful breadth, for it had been decades since he hoisted the heavy sets of lead type that were the printer's daily burden, and longer since he had swum for exercise; but still they conveyed an impression of strength. His stoutness had increased with the years; cloaked today in a brown, knee-length coat of Manchester velvet, it connoted gravity. He eschewed the wigs that decorated nearly every head present, male and female; his thin gray hair fell over and behind his ears to his shoulders. His face had never been expressive; today it was a mask. Not the slightest frown or grimace greeted the diatribes rained down upon him. When instructed to submit to questions, he silently refused—a refusal that seemed to seal his humiliation.

But he was not humiliated; he was outraged. The mask concealed not mortification but anger. Who did these people—this bought solicitor, these smug lords, the corrupt ministers that made the proceeding possible—who did they think they were? Who did they think *he* was?

It was the question of the hour; generalized, it was the question on which hung the fate of the British empire. Who were these Americans? To the British they were Britons, albeit of a turbulent sort. The Americans might live across the ocean, but the colonies they inhabited had been planted by Britain and were defended by Britain; therefore to the government of Britain—preeminently, to the British Parliament—the Americans must submit, like any other Britons. To the Americans, the question was more complicated. Nearly all Americans considered themselves Britons, but Britons of a different kind than lived in London or the Midlands or Scotland. Possessing their own assemblies—their own parliaments—the Americans believed they answered to the British Crown but not to the British Parliament. At its core the struggle between the American colonies and the British government was a contest between these competing definitions of American identity. Put simply, were the Americans truly Britons, or were they something else?

Franklin came to the questioning with decades of experience. For his whole life he had been asking himself who—or what—he was. As a boy he had been a Bostonian. Yet the theocratic orthodoxy of Boston's Puritans eventually became more than he could stand, and, linked to the legal and familial orthodoxy of an apprenticeship to an overbearing elder brother, it drove him away. He broke his apprenticeship, defied law and family, and fled Boston.

He landed in Philadelphia, a comparative haven for freethinkers like himself. During the next forty years he earned an honorable name and substantial wealth as the publisher of the *Pennsylvania Gazette*, the author of *Poor Richard's Almanack*, and the originator of numerous public improvements in his adopted home. By all evidence he was the model Philadelphian.

Yet gradually Philadelphia, like Boston before it, began to chafe. The political framework that had suited Pennsylvania at its founding—the charter granted by Charles II to William Penn and his heirs—hindered the growth of the province at maturity. For his first two decades in Philadelphia, Franklin scarcely noticed politics; but the wars that accompanied colonial life during the eighteenth century enforced attention. And they drove home the anachronistic nature of rule by a single family. Initially he battled the Penns from Philadelphia; when that failed, he carried the fight to England as the agent of the Pennsylvania assembly.

Yet there was more than politics in his departure. Like Boston before it, Philadelphia had become too small for him. The budding genius of his Boston youth had blossomed in the tolerant atmosphere of Philadelphia; but Philadelphia, and finally even all of America, afforded insufficient scope for the talents he discovered in himself and the world discovered in him. Kindred scientific spirits were few in America; kindred intellectual gifts still fewer.

Britain at first seemed everything Franklin desired. Electricians and others who had admired him from afar found him even more admirable in person. His admirers became his friends; his friends became his sponsors, introducing him to influential figures throughout the country. His journeys across England and Scotland turned into triumphal processions. The best houses opened their doors to him; cities and towns made him an honorary citizen. The Royal Society embraced him and provided a venue through which he communicated with the most learned and ingenious men of Britain and Europe—the Scotsman Hume, the Irishman Burke, the German Kant, the Italian Beccaria, the Frenchman Condorcet. London was soon his spiritual home. It would have been his actual and permanent home if he had succeeded in persuading his wife, Deborah, to leave Philadelphia. As it was, despite her refusal, he took up semipermanent residence in London, in Craven Street.

Franklin proudly called himself a Briton. In doing so he did not deny his American birth, for he conceived Americans to be as fully Britons as the English, Scots, and Welsh. He delineated for all who would listen the glorious future of Britain in North America, a future joining American energy to the English tradition of self-government. As a measure of his faith in the future of America within the British empire, he employed his influence to help his son William win appointment as royal governor of New Jersey.

But then things began to go wrong. A foolish ministry ignored that tradition of self-government and started treating the Americans as subjects—not subjects simply of King George but of Parliament. The Stamp Act attempted to put this novel interpretation into effect and touched off the first round of rioting in America. Franklin sought to calm the turmoil by persuading Parliament of its error; this was the purpose of his appearance before Commons in 1766. Yet though the Grenvillites were compelled to retreat at that time, the lesson never took hold, and distrust between the colonies and the mother country grew.

All the same, for several years civil discussions of the differences between the American and British views of the English constitution remained possible. Franklin, the most civil of men, did his best to promote these discussions, at peril to his political reputation in America, where the radicals spoke of him as residing in the pocket of the British ministry.

And what had his efforts accomplished? The answer came in the Cockpit: nothing but abuse and condemnation from an arrogant people maliciously led. Wedderburn and the ministry ignored the crucial issues between Britain and America, the high constitutional questions that would hold the empire together or tear it apart, in order to indulge personal vanity and satisfy corrupt ambition. At this moment of truth, all the British government could do was vilify the character of one who had been Britain's most loyal subject, its best friend among the Americans. Franklin had thought Britain could be his home; now he realized his only home was America. In the Cockpit it was Wedderburn insulting Franklin, but it was also Britain mocking America.

Franklin left the Cockpit seething—yet enlightened. Wedderburn had answered the question that Franklin had been asking all his life, and that his fellow Americans had been asking of late. Who were they? They must be Americans, for they could not be Britons.

Revolutions are not made in a morning, nor empires lost in a day. But Britain did itself more damage in those two hours than anyone present imagined. By alienating Franklin, the British government showed itself doubly inept: for making an enemy of a friend, and for doing so of the ablest and most respected American alive. At a moment when independence was hardly dreamed of in America, Franklin understood that to independence America must come.

He sailed for home—his real home—still burning with anger and disgust, and immediately took a place at the head of the opposition to British rule. Once the most loyal of Britons, now he became the most radical of Americans, demanding independence and driving the rebellion to a genuine revolution. He helped draft the Declaration of Independence; when that manifesto of American identity won the approval of the Continental Congress, he helped organize the government of the new republic. He guided American diplomatic efforts and sent secret American agents to Europe. Traveling to Paris himself, he negotiated the treaty with Britain's nemesis, France, that gave the revolution its first real hope of success. From Paris he directed the American war effort abroad, securing the gifts and loans that kept American soldiers in the field and managing the system of alliances that finally delivered America's freedom. In the eyes of much of Europe, Franklin *was* America, and the enormous respect accorded Franklin extrapolated to the American cause.

Of those patriots who made independence possible, none mattered more than Franklin, and only Washington mattered as much. Washington won the battle of Yorktown, but Franklin won the European support that allowed Washington his victory.

At war's end, Franklin artfully headed negotiation of the peace settlement that guaranteed America's future by doubling the American domain and tying the interests of the European powers to America's continued success. Returning in triumph to Philadelphia, he was elected president of Pennsylvania, and in that capacity hosted the Constitutional Convention of 1787. Throughout the convention he offered sage advice, keeping the delegates at their tasks when attention wandered, proposing the essential compromises that made the final consensus possible. As the sun set on his own life, he had the unparalleled pleasure of watching it rise on the life of the new American nation.

Franklin's story is the story of a man—an exceedingly gifted man and a most engaging one. It is also the story of the birth of America—an America this man discovered in himself, then helped create in the world at large.

1

Boston Beginnings

1706–23

〜 Cotton Mather was the pride of New England Puritanism.
As a boy he had shown a curious, inquiring mind; he studied
science toward a career in medicine. But the pull of religion
was too strong, as might have been expected of the
grandson of Puritan pillars John Cotton and Richard
Mather and the son of Increase Mather, a column of
Congregationalism of comparable diameter. Shortly after
ordination in 1685, Cotton Mather joined his father at
Boston's Second Church and commenced an astonishingly
prolific career as a publicist of Puritanism. Some 450 books
and pamphlets poured from his pen during his lifetime;
although the majority dealt with religious topics, many
revealed a continuing affinity for such secular subjects as
natural history and music.

But nothing was truly secular for Cotton Mather. An unchurched neighbor fell from a rooftop and for weeks lay in a coma; Mather remembered having told the man that if he did not get religion soon, God would lay him low. "Coming to himself," Mather recorded in his diary, "one of the first things he thought on was what I had said unto him, under the sense whereof he quickly went and joined himself unto the South church"—which, perhaps significantly, was *not* Mather's church. On another occasion an even more mundane matter prompted musings on man's place in God's order. "I was once emptying the cistern of nature, and making water at the wall. At the same time, there came a dog, who did so too, before me. Thought I: 'What mean and vile things are the children of men, in this mortal state! How much do our natural necessities abase us, and place us in some regard, on the same level with the very dogs!' " Additional reflection inspired a determination to transcend the gutter in which men's bodies were consigned to live. "My thought proceeded: 'Yet I will be a more noble creature, and at the very time when my natural necessities debase me into the condition of the beast, my spirit shall (I say, at that very time!) rise and soar and fly up towards the employment of the Angel.' " Never again, Mather vowed, would he answer the call of nature without consciously evoking "some holy, noble divine thought." Looking back on the matter later, he was happy to report: "And I have done according to this resolution!"

With his Puritan contemporaries, Mather perceived the cosmos as a battleground between good and evil. God led the army of good, whose ranks included those humans his grace had inspired with biblically enlightened reason; Satan spearheaded the legions of evil, which counted unbridled passion and unrelieved ignorance among their principal weapons. To Mather and his fellow Puritans, God was a pervasive and all-but-tangible presence; Satan still more so. "That there is a Devil, is a thing doubted by none but such as are under the influence of the Devil," Mather declared. Not only was Satan real, but he was actively involved in people's lives. "The Devil, in the prosecution and execution of his wrath upon them, often gets a liberty to make a descent upon the children of men." And nowhere was this more true than in New England, which the Evil One had had all to himself and his red children—"the Tawnies"— until lately, when the arrival of the Christian Gospel had roused him to terrible anger. "I believe there never was a poor plantation more pursued by the wrath of the Devil than our poor New England."

Mather rarely indulged in idle scribbling (although weary readers of those 450 titles might have been forgiven for occasionally thinking so); at the time that he inscribed these words, Massachusetts was writhing under what seemed Satan's latest assault. The Salem witch trials of 1692 convulsed the colony as nothing before or after. No man or woman of consequence doubted that witches existed; Satan, according to the consensus, frequently acted through individuals who entered into demonic pacts with him. The only question was whether the nineteen people executed were actually the demonic agents they were alleged to be by their accusers, principally teenage girls given to an unsettling emotionalism.

Cotton Mather's attitude toward the accusations and the accused was typical—for him, and for his time and place. "The Devil, exhibiting himself ordinarily as a small black man, has decoyed a fearful knot of proud, froward, ignorant, envious and malicious creatures, to list themselves in his horrid service, by entering their names in a book by him tendered unto them. These witches, whereof above a score have now confessed and shown their deeds, and some are now tormented by the devils, for confessing, have met in hellish rendezvouzes, wherein the confessors do say, they have had their diabolical sacraments, imitating the Baptism and Supper of our Lord." The witches laid hold of innocent men and women and carried them out of their houses, over trees and hills for miles through the air. "They seize poor people about the country with various and bloody torments; and of those evidently preternatural torments there are some have died. . . . The people thus afflicted are miserably scratched and bitten so that the marks are most visible to all the world, but the causes utterly invisible; and the same invisible furies do most visibly stick pins into the bodies of the afflicted and scald them and hideously distort and disjoint all their members, besides a thousand other sorts of plagues beyond these of any natural diseases which they give unto them."

With such awesome evil abroad in the land, Mather could only endorse the action of the Salem court that condemned the witches to death. Indeed, at one hanging he all but tied the noose himself. The condemned man, pleading innocence, recited the Lord's Prayer in a powerful and moving voice. A wave of sympathy surged through the gathered throng, which reasoned that the devil would never suffer one of his servants to turn coat at the very gate of hell. But Mather stood against the tide, reminding the crowd that the Evil One was never so dangerous as when he took on the trappings of righteousness. The merciful mood passed, and the rope snapped taut.

Yet even Mather began to worry about the nature of some of the evidence accepted by the court. This "spectral evidence" consisted of statements by the accusers that they had seen the fiendish "specters" of the accused performing satanic acts. Mather did not doubt the veracity of many such statements; certainly the devil frequently incited his agents to such acts. But might his catalog of destruction not also include planting false evidence in unwary and weakened minds, thereby engineering the conviction of innocent people—good and upstanding people, people like Mather himself, even? Mather believed that his name ranked high on Satan's roster of enemies; he constantly ascribed diabolical intervention to the mishaps of his life. The manuscript of a particularly potent sermon disappeared on the eve of delivery; Mather concluded that the devil had stolen it. It turned up afterward; Mather interpreted the return as satanic taunting.

Mather did not deem it beyond the Evil One, in his current ferocious descent upon Massachusetts, to try to bring down a formidable foe like himself by conjuring spectral evidence pointing his way. He suggested that Satan and his fellow fallen angels had "obtained the power to take on them the likeness of harmless people"; he reiterated, "Many innocent, yea, and some virtuous persons are by the Devils in this matter imposed upon."

It was this fear in Mather, shared among other ministers and magistrates of the district, that eventually brought the witch-hunt to a halt. To accept spectral evidence was to hand enormous power to people who might be the devil's tools—which was to say, to the devil himself. After worried reconsideration, the court threw out uncorroborated spectral evidence, and after the specters were barred from the court, other evidence evaporated. The hysteria waned; in time some of those at the center of the proceedings regretted their actions. Five years after the fact, Judge Samuel Sewall stood up before his fellows in the congregation at Boston's South Church and acknowledged the "blame and shame" of his role in the witch trials. He requested the congregation's forgiveness and their prayers on his behalf for God's mercy. Cotton Mather did not go so far as a public recanting, but he later conceded, speaking of the man whose death he had guaranteed by his gallows intervention, that he wished he had never encountered "the first letters of his name."

⌐ Josiah Franklin almost certainly heard Samuel Sewall's confession on that January day in 1697. Josiah was a member of the South Church (also called the Third Church, being the third congregation established in Boston) and a friend of Sewall. Neither the friendship nor the membership was of especially long standing, for Josiah was a comparative newcomer to New England. In old England the Franklin family had lived in Ecton in Northamptonshire for at least three hundred years (where they may have known the forebears of George Washington, whose ancestry also ran to that county). The Franklin family held a farm of thirty acres; in addition the eldest son of each generation inherited and operated the family blacksmith shop. Josiah, being the fourth surviving son of his father Thomas Franklin, inherited neither farm nor smithy, and when the older man retired and went to live with Josiah's elder brother (Thomas's second adult son) John in Banbury, Oxfordshire, Josiah accompanied him. John had solved the younger-son problem by taking up dyeing; it was in this occupation that Thomas apprenticed Josiah to him.

Josiah learned the trade well and might have remained a dyer and an Englishman of the Midlands for the rest of his life had not Charles II turned the Church of England in a popish direction Josiah's dissenting conscience could not abide. Josiah was not a confrontational type, and having acquired a wife—Anne—and three children, he felt the responsibilities of family. But ultimately he determined that England was unsafe for dissent, and he followed the thousands of nonconformists who had decamped to America before him.

He arrived in Boston in 1683. As expected, he found the theology of his new home congenial, and after some asking around and sampling of sermons, he applied to join the South Church. Attaining full membership would take several years, but with eternity at issue he was in no hurry.

The economics of the move were more jarring. Boston was a small town and already had as many dyers as it could support. Consequently Josiah had to find a new occupation. More soundings directed him to the chandler trade: that of making candles and soap. The business was always hard, often hot (although in winter this aspect was not unwelcome), frequently smelly (the primary raw material of both candles and soap was tallow rendered from animal carcasses). But it afforded a regular income to those unafraid to work, and, being labor-intensive, it furnished early employment for as many children as came along. It also brought Josiah into contact with a broad spectrum of the inhabitants of his new home. All but the most slovenly needed soap; only the poorest made do without candles. In time Josiah won a contract to furnish candles for the night watch of the town, a concession that provided both a nice profit and additional access to community leaders.

By all evidence Josiah was a man of solid character, robust intelligence, and natural good judgment. The demands of his business kept him from taking public office, but his neighbors often sought his counsel on matters civic and personal. "I remember well," Benjamin Franklin recollected later, "his being frequently visited by leading people, who consulted him for his opinion in affairs of the town or of the church he belonged to and showed a good deal of respect for his judgment and advice. He was also much consulted by private persons about their affairs when any difficulty occurred, and frequently chosen an arbitrator between contending parties."

Josiah had additional gifts. Though not tall, he was well built and strong. His hard work agreed with him; until his death at eighty-seven he lost scarcely a day to illness. He wrote in a confident hand and, according to his son, "could draw prettily." Lacking formal training in music, he cultivated his native musicality himself. "When he played psalm tunes on his violin and sung withal as he sometimes did in an evening after the business of the day was over, it was extremely agreeable to hear."

It may have been that voice that first attracted Abiah Folger, sitting a few rows from Josiah and Anne in the South Church. Abiah was the daughter of Peter Folger, who had emigrated to Massachusetts in 1635 in the first wave of Puritan refugees from Charles I and Bishop Laud, and on the same ship as the son of Governor John Winthrop. Peter Folger, eighteen years of age on arrival, grew up with the new land, albeit restively. From Boston he went straight upriver to Dedham; at twenty-five he joined an expedition to establish a new settlement on Martha's Vineyard. He subsequently moved to Nantucket, in part because the Puritan theocracy of Boston sat about as uncomfortably on his shoulders as had the Anglican authoritarianism of Charles and Laud. But he got along barely better with the representatives of Governor Edmund Andros of New York, the colony that claimed jurisdiction over Nantucket. In his position as clerk of the court adjudicating a dispute among settlers of the island, Folger refused to release records that presumably would have supported the position favored by the governor. For his refusal he was arrested and imprisoned—in "a place where never any Englishman was put," he complained in a petition to Andros, "and where the neighbors' hogs had layed but the night before, and in a bitter cold frost and deep snow." While Folger managed to defeat this prosecution, the experience only confirmed his disdain for authority. He became a Baptist; he took the side of local Indians against English encroachment; when the Indians forcibly resisted, he castigated colonial officials in a searing diatribe that he set to verse and sold in pamphlet in the heart of the enemy camp: Boston.

While not in custody, Folger was equally busy at home. He and his wife, Mary, had nine children, of whom Abiah was the last. Despite her father's distaste for entrenched power, she moved to Boston as a young adult. There she met Josiah and Anne Franklin, who welcomed her into communion with their church. When Anne died in 1689 bearing Josiah's seventh child, the father—after the practical, if unromantic, fashion of the age—wasted little time mourning her; within six months he was married to Abiah. He was thirty-two; she was ten years younger.

~ Josiah and Abiah had ten children together. Nine of these ten survived childhood; one—Ebenezer—accidentally slipped under the surface of a soapy washtub at sixteen months and was missed too late to be revived.

Benjamin, who was named for his father's next-older and favorite brother, was the eighth child of his mother and the fifteenth of his father. He was born on January 6, 1705, by the calendar then in use; this would translate to January 17, 1706, when the calendar was reformed halfway through his life. His birthplace was the small house his parents were leasing on Milk Street just across from the South Church. The convenience of the location, coupled with the fact that the birth occurred early on a Sunday, when the congregation would be in church anyway, prompted Josiah to swaddle the newborn in thick blankets against the January wind and carry him across the street for baptism within hours of the birth.

The father returned the baby to the Milk Street house immediately after the christening; there Ben lived for the next six years, until Josiah purchased a larger dwelling at the corner of Union and Hanover streets. Even the larger house overflowed with all those children. The number actually in residence varied as the older ones came and went; Ben later recollected sitting down at the dinner table with an even dozen of his siblings. Other relatives, including Uncle Benjamin, spent stretches of various length under Josiah's roof.

As one of the youngest, Ben necessarily learned to get along with others; outnumbered and outweighed by his elder siblings, he relied on wits where force failed. Often insight came after the fact. "When I was a child of seven years old," he recounted several decades later, "my friends on a holiday filled my little pocket with half-pence. I went directly to a shop where they sold toys for children, and being charmed with the sound of a whistle that I met by the way, in the hands of another boy, I voluntarily offered and gave all my money for it. When I came home, whistling all over the house, much pleased with my whistle, but disturbing all the family, my brothers, sisters and cousins, understanding the bargain I had made, told me I had given four times as much for it as it was worth, put me in mind of what good things I might have bought with the rest of the money, and laughed at me so much for my folly that I cried with vexation; and the reflection gave me more chagrin than the whistle gave me pleasure." With the wisdom of age, Franklin added, "As I came into the world, and observed the actions of men, I thought I met many who gave too much for the whistle."

Ben's facility with the written word manifested itself early. "I do not remember when I could not read," he said afterward—which in another person might have meant a weak memory but in his case indicated real precociousness. This inclined his father to train him for the ministry, as did the circumstance that Ben was the tenth—the "tithe"—of Josiah's sons. At eight years Ben was enrolled in the town's grammar school (which would become the Boston Latin School). He quickly went to the head of his class and was promoted midterm to the next class. But his academic career was cut short when Josiah, reflecting on the expenses of feeding, clothing, housing, and educating his large brood, and reckoning the meager income a minister might command, decided that God would have to be satisfied with the sons of the well-to-do. Josiah briefly enrolled Ben in a school run by one George Brownell, specializing in arithmetic and writing; Ben's way with words continued to distinguish him, but numbers proved mystifyingly perverse, and the experiment was canceled. At ten, Ben entered the chandler trade, cutting wicks for candles, filling molds, waiting on customers, and running errands about the town.

⌒ It was an entrancing town for a boy to run about. Boston may have begun life as a religious refuge for nonconformists, but by the beginning of the eighteenth century it was looking like any number of secular seaports that dotted both shores of the North Atlantic. It was by far the busiest port in English America. More than a thousand ships were registered with Boston's harbormaster—these in addition to the many more that were registered elsewhere but made Boston a regular stop on the trade routes between the New World and the Old. This merchant armada brought cargoes of silk and spices from the Orient, slaves from West Africa, rum and molasses from the West Indies, manufactured goods from Britain, and foodstuffs and other raw and partially processed materials from elsewhere in North America. Only when the coldest weather encased the harbor in ice did the traffic cease. Scores of wharves lined the waterfront at the eastern edge of the town; the most magnificent of these was the fittingly labeled Long Wharf, which extended from the foot of King Street nearly a quarter mile into the harbor. This remarkable structure contained both a wooden roadway thirty feet wide and a string of warehouses perched on pilings above the waves.

Boston did not merely service ships; it also built them. A dozen shipyards employed hundreds of skilled artisans and unskilled laborers—brawny men with arms as thick as hawsers from sawing oak logs into keels and ribbing for the hulls that would have to withstand the tempests of all the world's oceans, dextrous men who wove those hawsers and sewed the sails that turned those tempests to propulsion and profit, clever men who adapted standard ship designs to suit the diverse needs of this India trader, that coaster, those lobstermen. Every week or so a new hull would groan down the ways and, amid a stupendous splash and that irrepressible frisson of uncertainty as to whether she would go down to the sea or down to the sea floor, add another bottom to Boston's navy.

The ocean's call tantalized every Boston boy of Ben Franklin's generation. The salt smell permeated the entire town, not least the house on Union Street, which was but a block back from the water. From his doorstep he could see the masts of the Indiamen as they lay beside the Long Wharf; in the mornings before rising he could hear the metal moanings of the anchor chains as the ships in the harbor made ready to run out on the ebb tide. He knew they would visit the most exotic places on earth before returning to Boston two or three or ten years hence; he could imagine the strange and wonderful people who inhabited those exotic locales.

The call of the sea had been too much for Ben's eldest brother, Josiah. Two years before Ben was born, the younger Josiah had turned his back on the terrestrial world of his father—the world of the chandlery, of the house on Milk Street, of the South Church, of the probing gaze of the Puritan elders—and shipped out on a merchantman bound for the Indies. He never returned. For years his father assumed he would eventually find his way back to Boston, if only for a stopover. But in 1715, when Ben was nine years old, the grim word arrived that Josiah's vessel had been lost at sea.

Thus it was with worry and fear that the elder Josiah observed his youngest son being drawn to the waterfront. Ben later recorded that he had "a strong inclination for the sea," which he indulged to the extent a young boy could against his father's disapproval. "Living near the water, I was much in and about it, learned early to swim well, and to manage boats, and when in a boat or canoe with other boys I was commonly allowed to govern, especially in any case of difficulty."

The lure of the water—joined to Ben's emerging mechanical curiosity and inventiveness—prompted an early experiment. One windy day he was flying a kite on the bank of the Mill Pond, an artificial enclosure that had been constructed to trap the high tide and release it through the race of a gristmill. Notwithstanding the wind, the afternoon was warm and the water inviting. Ben tied the kite to a stake in the ground, doffed his clothes, and dove in. The water was pleasantly cool, and he was reluctant to leave it, but he wanted to fly his kite some more. He pondered his dilemma until it occurred to him that he need not forgo one diversion for the other. He clambered out of the pond, untied the kite from the stake, and returned to the water. As the buoyancy of the water diminished gravity's hold on his feet, he felt the kite tugging him forward. He surrendered to the wind's power, lying on his back and letting the kite pull him clear across the pond—"without the least fatigue and with the greatest pleasure imaginable." Writing from France decades later, he added, "I think it not impossible to cross in this manner from Dover to Calais." On other occasions the youngster experimented with hand paddles to augment the power of his swimming stroke, and wooden flippers for his feet. Neither innovation was as successful as the sail-kite: the paddles overly fatigued his wrists, while the flippers, being stiff, failed to mimic a fish's tail sufficiently.

The Mill Pond was the location of at least one adventure that turned out ill. Next to the pond was a salt marsh where Ben and the boys liked to hunt small fish. But their stalking stirred up the mud and clouded the water, frustrating their efforts to capture lunch. To mitigate the murkiness, Ben proposed that they build a jetty extending into the marsh. The only convenient building material consisted of stones recently delivered to a building site nearby. Ben suggested that the gang wait until the masons at the site went home for the evening, at which point the stones might be put to the purpose of improving the fishery. The boys waited, the men departed, and the construction commenced. After several hours and much struggling, the jetty was completed, to the boys' satisfaction and pride. The foreman of the building crew, arriving next morning, was less admiring. A cursory investigation revealed the whereabouts of the missing stones, from which the foreman deduced the identity of those responsible for their removal. The boys were remanded to their parents' custody and chastisement; although Ben pleaded the civic usefulness of the construction, Josiah pointed out that the first civic virtue was honesty.

Ben might have added that this transgression was decidedly venial compared to what other lads of the town regularly engaged in. Boston's boys had long evinced an ebullient streak, especially on Guy Fawkes Day, the November anniversary of the aborted Gunpowder Plot against Parliament in 1605. Clusters of youths from the South End of town would swarm past the Franklin house—which lay not far from Mill Creek, the line of demarcation between the southern and northern neighborhoods—into the North End looking for trouble. More often than not, they found it. When they failed, they could count on discovering it back in their own neighborhood when the northerners repaid the visit. Over time the fun grew more frequent; at the end of the eighteenth century, Edward Reynolds—who happened to be the great-great-grandson of Josiah Franklin's landlord on Milk Street—explained that "the old feud between the Southenders and Northenders," which he described as being "as old as the town itself," was "the occasion of a regular battle every Thursday and Saturday afternoon." Reynolds added that the clashes were "not infrequently the occasion of very serious injury to wind and limb." They were also practice in the arts applied against the agents—and then the soldiers—of King George III.

⌘ Josiah Franklin was fifty-eight when he brought Ben into the shop, and by this time of his life he was content with the predictability and security his business afforded him and his family. But the candle shop held little appeal for the boy, who found the endless pouring, trimming, cutting, and packing hopelessly dull next to the far more exciting activities happening all over town. His dissatisfaction only increased—indeed, approached something akin to despair—when his elder brother John left the family firm to set himself up independently in Rhode Island, and Josiah gave every indication of commanding Ben to take his place as apprentice and future partner.

The scope for rebellion by a twelve-year-old boy was limited. But there was always the threat of running off to sea—a real threat even for one as young as Ben, considering the demand of the shipping trade for cabin boys. Josiah had lost his namesake this way, and he could hardly bear the thought of losing his youngest son similarly. Consequently, in a strange way Ben gained an advantage over his father in this early contest of wills. Josiah abandoned the notion of making a chandler out of the boy and began taking him around the town to observe the other craftsmen at work, in the hope that some honest calling less dangerous than the sea would satisfy his taste for novelty and excitement.

Although no single craft commended itself above all others, cutlery appeared promising. Ben had shown some cleverness with his hands and with tools; making and repairing knives might put that cleverness to use. Moreover, his cousin Samuel—Uncle Benjamin's boy—who had been a cutler in London, had recently relocated to Boston; Ben could apprentice with him. And so Ben was sent to live and work with Samuel on a trial basis. But Samuel demanded a maintenance fee Josiah judged excessive, not least in light of the fact that Josiah had been maintaining Samuel's father for years with no remuneration. The cutlery apprenticeship collapsed.

Josiah then consulted a son of his own. James Franklin, nine years Ben's elder, had recently returned from London, where he had learned the printer's trade. He had established a shop on Queen Street, just three blocks from Josiah's house; there he was attempting to find a niche among the town's four other printers. The business began slowly, but in an era when printing provided the only feasible means of reproducing the written word on any but the most limited scale, and in a community devoted to the study of the Scriptures, an activity that required and indeed produced nearly universal literacy among adult males and substantial literacy among females, James had reason to anticipate success. He believed that from a small start printing sermons and broadsides—those all-purpose posters conveying information on everything from politics to the price of peas—he might graduate to books and other more profitable assignments. He needed a helper. Ben could serve as well as any other.

In fact Ben served very well. Printing turned out to be ideally suited to his peculiar combination of manual and intellectual dexterity. The physical process of printing was straightforward, if somewhat involved. The printer set the handwritten text in type, placing the cast-metal letters (imported, during this period, from England) in rows that would yield the lines of printed text. These lines were held in place by rectangular frames corresponding to the printed pages; typically four pages were set and framed at once. The letters were inked, paper was laid over them and pressed against them, and the sheet of four pages was hung or laid aside to dry. As many sheets were pressed as copies the customer ordered. After the last impressions were made and had dried, the sheets were cut into their separate pages, which were collated and bound.

The mental aspect of the craft was no less significant than the physical. Printers doubled as editors, proofreading their patrons' prose (and their own typesetting) and suggesting improvements in style. In some instances they served as coauthors or ghostwriters, filling gaps in imagination or knowledge. In addition, the printing trade shared certain activities with all businesses: accounting, marketing, inventory control, customer relations.

From the beginning Ben showed himself adept at both the physical and mental aspects of printing. His fingers flitted from type rack to frame, plucking the letters he needed and slipping them into their places. He had inherited a good set of shoulders from Josiah; as he matured, and as he continued to swim at every opportunity, these grew strong enough to sling around the heavy sets of lead type and to operate the manual presses for hours at a time. His facility with language eased the chores of editing and proofing; his early-acquired and always-widening reading habits attuned his ear to felicitous phrasing and his eye to orthodox orthography. His failure at arithmetic proved to have been Mr. Brownell's doing more than his own; a subsequent self-study course yielded rapid progress to a mastery more than adequate for any tradesman.

It did not take James long to appreciate what Ben could bring to the printing business. He soon struck an agreement with Josiah that Ben would serve as his apprentice. The term—nine years—was longer than that of most apprenticeships, but printing required greater skill and longer training than most trades. In other respects the apprenticeship fit the custom of the day, which was summarized in a typical indenture document:

> The said Apprentice his Master faithfully shall or will serve, his secrets keep, his lawful commands everywhere gladly do. . . . The goods of his said Master he shall not waste, nor the same without license of him to any give or lend. Hurt to his said Master he shall not do, cause, nor procure to be done. . . . Taverns, inns, or alehouses he shall not haunt. At cards, dice, tables or any other unlawful game he shall not play. Matrimony he shall not contract; nor from the service of his said Master day or night absent himself; but in all things as an honest and faithful apprentice shall and will demean and behave himself towards his said Master and all his during said term.

Beyond this boilerplate, James agreed to pay Ben the wages of a journeyman printer during the final year of his indenture.

Although Ben deemed printing preferable to cutlery, and certainly to chandlery, and while he could see that printing was something he might be good at, he had reservations about the apprenticeship. Nine years looked an eternity to a twelve-year-old, and, as he recalled later, he "still had a hankering for the sea." But this hankering simply intensified Josiah's determination to seal the arrangement, and through a combination of cajolery and threat—legally, a father did not require his son's approval for an apprenticeship—he induced Ben to sign the indenture papers.

∼— **Before long,** Ben began to appreciate the advantages of his new line of work. His appetite for reading had always grown with the eating; of late he had devoured *Pilgrim's Progress* and other works by Bunyan, Burton's *Historical Collections*, Plutarch's *Lives*, Defoe's *Essay on Projects*, and various of Cotton Mather's preachments. Now that he was thrown into regular contact with the most literate element in a highly literate society, he discovered that an even wider array of literature fell open to him. As apprentice to a printer, he daily dealt with apprentices to the town's booksellers; he formed an alliance with one in particular, who allowed him to borrow books from his master's collection to read after hours. "Often I sat up in my room reading the greatest part of the night, when the book was borrowed in the evening and to be returned early in the morning lest it should be missed or wanted." One of James's customers, Matthew Adams, remarked this inquisitive lad and gave him direct access to the Adams family library, an impressive if quirky collection.

James did not object to his younger brother's campaign of self-improvement, so long as it did not diminish his productivity in the press room, which it did not. "In a little time I made great proficiency in the business, and became a useful hand to my brother," Ben wrote, quite believably. Indeed, James soon found a way to capitalize on the boy's literary bent. A common entertainment in those days consisted of poems struck off on the occasion of important or otherwise noteworthy events. Ben had been reading verses from the Adams library, and he determined to have a try at the genre. An early effort memorialized the sad drowning of the keeper of a local lighthouse, his wife and daughter, and a friend and a slave. Beyond the basic human appeal of a story of the untimely death of loved ones, especially including a sweet and innocent young girl, the tragedy had special resonance in a society that lived by the sea—and consequently too often died by the sea. Whether or not Ben comprehended all the facets of his tale, he knocked out a piece called "The Lighthouse Tragedy," which he and James quickly printed up. A much older, more sophisticated Franklin called it "wretched stuff, in the Grub-street ballad style," but had to admit that it "sold wonderfully." He added frankly, "This flattered my vanity."

The plaudits and the profits inspired another venture into verse, a ballad commemorating the recent killing of the notorious pirate Edward Teach, commonly called Blackbeard.

> *Will you hear of a bloody battle,*
> *Lately fought upon the seas,*
> *It will make your ears to rattle,*
> *And your admiration cease.*
> *Have you heard of Teach the Rover*
> *And his knavery on the main,*
> *How of gold he was a lover,*
> *How he loved all ill-got gain.*

There were several more stanzas, climaxing on the quarterdeck:

> *Teach and Maynard on the quarter,*
> *Fought it out most manfully;*
> *Maynard's sword did cut him shorter,*
> *Losing his head he there did die.*

Perhaps because this poem lacked the romantic-tragic element, it sold less well than Ben's first. (Closer comparison is impossible, as the first does not survive). Josiah had frowned on his son's poetic efforts, ridiculing them and warning that verse-makers were generally beggars, but as long as the lighthouse tale belied the warning, Ben ignored the criticism. Yet now the ridicule stung more sharply and the warning rang louder, and the boy abandoned balladic Grub Street for more respectable precincts of prose.

❧ By a matter of luck and untutored good taste, his guides to those precincts turned out to be some of the finest prose stylists of the day. Previously Ben had honed his argumentative skills on a friend of similarly bookish bent. On one occasion Ben and this John Collins disputed the prudence and appropriateness of educating girls beyond basic literacy. Ben, who took the affirmative, believed he had the better of the argument on merits but conceded that Collins was the more persuasive presenter. Ben hoped to gain an advantage by shifting ground from the spoken word to the written, but here again he discovered that his arguments lacked the eloquence and power of his opponent's. Josiah, who happened across some of Ben's papers, concurred, pointing out particular deficiencies in style and approach.

Frustrated and now somewhat embarrassed, Ben determined to remedy the situation. He had recently encountered an early issue of *The Spectator*, the London journal soon to be famous for the essays of Joseph Addison and Richard Steele. Ben read this number front to back, then back to front and all over again. Entranced by the authors' ease of exposition, he adopted the *Spectator*'s style as a model for his own. He devised elaborate exercises to absorb the principles that underlay its phrases. He would read passages, then try to recapitulate them from memory. On the reasoning that poetry demands a larger vocabulary than prose—a given meaning must also fit the pattern of rhyme and meter—he reworked the *Spectator* essays into verse, and subsequently back into prose again. He took notes on the essays, then deliberately scrambled the notes before attempting to reconstruct the original order, the better to appreciate the art of rhetorical organization. He shunned sleep, sitting up late with his quill pen and a sheaf of papers salvaged from the printing shop's scrap pile, then rising early to fit in a few more exercises before James entered the shop and the real work of the day commenced. He exploited James's relative unconcern at the state of his younger brother's soul to steal Sundays from the South Church and its sacred texts for the print shop and his secular volumes. Josiah, missing his youngest son at services, disapproved but declined to intervene between master and apprentice; perhaps he already recognized that Ben's zeal for the word of man would forever outstrip his zeal for the word of God. The former sentiment was a powerful motivator; referring to his efforts to make himself a writer, Ben admitted afterward, "I was extremely ambitious."

He had a chance to gratify that ambition, and to measure his literary advancement, after James began publishing the *New England Courant* in 1721. During the previous two years James had been the printer—but not the publisher—of the *Boston Gazette*, which, like other papers of that era, was something of an adjunct to and perquisite of the office of the Boston postmaster. Postmasters had first knowledge of most of the news that came in—by post frequently—from the outside world; this news could be recycled in one's own paper. Moreover, a postmaster could exploit his command of the outgoing mails to arrange distribution of his paper in preference to—or to the exclusion of—competitors' publications.

But because the postmastership was a public office, postmasters' papers (including the *Gazette*) tended to tread lightly on issues relating to government. The *Gazette* boasted that it was published "by authority"; it read as though it were published by the authorities. James Franklin thought Boston deserved better, and after his printing contract with the *Gazette* ran out, he determined to start his own paper. This one would be lively, opinionated, and not averse to challenging the establishment.

No one so represented the establishment as Cotton Mather; James's new paper, the *New England Courant*, announced its birth with a scathing attack on Mather. The occasion of the attack was an epidemic of smallpox, the first in nearly two decades—which hiatus was a primary cause of the virulence of this outbreak, in that an unexposed generation had little or no resistance to the disease. For all his obsession with the supernatural, Mather had maintained his youthful interest in the natural, and he advocated the novel technique of inoculation to combat the contagion.

James Franklin knew next to nothing of the etiology of smallpox, but he knew he despised Mather for what James judged the eminent minister's smugness and his inordinate influence over the life of Boston. If Mather advocated inoculation, the *Courant* must oppose it—and did. The campaign of opposition accomplished no good for the health of the community; nearly 10 percent of the population died before the disease ran its course. In fairness to James, the preponderance of medical knowledge at the time was on his side regarding the inefficacy of inoculation; one of his collaborators in opposition was William Douglass, a physician educated at the best English and continental European universities. But whatever its effects on public health, the anti-inoculation campaign served James's purpose of shaking the status quo.

The status quo shook back. Increase Mather publicly denounced the "vile *Courant*" and said he "could well remember when the Civil Government would have taken an effectual course to suppress such a cursed libel." Samuel Mather, Cotton's son and an apparent beneficiary of inoculation, wrote semianonymously (and that not for long) in the *Gazette* that the *Courant* was trying "to vilify and abuse the best men we have"; he warned that "there is a number of us who resolve that if this wickedness be not stopped, we will pluck up our courage and see what we can do in our way to stop it." Many readers heard the voice of Cotton Mather in an unsigned complaint to the *Boston News-Letter* decrying the "notorious, scandalous paper called the *Courant*" and charging said screed sheet with purveying "nonsense, unmanliness, railery, profaneness, immorality, arrogance, calumnies, lies, contradictions, and what not all tending to quarrels and divisions, and to debauch and corrupt the minds and manners of New England." Whether or not those precise words were Cotton Mather's, the sentiments surely were; in his diary Mather wrote of "the wicked printer and his accomplices who every week publish a vile paper to lessen and blacken the ministers of the town, and render their ministry ineffectual."

⌒— With the battle joined, James Franklin sought allies. At this early stage the list of *Courant* contributors comprised only James and a few kindred skeptics; to create the illusion of numbers, the publisher-editor and his friends employed the common journalistic tactic of writing under noms de plume—"Abigail Afterwit," "Timothy Turnstone," "Harry Meanwell," "Fanny Mournful" and others. These fictitious personages graced the paper with sharp-penned commentary on issues of the day; not surprisingly they tended to endorse the paper's editorial views.

Consequently it was with pleasure that James awoke one morning to discover beneath the door of the print shop a contribution from a genuine outsider. Actually, this contributor was not an outsider at all; it was Ben Franklin, who had observed the genesis of the *Courant* and its challenge to Mather and the Massachusetts hierarchy but who conspicuously had not been invited to join the undertaking. Because he had not—and because he realized that James might be less than enthusiastic about his younger brother's participation in the new project—Ben carefully disguised his handwriting and signed the letter "Silence Dogood." James read the missive with growing delight—which increased the more from his appreciation that the author's very name tweaked Cotton Mather, whose recently published *Silentarius* followed his earlier *Bonifacius, or Essays to Do Good.* James shared the Dogood letter with his colleagues; they registered equal approval. James ran it in the April 2, 1722, issue of the *Courant.*

Mrs. Dogood introduced herself to *Courant* patrons by chaffing them for the contemporary unwillingness "either to commend or dispraise what they read until they are in some measure informed who or what the author of it is, whether he be poor or rich, old or young, a scholar or a leather apron man." She (or Ben Franklin, rather) proceeded to mock this timidity by fabricating a fanciful background for herself. She had, she said, been born at sea en route from the old England to New England. But the joy surrounding her birth had turned to sorrow almost at once when a huge wave swept across the deck of the vessel and carried her celebrating father to his watery doom. It was a misfortune, Silence said, "which though I was not then capable of knowing, I shall never be able to forget."

The death of her father had made an indigent of her mother, with the result that the infant Silence was placed in foster care outside Boston, where she passed her childhood "in vanity and idleness" until being bound over to a country minister, "a pious good-natured young man and a bachelor." This godly fellow instructed the girl in all that was necessary for the female sex to learn—"needlework, writing, arithmetic, &c." (Had James known of Ben's earlier defense of education for girls, he might have guessed the identity of Silence Dogood at this point.) Because she displayed a head for books, the minister allowed her the run of his library, "which though it was but small, yet it was well chose to inform the understanding rightly and enable the mind to frame great and noble ideas." This bucolic idyll was interrupted briefly by the news that her poor mother had died—"leaving me as it were by my self, having no relation on earth within my knowledge"—but soon enough it resumed. "I passed away the time with a mixture of profit and pleasure, having no affliction but what was imaginary and created in my own fancy; as nothing is more common with us women than to be grieving for nothing when we have nothing else to grieve for."

Almost certainly none of the readers of the *Courant* guessed that this ironically knowing voice belonged to a sixteen-year-old boy; neither did James, who inserted after Silence Dogood's first epistle an invitation for more. Any such additional missives could be delivered to the printing house or to the candle shop of Josiah Franklin. "No questions shall be asked of the bearer."

Ben later said he felt "exquisite pleasure" at the approbation this first effort in journalism elicited; he took particular satisfaction from listening to James and the others guess who the anonymous author might be. "None were named but men of some character among us for learning and ingenuity." During the next six months Ben continued his correspondence, delivering fifteen Dogood letters in all.

His topics ranged from love to learning to lamenting the death of dear ones. As in the first letter, insight and irony were evenly matched. Silence related how, to her astonishment, her ministerial benefactor presently essayed to woo her. "There is certainly scarce any part of a man's life in which he appears more silly and ridiculous than when he makes his first onset in courtship." (As Ben was of an age, if not an economic condition, to consider courtship, the reader who knows the identity of Silence Dogood discerns a certain dawning in him of the difficulties of the endeavor.) But gratitude inclined Silence to accept his suit, leading to wedlock and "the height of conjugal love and mutual endearments," not to mention "two likely girls and a boy." Tragically, her husband was carried off by illness almost as suddenly as her father had been swept away by the ocean, and Silence was left to look after herself and her offspring. Yet, as she assured readers, especially the men among them: "I could be easily persuaded to marry again. . . . I am courteous and affable, good humoured (unless I am first provoked) and handsome, and sometimes witty."

Silence satirized the state of higher education in Boston, lampooning Harvard College—the alma mater of Cotton Mather, among other establishment influentials—as a snobbish ivory tower where students "learn little more than how to carry themselves handsomely and enter a room genteelly (which might as well be acquired at a dancing school) and from whence they return, after abundance of trouble and charge, as great blockheads as ever, only more proud and conceited." She chided men for being as foolish as the women they criticized for idleness and folly: "Are not the men to blame for their folly in maintaining us in idleness?" She scoffed at women for silliness equal to men's—how else to explain hoop petticoats, those "monstrous topsy-turvy mortar pieces" that looked more like "engines of war" than ornaments of the fair sex. Having experienced multiple deaths in her family, she offered a formula for eulogizing departed loved ones, pointing out that tears were the easier to elicit the more unexpected and violent the demise. "It will be best if he went away suddenly, being killed, drowned, or froze to death." The address in such a case ought to include a litany of melancholy expressions such as "dreadful, deadly, cruel cold death, unhappy fate, weeping eyes." An experienced speaker would wring the maximal lachrymation from an audience, but in a pinch anyone could deliver the doleful sentiments. "Put them into the empty skull of some young Harvard (but in case you have ne'er a one at hand, you may use your own)." Rhymes were nice: "power, flower; quiver, shiver; grieve us, leave us." A concluding flourish was the mark of a really distinguished graveside encomium. "If you can procure a scrap of Latin to put at the end, it will garnish it mightily."

Had they come from the pen of a mature writer, the Dogood letters would deserve to be considered a delightful example of social satire. Coming as they did from the pen of a mere youth, they reveal emerging genius. Some of what Franklin wrote he might have experienced indirectly; some he extrapolated from his reading; much he must simply have imagined. But the tone is uniformly confident and true to the character he created. Silence is irreverent and full of herself, yet she brings most readers—the proud and powerful excepted—into the realm of her sympathy. They laugh when she laughs, and laugh at whom she laughs at. She is one of the more memorable minor characters of American literature, and all the more memorable for being the creation of a sixteen-year-old boy.

 Silence Dogood's early offerings afforded distraction from the controversies that continued to roil the town. A visitor to Boston had limned the environs and their inhabitants: "The houses in some parts join as in London—the buildings, like their women, being neat and handsome. And their streets, like the hearts of the male inhabitants, are paved with pebble."

Many of those pebbled hearts agreed with James Franklin that the public pietism of the Mathers and their ecclesiastical allies had grown intolerable. One anticlerical militant, perhaps still sore from the witch trials, went so far as to throw a bomb into Cotton Mather's house. The explosive device failed to detonate, leaving the target to intone, "This night there stood by me the angel of the God, whose I am and whom I serve." The failure also allowed Mather to read the appended message: "COTTON MATHER, You Dog, Damn You: I'll inoculate you with this, with a Pox to you."

James Franklin preferred bombs of the printed sort; oddly, it was one of his lesser fireworks that triggered the strongest reaction. In June 1722 James printed a faked letter to the editor, in which the writer (that is, James himself) suggested that the authorities were remiss in failing to pursue with adequate vigor pirates who were afflicting the New England coast that season. Of the captain named to head the posse, the *Courant* said sarcastically, " 'Tis thought he will sail sometime this month, if wind and weather permit."

For this disrespect the Massachusetts General Court ordered that James be jailed. Many observers judged the reaction disproportionate to the provocation. A commonly accepted explanation was that ever since the smallpox scuffles, the court had been seeking an excuse to silence the turbulent pressman; this was simply the excuse that fell to hand. In connection with his brother's arrest, Ben was briefly detained and questioned. But on the reasoning that as an apprentice he was legally required to follow his master's orders, the magistrates released him.

As a result of James's imprisonment, Ben found himself the acting publisher and managing editor of the *Courant.* Josiah Franklin earlier had implicitly acknowledged Ben's strong-headedness in releasing him from the candle shop; James had encountered some of that same independence of mind in the four years following. Ben's recent surreptitious success with Silence Dogood had not reduced his opinion of himself; now he was in charge of the whole printing and publishing operation. It was enough to swell the vanity of any sixteen-year-old.

"I made bold to give our rulers some rubs," he boasted afterward. On behalf of freethinkers everywhere—not to mention James, languishing in jail—Silence Dogood contradicted her Christian name. "Without freedom of thought there can be no such thing as wisdom," she quoted from an English paper; "and no such thing as public liberty without freedom of speech, which is the right of every man. . . . Whoever would overthrow the liberty of a nation must begin by subduing the freeness of speech, a thing terrible to public traitors." This talk of traitors was strong stuff, but Silence had not finished. "It has been for some time a question with me, whether a commonwealth suffers more by hypocritical pretenders to religion or by the openly profane? . . . Some late thoughts of this nature have inclined me to think that the hypocrite is the most dangerous person of the two, especially if he sustains a post in the government." The openly profane person deceived no one and thereby limited the damage he could cause; but the godly hypocrite enlisted the unwitting many into his malign service. "They take him for a saint and pass him for one, without considering that they are (as it were) the instruments of public mischief out of conscience, and ruin their country for God's sake."

James won his release from jail after a month, following a public apology and a physician's report that confinement was harming his health. Yet he reconsidered his repentance about the same time he recovered his health, and by the beginning of 1723 the *Courant,* again under his direction, was taxing the council in language like that which Ben had placed in the mouth of Mrs. Dogood. "Whenever I find a man full of religious cant and pellaver," the January 14 issue opined, "I presently suspect him of being a knave. Religion is indeed the principal thing, but too much of it is worse than none at all. The world abounds with knaves and villains, but of all knaves, the religious knave is the worst; and villainies acted under the cloak of religion are the most execrable."

Once more the hammer of authority fell. Declaring that the tendency of the *Courant* was "to mock religion and bring it into disrespect," the General Court ordered that "James Franklyn, the printer and publisher thereof, be strictly forbidden by this court to print or publish the New England Courant" unless he submitted each issue of the paper to the censor for prior approval.

Briefly James defied the order, publishing additional provocations; but when the sheriff came round with a warrant for another arrest, he fled his shop and went into hiding. From underground—not far underground, as it happened; the sheriff did not look very hard—he arranged to continue the *Courant*'s crusade. The court's order applied to James Franklin; it said nothing about Benjamin Franklin. James told Ben to keep publishing but under his own name. In order to prevent the court from acting against Ben as James's apprentice, James released Ben from his indenture, signing the back of the original agreement and discharging his brother from all obligations. Ben was to keep the endorsed document handy to show the sheriff and anyone else who doubted that Ben was really his own man.

But in fact Ben was *not* his own man. As a secret condition of his release from the original indenture, James made his brother sign a new, sub rosa agreement covering the scheduled last years of the apprenticeship. In public Ben was free; in private he remained bound.

Yet he was in charge, which counted for something. The February 11, 1723, issue of the *Courant* explained that James Franklin had "entirely dropped the undertaking"; this was not quite true, but it grew truer by the week. With each issue the paper lost a little of James's character and took on more of Ben's. Where James swung his pen like a broadsword, Ben wielded a rapier. His satire was always light, never ponderous; it usually brought smiles to objective lips and must occasionally have turned up the corners of even Cotton Mather's mouth. With his own name now on the masthead, Ben refrained from labeling the colony's notables hypocrites; instead he spoofed their obsession with titles. "Adam was never called *Master* Adam; we never read of Noah *Esquire*, Lot *Knight* and *Baronet*, nor the *Right Honourable* Abraham, *Viscount Mesopotamia*,

Baron of Carran. . . . We never read of the *Reverend* Moses, nor the *Right Reverend Father in God,* Aaron, by Divine Providence, *Lord Arch-Bishop of Israel.*" He got his point across, less dramatically but more effectively than James had.

∼ To some extent Ben's oblique style reflected a rhetorical technique he had picked up from his reading. Xenophon and other authors had introduced him to the Socratic method of argument by inquiry; Ben quickly divined that this would be more effective than the confrontational approach he had been accustomed to use against the likes of John Collins. "I was charmed with it," he said of the indirect method, "adopted it, dropped my abrupt contradiction, and positive argumentation, and put on the humble inquirer and doubter." Applied to assorted questions philosophical, theological, and political, the new approach exceeded his fondest expectations. "I took a delight in it, practised it continually and grew very artful and expert in drawing people even of superior knowledge into concessions the consequences of which they did not foresee, entangling them in difficulties out of which they could not extricate themselves, and so obtaining victories that neither my self nor my cause always deserved."

But to some extent Ben's decision to deescalate the *Courant*'s confrontation with council and court reflected tactical matters touching his personal standing vis-à-vis James. At twelve Ben had been willing, if grudgingly, to accept the terms of his apprenticeship to James; a boy with neither skills nor capital could hardly make his way in the world alone. But at seventeen his circumstances were decidedly different. Although technically not even a journeyman printer, he was as proficient in the craft as many masters. He was at least as clever a writer as James—as James himself had implicitly admitted by the praise he lavished on Silence Dogood before discovering, as he eventually did, who the widow was, when his praise suddenly ceased. Yet James's colleagues continued to applaud Ben after he dropped his veil of Silence, which irritated James the more. "He thought, probably with reason, that it tended to make me too vain." When the two brothers took their differences to their father, the old man sided with his younger son—because "I was either generally in the right, or else a better pleader." This made James all the angrier; in his anger he frequently beat Ben, who took this physical form of insult "extremely amiss." (He added, parenthetically, from amid the American challenge to British colonial rule during the early 1770s: "I fancy his harsh and tyrannical treatment of me might be a means of impressing me with that aversion to arbitrary power that has stuck to me through my whole life.")

Ben had little doubt he could manage on his own by now. Better than most apprentices, he knew how much it cost to support himself. James was unmarried and for this reason did not keep house himself but boarded with another family. He paid that family for meals; when he took Ben on as apprentice, he paid them for Ben's board too. After Ben happened upon a book extolling the virtues of vegetarianism, the boy decided to try it. This occasioned some inconvenience with his hosts and provoked additional upbraiding from James. So Ben, after calculating the cost of beef and pork as compared to potatoes and rice, offered to board himself for half the amount James was paying their hosts. James agreed, freeing Ben to discover that even this half was twice what it really cost to feed himself. The balance he spent on books.

"I had another advantage in it," Ben remarked of his new regimen. "My brother and the rest going from the printing house to their meals, I remained there alone, and dispatching presently my light repast (which often was no more than a biscuit or a slice of bread, a handful of raisins or a tart from the pastry-cook's, and a glass of water) had the rest of the time till their return for study, in which I made the greater progress from that greater clearness of head and quicker apprehension which usually attend temperance in eating and drinking."

By the evidence of his recurrent arguments with James ("I was frequently chid for my singularity"), Ben made little effort to disguise the feeling of moral superiority his discovery of vegetarianism afforded him; together with the intellectual superiority he felt after the triumph of Silence Dogood, he must have seemed insufferable to his older brother. He himself admitted as much after the fact. "Perhaps I was too saucy and provoking."

Wherever the demerits lay, Ben decided that his situation with James had grown intolerable—and this conclusion, along with the other reasons, cautioned him against unnecessary affront to the ministerial-magisterial axis of Boston. Several months after his seventeenth birthday he determined to break his indenture to James. This would be illegal; his second contract with James bound him for three years more. But because this contract was secret, Ben reasoned, James would have difficulty enforcing it. Ben could deny its existence; for James to affirm it in any court of law would reveal the sham by which he had evaded the General Court's cease-and-desist order and open him to contempt charges. By now James had come out of hiding but had posted a sizable bond for good behavior; Ben reckoned that the bond money was his own guarantee of James's silence on the indenture issue.

It seemed a sound plan, but Ben could not place too much trust in it. James had friends who disliked the censorious ways of the Mather clique as much as he did; already one grand jury had refused to indict him on contempt charges. It was conceivable that opinion's wheel would turn and James would be hailed as a free-speech hero. Such circumstances might embolden him to press his indenture claim against Ben. From Ben's perspective the safest course appeared to be to make no more enemies than necessary.

James guessed what his brother was thinking, and even before Ben began inquiring around town for other printing work, James preempted him by pledging his fellow printers to eschew his brother's services. He also enlisted Josiah, who, while sympathetic to his youngest boy on minor points within the framework of the indenture pact, sided with James on the moral and civic necessity of preserving the framework as a whole.

Consequently Ben saw no recourse but flight—which recommended itself on other grounds as well. To a curious boy, Boston had been an exciting place; to an independent-minded young man, it was starting to stifle. The Mathers did not say such threatening things about Ben as about James, but it was clear they and their supporters had doubts about the younger Franklin too. Reports of his inquiring and skeptical mind were circulating. "My indiscreet disputations about religion began to make me pointed at with horror by good people, as an infidel or atheist." Ben added that he had become "obnoxious to the governing party." Now might be a good time to leave, before the clerics and judges came after him as they had come after James. "It was likely I might if I stayed soon bring myself into scrapes."

So he plotted his flight. Selling some of his books to raise money for ship passage to New York, he sent his friend John Collins to tell the captain that he needed to board the boat secretly because he had got a girl pregnant and was being pressed to marry her. The captain, evidently a man of the world, understood. He pocketed Ben's money and found something to examine at the opposite rail of the ship while Ben slipped aboard. On an outgoing tide and a fair September wind, Ben Franklin fled the town of his birth and youth, carrying only the few shillings in his pocket and all the self-assurance of his nearly eighteen years.

2

Friends and Other Strangers

1723–24

⌒ Only later, with age and distance, would Franklin learn to
appreciate the more admirable aspects of Cotton Mather's
character and thinking. Now, upon leaving Boston, he
landed in a city established by a contemporary of Mather's,
but a man whose view of the proper relation between
ministers and magistrates could hardly have been more
different from Mather's—or more congenial to Franklin,
both then and during the rest of Franklin's life.

William Penn first ran afoul of religious authority at about the same age as Franklin (and at about the same time as Josiah Franklin, then still in England). Attending university in Oxford, Penn fell under the sway of the Quaker Thomas Loe, and when Charles II restored strict enforcement of Anglican orthodoxy, Penn resisted. Whether he was thrown out of Oxford or departed of his own disgust at what now seemed to him "a den of hellish ignorance and debauchery" was perhaps a fine point; in either case he left. His father, the formidable Admiral Sir William Penn, was not any more pleased than the boy's tutors at his strange beliefs; he greeted the lad with blows, turned him out of the house, and threatened to disown him. (Paternal displeasure aside, Sir William may simply have been a difficult man to get along with; his neighbor and navy colleague Samuel Pepys had to put up with him for professional reasons but declared in his diary, "I hate him with all my heart." On the other hand, it may have been Pepys who was the difficult one. Although he did not disdain his neighbor's invitations to dinner, he complained confidentially that Mrs. Penn's cooking "stank like the very Devil.")

The threat of disownment triggered a temporary lapse from Quaker conscience; young William reconciled with his father and went off to the Continent for a holiday at the court of Louis XIV. He did not stay long and by 1667 was securely back within the fold of his English Friends. He published a series of tracts contending for freedom of conscience; he preached the same doctrine before crowds large and small. In 1670 he was arrested for unlawful address to an unruly assembly. At the trial he argued eloquently that a man's mind and soul must remain beyond the reach of the magistrate; the jury voted to acquit—whereupon the judge ordered the jury arrested. (The latter arrests were subsequently overturned in a case that became a landmark in the evolution of the common law.)

At about this time Penn's father died. The admiral had learned to accept his son's sincerity if not his beliefs, and he left young William a sizable fortune. This included an annuity of £1,500 and, more portentously for English and American history, a claim of £16,000 upon the impecunious Charles for loans outstanding. The younger Penn was in and out of prison during this period—for declining to doff his hat in court, for further unauthorized preaching, for refusing to take an oath of allegiance to the Crown. When he was not behind bars, he spent extended periods in Europe disseminating Quaker ideas and values. In court, in prison, and on the Continent, he sharpened his arguments for religious toleration, and when a Quaker friend who had an interest in what would become the colony of New Jersey ran into financial trouble and needed rescue, Penn took the opportunity to draft a set of "concessions and agreements" for the venture, guaranteeing to settlers the most sweeping religious liberty anywhere in England's empire. Unfortunately for freedom of conscience in New Jersey, the concessions never went into effect, being swallowed up in some further commercial restructuring of the colony.

Disappointed but determined to try again, Penn pressed Charles to redeem his debt to him by granting him a large tract of land west of New Jersey. Charles consented, and after some haggling Penn became the proprietor of what may have been the largest single piece of real estate ever legally held by someone other than a monarch. Penn wanted to call the well-forested territory "Sylvania," but Charles insisted on honoring the admiral—not the son—by prefixing "Penn." Both parties were happy to portray the transaction as a case of balancing the royal books, but both understood that there was more involved. Speaking of himself and his fellow Friends, Penn observed, "The government was anxious to be rid of us at so cheap a price."

As proprietor of Pennsylvania, Penn enjoyed sweeping powers subject only to the constraints of the common law, applicable Parliamentary measures such as the navigation acts, and the sensitivities of imperial politics. This left a great deal of latitude in all his longitude. He immediately prescribed the closest thing to democracy within the empire, allowing the election of a representative council based on broad manhood suffrage. Not surprisingly, in light of his convictions—both the theological kind and those handed down by the courts—he guaranteed freedom of religion. Equally predictably, in light of the pacifism of the Quakers, he called for amicable relations with the Indian tribes that occupied his new possessions.

⌒ **In the autumn** of 1682, just several months before Josiah Franklin left England for Boston, Penn traveled to America for the first time. He wished to see the forests and streams he had heard so much about; he also wanted to walk the streets—notional though they yet were—of the "large town or city" he had directed be laid out on the west bank of the Delaware River. Philadelphia—the name was a neoclassical rendering of "brotherly love"—was the first planned city in America and among the first in the world; its plan reflected Penn's desire to mitigate the ills attached to Old World cities. The great plague and fire of the 1660s still seared the memories of Londoners; Penn would combat these egregious civic afflictions by making Philadelphia airy and open, "a green country town, which will never be burnt, and always be wholesome." The main streets would be one hundred feet across—wider than anything in London—and the lesser avenues fifty feet, all arranged in a regular, rectangular grid. Lots would be large—half an acre or an acre—with room enough for gardens and orchards to surround houses set well back from the street. Four squares of several acres each and a central square of ten acres would guarantee additional open space to the city's inhabitants. Unlike Boston, New York, and other colonial towns, Philadelphia would have no walls or fortifications; Penn's enlightened Indian policy would provide all the protection necessary.

Reality on the American frontier did not immediately match Penn's vision. Early inhabitants dug dwellings out of the steep banks of the Delaware River, living alternately amid the mud and dust of wet seasons and dry. Pigs, goats, chickens, dogs, and the occasional cow ran loose through the streets of the town, feeding on, in some cases, and contributing to, in all cases, the garbage and filth that made the summer air excruciatingly pungent. Front Street was a standing cesspool.

But time softened the rough edges, and by the beginning of the eighteenth century the town was starting to approach Penn's blueprint. The inhabitants numbered somewhat more than two thousand, and they gave evidence of having been busy. A recent arrival from Sweden declared, "If anyone were to see Philadelphia who had not been there, he would be astonished beyond measure that it was founded less than twenty years ago. . . . All the houses are built of brick, three or four hundred of them, and in every house a shop, so that whatever one wants at any time he can have, for money."

Money, however, was a problem. Philadelphia—like Boston, New York, and other North American cities—suffered from the chronic affliction of colonial commerce: a lack of money. The early eighteenth century was the heyday of mercantilism in British imperial thought and practice; according to the mercantilists, the measure of imperial power was ready cash (to build navies, outfit privateers, and pay mercenaries, besides less martial purposes). The function of colonies was to foster a favorable trade balance, which would funnel cash—most liquidly (or solidly, rather) in the form of gold and silver—into the treasury of the monarch, and into the pockets of his inhabitants in the metropolis (from whom it could be extracted when necessity arose). The maturity of the English economy relative to that of the American colonies, augmented by the navigation (that is, trade) laws passed by Parliament during the seventeenth century, ensured that money would flow into England with ease, in payment for high-value manufactured goods, and flow out, in payment for low-value raw materials, with difficulty. The result was a perennial shortfall of cash among colonial merchants and their customers.

As a result the colonists were often reduced to barter. One Philadelphia shipbuilder, James West, recorded charging £39 for building a sloop. His customer lacked cash, so West accepted payment in flour, butter, sugar, raisins, and beer. Partly because this was a recurrent problem, he had gone into the sideline of operating a tavern; he served the proceeds from his ship contract to his patrons. As part of this redefinition of liquidity, West boarded his boatwrights at the tavern and paid them their wages in beer.

In good times the dearth of money was merely annoying; in bad times it threatened to strangle the colonial economy. And times were rarely worse than following the collapse of the South Sea bubble in 1720. The South Sea Company had been chartered in 1711 and granted a monopoly of British trade with South America and the islands of the Pacific Ocean (formerly and still sentimentally the "South Sea"). During the next several years this monopoly rewarded shareholders handsomely, prompting wealthy and influential individuals, including King George I and many close to the court, to purchase stock. To tighten the company's connections to the Crown still further, the directors made George a governor of the company in 1718. A year later the directors concocted a scheme to privatize the national debt; they would assume the Crown's obligations in exchange for an annual payment—and, most significantly, the chance to persuade the Crown's creditors to exchange their notes for stock in the South Sea Company. With the company's stock appreciating rapidly, the task of persuasion was easy enough, which made the stock rise all the faster. Between January and July of 1720 it octupled in value, sucking in all manner of speculators and inspiring no end of imitators. In August the inevitable occurred: the price broke. By November nearly nine-tenths of the stock value of the company had vanished, shaking such rocks of the establishment as the Bank of England, disgracing the directors of the company (who proved to have collaborated in assorted

other shenanigans with the company's accounts), ruining thousands
of investors, and wreaking havoc on the finances of the entire British
empire.

~ Philadelphia was still reeling when Ben Franklin arrived in October 1723. If he had known how bad things were, he might not have
come. In any event, Philadelphia was not his first choice. Franklin's original plan upon leaving Boston was to settle in New York, the thriving
town on the island at the mouth of the Hudson River that retained the
Dutch character of its founders, including the burghers' ambitions of
worldly success. In such a setting a young man of similar ambition ought
to have no difficulty finding work, unbothered by the formalities of an
unfulfilled contract back in Boston.

But once out of Boston, Franklin found himself at the mercy of
forces beyond his control. After two days at sea the fair wind that had
swept his escape vessel south failed, leaving the fugitive and his shipmates becalmed near Block Island, off the mouth of Narragansett Bay.
The ship's hands, accustomed to the vagaries of sea travel, employed the
time to fish for the cod that had drawn seafarers to the northeastern
coast of America for more than two centuries. The fish were thick, and
the crew hauled them up by the hundredweight. The smaller ones were
cleaned, boned, and tossed into a pan of hot oil, emerging moments later
golden brown, steaming hot, and exuding an aroma that enclouded the
ship and stirred the digestive juices of all hands and passengers.

When he had entered the ship, Ben Franklin still held to his vegetarian philosophy. One leg of this philosophy—which proscribed both
flesh and fish—was economic; the other was moral. The essence of the
latter was that the creatures to be eaten had done nothing to deserve
death at the hands of humans and therefore ought to be allowed to live
out their innocent lives. Franklin continued to reason thus as the first
codfish were pulled up over the ship's gunwales. But his reason wavered
as the smell of the frying fish wafted across the deck. Before his vegetarian days he, like most Bostonians, had loved fish: fried, steamed,
boiled, stewed. The present smell conjured recollections of memorable
meals past, and he decided to revisit the argument for interspecies pacifism. To his delight he discovered a loophole. "I recollected that when
the fish were opened, I saw smaller fish taken out of their stomachs; then
I thought, if you eat one another, I don't see why we mayn't eat you."

And so he did, dining "very heartily" with the rest of the passengers and crew. This was the beginning of the end of Ben Franklin's vegetarianism; he remarked later, with signature irony, "So convenient a thing it is to be a *reasonable creature*, since it enables one to find or make a reason for every thing one has a mind to do."

The ship's eventual arrival in New York overturned Franklin's expectations in another respect. For all their commercial energy—perhaps because of it—the Dutch merchants and tradesmen in Manhattan evinced scant interest in the services of printers. The town lacked a newspaper, the merchants evidently being too busy to read about the world they lived in. And sermons had no such sale as in Boston, the merchants being equally unable to focus on the world to which they were going. The single printer who kept a shop in New York, William Bradford, had no difficulty supplying the town's needs with the helpers he already had. There was no room for Franklin.

But Bradford had a son, Andrew, who operated a print shop in Philadelphia. Andrew had just lost a journeyman, a promising and engaging young fellow who had died suddenly. A replacement was needed. William Bradford thought it worth Franklin's time to explore the possibility.

Franklin could see little alternative. The money that remained from the sale of his books would not last more than several days, and he had no marketable skill but what he had learned in James's print shop. Philadelphia had the added attraction of being even farther from Boston. It seemed unlikely that James would send someone after him, but it would not hurt to put another hundred miles between himself and what he owed on his apprenticeship.

 The first fifteen of those miles proved to be the hardest. Husbanding his shrinking supply of cash, Franklin boarded the cheapest boat he could find to carry him across the estuary of the Hudson to Perth Amboy. But an autumn squall caught the craft midpassage and tore away its rotted sail, preventing it from entering the sheltered strait west of Staten Island, driving it instead east across the Hudson's mouth toward Long Island. Amid the pitching of the small vessel, a drunken Dutch passenger was hurled overboard; Franklin, the most alert and active person on the boat, pulled him back in by the scruff of his shaggy head. The fellow, sobered only slightly by his close brush with a watery death, proceeded to fall asleep in the scuttle.

As the wind drove the stricken vessel closer to Long Island, Franklin and the others looked for a suitable landing. But the beach was rocky and the surf high, and to risk both was more than the ferryman was willing. So they dropped anchor to ride out the storm. By now the drunken Dutchman clearly had the better part of the bargain; the spray from the water had doused everyone almost as thoroughly as his ducking had wetted him, but at least he was unconscious. Some villagers on shore saw the boat bouncing beyond the breakers; the ferryman, Franklin, and the others shouted for them to come fetch them in smaller boats they could see lying by. But the villagers chose not to hazard their lives for these strangers and went back to their houses.

Although the wind gradually abated, Franklin and the others spent a most uncomfortable night on the water—cold, wet, hungry, and thirsty. A single dirty bottle of rum had to sustain them as what should have been a passage of a few hours stretched well beyond twenty-four. The next morning, with the storm over and the wind shifting again to the east, the master of the craft jury-rigged a sheet that carried them by nightfall on the second day to Perth Amboy.

Franklin, feverish from the strain and the exposure, collapsed into the first bed he could find. Just before passing out, however, he remembered reading somewhere that a large dose of water at the onset of a fever could forestall it. So he quaffed several glasses, then collapsed again. During most of the night he tossed fitfully, sweating profusely, but finally he fell asleep, and he awoke feeling as hale as healthy seventeen-year-olds generally do.

He made another ferry passage, uneventful this time, across the Raritan River and set out on foot in the direction of Burlington. There he hoped to catch a boat down the Delaware for Philadelphia. The storm of two days earlier had given way to a hard rain, which, after what he had already experienced, dampened his spirits as much as his body. "I was thoroughly soaked, and by noon a good deal tired, so I stopped at a poor inn, where I stayed all night, beginning now to wish that I had never left home." Moreover, in his bedraggled condition he looked the fugitive he was, or something similar. "I found by the questions asked me I was suspected to be some runaway servant, and in danger of being taken up on that suspicion." But he kept to himself, found a dark corner to the side of the fire, and retired early.

The next morning he headed out with the first travelers and made it almost to Burlington by nightfall. This evening passed more pleasantly than the previous; his host, a Dr. Brown, delighted to find a guest whose reading and interests approached his. Franklin and the physician spent hours conversing on various topics. (The acquaintance struck up on this occasion continued, as it happened, for the rest of Brown's life.)

Rested and with his spirits revived, Franklin walked the remaining several miles to Burlington the following morning, a Saturday. To his renewed discouragement, however, he discovered that he had just missed the regular packet boat to Philadelphia and that the next would not be leaving until Tuesday. An elderly matron of the village took pity on him, fed him a dinner of ox cheek, and offered to lodge him till the boat came. He accepted the invitation and resigned himself to a long weekend in the hinterlands of New Jersey. But that evening after supper, while stretching his legs by the bank of the Delaware, he spied a boat that appeared to be headed decisively downstream. His inquiries revealed that it was indeed bound for Philadelphia, and, yes, there was room for one more. With no time to beg leave of his hostess, he climbed aboard, and off they went. The current was nearly slack in this part of the river, and the wind afforded little help, so the young and strong among the passengers took turns at the oars. Franklin, younger and stronger than most, pulled more than his share.

They rowed for several hours through the darkness until some on board wondered whether they had passed their destination by mistake. Tired and uncertain, the rowers refused to pull anymore. A collective decision was made to put in to shore, where several of the passengers started a fire of old fence rails they stumbled upon, to ward off the cold of the October night. At daylight one of them recognized their campsite as being only a short distance above Philadelphia. They wearily clambered back into the boat and finished their voyage, landing early on Sunday morning at the wharf at the foot of Market Street.

~ As Franklin walked up from the dock, the ravages of the South Sea collapse remained everywhere apparent. "I saw most of the houses in Walnut Street between Second and Front Streets with bills on their doors, to be let," he recalled; "and many likewise in Chestnut Street and other streets, which made me then think the inhabitants of the city were one after another deserting it."

At the time, Franklin could not connect the empty houses and shuttered shops with the collapse of the money supply in London. The money supply that worried him was his own. He touched shore in Philadelphia with a single Dutch dollar in his pocket, received in change in

New York. He also had a hole in his belly from four days on the road and a long night of rowing and shivering.

He got his first lesson in imperial economics when he tried to purchase breakfast and discovered, to his relief and gratification, that one Dutch dollar went further in Philadelphia than it did farther north. Upon meeting a boy carrying a basket of bread, he inquired as to the loaves' provenance. The boy pointed in the direction of Second Street; Franklin's hunger-sharpened senses guided him the rest of the way to the bakery. He asked for biscuit, the sort of thing Boston's bakers produced by the barrel for the ship trade. Philadelphia's bakers made nothing of the sort, he was told. He requested a threepenny loaf—in Boston a step up from biscuit. He learned that threepenny loaves were not made in Philadelphia either. At a loss, he asked for threepence' worth of whatever they *did* make in this city. The baker handed him three large, puffy rolls, each the size of the threepenny loaves he had been accustomed to purchase in Boston. The rolls were too big to fit in his pockets, and he had no bag to carry them—customers being expected to supply their own. So he tucked one under his right arm, one under his left, and walked out the door taking large bites from the third.

As he proceeded up Market Street, munching his breakfast, he began to feel both conspicuous and out of place. He had not bathed in several days. He was wearing the same clothes that had been soaked by the salt water of the Hudson estuary and the rain of New Jersey; from his pockets hung dirty stockings, shirts, and underwear. He knew no one in the town, nor where he was going. Years later he remembered the "most awkward ridiculous appearance" he made.

Another person who evidently thought so was a girl somewhat younger than he, standing in the door of her father's house on the city's main thoroughfare. Ben did not know her name, nor she his. But he noticed her, and she him—which made him feel all the more awkward.

He turned and headed back toward the river, where at least he had the passing acquaintance of those he had come downstream with, some of whom were continuing on shortly. Although the first roll merely dulled his hunger, he decided to stop advertising his poverty and gave the other two to a woman and her child in the boat. The bread had made him thirsty; he helped himself to water from the river and freshened his face at the same time.

By now the inhabitants of the town were up and about. As a group they were clean and well dressed—which again reminded Franklin that he was neither—and as a group they seemed to be walking in a single direction. He fell into step and was carried along to the Friends' meeting house. No one questioned him at the door, and he allowed himself to be swept on in. As he had not been a regular at Boston's South Church for years, he may or may not have expected a learned disquisition on the Scriptures or a soul-stirring description of the fate that awaited those who spurned God's grace; what he did get was decidedly lower-key, in the Quaker fashion. After being up all night, and now warm and with at least a little food in his stomach, he soon grew drowsy and fell asleep. His hosts did not take his fatigue amiss; they let him slumber and gently woke him when the service was over.

Franklin followed the congregation out and, propelled as much by gravity as by any notion of where he was going, wandered back down toward the waterfront. A friendly-faced young man in the sober dress of a Quaker caught his eye; Franklin inquired as to where a stranger might find lodging. They were standing almost under the sign of the Three Mariners' inn; how about this place? he asked. The Quaker replied that strangers did indeed lodge there, but not the sort a decent fellow ought to share a table or a bed with. If Franklin would follow him, he said—employing the thees and thous of his sect—he would point out a more reputable establishment. Together they walked a short way to the Crooked Billet on King Street, next to the river.

Franklin's morning bread had lost its effect by now, and he ordered dinner. The host and patrons were accustomed to sailors and other strangers, but this one particularly engaged their attention. From his worn and tattered clothing and his beardless, dirty face, he gave every indication of being a runaway. No one challenged him directly; his host was too canny a businessman to allow his patrons to frighten off other paying customers on mere suspicion. But by oblique queries—Been traveling long? Whither bound?—they probed to discover who might be chasing him and why. Franklin answered civilly but unforthcomingly; he kept his head in his plate and finished his meal as quickly as he decently could. He may have aroused additional suspicion when he asked about a bed where he could sleep the afternoon—and, as it must have seemed, hide out. But no one gainsaid him, and he recouped several hours more of the slumber he had missed the previous two nights. His host roused him for supper, which he ate as discreetly as dinner, before returning to bed. He slept the night through, waking the next morning almost as fit as when he had left Boston.

—

∿— As he gathered himself for his interview with Andrew Bradford, Franklin may have reflected that it was a good thing his beard had not yet begun to grow. At least he did not need a shave. But he could have used a bath—and some clean clothes, and breakfast. His money, however, was nearly gone, and he chose to husband what he had. So, without bathing or changing his clothes or eating, he headed off for the printing shop of Bradford the younger.

To his surprise he was greeted there by Bradford the elder. William Bradford had practiced his craft in Philadelphia before moving to New York; now he had returned—on horseback, a more reliable but more expensive mode than Franklin could afford—to see old friends and check on his son. Franklin, after his friendly encounter with the father in New York, doubtless hoped that the older man's presence would work to his benefit. It did, but not to the degree he desired. William Bradford made the introductions, and Andrew appeared favorably disposed, asking Franklin about himself and insisting that he join the two of them for breakfast. Unfortunately, he said, he had just engaged a journeyman to replace his untimely-departed assistant, and business did not allow adding another hand. He expected some special orders presently; when these arrived, he *would* need more help and could offer Franklin piecework.

But there was another printer in town, he continued, a new man who might well desire a second. Franklin should call on him. If something worked out there, all the good; if not, Franklin was welcome to come back and lodge at the Bradford house till business warranted hiring him.

Franklin finished his breakfast and extended thanks for the advice and the offer. As he headed out the door to the other printer's, William Bradford accompanied him, saying he would show the boy the way. On arrival Bradford introduced himself and Franklin to Samuel Keimer. Neighbor, he said, here is a young man about your own business; perhaps you have work for him?

Keimer may have been puzzled as to why this stranger should bring him a second stranger to hire, but he marked it up to the friendliness of the City of Brotherly Love. A voluble sort, Keimer began telling Bradford his plans for capturing the bulk of the printing business in Pennsylvania. Bradford, not wishing to interrupt the flow of useful intelligence, declined to reveal his own background or his connection to Keimer's only rival. Instead he drew Keimer out by the artful question and the quizzical glance, till Keimer had divulged his entire business agenda and strategy. Franklin observed the performance with interest and no little admiration. It was apparent to Franklin—though obviously not to Keimer—"that one of them was a crafty old sophister and the other a mere novice."

What Franklin heard caused him to wonder whether he wished to work for such a novice; what he saw while walking around the shop as Keimer and Bradford talked doubled his doubts. The equipment was far inferior to what he had employed at James's; it consisted of a broken-down press and a single worn-out font. Keimer was clearly unfamiliar with its operation and was currently engaged in the woefully inefficient method of composing directly into type—which precluded anyone's assisting him. His project was an elegy to Aquila Rose, Andrew Bradford's late journeyman, whose contributions to local civic life had transcended his print work. Rose operated a ferry on the Schuylkill River, served as clerk of the colonial assembly, and wrote well-received poems. If Franklin thought it at all odd that Keimer was eulogizing the former assistant of his rival, the thought simply added to the conception he was forming of Keimer as eccentric.

But Franklin needed work and indicated he would be happy with whatever Keimer could offer. Keimer handed Franklin a composing stick and asked him to demonstrate; impressed by Franklin's efforts, he said he would have work for him soon, although not just now. Franklin put the press into such working order as it was capable of, and said that when Keimer had finished setting the type for the elegy he would come back and print it. He left, shaking his head, if only to himself.

He returned to Andrew Bradford's and took up the invitation to lodge there. In the next few days Bradford found odd jobs for him, but not so many that when Keimer belatedly accepted his offer to print the Rose elegy, Franklin was inclined to say no. By then Keimer had acquired additional type and an order for some pamphlets; together these allowed him to hire Franklin on a regular basis.

Briefly Franklin continued to live with Bradford while working for Keimer. The arrangement enabled him to form an opinion of the state of the printing craft in Pennsylvania, and he quickly judged it less than he was accustomed to. Bradford was "very illiterate"—an obvious handicap for one who lived on letters. Keimer was better read and indeed fancied himself a scholar. But in fact he was "very ignorant of the world"—including the printer's craft. In addition he professed a strange variant of

French Protestantism, one given to mystical trances and alarming revelations of the messianic age to begin at any moment. Having discovered too late the true identity of William Bradford—from Franklin—Keimer was suspicious of spies in his shop, and he announced one day that Franklin must cancel his housing arrangement with his rival or find other work. Franklin would have been happy to find other work had such existed, but none did. He inquired whether he might lodge with Keimer, who owned a house. But though Keimer had a house, he had no furniture, and no plans to purchase any; Franklin could not stay with him, he said. Instead the young man should seek a room with John Read, a carpenter who lived on Market Street.

ᐁ Franklin presented himself at the Read house, where he encountered the fifteen-year-old girl he had noticed, to his embarrassment, on his first morning in Philadelphia. By now, though, his trunk had arrived from New York, and with clean clothes and a few recently earned coins in his pocket, he felt much better able to stand scrutiny by the fair sex. "I made rather a more respectable appearance in the eyes of Miss Read than I had done when she first happened to see me eating my roll in the street."

Deborah Read evidently thought so too, either at once or shortly thereafter. Nor was she alone in her opinion. During the winter of 1724–25 Ben Franklin began forming a circle of friends, acquaintances, and admirers. He was a pleasant-looking young man, with a broad forehead, firm nose, and square jaw. On the tall side of average, he was thick through the shoulders and chest. His eyes were lucid, suggesting a lively intelligence; his well-formed mouth pursed when he was concentrating but smiled easily and often, revealing an equally well formed sense of humor. His self-confidence—never lacking—had grown since his arrival in Philadelphia. Having measured himself against the printers of a second city, he appreciated his skills more than ever. As much to the point, he had discovered—as every young person does who successfully leaves home—that he could make his way in the world. His native intelligence and common sense served him well; so too the social skills absorbed in the crowded bosom of the family he had left behind. The former gifts gave him the ascendancy in nearly any group he joined; the latter prevented that ascendancy from annoying any but the most envious in the group.

As was the case throughout the American colonies, the population of Philadelphia was growing rapidly, and had been for some time; one result was the large number of young people Franklin found to socialize with. His work with Keimer threw him into contact with the more literary-minded of the city; he was delighted to find a cohort of contemporaries who shared his interest in reading, questioning, and exploring the life of the mind generally. They debated topics classical and literary, current and political. Most were just starting on careers in the crafts or professions; few had much more to spend on books or beer than Franklin did. So they swapped books as they swapped arguments, and as long as they enlivened the conversation at one tavern or another, the proprietors did not mind that they nursed their glasses longer than was strictly profitable.

In feudal times arose a saying that city air made a man free; Franklin certainly felt that way during his first winter in Philadelphia. To be sure, Philadelphia was no more a city than Boston, but in Boston he had borne the double burden of Puritan clerisy and sibling jealousy. The tolerant spirit of William Penn still protected Penn's city half a decade after his death, and to a person of Franklin's questioning temperament it was infinitely more congenial than the forced certitude of the Mathers.

If Franklin was pleased to put Puritanism behind him, he was no less happy to be beyond the reach of his brother James. With James, Ben's life had always been an emotional—and sometimes a physical—struggle. Ben was smarter than James and more talented, as James and Ben both knew. James had resented this, and in his resentment insisted on his prerogatives as master—not to mention older brother—all the more. But James's insistence backfired. Ben, as the younger brother, naturally had to assert his independence; James's attempts to suppress that independence simply provoked Ben to rebellion. Keimer was not half the printer James was, but because Ben's relationship with Keimer was strictly business, he could accept his boss's odd ways for the harmless idiosyncrasies they were. Acceding to idiosyncrasy for the sake of wages did not touch Ben's self-esteem the way bending to brotherly dictate had.

As a result, Franklin's first winter in Philadelphia marked a vast improvement over recent circumstances in the city of his birth. "I lived very agreeably, forgetting Boston as much as I could and not desiring that any there should know where I resided, except my friend Collins who was in my secret and kept it when I wrote to him." By chance a brother-in-law, Robert Homes, who sailed a commercial sloop between Massachusetts and the Delaware region, heard that his wife's brother had landed in Philadelphia. Homes wrote Franklin a letter explaining the family's distress at his disappearance and assuring him that all would be put right if he returned to Boston. Ben did not question Homes's worthy intentions, but he replied that he had left Boston for good cause, was quite happy in Philadelphia, and had not the slightest desire to go back.

⌒ Yet this seventeen-year-old master of his fate discovered he was not so independent as he thought. On the day Robert Homes received Franklin's letter at New Castle, Delaware, the provincial governor of Pennsylvania, William Keith, happened to be present. Captain Homes evidently made some remark about Franklin, perhaps about the boy's obduracy, and shared the letter with the governor. Keith was surprised and impressed to learn that the author of the letter was not even a man yet. Keith had arrived independently at the same opinion Franklin was forming of Philadelphia's two printers: that they were a sorry pair for a province of promise and ambition. On the spot, apparently, Keith conceived a plan to keep Franklin in Philadelphia and encourage him in his craft.

The governor returned to Philadelphia and paid a visit to Keimer's print shop. Keimer and Franklin were working together in the window of the shop; both saw the governor and an obviously important friend approaching from across the street. Keimer had been hoping to win the official business of the province; here it came, he thought. He greeted the governor and the friend at the door and invited them in. To his chagrin they scarcely acknowledged him, instead seeking out Franklin. The governor belatedly welcomed Franklin to Philadelphia, kindly blamed him for hiding in the print shop and not presenting himself at the governor's house, praised his skill and intelligence, and invited him to join Colonel John French of Delaware and himself for a glass of excellent Madeira kept by the proprietor of a tavern just down the street. Franklin wondered at the cause of this benign attention; his boss was stunned. "Keimer stared like a pig poisoned," Franklin recalled.

Over the wine, the governor again praised Franklin's gifts and urged him to start his own printing business. Such a venture, he said, would have every chance of success, including his own support in procuring the public business of the province. Colonel French endorsed the governor's comments and added, in tones that sounded authoritative, that he would similarly recommend that Franklin receive the public printing business of Delaware. (Delaware at this time was administratively attached to Pennsylvania, under a 1682 lease—of ten thousand years' duration!—from the Duke of York to William Penn. The "lower counties," as Delaware was called by Pennsylvanians, had their own legislature and executive council but shared Pennsylvania's governor, currently Keith.)

The notion of his own print shop certainly had occurred to Franklin—probably as soon as he sized up Bradford and Keimer. He may or may not have asked himself *why* Philadelphia was so deficient in the printing and allied trades. He had not been in town long enough to agree or disagree with the opinion given some years earlier by one disgusted scholar: "The reason there are no bookbinders here, where all sorts of other craftsmen are found, is that there is no scholarship here, and nothing counts but chopping, digging, planting, plowing, reaping." Even at first glance Franklin could tell that the printed word mattered less in Philadelphia than in Boston, but that might simply reflect the deficiencies of the local printers. An enterprising and talented young man need not be discouraged by present conditions. Such, at any rate, was the expressed opinion of Governor Keith, who was placed to know.

Franklin did not doubt his own talents, but he painfully felt his lack of capital. Without money for a press and related equipment, not even the most gifted printer could set up shop. At his present pay he might put aside sufficient funds to purchase equipment in several years, but hardly before then. An older man with an established reputation might borrow money, but who would lend to a lad just arrived from distant parts—a lad who, as the governor evidently knew from Robert Homes, had fled his contractual obligations there?

Keith conceded that capital was a problem. Perhaps a relative could supply the initial funds? How about Franklin's father?

Franklin was dubious. He had no desire to return to Boston, certainly not to ask for money. For all he knew, James might try to enforce the apprentice agreement—out of jealousy if nothing else.

But Keith refused to be deterred by Franklin's family problems. He offered to write Josiah Franklin a letter laying out the plan he had just described and underscoring the bright prospects of the venture. Surely no father would deny his son the chance to pursue such an opportunity.

The governor's enthusiasm proved infectious. Reflecting, Franklin could scarcely believe his good fortune. Only weeks before, he had hauled himself up on Philadelphia's wharf hungry, ragged, and all but penniless, a runaway apprentice. Now the governor of Pennsylvania, and another man who evidently spoke for Delaware, were promising every assistance in the establishment of his own print shop. How *could* his father say no?

Franklin agreed to make the request. Winter weather had suspended most shipping to New England, but come spring he would take the first vessel for Boston. Meanwhile, as Keith suggested, prudence dictated keeping their plan to themselves; otherwise Franklin might run into trouble with his employer.

Franklin returned to Keimer's shop, where his still-stunned boss queried him as to what he and the governor had spoken of. Nothing of importance, Franklin replied; the governor was simply being polite. Keimer probably doubted he was hearing the whole story, and his doubts likely increased during the next several weeks, when Franklin accepted several invitations to dine with the governor. Franklin did not share with his employer how Keith conversed with him in the "most affable, familiar, and friendly manner imaginable," and certainly not how the governor reiterated his support for an independent Franklin shop. If Keimer suspected that competition was afoot, he suppressed his suspicions sufficiently to keep Franklin on. The boy was a good printer and could not easily be replaced.

By the time the shipping lanes reopened in April 1724, Franklin was more than ready to sail for Boston. His return voyage proved less eventful than his departing voyage had been, although the vessel he sailed on hit a shoal going down the Delaware Bay and began taking on water. The captain declined to stop for repairs, instead putting the pumps to work and putting the passengers to the pumps. Franklin did not begrudge the exercise, which warmed him against the chill of the North Atlantic spring. After two weeks they spied the heights of Beacon Hill; after a few more hours they landed at the Boston waterfront.

~ Franklin had been gone seven months, and because Robert Homes had not been back since discovering his presence in Philadelphia, none of his family or friends—with the exception of the discreet Collins—had any idea where he was, or even if he was alive. To some considerable degree his deliverance from the dead, as it appeared, absolved him of whatever guilt remained from his running away. His father and mother embraced him; his siblings marveled at his fine suit of clothes, his watch and fob, and the pocketful of silver he dispensed so freely. If such was Philadelphia, it must be a fine place.

The conspicuous exception to the general delight over the return of the runaway was James. Having resented Ben's talents, now he envied him his success. "He received me not very frankly," Ben noted, "looked me all over, and turned to his work again." James's journeymen were more inquisitive; they wanted to know all about Philadelphia, what life was like there, whether printers found employment. When they asked what wages workingmen made in Pennsylvania, Ben spread his silver coins before them. Such solid currency was rare in Boston, where paper notes were the norm. He displayed his watch, impressing them the more, then gave them a piece of eight to drink his health.

James, across the room, affected not to notice. But to Ben he seemed "grum and sullen," and, as Ben heard from his mother later, felt so insulted at Ben's carrying on in front of his workers that he could never forgive the offense.

When Ben broached to his father the purpose of his visit, producing the letter from Governor Keith extolling Ben's talents and prospects and forecasting wonderful success for the printing venture, Josiah could not help feeling proud. Imagine such an exalted personage taking an interest in his boy! But having worked long for his money, he was loath to part with it lightly. He asked himself, then asked Robert Homes when the latter arrived in Boston, what sort of person—governor or no—would have him place such faith in a boy still three years from legal manhood. Homes could not entirely vouch for Keith's judgment but said what he could in favor of Ben and the project. Yet Josiah would not be moved. He wrote a letter to Keith expressing gratitude for the patronage the governor was offering his son, but said the money involved and the responsibilities to be incurred were more than should be placed on the shoulders of a boy.

All the same, he did not leave Ben bereft. He had hoped for a reconciliation between Ben and James; seeing the impossibility of this, he granted Ben his paternal blessing to return to Philadelphia. He enjoined his youngest son to work diligently and keep a rein on his rebellious streak. If Ben stuck to his task for three years and lived frugally, he would be able to save most of what he needed to establish himself in business; if at that time he fell short, he should come back to Boston for the balance.

This was less than Ben wanted but more than he had right—or reason, really, knowing his father—to expect. When he left his parents' house now, he did so in the light of day and full public view. James remained angry, but the rest of the family wished him Godspeed and continued success.

He also received a parting gift from Cotton Mather. To Franklin's surprise the minister evinced a desire to see the young man. Franklin visited his library, where Mather indicated that all was forgiven. But not quite forgotten: on showing Franklin out via a side passage, he suddenly said, "Stoop, stoop!" Franklin did not understand him and ran into a low beam. Never one to let a sermonizing moment pass, Mather explained, "You are young and have the world before you. *Stoop* as you go through it, and you will miss many hard thumps."

⌒ Franklin's education in life continued on the journey south. His sloop called at New York, where his Boston friend John Collins awaited him. Collins, having seen how Franklin prospered in Pennsylvania, had determined to join him in the city of the Friends. Collins traveled overland to New York, where he joined Franklin for the rest of the trip.

Franklin had known Collins as an industrious and sober scholar, but lately his friend had acquired a taste for brandy. Like many another young man suddenly unsupervised in unfamiliar surroundings, Collins found his freedom more than he could manage; he descended into a state of constant inebriation. He compounded his problem by frequent visits to gaming tables. When Franklin reached New York, he found his friend drunk, broke, and just ahead of the sheriff. Franklin paid Collins's bills and resigned himself to paying the rest of Collins's way to Philadelphia.

Despite his friend's antics, Franklin's New York stopover was not a dead loss. On this trip south, Franklin was transporting some books he had left behind in Boston when he departed covertly the previous year; he was also carrying Collins's small library. The captain of the sloop evidently did not have regular contact with bookish types, and in a casual conversation with William Burnet, the governor jointly of New York and New Jersey, he remarked on his learned passenger. The governor, himself a scholar, and feeling isolated in an intellectual wasteland, invited Franklin to pay him a visit. Franklin was flattered at this attention from another governor, and he accepted the invitation with pleasure. The two conversed about books and authors; the governor doubtless had his favorable indirect impression of Franklin confirmed firsthand.

Upon arrival in Philadelphia, Collins continued to cost Franklin. Collins's alcoholic habit prevented his obtaining employment, and Franklin saw no alternative to paying his room and board till his circumstances improved. Unfortunately, they did not. Collins found new gambling partners among the Pennsylvanians and ran into debt again. He pleaded with Franklin for loans, which Franklin provided, against his better judgment. Franklin lectured Collins to mend his affairs; Collins told him to mind his own. Sharp words gave way to physical violence on at least one occasion. Franklin and Collins were in a boat on the Delaware River with some other young men; Collins was drunk as usual. When it came his turn to row, he refused. He was in no shape to pull an oar, he said. Franklin declared hotly that he must row, as everyone else had done. Collins replied that he would not; they could spend the entire night on the water for all he cared. The others in the boat told Franklin to let it go; they simply wanted to get home. But Franklin would not drop the matter, nor would he let the others row. Collins thereupon took the offensive; vowing to throw Franklin overboard, he charged at his friend. Franklin side-stepped the attack, grabbed Collins under the crotch, and hurled him headlong into the river. This sobered him only slightly, for as he swam back toward the boat he responded to queries as to whether he would finally agree to row by cursing them all and declaring that he would never do so. Franklin, happy enough now to take an oar, pulled the boat beyond Collins's reach. Again those in the boat asked whether Collins would row; again he profanely refused. Again Franklin pulled the boat ahead of Collins. This continued for some time. Eventually, fearing that Collins might drown, the others convinced Franklin to let him be hauled up.

This episode ended what was left of the friendship. Not long afterward Collins shipped out to Barbados to serve as tutor to the sons of a planter there. In one of his rare clearheaded and remorseful moments he promised to pay Franklin what he owed him with the first money he received in his new post. But he never did, and Franklin never heard from him again.

~ **William Keith** was disappointed on learning of Josiah Franklin's refusal to stake his son as a printer. The old man was entirely too cautious, Keith said; mere youth was no warrant of indiscretion, financial or otherwise, just as age was no guarantee of judgment. Perhaps afraid that Philadelphia would lose this bright lad, perhaps swept away by his own vision and magnanimity, Keith declared that if Josiah Franklin of Boston would not back his boy, William Keith of Philadelphia would. Pennsylvania needed printers, and the governor would see that it got them. He told Franklin to draw up a list of the equipment and supplies he would require from England, and they would be ordered at once. Franklin could repay the debt when he was able; the important thing was to put the project in motion.

Franklin's head had been turned by Keith's previous solicitude, then turned further by the flattering attention of Governor Burnet; now this offer sent it fairly spinning. The greatest man of the city and the province was putting his own money into a venture whose sole source of promise was the intelligence and skill of eighteen-year-old Ben Franklin. The young man's future was assured. Philadelphia was a wonderful city.

Walking home from this interview, Franklin began calculating what he would require to commence business. A quick tally brought the total to £100. Keith found the inventory entirely acceptable when Franklin explained it; he asked, in a manner that presupposed a positive answer, whether the venture would benefit from Franklin's presence in London when the fonts and other items were selected. Besides, he intimated, Pennsylvania's leading printer must make acquaintances among his counterparts in the imperial capital. The outset of the project was the obvious occasion to do so. Franklin could sail in the autumn on the annual ship— at provincial expense, of course.

Once more Franklin was amazed at how marvelously his career was progressing. The governor had endorsed his business judgment by accepting his proposal; now he was sending him off to London as the all-but-official printer of the province. To be sure, the ship would not be sailing for some months; but that would simply allow time to perfect his plans.

⌒ **Frustratingly,** he could not share those plans with anyone— least of all Keimer, with whom he continued to spend his working hours. "He suspected nothing of my setting up," Franklin later asserted. One wonders. Franklin paid frequent visits to the governor's house; Keimer must have asked himself—although he apparently did not ask Franklin— what the young man and the governor talked about. Further, Franklin was obviously too talented to remain a journeyman forever. Unless he relocated again he must one day set himself up as Keimer's competitor.

Quite possibly Keimer thought he could keep Franklin till the boy turned twenty-one; only then would Franklin be fully able to conclude contracts and do all the other things necessary to direct a business. And it was entirely possible Keimer thought he himself might be out of the printing business by that time. Other enthusiasms beckoned. Foremost of these was a dream to found a new religious sect, one that embodied his own peculiar interpretation of the Scriptures. Keimer loved disputation; since Franklin did too, the pair spent many hours over their frame and fonts arguing the finer points of theology and philosophy. Franklin employed the indirect style he had learned in Boston and regularly used it to tie Keimer in intellectual knots. Keimer eventually discovered the equally venerable rhetorical device of refusing to accept any premise whatever—in his case from a plausible fear Franklin would find a devious path from premise to refutation. Whether or not the experience shook Keimer's beliefs, it heightened his regard for Franklin's forensic skills. He offered Franklin a place next to the throne in his new order. Keimer would dispense doctrine; Franklin would defend it by confounding their opponents.

To himself, Franklin laughed at Keimer's delusions—the more easily now that he saw the terminus of his dependence on his employer approaching. To Keimer, he put on a grave face and indicated he was flattered at the invitation but wondered if he might have some say about the sect's practices. A vegetarian diet, for example, would benefit both body and soul. Keimer was skeptical, but when Franklin agreed to accept Keimer's teaching on the proper observance of the Sabbath (Saturday instead of Sunday) and the Levitican ban on cropping beards (prospectively a problem once Franklin's whiskers started seriously growing, but not yet), the elder man agreed to give vegetarianism a test. Franklin supplied a neighbor woman with a list of forty dishes containing neither meat nor fish nor fowl; for eighteen pence per week she would cook from this list.

Franklin experienced no difficulty reacquainting himself with a non-sanguinary regime, but Keimer suffered—as Franklin knew he would. "He was usually a great glutton, and I promised myself some diversion in half-starving him." For three months Keimer held out, dreaming day and night of beefsteaks, lamb chops, and fried ham. Though the spirit remained willing, the flesh finally succumbed. He ordered a roast suckling pig and invited Franklin and two women friends to celebrate his delivery from this ill-advised experiment. But the pig arrived before the guests did, and Keimer, unable to wait fifteen minutes more, ate the whole thing himself.

◇— Keimer was not the only person who found himself the object of Franklin's amusements. Collins having departed in disgrace, Franklin devoted more time to his Philadelphia friends. Three in particular—Charles Osborne, Joseph Watson, and James Ralph—formed his literary circle.

The group met regularly for Sunday walks; these provided a peripatetic forum for discussions of this author or that. Occasionally one or another would produce a piece of writing and submit it to the group for critique.

Of the four, James Ralph had the highest ambitions for a career in writing—poetry, to be specific. Charles Osborne likewise had poetic pretensions, but he also possessed the askant eye of the critic—especially toward Ralph's poetry and hopes of making a living by it. Franklin, recalling his own humbling efforts at versifying, shared Osborne's opinion that a career in poetry was a fool's quest, although he allowed that if Ralph wanted to write poetry merely to please himself, that was his affair. Franklin added the opinion he had formed some years earlier that even poetry that did not rise to art could serve as a tool for the improvement of one's prose. The others concurred in this sensible opinion, and an assignment—setting the Eighteenth Psalm to verse—was agreed upon.

Just before the next meeting, Ralph approached Franklin, his updating of David in hand. Franklin read the piece and registered approval. Ralph thereupon asked him to take part in a deception. Osborne, Ralph complained, would never say anything positive about his—Ralph's—poetry; he could not stand that someone—specifically Ralph—might write more gracefully than he. Would Franklin be willing to present Ralph's piece as his own? Only by such a subterfuge could Ralph get an objective opinion.

Franklin's schedule at Keimer's that week had prevented his writing a poem himself, and he consented. He cribbed Ralph's work into his own hand and read it to the group. Osborne praised it extravagantly. Ralph suggested a few revisions; Osborne told him he was as dull a critic as a poet and did not know what he was talking about. After the meeting, while Osborne and Ralph were walking home together, the former continued to effuse over the purported Franklin poem. Such imagery! Such power! He confided to Ralph that he had not earlier praised the piece as fully as he might have; he did not want to seem a flatterer. He wondered aloud how a person who spoke so indifferently could write with such passion and fire.

The confusion provoked laughter, at Osborne's expense, when the ruse was revealed at the next meeting. The episode did not estrange Osborne from Franklin; the two remained friendly enough to pledge a pact that whichever of them predeceased the other should, after having surveyed the ground on that farther shore, return and apprise the living one of the landscape there. The obligation fell to Osborne, who died relatively young. "He never fulfilled his promise," Franklin noted at sixty-five.

—————

~ Debating with his friends and dreaming of his future success filled most of Franklin's leisure time during that summer of his nineteenth year; but not all. Love occupied him as well.

The object of his affections was Deborah Read, with whom he had grown increasingly familiar since that inauspicious morning of his arrival the previous autumn. She had watched his career prospects improve with Keimer; partly in consequence he saw his romantic prospects improve with her. Ten months earlier, unknown and unemployed, he was the sort no father would have let near his daughter. Now, well placed in his craft, surrounded by friends hardworking and respectable, and waited upon by Governor Keith, he was one of the more eligible young men in town.

Precisely what Franklin saw in Deborah Read is more difficult to discern. No one painted her portrait during that period, and the only surviving one from later years shows a woman with a not unpleasant but neither notably appealing face. She was two years younger than he, which especially in that age meant that she might physically have been hardly more than a girl. Yet he seems to have been quite attracted to her, for they spoke of marriage. Her father and mother did not dismiss the idea. They had been searching for a good match, not least because John Read had lately run into financial difficulties. The search grew more pressing that September, when Read suddenly died, leaving his debts and his daughter—among other children—to his wife. At this point Sarah Read must have listened carefully as Ben Franklin made his suit.

Yet careful she was, and reflecting on Ben's youth, she told them to wait until his return from England. Perhaps she wished to gauge the seriousness of his intentions. Perhaps she wished to see whether the print shop he spoke of with such enthusiasm—to Debbie and her, yet still to almost no one else—actually materialized. Her husband's money troubles had resulted from his lending credence, and cash, to glib retailers of fraudulent promises. A modest skepticism would become his widow and safeguard his daughter.

Franklin could not gainsay this prudence in a mother-in-law. Nor was there much he could do about it if he had, for Sarah Read was not the sort to be trifled with. Love would have to wait the six months or so the crossing to England and the return would require. Then he would be older, and, with printing equipment in hand, his success would be assured. At that point Sarah Read could not deny him, and Debbie would not.

3

London Once

1724–26

ço— It is a truism that one travels to learn about home, but Franklin was young, and consequently it came as a surprise that the most important lesson he learned in going to London was what sort of person William Keith was. The lesson commenced before his ship cleared the Delaware River. Right down to the dock the governor continued to pledge full support for Franklin's printing project; he would provide not merely the letter of credit for the £100 Franklin's inventory required but reference letters to friends well placed to see the project profitably started.

Repeatedly Franklin called at the governor's house to receive the letters; repeatedly he was told that the demands of duty had prevented the governor from drafting them. Come again next week and they would definitely be ready.

He did; they were not. He did again; they were not. Understandably, he began to worry. As luck would have it, the departure of the annual ship was several times postponed. Though this afforded more time for the governor to fulfill his pledge, it threw a cloud of additional uncertainty over the entire venture.

Finally on November 5, 1724, the *London Hope* cast off and drifted down the Delaware. The governor's promised letters still had not appeared. Franklin boarded at the last moment only on the express assurance of the governor's personal secretary that the letters would be supplied at New Castle, a downstream destination for which the governor himself was about to depart and which he would reach before the ship did. Even as the ship was tying up at New Castle, Franklin leaped ashore in search of the governor. Once more the governor's secretary intercepted him, saying again the governor was extremely busy. But he would include the letters with the rest of the official correspondence, to be loaded at the last moment.

This seemed a plausible, if not persuasive, explanation, and was made the more so when Colonel French, the governor's Delaware friend, personally carried the official packet aboard. He greeted Franklin warmly; this had the double effect of reassuring Franklin about Keith's bona fides and elevating the young man in the opinion of the other passengers, who heretofore had deemed him unworthy of notice. He would have been even more reassured had he been allowed to *see* the letters, but the captain, concerned that their numerous delays would place them in mid-Atlantic when the gales of winter began to blow, refused to risk any further delay. Franklin could not go through the packet now. But if he would be patient, he would have any letters meant for his hand long before they landed at London. "I was satisfied for the present," Franklin recalled, "and we proceeded on our voyage."

Franklin's first ocean crossing was a tempestuous one. The winter weather did indeed catch them out; wind, rain, sleet, and snow battered the vessel and kept the passengers below decks most of the way. To his satisfaction—and, as it turned out, his lifelong convenience—Franklin discovered that stormy seas had little effect on his stomach or head. He employed the time and the close quarters to improve his acquaintance with certain individuals who had taken notice of him when Colonel French did. Indeed, these men called him out of steerage to berth with them in the cabin; they shared their victuals and all made merry together. "We had a sociable company . . ." Franklin said, "and lived uncommonly well."

As the craft entered the English Channel the captain kept his promise and allowed Franklin to sort through the Pennsylvania pouch. To his surprise he found no letters bearing his name. Thinking this an oversight, he selected several addressed to individuals evidently connected to the governor's pledge and to the errand that had brought him hither. One such letter was to the king's printer, another to a London stationer. Franklin could not well open the letters and discover for certain, but he assumed that the governor therein explained this fine young man's mission and pledged political and financial support.

Upon landing at London on Christmas Eve of 1724, Franklin looked up the addressees. The first he chanced upon was the stationer, to whom he delivered the missive as from Governor Keith. The stationer looked puzzled. I don't know the man, he said—thereby puzzling Franklin. Opening the letter, the stationer exclaimed, "Oh, this is from Riddlesden."

William Riddlesden, as Franklin probably did not know, was a convicted felon who had been transported to Maryland in lieu of prison; as Franklin knew full well, Riddlesden had continued in his conniving ways in America, sucking John Read into one of his confidence schemes, to the persisting detriment of Sarah and their children. The Maryland assembly had conferred upon him the distinction of being officially proclaimed "a person of a matchless character in infamy."

This opinion was shared by the stationer who now read the letter Franklin delivered. "I have lately found him to be a complete rascal," he said (in Franklin's reconstruction of the conversation), "and I will have nothing to do with him, nor receive any letters from him." With this he thrust the letter back into Franklin's hand and turned to greet a customer.

As he left the stationer's shop, Franklin looked closely at the other letters. He realized that these were not from the governor either. For the first time he began seriously to doubt whether the mailbag contained any letters from Keith on his behalf, or even whether Keith had ever intended to write any such letters. Consulting Thomas Denham, one of his cabinmates and a prosperous Pennsylvania merchant who had known Keith for some time, Franklin learned that the governor had a habit of promising much and delivering little. Denham laughed aloud when Franklin mentioned the letter of credit Keith was to have sent. Sir William, Denham said, had no credit to give.

This lesson in human nature came as a shock. When he had awakened that morning, Franklin fancied himself an independent artisan about to embark on a brilliant career. Now he was simply an out-of-work journeyman a very long way from home, with no place to stay and no friends within three thousand miles.

∼ Actually, he did have one friend, although this friend soon proved more trouble than any enemy. James Ralph had accompanied Franklin to London, determined, after his success in the small charade he and Franklin had committed against Charles Osborne, to seek artistic fame in the capital of English letters. He did not confide his plans to his wife, who remained in Philadelphia with their small child; instead he told her he was going to London to establish commercial connections that would allow him to set up a merchandising business upon his return. She and her relatives doubtless deemed this an improvement over idle versifying and bade him bon voyage. But no sooner had the *London Hope* arrived at the city of its name than Ralph informed Franklin he was not going back. He could not abide his in-laws, he said. His future lay in England.

Disappointingly for Ralph, and unluckily for Franklin, that future was slow to unfold. He initially thought to broaden from written art to performance; approaching a local theater troupe, he inquired about acting. The director auditioned him briefly before pronouncing that literature could not spare his gifts. Ralph thereupon proposed to write a weekly paper, a competitor to the *Spectator*, for a rival publisher. The publisher, however, could not be convinced that Ralph's talent warranted the terms he was demanding. Ralph lowered his sights again, applying for work as a clerk and copyist for the stationers and lawyers who crowded London's Temple district. He was told no openings existed.

Ralph had arrived in London with empty pockets, having spent his last on the passage from America. His failure to find work extended his impecunious period. So he imposed on Franklin to underwrite his portion of a room they shared on the street called Little Britain, to the north of St. Paul's Cathedral. One of their neighbors was a young woman they both found attractive; Ralph, the older and more worldly of the two, beat Franklin to her favors. When she moved to other quarters, Ralph moved in with her. For a time he lived off her earnings as a milliner, but when these proved insufficient to support him, her, and her young daughter, he resolved once more to get work. He advertised himself as a schoolmaster and indeed set up an establishment of learning in the countryside, in Berkshire. He acquired some dozen pupils, a modest income—and a new name. He had not abandoned his literary ambitions, and, evidently fearing that such a low post as schoolmaster might be held against a budding genius, he borrowed his friend's name. Franklin learned this fact upon receiving a letter from Ralph in which the latter explained his circumstances and requested that any reply be addressed to "Mr. Franklin, Schoolmaster."

His family name was common enough that Franklin did not feel obliged to object to its borrowing—any more than he had objected to Ralph's borrowing of his money. He calculated that he would eventually get his name back; as for the money, that seemed to have slipped down the same hole that had swallowed the generosity he extended to John Collins.

Yet Ralph was not without collateral of sorts. His absence in Berkshire left his paramour, the madam milliner, in distress both emotional and financial. Her relationship with Ralph had cost her friends and a job. She knew Franklin as an easy mark for a hard tale; with tears, sighs, and doubtless the well-timed coquettish glance, she took up where Ralph had left off fishing in Franklin's purse.

Yet Franklin was not a complete naïf, at least not on this point. He favored her requests for money, then made a request of his own. As he phrased it later: "Presuming on my importance to her, I attempted familiarities."

The vigor of his attempt exceeded its welcome. The initiative was "repulsed with a proper resentment," forcing Franklin to withdraw. The miscue cost him more than embarrassment. The woman informed Ralph of the real Mr. Franklin's improper advance, prompting Ralph to declare his friendship with Franklin ended and his financial obligations canceled.

Franklin felt himself in no position to make an issue of his loss. As he was learning to do, he philosophized that this was all for the best. He never would have seen the money anyway; nothing had been sacrificed save his good reputation in the eyes of a woman whose own reputation was hardly the finest, and of a friend who was no true friend. "In the loss of his friendship," Franklin concluded of Ralph, "I found myself relieved from a burden."

～ With almost equal ease Franklin dispensed with the burden of his relationship with Deborah Read. Perhaps his eyes were opened by Ralph's flippant abandonment of his wife and child; perhaps the allure of the millineress distracted him; perhaps London simply enticed him in a way staid Philadelphia never had. Certainly he was stunned by his abrupt return to poverty; after the promises, explicit or otherwise, he had made about his imminent success, he probably did not want to face Sarah Read, let alone Debbie. Finally, as much of his adult life would demonstrate, Franklin possessed a lively libido, which now hindered faithfulness to one so far away, when other females were close at hand. Debbie soon slipped from his mind. During his entire stay he wrote her only once, and then merely to inform her that he would not be returning soon.

London in the early eighteenth century was enough to turn the head of any young man. The city that would play a central role in Franklin's life still carried scars and memories from its twin scourges of the 1660s, the plague and the great fire. Puritan types (the Cotton Mathers who stayed in old England) attributed the pestilence and the holocaust to the ungodly and often downright lewd celebrations that greeted the restoration of the Stuarts after the death of the Lord Protector, Oliver Cromwell. The plague began during the spring of 1665, creeping out of the slums of the city and spreading silently—except for the wailing of friends and relatives, before they themselves succumbed—across every district and neighborhood. By summer thousands of men, women, and children were dying each week. Those who could fled the city for the countryside in hopes of eluding the invisible destroyer. (Isaac Newton, sitting out the plague in Woolsthorpe, watched an apple fall from a tree and extrapolated its trajectory into a theory of universal gravitation.) Persons too poor to leave kept to their houses, fearing contact with carriers of the disease. Taverns, inns, and theaters were closed by decree of the frantic civic authorities; a curfew reinforced the popular desire to avoid unnecessary contact with anyone who might be a carrier.

A hundred thousand souls went to their reward, and grass was growing in the streets by the time the great fire of 1666 brought the plague to an end. The sight of this new disaster turned discouragement to despair. "Oh, the miserable and calamitous spectacle!, such as happily the world had not seen the like since the foundation of it, nor be outdone till the universal conflagration of it," wrote an eyewitness.

All the sky was of a fiery aspect, like the top of a burning oven, and the light seen above forty miles round about for many nights. God grant mine eyes may never behold the like, who now saw above 10,000 houses all in one flame. The noise and cracking and thunder of the impetuous flames, the shrieking of women and children, the hurry of people, the fall of towers, houses and

churches, was like an hideous storm, and the air all about so hot
and inflamed that at the last one was not able to approach it. . . .
The stones of Paul's flew like granados, the melting lead running
down the streets in a stream, and the very pavements glowing with
fiery redness.

Its horrible destructiveness apart, the fire had two positive consequences. The first was the sterilization of the city against the plague, in
what was an inadvertent and extreme but nonetheless successful application of the principle of burning down the house to get rid of the rats.
The second was the creation of an elaborate system of men and ma-
chines to fight future fires. As Daniel Defoe observed in his *Tour Thro' the
Whole Island of Great Britain*, written during the period of Franklin's stay
in England, "No city in the world is so well furnished for the extinguish-
ing fires when they happen." Trained firemen, organized into squadrons
with special uniforms and insignias, operated pumping engines that drew
water from the Thames and other streams and directed it through hoses
onto the flames. Iron hooks on ropes were employed to pull down burning buildings; in stubborn cases gunpowder was detonated to blast the
fuel beyond the fire's reach.

The performance of the firefighters obviously impressed Franklin,
who after his return to Philadelphia set about organizing similar crews.
Other aspects of city life were less worthy of imitation but hardly less
fascinating to a lad from the provinces. London afforded endless amusements, some innocuous, others dangerous, still others indicative of the
often brutal nature of life in that era. In the category of the at-least-
potentially harmful—to body and perhaps to soul—were the prostitutes
who put in the shade any on offer in Philadelphia (let alone Boston). "As
we stumbled along," wrote a chronicler of the period, "my friend bid me
take notice of a shop wherein sat three or four very provoking damsels,
with as much velvet on their backs as would have made a burying-pall for
a country parish, or a holiday coat for a physician, being glorified at bottom with gold fringes, that I thought at first they might be parsons'
daughters, who had borrowed their fathers' pulpit-clothes to use as
scarfs, and go a-visiting in; each with as many patches in her market-place
as are spots in a leopard's skin or freckles in the face of a Scotchman."
The writer inquired of his friend who or what these ladies were. He answered that "they were a kind of first-rate punks by their rigging, of
about a guinea purchase." The writer asked his friend how he knew they

were prostitutes ("lechery-layers," was the term he used). "He replied, because they were sitting in a head-dresser's shop; which, he says, is as seldom to be found without a whore as a bookseller's shop in Paul's Churchyard without a parson."

Leisured gentlemen partook of the services of such entrepreneurs of intimacy; when satisfied in this regard they might, along with persons of lesser means, seek diversion at the justice court at Bridewell, where they would watch assorted transgressors—including women and girls— being flogged for their poverty and related misdeeds. Another favorite stop was the royal hospital at Bedlam—a corruption, in at least two regards, of "Bethlehem"—where guests would laugh at the antics of the lunatics. So popular was mental illness as a spectator sport that rules for visitors had to be posted: "No person do give the inmates strong drink, wine, tobacco, or spirits; nor be permitted to sell any such thing in the hospital." Public pillories at Charing Cross and executions at Newgate drew consistent and enthusiastic crowds; persons unlucky enough to miss the judicial killings could examine the decorporated heads displayed on Temple Bar, otherwise known as London's Golgotha.

Spectators who preferred their cruelty inflicted on nonhuman species could take in the combat among various animals at Hockley-in-the-Hole. A handbill forecast the fun:

> This is to give notice to all gentlemen, gamesters, and others, that on this present Monday is a match to be fought by two dogs, one from Newgate market, against one from Honylane market . . . Likewise a green bull to be baited, which was never baited before; and a bull to be turned loose with fireworks all over him; also a mad ass to be baited, with variety of bull-baiting and bear-baiting, and a dog to be drawn up with fireworks. Beginning exactly at three of the clock.

Even unintentionally, London life could be cruel. At inns and public houses the guests ate out of a common dish; armed with their own cutlery, they speared for the choicest morsels on what occasionally turned out to be a first-come, first-severed basis. The *Grub Street Journal* reported, "Last Wednesday a gentleman met with an odd accident in helping himself to some roast chicken. He found that he had conveyed two joints of another gentleman's forefinger to his plate together with the wing which he had just taken off."

That the digit-deprived gentleman did not complain more loudly may have owed to the anesthetizing effect of the alcohol in which Londoners swam from morning till night. Like all large cities, London suffered serious problems of public sanitation, exemplified perhaps most odiously, although hardly uniquely, by the Fleet River, which ran as an open sewer to the Thames. The authorities regularly railed against the popular habit of discharging human, animal and vegetable waste into the stream; that they had to do so on such a regular basis betrayed their lack of success at compelling compliance. Not until the 1760s was the problem solved, or at least covered over, when the Fleet River became Fleet Street.

Partly as a health measure—to avoid drinking contaminated water—Londoners quaffed alcoholic beverages of all proofs and flavors. They drank beer with breakfast, perhaps following a dram of sherry as an eye-opener; more beer as the morning progressed, perhaps interspersed with brandy to ward off the English chills; ale with lunch; raisin or elder wine with afternoon tea (which was a relative novelty and the principal alternative to alcoholic beverages, with the boiling of the water serving to kill the microorganisms that infested the water supply); grape wine with dinner, followed by punch and liqueurs of one sort or another—"White and Wormwood," "Ratafia," "Nectar and Ambrosia," "Rosolio"—till bedtime.

Not surprisingly, public intoxication was common. "We continued drinking like horses, as the vulgar phrase is," wrote one diarist, "and singing till many of us were very drunk, and then we went to dancing and pulling of wigs, caps, and hats; and thus we continued in this frantic manner, behaving more like mad people than they that profess the name of Christians. Whether this is inconsistent to the wise saying of Solomon let anyone judge, 'Wine is a mocker, strong drink is raging, and he that is deceived thereby is not wise.'"

Often the sots found their way to the theater, where they behaved no better. Crowded into the galleries and the pit, they made ribald jokes at the expense of the actors and, purchasing apples and oranges from the barker-women strolling the aisles between acts, hurled the fruit onto the stage. Alexander Pope, who was busy editing Shakespeare during Franklin's London stay, decried the presence of the rabble:

> *The many-headed monster of the pit,*
> *A senseless, worthless, and unhonour'd crowd,*
> *Who, to disturb their betters mighty proud,*

Clatt'ring their sticks before ten lines are spoke,
Call for the farce, the bear, and the black-joke.

꙳ Franklin frequented the theater and London's various other diversions, initially in the company of James Ralph. In his own words, he "spent with Ralph a good deal of my earnings in going to plays and other places of amusement." The velveted prostitutes were beyond his means, but he evidently engaged in what he afterward characterized vaguely as "foolish intrigues with low women." (Even this characterization struck him, on second thought, as too concrete: having written it in the first draft of his autobiography, he proceeded to cross it out. That it referred specifically to prostitutes may be gleaned from the rest of the deleted description of his encounters with these "low women": "which from the expence were rather more prejudicial to me than to them.") If he visited the bear-baiting dens, it was probably as an onlooker rather than a player; neither then nor later did he manifest a gambling streak. As curious as the next person, he certainly saw prisoners in the pillory and convicts swinging from the scaffold. He retained all his fingers, a fact that attested either to his diffidence in the public pot or his dexterity.

The English affinity for alcohol he encountered on the streets, in the theaters, and especially in the workplace. Upon discovering the emptiness of Governor Keith's promises, Franklin sought employment in the printing trade. Because London supported far more printers than all the American colonies together, there was no lack of work, and he soon accepted an offer from a man named Palmer, who had a shop in Bartholomew's Close. There he remained for nearly a year, making a strong and favorable impression on his employer. Yet Palmer was unable to provide Franklin sufficient opportunity for advancement, and he left to take up with another printer, one who did a larger business.

This second house employed more than fifty men, allowing the proprietor, one Watts, to practice the sort of specialization that would be one hallmark of the industrial revolution, about to begin. Certain men specialized in press work, others in composing, still others in collating, binding, and so on. Franklin's skills were sufficiently obvious that he had his choice of specialties; he initially chose the pressroom as a means of getting the physical exercise he was accustomed to as an everyday aspect of the work of print-shop employees in the less diversified colonial trade.

Partly on account of his youth, partly because of his well-muscled shoulders and back, partly because he sought out the heavy lifting where others did just the opposite, Franklin soon gained a reputation for strength. He typically carried two sets of heavy lead type, one in each hand, running up and down the stairs of Watts's shop, where the other pressmen carried one at a time. Making this feat all the more remarkable in English eyes was that the young American accomplished it without the fortifying aid of the beer the others considered essential to their work. Franklin's partner at the press drank a pint of beer before breakfast, a pint with breakfast, a pint at midmorning, a pint with the midday meal, a pint in the afternoon, and a pint at day's end.

Franklin later described this as "a detestable custom"; whether or not he thought it so at the time, he avoided it, on grounds of expense if nothing else. He rejected the argument that hard work required strong beer, saying that this was silly, that the food value of the beer could be no greater than the barley that went into it. And this food value could be obtained far more cheaply by eating bread, washed down with water. He pointed to himself as proof.

Franklin's fellows in the pressroom could not deny that bread and water worked for him, but they declined to hazard their own health repeating his experiment. For some of them the resistance to change doubtless reflected what they took to be the positive side effects of perpetual semi-inebriation. To a certain extent the resistance revealed an unconscious wisdom that was greater than Franklin's uninformed theorizing. Both Boston and Philadelphia were much smaller than London and had far fewer problems with public sanitation. Franklin had no idea of the risk he was taking drinking plain London water; those who refused to join him had a better idea, even if it was uneducated and informed by custom rather than science. (No one in London who valued health would have drunk out of the Thames the way Franklin drank out of the Delaware on his first day in Philadelphia.) By the evidence of his long and relatively infection-free life, Franklin had an immune system superior to most of what nature or society could throw in his face; despite the warnings of the other pressmen he thrived on his bread and water. They were not all so blessed; it was probably just as well they stuck to their beer.

Franklin's arguments did not fail completely of effect. His employer Watts, having decided that as literate a fellow as Franklin was wasted slinging type sets and swinging the handles on the presses, decreed that Franklin must come upstairs to the composing room. Franklin did so, only to be greeted by the request, which soon became a demand, that he contribute five shillings to the common beer fund of the compositors. He refused on the dual ground that he did not drink the beer and that he had already paid below. His new fellows nominally accepted his refusal, not least since it was supported by Watts. But they engaged in constant mischief upon Franklin's work, inserting errors into pages he had already proofed, misplacing his letters, and generally making his life trying and unproductive. When he complained, as a man they denied knowledge of his misfortunes, beyond attributing it to the "chapel ghost," a mysterious being that haunted those not fully admitted to the local congregation, or "chapel," of compositors. And sure enough, as soon as Franklin gave in—"convinced of the folly of being on ill terms with those one is to live with continually," his older self said—and paid up, the appeased spirit ceased its vexing.

Yet no sooner was Franklin admitted to full membership in the chapel than he began preaching heterodoxy. He convinced some of his colleagues to join him in swearing off beer (at least at work) and replacing it with hot-water gruel supplied by an inn nearby. (That the gruel was boiled may well have been significant in the success of Franklin's experiment.) Not only did this save most of the money the men had been spending on beer, it left them clearheaded for their work (a more critical matter for compositors than for the pressmen). Between the muddle of the beer and its expense, those who resisted Franklin's teaching often fell into debt, with several of them agreeing to pay him interest on money borrowed toward their brew. Thus he gained the twinned benefit of his prudence and their folly, and on Saturday nights collected not only his own wages but substantial portions of theirs. This evidence of his prudence, combined with his reliability (unlike his beer-drinking colleagues he never required a "St. Monday" holiday) and his facility at composition, prompted Watts to put him on the most important printing tasks, which carried a better piece-rate. "I went on now very agreeably," Franklin remarked.

⁓ **The impression** Franklin made extended beyond the community of printers. At his first job, with Palmer, he received the assignment of setting the type for a new edition of William Wollaston's *The Religion of Nature Delineated*. In the dawning Enlightenment, when enthusiasm for Newton was undermining reverence for revelation, Wollaston essayed to defend orthodoxy with the weapons of the skeptics. Nature, far from contradicting the essential teachings of received religion, in fact confirmed them, he said. An ungospeled savage, merely attuned to the natural order, would arrive at a moral code that differed in no fundamental from the code promulgated in the most learned pulpit.

Franklin, weighing Wollaston's argument while he weighed the letters in which he set the book, judged that it failed at certain points. Not every nineteen-year-old would have felt moved to join such a metaphysical dispute, but Franklin by now clearly did not consider himself an ordinary nineteen-year-old. He wrote and printed an essay—*A Dissertation on Liberty and Necessity, Pleasure and Pain*—correcting Wollaston.

Franklin approached his subject syllogistically, after the fashion of philosophers since Aristotle. God was reckoned to be "all wise, all good, all powerful." "If He is all powerful, there can be nothing either existing or acting in the universe *against* or *without* his consent; and what He consents to must be good, because He is good; therefore evil doth not exist." Franklin did not deny the existence of pain and suffering in the world, but rather than interpreting these as evil, he deemed them essentially figments of the human imagination. In a passage that reflected both his reading and his experience, Franklin dismissed the notion of happiness detached from unhappiness:

> It is owing to their ignorance of the nature of pleasure and pain that the ancient heathens believed the idle fable of their Elysium, that state of uninterrupted ease and happiness. The thing is entirely impossible in nature! Are not the pleasures of the spring made such by the disagreeableness of the winter? Is not the pleasure of fair weather owing to the unpleasantness of foul? Certainly. Were it then always spring, were the fields always green and flourishing, and the weather constantly serene and fair, the pleasure would pall and die upon our hands; it would cease to be pleasure to us, when it is not ushered in by uneasiness.

Franklin went on to say something more striking. Not only were pleasure and pain, happiness and unhappiness, indissolubly connected to each other, they were equally allocated among men. "Since pain naturally and infallibly produces a pleasure in proportion to it, every individual creature must, in any state of life, have an equal quantity of each." From this it followed that no one was happier or unhappier than anyone else. "The monarch is not more happy than the slave, nor the beggar more miserable than Croesus." More striking still, in the calculus of pleasure and pain the monarch and the slave were both on an equal footing with a rock. "Suppose A, B, and C, three distinct beings; A and B animate, capable of pleasure and pain, C an inanimate piece of matter, insensible of either. A receives ten degrees of pain, which are necessarily succeeded by ten degrees of pleasure; B receives fifteen of pain, and the consequent equal number of pleasure; C all the while lies unconcerned, and as he has not suffered the former, has no right to the latter. What can be more equal and just than this?"

To the obvious objection that the most cursory glance at human society showed some people to be happy while others were unhappy, Franklin rejoined that appearances deceived. "When we see riches, grandeur and a cheerful countenance, we easily imagine happiness accompanies them, when oftentimes 'tis quite otherwise; nor is a constantly sorrowful look, attended with continual complaints, an infallible indication of unhappiness."

Having disposed of happiness and unhappiness, Franklin attacked the notion of the immortality of the soul. He identified the soul with consciousness and the ability to treat ideas absorbed by the senses ("The soul is a mere power or faculty of contemplating on and comparing those ideas"), and then argued that when consciousness ended, the soul ceased to exist. Perhaps the soul in some way attached itself to a new body and new ideas. "But that will in no way concern us who are now living, for the identity will be lost; it is no longer that same self but a new being."

If temporal happiness was an illusion, and eternal happiness an impossibility, why should anyone strive for anything? Merely to avoid pain. The soul of an infant did not achieve consciousness ("it is as if it were not") until it felt pain.

> Thus is the machine set on work; this is life. We are first moved by pain, and the whole succeeding course of our lives is but one continued series of action with a view to be freed from it. As fast as we have excluded one uneasiness another appears; otherwise the motion would cease. If a continual weight is not applied, the clock will stop. And as soon as the avenues of uneasiness to the soul are choked up or cut off, we are dead, we think and act no more.

Like most such attempts to prove the unprovable, Franklin's effort revealed more about the author than about the subject. Indeed, it revealed more about the author than he cared to have revealed. Although his employer, Palmer, was impressed by the ingenuity of Franklin's argumentation, he decried Franklin's conclusions as abominable. This reaction prompted Franklin to reconsider. In his autobiography he characterized various mistakes of his life as "errata"; regarding this episode he asserted, "My printing this pamphlet was another erratum." Long before then he had burned all but the few copies already delivered to friends.

It was meaningful that Franklin said his *printing* the pamphlet, rather than the *reasoning* of the pamphlet, was the erratum. The pamphlet was a tour de force of logic, another indication of the emerging genius of the author. Some of its premises were open to question—which simply indicated that the genius was self-taught and lacked some life experience and the judgment it brings. But the reasoning placed Franklin on par with men much older than himself and more versed in the argumentative arts.

✄ In time he would recant his conclusions about the nonexistence of evil and futility of striving for happiness. But at the moment what bothered him was the bad impression his essay made. A young man alone in the world, dependent on the goodwill of others, could not afford the stigma of gross unorthodoxy, however grossly unorthodox his beliefs might be. A reader of the *Dissertation on Liberty and Necessity* could readily conclude that if the author were not already an atheist, he would be soon. God was less a real presence in this tract than a rhetorical device. In many ways London in the 1720s was more tolerant than Philadelphia, which in turn was more tolerant than Boston. But London's tolerance had its limits, and Franklin was in no position to push them.

Others were, however, and they found much to praise in Franklin's pamphlet. A surgeon named William Lyons, who in his spare time practiced philosophy, read Franklin's essay and at once demanded to meet this brilliant young fellow. On doing so, he escorted Franklin to his favorite alehouse and introduced the lad to his circle of intellectual friends. Among these was Bernard Mandeville—"a most facetious entertaining companion," in Franklin's words—who had written *The Fable of the Bees, or Private Vices Public Benefits*. This work outraged moralists and made Mandeville a minor hero among those who liked to tweak conventional conscience; not surprisingly, its author saw in Franklin a kindred spirit who might carry the fight forward. Another member of the circle was

Henry Pemberton, a friend of Isaac Newton. Pemberton delighted Franklin by promising to introduce him to the great scientist; he disappointed Franklin by failing to fulfill his promise.

Even as he gained a reputation as a philosophical wunderkind, Franklin made friends by his other gifts. One of his printing colleagues at Watts's was a young man named Wygate, a lover of knowledge after Franklin's heart and a bit of a linguist as well. But certain practical arts escaped him, including the art of swimming. He engaged Franklin to teach him and another friend. The pupils were apt and in a short time exhibited remarkable proficiency. Word spread of Franklin's skill as a teacher and his prowess in the water; one day, returning by boat from Chelsea, several acquaintances insisted that Franklin demonstrate. He stripped, dove into the water, and put on a bravura performance. He showed off various strokes and positions, behaving, to all appearances, as though he had been born in the water. Matching the speed of the boat, he covered more than three miles before taking his watery bow.

After this feat word spread still farther about the talented American. A Sir William Wyndham sent for Franklin and offered a handsome fee for teaching his two sons, about to embark on a long journey, to swim. Franklin was flattered and said yes in principle, but a scheduling conflict prevented the lessons from actually taking place. Despite this disappointment, Franklin inferred that if he so wished, he might make a fair living introducing the sons of the gentry to water sports.

Meanwhile Franklin showed a knack for ingratiating himself to the fairer sex—or rather, considering his failure with James Ralph's lover, to that segment of the sex that had once been fairer but now was less so. After leaving Palmer's print shop for Watts's, Franklin moved to a more convenient residence in Duke Street. His landlady was an elderly widow who reduced his rent on account of his being a strong young man whose presence might ward off intruders. She soon became smitten with Franklin. For his part, he found her delightful. She knew "1000 anecdotes as far back as the times of Charles the Second," he explained. "She was lame in her knees with the gout, and therefore seldom stirred out of her room, so sometimes wanted company; and hers was so highly amusing to me that I was sure to spend an evening with her whenever she desired it." The two would split an anchovy for dinner, laid out on a piece of bread with butter; they would wash this down with a shared pint of ale. As Franklin gradually formed a plan to return to Philadelphia, he desired to save money for his passage; he told her of cheaper lodgings he knew where he would have to pay but two shillings per week. She would not hear of his leaving, and reduced his rent from three shillings six pence to one shilling six. He stayed.

In the garret of this same house lived another old woman, of seventy years and never married. A Roman Catholic, she had been sent abroad to become a nun—there being no nunneries in England since the time of Henry VIII. But her destination did not agree with her, and she returned home, resolved to be a conventless nun. She donated her inherited estate to the poor and learned to subsist on the scantest pension. Her diet consisted of gruel; the only fire she allowed herself in her chilly attic was that required to cook the gruel. Despite the deprivation, she was healthy and by all appearances quite content. Franklin found her a most pleasing conversationalist. He also found her an object lesson in the virtues of frugality—"another instance on how small an income life and health may be supported."

Frugality was more on Franklin's mind than ever as the months passed. London's undeniable excitements lost their appeal upon continued exposure, and America beckoned. "I was grown tired of London, remembered with pleasure the happy months I had spent in Pennsylvania, and wished again to see it." He began saving every farthing and seeking other means of speeding his return. One of his shipmates from the eastward passage, Thomas Denham, the Quaker merchant, explained that he was about to head back with a cargo of merchandise. Knowing Franklin to be an enterprising fellow with a good head, he offered to employ him as a clerk and potential partner. Initially Franklin would keep the books; later he might venture forth and earn commissions of his own. The prospect appealed to Franklin, both for the future profits and for the sooner arrival home. He quit his printing job at Watts's and helped Denham gather his goods for export.

⌐ They shipped out in late July 1726, aboard the *Berkshire*, a vessel in which Denham had a half share. Riding down the Thames, they anchored overnight at Gravesend, where Franklin took the opportunity to go ashore and inspect the countryside, which was agreeable and open, and meet the people, who were neither. "This Gravesend is a *cursed biting place*," he recorded in his journal of the voyage, "the chief dependence of the people being the advantage they make of imposing upon strangers. If you buy any thing of them, and give half what they ask, you pay twice as much as the thing is worth. Thank God we shall leave it tomorrow."

The Gravesenders presumably would have disputed Franklin's characterization; its significance lies less in its accuracy (or inaccuracy) than in the sharpness of its tone. This in turn follows from the fact that the journal of this voyage affords the student of Franklin's life the first unedited, unfiltered rendition of Franklin's voice. Save a couple of inconsequential notes, the journal is the oldest surviving work of Franklin's hand written not for publication but for himself. Most of what is known of Franklin's early years comes from his autobiography, which, like all memoirs, bears the imprint of subsequent experience, reflection, and reconsideration. Franklin the mature memoirist would have found cause to excuse the Gravesenders' inhospitability; Franklin the twenty-year-old traveler did not even try.

Franklin's opinions were not all as harsh as his view of Gravesend. From the Thames the ship turned south through the Strait of Dover.

> Whilst I write this, sitting on the quarter-deck, I have methinks one of the pleasantest scenes in the world before me. 'Tis a fine clear day, and we are going away before the wind with an easy pleasant gale. We have near fifteen sail of ships in sight, and I may say in company. On the left hand appears the coast of France at a distance, and on the right is the town and castle of Dover, with the green hills and chalky cliffs of England, to which we must now bid farewell. Albion, farewell!

Yet Albion would not release them so readily. For nearly a fortnight the wind blew hard from the west, forcing them to take refuge at various anchorages along England's southern coast. The delay allowed Franklin the chance to examine the harbor and fortifications at Portsmouth, and to reflect on the nature of military leadership. A recently departed lieutenant governor of Portsmouth had fairly earned a reputation for severity in enforcing military discipline; for the slightest misdemeanor soldiers were thrown into the dungeon, called "Johnny Gibson's Hole" when said martinet was beyond earshot. Franklin—with the self-assurance of his twenty years and utterly innocent of military life, beyond what he had read—pronounced that fear might indeed be required by lesser commanders to govern such rabble as commonly filled barracks. "But Alexander and Caesar, those renowned generals, received more faithful service, and performed greater actions by means of the love their soldiers bore them, than they could possibly have done, if instead of being beloved and respected they had been hated and feared by those they commanded."

Another delay allowed a tour of the Isle of Wight; here Franklin heard the tale of a local governor who had been esteemed a saint in most of his lifetime by nearly all men, but who turned out to have been a great villain. What struck Franklin was that the man's true character had been discerned by a "silly old fellow" Franklin met, who currently kept the castle and otherwise had little sense about life. The moral? No man, though he possessed the cunning of a devil, could live and die a rogue yet maintain the reputation of an honest man; some slip, some accident, would give him away. "Truth and sincerity have a certain distinguishing native lustre about them which cannot be perfectly counterfeited; they are like fire and flame that cannot be painted." While on the subject of reputation, Franklin noted a statue of Sir Robert Holmes, formerly governor of Wight, who built a monument to himself, with an autobiographical, and highly flattering, inscription. Franklin observed wryly, "One would think either that he had no defect at all, or had a very ill opinion of the world, seeing he was so careful to make sure of a monument to record his good actions and transmit them to posterity."

On this same excursion Franklin and two others took a walk inland, then returned to the coast at nightfall, only to find themselves across a creek from their starting point. A boy operated a ferryboat during the day but now was in bed and refused to get up to put Franklin and his companions across. Franklin thereupon determined to commandeer the boy's boat and do the job the "lazy whelp" should have done himself. Despite Franklin's experience with watercraft, he and the others bungled the crossing, breaking an oar and thoroughly soaking and chilling themselves. As a belated gesture to the owner, they tied up the boat on the opposite shore, less the ruined oar.

Not till the twentieth day out from London did the *Berkshire* leave the Lizard—the promontory that marks England's southmost point—and enter the open ocean. The Atlantic treated the vessel hardly better than the Channel had; the winds of August held stubbornly out of the west, making every league toward America a struggle. Franklin was in too much of a hurry, too much the improver, at this stage of his life to waste time playing games while ashore, but aboard the slow-moving vessel he joined the other passengers in whatever diversions came to hand. He developed a theory of draughts (checkers) that in turn revealed more of his thinking on human nature. "The persons playing, if they would play well, ought not much to regard the *consequence* of the game, for that diverts and withdraws the attention of the mind from the game itself. . . . I will venture to lay it down for an infallible rule, that if two persons equal in judgment play for a considerable sum, he that loves money most shall lose; his anxiety for the success of the game confounds him."

One of Franklin's shipmates accused another of cheating at cards. The accused was English, the accuser Dutch; Franklin accounted the national difference partly responsible for the fraud. "We are apt to fancy the person that cannot speak intelligibly to us, proportionately stupid in understanding. . . . Something like this I imagine might be the case of Mr. G——n; he fancied the Dutchman could not see what he was about because he could not understand English, and therefore boldly did it before his face." An ad hoc court of justice heard the matter; the accused was convicted and sentenced to pay a fine of two bottles of brandy and to be placed in the round top for three hours, there to be subject to public ridicule. The prisoner resisted his punishment, prompting one of the sailors to lower a rope from aloft, which was forcibly fastened about the prisoner's waist and used to hoist him off his feet. Suspended above the deck, the man kicked and pitched wildly, cursing in a loud voice. After about fifteen minutes he began to turn black in the face. Murder! he cried. Concerned that death, if not murder precisely, might indeed be the consequence, the others relented and lowered him. Yet they excommunicated him from their company till he consented to pay his fine. He held out for a few days, then gave in and was received back into the group.

This outcome elicited another Franklin reflection on human nature:

> Man is a sociable being, and it is for aught I know one of the worst of punishments to be excluded from society. I have read abundance of fine things on the subject of solitude, and I know 'tis a common boast in the mouths of those that affect to be thought wise, *that they are never less alone than when alone*. I acknowledge solitude an agreeable refreshment to a busy mind; but were these thinking people obliged to be always alone, I am apt to think they would quickly find their very being insupportable to them.

He contradicted another bit of conventional wisdom, one he placed in the mouths of "the ladies," that alcohol provided the best test of men's true nature and disposition. "I, who have known many instances to the contrary, will teach them a more effectual method. . . . Let the ladies make one long sea voyage with them, and if they have the least spark of ill nature in them and conceal it to the end of the voyage, I will forfeit all my pretensions to their favor."

Franklin did not confine his observations of nature to the human species. On this voyage he commenced his study of the natural sciences, discovering an interest that would make him famous in middle age. Now, as in some of his other early intellectual endeavors, his inexperience showed beneath his analytical power. When a storm stirred up some seaweed, he employed a boat hook to pull samples aboard; among the tangled branches (in some cases attached to the branches) he found tiny crabs. No one in that era knew much about the life cycle of crabs, and Franklin guessed—incorrectly—that the crabs were in fact the progeny ("a fruit of the animal kind") of the seaweed. He attempted to test his hypothesis by taking some seaweed without crabs and placing it in a bucket of seawater on board the ship. He watched to see whether new crabs emerged. Unfortunately, the seaweed died, terminating the experiment.

He made numerous observations of the finned fish of the Atlantic. Most striking were the flying fish and the dolphins (the gilled kind, not the mammals). The reason the flying fish took to the air was to escape the dolphins, which raced beneath them, ready to gobble them up as soon as they touched down. Franklin confirmed this by noting that whenever dolphins were caught by persons on the ship—for food, and tasty food at that—they invariably had flying fish in their bellies. Moreover, the dolphins responded to no other bait the shipboard fishermen had to offer.

Franklin observed the heavens as well. A night with a full moon and intermittent rain showers yielded the first rainbow-by-moonlight he had ever seen. He witnessed two eclipses: a nearly complete one ("at least ten parts out of twelve") of the sun, and a half-eclipse of the moon. Not till late in Franklin's life would precise chronometers allow regularly accurate measurements of longitude at sea; in 1726 eclipses furnished one of the few methods by which a ship's east-west position might be charted. Franklin sat up the night of September 30 to time the eclipse. A calendar informed him that the eclipse would reach its maximum extent at 5 A.M. London time; his own measurement indicated the maximum at half-past midnight local time. From this he deduced that the ship was four and a half hours, or 67 degrees 30 minutes, west of London. By subtraction, landfall lay little more than one hundred leagues to the west.

This news prompted all aboard to scan the western horizon for any sign of shore. "I cannot help fancying the water is changed a little, as is usual when a ship comes within soundings," Franklin wrote on October 2, before adding a disclaimer: "But 'tis probable I am mistaken, for there is but one besides myself of my opinion, and we are very apt to believe what we wish to be true." When five more days brought no sight of land, Franklin employed irony to alleviate the anticipation: "Sure the American continent is not all sunk under water since we left it."

Finally, on October 9, the call "Land! Land!" came from the lookout. "In less than an hour we could descry it from the deck, appearing like tufts of trees. I could not discern it so soon as the rest; my eyes were dimmed with the suffusion of two small drops of joy." Even calculating latitude, while in principle far easier than longitude, was imprecise enough that the captain could not initially tell just what part of the coast the ship had reached; soon, however, someone suggested that the promontory in view was Cape Henlopen at the mouth of Delaware Bay, a judgment confirmed by a pilot-boat that came out to greet them. The pilot brought aboard a peck of apples. "They seemed the most delicious I ever tasted in my life," wrote Franklin, weary of a diet of salt meat, biscuit, and dolphin.

The *Berkshire* ran up the Delaware toward Philadelphia. Most of the passengers, eager to end their confinement as soon as possible—it was now nearly twelve weeks since they had left London—jumped ship at Chester to finish the journey on land. Franklin, reckoning that the long voyage had weakened him, preferred to stay with the vessel. But even he changed his mind at Redbank, where the ship anchored just six miles out from Philadelphia. A pleasure boat bound for the city offered him and the three other remaining passengers a ride. "We accepted of their kind proposal, and about ten o'clock landed at Philadelphia, heartily congratulating each other upon our having happily completed so tedious and dangerous a voyage. Thank God!"

4

An Imprint of His Own

1726–30

∾ Ben Franklin had left Philadelphia a journeyman printer
intent on opening a shop of his own; he returned a budding
merchant, engaged for £50 a year and with every prospect
of earning more, perhaps much more. Franklin's London
stay had not diminished his ambition; if anything, his
experience with Governor Keith afforded a reminder that a
young man who had chosen to strike his own way in the
world could count on nothing but his own efforts and
abilities. The promises of others, however pleasing
to the ear, were trusted at peril.

Franklin took up his new job with customary industry. Thomas Denham opened a store on Water Street with his cargo of merchandise; Franklin served in the store as clerk, accountant (an aspect of the job he quickly mastered), and salesman. As in all branches of the retail trade, the key to success was skill at sales. Franklin possessed the tools of the salesman: he was intelligent, well spoken, a student of human behavior, and determined to get ahead. By his own entirely credible account—an account corroborated by the persuasiveness he demonstrated during the rest of his life—he quickly became "expert at selling." Denham, himself an astute salesman and a proven success in the business, doubtless congratulated himself on acquiring such a promising assistant, one who would rapidly make the transition to partner.

Nor was this the end of Denham's plans for Franklin. With no obvious successor in the business, the elder man took the younger as not merely a protégé but a surrogate son. Franklin, needless to say, had a father of his own, but Josiah remained in Boston, had numerous other children, and had nothing to offer in career terms that approached what Denham was making available to Ben. Future prospects apart, Denham had a hold over Franklin from the (recent) past: the cost of Franklin's passage from London, which the young man was working off in the store.

For his part, Franklin warmed to Denham in a way he found difficult with his own father. "I respected and loved him," Franklin wrote. He certainly might have written similar words about Josiah, if only because he felt he ought to. But Denham was a man of the world, a man of substance, a man who understood success in terms with which Franklin increasingly identified. As Franklin had outgrown Boston, so he had outgrown his father. There was nothing unusual about this; it is a fundamental task of growing up. But the precocious Franklin, having grown up sooner than most sons, still felt the need for a father figure. Thomas Denham filled the need.

From this mix of emotional and pecuniary motives, the two developed a close relationship. Franklin lodged and boarded with Denham; Denham instructed him as a father tutored his son. In the store, over dinner, before bed the two spoke of how Franklin might advance in the business by taking a cargo of foodstuffs to the West Indies to be traded for cash or molasses, or by leveraging his time and contacts by accepting goods on commission from other merchants. Thoughts of the printing trade, which offered no such straightforward path to financial success, dimmed with each passing week. Franklin came to see himself as a merchant.

Fate saw things differently. The winter of 1726–27 brought its usual coughs, colds, and fevers to the Delaware Valley; amid the general ill feeling, Franklin developed a case of what he identified as pleurisy. Pleurisy is characterized by an inflammation of the pleura, the membrane that covers the lungs and lines the chest cavity, and it comes in two forms: dry pleurisy and pleurisy with effusion. The latter involves a fluid (the effusion) that fills the chest cavity outside the lungs and makes breathing difficult; it typically accompanies chronic lung conditions, such as tuberculosis. Franklin had no such chronic condition; consequently his pleurisy was probably the dry kind, which is usually a response to a bacterial infection. In an otherwise healthy person it is rarely life-threatening; this was true even in the days before antibiotics. Yet it can be quite uncomfortable, as it was with Franklin. "I suffered a good deal," he recalled. In fact, he felt as though he might die. The illness "very nearly carried me off," he wrote. He added that he "gave up the point in my own mind, and was rather disappointed when I found myself recovering, regretting in some degree that I must now some time or other have all that disagreeable work to do over again." In this passage, even more than was usual in his autobiography, the sexagenarian author was speaking rather than the twenty-one-year-old subject. Possibly the young Franklin, who had never been badly sick before, mistook his malady for something fatal; but no young man making a full recovery, which Franklin quickly did, ever regretted missing an early opportunity to exit this life.

More critical for Franklin was the simultaneous sickness of Thomas Denham. The precise nature of Denham's disease is unknown, except that it lasted long and finally proved fatal. In time, perhaps, Denham might have left the business to Franklin; quite possibly that prospect had entered Franklin's mind. But all he left in the event was an oral statement releasing Franklin from his debt of ten pounds, three shillings, and five pence—the ten pounds being the price of Franklin's passage from London, the balance an amount forwarded against wages. (It may have been an indication of Franklin's high hopes for his future with Denham that for one of the very few times in his life he lived beyond his means.) Denham's executors and heirs honored the deceased's wishes in dropping the debt, but apart from this they had no desire to share their new wealth with an interloper, however worthy he might be. Franklin was informed that his services were no longer needed, and he was left once more to the wide world and his own wits.

～ **Briefly** Franklin attempted to pursue his new calling as a merchant. But as he might have guessed, a city as attuned to business as Philadelphia had more merchants than it could well support, and, lacking the kind of personal connection Denham provided, he had no luck finding work.

Friends and his brother-in-law Robert Homes, happening to be in Philadelphia on his commercial travels, recommended a return to the printing craft. This course had obvious advantages but required a lowering of the expectations Franklin's taste of the mercantile trade had raised. Philadelphia not being London, it also required accommodation with one of the city's two printers: Keimer and Andrew Bradford. Franklin knew Keimer's eccentricities and Bradford's intellectual limitations. He may have entertained the idea of setting himself up in the printing business, but, lacking capital, he would have had to find investors. His father had mentioned assistance upon his turning twenty-one, which he did in January 1727. But that assistance had supposed steady progress in the craft—and it came with an implicit warning about people like William Keith, a warning that had proved all too true. Franklin could guess that his London adventure fell outside what Josiah judged steady progress, and in any event he had no desire to give his father the satisfaction of being right.

By this time Franklin had severed nearly all ties with his family. He encountered Robert Homes periodically, and he took the occasion of his twenty-first birthday to write a letter to his youngest sister, Jane, now fifteen, said to be a beauty (though Franklin himself had no way of knowing this, not having seen her since she was a girl) and engaged to be married. Without indicating any inclination to attend the wedding, Franklin pondered what he might send her by way of a gift. "I had almost determined on a tea table," he said, in a tone that must have sounded to Jane as patronizing; "but when I considered that the character of a good housewife was far preferable to that of being only a pretty gentlewoman, I concluded to send you a spinning wheel." He went on to deliver a small homily about vanity. "Remember that modesty, as it makes the most homely virgin amiable and charming, so the want of it infallibly renders the most perfect beauty disagreeable and odious. But when that brightest of female virtues shines among other perfections of body and mind in the same person, it makes the woman more lovely than an angel." Beyond this distant and diffident connection, Franklin had rendered himself essentially a stranger to his family, and as a result did not feel he could call on Josiah or other family members for financial assistance.

Consequently, when Keimer, somewhat to his surprise, offered employment on attractive terms, Franklin was in no position to decline. Keimer evidently had followed Franklin's career, at least sufficiently to appreciate the business sense the young man acquired under Denham; he now asked Franklin to take over management of the operations of his print shop. Keimer said he wished to devote his own full attention to the stationery store he ran as an adjunct to the printing business. Franklin would receive an annual salary, rather than the weekly wage common among journeymen; he would supervise and train the others on Keimer's staff.

Thus Franklin assumed his first managerial post. He directed the activities of five men. The oldest, at thirty, was Hugh Meredith, a man of Welsh descent and rural upbringing who had a strength for hard work and a weakness for hard liquor; he also had an inquisitive mind and, except when clouded by drink, good sense. Stephen Potts was another country boy, likewise older than Franklin. Possessed of wit and humor, he showed flashes of promise between bouts of laziness. Beyond these two waged workers, Franklin oversaw three bound workers. David Harry, yet another with hay behind his ears, was Keimer's apprentice. A rambunctious Irish lad named John was an indentured servant who had sold several years of his life to a ship's captain in exchange for passage to America; the captain in turn had sold the indenture to Keimer. George Webb was also indentured but had arrived at that state by an unusual route. Born in Gloucester in old England, he had shown real literary and dramatic promise as a schoolboy, with the result of a scholarship to Oxford. That venerable institution had not suited him, however; he ached for fame on the stage. He took the fifteen guineas scholars were allotted quarterly, abandoned his studies, stashed his gown in a bush, and set out for London afoot. Unable to obtain work as an actor, however, and unused to the deceits of the city, he presently found himself destitute and starving. In his extremity he accepted an offer of transport to the American plantations in exchange for four years' service. He was taken to Philadelphia, where Keimer purchased his indenture, thinking the lad likely to be useful in the literary trades. So he was, although his usefulness suffered from an idle streak and his innate imprudence.

Franklin initially puzzled over the fact that Keimer had hired him, when, with these other hands, he already had more labor than he had work. Needing employment, however, Franklin put aside his puzzlement and accepted the job. Once in charge, he soon guessed the proprietor's purpose: to have Franklin train these novices, better than Keimer himself could do, and then to let Franklin go. Rather than confront Keimer, Franklin joined the game of indirection. He carried on cheerfully yet improved every opportunity to prepare himself for something better. He reacquainted himself with old customers and introduced himself to new. He scrutinized the performance of each of those beneath him, estimating which might make suitable partners. He took advantage of Keimer's sabbatarianism to lengthen his weekends, and with them the time he could devote to his literary and other studies. He experimented with casting types, alleviating the need to send to England for replacements. He taught himself engraving and ink-making.

Perhaps Keimer divined Franklin's strategy; perhaps he simply decided that Franklin had served his purpose. In either case, after a few months he contrived an excuse to break with his manager. One day a commotion near the courthouse, up the street from Keimer's shop, prompted Franklin to look out the window to investigate. Keimer, seeing Franklin not at his task, berated him for neglecting business; he added a few insults that Franklin took the more amiss for being broadcast to the entire street. Keimer continued the abuse upon coming inside, provoking Franklin to respond in kind. Keimer escalated the quarrel; he cursed the day he had consented to give three months' notice in the event of deciding to terminate Franklin's employ. Franklin, angry at Keimer's rude treatment of him and, in any event, anticipating Keimer's next move, retorted that notice would be unnecessary. He would leave that very moment. Which he did, taking only his hat.

⁓ As his anger subsided, Franklin examined his options. They appeared bleak—so bleak, in fact, that he briefly considered returning to Boston. But Hugh Meredith would hear no such defeatism. He reminded Franklin what a poor businessman Keimer was: how he ran chronically into debt and could not, or would not, even keep track of what he was owed. Keimer's creditors doubtless would press him for payment as soon as they discovered he had lost his most talented employee. Keimer's business must fail, and probably soon. The failure would open a way to Franklin's success.

Similar considerations must have occurred to Franklin, yet they ran up against the problem that had vexed him from before his trip to England: his lack of capital. The printing trade was comparatively capital-intensive, requiring specialized equipment that had to be purchased. Whether he bought an existing business—Keimer's, for instance—or started his own from nothing, he would have to find the funds to purchase the equipment. Such funds were precisely what he lacked.

Meredith evidently had been thinking over this problem too. He declared that his father had formed a high opinion of Franklin, and that between this high opinion and his paternal desire to see his son succeed, he gave every indication of willingness to underwrite a partnership between the two of them. Intrigued, Franklin followed Meredith's suggestion to meet the father, who indeed registered willingness to stake the two young men to a start in the trade. Pulling Franklin aside, he added a personal element to the business reckoning. He said he was most grateful that his son, under Franklin's guidance, had sworn off spirits; he earnestly desired that the good influence continue.

Thus it was agreed that Franklin and Hugh Meredith should enter into a partnership, Franklin providing the expertise and Meredith, from his father, the financing. Because the younger Meredith remained committed to Keimer for several months more, the partnership would not commence operations until the spring of 1728. This was just as well, as it would allow time to procure the requisite types and press from London. Meanwhile Franklin and the Merediths would keep their plans to themselves. Franklin might take such printing work as he could find—presumably with Keimer's rival, Bradford.

Yet Keimer was cannier than Franklin or the Merediths allowed. Recognizing that Franklin was the best printer in the province, and not wishing to lose him to his competitor, he parleyed for peace. He sent what seemed to Franklin "a very civil message" that old friends ought not to part on account of a few words spoken in heat. Would not Franklin return, that they might resume their former relation?

Franklin doubted that a change of heart informed Keimer's change of tone. Investigating, he discovered that Keimer was trying to secure a contract to print paper money for New Jersey. The contract specified a quality of notes beyond anything Keimer himself could supply; the only man he knew who could was Franklin. Andrew Bradford also wanted the New Jersey contract; like Keimer, he recognized that Franklin was the one who might bring the contract home. It was to preempt Bradford and win the New Jersey job that Keimer was offering amends.

Franklin hesitated. If he waited, perhaps Bradford would make him a better offer. Certainly Keimer was no joy to work for. Yet he could not afford to wait long, as his cash reserves were essentially at zero. What appears to have decided the issue was Hugh Meredith's observation that if Franklin came back to Keimer, he—Franklin—might continue to instruct Meredith in the printing art, to the benefit of their partnership once they struck out on their own.

Displaying what would prove to be one of his trademark gifts—making virtue of necessity—Franklin returned to Keimer's shop. He improved Meredith's skills, at Keimer's expense; he also taught himself some new techniques. The perennial problem with paper money was that paper, unlike specie—gold and silver—might be multiplied at the squeeze of a printing press. This was a temptation to the legislatures and other bodies charged with directing the printing process; it was equally a temptation to counterfeiters. Shortly Franklin would address the former temptation; for the moment the latter was what concerned him. The chief means of frustrating counterfeiters was to produce bills of such quality as could not be readily reproduced. Governments were willing to pay well for quality of this sort, as New Jersey was paying Keimer—and Keimer, less his own profit, was paying Franklin.

To achieve the requisite quality, Franklin contrived the first copperplate press in America. He had observed the method in London and now repeated what he had observed. He carved curlicues and other ornamentation into the soft copper plates, along with the necessary information about the value of the notes and the authority of the government of New Jersey to print them. After a few intervening steps these were transferred to the sturdiest paper available. The product pleased the New Jersey authorities, who extended Keimer's contract.

Besides enhancing Meredith's skills and his own, Franklin's continuation with Keimer enlarged Franklin's circle of important acquaintances. Security—to wit, a close count on the number of notes run off—required that the printing be done in New Jersey, in Burlington. Franklin made no effort to hide from those authorities looking over his shoulder that his skill, not any attribute of Keimer's, was responsible for the high quality of the product. In this regard Keimer's personal eccentricities inadvertently assisted Franklin. His theological innovations put off more than a few of the establishment types who held positions of political authority in New Jersey; his obstreperousness, inattention to the most basic personal hygiene (he was "slovenly to extreme dirtiness," Franklin recalled), and overall air of untrustworthiness cast Franklin, who cultivated just the opposite qualities, in all the more favorable comparative light.

The social skills Franklin had learned around Josiah's crowded table now helped him ingratiate himself to New Jersey's influentials. He became a prized dinner guest, with his wide reading, his recent experience of London, and his general good manners. He charmed government officials and their wives; the approbation of the latter confirmed the judgment of the former that this young man would go far. He listened with attention and pleasure when the surveyor general of New Jersey took him aside, explained how he himself had sprung from the humblest beginnings to his present affluent estate, predicted that Franklin would soon work Keimer out of the printing business, and forecast that he would make a fortune in the process. "These friends were afterward of great use to me," Franklin recalled candidly, "as I occasionally was to some of them."

❧ **The New Jersey job** ended about the time Hugh Meredith's contract with Keimer ran out and the ordered equipment arrived from England. Keimer, pleased with the profit he had garnered, and evidently not suspecting any new competition, shook hands with Franklin and Meredith and amicably sent them on their way. For some time the covert partners had been scanning Philadelphia real estate; with the partnership now able to come out in the open they leased a house on Market Street, just below Second. The modest rent—£24 per year—was still more than they could shoulder alone; to help with the burden they rented part of the building to Thomas Godfrey, a glassman, and his family. In turn Mrs. Godfrey cooked for the two bachelors.

Almost before they had set up their press and sorted their types, the partners greeted their first customer. Franklin's reputation was abroad in the city, and when a stranger to town inquired on the street where he might find a printer, an acquaintance of Franklin's directed him to the new shop. Expressing a sentiment repeated by many other successful entrepreneurs, Franklin remembered, "This countryman's five shillings being our first fruits, and coming so seasonably, gave me more pleasure than any crown I have since earned."

Other friends and acquaintances sent more business Franklin's way. Joseph Breintnall, a well-connected Quaker merchant, scrivener (that is, copyist), conversationalist, and occasional poet, procured for Franklin and Meredith the printing of forty sheets (comprising 160 pages) of the authorized history of the Quakers. Franklin devoted particular diligence to this job, as Keimer had the contract for the balance of the book, and a certain spirit of competition entered into the work. Franklin resolved to print a sheet a day, beyond the smaller jobs that walked through the door. Quite often this required working till nearly midnight; in at least one instance, when a slip reduced two set pages to ruin, he worked well into the next morning.

Besides the benefit of finishing the job on schedule, Franklin appreciated the positive impression he was making on the sober and hard-working Quakers. "This industry visible to our neighbors began to give us character and credit," he remembered. Many of the merchants, who gathered for refreshment and the exchange of business intelligence at the Every-Night Club, wondered at Franklin and Meredith's boldness in beginning their business when Philadelphia already had two printers and was hardly clamoring for a third. Those without personal knowledge of Franklin asserted that the new enterprise must surely fail. Yet individuals who observed Franklin at work argued a contrary view. Patrick Baird, a surgeon who passed Franklin's shop regularly, explained that Franklin's devotion to work excelled anything he had ever seen. The earliest risers found Franklin at his frame before dawn; the latest revelers saw him there after everyone else had retired.

Unfortunately, even as Franklin was earning credibility for the new partnership, Hugh Meredith was squandering it. Perhaps Franklin became distracted by the effort required to meet his quota of four pages of Quaker history per day and had less time to devote to the cure of Meredith's character; perhaps Meredith listened less to Franklin's advice now that he was a partner rather than a subordinate. Whatever the cause, Meredith resumed his alcoholic habits and soon proved a burden and an embarrassment. Franklin's friends advised him to dissolve the partnership. Franklin demurred, partly from a feeling of responsibility to Meredith and his father, who had made this venture possible, and partly from a lack of funds to buy out his partner.

Franklin may well have reflected—thinking back on his experiences with John Collins and James Ralph—that his choice of associates was not always the best. He doubtless weighed various devices for ending his relationship with Meredith. In the meantime he redoubled his efforts in the shop, both to make up for what Meredith was not doing and to make clear to those merchants at the Every-Night Club which member of the partnership was doing all the work.

∾ Yet business hardly filled Franklin's world, even in these difficult early days. Always the improver, in the autumn of 1727 he organized a club of inquirers into matters moral, political, and scientific. Many years later Franklin told Samuel Mather, Cotton's son, that Cotton Mather's *Essays to Do Good* provided the model for the Junto, as Franklin's clique called itself. If so, Franklin borrowed the model but left the content back in Boston, for rather than the stern religiosity that informed Mather's intellectual world, a skeptical secularism marked the proceedings of the Junto. New members were required to answer four questions: whether they had any disrespect for current members (a negative answer was anticipated); whether they loved mankind in general, regardless of religion or profession (yes); whether anyone ought to be harmed in his person, property, or reputation, merely on account of his opinions or way of worship (no); and whether they loved and pursued truth for truth's sake and would impartially impart what they found of it to others (yes). Topics of discussion included why fog formed on the outside of a tankard of cold water in the summer, whether the importation of servants advanced the wealth of America, how far temperance in diet ought to be taken, and in what consisted human happiness.

The group met on Friday evenings, first at a tavern, later at a house hired for the purpose. To guide discussions, Franklin formulated a set of queries. Had members encountered any citizen failing in his business, and if so, what was the cause? Conversely, were certain citizens thriving, and why? Had any citizen accomplished a particularly praiseworthy feat? How might it be emulated? Were there any egregious errors that ought to be avoided? Had members met any persons suffering from the ill effects of intemperance or passion? Any persons benefiting from the virtuous opposites of those vices? Was anyone departing on a voyage, and might such person transport a message or material item for someone staying home? Had any strangers arrived in town, and had they been welcomed? Were there any young tradesmen who might be encouraged by the Junto's patronage? Were there any worthy citizens to whom one Junto member might be introduced by another?

The group also cultivated the literary arts. Common readings were assigned; these provided the grist for debate. By turns the members raised particular issues of morals, philosophy, and civic life. Every three months each member was required to read an essay of his own composition on a subject of his choosing. Other members would critique the content and form of expression. In order to maintain a constructive atmosphere, the rule Franklin had established for himself—to avoid overly assertive or directly contradictory expressions, in favor of suggestions, hypotheses, and polite questions—was eventually applied to the group as a whole. Failure to follow the rule resulted in small but embarrassing fines.

Franklin's mates in the Junto were a diverse crew united chiefly by an inquiring spirit and a devotion to self-improvement. Joseph Breintnall, the merchant and scrivener, was substantially older than Franklin; outside his work he loved poetry and natural history. Thomas Godfrey, the glazier, was also a mathematician and inventor; he devised an improvement on the quadrant then commonly in use. Nicholas Scull and William Parsons might have employed Godfrey's quadrant, for each became surveyor general of the colony. Otherwise Scull was a bibliophile, Parsons a cobbler and astrologer. William Maugridge was a cabinetmaker, William Coleman a merchant's clerk. Robert Grace was a gentleman, which meant that, unlike the others, he did not have to work for a living. Hugh Meredith, Franklin's partner, was also a Junto member, as were Stephen Potts and George Webb, his former protégés at Keimer's.

However much the Junto drew on the interests and talents of its membership, it clearly was Franklin's creation. His was the initiative that started it, his the spirit that informed it. Franklin took pains not to dominate the discussions; those fines for unseemly self-assertion were reminders to him as much as to the others. Yet if any group ever reflected the philosophical outlook and social sensibilities of one of its members, the Junto reflected Franklin's. This was all the more remarkable—and perhaps the plainest testament to his emerging leadership skills—in that he was nearly the youngest member of the group, with no claim to primacy but intellectual and moral force. Lacking wealth or other sources of conventional influence, Franklin led by example.

～ The more metaphysical of the Junto's discussions drew Franklin back to the issues he had examined in his *Dissertation on Liberty and Necessity*. At that time the harsh reaction of his employer Palmer had caused him to question the practicality of his conclusions, if not their veracity;

yet the more he thought about it, the more difficulty he had separating truth from practicality. Franklin was an original and independent thinker, but he never flouted conventional opinion for the thrill of the flouting—as his brother James did, for example. Having made his youthful statement of rebellion by fleeing Boston, Franklin felt no compulsion to redundancy.

Temperamentally, Franklin was a skeptic rather than a rebel. Indeed, his skepticism made him suspicious of many rebels, who were often as zealous in their quest for change as the most ardent defenders of the status quo were in their defense of what was. His skepticism was probably congenital; such central traits of personality typically are. When it surfaced during his teens, at a time when his reading was rapidly expanding his intellectual horizons, it made him increasingly dubious of biblical revelation. Why should God speak to one insignificant desert tribe, to the exclusion of the vast majority of the human race? Yet unwilling—and in those pre-Darwinian days intellectually unable—to dispense with divinity entirely, Franklin gravitated toward the mechanistic approach of deism. One book written against deism by the chemist Robert Boyle in fact pushed Franklin further in a deistic direction. "The arguments of the deists which were quoted to be refuted," he wrote, "appeared to me much stronger than the refutations."

Franklin's skeptical soul, however, was not really attuned to theology; it resonated less to first causes than to secondary effects. And the effects of deism struck him as unsettling. Deism, he said in his autobiography, had "perverted" his former friends John Collins and James Ralph and had contributed to his abandonment of his betrothal to Deborah Read, in favor of his "foolish intrigues with low women." (This infidelity "at times gave me great trouble," he said, though he did nothing then to rectify it.) In any event, the more he reflected on deism, the less it appealed to him. "I began to suspect that this doctrine, though it might be true, was not very useful." Reflecting further, he guessed that his dismissal of right and wrong in his *Dissertation on Liberty and Necessity* had been too clever, which was to say not clever at all. Truth, sincerity, integrity, and other virtues did indeed exist; they were what made human happiness possible—and the fact that human happiness *was* possible was something anyone not blinded by his own rhetorical virtuosity could see. Franklin remained too much the skeptic to return to revelation as understood by the Cotton Mathers of the world, but now he conceded that if what passed for revelation revealed little about God, it might reveal much about man. "I entertained an opinion, that though certain actions might not be bad *because* they were forbidden by it, or good *because* it commanded them, yet probably those actions might be forbidden *because* they were bad for us, or commanded *because* they were beneficial to us."

This inversion of moral cause and effect came as an epiphany to Franklin. It allowed him to reconcile his skepticism with his practicality. A man had to conform his conduct to prevailing mores if he wished to get ahead; he did *not* have to conform his convictions to the prevailing theology. With a sigh of relief almost audible from a distance of nearly three centuries, Franklin codified his new thinking in what he called his "Articles of Belief and Acts of Religion," dated November 20, 1728. Borrowing from Cato, he declared, "I hold: If there is a Power above us (and that there is all nature cries aloud, through all her works), He must delight in virtue, and that which He delights in must be happy." As the deists did, Franklin measured the immensity of the universe against the minusculity of the earth and the inhabitants thereof, and concluded from this that it was "great vanity in me to suppose that the Supremely Perfect does in the least regard such an inconsiderable nothing as man." Moreover, this Supremely Perfect had absolutely no need to be worshipped by humans; He was infinitely above such sentiments or actions. Yet if worship filled no divine purpose, it did serve a human need. "I think it seems required of me, and my duty as a man, to pay divine regards to *something*."

As to virtue in humans, the Supreme Being valued it not for what it did for Him—since humans, again, could do nothing for One so far above them—but for what it did for *them*. "Since without virtue man can have no happiness in this world, I firmly believe He delights to see me virtuous, because He is pleased when he sees me happy." This same pragmatic calculus prescribed the appropriate use of all things. "Since He has created many things which seem purely designed for the delight of man, I believe He is not offended when He sees His children solace themselves in any manner of pleasant exercises and innocent delights, and I think no pleasure innocent that is to man hurtful."

Thus Franklin, having previously wandered from the pietistic moralism of his Boston upbringing to the agnostic—almost atheistic—amoralism of his London days, now found his way to a pragmatic moralism that made man the measure of virtue rather than virtue the measure of man. The good was what rendered men happy. A more practical philosophy, or one better suited to success in tolerant but sober Philadelphia, was hard to imagine.

‮ Having settled the philosophical issue—essentially once for all, though he had no way of knowing this—Franklin turned to implementing his conclusions. On the voyage back from London he had filled that part of the time not devoted to playing draughts, conjecturing the ontogeny of crustaceans, or making astronomical observations, with formulating a plan of conduct for his life. Throughout his career Franklin would employ metaphors from the literary world to convey lessons about life; he started early. "Those who write the art of poetry," he explained, "teach us that if we would write what may be worth the reading, we ought always, before we begin, to form a regular plan and design of our piece; otherwise we shall be in danger of incongruity. I am apt to think it is the same as to life." He chided himself for the irregularity of his life to date, which consisted of a "confused variety of different scenes." Now that he was entering on a new phase of his life, he felt obliged to make certain resolutions and form a scheme of action "that henceforth I may live in all respects like a rational creature."

His resolutions were straightforward and eminently practical.

1. It is necessary for me to be extremely frugal for some time, till I have paid what I owe.

2. To endeavor to speak truth in every instance; to give nobody expectations that are not likely to be answered, but aim at sincerity in every word and action—the most amiable excellence in a rational being.

3. To apply myself industriously to whatever business I take in hand, and not divert my mind from my business by any foolish project of growing suddenly rich; for industry and patience are the surest means of plenty.

4. I resolve to speak ill of no man whatever, not even in a matter of truth; but rather by some means excuse the faults I hear charged upon others, and upon proper occasions speak all the good I know of every body.

Franklin was proud of this plan, and prouder still, with the passing years, of making it the basis for his life's conduct. Writing almost half a century later, he said, "It is the more remarkable, as being formed when I was so young, and yet being pretty faithfully adhered to quite through to old age."

Having formulated his four commandments on the high seas, Franklin proceeded after landing to identify thirteen cardinal virtues. In typical orderly fashion (number three on the list), he enumerated them, with a thumbnail description of each:

1. Temperance

   Eat not to dullness.

   Drink not to elevation.

2. Silence

   Speak not but what may benefit others or yourself. Avoid trifling conversation.

3. Order

   Let all your things have their places. Let each part of your business have its time.

4. Resolution

   Resolve to perform what you ought. Perform without fail what you resolve.

5. Frugality

   Make no expense but to do good to others or yourself: i.e., Waste nothing.

6. Industry

   Lose no time. Be always employed in something useful. Cut off all unnecessary actions.

7. Sincerity

   Use no hurtful deceit.

   Think innocently and justly; and if you speak, speak accordingly.

8. Justice

   Wrong none, by doing injuries or omitting the benefits that are your duty.

9. Moderation

   Avoid extremes. Forbear resenting injuries so much as you think they deserve.

10. Cleanliness

    Tolerate no uncleanness in body, clothes or habitation.

11. Tranquillity

    Be not disturbed at trifles, or at accidents common or unavoidable.

12. Chastity
    Rarely use venery but for health or offspring; never to dullness,
    weakness or the injury of your own or another's peace or
    reputation.

Franklin's list originally stopped at a dozen. But a Quaker friend
gently pointed out that certain of Franklin's neighbors thought him
proud. Franklin expressed surprise, thinking he had tamed that lion.
After the friend cited examples, however, Franklin conceded that he required more work in this area. He added a thirteenth virtue:

13. Humility
    Imitate Jesus and Socrates.

Other young men—albeit not many—might have compiled such a
list; what truly set Franklin apart was the program he inaugurated to inte-
grate his thirteen virtues into his daily life. The program was straightforward. In successive weeks he would concentrate on mastering particular virtues. There was a method (that is, order: number three again) to
his approach. During the first week he would focus on temperance, letting the other virtues fend for themselves. Once he conquered temperance (in his early optimism, a week appeared sufficient), his steady head
would allow him to move on to silence. Silence would clear his mind the
way temperance cleared his brain; together they would enable him to perfect order. Order would facilitate resolution, which in turn would render
resolution easier. And so on.

To chart his moral progress Franklin compiled a kind of scorecard,
consisting of a small notebook of nearly identical pages. Each page was
blocked out in seven columns of thirteen rows each. The columns were
labeled for the days of the week, Sunday through Saturday. The rows
were labeled for the thirteen virtues, temperance down to humility. The
pages differed only in the headings; the page for week one was headed
"Temperance: Eat not to dullness. Drink not to elevation." The second
page featured silence, the third order, and so on.

At the end of every day Franklin evaluated his progress—or rather
lack of progress—toward making a habit of his virtues. Each failure received a black mark in the appropriate position. During the first week he
aimed to keep the row for temperance devoid of spots. During the second week the silence row should be spotless (as, presumably, would be
the row above it, for temperance, which by then would have become a

habit). At the end of thirteen weeks he would have mastered all the virtues. To allow for stubborn imperfection, and to prevent backsliding, he would then repeat the process—indeed make it a regular and continuing part of his daily regimen. (In this regard the addition of the thirteenth virtue proved convenient, for now the fifty-two weeks of the year neatly comprised four repetitions of the self-improvement process).

Franklin was an idealist of a very practical sort. In this case his practicality guided his choice of virtues, which were well suited to the worldly success he aimed to achieve; his idealism appeared in his belief that mastering these virtues might be so simply accomplished.

He shortly discovered, however, as had countless others before him, that virtue was *not* so simply accomplished. Surprisingly—considering how far the project had already progressed—Franklin found order to be the most elusive virtue. To some degree he attributed this to the circumstances of his daily life. His position as a tradesman required him to be, to a not insignificant extent, at the disposal of others. A customer required a job done immediately; this threw an entire day's schedule into confusion. Franklin's attempts at order also suffered from what others might have considered a virtue—or at least a gift—in itself. With an excellent memory, his failure to keep things in their places, both spatial and temporal, hindered him only minimally in his work.

For a time his inability to maintain order vexed him greatly. But soon he began to rationalize his deficiency. He afterward told a story on himself, of a man who wanted to buy an ax from a smith. The man agreed to pay the advertised price only on the condition that the smith grind the ax until the entire surface of the head shone as brightly as the cutting edge. The smith accepted, on a condition of his own: that the purchaser power the grinding wheel. The man consented and the work began. After a time the man inquired how the polishing was progressing. Steadily, said the smith. The man turned the wheel some more and inquired again. Steadily, said the smith. Again more turning, again the inquiry. Again: Steadily. Finally, exhausted from his labors, the man said he would take the ax as it was. No, no, said the smith; keep turning and we shall have the whole head like a mirror by and by. So we might, said the man, but I think I like a speckled ax best.

Not content simply to accept his speckles, Franklin explained they were better than a polished moral finish. "Something that pretended to be reason was every now and then suggesting to me that such extreme nicety as I exacted of myself might be a kind of foppery in morals, which if it were known would make me ridiculous; that a perfect character might be attended with the inconvenience of being envied and hated; and that a benevolent man should allow a few faults in himself, to keep his friends in countenance." Yet even as he embraced imperfection—he abandoned his project before the end of the first thirteen-week course—he judged that the mere attempt made him a better and happier man than he would have been otherwise—"as those who aim at perfect writing by imitating the engraved copies, though they never reach the wished for excellence of those copies, their hand is mended by the endeavour."

◦— While Franklin's moral calisthenics reflected a sincere pursuit of virtue, he hardly insisted that virtue be its own reward. On the contrary, whatever the virtuous might earn for themselves in the hereafter (a time and place of which Franklin remained skeptical), they could hope to realize material benefits in the here and now. Of course, to do so, they must take care not to hide their virtue under a bushel basket. "In order to secure my credit and character as a tradesman," he explained, "I took care not only to be in *reality* industrious and frugal, but to avoid all *appearances* of the contrary. I dressed plainly; I was seen at no places of idle diversion; I never went out a-fishing or shooting; a book, indeed, sometimes debauched me from my work; but that was seldom, snug, and gave no scandal." Even after he hired an assistant and took an apprentice—this latter the son of the late Aquila Rose—he continued occasionally to do the most menial tasks himself. "To show that I was not above my business, I sometimes brought home the paper I purchased at the stores, through the streets on a wheelbarrow." (This may have had a second purpose. Paper was expensive in America, and Franklin would not have wanted to take a chance on having suppliers shortchange his apprentice or assistant.)

Moral credit in the eyes of his fellow Philadelphians mattered a great deal to Franklin, especially in that no sooner had he opened his print shop than he started to think about expanding operations. In one direction expansion led to the establishment of a stationery store, which required a customer base different from that of the print shop per se; in another it carried him back to newspaper publishing. Franklin pursued printing as a craft and a trade, but simply setting others' words into type left the creative part of him unfulfilled. From the first Silence Dogood letters he had been an author as well as a printer; as soon as the opportunity offered, he would become an author again.

Yet Franklin was never content to let opportunity find him. Andrew Bradford printed a paper, the *American Weekly Mercury*—"a paltry thing, wretchedly managed, and no way entertaining," remarked Franklin, evidently after the expiration of the statute of limitations on his speak-no-evil policy. Equally to the point, despite its deficiencies it turned a profit for its owner. Franklin had no doubt he could do better, in regard to both quality and profitability, and he determined to do so.

But Franklin sinned against silence, and paid the cost. Keimer's apprentice George Webb had found a female friend willing to lend him the money to purchase his remaining time; he told Franklin he would like to join the Franklin-Meredith shop. Franklin lacked sufficient present work to take Webb on at once, but to keep him interested let slip that he was going to start a newspaper. Webb, by accident or design, relayed the intelligence to Keimer, who immediately announced that *he* would be opening a paper. Franklin was short the capital to start a paper at once; he could only watch with annoyance—at Keimer for stealing his idea, at Webb for being the accessory to the theft, at himself for leaving the idea unguarded—as Keimer commenced publication of *The Universal Instructor in All Arts and Sciences; and Pennsylvania Gazette*.

Had patience been one of Franklin's thirteen cardinal virtues, he might simply have waited until he was ready to launch his own paper, then let quality speak for itself. Instead he linked up with Andrew Bradford and wrote for the *Mercury* in a tone that mocked Keimer's pretensions at putting out a paper. In this case Franklin hewed to the letter, although not the spirit, of his speak-no-evil policy, by hiding behind the mask of anonymity. His first salvos came from "Martha Careful" and "Caelia Shortface." In keeping with the *Universal Instructor* promise of his title, Keimer was essaying to reprint the Chambers *Cyclopaedia*, starting with A. Perhaps he was not thinking clearly—a recurrent problem with Keimer, as Franklin knew—or perhaps he was thinking *very* clearly, about how controversy could be employed to sell papers. Whichever was the case, he ran the Chambers article on "Abortion." Franklin, as Franklin, never evinced excessive delicacy on such matters, but Martha Careful, speaking "in behalf of myself and many good modest women in this city," warned Keimer "that if he proceed farther to expose the secrets of our sex in that audacious manner . . . my sister Molly and myself, with some others, are resolved to run the hazard of taking him by the beard, at the next place we meet him, and make an example of him for his immodesty." Caelia Shortface helpfully sent Andrew Bradford a letter actually addressed to Keimer; Bradford with equal helpfulness printed it. "If thou proceed any further in that scandalous manner," she said, "we intend very soon to have thy right ear for it." Mrs. Shortface went on to advise Keimer, "If thou hath nothing else to put in thy *Gazette*, lay it down."

Subsequent articles in Keimer's paper offered Franklin a less obvious opening; consequently his strategy for undermining his old employer took a different turn. The week after the Careful and Shortface letters appeared, Bradford published another anonymous Franklin piece, this one over the signature "Busy Body." Here the assault on Keimer was oblique. "Let the fair sex be assured that I shall always treat them and their affairs with the utmost decency and respect," Busy Body wrote, leaving readers to recall whose paper did not. Perhaps Franklin feared making Bradford, soon to be his rival, look *too* good; in any event, he leveled criticism at the publisher of the *Mercury* as well. "I have often observed with concern that your *Mercury* is not always equally entertaining. The delay of ships expected in, and want of fresh advices from Europe, make it frequently very dull; and I find the freezing our river has the same effect on news as on trade." Yet journalistic criticism was simply a sideline for Busy Body. Gossip was far more interesting. The author cited the proverb that what is everybody's business is nobody's business, then declared, "I, upon mature deliberation, think fit to take nobody's business wholly into my own hands, and out of zeal for the public good, design to erect myself into a kind of *censor morum*." This should afford general, albeit not universally uniform, enjoyment. "As most people delight in censure when they are not the objects of it, if any are offended at my publicly exposing their private vices, I promise they shall have the satisfaction, in a very little time, of seeing their good friends and neighbours in the same circumstances." A typical closing for first letters to editors declared that if this introduction met general approbation, more letters would follow. Busy Body disdained such ephemeral encouragement in favor of something more substantial. "If you send me a bottle of ink and a quire of paper by the bearer, you may depend on hearing further."

Additional Busy Body letters followed. Some satirized Keimer; others delivered wry observations on relations between the sexes, on the pretensions of the learned, and on assorted other topics intended to engage the lighthearted attention of readers. Franklin wrote four Busy Body letters by himself; he contributed parts of two others; the balance of these two, and the whole of several more, were the work of Franklin friend and fellow Junto member Joseph Breintnall. The letters continued until the early autumn of 1729, at which time—not coincidentally—Franklin and Meredith commenced publishing a paper of their own.

◦— The paper they published was actually the one Keimer had started but never managed to make profitable. Franklin's covert campaign against Keimer may have played a part in his paper's failure, but the greatest responsibility lay with the publisher. Keimer's chronic inability to stick to business both limited his clientele—Franklin, who later had a look at Keimer's accounts, reported that the subscription list never topped ninety—and unnerved his creditors, who successfully petitioned the Pennsylvania authorities to have him arrested for debt. This daunted him hardly at all, perhaps because he had been in debtors' prison in London before emigrating to America; upon his release he determined to move along again, this time to Barbados. On his way to the dock he divested himself of his paper, to Franklin and Meredith. Neither party disclosed the sale price; Franklin called it "a trifle"—which was about what the new owners got for their money: a few score subscribers and a name.

Of the name they kept only part. Lest they too be dragged down by the weight of Keimer's failure, they jettisoned all but *Pennsylvania Gazette* from his unwieldy title. Under this name Franklin informed readers on October 2, 1729, that the paper was "now to be carried on by new hands." He announced the abandonment of Keimer's design of printing all the articles from the Chambers cyclopedia. "Besides their containing many things abstruse or insignificant to us, it will probably be fifty years before the whole can be gone through in this manner of publication." Franklin did not think his readers were willing to wait that long. He certainly was not.

Having dispatched Keimer, he proceeded to give Andrew Bradford the back of his hand: "There are many who have long desired to see a good newspaper in Pennsylvania." Franklin proposed to fill the need. The task was difficult. "We ask assistance, because we are fully sensible that to publish a good newspaper is not so easy an undertaking as many people imagine it to be"—here Franklin slapped both Bradford and Keimer. "The author of a gazette (in the opinion of the learned) ought to be qualified with an extensive acquaintance with languages, a great easiness and command of writing and relating things cleanly and intelligibly, and in few words; he should be able to speak of war both by land and sea; be well acquainted with geography, with the history of the time, with the several interests of princes and states, the secrets of courts, and the manners and customs of all nations." As those who saw through

Franklin's cloak of modesty guessed, he judged himself nearer this ideal than anyone else in Philadelphia who might think of putting out a paper. At all of twenty-three years he was probably right. But he demurred from any such claim and instead called upon his readers for help. "It would be well if the writer of these papers could make up among his friends what is wanting in himself." Help or no, readers could count on the new *Gazette* to be "as agreeable and useful an entertainment as the nature of the thing will allow."

One person to whom Franklin did *not* look for help in editing the *Gazette* was his partner, Meredith. With each passing month Meredith discovered further that he was not suited to the literary line. Some of his difficulty may have stemmed from the high standard Franklin set; working beside one of such talents could not have been easy. That Franklin was almost ten years his junior merely made matters worse. Meredith continued to seek solace in drink—again perhaps indulging an inferiority complex vis-à-vis the abstemious Franklin.

The problem came to a head when Meredith's father, obviously disappointed at his son's downward spiral, failed to forward the second installment of the £200 he had pledged toward the initial expenses of the Franklin-Meredith shop. The creditors of the two young men—some of whom may well have lost money on Keimer and were understandably reluctant to be burned again—sued Franklin and Meredith. Unlike Keimer, the two managed to avoid jail, but the suit nonetheless threatened to ruin an enterprise that seemed so promisingly started.

Amid Franklin's distress, two of his friends from the Junto came to his aid. Robert Grace, the young gentleman, and William Coleman, the merchant's clerk, separately offered to advance Franklin the money he needed to satisfy his creditors. But each strongly advised him to sever his relationship with Meredith, who was often seen drunk and gambling, much to the discredit of the partnership.

These unsolicited offers showed Franklin a way out of both of his problems—the one with his creditors and the other with Meredith. Although he hesitated to force Meredith aside, feeling obliged for the opportunity father and son had brought his way, he determined that if the survival of the business demanded dissolution of the partnership, he would take that step.

Before long it did, and Franklin acted. He broached the subject by asking Hugh Meredith if he—Franklin—were the cause of Hugh's father's failing to furnish the rest of the money. Would his father advance the money to Hugh alone? If so, Franklin would bow out of the partnership.

Franklin may have been merely polite in making this gesture; he knew that the elder Meredith was not so blind as to think Franklin was the problem with the partnership. Yet even in the unlikely event the Merediths accepted Franklin's resignation, Franklin would emerge in better condition than he was currently in. He would be free of Hugh Meredith and would be able to take up one or both of the offers of funding he had received. He had dispatched Keimer as a competitor; if necessary he could dispatch Meredith.

Meredith did not accept Franklin's offer. Instead he tendered his own resignation. Sadder but wiser, he said he saw now that the printing trade was not for him. He had been bred a farmer, and a farmer he should be. Some friends were going to North Carolina, where land was plentiful and cheap; he wanted to go with them. If Franklin would assume the debts of the partnership, reimburse his father the £100 he had supplied already, pay some small personal debts of Meredith himself, and give him thirty pounds and a new saddle, the business would be his.

Franklin accepted at once. He reckoned he would be responsible for the debts to the merchants and to Meredith's father in any event, so long as the business continued. Consequently the price of the purchase came to a saddle plus £30 and change. This he got from the two friends who had offered him loans; in addition he borrowed enough from them to satisfy his creditors and to pay back Meredith's father.

The document of the partnership's dissolution was dated July 14, 1730. Although Meredith's name remained on the *Gazette* for some time longer, out of inertia as much as anything else, on that date the twenty-four-year-old Franklin gained his professional independence.

5

Poor Richard

1730–35

∾ Two months later Franklin gained independence of

another sort—even if many persons taking the

same step have interpreted it as just the opposite.

In September 1730 Ben Franklin married.

∾ Love's pathways are rarely straight; in the case of

Franklin and Deborah Read they were more crooked

than usual. He lost her once by his distraction and

neglect while he was in London. Tired of waiting,

she married another, a potter named John Rogers. Rogers

was a competent ceramicist but rather loose with

promises to pay—and, as rumors that

succeeded the wedding suggested, loose with other promises as well. Someone heard from someone else who knew secondhand that Rogers already had a wife, abandoned in England. Needless to say, this upset Debbie considerably. Rogers must have been a charming fellow to cause both Debbie and the vigilant Sarah to overlook his lack of references; almost certainly heartache accompanied the embarrassment Debbie felt at falling for someone so unworthy. Beyond the bigamy, his free spending threatened them both with debts that could not be paid. Debbie, disgusted, left him and returned to her mother's house, where she refused to have anything to do with men or most women either.

Not surprisingly, it was with mixed feelings that she subsequently learned that he had left Philadelphia for the West Indies. No one knew when he would return, or whether. Was he doing to her what he had done to his first wife? (Was that other woman even the first?) His creditors wanted to know, even if Debbie, who wished him good riddance, did not.

Yet the uncertainty of his whereabouts, combined with the importunities of his creditors, left Debbie in a more tenuous position than ever. If Rogers indeed still had a wife in England, then Debbie would have no difficulty getting her marriage annulled, freeing her from his debts and likewise liberating her to enter another marriage, should the occasion arise. But no one knew where this said first wife lived, and Debbie and Sarah certainly lacked the resources to conduct an investigation to confirm her existence. If the first wife did not exist, Debbie was stuck with Rogers, for Pennsylvania law did not allow divorce for mere desertion. The situation grew only more complicated when unconfirmable reports arrived from the Caribbean that Rogers had died. With no body or death certificate, Debbie would have to wait years for legal release from a union that may have been illegal from the start.

Franklin carried some of Debbie's misfortune upon his own conscience. At least so he said in his autobiography, written four decades after the fact. "I considered my giddiness and inconstancy when in London as in a great degree the cause of her unhappiness." This was the noble pose for the world-famous man; it was also rather self-centered. As noted, such guilt as Franklin felt about Debbie at the time of which he spoke was slow to surface. This is hardly surprising in a young man with much on his mind, however poorly it matched the persona the older Franklin projected back onto his past.

Whatever portion guilt played in his thinking, Franklin decided to resume his courtship of Debbie. His primary reasons were far from romantic. A journeyman printer might sow wild oats with little care for the opinion of others, and Franklin, by his own admission and by subsequent undeniable evidence, had continued to do so upon his return from London. "That hard-to-be-governed passion of youth had hurried me frequently into intrigues with low women that fell in my way." But a man of business, one who hoped to win the approval of the respectable element of Philadelphia, could hardly continue such illicit liaisons. Besides, money was tight and time tighter in the new business, and these liaisons "were attended with some expence and great inconvenience"—not to mention "a continual risque to my health by a distemper which of all things I dreaded, though by great good luck I escaped it." Unwilling to press his luck further, or to offend propriety any longer, Franklin determined to wed.

Debbie Read was not his first choice. A young man with promise might expect a dowry as accompaniment to his bride, and Franklin, judging his promise to be as bright as that of anyone else in the city, chose to test the marriage market. His housemate and fellow Juntoist, Thomas Godfrey, and especially Godfrey's wife encouraged a courtship between Franklin and the daughter of one of Mrs. Godfrey's relatives. Franklin took the encouragement and initiated the suit. As the matter grew more serious, Mrs. Godfrey inquired as to what Franklin would need in the way of a dowry. Franklin, feeling quite full of himself, said he would like to retire his debt in the print shop, at that time somewhat less than £100. When Mrs. Godfrey responded that the girl's parents had no such sum on hand, he suggested that they mortgage their house.

After some research the parents rejected Franklin's terms. The printing business, they said, was not so profitable as Franklin supposed— certainly not so profitable that they would risk their house to marry their daughter to a printer who had yet to prove himself. Rather than make a counteroffer, they abruptly broke off relations, shutting up their daughter and forbidding Franklin to see her.

Franklin was shocked. Reasonable and honest people would have met him halfway; these parents, he suspected, having lured him into a relationship with their daughter, now hoped to exploit the strength of his feelings for her by provoking him to elope with her—in the event of which they would have to supply no dowry whatsoever. He resolved to have nothing to do with them. His suspicions seemed confirmed when, sometime later, the parents—evidently judging that their bluff had been called—indicated they would be willing to entertain his suit once more.

Franklin stood on his pride, repeating that he would have nothing to do with that family. In his anger he managed to alienate the Godfreys, who packed their belongings and left his house. Subsequently Thomas Godfrey left the Junto as well. (Franklin gave another reason for Godfrey's withdrawal from the discussion club: "He knew little out of his way, and was not a pleasing companion, as like most great mathematicians I have met with, he expected unusual precision in every thing said, or was forever denying or distinguishing upon trifles, to the disturbance of all conversation.")

Yet as Franklin's anger cooled and he surveyed the situation further, he discovered that the opinion that printing was an unpromising trade was hardly unique to the Godfrey's relations. He might get a dowry, but only attached to an unattractive or otherwise disagreeable woman. Practical though he was, he was not so calculating as to consign himself to life with a woman he did not desire nor think he could learn to love.

So he settled for Debbie Read. She was happy to see him again, if only because he appeared her one escape from the predicament into which she had fallen. Sarah Read likewise approved the suit, for similar reasons.

But the complications of Debbie's predicament seemed almost overwhelming. If John Rogers really was dead, Franklin might inherit his debts along with his wife. If alive, he might return and charge Franklin and Debbie with bigamy. The same mores that prevented Debbie's divorce took an even sterner view of bigamy. Upon conviction both parties might receive thirty-nine strokes of the lash upon their bare backs, followed by life imprisonment at hard labor.

These perils persuaded the prospective newlyweds to postpone their union many months. But with each turn of the calendar leaf the likelihood of Rogers's reappearance diminished, and in the summer of 1730 Franklin and Debbie decided to go through with their plan. Yet even then they adopted an expedient: rather than celebrate a formal wedding, they simply set up housekeeping as husband and wife. This kind of common-law arrangement had evolved for precisely such ambiguous situations; the official sanction it bestowed on relationships grew out of their durability and demonstrated success. Franklin had no relatives nearby to raise objections to such an irregular, if not exactly unusual, approach to marriage. Debbie's relations understood her plight and recognized this as the best, perhaps only, remedy. From September 1, 1730, they presented themselves to a largely approving community as husband and wife.

⌐ The marriage was tested almost at once, in a manner many wives would have found unendurable. Sometime in late 1730 or early 1731 a son was born to Benjamin Franklin by a woman other than Deborah Read Franklin.

The timing of events suggests that Franklin already knew, when he and Debbie decided to marry, that his child was on the way. He would have been unthinkably imprudent not to tell her of such a significant impending occurrence. Perhaps he also knew at that time that he, rather than the child's mother, would take charge of the infant; perhaps not. If he did know, he must have obtained Debbie's consent, since she would be the child's stepmother and, in light of contemporary customs and Franklin's heavy workload, primary caretaker. If he did not know ahead of the birth that he would assume custody of the child, Debbie's consent must have been obtained after the fact—a circumstance fraught with potential for anger and resentment.

The identity of the mother of Franklin's son has been a mystery for nearly three centuries. Because there evidently was no question as to Franklin's paternity, she must not have been a prostitute or someone otherwise particularly promiscuous (at least not around the time of conception). Debbie must have known who she was—as Franklin's fiancée and then wife she certainly would have asked if she did not know already. Therefore Sarah must have known also. Doubtless some other people close to Franklin or Debbie must have wondered where this child came from; the nosiest would have pried the secret out. Some authors have suggested that the boy—named William—was actually Debbie's child, conceived before her marriage to Franklin. By this argument the refusal of the couple to acknowledge her maternity reflected their continuing concern that John Rogers might return and that one or both of them would be charged with bigamy or adultery. Though the child could not well be hidden, the mother might be, shielding all concerned from the harshest consequences.

The initial reasonableness of this argument fails upon the protracted, and finally permanent, absence of Rogers. Even after the passage of years precluded any further concerns about Rogers, Debbie declined to claim William as her own—an omission impossible to imagine in any mother, let alone one who had to watch from close at hand while her son spent his life labeled a bastard. Besides, Franklin's friends all assumed that Debbie was not the mother. " 'Tis generally known here his birth is illegitimate and his mother not in good circumstances," wrote George Roberts, albeit thirty years after the fact. Apparently Franklin had a financial arrangement of sorts with the mother, who was content to remain anonymous. "I understand some small provision is made by him for her," Roberts said, "but her being one of the most agreeable of women prevents particular notice being shown, or the father and son acknowledging any connection with her."

(In the 1760s one of Franklin's political rivals anonymously put out that William's mother was a woman servant named Barbara, who worked in the Franklin household for years, at £10 per annum, until her recent death. There is no reason to credit the story and much to discredit it, starting with the fact that it boggles the mind to think that Deborah would have tolerated the continuing presence of her husband's former paramour. William she could not turn out, though she was frequently tempted; "Barbara" she could have, and certainly would have.)

By all evidence, marriage to Debbie settled Franklin down. This, of course, was much of the point of the match from his perspective, but Debbie could have been forgiven for wondering. For several years his passion had ruled him, with little William being only the most obvious evidence. Whether Franklin could rule his passion remained to be seen. Debbie must have kept close watch.

In the second year of their marriage she discovered, doubtless to her joy and satisfaction, and likely to his joy and relief, that she was pregnant. No longer would that other woman's brat be the only child in the house; this new child would bond Ben to her in a way mere (common-law) marriage could not. On October 20, 1732, Francis Folger Franklin was born. Debbie may have chosen the boy's Christian name, since obviously Ben selected his own mother's family name as the baby's middle name. Sarah, who had joined her daughter and son-in-law in the house on Market Street that served as both domicile and workplace, assisted in the delivery and in the care of the newborn. In addition, Sarah almost certainly tended to little William while Debbie nursed and otherwise doted on Franky. Downstairs, Ben hoped for an extrapolation of Debbie's maternal good feelings from Franky to William.

∽ **Marriage** and the birth of two sons, coming after the establishment of his own printing business, fairly well rooted Franklin in Philadelphia.

Much of his life to this point had been a search for a place that suited his temperament and talents. Boston was too confining, London too loose. Eventually Philadelphia would grow too small for him—or rather he would grow too large for Philadelphia. But during the three decades that spanned his twenties, thirties, and forties, Philadelphia provided a congenial home.

Of course, the congeniality was as much Franklin's doing as Philadelphia's. His founding of the Junto was a first step in this direction. The club allowed Franklin to surround himself with individuals of similar intellectual interests; in time, as the members of the group assumed positions of leadership in the city, its influence leavened the community as a whole.

A second step was the organizing of the Library Company of Philadelphia. Private libraries were common enough among men of wealth in the colonies; Franklin had taken advantage of a few himself. Nor were institutional libraries unheard of; these were usually joined to churches or other bodies heavenly bent. A secular subscription library, however, was something new. Subscribers would pool their resources to buy books all would share and from which all might benefit. Franklin floated the idea in the Junto; upon favorable reception he drew up a charter specifying an initiation fee of forty shillings and annual dues of ten shillings. The charter was signed in July 1731, to take effect upon the collection of fifty subscriptions.

Franklin led the effort to obtain the subscriptions. At first, in doing so, he presented the library as his own idea, as indeed it was. But he encountered a certain resistance on the part of potential subscribers, a subtle yet unmistakable disinclination in some people to give credit by their participation to one so openly civic-minded. They asked themselves, if they did not ask him, what was in this for Ben Franklin that made him so eager to promote the public weal. To allay their suspicions, Franklin resorted to a subterfuge. "I therefore put myself as much as I could out of sight, and stated it as a scheme of a *number of friends*, who had requested me to go about and propose it to such as they thought lovers of reading."

Within four months the Library Company had its requisite two score and ten commitments. Compiling the initial book order involved identifying favorite titles and consulting James Logan, the most learned man in Pennsylvania. Logan knew Latin, Greek, Hebrew, French, and Italian and was said to be the only person in America sufficiently conversant with mathematics to be able to comprehend Newton's great *Principia Mathematica*. Before Franklin's emergence, Logan—who was thirty years the elder and had been the personal protégé of William Penn—was the leading figure of Pennsylvania letters (and numbers). Naturally Franklin cultivated him as source of advice, patronage, and civic goodwill. Logan listed several items essential to the education of any self-respecting person; between these and the titles Franklin and the other library directors chose on their own, early purchases covered topics ranging from geometry to journalism, natural philosophy to metaphysics, poetry to gardening.

Louis Timothée, a journeyman in Franklin's shop, was hired as librarian, and a room to house the collection was rented. Franklin and the other directors of the library instructed Timothée to open the room from two till three on Wednesday afternoons and from ten till four on Saturdays. Any "civil gentlemen" might peruse the books, but only subscribers could borrow them. (Exception was made for James Logan, in gratitude for his advice in creating the collection.) Borrowers might have one book at a time. Upon accepting a volume each borrower must sign a promissory note covering the cost of the book. This would be voided upon return of the book undamaged. The borrower might then take out another, building his edifice of knowledge, as it were, one brick at a time.

⌒ **Franklin** was twenty-seven when the Library Company was founded, twenty-eight by the time the first shipment of books arrived from London. Colonial life was noteworthy for the opportunities it afforded able and ambitious young men, but few took such advantage of these opportunities as Franklin—not least since none were more able and not many more ambitious. The skeptics on the subject of the library were right to wonder what Franklin stood to gain from the project; he expected to gain from everything he did. But his gain, as he interpreted it, would be the community's gain, and the community's gain his.

In February 1731 Franklin became a Freemason. Shortly thereafter he volunteered to draft bylaws for the embryonic local chapter, named for St. John the Baptist; upon acceptance of the bylaws he was elected warden and subsequently grand master of the lodge. Within three years he became grand master of all of Pennsylvania's Masons. Not unforeseeably—indeed, this was much of the purpose of membership for everyone involved—his fellow Masons sent business Franklin's way. In 1734 he printed the *Constitutions*, the first formally sponsored Masonic book in America; he derived additional work from his brethren on an unsponsored basis.

Masonic connections may have been behind Franklin's success in winning work from the provincial government. On the other hand, when the Assembly selected him to print the colony's paper money, the legislators may simply have based their decision on the quality of his product— as demonstrated, on this topic, by the New Jersey notes he had printed while with Keimer. Success bred success; soon he became the official printer to the Assembly. This provided the print shop with steady work and a predictable income, which in turn allowed Franklin to expand his other activities. The stationery store was enlarged; under Debbie and Sarah's supervision new items were ordered and new business solicited. Franklin sent one of his journeymen, Thomas Whitmarsh, to South Carolina to open a print shop there after the South Carolina assembly offered a bounty for a printer. Following Whitmarsh's death of yellow fever in September 1733, Franklin dispatched Louis Timothée to replace him, presumably with a warning about staying clear of low-lying areas during hot weather.

⌒ Meanwhile the *Pennsylvania Gazette* grew into the leading paper of the province. It printed news of Philadelphia and the rest of the province, gleaned from official notices, Franklin's conversations with persons of high station and low, and sundry other sources. It reprinted articles and notices from papers elsewhere in America and from those London papers and magazines that found their way across the Atlantic.

It also published opinion. Some journalists enter their profession from a zeal to right wrong and oppose entrenched authority; this was what had motivated Franklin's brother James—and landed James in jail. Ben Franklin certainly learned from James's experience and from his own experience on James's paper. He had no desire to publish from prison, and even less desire to *not* publish from prison or anywhere else. Journalism for him was a business rather than a calling, or perhaps it was a calling that could call only so long as the business beneath it flourished. Unlike James, Ben Franklin would not provoke the authorities into closing him down. If nothing else, such rashness would lose him his printing contract with the provincial government.

In another person such an attitude might have seemed opportunistic, even cynical. Although Franklin was not cynical, it *is* true that few opportunities escaped him. Yet his attitude toward journalism honestly reflected his personality, to wit, his innate skepticism. No argument ever so convinced him as to preclude his entertaining the opposite. Many people find uncertainty unsettling and insist on definite answers to the large and small questions of life. Franklin was just the opposite, being of that less numerous tribe that finds certainty—or certitude, rather—unsettling. Doubtless this reflected, at least in part, his experience of the stifling certitude of the Mathers in Boston. It also reflected his wide, and ever-widening, reading, which exposed him to multiple viewpoints. Above all, it probably reflected something innate: an equipoise that nearly everyone who knew him noticed and that many remarked upon. It could make him seem smug or shallow; while others agonized upon life's deep issues, Franklin contented himself with incomplete answers, maintaining an open mind and seeming to skate upon life's surface.

In short, Franklin possessed the ideal temperament for a newspaper editor who hoped to make money, rather than win converts. He opened the columns of the *Gazette* to opinions of all kinds, thereby attracting readers of all kinds and allowing the paper to thrive.

Occasionally his broad-mindedness brought him trouble. An outbreak of criticism prompted him to explain his philosophy in an "Apology for Printers," published in the *Gazette* in June 1731. The apology began with a subapology for not crafting his case better, but "I have not yet leisure to write such a thing in the proper form, and can only in a loose manner throw those considerations together which should have been the substance of it."

Franklin was being modest, if not coy. In fact a single sentence summarized his case and that of printers everywhere, while adding the characteristic twist that readers would learn to expect of him. "Printers are educated in the belief that when men differ in opinion both sides ought equally to have the advantage of being heard by the public; and that when truth and error have fair play, the former is always an overmatch for the latter: Hence they cheerfully serve all contending writers that pay them well, without regarding on which side they are of the question in dispute."

As usual with Franklin, the twist wound to the heart of the argument. Readers needed to remember that printing was a business, not that different from any other. Smiths dealt in iron, cobblers in leather, printers in opinions. Yet this was what got the printers in trouble. "Hence arises the peculiar unhappiness of that business, which other callings are no way liable to; they who follow printing being scarce able to do any thing in their way of getting a living which shall not probably give offence to some, and perhaps to many, whereas the smith, the shoemaker, the carpenter, or the man of any other trade may work indifferently for people of all persuasions without offending any of them; and the merchant may buy and sell with Jews, Turks, heretics and infidels of all sorts, and get money by every one of them, without giving offence to the most orthodox." If other tradesmen were required to vouch for the convictions of their customers, there would be little trade transacted. So with printers. "If all printers were determined not to print anything till they were sure it would offend nobody, there would be very little printed."

Franklin remarked that in fact much presented to him did not find its way into his paper. Here he cited a couplet from one of the more forgettable books the Junto had recently received from London:

> *Poets lose half the praise they would have got*
> *Were it but known what they discreetly blot.*

He regularly refused anything that might promote vice or other immorality; likewise letters and articles that might do real injury to individuals.

Occasionally something slipped through—as with that which occasioned this defense of printers. Franklin had published an advertisement of a ship about to sail for Barbados; appended to the notice was an N.B.: "No Sea Hens nor Black Gowns will be admitted on any terms." Franklin, busy as usual, paid little attention to the wording of what, in any event, was obviously someone else's copy. "I printed it, and received my money, and the advertisement was stuck up round the town as usual."

At once Franklin found himself excoriated for malice against the clergy and religion. "Black gowns" was an unmistakable reference to priests of the Church of England; sea hens were raucous birds with whom no decent person would wish to be associated.

Franklin conceded error in printing the line. He knew what "black gowns" referred to, although he said he had never encountered "sea hens" before. Could he do the thing over, he would refuse to print the notice. "However, 'tis done and cannot be revoked." In his defense he adduced some mitigating factors: that he harbored no ill will toward those allegedly slandered, and in fact claimed customers and friends among the Anglican clergy; that he had printed more than a thousand advertisements since opening shop, and this was the first that had given such offense; that if he had intended injury against the clergy, this was an exceedingly foolish way to accomplish it, as the backlash demonstrated;

and—not incidentally—"that I got five shillings by it" and "that none who are angry with me would have given me so much to let it alone."

He recited a fable illustrating his predicament:

> A certain well-meaning man and his son were travelling towards a market town, with an ass which they had to sell. The road was bad, and the old man therefore rid [rode], but the son went afoot. The first passenger they met asked the father if he was not ashamed to ride by himself and suffer the poor lad to wade along through the mire; this induced him to take up his son behind him. He had not travelled far when he met others, who said they were two unmerciful lubbers to get both on the back of that poor ass, in such a deep road. Upon this the old man gets off and let his son ride alone. The next they met called the lad a graceless, rascally young jackanapes to ride in that manner through the dirt while his aged father trudged along on foot; and they said the old man was a fool for suffering it. He then bid his son come down and walk with him, and they travelled on leading the ass by the halter; till they met another company, who called them a couple of senseless blockheads for going both on foot in such a dirty way when they had an empty ass with them, which they might ride upon. The old man could bear no longer. My son, he said, it grieves me much that we cannot please all these people. Let us throw the ass over the next bridge, and be no farther troubled with him.

Franklin noted that should the old man have been seen acting on this resolution, he would have been judged even more the fool for trying to please everyone. "Therefore, though I have a temper almost as complying as his, I intend not to imitate him in this last particular. I consider the variety of humours among men, and despair of pleasing everybody; yet I shall not therefore leave off printing. I shall continue my business. I shall not burn my press and melt my letters."

 Franklin's slip with the sea hens and the black gowns caused him to be more circumspect but no less energetic in soliciting the business of all and sundry. On the contrary, he reached out in every direction he could imagine. He printed notices in Welsh for his small Welsh readership and in German for the larger German community growing up in Pennsylvania. For the latter group he went so far as to launch an entire newspaper in German. Unfortunately, the combination of Germans and their money had yet to yield the critical mass necessary to sustain a paper, and the *Philadelphische Zeitung* expired after two issues.

The *Gazette* advertised a diverse array of goods and services. "A considerable quantity of fresh drugs just imported from London are to be sold in large or small parcels," announced Samuel Chew and Thomas Bond, who kept a shop on Market Street near the market. "Where also may be had most kinds of chemical and galenical medicines duly and honestly prepared, all at very reasonable prices." The Davis family proposed to sell "a plantation containing 400 acres of very good land . . . about 120 acres of cleared land, with a good dwelling house, a large barn and a good orchard, a good meadow ready made, and more may be made; the said tract of land may be made into three settlements." John Parsons offered "a very good new brick house well finished, thirty foot front, two story high, besides a very large cellar, and garret, a good new brick kitchen, stable, and a large garden."

The traffic in labor was equally lively. "A boy about four years of age to be bound out till he is twenty-one, and a likely young woman's time to be disposed of, for between two and three years," advertised Thomas Parry and Isaac Williams, overseers of the poor for the city of Philadelphia. Franklin, either for himself or for a patron who wished to remain anonymous, offered "a likely servant maid's time for four years. . . . She works well at household work, and with her needle."

Traffic in labor included traffic in slaves. "To be sold by Capt. Palmer, two young likely Negro men, country born, bred up in a farm, and can do all manner of plantation work." Another ship's captain, Thomas James, advertised "a young Spanish Indian woman . . . about 20 years of age, and very fit for all household business."

In later life Franklin would come to view slavery as a pernicious institution incompatible with justice, humanity, or emerging republican values. But in the 1730s, at a time when slavery existed in all of England's American colonies, when none but the most radical Quakers considered it exceptional, and when bound labor included large numbers of whites as well as blacks (although the whites were bound for a fixed term rather than life), Franklin's conscience apparently pained him little on the subject. Even as the *Gazette* carried advertisements for slaves, he participated in the slave trade himself, quite matter-of-factly. "To be sold: A likely Negro girl, about 14 years of age, bred in the country but fit for either town or country business. Enquire of the printer hereof." On another occasion he offered "a likely young Negro fellow, about 19 or 20 years of age. . . . He is very fit for labour, being used to plantation work, and has had the small-pox." And again: "A very likely Negro woman aged about thirty years who has lived in this city from her childhood and can wash and iron very well, cook victuals, sew, spin on the linen wheel, milk cows, and do all sorts of house-work very well. She has a boy of about two years old, which is to go with her. . . . And also another very likely boy aged about six years who is the son of the abovesaid woman. He will be sold with his mother, or by himself, as the buyer pleases."

Other notices were more personal. "Whereas Christiana, the wife of John Rubbel of Lancaster County, hath eloped herself from her said husband, and left five young children at home with their father her said husband, these are to give notice to all manner of people that they give no credit nor trust for any manner of goods to the said Christiana on account or with expectation to make any demand on her said husband for anything she buyeth." Nathaniel Lamplugh gave similar notice when his wife Abigail ran off: "He will not pay any debts she may contract."

Masters regularly posted notices of runaway servants. Thomas Mills offered a twenty-shilling reward for "a servant man named John Homer, by trade a shoemaker, of short stature, pale complexion, one of his feet hath been half cut off, and three toes off the other. He had on a light double-breasted coat with light-coloured buttons, and he rode on a small dark bay horse." Christian Grassholt promised a similar reward for "a Dutch servant man, by trade a tailor, talks little or no English, named Hans Wulf Eisman, no hair, about 22 years old, wears a white cap under his felt-hat, white hatband, an old olive-green duroy coat, one sleeve a little torn, a black cloth waistcoat and breeches, white yarn stockings and dark stockings, square-toed shoes with large brass buckles, coarse linen shirt."

Sometimes it was the inanimate that got away. "Lost on Tuesday night last, on the road between Marcus Hook and Chester, a pocket book with 30s. money and some notes. The finder is desired to leave the book and notes with the printer hereof, and take the money for his pains."

Useful or simply curious facts filled the odd column-end. "The small-pox has now quite left this city. The number of those that died here of that distemper is exactly 288 and no more. 64 of the number were Negroes; if these may be valued one with another at £30 per head, the loss to the city in that article is near £2000." "From Newcastle we hear that on Tuesday the 8th instant, the lightning fell upon a house within a few miles of that place, in which it killed 3 dogs, struck several persons deaf, and split a woman's nose in a surprizing manner."

When he took over the *Gazette* from Samuel Keimer, Franklin had promised entertainment as well as information. The two were hard to tease apart on those slow news days when he retailed the latest gossip.

> Sure some unauspicious cross-grained planet, in opposition to Venus, presides over the affairs of love about this time. For we hear that on Tuesday last, a certain C-n-table having made an agreement with a neighboring female, to *watch* with her that night, she promised to leave a window open for him to come in at; but he going his rounds in the dark, unluckily mistook the window, and got into a room where another woman was in bed, and her husband it seems lying on a couch not far distant. The good woman perceiving presently by the extraordinary fondness of her bedfellow that it could not possibly be her husband, made so much disturbance as to wake the good man; who finding somebody had got into his place without his leave, began to lay about him unmercifully; and 'twas thought that had not our poor mistaken gallant called out manfully for help (as if he were commanding assistance in the king's name) and thereby raised the family, he would have stood no more chance for his life between the wife and husband than a captive l[ouse] between two thumb nails.

In the spirit of Silence Dogood and Caelia Shortface, Franklin fabricated letters to the editor. Anthony Afterwit related how his father-in-law had tricked him out of a £200 dowry he had been led to expect, and how his wife, taking after her father, had gulled him into spending the two of them into debt on a lifestyle well beyond their means. Only after his wife had gone to visit relatives had he regained control of himself; he dismissed their maid, sold their fine furniture, traded their ornate clock for an honest hourglass and their pacing mare for a milk cow. He had not yet told her of the changes, however—which was why he was writing to the *Gazette*. "I expect my Dame home next Friday, and as your paper is taken in at the house where she is, I hope the reading of this will prepare her mind for the above surprizing revolutions."

Alice Addertongue was of the direct lineage of Busy Body. As her own existence was rather quiet ("I am a young girl of about thirty-five, and live at present with my mother"), she relied for entertainment on the follies of others, which she duly repeated to any who would listen. "By industry and application, I have made myself the center of all the scandal in the province; there is little stirring but I hear of it." Occasionally she encountered a person of whom no ill was spoken; this she attributed to defective intelligence, which she remedied at once. "If she is a woman, I take the first opportunity to let all her acquaintance know I have heard that one of the handsomest or best men in town has said something in praise either of her beauty, her wit, her virtue, or her good management." This invariably evoked observations on the faults of the woman in question. "To the same purpose, and with the same success, I cause every man of reputation to be praised before his competitors in love, business, or esteem on account of any particular qualification." Particular occupations facilitated her task. Politics, for example, brought forth if not the worst in men, at least the worst in what people said about men. Recalling a recent golden moment of scandal, which she had recorded faithfully, she predicted that "whoever peruses my writings after my death may happen to think that during a certain term the people of Pennsylvania chose into all their offices of honour and trust the veriest knaves, fools and rascals in the whole province." Miss Addertongue urged the editor of the *Gazette* to do his part in disseminating scandal; she predicted a doubling of subscriptions if he complied. To get him started, she included with her letter no fewer than sixteen items guaranteed to besmirch the reputations of those involved. The editor thanked her for her goodwill but declined to print them.

✒— The most famous of Franklin's alter egos was Richard Saunders. Had Franklin known what a lasting success Richard Saunders would be, he probably would have chosen the name with greater care, for the confusion that arose in readers' minds—was this Ben Franklin speaking or Richard Saunders?—was compounded by the existence of a real Richard Saunders, a physician and astrologer who had produced an almanac in London for two decades during the latter part of the seventeenth century. Franklin certainly knew of Saunders; he may have read surviving copies of Saunders's almanac. Yet even if Saunders's publication physically escaped him, the success of Saunders's almanac—and of almanacs generally—did not.

Almanacs had existed in one form or another for several centuries.

The word was said to derive from the Spanish-Arabic term *al manakh*, for "calendar"—although other etymologies were forwarded by imaginative scholars, not excluding the almanac-makers themselves. Samuel Ellsworth, a contemporary of Franklin, solved the mystery once for all, and simultaneously applauded the superlative, but not unlimited, talents of himself and others of his vocation:

> As to the abilities requisite for composing an ALMANACK, the obvious etymology of the word is sufficient to convince us that in the opinion of the ancients they must be very extraordinary; ALMANACK, an evident abbreviation of ALL MY KNACK, or ALL MAN'S KNACK, plainly intimating, in the most expressive and laconic manner, that ALMANACK was the *ne plus ultra* of human genius, that this astonishing art engrossed all the powers and faculties of the mind, to that degree that a man that had a KNACK at this could not have had a KNACK at anything else.

As the more pedestrian Arabic origin suggested, almanacs were constructed around a calendar. Samuel Atkins, who produced an almanac in Pennsylvania half a century before Franklin, explained that on his journeys through the mid-Atlantic provinces he found "the people generally complaining that they scarcely knew how the time passed, nor that they hardly knew the day of rest, or Lord's day, when it was, for want of a diary, or daybook, which we call an *Almanack*."

Calendar-keeping was complicated in Franklin's era by the confusion that attended the changeover from the Julian calendar to the Gregorian. Catholic Europe had accepted Pope Gregory XIII's reform in the late sixteenth century, but Protestant Europe, including England, remained behind the times—literally, by about eleven days. The question of when the year started also occasioned confusion: in March, according to the old style, or January, by the new? A person happening upon an antique newspaper bearing such date as "January 6, 1705" needed to know whether this was old style or new, since the difference amounted to nearly a whole year. (Thus Franklin, born January 6, 1705, by the old calendar, was born January 17, 1706, by the new.) Conscientious date-writers solved the problem by the device of "January 6, 1705/6." Not till 1752 would the British government formally decree the changeover within the British empire.

Beyond mere enumeration of days, almanacs noted fixed holidays and such movable feasts as Easter. They charted the phases of the moon, which constituted essential intelligence for travelers and others in an era before extensive artificial lighting, and the related timing of tides, upon which sailors and fishermen, as well as seafaring travelers, depended. Farmers relied on the almanacs' identification of likely latest and earliest frosts. Citizens with legal business took note of the court-meeting days.

No one, of that age or later, could deny the influence of the sun and moon on human existence; from this incontrovertible fact it was a small step to the belief that other heavenly bodies also influenced life on earth. Although Newton was demystifying the mechanism of the cosmos, astrology retained a hold over many people who knew no better explanation for myriad misfortunes large and small, for wondrous and mundane delights, and for all those other things that remained inexplicable in a prescientific time. Almanac-makers may have placed more or less importance on planetary conjunctions and transits than almanac readers, who themselves varied greatly in the store they put in such things. But readers expected astrology with their equinoxes and eclipses, and publishers did not disappoint them.

Readers expected other expert information as well. For centuries astrologers had doubled as physicians, and vice versa—the real Richard Saunders being a recent example. Moreover, an age that swallowed the idea of witches hardly choked on a magical connection between the macrocosm of the stars and planets and the microcosm of the liver and bowels. Almanackers made the connection explicit; the "man of signs," a woodcut or engraving identifying various organs with signs of the zodiac (the two arms with Gemini, the heart with Leo, the bowels with Virgo, and so on), was a standard feature of nearly every almanac. On a more practical plane, almanacs included recipes for poultices, emetics, and potions that ranged from the rankly superstitious to the semiscientific. What a later era would call psychological counseling was included as well; this completed a circle with the astrological element by identifying particular days as good for this activity or bad for that.

Style, naturally, counted. Indeed, it counted for a great deal, since most of the substance of what went into almanacs was common knowledge—or common ignorance, as the case happened to be. The very familiarity of almanacs made them old friends to their readers; to tamper too much with the formula would disappoint—and damage sales. In consequence, such differentiation as took place between almanacs took place within relatively narrow constraints. What an almanacker said often mattered less than how he—or she, in a few cases (including that of James Franklin's widow and Ben's sister-in-law, Ann, who took over the printing business upon her husband's death in 1735)—said it.

In short, almanacs attempted to be all things to all people. One English almanacker summarized the craft:

> *Wit, learning, order, elegance of phrase,*
> *Health, and the art to lengthen out our days,*
> *Philosophy, physic and poesie,*
> *All this, and more, in this book to see.*

The best of the almanacs succeeded famously. Sales figures are elusive, but such as survive indicate that in England in the 1660s, total sales averaged about 400,000 annually. Even after the government, remarking the plumpness of this goose, levied a fat tax, sales topped 450,000 a century later. In America, almanac publications outstripped those of all other books combined during the seventeenth and eighteenth centuries. The most popular of the American almanacs, produced by Nathaniel Ames, sold between 50,000 and 60,000 per year. A man could get rich by almanacs.

⁓ Franklin intended to do just that. He had already been in the business of publishing almanacs, starting with Thomas Godfrey's *Pennsylvania Almanack* in 1729 (for 1730) followed by John Jerman's *American Almanack* the next year. Either Jerman was hard to please or he liked to keep his printers off balance; he had been with Andrew Bradford before coming to Franklin, and he returned to Bradford in 1732. Godfrey too abandoned Franklin for Bradford that year, perhaps for economic reasons, perhaps as part of the general falling-out between his family and Franklin. Whatever the reasons, Franklin found himself staring at the final months of 1732—prime almanac season—with nothing to offer his customers.

So he decided to write his own. He stole the name of Richard Saunders from the deceased astrologer-doctor. He borrowed—apparently without asking—and adapted the title of an almanac his brother James was publishing at Newport: *Poor Robin's Almanack* (itself appropriated from a seventeenth-century almanac published under the same title in London). His format followed any number of other almanacs. His facts were public property or easily deducible therefrom.

What was peculiarly Franklin about *Poor Richard* was the pushy manner in which he marketed it and the distinctive voice in which its author spoke. "Just Published for 1733," declared the *Gazette* on December 28, 1732:

> Poor Richard: An Almanack containing the Lunations, Eclipses, Planets' Motions and Aspects, Weather, Sun and Moon's Rising and Setting, High Water, &c., besides many pleasant and witty Verses, Jests and Sayings, Author's Motive of Writing, Prediction of the Death of his friend Mr. Titan Leeds, Moon no Cuckold, Batchelor's Folly, Parson's Wine and Baker's Pudding, Short Visits, Kings and Bears, New Fashions, Game for Kisses, Katherine's Love, Different Sentiments, Signs of a Tempest, Death a Fisherman, Conjugal Debate, Men and Melons, H. the Prodigal, Breakfast in Bed, Oyster Lawsuit &c.

Gazette readers intrigued enough to buy the bound version (priced at three shillings sixpence per dozen, obviously intended for resale) or the broadsheet edition (two shillings sixpence the dozen) were introduced to Richard Saunders, Philomath—a standard honorific for almanacmakers—by Saunders himself. "Courteous Reader, I might in this place attempt to gain thy favour by declaring that I write almanacks with no other view than the public good; but in this I should not be sincere, and men are nowadays too wise to be deceived by pretenses how specious soever." Like the printer Franklin apologizing for the advertisement that gave offense to certain customers, Saunders confessed to monetary motives. "The plain truth of the matter is, I am excessive poor, and my wife, good woman, is, I tell her, excessive proud. She cannot bear, she says, to sit spinning in her shift of tow while I do nothing but gaze at the stars, and has threatened to burn all my books and rattling-traps (as she calls my instruments) if I do not make some profitable use of them for the good of my family. The printer has offered me some considerable share of the profits, and I have thus begun to comply with my Dame's desire."

Twenty-five years earlier Jonathan Swift, writing as Isaac Bickerstaff, had drawn attention to his own almanac by solemnly predicting the death of his rival John Partridge. Lampooning those who took astrological predictions seriously, Swift supplied the precise day and hour of Partridge's demise: 11 P.M. on March 29, 1708. The dread day arrived, and was followed shortly by printed accounts, written in a style suspiciously Swiftian, of Partridge's passing. Partridge, outraged, protested that he remained very much alive. Swift dismissed the protests as a hoax perpetrated by persons intent on deceiving the public.

Franklin knew of the Swift stratagem—and knew that most readers in America did not. So he had Richard Saunders declare that the only reason he was commencing publication of his almanac just now—he had long been excessive poor and his wife excessive proud—was that his good friend and fellow student of the stars, Mr. Titan Leeds, was about to expire. Mr. Leeds (really) published an almanac of his own each year, and Saunders said he had not wished to injure him in any regard. "But this obstacle (I am far from speaking it with pleasure) is soon to be removed, since inexorable death, who was never known to respect merit, has already prepared the mortal dart, the fatal sifter has already extended her destroying shears, and that ingenious man must soon be taken from us."

Typically, Franklin twisted the template he employed; he injected an element of competition into his forecast of impending doom. As colleagues in the astrologic art, Saunders said, both he and Mr. Leeds had cast the latter's horoscope. By Saunders's calculation, death would come for Leeds at 3:29 P.M. on October 17, 1733. By Leeds's calculation (Saunders said), it would tarry till the 26th of the same month. "This small difference between us we have disputed whenever we have met these 9 years past. . . . Which of us is most exact, a little time will now determine." Yet whether Leeds's days were the few more or the few less, they were, by Saunders's reckoning, irretrievably delimited. "As therefore these provinces may not longer expect to see any of his performances after this year, I think myself free to take up the task, and request a share of the public encouragement." The reader—purchaser, rather—who provided such encouragement might consider himself "not only as purchasing an useful utensil but as performing an act of charity to his poor friend and servant, R. Saunders."

A principal advantage of being one's own printer lay in the opportunity to wait till the last moment to put thought to type; Franklin waited for Titan Leeds to publish his response, in his own almanac for 1734, before taking his hoax to the next step. Leeds upbraided Franklin for Saunders's "false prediction," noting for the benefit of his readers that "I have by the mercy of God lived to write a Diary for the year 1734, and to publish the folly and ignorance of this presumptuous author." Leeds was especially incensed at Franklin's "gross falsehood" in asserting that he—Leeds—had had the temerity to forecast his own death. "I do not pretend to that knowledge, although he has usurped the knowledge of the Almighty herein, and manifested himself a fool and a liar." Carefully dating and timing his authorship of this preface as precisely 3:33 P.M. on

October 18, 1733, safely past Saunders's alleged hour of doom, Leeds reminded readers that he had been providing almanacs for many years before Franklin ever appeared, and concluded, "So perhaps I may live to write when his performances are dead."

By responding so, Leeds delivered himself into Franklin's hands. Saunders rejoined, in the preface to *Poor Richard* for 1734, that although an illness in his own family had prevented him from being present at Mr. Leeds's mortal moment—"to receive his last embrace, to close his eyes, and do the duty of a friend in performing the last offices to the departed"—the woeful event must indeed have occurred.

> There is the strongest probability that my dear friend is no more, for there appears in his name, as I am assured, an almanack for the year 1734, in which I am treated in a very gross and unhandsome manner, in which I am called *a false predicter, an ignorant, a conceited scribbler, a fool, and a liar.* Mr. Leeds was too well bred to use any man so indecently and so scurrilously, and moreover his esteem and affection for me was extraordinary. So that it is to be feared that pamphlet may be only a contrivance of somebody or other, who hopes perhaps to sell two or three years' almanacks still, by the sole force and virtue of Mr. Leeds's name.

Notwithstanding his distress at this unfortunate turn of events, Saunders explained to readers that his life on the whole was much improved from the previous year:

> Your kind and charitable assistance last year, in purchasing so large an impression of my almanacks, has made my circumstances much more easy in the world, and requires my grateful acknowledgment. My wife has been enabled to get a pot of her own, and is no longer obliged to borrow one from a neighbor, nor have we ever since been without something of our own to put in it. She has also got a pair of shoes, two new shifts, and a new warm petticoat; and for my part, I have bought a second-hand coat, so good that I am now not ashamed to go to town or be seen there. These things have rendered her temper so much more pacific than it used to be, that I may say I have slept more, and more quietly within this last year, than in the three foregoing years put together. Accept my hearty thanks therefor, and my sincere wishes for your health and prosperity.

Leeds learned only a little from his first encounter with Franklin. He congratulated Saunders for his good fortune and that of his wife; yet he could not help asking, for the sake of his readers, "If falsehood and ingenuity be so rewarded, what may he expect if he ever be in a capacity to publish that that is either just or according to art?" Leeds then attempted to brush away this pesky fly: "I shall say little more about him than, as a friend, to advise he will never take upon him to predict or ascribe any person's death till he has learned to do it better than he did before."

Franklin refused to let Leeds off so easily. "Whatever may be the music of the spheres, how great soever the harmony of the stars, 'tis certain there is no harmony among the stargazers; but they are perpetually growling and snarling at one another like strange curs, or like some men at their wives." Of course, it was Franklin who had upset the harmony of the stargazers by trying to break into the almanac market, yet the device of Saunders allowed him to massage the truth with impunity and imagination:

> I had resolved to keep the peace on my own part, and affront none of them; and I shall persist in that resolution. But having received much abuse from Titan Leeds deceased (Titan Leeds when living would not have used me so!) I say, having received much abuse from the Ghost of Titan Leeds, who pretends to be still living, and to write almanacks in spite of me and my predictions, I cannot help saying, that though I take it patiently, I take it very unkindly.
>
> And whatever he may pretend, 'tis undoubtedly true that he is really defunct and dead. First because the stars are seldom disappointed, never but in the case of wise men, *sapiens dominabitur astris,* and they foreshowed his death at the time I predicted it. Secondly, 'twas requisite and necessary he should die punctually at that time, for the honour of astrology, the art professed both by him and his father before him. Thirdly, 'tis plain to everyone that reads his last two almanacks (for 1734 and 35) that they are not written with that *life* his performances used to be written with: the wit is low and flat, the little hints dull and spiritless, nothing smart in them but Hudibras's verses against astrology at the heads of the months in the last, which no astrologer but a *dead one* would have inserted; and no man *living* would or could write such stuff as the rest.

Franklin—Saunders, rather—then employed, or misemployed, the words of Leeds himself to deliver the coup de grâce:

In his preface to his almanack for 1734, he says, "Saunders adds another *gross falsehood* in his almanack, viz., that by my own calculation I shall *survive* until the 26th of the said month October 1733, which is as *untrue* as the former." Now if it be, as Leeds says, *untrue* and a *gross falsehood* that he survived till the 26th of October 1733, then it is certainly true that he died *before* that time. And if he died before that time, he is dead now, to all intents and purposes, anything he may say to the contrary notwithstanding.

Franklin milked the ploy shamelessly. In the preface to *Poor Richard 1736* he registered his utter indignation that persons envious of his ability to forecast a man's death should try to steal his reputation by asserting that he—Richard Saunders, Philomath—did not exist. "If there were no such man as I am, how is it possible I should appear publicly to hundreds of people, as I have done for several years past, in print?" Saunders said he would not have deigned to notice these slanders but for the sake of his printer, "to whom my enemies are pleased to ascribe my productions, and who it seems is as unwilling to father my offspring as I am to lose the credit of it."

When Titan Leeds really *did* die, Franklin refused to let him rest in peace. Speaking of Leeds's publishers, Saunders reminded his readers how for several years the Bradfords (William Bradford printed a New York edition to complement Andrew's Philadelphia version) had refused to admit that Leeds was dead. "At length when the truth could no longer be concealed from the world, they confess his death in their Almanack for 1739, but pretend that he died not till last year, and that before his departure he had furnished them with calculations for 7 years to come. Ah, *My Friends,* these are poor shifts and thin disguises." As it happened, Saunders said, just three days earlier Titan Leeds himself had communicated in writing with him from that place where all philomaths must go sooner or later. In this letter, which Saunders helpfully included with his preface, so that readers might know the truth, Leeds reported that Saunders's original prediction had been accurate—"with a variation only of 5 min. 53 sec. which must be allowed to be no great matter in such cases."

◦— As was apparent to the least attentive reader, Franklin thoroughly enjoyed adopting the guise of Richard Saunders. Where Franklin the businessman had to be circumspect, careful not to offend, Saunders the almanacker could be outrageous—indeed, the more outrageous the better. Franklin as Franklin often had to hide his gifts to avoid inspiring envy; Franklin as Saunders could flaunt his wit, erudition, and general brilliance. In time—as his position in the community grew more secure—Franklin would no longer require Richard Saunders; till then the alter ego helped keep him sane.

Readers enjoyed *Poor Richard* as much as Franklin did. Copies went out the door by the single and the gross. In one year John Peter Zenger of New York (lately the defendant in a celebrated libel trial) took eighteen dozen in a batch, then another sixteen dozen. Louis Timothée (who now generally went by Lewis Timothy) in South Carolina ordered twenty-five dozen; Thomas Fleet in Boston also took twenty-five dozen. James Franklin's widow, Ann, in Newport bought one thousand. These numbers hardly made *Poor Richard* the bestselling almanac in America; where *Poor Richard* sold an average of about ten thousand per year, Nathaniel Ames's *Astronomical Diary* sold five to six times as many. But *Poor Richard* had a unique persona, and it developed a loyal readership.

While readers may have come for the quarrels Franklin provoked, they stayed for the advice he dispensed—and the way he dispensed it. Every almanac offered pearls of wisdom on personal conduct and related matters of daily life; that the pearls had been retrieved from other oysters bothered no one except perhaps the owners of those other oysters, who in any event had no recourse in the absence of applicable copyright law. The trick for writers like Franklin was to polish the pearls and set them distinctively; in this he had no peer. What came to be called "the sayings of Poor Richard" first surfaced as filler on the calendar pages of the almanac; the limitations of space, together with Franklin's inherent economy, taught him to distill each message to its morsel. "Great talkers, little doers" broke no philosophical ground, but for pith it trumped nearly every alternative. "Hunger never saw bad bread"; "Light purse, heavy heart"; "Industry need not wish"; and "Gifts burst rocks" fell into the same category.

Sometimes succinctness yielded—slightly—to sauciness. "Neither a fortress nor a maidenhead will hold out long after they begin to parley."

"Marry your son when you will but your daughter when you can." "Tell a miser he's rich, and a woman she's old, you'll get no money of one nor kindness of t'other." "Prythee isn't Miss Cloe's a comical case?/She lends out her tail, and she borrows her face." "The greatest monarch on the proudest throne is obliged to sit upon his own arse." "Force shits upon reason's back."

Poor Richard jabbed at both sexes about equally, and at the professions ecumenically. "One good husband is worth two good wives, for the scarcer things are, the more they're valued." "When man and woman die, as poets sung/His heart's the last part moves, her last the tongue." "He's a fool that makes his doctor his heir." "God heals, and the doctor takes the fees." "God works wonders now and then/Behold! a lawyer, an honest man!" "A countryman between two lawyers is like a fish between two cats." "Never spare the parson's wine, nor the baker's pudding." "Eyes and priests bear no jests."

The success of *Poor Richard* would eventually cause Franklin to temper his tone, as the author became increasingly identified with—and therefore publicly responsible for—his creation. But meanwhile Richard Saunders remained "Poor Dick" (as Deborah Franklin liked to call him), irreverent and earthy. "Ignorant men wonder how we astrologers foretell the weather so exactly, unless we deal with the old black Devil," he wrote.

Alas! 'tis easy as pissing abed. For instance: the stargazer peeps at the heavens through a long glass; he sees perhaps Taurus, or the great bull, in a mighty chase, stamping on the floor of his house, swinging his tail about, stretching out his neck, and opening wide his mouth. 'Tis natural from these appearances to judge that this furious bull is puffing, blowing, and roaring. Distance being considered, and time allowed for all this to come down, there you have wind and thunder.

He spies perhaps Virgo (or the Virgin); she turns her head round as it were to see if anybody observed her; then crouching down gently, with her hands on her knees, she looks wistfully for a while right forward. He judges rightly what she's about; and having calculated the distance and allowed time for its falling, finds that next spring we shall have a fine April shower.

6

Citizen

1735–40

❧ Although Richard Saunders could say things Benjamin Franklin could not, the sustained success of the almanac afforded Franklin a financial security that allowed him— indeed, given his self-confidence in his own judgment, encouraged him—to test the waters of political controversy. One whirlpool surrounded the perennial problem of money—that is, currency. During the half decade after his arrival in Philadelphia, the economy of Pennsylvania improved dramatically. The boarded windows that had greeted him on his first morning there had reopened, with new and newly active merchants and tradesmen announcing their intention to do business, and customers responding with alacrity and cash.

The alacrity reflected the rapid growth of the population of the colony, as thousands of immigrants, including a large contingent of German Pietists, accepted the promise handed down from William Penn to his heirs, of free religion and cheap land. The filling-in of the hinterland spurred demand for the myriad things the farmers required and the city sold.

As for the cash, that was the consequence of an experiment in liquidity begun by the Pennsylvania Assembly in the year of Franklin's arrival. Following the lead of Massachusetts and other colonies, Pennsylvania in 1723 authorized the issue of paper currency—actually, bills of credit backed by real estate—to the amount of £45,000. A similar law of 1726 extended the idea of a paper issue, eliciting an enthusiastic response from the business class, which accounted the currency responsible for lubricating the gears of commerce and thereby promoting the prosperity of the province.

Yet lunch was no freer in the eighteenth century than before or since, and what pleased merchants and debtors dismayed landlords and creditors. The latter groups alleged trickery, even fraud, in the issue of paper; the inflation that inevitably followed flimsy money, they said, was nothing but theft.

Franklin entered the fray in 1729. He wrote and printed *A Modest Enquiry into the Nature and Necessity of a Paper-Currency*, a treatise that combined what he read with what he saw and heard. Most important of his reading was the work of William Petty, an early advocate of the labor theory of value later adopted by Marxists and others; Petty's views would color Franklin's thinking on political economy his whole life. As for his personal observations, these included his experiences as a businessman and the intelligence he gathered as a newspaper editor and a generally aware individual.

As with his earlier essay on metaphysics, his argument for a paper currency was less noteworthy for what it said about its subject than for what it said about its author. Franklin was not an original economist and would never become one, although his observations in other areas—population growth, for instance—would greatly influence the work of economists. Yet at twenty-three he did not hesitate to engage the theorists on their own ground, and if his insights gave little instruction to the experts, they conveyed the subject to the amateurs who formed his true—and growing—audience.

The gist of his argument was that a scarcity of circulating money elevated interest rates and thereby retarded trade. Merchants had to borrow to finance inventories; the greater the cost of the borrowing, the smaller the inventories financed. High interest rates also discouraged land sales by pricing potential buyers out of the market. The general phenomenon was at once an obvious application of the law of supply and demand and an observed inference from the behavior of the Pennsylvania economy. The opposite was equally obvious and observable. "We have already experienced how much the increase of our currency by what paper money has been made, has encouraged our trade." The single example of shipbuilding illustrated the point:

> It may not be amiss to observe under this head what a great advantage it must be to us as a trading country that has workmen and all the materials proper for that business within itself, to have ship-building as much as possible advanced: For every ship that is built here for the English merchants gains the province her clear value in gold and silver, which must otherwise have been sent home for returns in her stead; and likewise every ship built in and belonging to the province not only saves the province her first cost but all the freight, wages and provisions she ever makes or requires as long as she lasts, provided care is taken to make this her pay port, and that she always takes provisions with her for the whole voyage, which may easily be done.

By other examples Franklin elaborated his pro-paper argument. A plentiful currency would attract workmen drawn to high wages, as most workmen were. It would diminish dependence on imports from England as local manufacturers found markets for their goods, thereby righting the chronic imbalance in trade and cash flows with the motherland. It would improve social relations throughout the province as men of various stations found outlets for their talents and energies.

The opposition to paper often reflected an unwarranted reverence for specie, Franklin said. Gold and silver were nothing more than convenient measures of something more intrinsic: the amount of human labor that went into any commodity. "Suppose one man employed to raise corn, while another is digging and refining silver; at the year's end, or at any other period of time, the complete produce of corn, and that of silver, are the natural price of each other; and if one be twenty bushels and the other twenty ounces, then an ounce of that silver is worth the labor of raising a bushel of that corn." This fundamental principle had an important corollary: "The riches of a country are to be valued by the quantity of labor its inhabitants are able to purchase, and not by the quantity of gold and silver they possess."

Franklin acknowledged the temptation inherent in paper issues—namely, to print too much of the stuff. Current Pennsylvania practice avoided this pitfall by securing the notes with land. Franklin succinctly explained, "As bills issued upon money security are money, so bills issued upon land are in effect *coined land*." The value of land was rising with the prosperity of the province and the growth of its population; this was the best security of all.

Franklin doubtless hoped that if the Assembly could be persuaded to authorize another paper issue, he would receive the contract for the printing; as always, he expected that what was good for Pennsylvania would be good for him. In fact his arguments, joined to those of others of like mind, did carry the day, and although Andrew Bradford got the first contract, Franklin received a subsequent one: for £40,000 of notes, on which his fee was £100.

~ Civic-mindedness and self-interest intersected in another area, though not so directly. No city in America had ever suffered a fire on the scale of the London fire of 1666, but that had less to do with American circumspection than with the lesser combustible density of American urban life. As noted, the original plan of Philadelphia had taken the London disaster to heart and specified wide streets and ample spacing of buildings; but with time and prosperity the open spaces of Penn's "green town" filled in. As they did, one person's carelessness became his neighbors' hazard, and consequently their concern.

Franklin employed one of his tested methods to register this concern. At the beginning of 1735 he assumed yet another literary persona; this "A.A." wrote a letter to the editor of the *Gazette*, which Franklin obligingly published. A.A. was, by his own account, "old and lame of my hands, and thereby uncapable of assisting my fellow citizens when their houses are on fire"; all he had to offer was the wisdom of his years. "An ounce of prevention is worth a pound of cure," he said, sounding oddly like Poor Richard. Prevention was particularly important in matters inflammatory. Citizens ought to take care how they transported hot embers and coals from one room to the next—"for scraps of fire may fall into chinks and make no appearance till midnight; when your stairs being in flames, you may be forced (as I once was) to leap out of your windows and hazard your necks to avoid being over-roasted."

Other points of prevention called for collective effort. The city currently regulated bakeries and coopers' shops; A.A. suggested appending to those regulations a measure proscribing all hearths that lacked sufficient depth to keep the flames within, and a similar ban on the practice of framing the fronts of fireplaces in wood molding, which frequently was fashioned of the heartwood of pine and therefore oozed flammable resins. Under present practice anyone could call himself a chimney sweep, whether or not he knew the first thing about ridding chimneys of creosote and other combustible buildup. For civic safety, chimney sweeps ought to be licensed by the mayor and fined for any chimney that caught fire within fifteen days after exercise of their services.

An ounce of prevention might be worth a pound of cure, but sometimes civic safety had to be purchased in larger lots. A.A. explained that "a city in a neighboring province"—the well-traveled among his readers would recognize Boston—had formed clubs of active men to combat fires. Each club commanded a fire engine, with which the members practiced regularly; each included specialists in the use of other equipment, including axes and hooks; each was led by an officer who directed their efforts and could compel obedience of the citizenry in times of fire emergency. Prior to the establishment of this system, fire had scourged their city; since then the flames had been kept in check. Philadelphia should learn from the example. To date, no extraordinary fire had ever raked the city on the Delaware, but given a hardly unthinkable combination of drought, wind, and place of outbreak, a small fire might easily become extraordinary in the absence of preparations to suppress it.

Franklin had already circulated these ideas in the Junto; after airing them in the *Gazette*, he took the obvious next step of organizing a fire club. Combining what he knew of Boston with what he had seen in London, the Union Fire Company incorporated itself in December 1736. Each member pledged to provide two leather buckets for carrying water and four cloth bags for rescuing goods, to be devoted exclusively to the activities of the fire company and marked accordingly. Failure to have this equipment at the ready would result in a fine of five shillings per missing piece—although any equipment lost fighting a fire would be replaced at the expense of the company. Members would meet monthly for inspection and consideration of policies (and socializing); absent members would be fined one shilling. As to the business of fire fighting:

We will all of us, upon hearing of fire breaking out at or near any of our dwelling houses, immediately repair to the same with all our buckets and bags, and there employ our best endeavours to preserve the goods and effects of such as shall be in danger. . . . And if more than one of us shall be in danger at the same time, we will divide ourselves as near as may be to be equally helpful. And to prevent suspicious persons from coming into, or carrying any goods out of, any such house, two of our number shall constantly attend at the doors until all the goods and effects that can be saved shall be secured in our bags, and carried to some safe place.

The twenty-five charter members included Franklin and friends from the Junto and Library Company, also merchants, city and provincial officials, and various other persons hoping to protect their property from fire. Significantly—and perhaps realistically—the members pledged to protect their own houses, not those of nonmembers. Accordingly, many of those nonmembers formed companies of their own, until much of the city fell under the protection of one company or another. Franklin's company devoted the fines it collected to purchasing equipment; in 1743 it bought a fire engine like those he had seen in London.

Franklin took as much pride in encouraging the creation of the Philadelphia fire companies as in nearly anything else he did. Writing late in life, after he had visited every city in America and many of those in Europe, he said, "I question whether there is a city in the world better provided with the means of putting a stop to beginning conflagrations; and in fact since those institutions, the city has never lost by fire more than one or two houses at a time." By then Franklin was a world-renowned scientific and political figure, feted for taming lightning and tyrants; that such a mundane improvement as fire prevention gave him such pleasure reflected his solid grounding in the affairs of ordinary life.

෨ **Another** contribution to civic betterment began as an undiluted expression of self-interest. Although Franklin's *Gazette* was the livelier paper, Bradford's *Mercury* benefited from its publisher's second job as postmaster. Not only did this give Bradford first view of news from beyond the city, but his assured circulation via the mail attracted advertisers, who—then as later—supplied a crucial portion of any paper's revenues.

As if this double advantage were not enough, Bradford forbade his carriers from delivering the *Gazette*.

Franklin resented this last measure as pushing competition too far; consequently he felt no compunction about bribing the carriers to disobey their boss and tuck copies of the *Gazette* beneath their saddlebags. For a time he and Bradford engaged in a game of cat and mouse. Eventually, however, the cat got snarled in his own ball of yarn, as Bradford hopelessly tangled the post-office accounts. Bradford's boss, the postmaster general for America, demanded his resignation. The postmaster general offered the job to Franklin, who accepted readily.

The position paid little directly, and in fact left Franklin liable for the debts of his customers. In those days of uncertain delivery, recipients rather than senders paid the postage on letters. Or did *not* pay: Franklin kept hundreds of customers on credit. Meanwhile *he* had to pay the colonial post office for the charges incurred. Collecting from such a crowd was a headache; more than a few ran years behind.

Franklin had no idea when he took the job in 1737 what he was getting into—in particular, how the post office would pull him into American and then imperial politics. All he knew then was that the job would boost his newspaper business, which it soon did. "Though the salary was small, it facilitated the correspondence that improved my newspaper, increased the number demanded, as well as the advertisements to be inserted, so that it came to afford me a very considerable income."

⌐ **As postmaster,** Franklin was among the first to hear of a tempest sweeping across the Atlantic from England, a tempest about to turn much of American life upside down. At the eye of the storm was the most charismatic man Franklin ever met—perhaps the most charismatic man to speak the English language during Franklin's lifetime. It was said of George Whitefield that he could reduce listeners to tears merely by uttering the word "Mesopotamia." Charles Wesley wrote of their first meeting, "I saw, I loved, and clasped him to my heart." An eyewitness described "the awe, the silence, the attention" with which audiences listened to Whitefield. "Many thought, *He spoke as never a man spoke,* before him. So charmed were people with his manner of address, that they shut up their shops, forgot their secular business, and laid aside their schemes for the world." Another observer was moved to meter:

See! See! He comes, the heav'nly Sound
Flows from his charming Tongue;
Rebellious Men are seiz'd with Fear,
With deep Conviction stung.

The object of these effusions was a young man, a few weeks shy of his thirtieth birthday when Franklin met him in 1739. He was "graceful and well-proportioned," in the opinion of one who knew him: "his stature rather above middle size. His complexion was very fair. His eyes were of a dark blue colour, and small, but sprightly. He had a squint in one of them, occasioned either by ignorance or the carelessness of the nurse who attended him in the measles, when he was about four years old." This observer, a Whitefield partisan, took pains to characterize his countenance as "manly"; this may have been a reaction against those who found his features delicate, even effeminate. Whitefield himself was sensitive on this score. Recalling a school play in which he was cast as a girl, he declared, "The remembrance of this has often covered me with confusion of face, and I hope will do so, even to the end of my life."

By his own account, perhaps magnified for effect, Whitefield spent a dissolute boyhood and youth. He lied, talked dirty, stole from his mother, and indulged in "abominable secret sin." Yet salvation, of a secular sort, beckoned when he learned of the possibility of attending university at Oxford as a servitor, a student who worked to earn his way. "Will you go to Oxford, George?" his mother implored. He would.

Yet Oxford initially attempted to corrupt him. His classmates habitually engaged in an "excess of riot" and encouraged him to come along. By now at least aware of the evil nature of such a life, Whitefield prayed for the strength to resist temptation.

God answered his prayers by leading him to the brothers Wesley, John and Charles, who had formed a small group devoted to piety, prayer, and an ascetic "method" of living. These "Methodists" were the butt of ridicule of most of Whitefield's classmates, and at first he attempted to keep his connection secret. But, driven by a deep conviction that he was unworthy of salvation, he soon became more methodical—indeed fanatical—than the Wesleys. He fasted for days at a time and deprived himself of everything that gave him pleasure, thinking that somehow this mortification of the flesh would save him. Yet the more he strove, the more convinced he grew of his sinfulness.

One day revelation came to him in the form of a desperate woman.

For some time Whitefield had been carrying the message of the gospel to prisoners in the local jail; this woman was the wife of one of the prisoners. Distraught at her inability to support her children with her husband behind bars, she had attempted to escape their hungry cries by the sole expedient she knew: to hurl herself into the river and drown. The chance intervention of a passerby had prevented her from carrying out her plan; now she turned to the only one she could think of who might help her, the one who had visited her husband in jail. Whitefield comforted her as best he could at the moment, and told her to meet him at the jail that afternoon. She did so. He read to the woman and her husband from the Gospel of John, and suddenly, as he later described it, "God visited them both by his free grace." The woman was "powerfully quickened from above"; the man, trembling and crying out, "I am upon the brink of hell!" likewise felt the powerful rush of salvation. "From this time forward, both of them grew in grace."

Having now witnessed this instantaneous rebirth through grace, Whitefield longed to experience it himself. He mortified the flesh more than ever, increasing his fasts, taking long walks on cold mornings till his fingers turned black from the frost. His health began to fail and his body to break down.

> One day, perceiving an uncommon drought and disagreeable clamminess in my mouth, and using things to allay my thirst, but in vain, it was suggested to me that when Jesus Christ cried out, "I thirst," His sufferings were near at an end. Upon which I cast myself down on the bed, crying out, "I thirst! I thirst!" Soon after this, I found and felt in myself that I was delivered from the burden that had so heavily oppressed me. The spirit of mourning was taken from me, and I knew what it was truly to rejoice in God my Saviour. . . . Now did the Spirit of God take possession of my soul, and, as I humbly hope, seal me unto the day of redemption.

Having felt for himself what he soon took to calling "the new birth," Whitefield set to sharing the experience with others. In 1736 he was ordained at Gloucester; he shortly began preaching the message of the new birth. Despite his inexperience and his youth (he was only twenty-one), he vowed to speak the truth as it had been revealed to him. "I shall displease some, being determined to speak against their assemblies," he confided to a friend on the eve of his inaugural sermon. "But I must tell them the truth, or otherwise I shall not be a faithful minister of Christ."

The "boy parson," as he was dubbed, made a sensation from the start—a matter not lost on the parson himself. "I preached at Bishopsgate Church, the largeness of which, and the congregation together, at first a little dazed me," he wrote, regarding his initial appearance in London. But God saw him through. "My mind was calmed, and I was enabled to preach with power. The effect was immediate and visible to all; for as I went up the stairs almost all seemed to sneer at me on account of my youth; but they soon grew serious and exceedingly attentive, and, after I came down, showed me great tokens of respect, blessed me as I passed along, and made great enquiry who I was."

The clergy did not all bless Whitefield. Some were simply jealous of his oratorical brilliance; others questioned the orthodoxy of his message. Consequently, few men of the cloth—although many of the laity—lamented the news that he intended to take his message to America, to pursue his ministry among the debtors and other poor of James Oglethorpe's new colony in Georgia. The Wesleys had already gone; Whitefield would follow.

His first American mission lasted four months. He generated as much excitement in Georgia as he had at home. "Mr. Whitefield's auditors increase daily," wrote one who saw him in Savannah. "And the place of worship is far too small to contain the people who seek his doctrine." That doctrine was the doctrine of the new birth; Whitefield called on his hearers to cast aside their sinful ways and take God directly into their lives.

He returned to England to even more popular acclaim than before, and even more clerical disapproval. One by one the churches closed their pulpits to him. Yet the people demanded to hear him, so he began preaching in the open fields. His first outdoor sermon was heard by some two hundred coal miners on a hill near Bristol. Within weeks the crowds numbered twenty thousand. What even Whitefield at first characterized as the "mad trick" of preaching in the fields became the centerpiece of his ministry. "Blessed be God that I have now broken the ice!" he recorded after the Bristol performance. "I believe I never was more acceptable to my Master than when I was standing to teach those hearers in the open fields. Some may censure me; but if I thus pleased me, I should not be the servant of Christ."

○— **While Whitefield** was learning to antagonize established religion in England on the way to his sermon on the mount, Franklin was engaged in a similar dispute in Philadelphia. Not since Boston had he attended church regularly, although he judged the institution of religion conducive to civic welfare and, accordingly, contributed to its upkeep. The object of his subscription was the Presbyterian congregation in Philadelphia, which, encompassing a congeries of dissenters from both the Church of England and the Society of Friends—Congregationalists, Baptists, English Nonconformists, in addition to Presbyterians—was the closest thing Franklin could call to a church of his own. The pastor of the Presbyterians since before Franklin's arrival in Philadelphia was Jedediah Andrews, an able organizer and energetic proselytizer. Andrews engaged in a running contest with an Anglican minister, Thomas Clayton, to capture the loyalty, or at least the attendance, of those souls not irretrievably lost to Quakerism. Andrews had observed the emergence of Franklin as one of the city's leading citizens, and he determined to bring him into his fold. From either his own persuasive skills or some lingering sense in Franklin that he ought to attend church, Andrews got Franklin to agree to come to service for five successive Sundays. If Franklin remained disinclined to join the church after that time, presumably Andrews would bother him no more.

Andrews may have been persuasive, but he was not eloquent. "His discourses were chiefly either polemic arguments or explications of the peculiar doctrines of our sect," Franklin said, "and were all to me very dry, uninteresting and unedifying, since not a single moral principle was inculcated or enforced, their aim seeming to be rather to make us Presbyterians than good citizens." Franklin served out his time, then left in disappointment and no little disgust.

He stayed away until the arrival of a new preacher. The growth of population in the colony more than offset Andrews's inadequacy in the pulpit, and the pastor's workload increased. In 1733 he called across the Atlantic for an assistant, who arrived in the latter part of 1734. For all its amenities, Philadelphia was not the first choice of every promising young minister in the British Isles; as a result, Andrews and the Presbyterian synod had to take whom they could get. Whom they got was Samuel Hemphill, lately of Ireland, oratorically gifted but, according to his critics, doctrinally suspect. A fellow minister who knew him in Ireland called him a "new-light man"—a term denoting an unsettling latitudinarianism, either theological or institutional or both—as well as, more specifically, "a vile heretic, a preacher of morality rather than dogma."

Franklin cared nothing for the purity of Presbyterian dogma, and if Hemphill preached morality rather than dogma, he was probably worth a hearing. Franklin returned to Sunday services and enjoyed "most excellent discourses," which "had little of the dogmatical kind, but inculcated strongly the practice of virtue, or what in the religious style are called good works." Franklin was not alone in his enthusiasm for the new man; according to Andrews, who was now having second thoughts about Hemphill, "free-thinkers, Deists, nothings, getting a scent of him, flocked to him."

Hemphill's popularity with this unholy mob was prima facie evidence of his irregularity. At Andrews's urging, the Presbyterian synod conducted an investigation, which culminated in a trial. Franklin might have let the matter alone, as being solely the concern of narrow-minded sectarians, but he believed that Hemphill's emphasis on good works could have only a beneficent influence on civic life, and he was loath to lose it. Besides, the actions of Andrews and the synod struck the same anti-authoritarian nerve in Franklin that had made it impossible for him to remain in Boston. Let the dogmatists speak their piece, he believed, but do not let them stifle the opinions of others.

Franklin joined the fray, though he had no standing in the matter. The week before Hemphill's trial Franklin published an imagined dialogue between two Presbyterians on the streets of Philadelphia. One defends the position of the Presbyterian synod; the other—clearly speaking for Franklin—dismantles the synod's arguments. When the first complains that the new minister preaches morality rather than faith, the second says, "What is Christ's Sermon on the Mount but an excellent moral discourse?" The first replies that, regardless, the Presbyterians have the right to determine who will preach from their pulpit; anyone who will not subscribe to the Westminster Confession should be barred. The second answers that just as Luther had found error in the practices of the Church of Rome, and Calvin been obliged to modify Luther, so might synods today correct Westminster. "Why must we be for ever confined to that, or any, Confession?" The first says that most Presbyterians are perfectly happy with the Westminster Confession; this being so, they have every right to prohibit their pulpit to an innovator. The second responds that a majority can be mistaken. At the beginning of the Reformation, the reformers were in a distinct minority. Besides, Presbyterians deem it their right to preach their version of the Gospel to unbelievers; they ought to accord a similar right to others, even if they think those others misguided. They might learn something. "We have justly denied the infallibility of the Pope and his councils and synods in their interpretations of scripture, and can we modestly claim infallibility for our selves or our synods?" None can know, this side of heaven, where lies true orthodoxy. In the meantime, "No point of faith is so plain as that morality is our duty, for all sides agree in that. A virtuous heretic shall be saved before a wicked Christian."

Franklin must have realized this last statement made him sound almost like a papist; the crux of the Reformation had been Luther's conviction that faith, not good works, was what allowed a person to be saved. Whether he expected that his little dialogue would help Hemphill before the synod is unclear; in the event, that body voted unanimously to censure the preacher and suspend him from his ministerial office. It did not help Hemphill's case that he was caught having cribbed his sermons from others. He explained to Franklin that he had an exceedingly retentive memory; he needed to read a text only once and he knew it by heart. Franklin, embarrassed at seeming to defend plagiarism, nonetheless made the best of things. "I rather approved his giving us good sermons composed by others, than bad ones of his own manufacture."

In fact, by now Hemphill was almost the least of Franklin's concerns. Franklin could hardly contest the *right* of the synod to dismiss Hemphill, but he *could* challenge their *wisdom* in doing so. He did precisely this, in language that grew more vehement as the controversy continued. In July 1735 Franklin published a pamphlet dissecting the proceedings to date. He rebutted, article by article, the prosecution's charges and evidence. He alleged "malice and envy" in certain of the accusers, "hot distempered zeal" in others, and he likened the entire affair to the Inquisition. When the synod responded with a defense of its actions, Franklin put out another pamphlet, in which such slight circumspection as his first one exhibited had evaporated entirely. He called the camp of the synod "the dominion of bigotry and prejudice"; their evidence showed "pious fraud." Of those who defended Andrews against the allegation of bringing false evidence, he declared, "Vain is their endeavour to wipe out the indelible stain he has fixed upon his character by his conduct in that affair. They flounder and wallow in his quagmire, and cover themselves with that dirt which before belonged to him alone." One charge by Andrews was "ridiculous, false and absurd"; another was "abominably ridiculous and absurd" and "absolutely a stranger" to Holy Scripture. To what he judged an especially egregious lapse of logic in the prosecution's case, Franklin responded sarcastically, "Admirable reasoning! To which I answer that

> *Asses are grave and dull animals,*
> *Our authors are grave and dull animals; therefore*
> *Our authors are grave, dull,* or if you will, *Rev. Asses.*

Lest calling the Presbyterian clergy "asses" was insufficient insult, Franklin asserted that those involved in the Hemphill prosecution fell into three categories: "first, the men of honesty who wanted sense; secondly, the men of sense who wanted honesty; and lastly, those who had neither sense nor honesty." The instigators of the investigation were of the last sort. "Malice, rancour and prejudice" motivated their actions; "animosity" and "false zeal" gave rise to "injustice, fraud, oppression"; the prosecution was already deep and appeared about to go deeper into "the dirt and filth of hypocrisy, falsehood and impiety."

↶ Franklin's outburst of anticlericalism was unlike him—or rather, unlike the side of him he preferred to present to the world. The sweet reasonableness with which he normally cloaked his actions withered before his anger at the suppression of a dissenting voice in the Presbyterian pulpit. In this regard the Presbyterians of Philadelphia were as closed-minded as the Puritans of Boston; the struggle over Hemphill aroused the same emotions in Franklin that had driven him from the city of his birth. He was not proud of his performance in the Hemphill case; in his autobiography he glossed it over almost to the point of prevarication.

Yet in this, as in so many other things, Franklin was a man of his times. Matters of religion were provoking people all across the American colonies to unusual emotions. During the late 1730s and early 1740s a religious eruption occurred, rending congregations from New England to the Carolinas. This "Great Awakening" grew out of the pietistic preaching of Theodore Frelinghuysen among his Dutch Reformed flock in New Jersey in the 1720s, and of William and Gilbert Tennent among Presbyterians in the same province. Gilbert Tennent was a particularly compelling character: brawny, earthy, and direct. Where many other preachers appealed to the intellects of their congregants, Tennent spoke to their emotions in a language to which they were unused but which they could not resist. He preached "like a boatswain of a ship, calling the sailors to come to prayers and be damned," said one witness, who did not entirely approve. The sailors—congregants, rather—came, were damned, and came back for more.

Equally compelling, though in a style oratorically opposite to Tennent's, was Jonathan Edwards. Two years older than Franklin, Edwards was an intellectual prodigy. He entered Yale before his thirteenth birthday and finished by his seventeenth. At twenty he was the head tutor at the college and, in effect, president. His early interests were as varied as those of Franklin—or more aptly, Cotton Mather—and he speculated on atoms, rainbows, and the lives of spiders. He never forgot about those spiders, but in time he narrowed his focus to the cure of the souls he inherited from his grandfather, Solomon Stoddard, at the Congregational Church in Northampton, Massachusetts.

Edwards's devotion to his calling soon became legendary. He rose by four on summer mornings, by five in winter. He ate sparingly, to keep his mind clear and sharp. He devoted fully half of each twenty-four hours to the study of the Scriptures and other volumes conducive to holiness. He chopped wood and rode horseback for exercise, yet with each fall of the ax he reflected on Adam's fall, and with each hill his horse ascended he thought of the uplifting power of God's grace. Like Franklin—and Mather—he sought moral self-improvement; in his case he vowed "never to do anything which I should be afraid to do if I expected it would not be above an hour before I should hear the last trump."

To say Edwards walked in the fear of God would be to put matters mildly (and here he walked away from Franklin); to say that he attempted to instill this same fear in his congregation would be equally bland. Unlike Gilbert Tennent or George Whitefield, Edwards spoke without gestures. His eyes did not search his audience but stayed fixed on the bell-rope at the back of the meeting hall; his words came out in a flat monotone that would have put his listeners to sleep had the message not been so hair-raising:

> The God that holds you over the pit of hell, much as one holds a spider or some loathesome insect over the fire, abhors you, and is dreadfully provoked; his wrath towards you burns like fire; he looks upon you as worthy of nothing else but to be cast into the fire; he is of purer eyes than to bear to have you in his sight; you are ten thousand times so abominable in his eyes as the most hateful and venomous serpent is in ours.
>
> You have offended him infinitely more than ever a stubborn rebel did his prince; and yet it is nothing but his hand that holds

you from falling into the fire every moment; it is ascribed to nothing else that you did not go to hell the last night; that you were suffered to wake again in this world after you closed your eyes to sleep; and there is no other reason to be given why you have not dropped into hell since you arose in the morning, but that God's hand has held you up. There is no other reason to be given why you have not gone to hell since you have sat here in the house of God, provoking his pure eyes by your sinful wicked manner of attending his solemn worship. Yea, there is nothing else that is to be given as a reason why you do not this very moment drop down into hell.

Edwards may have remained calm, but his auditors shrieked and moaned, their horror exceeded only by the exquisiteness of their agony. Periodically their wailing compelled the speaker to pause, lest his message be lost in the din. At least one listener was so moved that he decided to end his life rather than continue his torment. (As it happened, this lost soul was married to Edwards's aunt Rebekah Stoddard, who showed true Stoddard grit when, informed in the buttery that her husband had fatally cut his throat, she finished her cheese work before seeing to her dead husband.)

Such excesses merely underscored the excitement the new preachers brought to the religious and social life of the colonies. The persecutions that had driven the colonial founders from England were history, and tired history, to the third and fourth generations. Meanwhile an insidious rationalism—the work of Newton and the other apostles of the Enlightenment—had driven the center of religious gravity from the bowels of believers up toward their brains. In meeting halls in every province, congregants nodded assent to received doctrines but knew that something was missing from their experience of the divine. The new preachers—the awakeners—supplied that missing element.

~ And none with such impact as George Whitefield. Returning to America in 1739, Whitefield set the colonies on fire. "The multitudes of all sects and denominations that attended his sermons were enormous," Franklin reported of Whitefield's visit to Philadelphia, "and it was a matter of speculation to me, who was one of the number, to observe the extraordinary influence of his oratory on his hearers, and how much they

admired and respected him, notwithstanding his common abuse of
them, by assuring them they were naturally *half beasts and half devils*." The
Gazette described the effect:

> The alteration in the face of religion here is altogether surprising.
> Never did the people show so great a willingness to attend ser-
> mons, nor the preachers greater zeal and diligence in performing
> the duties of their function. Religion is become the subject of
> most conversations. No books are in request but those of piety
> and devotion; and instead of idle songs and ballads, the people are
> everywhere entertaining themselves with psalms, hymns and spiri-
> tual songs. All which, under God, is owing to the successful
> labours of the Reverend Mr. Whitefield.

Theologically, Franklin held aloof from the excitement. He was fairly
certain he was neither beast nor devil, and his view of fire and brimstone
was purely scientific—as indeed was his view of the Whitefield phenomenon generally. For the same reasons as in England—to wit, the
disapproval of the regular clergy and the magnitude of his audiences—
Whitefield preached in the open air. One evening he spoke from the top
of the steps of the Philadelphia courthouse, in the middle of Market
Street on the west side of Second. "I had the curiosity to learn how far he
could be heard," Franklin wrote. Franklin was already at the rear of the
crowd; he walked slowly backward in the direction of the river. He could
hear Whitefield's "loud and clear voice" distinctly until he came to Front
Street, where some street noise obscured it. Taking the distance from
Front Street to Second as radius, he mentally constructed a semicircle
and filled it with listeners, allowing two square feet to each. In this way he
calculated that Whitefield might be heard by an audience of more than
thirty thousand. "This reconciled me to the newspaper accounts of his
having preached to 25,000 people in the fields, and to the ancient histo-
ries of generals haranguing whole armies, of which I had sometimes
doubted."

The businessman in Franklin spied an opportunity in the enthusiasm
for Whitefield. He arranged to publish Whitefield's sermons and journals; so favorable was the reception that Franklin ran off eight installments of the journals and nine of the sermons and other writings.
Subsequently he published Whitefield's memoirs, which proved equally
popular.

For Franklin this was principally a profit-making enterprise, yet, rationalist though he was, he was not immune to Whitefield's charm. Whitefield had conceived the idea of an orphanage in Georgia for children left parentless by the hardships of life in that lately founded penal colony. He undertook to raise money to cover the expense of construction. Franklin approved the orphanage in principle but suggested that the donations would be better spent bringing the orphans to Philadelphia than sending the construction materials and workers to Georgia. Whitefield stuck to his plan, causing Franklin to refuse to contribute.

Yet Whitefield was a hard man to resist, as Franklin recounted:

> I happened soon after to attend one of his sermons, in the course of which I perceived he intended to finish with a collection, and I silently resolved he should get nothing from me. I had in my pocket a handful of copper money, three or four silver dollars, and five pistoles in gold. As he proceeded I began to soften, and concluded to give the coppers. Another stroke of his oratory made me ashamed of that, and determined me to give the silver; and he finished so admirably that I emptied my pocket wholly into the collector's dish, gold and all.

To some extent Franklin's softening was a reaction to Whitefield's power; to some extent to the worthy cause he was promoting—even if that cause might have been better served, in Franklin's view, by relocation. There was yet another element as well. Though Franklin found Whitefield's hellfire-and-damnation message as much beside the point of living a good life as he did the sectarian sophistry of Jedediah Andrews, he appreciated the discomfort the silver-throated itinerant inflicted on the local religious establishment. Doubtless recalling the unsatisfactory—to him—outcome of the Hemphill case, Franklin helped arrange the construction of a new building (prosaically called the "New Building") for the express purpose of hosting preachers unwelcome in the regular pulpits of the city. Franklin spoke his desires rather than strict reality when he declared in his autobiography that "if the Mufti of Constantinople were to send a missionary to preach Mahometanism to us, he would find a pulpit at his service." (For all the uproar the Great Awakening caused among Protestants, they retained sufficient composure to band together against such irredeemably lost souls as Muslims, Catholics, and Jews.)

Yet though Franklin supported Whitefield's good works and defended his right to preach, he drew the line well short of his own conversion. Whitefield spared no effort on behalf of Franklin's soul, but Franklin rebuffed them all. He was as skeptical of organized religion as ever, even religion that challenged prevailing orthodoxy. And the enthusiasms of the awakeners left him as cold as enthusiasms generally did.

All the same, Franklin counted Whitefield a friend. He housed the preacher in Philadelphia and defended him against charges that he had siphoned funds from the collection plate for his own comfort. In this regard Franklin's unregeneracy worked in Whitefield's favor, at least marginally. Most of Philadelphia had sided theologically with Whitefield or against him; Franklin, having taken no position in the dispute between the "New Lights" and the "Old Lights," was well placed to offer objective testimony. "Ours was a mere civil friendship, sincere on both sides, and lasted to his death [in 1770]."

∽ If the Awakening was unsettling—many historians would see the roots of the American Revolution in the turmoil it produced— another affair of the period was downright bizarre. During the early summer of 1737 a gullible and perhaps mentally impaired apprentice named Daniel Rees fell in the way of several young Philadelphia rowdies, including one lapsed Freemason. Rees knew little of the Masons, but enough to think he wished to join the order. The rowdies, led by Rees's master, took the opportunity to have some diversion at his expense. They conducted a bogus but elaborate "initiation" ceremony, which included a satanic oath and the administration of a strong purgative and culminated in Rees's being required to kiss the buttocks of one of the initiators.

The ringleaders were acquaintances of Franklin's, and when they shared the story with him, he shared their laughter. " 'Tis true I laughed (and perhaps heartily, as my manner is)," he admitted afterward. He even asked for a copy of the oath, which he showed to friends.

Had the imposition on young Rees stopped there, it would have been merely cruel, after the cruel fashion of the age. But hoping to improve on their performance, Rees's taunters conducted a second ceremony, purporting to elevate him to a higher rank in the secret fraternity. On the night of June 13, in a dark and gloomy cellar, the group gathered about one of their number who was draped in a cowhide, with horns upon his head, pretending to be the devil incarnate. The only light in the room emanated from a bowl of brandy set alight. To intensify the terror, Rees's master raised the bowl and approached the boy. What happened next occasioned dispute. Either accidentally or on purpose, the master splashed the boy with the flaming spirits; this ignited his clothes and caused such injury that he died two days later.

"The coroner's inquest are now sitting on the body," the *Gazette* reported on June 16. That inquest, doubtless reflecting the testimony of those responsible for the death, found the tragedy to have been inadvertent. In the following few days, however, certain of the participants changed their story, causing the authorities to investigate further. A grand jury brought an indictment for murder against Rees's master and two others.

Franklin became involved in the matter at trial. The prosecution called him as a witness, for although absent from both mock ceremonies, he was known to have been familiar with the accused and presumably with their intentions. His testimony does not survive; it must not have been especially helpful to the prosecution, since two of the three were convicted only of the lesser charge of manslaughter and the third was acquitted.

But this was not the end of the story for Franklin. Andrew Bradford had never liked the Masons and from the moment of Rees's death had used the tragedy to attack them. He—or at least an anonymous writer in his *Mercury*—detailed Franklin's role in the sordid affair, suggesting that Franklin had through his approbation of the first prank encouraged the criminal behavior on the part of the accused, even if he did not participate in the homicide directly.

Franklin was familiar enough with printed controversy to know that any answer from him would probably prolong the scandal, but he deemed the allegations against him sufficiently grave as to require a response. He labeled the charges in the *Mercury* "very false and scandalous." He conceded that he had initially laughed at the discomfiture related of young Rees. "But when they came to those circumstances of their giving him a violent purge, leading him to kiss T's posteriors, and administering to him the diabolical oath which R———n read to us, I grew indeed serious, as I suppose the most merry man (not inclined to mischief) would on such an occasion."

Franklin subsequently undermined his own testimony on this point by admitting that he had asked to see the oath. Finding it "a piece of a very extraordinary nature," he said he wanted to show it to his friends, which he did until "so many people flocked to my house for a sight of it that it grew troublesome, and therefore when the mayor sent for it [as part of the investigation], I was glad of the opportunity to be discharged from it."

Far from encouraging additional ill treatment of young Rees, Franklin said, he had tried to prevent it. The boy happened into the tavern where the discussion of his initiation was taking place; his master pointed to Franklin and identified him as a Freemason. The master urged the lad to make the secret sign he had been taught. "Which whether he did or not, I cannot tell," Franklin declared, "for I was so far from encouraging him in the delusion, or taking him by the hand, or calling him brother, and welcoming him into the fraternity, as is said, that I turned my head to avoid seeing him make his pretended sign, and looked out of the window into the garden." The allegation that he—Franklin—had desired to attend the fatal session was "absolutely false and groundless." "I was acquainted with, and had a respect for the young lad's father, and thought it a pity his son should be so imposed upon, and therefore followed the lad down stairs to the door when he went out, with a design to call him back and give him a hint of the imposition; but he was gone out of sight and I never saw him afterwards."

It was hardly Franklin's finest hour, and he knew it. Of course he had no direct responsibility for the death of young Rees; he was righteously, and rightly, indignant at any intimation that he had. But he certainly might have done more to discourage those who were making inexcusable sport of the boy. His contention that he meant to warn him, but that he slipped away, was lame, as was his assertion—contradicted by his own words—that he had taken a serious view of the satanic oath. For years Franklin had been cultivating a pleasing personal style, one that accommodated others rather than confronting them. This style generally served him well, allowing his business to flourish and his reputation to grow. Some occasions, however, call for confrontation, as when a wrong demands to be righted, or at least addressed. This was one of those occasions, and here Franklin's style failed.

∽ As he surely guessed, Franklin's defense of his conduct did not put the matter to rest. Bradford's *Mercury* ran a rejoinder, and before long, papers in other cities had picked up the story. Josiah and Abiah Franklin read of Rees's death and of the trial at which their son testified. Abiah, especially, had long questioned this Freemasonry foolishness; her doubts now appeared confirmed. A letter to their son conveyed her worries, and Josiah's.

"They are in general a very harmless sort of people," Franklin replied, regarding the Masons, "and have no principles or practices that are inconsistent with religion or good manners." Unfortunately, Abiah would have to take her son's word for this, since the secrets of the order were not vouchsafed to women. "I must entreat her to suspend her judgment till she is better informed, and in the mean time exercise her charity."

Franklin took the opportunity of this letter to attempt to assuage his parents' concern over the larger and continuing issue of his lapse from orthodoxy. "I am sorry you should have any uneasiness on my account, and if it were a thing possible for one to alter his opinions in order to please others, I know none whom I ought more willingly to oblige in that respect than your selves." But such was not possible. "It is no more in a man's power *to think* than *to look* like another."

Franklin granted that some of his opinions were probably wrong. "When the natural weakness and imperfection of human understanding is considered, with the unavoidable influences of education, custom, books and company, upon our ways of thinking, I imagine a man must have a good deal of vanity who believes, and a good deal of boldness who affirms, that all the doctrines he holds, are true, and all he rejects, are false." The same applied to churches and councils, sects and synods. Yet though truth, in some transcendent sense, might elude mere mortals, efficacy need not. "I think opinions should be judged of by their influences and effects; and if a man holds none that tend to make him less virtuous or more vicious, it may be concluded he holds none that are dangerous; which I hope is the case with me."

Here Franklin missed the point, either inadvertently or by design. Devout Calvinists like his parents believed that truth—in matters of faith—was everything, works next to nothing. All their son's good works and all he might encourage others to perform would avail him nothing at the final judgment. Did he *believe?* That was the question. And by his own admission, if only oblique in this letter, he did not. They could hardly help being concerned.

Franklin anticipated their objections, which were the same ones he had been tilting against for years. "I think vital religion has always suffered when orthodoxy is more regarded than virtue. And the Scripture assures me that at the last day, we shall not be examined what we *thought*, but what we *did*; and our recommendation will not be that we said *Lord, Lord*, but that we did GOOD to our fellow creatures. See Matth. 26."

Josiah and Abiah knew their Gospels (better than Benjamin: the chapter he meant to cite was Matthew *25*), and they knew the appropriate Protestant riposte to his essentially Roman Catholic dependence on works. Franklin knew they knew, knew they would not be convinced, and threw himself on their love and understanding. "Methinks all that should be expected from me is to keep my mind open to conviction, to hear patiently and examine attentively whatever is offered me for that end; and if after all I continue in the same errors, I believe your usual charity will induce you rather to pity and excuse than blame me. In the mean time your care and concern for me is what I am very thankful for."

～ He might also have said he was thankful for their health and longevity, for such fundamental blessings were not bestowed upon all the members of his family. From birth, little Francis was his mother's darling and his father's delight. When he learned to crawl, and then walk, Franky doubtless followed his father from the upstairs bedroom to the downstairs print shop; he certainly marveled at the mysteries of composing, inking, pressing, and cutting. By all evidence Franklin indulged him; recollecting his own precocious curiosity, he was hardly one to chase his child away from the objects of such fascination. Besides, he almost certainly expected Franky to enter the printing trade, at least on a trial basis. The earlier he learned the basics, the better.

But fate, in the form of infectious disease, disrupted these plans. In 1736 Franky contracted smallpox. Since the days when Franklin had joined James to assault the Mathers for promoting inoculation against the disease, he had altered his view; he now advocated the practice as beneficial to private and public health. Yet he was a busy man, and Franky was not always in the most robust of health; between finding his own time and waiting for the boy to get stronger, he never got around to inoculating him. When the disease swept through the city in the autumn of the child's fifth year, it carried Franky off.

His father was devastated. "I long regretted bitterly and still regret that I had not given it to him by inoculation," he wrote a half century later. With a grim sense of civic duty, he noted in the *Gazette* that Franky had not died following inoculation, as was widely assumed of the son of a known supporter of the practice, but following failure to inoculate.

It was part of Franklin's credo to look forever forward, to dwell not on the past but on the future. On most subjects he followed this aspect of his own advice. For Franky he made an exception. The grieving father allowed himself—or perhaps he simply could not help it—to wonder what the boy would have become. For the rest of his life the sight of other boys caused him to reflect on Franky. In 1772 he responded to reports that one of his grandsons was growing up to be a fine lad, by declaring that such information "brings often afresh to my mind the idea of my son Franky, though now dead thirty-six years, whom I have seldom seen equaled in every thing, and whom to this day I cannot think of without a sigh."

What effect Franky's death had on Deborah can only be imagined. She did not keep a diary, and although she certainly shared her sorrow with her husband, and perhaps even more with her mother, still living with them, neither of them recorded her feelings for posterity.

The pain of losing a child is always excruciating, but for Debbie it was all the more excruciating from the fact that she confronted the real possibility that she might never have another. At the time of Franky's death she and Franklin had been married for more than six years. There is no reason to believe they were *not* trying to have more children; certainly Franklin, he of the dozen siblings plus two, looked forward to numerous progeny. (Debbie was one of seven children, four of whom died before reaching adulthood.) But in those six years the two had been able to produce just one child. And now that one was gone. In little more than a year Debbie would be thirty, her best childbearing years probably behind her. She might never see a child of hers grow up, might never have grandchildren. It was a bleak prospect.

The effect of Franky's death on Franklin's other son is harder to guess. Billy was six or nearly so at his half brother's passing. He may have been too young to appreciate that his situation was different from Franky's—specifically, that he was Franklin's son but not Debbie's. The loss of Franky likely made his father appreciate Billy more than ever, but the effect it had on Debbie's feelings toward Billy is problematic. She would have been more than human not to feel a certain resentment that *her* son had been taken but not that other woman's. In the close quarters of the crowded house—which sheltered not only Franklin, Debbie, Billy, and Sarah Read but also one or more apprentices and journeymen and, at various times, Debbie's siblings John and Frances—this resentment must have been palpable. Franklin would have felt it and understood. Billy would have felt and not understood.

~ Full as it was, the house would soon be fuller—but not of the children of Debbie. In 1733 Franklin had journeyed to New England to visit his parents and sister Jane (and Jane's children, including a son named Benjamin) in Boston, and his brothers John and Peter (the soap-makers) and James (who had finally given up on Boston) in Newport. A decade had diminished the antagonism between Ben and James; so also did a decline in James's health. Though not yet forty, James felt himself failing, and after evincing his love and affection for his younger brother, he implored Ben to look after his ten-year-old son and namesake when he was gone. In particular he wanted the lad brought up in the printing trade, to carry on his father's work—and his uncle's. Ben, who had never forgotten that he had absconded from James with time left on his indenture, could hardly refuse.

What Debbie thought of the arrangement when Ben got back to Philadelphia is open to speculation. Perhaps she judged that another body in the household—especially a relatively small one—would scarcely be noticed. On the other hand, it may have been Debbie who was behind the decision to send young James off to school for a few years following the elder James's death in 1735. Not till 1740 was he brought into the household as an apprentice. Ben duly taught him the trade while his mother, James's widow, Ann, carried on the business in Rhode Island. When the lad achieved the appropriate age and expertise, his uncle up-dated the Newport shop with new types and got him off to a fair start. "Thus it was that I made my brother ample amends for the service I had deprived him of by leaving so early."

7

Arc of Empire

1741 – 48

૭— "We have had a very healthy summer,
and a fine harvest. The country is filled with bread,
but as trade declines since the war began, I know not
what our farmers will do for a market."

૭— Franklin was writing to his parents in September 1744,
and the war he referred to was the fourth installment of
the colonial contest that formed the backdrop—and
frequently the foreground—to the history of the Atlantic
basin during Franklin's lifetime. The contest had roots in
the struggles of the rising nation-states of Europe for
control of the new discoveries across the seas. Portugal
and Spain were the early leaders, with the Portuguese
monopolizing the trade routes to the East via the South

(that is, around Africa) and the Spanish capitalizing on their conquests in the Americas, encountered accidentally while searching for trade routes to the East via the West. The English and French were slower to exploit the opportunities of expansion overseas, but after sorting out the squabbles surrounding the Reformation of the sixteenth century—a sorting that left France in the Catholic camp but put England among the Protestants—these northerners launched their own imperial ventures. The English defeat of the Spanish Armada in 1588 signaled the start of the eclipse of the Iberians; it was followed by the planting of English and French colonies in North America.

The English got the better of the planting, sowing the seeds of settlement in the relatively fertile soil and equable climates of the Atlantic seaboard between the middle thirties and low forties of northern latitude. The French put down roots, or tried to, in the rocky glacial leftovers of the St. Lawrence Valley. The French also tried to force their way into the Mississippi and Ohio valleys; this effort, superimposed upon the larger struggle between the English and French dynasties on the eastern shore of the Atlantic, was what led to the series of colonial wars in which Franklin eventually became involved.

The first of the series, named by the Americans for English King William, lasted eight years and entailed numerous atrocities, including one massacre in New Hampshire perpetrated by a raiding party that was, in Cotton Mather's characterization, "half Indianized French, and half Frenchified Indians." King William's War ended a decade before Franklin was born, and terminated in a treaty that restored the status quo, to the relief of the monarchs and ministers responsible but the disgust of most of those who did the actual fighting.

The second war was under way at the time of Franklin's birth and was christened for Queen Anne. (No one thought of naming wars after the French monarch, since for longer than most people lived in those days, specifically from 1643 to 1715, all the wars would have been named for the same person, Louis XIV). Queen Anne's War featured the seizure by Britain—as it was now properly called, following the recent unification of England and Scotland—of Gibraltar from France's ally Spain, and it ended during the seventh year of Franklin's life. The settlement confirmed the Gibraltar seizure, to the everlasting humiliation of the Spanish; awarded Acadia and Newfoundland to Britain, to the lasting, if not quite everlasting, vexation of the French; and made Britain's enterprising slave traders the exclusive (legal) suppliers of captured Africans for the Spanish American market (not to mention the British American market).

Had Louis XIV not finally died shortly after the conclusion of Queen Anne's War, the third round of fighting probably would have started sooner than it did. But the regents who ruled in the name of Louis's minor heir lacked the Sun King's sense of entitlement to primacy among nations, a sense that almost certainly would have provoked His Solarity to repudiate the Treaty of Utrecht. Meanwhile the Mississippi Valley absorbed more of France's expansionist energies than anyone had imagined, mitigating the hurt of the loss of territory in the northeast. As a consequence, an entire generation—Franklin's generation—grew up with the odd notion that peace was the rule among the imperial powers, and war the exception.

The error of this notion became apparent during Franklin's fourth decade. A British smuggler named Robert Jenkins was caught in the act by Spanish authorities, who chastised him by slicing off his ear. He retrieved the alienated part and for seven years carried it across the seven seas in a handkerchief in his pocket. Eventually he found his way to Westminster, arriving—not coincidentally—at a moment when English Protestant passions were again rising against the Spanish papists. He produced his leathery relic, to the professed shock of all the honorable members (who in fact saw far worse examples of human cruelty on the streets of London every day). It would be a few years yet before Samuel Johnson defined patriotism as the last refuge of scoundrels; perhaps the pioneer lexicographer was inspired by Jenkins, who declared that at the moment the Spanish sword was flashing down, "I commended my soul to God, and my cause to my country!"

Parliament and country rose in anger—however belated—and war ensued. The War of Jenkins's Ear was noteworthy for the massively stupid loss of British and American lives before the walls of Cartegena, Spain's Caribbean stronghold in New Granada. The American survivors began to form an opinion once commonplace but since forgotten: that they were pawns in Britain's imperial wars. And now it was evident that they were incompetently played pawns at that. (Whether from stubborn loyalty or as a reminder of what he had been through, an American captain named Lawrence Washington limped back to Virginia and called his hilltop plantation above the Potomac after the British admiral at Cartagena, Edward Vernon.)

The War of Jenkins's Ear segued seamlessly into King George's War when France joined the fight on the side of the Spanish. This conflict was the one Franklin referred to in his letter to Josiah and Abiah. The high point of the war, certainly from an American perspective, was the siege of Louisbourg, the French fortress on Cape Breton Island that commanded the entrance to the St. Lawrence River and harassed American fishing vessels on the Grand Banks. As far east as it was, Louisbourg received news of the formal declaration of war before that news reached New England; privateers out of Louisbourg exploited their informational advantage and swooped down upon American vessels, ultimately ranging as far south as the estuary of the Delaware River, where they seized ships almost within hailing distance of the docks of Philadelphia. The French military governor of Louisbourg meanwhile launched a surprise attack on an English fishing village on the Nova Scotian shore. The commander of the attack followed up his easy victory there with a fatal blunder: instead of transporting the prisoners straight to Boston as promised in the surrender terms, he stopped at Louisbourg on the way. This allowed the prisoners to observe that the fortress was poorly maintained and even less well manned. When they reached Boston they shared this intelligence with Governor William Shirley, who determined to put it to use. He advocated an offensive against Louisbourg to end forever the depredations of the French and their savage Indian allies upon the peace-loving and God-fearing people of New England. If the expedition made a hero of its sponsor, all the better.

Shirley struck a sympathetic nerve with his call for ships and troops and money. The maritime interests of Franklin's birthplace itched to be rid of the Gallic menace. Every New England family recalled horror stories of women and children being slaughtered by fiendish red men, provoked and provisioned by the French. The infamous massacre at Deerfield, Massachusetts, was forty years old but more horrible for the telling and retelling. Everyone knew that the Indian raids would never cease until the French were thrust out of Canada. The Massachusetts General Court—the same body that had chastised James Franklin for sedition—instructed Shirley to raise an army of 3,000 volunteers. He persuaded the popular and civic-minded merchant William Pepperell to lead the force and promised easy plunder to all who participated in storming the fortress and reducing the town it guarded. Shirley figuratively brought aboard local preachers, who literally brought aboard their lay brothers. George Whitefield provided a motto for what quickly assumed the trappings of a Protestant crusade: *"Nil desperandum Christo duce."* ("None despairing where Christ leads." Apparently the great revivalist was not bothered by the fact that Latin was the language of the papists.) Shirley invited the other colonies to join the crusade. Rhode Island promised a ship, sailors, and soldiers. Connecticut voted to dispatch a force of 500 men. New York sent cannon, vital for use against the walls of the French fort.

The response from Pennsylvania was less enthusiastic. Governor George Thomas spoke openly for the plan, commending the New Englanders' initiative to the Assembly. "The enterprise shows a fine public spirit in that people!" he declared. "And, if it succeeds, it will be greatly for the honour of His Majesty and the interest of all his colonies in North America." In private, however, he expressed reservations, which strengthened the skeptics in the Assembly. The theology of the Quakers had attenuated over time; pacifism was not as central to the self-conception of the third generation of Friends in America as it had been to William Penn's contemporaries. Yet there remained an uneasiness with war and war preparations, especially when they entailed expense and risk, as these did. Non-Quakers in the Assembly joined the party of the founders in objecting to the cost and hazard and in complaining that they had not been consulted by the New Englanders in advance of the decision to sail against Cape Breton. "We should not think it prudent," the Assembly concluded, "to unite in an enterprise where the expense must be great, perhaps much blood shed, and the event very uncertain."

☞ Franklin observed the Louisbourg debate as clerk of the Assembly. This extremely part-time job, which he had commenced in 1736, was hardly in demand, paying little in cash and less in honor. Its chief recommendation to Franklin was that it facilitated his work as printer of the Assembly's proceedings, which *did* make him some money. It also afforded a firsthand view of Pennsylvania politics.

What he witnessed in the debate over the Louisbourg expedition did not impress him. "When I compare the Governor's message to the House with his private conversation," Franklin noted to himself, "I cannot but admire at his insincerity, to commend the undertaking publicly, that he might gain the applause of the Governor and people of New England, and the Ministry at home [that is, in England], at the same time that he privately does all in his power to disappoint it." The Assembly was no more ingenuous. Remarking the enthusiasm of several members for New England's success, even while they precluded a role for Pennsylvania, Franklin asserted, "If it be against their consciences, they ought not by any means to encourage military proceedings in others more than themselves." To the faces of these same members he spoke more tartly.

"I told them those people [the New Englanders] were as much obliged to them for their good wishes as the poor in the Scripture to those that say, Be ye warmed and ye filled." Again speaking to himself, Franklin added, "I think they ought to be open and honest and give the true reason, and not trifle in the manner they do, by pretending, among other things, that they are offended in not being consulted in such an affair." Neither side had done itself credit. "The Governor and Assembly have been only acting a farce and playing tricks to amuse the world."

The Louisbourg offensive went forward without Pennsylvania's help—but not without Pennsylvania's attention. "Our people are extremely impatient to hear of your success at Cape Breton," Franklin wrote his Boston brother John a month after the expedition set sail. "My shop is filled with thirty inquiries at the coming of every post." Most of those who crowded into the Market Street shop were military innocents—this being Quaker country—and they wondered that the fortress had not already fallen. Franklin was scarcely surprised. "I tell them I shall be glad to hear that news three months hence," he reported to John. "Fortified towns are hard nuts to crack; and your teeth have not been accustomed to it. Taking strong places is a particular trade, which you have taken up without serving an apprenticeship to it. Armies and veterans need skilful engineers to direct them in their attack. Have you any?" Yet these objections hardly registered with many who watched the proceeding from afar. "Some seem to think forts are as easy taken as snuff."

Franklin could not resist a laugh at those who treated the expedition as a crusade and called upon God to guarantee its success. "You have a fast and prayer day for that purpose," he wrote John, "in which I compute five hundred thousand petitions were offered up to the same effect in New England, which added to the petitions of every family morning and evening, multiplied by the number of days since January 25th, make forty-five millions of prayers; which, set against the prayers of a few priests in the garrison, to the Virgin Mary, give a vast balance in your favor." There was serious theology at issue here, Franklin teased. "If you do not succeed, I fear I shall have but an indifferent opinion of Presbyterian prayers in such cases, as long as I live. Indeed, in attacking strong towns I should have more dependence on *works* than on *faith*, for, like the kingdom of heaven, they are to be taken by force and violence; and in a French garrison I suppose there are devils of that kind, that they are not to be cast out by prayers and fasting, unless it be by their own fasting for want of provisions."

ᕫ **Whatever** it did for popular piety, the Louisbourg expedition benefited Franklin's news business. The *Gazette* had gained readers each year since its establishment, although Andrew Bradford's *Mercury* fought a stubborn rearguard action. In November 1740 Bradford announced the inauguration of the first magazine to be published in the American colonies. Entitled *The American Magazine, or A Monthly View of the Political State of the British Colonies*, it would afford readers a broad perspective on public affairs, literature, and the arts and would cost twelve shillings in Pennsylvania currency for a year's subscription. Publication would commence in March 1741, assuming that sufficient subscribers paid their fee.

The following week Franklin's *Gazette* ran a notice of something strikingly similar. *The General Magazine, and Historical Chronicle, for All the British Plantations in America* would examine politics local and imperial, literature American and British, and sundry occurrences noteworthy and merely curious. Published monthly beginning in January, it would cost subscribers ninepence Pennsylvanian (or sixpence British sterling) per issue—that is, nine shillings per year.

To the reading public, Franklin appeared a shameless imitator. In fact he was an aggrieved originator, whose idea had been stolen—albeit through his own carelessness, which added anger at himself to his feeling of injury. And what made him even angrier at himself was that his mistake recapitulated his error of a dozen years earlier when he was planning to start his newspaper. Seeking assistance with the magazine project, he had revealed his plan to a person who, unsatisfied with Franklin's terms, took the idea to his competitor.

In his anger Franklin struck out. The person to whom he had tipped his hand was John Webbe, a lawyer and sometime contributor to the *Gazette*. Convinced that Webbe was behind Bradford's proposed magazine, Franklin—without explicitly naming Webbe—published a statement alleging breach of confidence and theft of ideas.

This provoked Webbe to identify himself, doubtless as Franklin intended. Webbe protested his innocence, saying Franklin was the wrongdoer. By making false, yet veiled, charges, Franklin practiced "the most mischievous kind of lying; for the strokes being oblique and indirect, a man cannot so easily defend himself against them." Webbe's complaint presaged many Franklin would hear in the future about his style of attack:

that there was something "more mean and dastardly in the character of an indirect liar than a direct one. *This* has the audacity of a highwayman, *that* the slyness of a pickpocket. Both indeed rob you of your purse, and both deserve a gibbet; but, were I obliged to pardon either, I could sooner forgive the *bold* wickedness of the one, than the *sneaking* villainy of the other."

The exchange did not cover Franklin in glory. His own indiscretion—not some betrayal by Webbe—was the cause of his preemption. But the nasty back-and-forth had the effect, as Franklin certainly anticipated, of drawing attention to his new magazine.

With the battle joined, both publishers pushed forward their initial issues. Franklin lost the race to Bradford by three days in February 1741. Yet being a step behind had its advantages, for it allowed Franklin to throw rocks at Bradford from the rear. Bradford advertised his magazine in the *Mercury* most elaborately; Franklin responded in the *Gazette* with ridicule. With the partial exception of the title—"Teague's Advertisement," likening Bradford to the infamous pirate—this lampoon was one of Franklin's less inspired offerings. He attempted to mimic the dialect of someone presumably German, but the result left confusion on that point. The wit fell short of the best of Richard Saunders—who in fact acquitted himself better in the contest against Bradford. "If you would keep your secret from an enemy," reminded the edition of *Poor Richard* appearing about this time, "tell it not to a friend."

As it turned out, all the sniping was wasted—or perhaps it was *too* effective. Bradford's magazine expired before its third month; Franklin's lasted but half a year. The competition between the two, by splitting the audience, may have contributed to the demise of both; more likely, Franklin (and Bradford, imitating Franklin) simply misjudged the market. For now—and for a long time—America lacked a literary culture like that which supported the successful *Gentleman's Magazine* of London, which served as the model for Franklin's *General Magazine*. (*Gentleman's* also served, to some extent, as Franklin's competition, as it was brought over the Atlantic and distributed by booksellers in America.) Perhaps the attention span of busy Americans was shorter than that of their English counterparts. Americans would read newspapers and almanacs, but not magazines.

⌁ **Another** part of Franklin's problem was that he was starting to stretch himself thin. The reason he approached John Webbe in the first place was that he lacked the time to produce the magazine himself. His basic business was better than ever. In 1742 he sponsored James Parker in a printing venture in New York. There was a certain historical symmetry here—although Andrew Bradford and his father might have taken it as additional evidence of Franklin's ingratitude. The young Parker had fled an apprenticeship with William Bradford in much the way Franklin had fled his commitment to James Franklin. Just as the elder Bradford had assisted the struggling Ben Franklin to find work, so Franklin took in James Parker and gave him a job as a journeyman. In February 1742 Franklin sent Parker, then about twenty-seven, back to New York to enter competition with William Bradford. Franklin would provide the press and letters and one-third of expenses; in return he would receive one-third of proceeds. At the end of six years Parker would have the option to purchase the press and letters and terminate the partnership.

This arrangement proved even more successful than the earlier one with Thomas Whitemarsh—succeeded by Lewis Timothy—in South Carolina. Franklin may have guessed that William Bradford was on the verge of retirement (Bradford was approaching eighty); he may have calculated that a nudge from Parker might push him over the edge. As events transpired, Bradford—perhaps unwilling to take on such an energetic rival as Franklin—did indeed put down his composition stick, leaving the best of the New York market to the Franklin-Parker combine. Parker succeeded Bradford as official printer of the colony of New York, and he started a newspaper that subsequently assumed the name and the small readership of Bradford's venerable but struggling *New York Gazette*.

The most successful of Franklin's protégés was David Hall. A native of Edinburgh who had followed the printing craft to London, Hall came to Philadelphia highly recommended by his latest employer, William Strahan. Franklin found the recommendation well warranted. "From the short acquaintance I have had with him," Franklin wrote Strahan in July 1744, "I am persuaded that he will answer perfectly the character you had given of him." Franklin hoped to send Hall out on the same kind of commercial colonization scheme as Whitmarsh and Parker—in this case to the West Indies. But a snag arose when Hall developed jaundice, perhaps from hepatitis contracted in the close quarters of the ship from England. Then he and Franklin found themselves at odds over the expense of Hall's passage west. Briefly it appeared that the partnership might founder before launch. Strahan, however, reassured Hall of Franklin's good faith. "Trust to his generosity . . ." Strahan told Hall, "and he will deal honorably by you." Strahan, who knew Franklin only by correspondence, added, "He seems to me by his manner of writing to have a very good heart, as well as to be a man of honour and good sense."

Hall eventually agreed, while Franklin learned to value Hall's talents so highly that he decided to keep him in Philadelphia. Hall became Franklin's foreman, handling the affairs of the shop with a skill and efficiency that not even the fastidious Franklin could fault. The printing business grew more profitable to its owner, yet he had to devote less time to it than ever.

⌁— In the two centuries after his death Franklin would be cited—in praise by some, in scorn by others—as a prototype of the American capitalist. The citation was misleading. Had Franklin possessed the soul of a true capitalist, he would have devoted the time he saved from printing to making money somewhere else. But he did not. For Franklin the getting of money was always a means to an end, never the end itself. No one worked harder at the printing business than Franklin during the years when his printing house had to be established and placed on a sound footing. But once the footing was assured, his interests and increasingly his energies went elsewhere.

The test of his attitude toward money was his handling of what he called the "Pennsylvania fireplace." For years Franklin had been convinced that fireplaces and stoves might be made more efficient; in hours borrowed from the printing business he tinkered with baffles and fireboxes to produce a better model. By the early 1740s he was satisfied with his design and arranged with Robert Grace, the Junto iron man, to manufacture and sell the new fireplace.

"In these northern colonies the inhabitants keep fires to sit by, generally *seven months* in the year," wrote Franklin in a promotional pamphlet published in 1744. "Wood, our common fuel, which within these 100 years might be had at every man's door, must now be fetched near 100 miles to some towns, and makes a very considerable article in the expense of families." Any method for economizing on fuel, by improving fuel efficiency, would benefit private citizens and the public at large. "The NEW FIRE-PLACES are a late invention to that purpose (experienced now three winters by a great number of families in Pennsylvania)."

Governor Thomas was so pleased with Franklin's innovation that he offered him a patent conferring exclusive rights to sell the fireplace within the province. Had Franklin accepted, he doubtless would have made a good deal of money (and if he had aggressively extended the patent to the other American colonies, he would have made a great deal of money), for the fireplace became very popular. And the colder the climate, the more popular it became. A correspondent to the *Boston Evening Post* could not speak highly enough of "the new-invented Philadelphia Fire Places, or as they ought to be called, both in justice and gratitude, Mr. Franklin's stoves." One cord, or at most one and a half cords, of quality firewood sufficed in Franklin's invention to warm the common room of an ordinary house the entire winter. The benefit was obvious. "Every body can calculate what a saving this must be in one of the most necessary articles of house-keeping, and I believe all who have experienced the comfort and benefit of them will join with me, that the author of this happy invention merits a statue from his countrymen."

Franklin would get his statues in time; for now he declined the offer of exclusive rights to his stove. His was not a patenting personality, one that perceived knowledge as the property of its discoverer. Rather he saw philosophy—broadly construed, as it was in those days—as a collective undertaking. What one investigator unearthed ought to become the common property of all. As it applied to patents, he explained, "That as we enjoy great advantages from the inventions of others, we should be glad of an opportunity to serve others by any invention of ours, and this we should do freely and generously."

Franklin's view was evident in his pamphlet describing the fireplace. The pamphlet was an advertisement only incidentally; its heart was a scientific treatise on the theory of combustion and on practical applications to domestic heating. He cited authorities classical (supplying one long source in Latin) and exotic (quoting, in translation, from a Chinese work). He explained the various means by which heat is transmitted (paying particular attention to convection, overlooked or misapplied in most fireplace designs). He contended, with evidence, that rooms heated with the new fireplace were more healthful than rooms heated conventionally, for the heat permeated the rooms more evenly. He included a schematic rendering of the fireplace, together with instructions as to how it ought to be installed (including a hint to mix rum with water in the paste used to seal the joints). Being Franklin, he closed with a verse of the sort Richard Saunders regularly penned, extolling the fireplace as a second sun:

> *Another sun!—'tis true—but not the same.*
> *Alike, I own, in warmth and genial flame.*
> *But more obliging than his elder brother,*
> *This will not scorch in summer, like the other,*

Nor, when sharp Boreas chills our shivering limbs,
Will this sun leave us for more southern climes;
Or, in long winter nights, forsake us here,
To cheer new friends in t'other hemisphere;
But, faithful still to us, this new sun's fire,
Warms when we please, and just as we desire.

It was characteristic of Franklin to combine theory and application in his pamphlet on the fireplace, for just as he did not have the heart of a modern capitalist, neither was he what the modern age would call a true intellectual. He had an inquisitive mind—ceaselessly inquisitive, in fact, as his whole life attested. But he found knowledge for knowledge's sake to be an unsatisfying formula. The kind of knowledge he prized was that which made life easier, more productive, or happier. In this regard his view of science mirrored his view of religion. Where faith was sterile if it failed to produced good works, so science was sterile—even if interesting—if it failed to produce good inventions.

In May 1743 Franklin printed *A Proposal for Promoting Useful Knowledge Among the British Plantations in America*. Others had bruited the idea before, chiefly John Bartram of Philadelphia and Cadwallader Colden of New York. But neither of them was a printer, which in this as in many of his other projects gave Franklin a crucial advantage. Bartram and Colden might—and did—communicate between themselves and with a small circle of correspondents, but Franklin could reach hundreds or thousands through his printing press. How many copies he produced of his broadside *Promoting Useful Knowledge* is unknown, but without doubt it spread the idea among a wider audience than had heard any such notion theretofore.

"The first drudgery of settling new colonies, which confines the attention of people to mere necessaries, is now pretty well over," Franklin wrote. "And there are many in every province in circumstances that set them at ease, and afford leisure to cultivate the finer arts and improve the stock of knowledge." To such as were of a philosophical turn of mind, curiosity and insight must from time to time produce discoveries "to the advantage of some or all of the British plantations, or to the benefit of mankind in general."

They would, at any rate, if properly encouraged and communicated. This was the purpose of Franklin's publication. He proposed "that one society be formed of Virtuosi or ingenious men residing in the several colonies, to be called *The American Philosophical Society.*" The society would be centered at Philadelphia, the city closest to the center of the colonies, where the post roads converged and where they intersected the sea-lanes to the settlements in the West Indies. In addition, Philadelphia already possessed a respectable and growing library, essential to any such endeavor.

At Philadelphia would reside the core of the society, consisting of a physician, a botanist, a mathematician, a chemist, a "mechanician," a geographer, and a natural philosopher of broad interests and expertise. The society's president, treasurer, and secretary would also be based in Franklin's home city. The group would meet at least once a month, and would discuss their own latest findings and those transmitted to them by members in other cities and colonies. A principal function of the Philadelphia nucleus would be to facilitate the flow of information among members with common interests but no common meeting ground. To this end the society would sponsor publication of the most noteworthy findings and hypotheses.

Topics suitable for investigation covered the range of human interests and needs. "All new-discovered plants, herbs, trees, roots, &c., their virtues, uses, &c., methods of propagating them. . . . Improvements of vegetable juices, as ciders, wines &c. New methods of curing or preventing disease. All new-discovered fossils in different countries, as mines, minerals, quarries, &c. New and useful improvements in any branch of mathematics. New discoveries in chemistry, such as improvements in distillation, brewing, assaying of ores, &c. New mechanical inventions for saving labour, as mills, carriages, &c." And so on, through geography, geology, animal husbandry, and more horticulture, and concluding with "all philosophical experiments that let light into the nature of things, tend to increase the power of man over matter, and multiply the conveniences or pleasures of life."

Franklin released this manifesto—characteristically, a roster of questions rather than of answers—to the world in May 1743. The reaction was slow but promising. Cadwallader Colden wrote from New York, "I long very much to hear what you have done in your scheme of erecting a society at Philadelphia for promoting of useful arts and sciences in America. If you think any thing in my power whereby I can promote so useful an undertaking I will with much pleasure receive your instructions for that end."

This response encouraged Franklin, especially as it came from one as distinguished as Colden. A physician by training, Colden was surveyor general of New York, and a man almost as catholic in his interests as Franklin would become. Colden refused to be intimidated by the awesome reputation of Isaac Newton, convincing himself that Newton had erred on certain important points. He devoted much of his adult life to correcting the mistakes. Yet the effort hardly exhausted him. He found time to write a history of the Indian tribes in and around the colony of New York, a taxonomy of the flora near his Orange County home (which he rendered in Latin and sent to the Swedish patriarch of plant science and Latin nomenclature, Linneaus, who duly published it), assorted treatises on moral philosophy, medical accounts of major diseases and lesser distempers, and a translation of Cicero's letters.

Franklin knew Colden by reputation and was flattered to hear from him. He replied at once. "I cannot but be fond of engaging in a correspondence so advantageous to me as yours must be," Franklin said. "I shall always receive your favours as such, and with great pleasure."

This exchange commenced a correspondence between Franklin and Colden that enlightened and delighted both parties. Colden encouraged Franklin in gathering the "Virtuosi" into his philosophical society. "I long to know what progress you make in forming your society," he inquired. "If it meet with obstruction from the want of proper encouragement or otherwise, I would have you attempt some other method of proceeding in your design, for I shall be very sorry to have it entirely dropped."

Franklin reported progress, but less than he would have liked. The charter membership included John Bartram as botanist; the disagreeable but ingenious Thomas Godfrey as mathematician; Thomas Bond, a medical doctor trained in Britain and France, as physician; his brother Phineas Bond as natural-philosopher-at-large; Samuel Rhoads, a master carpenter active in local politics, as mechanician; William Parsons, original member of the Junto, lately librarian of the Library Company, and currently surveyor general of Pennsylvania, as geographer; William Coleman, who underwrote Franklin's escape from his partnership with Hugh Meredith, as treasurer; and Thomas Hopkinson, a director of the Library Company and former city councilman, as president. Franklin served as secretary. Several meetings took place during the first half of 1744, and out-of-town members were added to the group. But most lacked Franklin's energy, to his frustration and annoyance. "The members of our Society here are very idle gentlemen," he complained to Colden. "They will take no pains."

⌖ **Franklin** did not guess when he floated the idea of the Philosophical Society that its establishment would mark a turning point in his life. What he envisioned was a more sophisticated and geographically in-clusive version of the Junto: a discussion group that brought together in-quiring minds from across the continent rather than across the city. What he got was a network of kindred spirits that spurred him to better and more original work than he knew he had in him. The expansion of Franklin's universe continued; his world came to include the best minds in America. And those minds came to recognize the preeminence of his.

With the letter to Colden in which he lamented the idleness of his fellow philosophers in Philadelphia, Franklin enclosed speculations on the flow of fluids throughout the human body. He granted that his ideas suffered from lack of opportunity for personal experimentation; he knew only what he had read and could infer therefrom. Yet he hoped to remedy the deficiency. He described an apparatus he had devised to test a hypothe-sis in hydrodynamics that had direct bearing on the flow of fluids through the human skin. "You shall know the success," he promised Colden.

In fact the experiment proved inconclusive. Franklin was disap-pointed but not discouraged. "I intend to try a farther experiment, of which I shall give you an account," he assured Colden.

Meanwhile the two men communicated on other topics. Franklin puzzled over Colden's comments on "fluxions," the infinitesimals de-vised by Newton as the basis for calculus and the physical theories that grew out of it; Franklin wished for a stronger background in mathe-matics and promised himself to acquire it. He shared some of Colden's reservations about current thinking in mechanical dynamics, including a theory of inertia that seemed to imply that a very small force could not move very large objects. Franklin countered this with a thought experi-ment. "Suppose two globes each equal to the sun and to one another, ex-actly equipoised in Jove's balance. Suppose no friction in the center of motion in the beam or elsewhere. If a mosquito then were to light on one of them, would he not give a motion to them both, causing one to descend and the other to rise?"

A more immediately practical problem motivated another letter to Colden. For centuries it had been noted that voyages from the Americas to England took less time than voyages in the opposite direction. Prevail-ing winds accounted for part of the discrepancy, but not all of it. Franklin wondered whether the rotation of the earth was involved. A ship at the equator was carried eastward by the earth's rotation faster—in an absolute, although not a longitudinal, sense—than a ship in the latitude of Philadelphia, which in turn was carried faster than a ship at the latitude of London. Was some residue of the rotational speed responsible for the more rapid transit from southeast to northwest, compared to the reverse? "I have not time to explain my self farther, the post waiting," Franklin wrote to Colden, "but believe I have said enough for you to comprehend my meaning." (Although he later would realize that the effect was more complicated than he supposed here, Franklin was definitely onto something, as the French mathematician Coriolis, after whom the effect was named, would make explicit a century later.)

 ⌐ Neither devoted capitalist nor pure intellectual, Franklin was not a strict scientist either. He accepted the unscientific and irrational for what it was—an inescapable aspect of human nature, and not necessarily ignoble for that. He could give a dozen reasons for restraining human passion but was not in the least surprised that it defied restraint. As a young man he had failed to restrain his own passions, irrational though they were; he fully expected that young men—and not a few older men, as well as women of various ages—would continue to succumb. Such was life; a person would be a fool to deny it.

Franklin was no fool, and no prude. In the summer of 1745 he wrote a letter—or perhaps an essay in the form of a letter—to "My dear Friend," an unnamed young man. The subject of this letter was so shocking to the sensibility of the several generations that followed Franklin's that the piece was effectively suppressed for nearly two centuries. Yet Franklin considered it matter-of-factly, as though it were a topic as fit for reflection and inquiry as any other.

The question was, what sort of mistress was best for an unmarried young man? Franklin prefaced his remarks by declaring that marriage was the proper condition for man. If Deborah had read this passage, she would have been touched:

> It is the most natural state of man, and therefore the state in which you are most likely to find solid happiness. . . . It is the man and woman united that make the complete human being. Separate, she wants his force of body and strength of reason; he, her softness, sensibility and acute discernment. Together they are more likely to succeed in the world. A single man has not nearly the value he would have in that state of union. He is an incomplete animal. He resembles the odd half of a pair of scissors. If

you get a prudent, healthy wife, your industry in your profession, with her good economy, will be a fortune sufficient.

Yet Franklin would not have been writing were his correspondent—whoever he was—likely to be swayed by such rational arguments. Male youth would sow its oats, whatever Franklin might say.

Accepting this, Franklin advised the young gent on the sort of mistress he should choose. "In all your amours, you should *prefer old women to young ones*," he said. He granted that this flew against inclination; consequently, on the premise that passion need not entirely banish practicality, he adduced eight reasons in favor of mature mistresses:

1. Because as they have more knowledge of the world and their minds are better stored with observations, their conversation is more improving and more lastingly agreeable.

2. Because when women cease to be handsome, they study to be good. To maintain their influence over men, they supply the diminution of beauty by an augmentation of utility. They learn to do 1000 services small and great, and are the most tender and useful of all friends when you are sick. Thus they continue amiable. And hence there is hardly such a thing to be found as an old woman who is not a good woman.

3. Because there is no hazard of children, which irregularly produced may be attended with much inconvenience.

4. Because through more experience, they are more prudent and discreet in conducting an intrigue to prevent suspicion. The commerce with them is therefore safer with regard to your reputation. And with regard to theirs, if the affair should happen to be known, considerate people might be rather inclined to excuse an old woman who would kindly take care of a young man, form his manners by her good counsels, and prevent his ruining his health and fortune among mercenary prostitutes.

5. Because in every animal that walks upright, the deficiency of the fluids that fill the muscles appears first in the highest part. The face grows lank and wrinkled, then the neck, then the breast and arms, the lower parts continuing to the last as plump as ever. So that covering all above with a basket, and regarding only what is below the girdle, it is impossible of two women to know an old from a young one. And as in the dark all cats are grey, the pleasure of corporal enjoyment with an old woman is at least

equal, and frequently superior, every knack being by practice capable of improvement.

6. Because the sin is less. The debauching a virgin may be her ruin, and make her for life unhappy.

7. Because the compunction is less. The having made a young girl *miserable* may give you frequent bitter reflections, none of which can attend making an old woman *happy*.

8thly and lastly. They are *so grateful!!*

↷ **Perhaps** Debbie did read this; if so, she must have had mixed feelings. At thirty-seven her face was starting to sag, her neck and arms to lose their tone. Yet here her husband was singing praise to the woman she was becoming—unless he was singing praise to some *other* older woman. How did he know that all women looked alike from the girdle down? It sounded as though he had done a survey. Was he complimenting *her* in declaring that the "knack" of lovemaking improved with practice? Or someone else? And who, precisely, was *"so grateful"* for an illicit liaison?

The other women in Franklin's life would occasion international comment, but there is little evidence of wandering at this stage in his life. On the contrary, he made much of his affection for Debbie. Franklin spent many, perhaps most, evenings in various taverns, meeting with members of the Junto and other associates. The distaste for alcohol he evinced in England had worn off; while never a lush, he hoisted a pint with his friends quite freely. As the tongues loosened, they often broke into song, to which Franklin contributed with voice and pen. One of his ditties he entitled "The Antediluvians Were All Very Sober":

> *The Antediluvians were all very sober,*
> > *For they had no wine, and they brewed no October [an autumn ale];*
> *All wicked, bad livers, on mischief still thinking,*
> > *For there can't be good living where isn't good drinking.*

> *'Twas honest old Noah first planted the vine,*
> *And mended his morals by drinking its wine.*
> *He justly the drinking of water decried,*
> > *For he knew that all mankind, by drinking it, died.*

> *From this piece of history plainly we find*
> *That water's good neither for body or mind;*
> *That virtue and safety in wine-bibbing's found,*
> *While all that drink water deserve to be drowned.*

The choristers often selected songs that spoke of relations between the sexes; frequently these extolled the virtues of women to whom the songs' narrators were not married. One of Franklin's friends remarked on the dearth of drinking music that made married life appear attractive. Franklin responded with another composition—the lyrics, anyway, for as with most such inventions, these were set to a tune the taverners already knew. The song praised his domestic existence with Debbie, who was discreetly rechristened as "My Plain Country Joan":

> *Of their Chloes and Phyllises poets may prate;*
> *I sing my plain country Joan.*
> *Now twelve years my wife, still the joy of my life;*
> *Blest day that I made her my own.*
>
> *Not a word of her face, her shape or her eyes,*
> *Of flames or of darts shall you hear.*
> *Though I beauty admire, 'tis virtue I prize,*
> *That fades not in seventy years. . . .*
>
> *Some faults we have all, and so may my Joan*
> *But then they're exceedingly small.*
> *And now I'm used to 'em, they're just like my own,*
> *I scarcely can see 'em at all.*

After 1743 Franklin had even more to be thankful to Debbie about. In the late summer of that year she gave birth to a daughter, named Sarah for her maternal grandmother. Eleven years after Franky's birth, seven years after his death, and almost certainly long past the time when she had despaired of having any children to survive her—and any children of her own to offset the presence of Benjamin's bastard William—Debbie delighted in little Sally. She insisted that the child be baptized at Christ Church, up Market Street past the market and around the corner on Fifth (next to the burial ground where young Franky lay). She did not have to insist that Sally be inoculated against smallpox; her husband's still-sore conscience made certain that his daughter would not suffer the fate of his second son. "Sally was inoculated April 18 [1746], being Friday at 10 o'clock in the morning," he noted to himself, as if to confirm in writing that he had done for Sally what he should have done for Franky.

Sally proved a true Franklin. "Your granddaughter is the greatest lover of her book and school of any child I ever knew," he wrote his mother just after Sally's fourth birthday. Precocity persisted through the next three years. "Sally grows a fine girl, and is extremely industrious with her needle, and delights in her book," he informed Abiah after Sally turned seven. "She is of a most affectionate temper, and perfectly dutiful and obliging, to her parents and to all. Perhaps I flatter my self too much; but I have hopes that she will prove an ingenious, sensible, notable, and worthy woman."

Such hopes led Franklin lightheartedly to consider a match between Sally and William Strahan, the son of Franklin's English correspondent, and increasingly his friend, of the same name. The idea appealed to William's father, offering the two fathers an excuse to share details of the development of their children. "I am glad to hear so good a character of my son-in-law," Franklin replied to one of Strahan's letters, written when young William was ten and Sally seven. "Please to acquaint him that his spouse grows finely, and will probably have an agreeable person. That with the best natural disposition in the world, she discovers daily the seeds and tokens of industry and economy, and in short, of every female virtue, which her parents will endeavour to cultivate for him." Talk of a dowry or other such arrangement was premature, but Franklin broached the subject obliquely, which was to say morally: "If the success [of his and Debbie's parenting efforts] answers their fond wishes and expectations, she will, in the true sense of the word, be *worth* a great deal of money, and consequently a great fortune."

Sally's arrival added a life to Franklin's universe; his father's death subtracted one. Josiah Franklin died in January 1745 at the age of eighty-seven. "By an entire dependence on his redeemer and a constant course of the strictest piety and virtue," the *Boston Weekly News-Letter* noted on his passing, "he was enabled to die, as he lived, with cheerfulness and peace." What Josiah in his last years thought of his youngest son is impossible to ascertain; the father was as frugal with his emotions as with his money. He must have been proud of Benjamin's worldly accomplishments, but he likely worried at Ben's lack of that piety Josiah's obituarist applauded in him. Father and son had never been close, and they were not close at the end. Needless to say, by the time Ben heard of the death, it was too late to travel to Boston for the funeral. Yet the death goes unremarked in Franklin's surviving correspondence. Although he must have written condolences to Abiah, the closest thing to an extant expression of feeling appears in a letter to his sister Jane, who lived near their father and mother. "Dear Sister, I love you tenderly for your care of our father in his sickness," he said.

∾ From Philadelphia it was often easy to forget there was a war going on in the north and on the western frontier. After its enthusiastic commencement, the Louisbourg expedition settled down to a difficult siege. The summer soldiers from New England could not help being impressed—indeed awed—by the "Gibraltar of the New World," with its thirty-foot-high stone walls; the 250 cannon protruding from the apertures in the ramparts; the curtain-wall that ran three-quarters of a mile across the neck of land that contained the town, anchored at one end in the harbor and buried at the other in the surf; the island battery commanding the harbor, positioned to blast any ships that slipped through the reefs jutting like the tines of a giant fork from the bottom, ready to rake the hulls of intruders ignorant of their exact position; the "Grand Battery" located a mile from the town, covering the entire harbor from mouth to head, eager to deliver a deadly crossfire against enemy forces.

Yet God was watching over the attackers, as their preachers had promised. At least so it seemed by the evidence of the first engagements. The French defenders fell for a feint that allowed the landing party to establish a beachhead with but minor casualties. Two days later Providence smiled again, persuading the French, who could see they were badly outnumbered, to consolidate their forces in the town itself. They abandoned the Grand Battery, spiking the guns there but unaccountably failing to blow up the magazine and destroy the structure. As it turned out, their spiking operation failed as well: the clever New Englanders had brought along blacksmiths and special tools, and dislodged the spikes from the powder holes of the guns. These they trained upon the walls of Louisbourg proper.

William Pepperell was no waster of human life; neither was Peter Warren, the commander of the squadron of the Royal Navy recently arrived to reinforce the Americans. "To prevent the effusion of Christian blood," as they put it, they called upon the French commander to surrender. The messenger sent to deliver the proposed terms was duly blindfolded at the gate of the town and conducted to the headquarters of Governor Louis du Chambon. The governor disdained these untested, untrained attackers, even if they had him cornered; equally to the point, he hoped for the arrival of a French naval squadron that would raise the siege. "The King of France, our King," he answered, having turned the blindfolded envoy around and sent him back out the west gate, "has given us the responsibility of defending this city; we cannot, except after the most vigorous attack, consider a similar proposition. The only reply we make to this demand is from the mouths of our cannon."

The Anglophone artillery spoke louder. The Americans heated their iron balls to glowing before firing them over the walls, where they set many of the wood-frame houses ablaze. Reports of the approach of several hundred French and Indian soldiers received credibility from the actual sighting of a French warship; together these developments caused Pepperell to escalate the siege into a direct assault. To secure his flank he ordered an attack on the island battery. The first such attack fizzled when the attackers bolstered their courage excessively with rum and arrived at the beach too drunk to make the crossing. A second landing, launched at night, clandestinely secured a beachhead on the island, but one hero spoiled the surprise by leading his comrades in a rousing cheer, which alerted the French sentries and triggered a near-massacre of the landing party.

Yet fortune refused to abandon the Americans. The continued pounding of the town, combined with some well-advertised preparations for a joint sea-land assault on the fortress, persuaded du Chambon to reconsider capitulation. He tested the idea on the leading merchants and citizens of Louisbourg, who urged him to surrender lest their property be destroyed. Satisfied he would not have to bear blame alone, he sued for peace. Pepperell and Warren accepted.

The news of the victory traveled fast. In Philadelphia, Franklin made it a lead item in the *Gazette*:

> Wednesday last, a great number of guns were distinctly heard in several places round this city, the occasion of which, as well as the place where they were fired, was unknown until the evening of the day following, when an express arrived with advice of the surrender of Louisbourg, which had caused great rejoicings at New York. 'Twas near nine o'clock when the express came in, yet the

news flying instantly round the town, upwards of 20 bonfires were immediately lighted in the streets. The next day was spent in feasting, and drinking the healths of Governor Shirley, Gen. Pepperell, Com. Warren, &c. &c. under the discharge of cannon from the wharfs and vessels in the river; and the evening concluded with bonfires, illuminations, and other demonstrations of joy. A mob gathered, and began to break the windows of those houses that were not illuminated, but it was soon dispersed, and suppressed.

Not surprisingly, the Americans acquired a high opinion of their prowess at war. Those who participated in the conquest itself took home a comment by the French port captain at Louisbourg, that he had first thought the New England men cowards but had changed his mind: "If they had a pick ax and spade, they would dig their way to hell and storm it." Echoes from across the Atlantic swelled the American heads still further. The *Gentleman's Magazine* threw laurels:

> *Hail, heroes born for action, not for show!*
> *Who leave toupees and powder to the beau,*
> *To war's dull pedants tedious rules of art,*
> *And know to conquer by a dauntless heart.*
> *Rough* English *virtue gives your deeds to fame*
> *And o'er the* Old *exalts* New England's *name.*

Although the greatest honor accrued to those who actually fought at Louisbourg, the glow warmed hearts all over America. It fostered a belief that England depended on America for defense—frontier defense, anyway—rather than vice versa. Americans could stand on their own.

From the belief they *could* stand on their own to the conclusion that they *should* stand on their own required another generation and a half, but the seeds of independence were germinating in the soil of colonial self-help. Although Ben Franklin, a city boy from birth, knew next to nothing of plowing and planting, on this subject he helped loosen the ground from which the shoots would emerge.

To the surprise of the myopic among the Americans, and to the disappointment of even the perspicacious, the victory at Louisbourg did not end the war. Indeed, it had little effect at all beyond demoralizing the

New Englanders who now had to garrison that chilly and forbidding rock, as the same task had demoralized the French. On the frontier, raiding parties of French and Indians beset isolated villages. In one notorious incident of November 1745, a band of three hundred French Canadians and two hundred Indians swept down upon the undefended village of Saratoga, New York, killing thirty, taking two or three times that many captive, and burning much of what could not be carried away.

Massachusetts Governor Shirley, whose wave of fame from Louisbourg had yet to break, advocated an encore: an invasion of Canada. The goal was to thrust the French finally out of America; with the French gone, their Indian allies would have to come to terms with the English, as the Iroquois, for example, had already done. When King George II bestowed his royal approval upon the project, the other colonies were obliged to participate. Pennsylvania's official cooperation came grudgingly; the Assembly loosened the purse strings with typical reluctance. Unofficially the Pennsylvanians betrayed greater eagerness. Four companies of volunteers rallied to the colors and prepared to march to Albany to join the rest of the invasion force.

Among the volunteers was William Franklin. Fifteen-year-old Billy was showing the same rebelliousness his father had evinced at that age. The boy's existence was, in material respects, easier than the father's had been. In previous years Benjamin had bought Billy a pony to ride; he engaged a tutor to instruct him in reading and writing and numbers; he sent him to study with the best teacher of mathematics in the city; he enrolled him in the academy where the sons of the city's gentry received the finest classical education.

But Billy grew bored and, like his father, found himself drawn to dockside. The ships that lined the Delaware waterfront, like those of Benjamin's Boston, came from all over the world; they promised adventures untold—or at least an escape from a life that weighed increasingly upon Billy's broadening shoulders. Much as Ben had longed to do but been dissuaded, Billy packed a small kit, walked the few blocks to the quay, and sought a vessel to ship out on.

It was Billy's good luck, or so it initially seemed, that there was a war in progress. The waterfront was full of privateers, licensed pirates who needed hands for their dangerous but potentially lucrative work. One first mate liked Billy's looks and signed him aboard. But before the craft weighed anchor, Ben discovered the boy's absence and hurried to the wharf. After a brief search he found the lad and unceremoniously fetched him home.

Franklin declined to blame himself for Billy's attempted escape. "No one imagined it was hard usage at home that made him do this," he explained to his sister Jane. "Every one that knows me thinks I am too indulgent a parent." Remembering his own youth, he attributed Billy's restlessness to his age and to the allure of what the privateers might win. "When boys see prizes brought in, and quantities of money shared among the men, and their gay living, it fills their heads with notions."

Franklin did not presume to banish those notions; such would be a fool's errand. Instead he sought to redirect them slightly, from the unforgiving sea to the somewhat safer land. He let Billy know he would not object if the boy enlisted among the volunteers for the Canada expedition. Billy happily took the offer. Delighted at putting whatever distance between himself and his home—yet unaware that in doing so he was simultaneously putting himself on a path that would lead to a terminal distancing from his father—Ensign William Franklin marched up the road toward Albany in the service of his king.

⌒ **At forty** Franklin felt no desire to head off to Canada himself. Yet he supported the idea of colonial defense, and when the Assembly continued to ignore the necessities of provincial security, he took up the weapon he had long since mastered: the printing press. In the autumn of 1747 he wrote and published a pamphlet entitled *Plain Truth: Or, Serious Considerations on the Present State of the City of Philadelphia and Province of Pennsylvania*. "War at this time rages over a great part of the known world," he declared. "Our news-papers are weekly filled with fresh accounts of the destruction it every where occasions." Heretofore Pennsylvania had been spared the worst of the violence, Franklin said, but this was due to an accident of geography—that Pennsylvania was surrounded by other colonies more directly in the line of fire—rather than the exertions of its inhabitants. Such safety as circumstance afforded could not be expected to last. Philadelphia's wealth supplied a strong inducement to attack by enemy privateers or warships, an inducement the city's defenseless condition only intensified. As for the countryside beyond the city, it lay open to assault by Indians allied to the French. To be sure, Pennsylvania's enlightened policies had won over the most important of the neighboring tribes, but the loyalty of those tribes could hardly be taken for granted when France aided their enemies and neither England nor Pennsylvania provided countervailing assistance.

Should the tissue of what passed for provincial defense be torn, the consequence for Philadelphians would be swift and brutal:

> On the first alarm, terror will spread over all; and as no man can with certainty depend that another will stand by him, beyond doubt very many will seek safety by a speedy flight. Those that are reputed rich will flee through fear of torture to make them produce more than they are able. The man that has a wife and children will find them hanging on his neck, beseeching him with tears to quit the city, and save his life, to guide and protect them in that time of general desolation and ruin. All will run into confusion, amidst cries and lamentations.

If such were the case in the event of advance alarm, what would happen if the blow fell by surprise?

> Confined to your houses, you will have nothing to trust to but the enemy's mercy. Your best fortune will be to fall under the power of commanders of king's ships, able to control the mariners, and not into the hands of *licentious privateers*. Who can, without the utmost horror, conceive the miseries of the latter! when your persons, fortunes, wives and daughters, shall be subject to the wanton and unbridled rage, rapine and lust, of *Negroes*, *Molattoes*, and others, the vilest and most abandoned of mankind. A dreadful scene!

The author of this lurid forecast identified himself only as "A Tradesman of Philadelphia," and it was as a tradesman that Franklin made his appeal. Neither the party of religion—the Quakers—nor the party of wealth—the rich merchants and their allies—had lifted a finger in defense of the city. Between the "mistaken principles of religion" of the former and the "pride, envy and implacable resentment" of the latter, the lives and fortunes of "the middling people, the farmers, shopkeepers and tradesmen of this city and country" were in the dire jeopardy they faced. Franklin called on the middling classes to seize control of their fate:

> At present we are like the separate filaments of flax before the thread is formed, without strength because without connection. But UNION would make us strong and even formidable. Though the *Great* should neither help nor join us, though they should even

oppose our uniting, from some mean views of their own, yet if we resolve upon it, and if it please GOD to inspire us with the necessary prudence and vigour, it *may* be effected.

Franklin's warning and appeal found a ready audience among ordinary Pennsylvanians, and to a lesser extent in other colonies. The first edition of this pamphlet—numbering two thousand—sold out quickly, requiring a second printing. A German translation soon appeared, for that growing community of German immigrants in the Pennsylvania backcountry. Selections from the pamphlet ran in newspapers in the leading cities of America.

Encouraged by this response, Franklin supplied specific recommendations for provincial defense. He drafted a charter for an "Association," or militia, of volunteers drawn from the public at large. Members would furnish their own weapons, form companies according to neighborhoods, choose officers by ballot of the men, and convene a general military council of representatives from each company. Civic virtue, rather than compulsion, would serve as the basis for the actions of all involved.

Franklin presented the plan at a meeting in the public hall built for George Whitefield and the awakeners. "The house was pretty full," Franklin recalled. "I harangued them a little on the subject, read the paper and explained it, and then distributed the copies." Public speaking had never been Franklin's forte and never would be; he felt obliged to elaborate his "harangue" in the *Gazette* in the following days.

Here the radical nature of his plan became apparent. Government having failed the people, he said, the people were entirely justified in assuming for themselves an essential role of government. "Where a Government takes proper measures to protect the people under its care, such a proceeding might have been thought both unnecessary and unjustifiable. But here it is quite the reverse." The insistence on organizing companies according to neighborhoods was intended "to prevent people's sorting themselves into companies according to their ranks in life, their quality or station." The tradesman-author was also a leveler. " 'Tis designed to mix the great and small together, for the sake of union and encouragement. Where danger and duty are equal to all, there should be no distinction from circumstances, but all be on the level." In the closest thing to an admission of the radicalism of his proposal, Franklin took pains to express "a dutiful regard to the government we are under." The Association was a wartime organization only. " 'Tis heartily to be wished that a safe and honourable peace may the very next year render it useless."

The plan was a stunning success and Franklin the hero of the hour. Five hundred men took the pledge at that first meeting; within days the number from the city alone surmounted one thousand; eventually some ten thousand subscribed from all over the colony. Soon the companies were drilling, converting the facility with firearms many American males (not to mention some females) acquired in childhood into something approximating military effectiveness. Women's auxiliaries complemented the work of the men, sewing flags for the different companies, often with colors and mottoes suggested by Franklin. He himself was voted colonel of the Philadelphia regiment, but, lacking any military experience, he declined the honor.

There was more to the scheme. Enlisting bodies in the defense of home and hearth was relatively easy, especially when actual fighting remained merely hypothetical. Arming those enlistees with rifles and other small weapons was scarcely harder, especially since many already owned such weapons. (For the weaponless, or those wishing to upgrade the household arsenal, Franklin advertised in the *Gazette*: "A parcel of good muskets, all well fitted with bayonets, belts and cartouch-boxes, and buff slings to cast over the shoulder, very useful to such as have occasion to ride with their arms; to be sold by B. Franklin.")

Artillery was another matter. Needed to defend the city against marine assault, cannons were not the sort of thing hanging in everyman's back room. Instead they had to be purchased, at a price commensurate with their scarcity.

Because the Assembly refused to appropriate the funds, Franklin proposed another extragovernmental scheme. He organized a lottery in which £20,000 of tickets would be sold; £17,000 would be paid out in prizes, with the balance of £3,000 being set aside for the purchase of cannons and the like. The idea of a lottery did not originate with Franklin; the practice had already come over from England and been employed in New England and New York. But he adapted it to Pennsylvania's circumstances. Many of the same persons who objected on pacifist grounds to buying weapons for the province now objected on anti-gambling grounds to a lottery. To overcome their objections, Franklin enlisted the support of the leading men of the city, including James Logan, whose Quaker credentials went back to William Penn. Logan once explained to Franklin the difference between his own and Penn's views on the legitimacy of self-defense. Queen Anne's War was on while Penn and Logan made the crossing to America; en route their ship encountered another vessel, which the prudent captain presumed to be an enemy. He ordered all hands and passengers to prepare to defend the craft and themselves, but he made special allowance for Penn and his Quaker company, knowing their scruples. They might retire belowdecks. James Logan, however, remained above and was assigned to a gun. After a tense half hour, the approaching ship turned out to be a friend, and Logan went below to share the welcome news with Penn and the others. To his surprise, Penn upbraided him for staying on deck and making ready to fight. Such was not the Quaker way. Logan, irritated at being chastised in front of the entire company, spoke more than he might have in private; he replied that it was rather late for Penn to be complaining. As he—Logan—worked for Penn, Penn might have ordered him below with the rest but had not, instead being willing to let Logan face the danger on behalf of those who would not.

Nearly a half century later, Logan continued to believe that while nonviolence was an ideal toward which humanity ought to strive, it need not be an altar on which pacifists must sacrifice themselves. "Thy project of a lottery to clear £3,000 is excellent," he wrote Franklin, "and I hope it will be speedily filled; nor shall I be wanting." Indeed he was not, putting down £250 toward the first issue of lottery tickets. Others followed Logan's lead, snatching tickets by the fistful for self-defense and civic pride—and in some cases for resale in other provinces. Fire companies purchased tickets in bulk—leading Franklin to suggest a ruse to one of his fellow firemen. If the lottery subscription appeared to be falling short, the two of them would propose to their company the purchase of a fire engine. "The Quakers can have no objection to that," Franklin explained. "And then if you nominate me, and I you, as a committee for that purpose, we will buy a great gun, which is certainly a *fire engine*."

Such shenanigans proved unnecessary, as the tickets disappeared as fast as Franklin could print them. Within a short while he was able to boast, in the name of his fellow citizens, that "the late lotteries in New-England and New-York have taken more *months* to fill than this has *weeks*."

Having raised the money for a battery of guns, Franklin now had to find the guns. This was the more difficult part of the task, as the absence of cannon foundries in America meant, in the short term (that is, until the arrival of reinforcements from England) that each piece added to Pennsylvania's arsenal subtracted a piece from New Jersey's or New York's or Massachusetts's. In the state of general alarm at the time, few governors or assemblies were willing to sell cannon that might be needed in their own colonies' defense; the most they would do was loan some ordnance.

Aware of the difficulty, Franklin led a committee of the Association north to negotiate with Governor George Clinton of New York. At first Clinton refused even to consider letting any guns out of his province. "But at a dinner with his council there was great drinking of Madeira wine," Franklin recounted, "as the custom of that place then was; he softened by degrees, and said he would lend us six. After a few more bumpers he advanced to ten. And at length he very good-naturedly conceded eighteen."

Though Franklin did not believe that God took sides in human quarrels, he was not above an appeal to Providence if such seemed necessary to solidify public opinion behind the defense effort. His activities had won him the confidence of Governor Thomas and the governor's council, and Franklin proposed to this group a public fast day. During these twenty-four hours the populace would entreat heaven for forgiveness of sins and for assistance in the colony's hour of need. No such occasion had ever been held in Pennsylvania, but the governor and council thought it a capital idea. Franklin remarked that such events were an annual occurrence in Boston, where he grew up; he would be happy to compose an appropriate proclamation. This he proceeded to do, with as much apparent fervor as ever Cotton Mather invested in a sermon. Speaking through the mouth of the governor and council, he recited past and current perils, and declared, "Unless we humble ourselves before the Lord, and amend our ways, we may be chastised with yet heavier judgments." The designated day of fasting and prayer—January 7, 1748—would allow all ministers and people of the city "to join with one accord in the most humble and fervent supplications, that Almighty God would mercifully interpose, and still the rage of war among the nations, and put a stop to the effusion of Christian blood; that he would preserve and bless our gracious king, guide his councils, and give him victory over his enemies."

Even for Franklin, his performance on behalf of his adopted city during the winter of 1747–48 was a tour de force. James Logan, probably the most respected person in Philadelphia, certainly thought so. "He it was," Logan wrote to Thomas Penn, son of William Penn and current proprietor of the colony, "that by publishing a small piece in the year 1747 with his further private contrivances, occasioned the raising of ten companies of near one hundred men each in Philadelphia and above one hundred companies in the province and counties. . . . He it was who set on foot two lotteries for erecting of batteries, purchasing great guns and to dispatch which he went himself to New York . . . and all this without appearing in any part of it himself, unless in his going to New York himself in company with others of whose going he was the occasion, for he is the principal mover and very soul of the whole."

8

Electricity and Fame

1748—51

∾ Thomas Penn read Franklin quite differently than James Logan did. "This Association is founded on a contempt to government," the proprietor declared, "and cannot end in anything but anarchy and confusion." Penn understood the implications of recent events, even if others did not.

Franklin had shown the people they could act independently of government; Penn asked, "Why should they not act against it?" Franklin's brainchild amounted to a "military commonwealth"; its creation was "little less than treason." As to its instigator, "He is a dangerous man and I should be very glad he inhabited any other country, as I believe him of a very uneasy spirit."

James Logan knew Franklin as a neighbor, a friend, a fellow philosopher, a political ally; Thomas Penn knew him solely by reputation. Yet, perhaps because he possessed keener intuition, perhaps because he had more to lose, Penn understood Franklin as Logan did not. Franklin was indeed dangerous—dangerous, that is, to the proprietary prerogatives Penn had inherited and was endeavoring to defend. And Franklin was indeed of an uneasy spirit, unwilling to leave well enough alone, insistent on asking whether well might be better, impatient to make it so.

In certain respects Penn knew Franklin better than Franklin knew himself. Franklin had not set out to undermine authority; he simply wanted to see his city defended. And he had chosen the same devices of voluntarism that had led to the creation of the Junto, the Library Company, the fire brigades, and the Philosophical Society. Yet as Penn recognized, even if Franklin did not, there was an obvious, almost inevitable, progression from acting independently of government to acting against government. Penn was the first defender of the imperial status quo to detect the danger in Franklin's restless intelligence; he would not be the last.

⌒ **If Franklin** had wanted to challenge authority, he could readily have exploited the favorable notice the Association's activities brought his way. He did not lack the time, for at the beginning of 1748 he retired from the printing business. David Hall continued to exceed Franklin's expectations for a foreman, being no less adept at the business side of his work than at the craft of the printer per se. Isaiah Thomas, a fellow printer who knew both men (and who wrote a comprehensive history of printing in America), said of Hall, "Had he not been connected with Franklin he might have been a formidable rival to him." Franklin thought so too, and determined to keep Hall from becoming a rival by making him a partner.

Besides, Franklin had enough money to allow him and Deborah to live quite comfortably. Wealth still failed to impress him; the purpose of money was to purchase one's freedom to pursue that which was useful and interesting. Accordingly, he decided sometime about midsummer of 1747 to turn the operation of the shop over to Hall, and on the first of January 1748 the agreement was concluded. For eighteen years the two men would be partners, should they both live that long. Franklin would supply the capital equipment and the inventory on hand; Hall would furnish the talent and diligence necessary to direct day-to-day operations. The two men would share expenses and profits equally. The agreement was essentially exclusive, although somewhat more on Hall's part than Franklin's. During the eighteen years of the contract, Hall would not engage in the printing business outside the partnership; Franklin was precluded only from practicing it in Philadelphia without Hall's leave. (This took account of the partnerships Franklin had planted elsewhere.) Hall was allowed to continue "occasional buying and selling in the stationery and bookselling way," which he did. At the end of the term of agreement, Hall would have the option of purchasing the equipment at its 1748 value less depreciation for wear and tear.

The partnership started splendidly and thrived with the passing years. "Mr. Hall continues well, and goes on perfectly to my satisfaction," Franklin wrote William Strahan, Hall's old employer, two years into the arrangement. Through the mid-1750s Franklin realized more than £650 per year, on average, from what his investment and Hall's efforts produced. At a time when a royal governor might earn £1,000 per year, this hardly made Franklin the richest man in America—or even Philadelphia, America's richest city. But it filled all his and Deborah's material desires. More to the point, it bought him time to pursue those other interests that always enticed him more than the getting of money.

◦— Franklin celebrated retirement by moving his home from Market Street to the quieter environs of Sassafras Street (also called Race Street, according to Philadelphians' confusing habit of naming certain streets twice). The neighborhood of the market had suited a diligent tradesman who wished, as any diligent tradesman should, to keep an eye on the business; but Franklin's new condition as silent partner called for a modest distancing from the hurly-burly. He was entering a more contemplative existence; quiet was what he sought.

In the early autumn of the first year of his retirement, he reported his state to Cadwallader Colden. "I am settling my old accounts and hope soon to be quite a master of my own time, and no longer (as the song has it) *at every one's call but my own.*" The future held only the pleasantest prospect. "I am in a fair way of having no other tasks than such as I shall like to give my self, and of enjoying what I look upon as a great happiness, leisure to read, study, make experiments, and converse at large with such ingenious and worthy men as are pleased to honour me with their friendship or acquaintance, on such points as may produce something for the common benefit of mankind, uninterrupted by the little cares and fatigues of business."

  ~ For a time, events—both those within his control and those beyond—followed Franklin's script. The most important of either category was the war with France and Spain, which drew to a close in 1748. If Franklin's efforts in forming the Association had proven more critical to the security of Pennsylvania, perhaps Thomas Penn would have taken less umbrage; but as things happened, the battery below Philadelphia was barely completed, and the militia had hardly started drilling seriously, before hints of peace began wafting across the Atlantic. The hints gained substance during the summer of 1748, and in October the Treaty of Aix-la-Chapelle officially concluded nearly a decade of conflict.

    Franklin later would say that there was never a good war or a bad peace, but in the aftermath of King George's War he would have had an argument, certainly in New England. Most disappointing—indeed infuriating—was the British restoration of Louisbourg to France. The Americans who captured the fortress, and the much larger number that fought vicariously, could hardly be expected to appreciate that in exchange for Cape Breton Island the British regained Madras in India, lost to the French at an earlier point of this global struggle. Nor did the Americans value the subtle shifts in European power the war produced. As they saw it, they had proved their superiority at arms to British regulars, only to be played fools by the British Crown. If someone had set a spark to this mixture of British arrogance and American resentment, it would have exploded.

  ~ Franklin was busy making sparks, but literally rather than figuratively. The return of peace, following his retirement from business, allowed him to indulge his interests, of which the most interesting—to himself and presently to others—was electricity.

    It was a stroke of either luck or genius that Franklin latched on to electricity when he did. Arguing for luck was his chance encounter with the subject; for genius, that he quickly appreciated that here was a field where an amateur from the provinces could do work rivaling the best-equipped institutions of Europe. At the mid-mark of the eighteenth century, the science of electricity was in its infancy; indeed, "science" was scarcely the name. Electrical phenomena were still encountered as often in the parlor and on stage as in the laboratory. Traveling "electricians" amazed audiences with demonstrations of this mysterious force. A standard trick involved suspending a boy from the ceiling with numerous silken cords, rubbing his feet with a glass tube, and drawing "electric fire"—that is, sparks—from his face and hands. The court electrician to Louis XV, the Abbé Nollet, once delighted an audience by arranging an electrical discharge through 180 soldiers of the guard who jerked to attention with an alacrity and a simultaneity unachievable by the most demanding drill sergeant. The French king, perhaps indulging an anticlericalism he could not own in public, laughed even louder when Nollet talked seven hundred monks into joining hands along short lengths of iron wire; Nollet connected the clerics to a condenser, which sent them leaping toward their Maker with a shriek.

But no one knew what accounted for such effects, and even the factual basis on which a theory of electricity might be erected was confused and contradictory. The field cried out for an investigator with the time and curiosity to pursue assorted leads down dead ends and live, with the manual dexterity and financial resources to fabricate or purchase necessary apparatus, with the personal connections to keep abreast of others' work, and with the literary facility to disseminate his own results in a timely and persuasive manner.

When Franklin encountered his first electrical demonstration, he had no idea he fit the job description as well as anyone alive. By his own recollection, in 1746 in Boston he met a "Dr. Spence," who put on an electric show Franklin found fascinating, if somewhat bumbling. In fact this Spence was probably Archibald Spencer, a native of Scotland who was between jobs as a male midwife and an Anglican clergyman, and the year was 1743. During the next few years Franklin queried Peter Collinson, the Library Company's agent in London and a man with wide scientific interests and acquaintances, regarding this intriguing subject. Collinson obliged by sending over a glass tube of the sort the electricians employed to create their effects, along with assorted remarks on the current state of the electrical art. "I eagerly seized the opportunity of repeating what I had seen at Boston," Franklin recalled, "and by much practice acquired great readiness in performing those also which we had an account of from England, adding a number of new ones."

Soon electricity became his passion. "I was never before engaged in any study that so totally engrossed my attention and my time as this has lately done," he told Collinson in March 1747. "For what with making experiments when I can be alone, and repeating them to my friends and acquaintances, who, from the novelty of the thing, come continually in crowds to see them, I have, during some months past, had little leisure for any thing else." It was just at this time that Franklin began negotiating with David Hall about taking over operation of the printing business; if a single influence can be said to have persuaded Franklin to doff his printer's apron, it was his desire to don the cloak of the electrician.

From this point forward, Franklin reported regularly to Collinson on the progress of experiments conducted by himself and his friends. In one of his first letters he supplied a novel terminology that became standard in analyzing electrical phenomena. Describing a particular apparatus, consisting of bodies labeled *A* and *B*, he wrote: "We say *B* (and other bodies alike circumstanced) are electrised *positively*; *A negatively*. Or rather *B* is electrised *plus* and *A minus*." He also recounted certain improvements in apparatus, for example the substitution of lead granules for water inside the glass vials used to generate electricity ("We find granulated lead better to fill the vial with than water, being easily warmed, and keeping the vial warm and dry in damp air"). He described an electric spider: a mannequin of cork and linen made to jump realistically when charged—"appearing perfectly alive to persons unacquainted." At a time when other electricians spoke of two different kinds of electricity— vitreous and resinous—Franklin unified the field by positing a single sort and explaining the opposite properties in terms of a surfeit or a deficit (that is, positive condition or negative) of this single electricity, with uncharged objects being in balance.

In his early enthusiasm Franklin occasionally conjectured more than he could prove. After additional experimentation caused him to question one of the assertions of his letters, he wrote Collinson expressing his new reservations. "I have observed a phenomenon or two that I cannot at present account for on the principles laid down in those letters, and am therefore become a little diffident of my hypothesis, and ashamed that I have expressed myself in so positive a manner." He proceeded to muse on the scientific enterprise. "In going on with these experiments, how many pretty systems do we build, which we soon find ourselves obliged to destroy! If there is no other use discovered of electricity, this, however, is something considerable, that it may *help to make a vain man humble*." He went on to request that Collinson not show his letters to others, or if he must, that he conceal the author's name.

Collinson had no intention of keeping Franklin's results confidential. Although a natural historian of some note—he debunked the common notion that swallows hibernated in the mud of streambeds—he in fact served science better as a communicator of other people's findings. He corresponded fruitfully with John Bartram, Franklin's botanist friend, and it was Collinson who brought Franklin to the attention of Britain's electrical experts. In April 1748 he wrote Franklin, regarding his earlier letters, "I have imparted them to the Royal Society, to whom they are very acceptable."

Franklin found Collinson's response encouraging. "I am pleased to hear that my electrical experiments were acceptable to the Society," he declared. Franklin hardly lacked confidence in fields he knew well, but he was the first to acknowledge his novice standing in electricity. Moreover, as one who had been attempting to establish a network of scientific communication in America, he appreciated the importance of word of mouth (or word of post) in keeping up with the latest discoveries. Philadelphia might be the hub of British North America, but it remained an ocean away from the scientific mainstream. Franklin could not help worrying that his best experiments were simply recapitulating work done in Europe, work he had not heard of yet.

But the approbation of the Royal Society, the most distinguished scientific body of its day (rivaled only by the French Academy of Sciences), gave Franklin every reason to carry on. In April 1749 he reported the creation of "what we called an Electrical Battery," a lead-and-glass arrangement that, once charged, could store electricity for use at will, as well as a "self-moving wheel," a primitive electric motor. In this and subsequent letters to Collinson, which he now knew were being read by an audience of experts, Franklin adopted a more formal tone than in his previous communications, numbering his paragraphs and leaving out most personal intelligence. But in his final sentences here he could not resist reporting how the electricians of Philadelphia proposed to conclude their current round of experiments:

Chagrinned a little that we have hitherto been able to discover nothing in this way of use to mankind, and the hot weather coming on, when electrical experiments are not so agreeable, 'tis proposed to put an end to them for this season somewhat humourously in a party of pleasure on the banks of the Schuylkill (where spirits are at the same time to be fired by a spark sent from side to side through the river). A turkey is to be killed for our dinners by the electrical shock, and roasted by the electrical jack, before a fire kindled by the electrified bottle, when the healths of all the famous electricians in England, France and Germany are to be drank in electrified bumpers under the discharge of guns from the electrical battery. [A note explained that "an electrified bumper is a small thin glass tumbler, near filled with water and electrified. This when brought to the lips gives a shock, if the party be close shaved and does not breathe on the liquor."]

Collinson duly delivered this letter to the Royal Society, where it was read aloud at the end of 1749 and assigned for critique to William Watson, a distinguished member and a recent winner of the society's Copley Medal for his electrical work. Joseph Priestley, who would become a renowned scientist in his own right, and a historian of electricity, characterized Watson as "the most interested and active person in the kingdom in every thing relating to electricity." When Watson reported back to the society, he described Franklin's work as "new and very curious" and conceded that he felt himself "not quite master of part of this gentleman's reasoning." He did question certain of Franklin's conclusions and made a few recommendations regarding how such questions might be resolved, yet he was particularly intrigued to know the outcome of one experiment projected in Franklin's letter but not completed at the time of writing. In the indirect reportage of the society's secretary, "Mr. Watson would further recommend to our worthy brother Mr. Collinson, in writing to his correspondent Mr. Franklin, to desire to know his success in attempting to kill a turkey by the electrical strokes."

∽ Franklin's triumphs in electricity marked the latest installment in a career of self-education that ran back to his eleventh year, when Josiah had pulled him out of school and into the candle shop. In light of the success he had achieved, and was still achieving, Franklin might have been thought an advocate of this method of schooling—or nonschooling. Teach children to read, provide them access to books (as through a library), and thereafter let them teach themselves.

In fact, Franklin's efforts to educate himself made him an enthusiast of formal education. Like many self-educated people, he was aware of the gaps in his education. He had filled most of them, better than they would have been filled in school. But it had required a great deal of work, more than ought to have been necessary. And it required a sense of discipline, a devotion to learning, and a knack for absorbing information that were not given equally to all. Though he deliberately downplayed it, Franklin understood his own exceptionality; unlike many self-made men, he did not set his own experience as a standard for others.

For some time Franklin pondered how to improve the educational opportunities available to the youth of Philadelphia. In 1743 he went so far as to draft a proposal for an academy, to be headed by Richard Peters, a scholar and Anglican clergyman who at the time happened to be underemployed. Peters approved the idea in principle but had higher ambitions for himself—as it turned out, in the service of the Penn family—and declined Franklin's offer.

The excitements of the war delayed further consideration of the academy, but in August 1749 Franklin announced he would soon offer a plan to educate the youth of Philadelphia, "free from the extraordinary expence and hazard in sending them abroad for that purpose." To whet the public appetite for his plan, he reprinted a letter by the younger Pliny extolling education rooted in one's homeland, received under the watchful and loving gaze of one's parents. In this letter Pliny proposed a subscription to establish an academy. "You can undertake nothing that will be more advantageous to your children, nor more acceptable to your country," the great Roman asserted. "They will, by this means, receive their education where they receive their birth, and be accustomed, from their infancy, to inhabit and affect their native soil."

Having enlisted Pliny on his side, Franklin proceeded to line up several other outstanding men of letters. In October he produced a pamphlet citing Milton, Locke, Francis Hutcheson, Obadiah Walker, and the current chaplain to the Prince of Wales on the benefits accruing to both individuals and society upon the appropriate education of youth and on the optimal method of that education. Franklin noted the common complaint that the present generation did not measure up to the generations that had gone before. He did not deny it, but rather explained it: "The best capacities require cultivation, it being truly with them, as with the best ground, which unless well tilled and sowed with profitable seed, produces only ranker weeds."

Franklin proposed the establishment of an "Academy for the education of youth." The academy would be situated in a house in or near the town ("if not in the town, not many miles from it; the situation high and dry, and if it may be, nor far from a river, having a garden, orchard, meadow, and a field or two"). A rector, "a man of good understanding, good morals, diligent and patient, learned in the languages and sciences, and a correct pure speaker and writer of the English tongue," would oversee the students, who would be taught a wide variety of subjects. "It would be well if they could be taught *every thing* that is useful, and *every thing* that is ornamental. But art is long, and their time is short. It is therefore proposed that they learn those things that are likely to be *most useful* and *most ornamental.*"

Arithmetic, geometry, astronomy, rhetoric, grammar, literature, history, drawing, handwriting, accounting, geography, morality, logic, natural history, mechanics, and gardening would be suitable subjects for study. Nor should the body be forgotten. "To keep them in health, and to strengthen and render active their bodies," the young scholars should be "frequently exercised in running, leaping, wrestling, and swimming." (On his favorite subject of swimming, Franklin quoted Locke quoting the Romans: *"Nec literas didicit nec natare,"* which, applied to some good-for-nothing soul, meant that he had learned neither to read nor to swim. In an age when surprisingly few persons learned to swim, Franklin added that swimmers freed themselves from the "slavish terrors many of those feel who cannot swim, when they are obliged to be on the water even in crossing a ferry.") In the same vein, the young scholars at the academy should dine together, "plainly, temperately, and frugally."

Franklin's proposal met with general approval, as measured by the nearly £2,000 in subscriptions it elicited within the first two months. A constitution for "the Public Academy in the City of Philadelphia" was drawn up by Franklin and Tench Francis, the attorney general of Pennsylvania. The subscribers selected a board of trustees, with Franklin as board president. In that position he oversaw negotiations leading to the acquisition and conversion of the great hall that had been built for George Whitefield a decade earlier but which had fallen into disrepair with the subsequent decline of religious fervor. Renovating the building required a year; the academy opened at the beginning of 1751.

"Our Academy flourishes beyond expectation," Franklin wrote a friend that fall. "We have now above 100 scholars, and the number daily increasing. We have excellent masters at present; and as we give pretty good salaries, I hope we shall always be able to procure such."

⁓ At the outset of his planning for the academy Franklin hoped his own son would benefit from it. But the delay in establishing the school, and Billy's insistence on leaving home, rendered his attendance impossible. At some point, however, he would have to resume his education.

Franklin had blessed Billy's enlistment as a soldier, but only in preference to his shipping out on a privateer. One campaign might be good for the lad: get him out of the house, let him see something of the world. But as a career option it had serious drawbacks. Colonials in the army were disdained by the socially connected Englishmen who decided promotions. And, of course, a young man might get killed. Franklin had lost one son; he did not want to lose his only other.

Consequently, it was with some dismay that Franklin saw his son take to soldiering with gusto. Six months under military discipline only increased its attractions. "Billy is so fond of military life that he will by no means hear of leaving the army," Franklin wrote his brother John. The winter of 1746–47 had been such as to discourage most would-be heroes; the projected invasion of Canada never took place, mired in bureaucratic bungling that stranded the soldiers in Albany, where they suffered from bitter weather, wretched rations, and miserable quarters. The ranks dwindled with each passing week as the part-timers deserted and went home.

William Franklin went home, too, in May 1747, but not as a deserter. Instead he was now a captain, charged with tracking down and capturing deserters thought to be in Philadelphia. He carried out his duty with an ardor that astonished his father—and dismayed him the more. When he learned that William was heading back to Albany, Franklin sent Cadwallader Colden a letter: "My son, who will wait upon you with this, is returning to the army, his military inclinations (which I hoped would have been cooled with the last winter) continuing as warm as ever." For the moment Franklin resigned himself to William's wishes and sought to help him make his way. He sent to London for some maps that would have military use and asked Colden to do what he could for the boy in Albany, should the forces be stationed there again.

The end of the war terminated, for the time at least, William's martial ambitions. Franklin wrote to London to cancel the map order; he explained to William Strahan, "It was intended for my son, who was then in the army, and seemed bent on a military life; but as peace cuts off his prospect of advancement in that way, he will apply himself to other business." The nature of that other business remained to be determined. William joined an expedition to the Ohio Valley to negotiate with the Indians there; upon the journey he kept a log and noted the bright prospects for the region and for those who would claim its lush lands.

William had never shown any more interest in his father's trade than Franklin had shown in *his* father's; this apparently inherited filial aversion was part of what prompted Franklin to turn the printing shop over to David Hall. William manifested somewhat more inclination toward a legal career. Despite Richard Saunders's repeated jabs at lawyers, Franklin considered the law an honorable enough calling—far preferable to the military. He arranged for William to read law in Philadelphia and asked Strahan to put William's name down for study at one of the Inns of Court in London.

⌒— In February 1750 Franklin responded to William Watson's query about killing turkeys. "Please to acquaint him that we made several experiments on fowls this winter," Franklin wrote Collinson. Recounting the details of charging the apparatus, he reported that a full charge sufficed to kill chickens outright. "But the turkeys, though thrown into violent convulsions, and then lying as dead for some minutes, would recover in less than a quarter of an hour." Not to be denied, Franklin linked several electrical jars together, which jointly succeeded. "We killed a turkey with them of about 10 lb. wt. and suppose they would have killed a much larger. I conceit that the birds killed in this manner eat uncommonly tender."

In the process of electrocuting birds, Franklin nearly electrocuted himself. The experience was enlightening, if jolting.

I found that a man can without great detriment bear a much greater electrical shock than I imagined. For I inadvertently took the stroke of two of those jars through my arms and body, when they were very near full charged. It seemed an universal blow from head to foot throughout the body, and was followed by a violent quick trembling in the trunk, which gradually wore off in a few seconds. It was some moments before I could collect my thoughts so as to know what was the matter; for I did not see the flash though my eye was on the spot of the prime conductor from whence it struck the back of my hand, nor did I hear the crack though the by-standers say it was a loud one; nor did I particularly feel the stroke on my hand, though I afterwards found it had raised a swelling there the bigness of half a swan shot or pistol bullet. My arms and back of my neck felt somewhat numb the remainder of the evening, and my breastbone was sore for a week after, as if it had been bruised. What the consequence would be, if such a shock were taken through the head, I know not.

Yet he could guess. From time immemorial humans had speculated on the nature and cause of lightning. That it was a form of fire—indeed, the first fire, the *fulmen fulminis*, as it came to be called—had seemed clear at least since the Greeks sang of Prometheus stealing fire from the heavens. The sulfurous smell that often accompanied lightning reinforced this view. As to the cause of lightning and the accompanying thunder, for long centuries most mortals were willing to account it supernatural. The gods were angry and in their anger hurled thunderbolts at each other or at the earth. The elder Pliny, one of the few ancients to look for a natural explanation, called thunder an "earthquake of the air"—which did not advance the discussion very far, since no one knew what caused earthquakes. The sulfurous smell of lightning reinforced this—spurious—connection, in that sulfurous flames were associated with Hades and the nether regions of the earth.

Not until the early eighteenth century, apparently, did anyone draw a connection between lightning and electrical phenomena. In 1716 Newton described an experiment in which a needle was brought close to a piece of amber that had been rubbed with silk. "The flame putteth me in mind of sheet lightning on a small—how very small—scale," he wrote. As electrical investigators learned to generate larger charges, and larger sparks, the similarity between the discharges in the heavens and the discharges in the laboratory grew more compelling. By the time Franklin took up the study of electricity, the notion that lightning was electric was commonplace among the cognoscenti.

But plenty of history's commonplace ideas—from the flatness of the earth to the faster falling of heavy objects—had proven, on closer examination, to be wrong; what remained in the puzzle of the lightning was for the electrical conjecture to be tested. This was precisely what Franklin proposed to do.

In April 1749 Franklin wrote a long letter to John Mitchell, a colleague of Peter Collinson and likewise a fellow of the Royal Society. In this letter he put forward a complex theory of lightning with a fairly simple essence: that particles of water in thunderclouds became electrically charged by their wind-borne jostling, and that lightning was nothing more than the discharge of the pent-up electrical force. This theory supported certain recommendations, which in turn comported with observation. For instance, a person caught out in a thunderstorm ought not to seek shelter beneath a lone tree, for the tree would tend to channel the electrical discharge to the ground—and to whoever happened to be at the base of the tree. "It has been fatal to many," Franklin noted. The unlucky person caught by the storm should remain in the open for a second reason. "When clothes are wet, if a flash, in its way to the ground, should strike your head, it will run in the water over the surface of your body; whereas if your clothes were dry, it would go through the body. Hence a wet rat can not be killed by the exploding electrical bottle, when a dry rat may."

Upon their arrival in London, these results won Franklin further praise from the Royal Society. "Your very curious pieces relating to electricity and thundergusts have been read before the Society," Peter Collinson reported back, "and have been deservedly admired not only for the clear intelligent style but also for the novelty of the subjects."

Franklin was delighted to hear this, as the piece was his most ambitious venture into the theory of electricity. The encouragement prompted him, during the next few weeks, to offer an exceedingly practical recommendation that followed from his theory. One aspect of the theory involved "points": sharp metal objects that could draw off electrical charges before they reached alarming levels. "The doctrine of *points* is very curious," Franklin told the Royal Society, through Collinson, "and the effects of them are truly wonderful; and from what I have observed on experiments, I am of opinion that houses, ships, and even towns and churches may be effectually secured from the stroke of lightning by their means." Customarily church spires and weathercocks were topped by round balls of brass or wood; these allowed the charge to build excessively. Let them be replaced by "a rod of iron, 8 or 10 feet in length, sharpened gradually to a point like a needle, and gilt to prevent rusting, or divided into a number of points, which would be better—the electrical fire would, I think, be drawn out of a cloud silently, before it could come near enough to strike. . . . This may seem whimsical, but let it pass for the present, until I send the experiments at large."

The experiments were designed to test aspects of Franklin's theory; the one that proved most important dealt directly with the fundamental question of whether lightning and electricity were the same. "To determine the question, whether the clouds that contain lightning are electrified or not, I would propose an experiment to be tried where it might be done conveniently." That is:

On the top of some high tower or steeple, place a kind of sentry box big enough to contain a man and an electrical stand. From the middle of the stand let an iron rod rise, and pass bending out of the door, and then upright 20 or 30 feet, pointed very sharp at the end. If the electrical stand be kept clean and dry, a man standing on it when such clouds are passing low, might be electrified, and afford sparks, the rod drawing fire to him from the cloud.

Franklin saw little danger in this test, but for apprehensive persons he suggested that the observer in the box hold a grounded wire by insulated handles; from time to time he could bring the wire close to the iron rod, drawing off any sparks without endangering himself.

By now Franklin was well known among the small community of English electricians; when Collinson published this paper and Franklin's letters on electricity in 1751, Franklin's circle of scientific admirers expanded swiftly. The circle encompassed King Louis of France, whose curiosity had progressed beyond dancing guardsmen and leaping monks. The monarch's interest inspired two intrepid French experimenters, Messieurs d'Alibard and de Lor, to put Franklin's conjecture to his test. In May 1752 d'Alibard reported just such sparks as Franklin had predicted; a week later de Lor recapitulated the test, with similar results.

Apparently both men eschewed the precautions Franklin prescribed for the faint of heart; by their good luck the storms they encountered were quite mild. At least three English experimenters were similarly fortunate, as, evidently, was an electrician in Berlin. In 1753, however, a Swedish scientist in St. Petersburg, Georg Wilhelm Richmann, suffered a fatal shock while conducting Franklin's experiment in a more severe storm.

Perhaps ironically, perhaps understandably, Richmann's death simply enhanced Franklin's growing fame. It demonstrated, if demonstration were necessary, that electricity was no mere plaything. It underscored the utility, indeed necessity, of Franklin's lightning rods. And it made Franklin out to be braver, in the pursuit of science, than he actually was.

Yet he was no coward. In June 1752, after the French trials were successfully performed but before the news of them reached America, Franklin himself conducted a variant of his experiment. He would have done so earlier had he not believed that the tower or steeple he spoke of needed to be quite tall—taller than anything in Philadelphia. As it happened, the vestrymen of Christ Church had decided to erect a new steeple; Franklin was waiting for the construction to be completed.

(Perhaps with an eye toward asking permission to tempt heaven from the steeple, nonmember Franklin was one of the first contributors to the construction fund. He subsequently managed a lottery to complete the fund-raising.)

Meanwhile, however, he conceived another route to the heart of the storm. Likely recalling the kite he had employed to pull himself across the Mill Pond in Boston, he proposed to fly another, this mounted with a miniature lightning rod. The kite would be made of silk rather than paper. "Silk is fitter to bear the wet and wind of a thunder gust without tearing," he explained. Hemp twine would run from the kite to the ground. Dry, hemp conducted electricity moderately well; wet, it would "conduct the electric fire freely." At the ground a large key was to be tied to the twine; this would absorb the electric charge that ran down the string. Lest the kite-flyer—Franklin himself—be jolted, a silk ribbon should be attached to the string at the bottom. This must be kept dry (the kite-flyer would stand in a doorway); if it was, it would insulate the flyer's hand from the wet twine and key.

Although Franklin could discern no flaws in the design of the experiment, he was insufficiently sure of himself to risk a public demonstration. So he surreptitiously enlisted William as his aide and found a lonely field, with a shed and the requisite doorway, where the two of them might hazard their lives but not their reputations.

Summer brought thunderstorms and the opportunity to test both his theory and his experimental design. A promising storm blew up one afternoon, with thunderheads rising high. Franklin and son launched their kite; it soared toward the base of the cloud. But nothing happened. The key gave no indication of absorbing an electrical charge. Franklin could not understand where he had miscalculated. Joseph Priestley, to whom Franklin related the afternoon's events, described what happened next:

> At length, just as he was beginning to despair of his contrivance, he observed some loose threads of the hempen string to stand erect, and to avoid one another, just as if they had been suspended on a common conductor. Struck with this promising appearance, he immediately presented his knuckle to the key, and (let the reader judge of the exquisite pleasure he must have felt at that moment) the discovery was complete. He perceived a very evident electric spark. Others succeeded, even before the string was wet, so as to put the matter past all dispute, and when the rain had wet the string, he collected electric fire very copiously.

~ Franklin appreciated the recognition that came with his growing scientific reputation, but there were times when he preferred anonymity. This preference had given birth to Silence Dogood; so also to Martha Careful and Caelia Shortface. None of these worthy women, however, became as famous as Polly Baker, who in the late 1740s embarked on a transatlantic career that for a time outshone Franklin's own.

Fame came late to Polly Baker. Her early life was obscure and hard— and made harder by what she (and Franklin) judged the unfair and counterproductive laws to which she was compelled to submit. Polly resided in Connecticut, where five times she was haled into court on charges of producing illegitimate offspring. She did not deny the charges but rather clung the evidence, quite literally, to her bosom. Yet having twice paid fines for her transgressions and twice been punished corporally for inability to pay, on the fifth occasion she stood her ground and denounced her accusers and the regime they had sworn to uphold. "Abstracted from the law," she declared, "I cannot conceive (may it please your Honours) what the nature of my offense is. I have brought five fine children into the world, at the risk of my life; I have maintained them well by my own industry, without burdening the township, and would have done it better if it had not been for the heavy charges and fines I have paid." Could there truly be any crime in adding to the king's subjects, in a country that sorely needed new inhabitants? "I should think it praise-worthy, rather than a punishable action." Polly was neither a home-wrecker nor a despoiler of youth; her liaisons were solely with unmarried men of mature judgment—if less than mature honor. The only complaint the magistrate might have against her was that by failing to marry, she deprived some justice or minister of his wedding fee.

Polly did not condemn marriage; indeed, quite the contrary. "You are pleased to allow I don't want sense; but I must be stupefied to the last degree not to prefer the honourable state of wedlock to the condition I have lived in. I always was, and still am willing to enter into it; and doubt not my behaving well in it, having all the industry, frugality, fertility [this went without saying] and skill in economy, appertaining to a good wife's character." She would have been married these many years had a faithless fiancé not got her—who trusted too readily in his promises—with child, only to abandon her as her belly swelled. Adding inequity to injury, this same fellow went on to a career at law, his reputation none the worse for the wear on hers. Even as Polly spoke, he sat as a distinguished magistrate, a man well known to every member of the present court. "I had hopes he would have appeared this day on the bench, and have endeavoured to moderate the Court in my favour; then I should have scorned to have mentioned it; but I must now complain of it as unjust and unequal." Yet even so, she forbore to mention his name.

He could walk away from his complicity in what the court insisted on calling her crime; *she* had to salvage what she could from a ruined reputation and lost hopes of honest matrimony. And still the court insisted on punishing her more. Some argued that she had flouted religion. If true, was not religion able to defend itself? Already she had been excluded from communion. If Heaven were offended, she would suffer eternal fire. "Will not that be sufficient?"

Yet she could not believe Heaven was truly offended. "How can it be believed that Heaven is angry at my having children, when to the little done by me towards it, God has been pleased to add his divine skill and admirable workmanship in the formation of their bodies, and crowned it by furnishing them with rational and immortal souls?" No, she had committed no crime; and if the court insisted on finding crime, let it look to those bachelors who refused to marry, and "by their manner of living leave unproduced (which is little better than murder) hundreds of their posterity to the thousandth generation." Was this not a greater offense against the public good than hers? "Compel them, then, by law, either to marriage, or to pay double the fine of fornication every year."

What must poor young women do, who were forbidden by custom to solicit men? The law made no provision to get them husbands yet punished them severely when they attempted to do their duty—"the duty of the first and great command of nature, and of nature's God: *increase and multiply*." Polly Baker, without denying her faults, was not embarrassed to own that she had done her duty in this regard. "For its sake, I have hazarded the loss of the public esteem, and have frequently endured public disgrace and punishment; and therefore ought, in my humble opinion, instead of a whipping, to have a statue erected to my memory."

~ Polly Baker had no statues erected to her memory, although her moving plea induced one of the judges in her case to marry her on the morrow of the trial. Instead it was Franklin who received, if not yet statues, other marks of public approbation. Perhaps Franklin felt that acknowledging his hoax—by explaining that Polly Baker was entirely the creation of his mind, a vehicle for complaining about certain of life's unfairnesses to women—would not go well with the sober mien of science he wished to convey to the Royal Society. Perhaps he simply wished to see how far Polly could travel. In either case he kept his secret, not revealing his authorship of the Polly Baker story till three decades later.

The same English journals—*Gentleman's* and *London* magazines—that carried Polly's story picked up the French reports of d'Alibard's and de Lors's confirmation of Franklin's design for the electrical experiment. Not long thereafter, the Royal Society read Franklin's own account of his kite experiment. Shortly after that, the society bestowed on Franklin its Copley Gold Medal for scientific achievement. "Though some others might have begun to entertain suspicions of an analogy between the effects of lightning and electricity," declared the society's president in announcing the award, "yet I take Mr. Franklin to be the first who, among other curious discoveries, undertook to shew from experiments, that the former owed its origin entirely to the latter, and who pointed out an easy method, whereby any one might satisfy himself of the truth of the fact which he had so advanced."

Others in England registered similar sentiments. Even before the lightning experiments succeeded, William Watson described Franklin as "a very able and ingenious man" blessed with "a head to conceive and a hand to carry into execution whatever he thinks may conduce to enlighten the subject matter of which he is treating." None knew more of electricity than Franklin, Watson told the Royal Society. Joseph Priestley was gathering information for his history of electricity; regarding Franklin's demonstration of the electrical nature of lightning, he wrote, "Every circumstance relating to so capital a discovery as this (the greatest, perhaps, that has been made in the whole compass of philosophy, since the time of Sir Isaac Newton) cannot but give pleasure to all my readers."

The French joined the chorus of praise to the brilliance of the American philosopher. The secretary to the Academy of Sciences at Paris, Abbé Guillaume Mazéas, wrote to the Royal Society describing how "universally admired" the "Philadelphian experiments" were in France. The king himself had expressed a desire to see them performed and had registered "great satisfaction" when they were. Speaking for the French Academy, and evidently for the French Crown, Mazéas declared that Franklin deserved the "esteem of our nation."

Franklin hardly knew what to make of his international fame. He could not help being impressed with himself; at the same time he tried not to be. He described his ambivalence to Jared Eliot, a friend and fellow philosopher, who had sent him congratulations on the honors coming his way.

> The Tatler tells us of a girl who was observed to grow suddenly proud, and none could guess the reason, till it came to be known that she had got on a pair of new silk garters. Lest you should be puzzled to guess the cause when you observe any thing of the kind in me, I think I will not hide my new garters under my petticoats, but take the freedom to show them to you in a paragraph of our friend Collinson's last letter viz.—but I ought to mortify, and not indulge, this vanity; I will not transcribe the paragraph.—Yet I cannot forbear.
>
> "If any of thy friends (says Peter) should take notice that thy head is held a little higher up than formerly, let them know: when the Grand Monarch of France strictly commands the Abbé Mazéas to write a letter in the politest terms to the Royal Society, to return the King's thanks and compliments in an express manner to Mr. Franklin of Pennsylvania, for the useful discoveries in Electricity, and application of the pointed rods to prevent the terrible effects of thunderstorms; I say, after all this, is not some allowance to be made if the crest is a little elevated? . . . I think now I have stuck a feather on thy cap, I may be allowed to conclude in wishing thee long to wear it."

Franklin closed this letter to Eliot with typical self-deprecation, adding a touch that flattered the recipient as much as the sender:

> On reconsidering this paragraph, I fear I have not so much reason to be proud as the girl had, for a feather in the cap is not so useful a thing, or so serviceable to the wearer, as a pair of good silk garters. The pride of man is very differently gratified, and had his Majesty sent me a Marshal's staff, I think I should scarce have been so proud of it as I am of your esteem.

9

A Taste of Politics

1751-54

~ In the late 1730s, while clerk of the Pennsylvania
Assembly, Franklin had often found the proceedings of that
body so wearisome that he filled his time with a minor form
of arithmetical amusement known as "magic squares."
These arrays of integers, invented in antiquity, contain an
equal number of rows and columns, with the property that
the sum of the numbers in each row equals the sum for
every other row, and also equals the sum for each column
and each diagonal. Franklin had encountered magic squares
as a boy; now, between his own cleverness and the dullness
of the legislative proceedings, he elaborated extensively
upon the basic idea. One square of his devising had eight rows

and eight columns with the defining properties but several others besides. Where the full rows and columns each totaled to 260, the half rows and half columns totaled to half of 260, or 130. Straight and bent diagonals summed to 260, as did truncated bent diagonals of six numbers, conjoined to the numbers in the closest corners. The four corner numbers, added to the four centermost numbers, summed to 260 as well.

James Logan, learning of Franklin's interest in magic squares, showed him an old book, written by one Michael Stifelius and published two centuries earlier in Nuremburg, containing a magic square of sixteen rows and sixteen columns. Logan, no mathematician himself, offered that this large magic square must have required enormous effort and time to construct. Franklin—"not wishing to be out-done by Mr. Stifelius," he later confessed—went home and that very night constructed a square of the same size but considerably greater complexity. Logan was amazed and told Franklin so. Franklin was proud of his work. After Logan wrote Peter Collinson about this unsuspected aspect of Franklin's genius, and Collinson inquired of Franklin for a sample, Franklin sent along his big square, with the partly jesting but partly serious comment, "I make no question but you will readily allow this square of 16 to be the most magically magical of any magic square ever made by any magician."

At the age of thirty, Franklin had found his numbers more compelling than the proceedings of the Assembly; at forty-five his priorities were shifting. Then he had been merely clerk, kept recorder of the sayings and doings of his betters. Now he was one of the most distinguished citizens of Philadelphia—an estimate confirmed by his selection to public office. In 1748 he was elected to the Philadelphia Common Council, in 1749 appointed justice of the peace for the city, in 1751 named city alderman. The first and last posts did not stretch him; in light of his civic activities of twenty years, he hardly noticed he was doing anything new. The post of justice of the peace was another matter, and for one of the few times in his life, he felt himself unequal to a task put before him. "More knowledge of the common law than I possessed was necessary to act in that station with credit," he related. Consequently he withdrew from the service of the court.

In the summer of 1751 Franklin was nominated for a seat in the Pennsylvania Assembly, and elected. He candidly described his feelings at this latest mark of recognition:

I conceived my becoming a member would enlarge my power of doing good. I would not however insinuate that my ambition was not flattered by all these promotions. It certainly was. For considering my low beginning they were great things to me. And they were still more pleasing, as being so many spontaneous testimonies of the public's good opinion, and by me entirely unsolicited.

No grand design motivated Franklin's entry into provincial politics; yet it did reflect important aspects of his character and circumstances. Starting with the success of Silence Dogood, Franklin had gradually come to see himself as the most capable individual he knew. The accuracy of this perception was confirmed by his assorted subsequent successes and the honors that came his way. He could look around Philadelphia—at the Junto, the Library Company, the fire companies, the Philosophical Society, the Association, the academy—and recognize his hand in making the city a more civilized place. Current projects included raising money for a hospital (he devised a scheme for what later would be called matching grants) and organizing a fire insurance company. Who had done more—who was doing more—for his adopted home than he?

Election to the Assembly allowed him to expand the scope of his activities. Though he represented Philadelphia in the legislature, he would be making laws for the whole province. At successive moments of his career, Franklin entered successively larger arenas. Mather's Boston became too small for him at seventeen; Philadelphia grew too small by forty-five. Pennsylvania was the obvious next venue.

There was another reason for the timing of his entry into provincial politics. As long as he had been in active business, Franklin felt obliged to observe the first rule of business relations: avoid gratuitous offense to potential customers. Ben Franklin, printer, was a man who generally kept his politics to himself, lest politics interfere with the printing business. With exceptions—his advocacy of paper currency, his defense of Samuel Hemphill—few enough merely to prove the rule, Franklin left political questions to the politicians.

But as the failure of the politicians to provide for defense during the late war demonstrated, the politicians could not be trusted to accomplish what needed to be done. Franklin knew he could do better; he had shown as much with the Association. His decision to leave the printing business to David Hall and his decision to enter Pennsylvania politics were closely linked. The former made the latter possible; the latter made the former desirable.

∿ **Pennsylvania** politics in the 1750s involved concentric circles of controversy. The innermost circle—at least by *their* thinking—comprised the proprietors, the heirs of William Penn. Unlike most British colonies in North America, proprietary Pennsylvania was ruled not by the Crown (at least not directly) but by the Penn family. Yet the family was not what it had been under William—or perhaps, considering the problems he had with *his* father, it was. William himself fell on hard times during his last years, to the point where Pennsylvania had to support the Penns, rather than the other way around. Times got harder after the great man's death, as the heirs squabbled over the estate. William Jr. had renounced the Quaker way for Anglicanism and then died shortly after his father, but neither action prevented William Jr.'s son from trying to break the will on grounds of his grandfather's septuagenarian senility. The assertion of mental incompetence was accurate enough, but it did not endear him to his father's siblings. For two decades the heirs tussled over who should get what; not until the mid-1740s did Thomas Penn, the founding William's son by his second wife, emerge as the controlling figure within the family and the prominent proprietor of the colony.

The quarrels were costly, for during that critical generation the initiative in Pennsylvania politics slipped from the proprietors to the Assembly, the second circle of controversy. The slippage started during the tenure of Franklin's notional patron, Governor William Keith, whose flippant attitude toward financial commitments was hardly confined to Franklin. Keith's many creditors lobbied to keep him in office, on the optimistic argument that a governor's salary provided them at least the prospect of being repaid. But the English Quakers close to the Penns contended that the behavior of Keith—who disported himself with ladies-not-his-wife in a decidedly un-Quaker manner—constituted an insult and an embarrassment. As the creditors eventually lost hope of seeing their money, the Quakers had their way, and Keith was forced out of the governorship.

Yet he was far from finished. He charged his expulsion to the aristocratic machinations of the proprietors, and immediately recast himself as the champion of the people, who constituted the third circle. Taking up his pen, Keith fabricated a character called Roger Plowman, who argued the case for the common folk against the learned and favored. "We are made of the same flesh and bone, and after the same manner with themselves," said Plowman, speaking to a character modeled on James Logan, "so that our sense and feeling of happiness and misery, justice and injustice, good fortune and ill fortune, are much the same with us all. And I appeal to you, Master, if a quiet enjoyment of, and equal support under these opposite states in life, respectively, be not the chief end, if not the whole business of civil government?"

The proprietors thought otherwise; the Penns expected their colony to provide them an income. And they understood that it would not do so if Keith won a following, as he appeared to be doing. Soon after his ouster as governor, the voters of Philadelphia elected him to the Assembly. His supporters celebrated their victory by burning the public pillory and stocks, which served as symbols of proprietary oppression of the ordinary people. (The collateral combustion of several stalls at the market was probably an accident.) Two weeks later, when Keith claimed his seat in the Assembly, he arrived leading a column of eighty horsemen, followed by a small army of the sweat-stained workforce—what a nervous Isaac Norris, the head of the Quaker party in the Assembly, scornfully called the "rabble butchers, porters and tag-rags."

But then, after sending shivers through the likes of Logan and Norris, Keith abruptly disappeared. Because his creditors were the first to complain of his absence, gossip congealed around assertions that he was fleeing to escape debtors' prison. As matters turned out, although he kept ahead of his American claimants, their English counterparts caught up with him, and he landed in a London jail. He never ceased spinning schemes for raising money, even when those schemes contradicted earlier-enunciated convictions. At one point, trying to curry favor with the imperial government, he proposed a plan for levying a stamp tax in the American colonies. Like most of his other concoctions, this one had come to naught by the time of his 1749 death.

The Keith phenomenon illuminated the overlap between the circles in Pennsylvania politics. Although the leaders of the Assembly often construed their interests in opposition to those of the proprietor, at times they found the proprietor an ally against challenge from below. Pennsylvania was far from a democracy, nor was it even a republic, but the limited suffrage it allowed to relatively ordinary people rendered the provincial status quo subject to disturbance by those who found the status quo unsatisfactory. The Penn family provided the focus of much of the dissatisfaction, especially when the proprietors insisted on their historic prerogatives, including exemption of their enormous land-holdings from taxation. Yet the first families of the colony—the Logans, Norrises, Pembertons (this last including merchant Israel and his brothers)—by standing on *their* historic prerogatives, notably control of the Assembly and other offices, often appeared equal impediments to needed reforms.

To some extent Pennsylvania provided a scale model of British North America at large. What the king was to the colonies together, the Penns, *mutatis mutandis,* were to Pennsylvania. What the London-linked ruling elites were to the British colonies, the Logan-Norris-Pemberton clique was to Pennsylvania. It was no accident that when revolution began to bubble in America against the king and his colonial officers, much of the bubbling could be traced to Pennsylvania. Pennsylvanians had been practicing for years.

&— Franklin practiced inconspicuously at first. Franklin was no political showman like William Keith; when he entered the Assembly in August 1751, he came not mounted but afoot, walking quietly up Chestnut Street to the State House. He made no large impression at first, possessing neither oratorical skills nor particular desire for attention. His legislative life consisted of committee work: a committee to locate a bridge across the Schuylkill River, a committee to report on expenditures relating to Indian affairs, a committee to revise the minutes of the Assembly, a committee to draft a message to the proprietors, a committee to prepare answers to the governor's messages, a committee to regulate the size of bakers' loaves, a committee to consider a tax on dogs.

Not all the work was so mundane. Perhaps in recognition of his earlier advocacy of paper currency, perhaps reflecting his experience printing the paper notes, Franklin gained appointment to a committee on the currency. Although the report submitted by the committee to the entire Assembly carried the signature of the five committee members, the substance and style of the report plainly indicate Franklin's authorship.

In this report Franklin evinced an even stronger conviction than he had in 1729 that more money meant a better future for Philadelphia and Pennsylvania. He described the moment in the early 1720s when the colonial economy had languished for want of means of exchange; in the prose of the report the reader can almost hear the echoing footsteps of the fugitive lad from Boston who was dismayed to discover the shops shut up in this city where he hoped to find a job. But then the Assembly had seen fit to print paper money, and "from that period both the city and country have flourished and increased in a most surprising manner." Franklin detailed the growth at considerable length, adducing evidence from tax rolls, customhouse accounts, and bills of mortality. He contended that the creation of new currency would allow the past growth to continue, principally by maintaining or increasing rates paid to laborers, which in turn would enable them, as it had their counterparts in the past, to become landowners. While acknowledging that this would harm employers of labor, Franklin argued that the benefits to society as a whole outweighed the costs to that small group. "By rendering the means of purchasing land easy to the poor, the dominions of the Crown are strengthened and extended; the Proprietaries dispose of their wilderness territory; and the British nation secures the benefit of its manufactures, and increases the demand for them. For so long as land can be easily procured for settlements between the Atlantic and Pacific Oceans, so long will labour be dear in America; and while labour continues dear, we can never rival the artificers, or interfere with the trade of our Mother Country."

Franklin's associates in the Assembly found his arguments convincing. The house resolved that an expansion of the currency was essential to the well-being of the province, and it directed Franklin and several other members with longer legislative service to draft a bill implementing the resolution. The bill passed the Assembly but then encountered objection from Governor James Hamilton, who declared that recent irresponsibilities on currency issues in other colonies made any application to the Crown "very unseasonable." The governor's veto touched off a battle with the Assembly that would busy Franklin for several years.

Other battles were more easily won. For nearly two decades Franklin had lamented the lack of safety on the streets of Philadelphia after dark. The Quakers' aversion to violence produced a criminal code decidedly less harsh than that of England or the other colonies; quite possibly for this reason, Philadelphia had a higher crime rate than other colonial cities. Franklin detected another reason as well: an inattention to policing that in itself was almost criminal. Householders in the city were liable for watch duty after dark but might buy their way out of this responsibility by paying the ward constable six shillings a year, with the fee ostensibly to be used to hire substitutes. In practice the money was more than necessary, and the watch fees became a profitable perquisite of the constables' office. They also undermined the security of the city. "The Constable for

a little drink often got such ragamuffins about him as a watch that reputable housekeepers did not choose to mix with," Franklin wrote. "Walking the rounds too was often neglected, and most of the night spent in
tippling."

Franklin first proposed a reform of the watch system to the Junto,
but after gaining approval there it failed to elicit the necessary official
support. Not until the early 1750s, following a continued deterioration of
street safety, was the Assembly persuaded to approve legislation enabling
Philadelphia to effect necessary improvements—in particular, to raise
the taxes required to light the streets and pay constables and watchmen
sufficiently to make them take their jobs seriously.

Franklin, having pondered the problem for years, and now both an
assemblyman and an alderman, was a natural to help draft orders for the
new system. The orders specified the hours of duty for constables (ten at
night till four in the morning from March to September, nine at night till
six in the morning from September to March). They identified the precise street corners on which the watchmen were to stand and the rounds
they were to walk ("Up Front-street, on the east side, to the first corner,"
for the watchman stationed at Front and Union, "thence down Water-
street, up Pine-street, down Second . . ."). They listed the sorts of trouble-
makers the constables and watchmen should be on the lookout for
("Night walkers, malefactors, rogues, vagabonds, and disorderly persons,
who they shall find disturbing the public peace, or shall have just cause to
suspect of any evil design"). And they characterized the duties of the
watch ("To prevent any burglaries, robberies, outrages, and disorders and
to apprehend any suspected persons who, in such times of confusion,
may be feloniously carrying off the goods and effects of others"). In addition the watchmen should immediately raise the alarm "in case of fire
breaking out or other great necessity."

~ Enhancing official vigilance addressed one aspect of the crime
problem, but it missed the problem's roots: the proliferation of criminals.
Since the seventeenth century the American colonies had been forced to
serve as a dumping ground for criminals convicted in England. Colonial
legislatures protested the practice of transportation of felons, only to
have their protests ignored. Colonial editors denounced the policy, appending to their editorials lurid descriptions of what the policy produced. The *Gazette* did its part in April 1751:

Last Thursday, a horrid murder was committed at Elk Ridge by Jeremiah Swift, a convict servant of Mr. John Harberley's, about 23 years of age. While himself and wife were gone to a funeral, this wretch quarreled with two boys in the field, both Mr. Harberley's sons, one about eleven, the other about nine years of age, and with a hoe knocked one of their brains out, and killed him on the spot; the other he knocked down and left him for dead. . . . After that he went to the house and murdered a young woman (Mr. Harberley's daughter) about 14 or 15 years of age, as is supposed, with an axe, for she was found dead and very much mangled. . . .

From Virginia we hear that six convicts, who were transported for fourteen years, and shipped at Liverpool, rose at sea, shot the captain, overcame and confined the seamen, and kept possession of the vessel 19 days; that coming in sight of Cape Hatteras, they hoisted out the boat to go on shore, when a vessel passing by, a boy they had not confined, hailed her, and attempted to tell their condition, but was prevented; and then the villains drove a spike up through his under and upper jaws, and wound spunyarn round the end that came out near his nose, to prevent his getting it out. . . .

From Maryland we hear that a convict servant, about three weeks since, went into his master's house, with an axe in his hand, determined to kill his mistress; but changing his purpose on seeing, as he expressed it, *how d—d innocent she looked,* he laid his left hand on a block, cut it off, and threw it at her, saying, *Now make me work, if you can.* (N.B. 'Tis said this desperate villain is now begging in Pennsylvania, and 'tis thought he has been seen in this city; he pretends to have lost his hand by an accident. The public are therefore cautioned to beware of him.)

The *Gazette*—meaning, at this time, David Hall—editorialized, "When we see our papers filled continually with accounts of the most audacious robberies, the most cruel murders, and infinite other villainies perpetrated by convicts transported from Europe, what melancholy, what terrible reflections it must occasion! What will become of our posterity! These are some of thy favours, Britain! Thou art called our Mother Country; but what good mother ever sent thieves and villains to accompany her children; to corrupt them with their infectious vices, and murder the rest?"

Franklin was as outraged as Hall (they certainly discussed the issue), yet he articulated his outrage with a lighter touch and sharper pen. Writing anonymously, Franklin asserted in all apparent seriousness that every argument adduced for sending convicts to the colonies argued equally for sending rattlesnakes from Pennsylvania to England. These serpents— "felons-convict from the beginning of the world"—were a hazard to public safety, to be sure, but this might be simply due to an unfavorable environment (as was said of the transported convicts). "However mischievous those creatures are with us, they may possibly change their natures if they were to change the climate." To test this hypothesis, Franklin proposed that a bounty be awarded to any enterprising person who collected rattlesnakes—he suggested the spring, when, heavy and sluggish, they emerged from their winter quarters and might easily be captured—and transported them to Britain. "There I would propose to have them carefully distributed in St. James's Park, in the Spring Gardens and other places of pleasure about London; in the gardens of all the nobility and gentry throughout the nation; but particularly in the gardens of the Prime Ministers, the Lords of Trade and Members of Parliament; for to them we are most particularly obliged [for the transport of felons to America]." The upper classes as a whole would benefit from proximity to Pennsylvania's slithering class. "May not the honest rough British gentry, by a familiarity with these reptiles, learn to creep, and to insinuate, and to slaver, and to wriggle into place (and perhaps to poison such as stand in their way), qualities of no small advantage to courtiers!"

Franklin noted that transport of felons to the colonies was treated by the British government as a trade, with the convicts' services being sold like other bound labor. Trade required returns. "And rattlesnakes seem the most suitable returns for the human serpents sent us by our Mother Country." Yet the trade in serpents would not be quite equal, for snakes posed fewer dangers than felons. "The Rattlesnake gives warning before he attempts his mischief, which the convict does not."

~ Felons posed an obvious threat to Pennsylvania; the threat from unchecked immigration was more subtle. At least this was Franklin's view. Certain of his neighbors were considerably more alarmed. Lutheran pastor Henry Muhlenberg declared, "It is almost impossible to describe how few good and how many exceptionally godless, wicked people have come into this country every year. The whole country is

being flooded with ordinary, extraordinary and unprecedented wickedness and crimes. . . . Our old residents are mere stupid children in sin
when compared with the new arrivals! Oh, what a fearful thing it is to
have so many thousands of unruly and brazen sinners come into this free
air and unfenced country!"

Such comments were striking, coming from Muhlenberg, himself a
recent immigrant (1742) and from the same region (Germany) where
most of the troublesome newcomers originated. German immigration to
Pennsylvania was as old as the colony itself, and it grew with each passing
decade, until by the mid-eighteenth century the Germans constituted
perhaps a third of Pennsylvania's population. Most of the Germans were
sober and industrious, yet some displayed an unsettling religious enthusiasm. A millennial sect of German Pietists known as the "Society of the
Woman in the Wilderness" built—or dug—a communistic colony in
caves above Wissahickon Creek, not far from Philadelphia, where they
ascetically awaited the Second Coming. Another group, led by Johann
Conrad Beissel, established a frontier village of the godly at Ephrata,
near the Susquehanna River some fifty miles west of Philadelphia. The
core of Beissel's sect was the "Spiritual Order of the Solitary," forty men
who devoted themselves to a rigorous regimen of work, fasting, and
prayer. Although avowedly celibate, the Ephratans admitted women, who
enrolled in the "Order of Spiritual Virgins."

By any reckoning, Beissel was a singular character. He denounced
marriage as the "penitentiary of carnal man," and he conjectured (and
repeatedly—but unsuccessfully—attempted to prove) that elimination
was not a necessary function of the body. He banned pork from Ephrata
on the unoriginal ground that it was unclean; he barred geese on the
slightly more imaginative reasoning that their feathers and down tempted
followers to sinful luxury. When he preached, he closed his eyes and spoke
very rapidly, saying he had to "hurry after the Spirit"; when at length he
stopped and discovered that most of his auditors had gone home, he
lamented their inability to endure "the Spirit's keenness." Beissel opened
his door and his heart to all who suffered and sought relief. These included unhappy wives who found him hypnotizing, and found his Order
of Spiritual Virgins about the only escape—in that era of prohibitively
difficult divorce—from unsatisfactory husbands. It did not help Beissel's
reputation with those husbands that he spent a surprising amount of time
in the quarters of the Virgins. He said he was consoling them and testing
his resistance to carnality; none but believers believed him.

Franklin knew Beissel chiefly as a customer. When the sect leader brought some of his writings to the print shop to be published, Franklin welcomed the business. He declined to get exercised about Beissel's religious or moral views, judging the unorthodoxy of the Ephratans and the other German cultists a harmless eccentricity.

At the same time Franklin wondered whether English Pennsylvania could well absorb large numbers of Germans. Many were ignorant, and though this by itself was no disqualifying trait, combined with their lack of English it made remediation difficult. "As few of the English understand the German language," Franklin told Peter Collinson, "and so cannot address them either from the press or pulpit, 'tis almost impossible to remove any prejudices they once entertain."

In days past, the Germans had kept to themselves, leaving public affairs to the English majority. No longer. "I remember when they modestly declined intermeddling in our elections, but now they come in droves, and carry all before them, except in one or two counties." Yet in joining the larger political community, the Germans refused to join the predominant cultural community. Halfway through the eighteenth century Franklin expressed a fear like those that would infuse American thinking about immigration until the twenty-first.

> Few of their children in the country learn English; they import many books from Germany. . . . The signs in our streets have inscriptions in both languages, and in some places only German. They begin of late to make all their bonds and other legal writings in their own language, which (though I think it ought not to be) are allowed good in our courts, where the German business so increases that there is continual need of interpreters; and I suppose in a few years they will also be necessary in the Assembly, to tell one half of our legislators what the other half say.

In peacetime the separateness of the Germans was troubling; in wartime it struck at the very safety of the province. Franklin suspected—mistakenly, it seems—that the French were deliberately encouraging German settlements in the Ohio Valley, as a means of containing the British colonies. Yet French strategy or no, the Germans already settled in Pennsylvania were doing the French king's work. When Franklin had been trying to summon support for the provincial militia, the Germans had been opposing it. "The Germans, except a very few in proportion to their numbers, refused to engage in it, giving out one among another, and even in print, that if they were quiet the French, should they take the country, would not molest them." Even where they were not actively seditious, the Germans complained against the cost of defense, forming a passive impediment to measures necessary for security.

Franklin did not wish the Germans barred entirely. "They have their virtues; their industry and frugality is exemplary; they are excellent husbandmen and contribute greatly to the improvement of a country." Nor were such changes in policy as the situation demanded especially great. "All that seems to be necessary is to distribute them more equally, mix them with the English, establish English schools where they are now too thick settled, and take some care to prevent the practice lately fallen into by some of the ship owners, of sweeping the German gaols to make up the number of their passengers." Yet absent such changes, the future could inspire only additional concern. "Unless the stream of their importation could be turned to other colonies . . ." Franklin told Collinson, "they will soon so outnumber us that all the advantages we have will not be able to preserve our language, and even our government will become precarious."

Collinson concurred with Franklin and forwarded several proposals for diluting the German influence in Pennsylvania. Franklin agreed with one, to invalidate all deeds and contracts written in a language other than English. The printer in Franklin demurred from another Collinson recommendation, to suppress German printing houses. The scholar and bibliophile in Franklin similarly resisted Collinson's suggestion that the importing of German books be banned. As to a recommendation that intermarriage between Germans and English be encouraged by government subsidy, Franklin simply thought it unworkable.

> The German women are generally so disagreeable to an English eye, that it would require great portions to induce Englishmen to marry them. Nor would German ideas of beauty generally agree with our women; *dick und starcke;* that is, *thick and strong,* always enters into their description of a pretty girl, for the value of a wife with them consists much in the work she is able to do. So that it would require a round sum with an English wife to make up to a Dutch man the difference in labour and frugality.

~ As a citizen, Franklin sought solutions to the German problem; as a philosopher, he sought its origins. Franklin conjectured why

Germans and English differed so deeply in character despite their common background. The English were the "offspring" of the Germans, he told Collinson, and the climate of England was similar to the climate of Germany. Therefore, he concluded, the differences in character between the two peoples must arise from differences in their institutions.

Among these institutions were the English statutes for the maintenance of the poor. Franklin asked himself whether these laws had not instilled in the poor "a dependence that very much lessens the care of providing against the wants of old age." He did not question the morality of aiding the poor, only the efficacy. "To relieve the misfortunes of our fellow creatures is concurring with the Deity; 'tis Godlike, but if we provide encouragements for laziness, and supports for folly, may it not be found fighting against the order of God and nature, which perhaps has appointed want and misery as the proper punishments for, and cautions against as well as necessary consequences of, idleness and extravagancy?"

Tampering with natural order was hazardous business. Franklin told a story of how an excess of blackbirds in New England's cornfields prompted the locals to pass laws encouraging the destruction of those pests. The blackbirds were duly diminished, but the New Englanders soon discovered their meadows engulfed in worms on which the blackbirds had fed. "Finding their loss in grass much greater than their saving in corn, they wished again for their black-birds." Drawing the moral, Franklin cautioned, "Whenever we attempt to mend the scheme of Providence and to interfere in the government of the world, we had need be very circumspect lest we do more harm than good."

Franklin told another story apropos of human motivation. A well-traveled and well-read individual from the Balkans, a Greek Orthodox priest, had passed through Philadelphia. Franklin, always eager to engage interesting people, sought him out.

He asked me one day what I thought might be the reason that so many, and such numerous, nations, as the Tartars in Europe and Asia, the Indians in America, and the Negroes in Africa, continued a wandering careless life, and refused to live in cities, and to cultivate the arts they saw practiced by the civilized part of mankind. While I was considering what answer to make him, I'll tell you, says he, in his broken English. God make man for Paradise, he make him for to live lazy; man make God angry, God turn him out of Paradise, and bid him work; man no love work; he want to go to Paradise again, he want to live lazy; so all mankind love lazy.

Franklin had doubts about the theology of this argument, but he agreed that certain groups of people were less inclined to toil than others. American Indians, for example, had resisted every effort by the English to teach them the arts of civilization. Franklin thought this striking, yet hardly inexplicable. "They visit us frequently," he told Collinson, "and see the advantages that arts, sciences, and compact society procure us. They are not deficient in natural understanding, and yet they have never shewn any inclination to change their manner of life for ours, or to learn any of our arts." The reason was plain enough: "In their present way of living, almost all their wants are supplied by the spontaneous productions of nature, with the addition of very little labour, if hunting and fishing may indeed be called labour when game is so plenty."

Significantly, when an Indian child was brought up in white ways, the education often failed to stick. "If he goes to see his relations and make one Indian ramble with them, there is no persuading him ever to return." More significantly, the opposite was not true. White children raised as Indians demonstrated no desire, after visits to English settlements, to stay there. "In a short time they become disgusted with our manner of life, and the care and pains that are necessary to support it, and take the first good opportunity of escaping again into the woods, from whence there is no reclaiming them." In one case an Englishman raised with the Indians inherited a substantial estate; he came home to test his new circumstances but soon abandoned them, leaving the estate to a younger brother and carrying off only a gun and a coat.

Franklin related yet another story that further illustrated his point. Some years earlier one of the colonies had concluded a treaty with the Six Nations (the Iroquois confederacy of the lower Great Lakes region). All that remained was the exchange of civilities. The English commissioners offered to underwrite the education of half a dozen of the brightest Indian lads at the College of William and Mary, the finest educational institution in the region. The Indians responded that they were most grateful for this kind offer but must decline. Some Indian youths had been educated in this way several years before and had returned good for nothing, being unable to hunt, trap, or fight. The Indians made a counteroffer: to take a dozen English children to the Indians' great council, where they would be raised as real and useful men.

◦— Franklin had special reason for thinking about Indians at just this time. In the autumn of 1753 he represented the province at an emergency meeting with the Indians of the frontier region, held at Carlisle, about halfway between Philadelphia and the Ohio River.

While William Penn had lived, relations between the provincial government and the local Indians were reasonably amicable. Penn interpreted his royal grant of Pennsylvania as giving him not title per se to the lands therein (after the custom of conquerors and other charter holders) but as conveying first right to purchase land from the Indians. Penn insisted that dealings in land be handled by the proprietor and his agents; individuals were generally prohibited from buying land directly from the Indians. For his own part—and therefore for the province's part—he was conscientious in adhering to the terms of purchases he negotiated with Indian leaders.

His heirs were less conscientious, in this as in other matters touching the founder's "holy experiment." The most notorious instance of proprietary overreaching was the "Walking Purchase" of 1737. By this time the predominance in western Pennsylvania of the Delaware Indians, the fluid confederation of Algonquin-speaking tribes that occupied territory from the Delaware Bay to the Hudson Valley, was being seriously challenged by the Six Nations, whose roots were in the north but whose ambitions stretched south into the Delaware lands. Meanwhile immigrants from Europe were pushing into the interior and onto Indian lands; this created friction between the settlers and the Indians and deprived the proprietors of revenue that would have been theirs had the immigrants purchased proprietary lands, as they were supposed to do.

To Thomas Penn this last was the critical consideration. The grandson of the founder always viewed Pennsylvania as a source of income rather than a venture in godly living. Calculating how he could increase his revenues, he resurrected a long-forgotten (some said fabricated) deed conveying Delaware Indian land to William Penn. The language of the deed was no more precise than that of other deeds of that bygone era, when land was limitless and the word of the Penn family was better than law; it gave the proprietor title to a tract starting at the Delaware River and extending into the woods "as far as a man can go in a day and a half."

Penn cared even less for Indian sensitivities than for Quaker conscience, and he determined to make the most of this vague description (which almost certainly had never been meant to be taken literally). He advertised for the fittest and fleetest men in the province, offering five hundred acres and five pounds money to the one who could cover the most territory in the specified time. Three men showed the greatest promise; this trio—Edward Marshall, James Yates, and Solomon Jennings—placed themselves at the starting line at dawn on the appointed day, which had been selected, as standard days often were, to fall near the autumn equinox.

Two Indians were to accompany the Englishmen; they expected the walk to be a leisurely stroll. To their surprise and dismay, Marshall and the others bolted west as the first shaft of sun lit the eastern sky, and set a killing pace. The feet of one Indian gave out early; asserting he would have brought better footwear had he known there was to be a race, he complained that the least the proprietor could have done was to provide decent shoes to the participants in the walk. Some English observers on horseback offered the Indians a ride; they gladly accepted, even as they grumbled about the miscarriage the walk was proving to be. Marshall maintained his pace throughout the day, leading the others till the country sheriff called time at sunset, twelve hours after the start. Marshall, belatedly admitting to exhaustion, clasped a sapling to keep from falling down.

At first light the next morning the race resumed. The Indians had gone home in disgust; one Delaware elder was heard to say, "No sit down to smoke, no shoot a squirrel, but run, run, run all day long." Marshall, clearly the fittest, or most determined, of the three walkers, plunged through the woods till the noon finish. By then he had covered some sixty-five miles, at least twice what William Penn and the Delawares probably contemplated when they put their marks to the contract (if indeed they did) fifty years before.

The episode won Thomas Penn a large tract of land but lost his family the friendship of the Delawares. Even the English settlers in the area, many of whom stood to gain from the younger Penn's duplicity, shook their heads. "The unfairness practiced in the walk," recalled one eyewitness, "both in regard to the way where, and the manner how, it was performed, and the dissatisfaction of the Indians concerning it, were the common subjects of conversation in our neighborhood for some considerable time after it was done." As dissatisfied in his own fashion as the Indians was Edward Marshall, who never received his promised reward, despite repeated assurances from the governor that he would.

Under other circumstances, the fiasco of the Walking Purchase might have alienated the Delawares from the Pennsylvanians permanently. But politics among the Indians was almost as competitive as politics among the Europeans—in no small part *because* the politics among the Europeans was so competitive. With the French pushing eastward from the Ohio Valley, even as English settlers moved west from the Delaware Valley, the various Indian tribes and confederations, including the Delawares, had to fashion alliances where they could.

Such alliance-fashioning carried Franklin to Carlisle in the autumn of 1753. For some time the Pennsylvania Assembly had been supplying what the Quakers called the "necessities of life"—and everyone else called guns and ammunition—to the Delawares and other Indian opponents of the French. As the French stepped up their pressure, instigating raids upon the pro-English Indians, the latter requested additional help. In September 1753 they informed Pennsylvania Governor Hamilton that they would send a delegation to Carlisle in a few days. If Brother Onas (a word meaning "quill" or "pen," and signifying the governor of Pennsylvania, at the same time that it served as a pun on the name of the proprietary family) wished to keep their loyalty, he had better act quickly. Hamilton immediately commissioned Richard Peters, the secretary of the provincial Council; Isaac Norris, at that time speaker of the Assembly; and Benjamin Franklin to head west to parley.

Peters and Norris supplied the political gravity in the Pennsylvania delegation; Franklin much of the common sense. For expertise on Indian affairs the group turned to Conrad Weiser, a German immigrant who had spent years living with and around various Indian tribes, learning their languages and customs, and making himself indispensable as a mediator between the Indians and the whites. Weiser was especially friendly with the Iroquois and had been largely responsible for winning the Six Nations to the English side. The Six Nations would be joining the Pennsylvanians at Carlisle; by way of preparing Franklin and the other commissioners for the negotiations, Weiser told of a recent conversation between himself and Canasatego, an important Iroquois chief. Canasatego had just returned from Albany, where he noticed that the white men there worked hard for six days, then shut up their shops on the seventh and retired to a great house. What were they doing in the great house?, he asked Weiser.

Weiser thought a moment, then replied that they learned "good things" in the great house.

Canasatego rejoined that he had no doubt they told Weiser so, but as for himself, he was skeptical. He explained why. He had taken a batch of skins to a merchant in Albany, with whom he had done business before. He asked the merchant, a man named Hanson, how much he would pay for the skins. Hanson answered that he could not give more than four shillings per pound, a price Canasatego considered so low as to be almost insulting. But Hanson could not talk business now, as it was the day when all the Europeans gathered at the great house to learn good things.

Canasatego, knowing there would be no business done that day, decided to go to the great house himself and learn firsthand what happened there. He was intrigued, after entering the building, to see everyone listening intently to a man dressed in black, standing in the front and speaking rapidly in an angry voice. Unfortunately, Canasatego's English could not keep up with the lesson, so he retired outdoors, where he smoked his pipe and waited for the meeting to end.

When it did, Hanson emerged, and Canasatego said he hoped the merchant had reconsidered his earlier offer. Four shillings a pound was much too low. Hanson said he had indeed reconsidered; he could not go higher than three shillings and sixpence. Surprised, Canasatego attempted to take his business elsewhere, only to hear every other fur buyer quote the same price: three and six. From this he concluded, as he explained to Weiser (and as Weiser related to Franklin), that the "good things" discussed in the great house were not good things at all but ways to cheat Indians on the price of beaver.

━ The Carlisle treaty—as the negotiation itself was called—was an education to Franklin. A strict and elaborate formality governed the speeches of both sides: the Pennsylvanians and the Six Nations on the one hand, and the Delawares, Twightwees, Shawonees, and Owandaets on the other. "Brethren," the Pennsylvania commissioners jointly declared, delivering a string of wampum, "by this string we acquaint you that the Six Nations do, at our request, join with us in condoling the losses you have of late sustained by the deaths of several of your chiefs and principal men."

This sentiment was seconded by Scarrooyady, the representative of the Iroquois. "Brethren, the Twightwees and Shawonees," he said (as interpreted by Weiser), "It has pleased Him who is above that we shall meet here today and see one another. I and my Brother Onas join together to speak to you. As we know your seats at home are bloody, we wipe away the blood, and set your seats in order at your council fire."

Handing over another string of wampum and several blankets, Scarrooyady added: "We suppose that the blood is now washed off. We jointly, with our Brother Onas, dig a grave for your warriors, killed in your country, and we bury their bones decently, wrapping them in these blankets, and with these we cover their graves."

After similar condolences to the Delawares and the Owandaets, Scarrooyady and the commissioners came to the point of the parley, which was to strengthen the tenuous alliance that currently obtained between the two sides. Speaking for both his own people and the Pennsylvanians, Scarrooyady addressed the others: "We, the English and Six Nations, do exhort every one of you to do your utmost to preserve this union and friendship, which has so long and happily continued among us. Let us keep the chain from rusting, and prevent every thing that may hurt or break it." The commissioners warned that the French were doing their utmost to break the chain, trying to turn friend against friend. This must not be allowed to happen. "Do not separate. Do not part on any score. Let no differences nor jealousies subsist a moment between nation and nation."

During the next four days the Delawares and the others indicated their willingness that the chain remain unbroken. But they and the other Indians, including the Iroquois, had some complaints they wished to air with the Pennsylvanians. Scarrooyady pointed out that the French governor of Canada blamed the English for the frontier troubles, contending that their advance toward the Ohio was the origin of all the conflict. Scarrooyady said the Six Nations did not take the French leader's statements at face value—"He speaks with two tongues"—but there was no denying that the arrival of the English from the east made matters worse. "Call your people back on this side of the hills," Scarrooyady said.

Of equal concern was the cost and quality of the trade goods the English merchants brought into the region. The English goods were too expensive and were not what the Indians wanted. The Indians wanted powder and lead, but the traders brought rum and flour. The rum was a curse, for the traders employed it to cheat the Indians. "These wicked whiskey sellers," Scarrooyady said, "when they have once got the Indians in liquor, make them sell their very clothes from their backs."

Franklin witnessed personally whereof Scarrooyady spoke. On their arrival at Carlisle the Pennsylvania commissioners forbade the sale of liquor by the merchants there. The embargo lasted the four days of the conference. At the end of that time the ban was lifted. Franklin described the result:

They were near 100 men, women and children, and were lodged in temporary cabins built in the form of a square just without the town. In the evening, hearing a great noise among them, the commissioners walked out to see what was the matter. We found they had made a great bonfire in the middle of the square. They were all drunk, men and women, quarreling and fighting. Their dark-coloured bodies, half naked, seen only by the gloomy light of the bonfire, running after and beating one another with firebrands, accompanied by their horrid yellings, formed a scene the most resembling our ideas of hell that could be imagined. There was no appeasing the tumult, and we retired to our lodging. At midnight a number of them came thundering at our door, demanding more rum; of which we gave no notice.

The next day, sensible they had misbehaved in giving us that disturbance, they sent three of their old counsellors to make their apology. The orator acknowledged the fault, but laid it upon the rum; and then endeavored to excuse the rum, by saying, "The Great Spirit who made all things made every thing for some use, and whatever use he designed any thing for, that use it should always be put to. Now, when he made rum, he said, 'Let this be for Indians to get drunk with.' And it must be so."

The rum did not merely corrupt the Indians. It also weakened the shield the Indians provided against the French. Franklin and his fellow commissioners emphasized this point in a scathing appendix to their report of the Carlisle proceedings. The quantities of liquor sold to the Indians, they said, had lately increased "to an inconceivable degree, so as to keep these poor Indians continually under the force of liquor." As a result the tribes had become "dissolute, enfeebled and indolent when sober, and untractable and mischievous in their liquor, always quarrelling, and often murdering one another." The actions of the traders, who acknowledged no obligation to anyone but themselves, threatened to "entirely estrange the affections of the Indians from the English, deprive them of their natural strength and activity, and oblige them either to abandon their country or submit to any terms, be they ever so unreasonable, from the French." In light of this "deplorable state" of the Indians, the commissioners advocated "that good and speedy remedies may be provided, before it be too late."

10

Join or Die

1754–55

◦— It was already too late. Almost as Franklin was heading
east with Richard Peters and Isaac Norris for Philadelphia,
carrying news of their apparent success in affirming
Pennsylvania's Indian alliances, a young Virginian—at
twenty-one years of age, not quite as old as William
Franklin—was heading in the opposite direction.
George Washington was a soldier in the Virginia militia;
he showed such promise at soldiering that he already held
the rank of major. And he was entrusted with an important
mission. The governor of Virginia, Robert Dinwiddie,
had ordered him to travel to the Ohio Valley and warn
the French commander there that he was trespassing
on English soil. The French commander must remove
his troops and withdraw to Canada.

The Washington mission followed many months of rising tension over the fate of the trans-Appalachian west. The peace treaty of 1748 may have silenced the guns in Europe and compelled the privateers to abandon their licensed piracy for less thrilling (and less profitable) pursuits, but it did nothing to settle the question of ownership of the Ohio Valley. Various of the English colonies claimed Ohio by virtue of their charters, which audaciously (and ignorantly—no one had any idea of the distances involved) granted them territory from sea to sea. The French asserted ownership by claiming (ignorantly or disingenuously—he never got that far) that their man La Salle had reached the Ohio River on his voyage up the Mississippi in the 1670s.

Beyond their historic claims, the two sides had continuing competing interests in Ohio. The English coveted the opportunity to expand from their seaside colonies; the colonies' growing agricultural populations made the rich bottomlands of the Ohio floodplain appear luscious almost beyond measure. Already, speculative land companies were surveying the region for subdivision and sale. Such surveying was what had propelled young Washington into the soldier's trade; with only modest formal education but a head for trigonometry and a hand for draftsmanship, Washington at seventeen had joined a survey of the Shenandoah holdings of Lord Fairfax, an in-law. The hardy life of camp and march agreed with Washington; at the first chance he made the natural transition to the Virginia militia.

As for the French, in their thinking Ohio formed the keystone in a strategic arch that spanned North America from the Gulf of Mexico to the Gulf of St. Lawrence. Ohio would connect Canada to Louisiana, guaranteeing French control of the great North American heartland and forever condemning the hated British to a precarious existence on the continent's eastern shore. More immediately, the French sought control of the Ohio fur trade, a commerce too small to support an empire but sufficient to incite the cupidity of corporations connected to government ministries.

News of the peace treaty had hardly reached America when the governor of Canada dispatched Captain Pierre Joseph Céloron de Blainville to Ohio to wave the French flag and plant lead plates bearing French territorial claims at strategic sites. In addition, he was to frighten off any English traders or settlers and convince the Indians of the region that their future lay with la belle France rather than perfidious Albion.

Céloron's mission was only partly successful. Burying the lead plates was straightforward; convincing the Indians that France was their future was more involved, not least since the easier access of English traders (who came straight over the mountains from the Atlantic, rather than circuitously via Canada) meant they could undersell their French rivals. This cost differential had given the English an edge in Ohio—an edge visible in the much larger numbers of English traders, as compared to French, Céloron encountered. His own chaplain was forced to admit that Ohio was "little known to the French, and, unfortunately, too well known to the English."

It was the French effort to alter this balance that led to the trouble that drew first Franklin and then Washington toward the Ohio. A new governor in Canada had sent several French traders to Logstown, located on the Ohio River in what would become the extreme western portion of Pennsylvania. One of the Virginia land companies—aptly named the Ohio Company—mobilized its merchants to counter the increased French presence. This triggered a minor competition between Pennsylvania and Virginia, as Pennsylvania traders hurried across the Alleghenies lest they lose the trade, and perhaps the land that supported the trade, to their southern cousins. The Pennsylvanians appealed to their provincial government for funds to build a fort at the Forks of the Ohio (where that river was formed from the Allegheny and Monongahela). But the Assembly was as stingy on frontier defense as it had traditionally been on every other form of defense, and the initiative remained with the Virginians.

The *English* initiative, that is. The French sponsored initiatives of their own. Most ominous of these was the construction of a line of forts running south from Lake Erie toward the Forks. This construction was what rang the alarm bells in the summer of 1753 and prompted Franklin's trip to Carlisle. It was also what lay behind Washington's expedition farther west just afterward.

Washington arrived at Venango (near what would become the town of Franklin) only to see a French flag flying over a trading post lately English. Here he encountered the same problem of Indian weakness for alcohol—and European exploitation of that weakness—that had so struck Franklin. At Venango, Washington tried to talk the Indians out of any attachment to the French. He initially had some luck with Tanachrison, a Seneca chief, who showed a desire to resume his alliance with the English after having been wooed away by the French. Tanachrison agreed to return the symbolic wampum he had received from French captain Philippe de Joincaire. Joincaire's first reaction, on learning of this double cross (or perhaps triple cross), was to mutter of Tanachrison, "He is more English than the English." But Joincaire masked his anger and insisted that Tanachrison join him in a series of toasts. By the time the keg was empty, Tanachrison was too drunk to hand back the wampum.

The rest of Washington's expedition was no more successful. Joincaire refused the letter Washington carried from Governor Dinwiddie; he told Washington to take it to Fort Le Boeuf, north near Lake Erie. Washington wearily pushed through the rain and snow of December, finally reaching the fort and finding someone willing to accept Dinwiddie's letter—albeit simply for forwarding to the governor of Canada. The French commander at Fort Le Boeuf politely informed Washington that evacuation of this French territory was out of the question.

Washington retired the way he had come. His horses failed on the way home, and he was reduced to walking. He came under Indian fire in the forest; he almost drowned in the Allegheny when a makeshift raft crashed against floes in the ice-laden stream. On several occasions he nearly succumbed to hypothermia. But his diary of the journey told a gripping story, which impressed Governor Dinwiddie and made Washington locally famous when the governor had it printed.

Washington's report encouraged Dinwiddie to mount a more serious effort against the French. The Virginia governor requested assistance from Pennsylvania. To no one's surprise, Franklin's fellows in the Assembly displayed their customary aversion to military spending and refused Dinwiddie's invitation. The Virginians were left to press on alone.

In the spring of 1754 Washington led two (rather skimpy) companies of militia toward the Forks of the Ohio, there to oversee construction of a fort. Unluckily for them, a larger French force had other ideas. The French troops scattered the English and leveled their unfinished handiwork. They then proceeded to lay the foundation for a more impressive French version, which they called Fort Duquesne.

Yet Washington did not discourage easily. After the embarrassment of the previous winter, he vowed to retake the Forks. He led his men on a swift night march and surprised a French scouting party, killing the commander and several others and capturing nearly all the rest. He then fell back to await reinforcements, which soon arrived.

These, however, created as many problems as they solved. They had outrun their supply train, which remained bogged in the woods behind; until the supplies arrived, the reinforcements simply ate the bread of Washington's men. Moreover, one company consisted of British regulars from South Carolina who refused to take orders from a colonial—even a colonial colonel, as Washington now was. Neither did they warm to the work of digging trenches and constructing other necessary defenses.

The French struck while the redcoats quarreled. In a July rainstorm French muskets raked the English lines; at nightfall the French commander ceased fire and urged Washington to surrender. After all, the Frenchman argued, their countries were not at war. Washington conceded this point, and, surveying his four dozen wounded and dozen dead and the enfeebled condition of many of the unwounded, he accepted the French terms.

Whereupon he came to wish he had learned French. The terms included a pledge to pull back across the mountains to Virginia; they also included an admission that the leader of the French scouting party had been "assassinated." Only later did Washington realize what he had signed; the knowledge mortified and angered him immensely.

Perhaps Washington's proud heart sensed that this defeat was but the beginning of a much longer and much more violent struggle. Perhaps, despite this second humiliation, he suspected that under arms he had found his calling. In a letter to his brother he described the first skirmish—the successful one: "I fortunately escaped without a wound, though the right wing where I stood was exposed to and received all the enemy's fire. . . . I can with truth assure you, I heard the bullets whistle, and believe me, there was something charming in the sound."

⌐ The response of King George to this comment (Washington's brother shared the letter) was reported to be "He would not say so if he had been used to hear many." Washington soon heard plenty, for the fighting on the banks of the Ohio that summer of 1754 escalated into a major war, in which Washington took a major part.

Franklin's part in what Americans called the French and Indian War involved fewer bullets but was no less significant for that. At least since he had begun pondering the problem of colonial defense during the previous war, Franklin had been struck by the inexcusable inefficiencies consequent to the several colonies' failure to coordinate actions. When France could count on Virginia's jealousies of Pennsylvania and New York's suspicions of New England, the far fewer Frenchmen in North America could effectively stymie the more numerous and otherwise more resourceful Englishmen. The example of their neighbors the Iroquois should shame those provincials who placed particular interest ahead of the common good. "It would be a very strange thing," Franklin wrote in 1751, "if six nations of ignorant savages should be capable of forming a scheme for such an union, and be able to execute it in such a manner as that it has subsisted for ages, and appears indissoluble; and yet that a like union should be impracticable for ten or a dozen English colonies, to whom it is more necessary, and must be more advantageous."

In this letter Franklin offered a blueprint for just such a colonial union. The several colonies should select delegates to a general council, which would be headed by a governor general appointed by the Crown. This council, acting with the governor general, would direct matters relating to Indian affairs and colonial defense.

Franklin acknowledged the political difficulties such a scheme would encounter. The separate provinces were possessive of their independence and privileges; anything essayed in common would tend to diminish these. Governors often mouthed approval of colonial coordination only to subvert it privately lest it undermine their authority or diminish their perquisites.

For this reason the initiative toward the union Franklin proposed ought to be entrusted to a handpicked cadre of perhaps half a dozen men of insight, public spirit, and persuasive skills. Such a group would travel from colony to colony explaining the benefits of union and rebutting criticism. "I imagine such an union might thereby be made and established, for reasonable sensible men can always make a reasonable scheme appear such to other reasonable men, if they take pains, and have time and opportunity for it." Like the Association Franklin had devised for Philadelphia, this should be an organization that grew upward from below, rather than downward from above. "A voluntary union entered into by the Colonies themselves, I think, would be preferable to one imposed by Parliament."

As did many other Franklin schemes, this one took time to mature. The provinces were then at peace, and Franklin's fellow provincials felt little inclination to accept the limitations on colonial autonomy his union entailed.

The resumption of hostilities on the Ohio frontier altered calculations. In June 1754 a convention of delegates from seven colonies gathered in Albany to discuss measures for intercolonial cooperation. The auguries were not especially promising; as a group the delegates were hardly the most influential men of their provinces, and such important provinces as Virginia shunned the proceedings entirely. Yet, for what it was worth, the convention had the blessing of the British Board of Trade, the London body that oversaw colonial affairs.

Franklin was selected to represent Pennsylvania, along with Richard

Peters, Isaac Norris, and John Penn, a grandson of William Penn. Planning for the event coincided with the setbacks suffered by the Virginians on the Ohio that spring. "Friday last an express arrived here from Major Washington," noted the *Gazette* on May 9, in a piece Franklin enclosed in a letter to a correspondent in England. Washington's dispatch described the French attack at the Forks, and it elicited reflection from the *Gazette* article's anonymous author on the need for unity among the English colonies. From the style of the writing, and from what is known of Franklin's views on the matter, the author quite likely was Franklin himself. To hear from Washington and other witnesses, the author said, the French were confident of success in their offensive. And why not? "The confidence of the French in this undertaking seems well-grounded on the present disunited state of the British colonies, and the extreme difficulty of bringing so many different governments and assemblies to agree in any speedy and effectual measures for our common defence and security, while our enemies have the very great advantage of being under one direction, with one council, and one purse." So long as the English colonies remained disunited, the French would retain their advantage. "They presume that they may with impunity violate the most solemn treaties subsisting between the two crowns, kill, seize and imprison our traders, and confiscate their effects at pleasure (as they have done for several years past), murder and scalp our farmers, with their wives and children, and take an easy possession of such parts of the British territory as they find most convenient for them; which if they are permitted to do, must end in the destruction of the British interest, trade and plantations in America."

Attached to the *Gazette* article was an illustration, a woodcut of a dismembered snake. The eight segments of the snake's body were labeled for the two Carolinas, Virginia, Maryland, Pennsylvania, New Jersey, New York, and New England. Beneath the illustration was the motto "Join, or Die." This illustration has often been characterized as the first original political cartoon printed in America; whether the artist was Franklin or someone else, the concept for the cartoon almost certainly was his. As the *Gazette* circulated through the mail, other papers reprinted the illustration, allowing readers to absorb the essence of Franklin's argument for unity at a glance.

Consequently it was to a collective mind preconditioned to union that Franklin addressed further thoughts on the nature of an American union. In New York City en route to Albany he began buttonholing fellow delegates and other influential persons. He showed an outline for a supracolonial government to Cadwallader Colden and James Alexander, requesting each man to supply suggestions for improvements.

Franklin's outline was just that; it supplied only sufficient detail to serve as a basis for discussion at Albany. Heading the union, in this conception, would be a governor general, a military man appointed and paid by the king and charged with executing measures adopted by a "grand council," except for those measures he vetoed. The grand council would consist of persons selected by the provincial assemblies; the smaller provinces each would send one member, the larger two, in rough proportion to the payments each colony made to a general treasury. Franklin suggested that the general treasury be funded by excise taxes collected by the several provinces; these excise taxes might be levied upon liquor or tea, items consumed at fairly equal rates across the land and therefore serving as a fiscal stand-in for population.

Franklin's was a federal system, its members answerable to the provincial assemblies that selected them, rather than to the people of the colonies. Its responsibilities lay in the realm of what might have been called foreign and defense policy: relations with the Indian tribes, construction and garrisoning of forts, outfitting of naval vessels for the protection of the coast and the security of trade in wartime.

While more specific than his plan of 1751, Franklin's 1754 version was an extension of the principles outlined in that earlier draft, with one important exception. Where previously he had preferred a confederation organized by the provinces on their own, without the involvement of London's Parliament, by now he recognized that the provinces would *not* act on their own. Accordingly he advocated that the commissioners at Albany debate his proposal and modify it as suited their perceptions of necessity, with the result "to be sent home [that is, to England], and an Act of Parliament obtained for establishing it."

༄ **Alexander** and Colden commented, as Franklin had requested, but another man played a larger part in persuading the Albany Congress to agree to Franklin's plan of union. Thomas Hutchinson was a Boston boy, like Franklin, born five years later; although there is no record of it, the paths of the two may well have crossed on the streets of the Massachusetts capital. Yet if they crossed they hardly coincided, for Hutchinson enjoyed all the advantages of birth and breeding Franklin lacked. Hutchinson's family was of the first generation of New Englanders;

Anne Hutchinson, Thomas's great-great-grandmother, out-Puritaned the Puritans in insisting that faith alone sufficed for salvation and that works were secondary. Ben Franklin later rejected this view; so too, for different reasons did Thomas Hutchinson.

What Hutchinson disliked about Anne's doctrine was that it earned her excommunication and exile (and ultimately death, inflicted by Indians who were seen by Anne's accusers as agents of divine wrath against the heretic). All his life Thomas Hutchinson was a man of the status quo. He described himself as "a quietist," believing "that what is, is best." He certainly looked so. The only surviving portrait of him, painted when he was thirty, shows a slender man ("Tommy, skin and bones," jibed his political opponents after he became controversial). He has a wide and high forehead, a large nose, eyes that bulge ever so slightly, and a mouth set in a careful but self-satisfied smile.

At thirty he had reason to be self-satisfied. The heretics and theologians of the family were on the female side; for several generations the males were merchants, conservatives who sought salvation through commerce. Thomas fit the male mold. His father staked him to a start in trade ("two or three quintals of fish," by Thomas's recollection); this he parlayed by "adventuring to sea" (that is, purchasing shares in ships) into the not inconsiderable sum of perhaps £500 sterling by the time he was twenty-one. An inheritance enlarged his fortune; the bequest included a magnificent house, the finest in Boston ("the first developed example of provincial Palladianism in New England," according to a later historian of architecture). This house became Hutchinson's pride and joy, the emblem of his earthly success.

Affluence—if not salvation—assured, Hutchinson entered politics. He was elected to the Boston town council and to the provincial House of Representatives. By the mid-1740s he had ascended to the speakership of the House and was one of the most influential figures in the public life of the colony.

The issues in Massachusetts mirrored some of those in Pennsylvania. While Franklin was promoting paper money in Philadelphia, Hutchinson—as might have been expected of a man who had made his fortune and was concerned with keeping it—championed hard currency in Boston. Through persistence and skill, and the canny employment of the gold and silver sent to Massachusetts by London in repayment for that colony's expenses in the Louisbourg expedition, Hutchinson and his hard-money allies carried the day. It helped that they had the strong arm of the government behind them, for when the partisans of paper became particularly rowdy, Governor Jonathan Belcher forcibly crushed the incipient insurrection. "They are grown so brassy and hardy as to be now combining in a body to raise a rebellion," Belcher said of the rioters, in words capturing Hutchinson's view. "I have this day sent the sheriff and his officers to apprehend some of the heads of the conspirators, so you see we are becoming ripe for a smarter sort of government."

The smarter sort of government Hutchinson had in mind in 1754 was one that encouraged common action among the several colonies. Hutchinson agreed with Franklin that the present disunity endangered the English colonies in North America, and that decisive action must be taken to knit the too-often-competing colonies into a coherent whole. The two men—the most capable public figures of Massachusetts and Pennsylvania—joined heads and pens on a committee appointed by the Albany Congress to consider means for effecting such a union.

With Franklin's approval, Hutchinson took the lead in drafting a report that made the arguments Franklin had been making for some time. The British colonies were suffering badly, the report said, from their lack of cooperation. "There has never been any joint exertion of their force, or counsels to repel or defeat the measures of the French." Each colony devised its own land policy, which typically conflicted with those of its neighbors. This produced "great uneasiness and discontents" among the Indians, who were either cheated by the competing colonies or caused to think they were being cheated. English traders, under the spur of the intercolonial competition, corrupted the Indians with rum "in vast and almost incredible quantities, the laws of the colonies now in force being insufficient to restrain the supply."

A reversal of direction was imperative, the report said. Common laws must be implemented to restrain the traders and the competition in land. Frontier forts must be constructed from a common fund. Most important, the colonies must be encouraged to establish "a Union of His Majesty's several governments on the continent, that so their councils, treasure, and strength may be employed in due proportion against their common enemy."

The Albany Congress found the argument compelling. The body accepted the report, unanimously approved the principle of union, and appointed Franklin, as the originator of the idea, to draw up a concrete proposal to lay before Parliament.

With his usual discretion, Franklin accommodated the suggestions of others. "When one has so many different people with different opinions to deal with in a new affair," he explained to Cadwallader Colden, "one is obliged sometimes to give up some smaller points in order to obtain greater." Under Franklin's revised plan the unified government would be headed by a "President General." The "Grand Council" would comprise seven members each from Massachusetts and Virginia, six from Pennsylvania, and so on down to two from Rhode Island and New Hampshire. The council would meet at Philadelphia, at least initially. On the critical matter of powers, the "President General with the advice of the Grand Council" would be responsible for making war and peace with the Indian nations, for regulating trade and land sales on the frontier, for raising soldiers and building forts, for levying taxes and other duties. The individual colonies would retain their own governments, which would continue to act in those areas not preempted by the common government.

Franklin's revisions provoked further discussion, at times heated. "We had a great deal of disputation about it, almost every article being contested by one or another," he told Colden. But finally the Congress strongly approved the union plan and referred it to the individual provinces and to Parliament.

Gratified though he was at this endorsement, Franklin appreciated that the hard work lay ahead. In the confines of the Albany gathering, Franklin's reasonableness, his understated style, his willingness to work through such others as Thomas Hutchinson, and his ability to accommodate varying viewpoints made his arguments almost irresistible. In the larger world, however—the world of the provincial assemblies and Parliament—the fate of the union plan might be far different. "How they will relish it," he said of the assemblies, "or how it will be looked on in England, I know not."

~ He did what he could to whet the pertinent appetites. In late July he produced an extensive explanation of the reasons and motives behind the union plan. This gloss answered objections already raised, anticipated others, and amplified the arguments for union made by Franklin himself, by Hutchinson, and by other advocates.

Subsequently Franklin parried alternatives to the Albany plan, explaining where and why they fell short. In December 1754 he took on Governor Shirley of Massachusetts, who proposed a scheme diluting the popular role of the provinces in selecting the members of the union government. Franklin judged such dilution deadly, and told Shirley so. One letter explicating his views revealed much not only about the Albany plan but about Franklin's developing theories of government and of the relation of the American colonies to the British homeland.

"Excluding the people of the Colonies from all share in the choice of the Grand Council would probably give extreme dissatisfaction," Franklin said. The people of the colonies considered themselves, with justice, "as loyal and as firmly attached to the present Constitution and reigning family as any subjects in the King's dominions." They were as willing as any Englishmen to furnish supplies for the defense of their country. But to be *required* to do so by a Council unanswerable to them contravened one of the most venerable English traditions. "It is supposed an undoubted right of Englishmen not to be taxed but by their own consent given through their own representatives."

To this, Governor Shirley responded with a proposal that the colonies receive representation in Parliament—effecting, in essence, a union of the colonies with Britain. Franklin thought the idea a good one, if correctly construed. "Such an Union would be very acceptable to the Colonies provided that they had a reasonable number of representatives allowed them, and that all the old Acts of Parliament restraining the trade or cramping the manufactures of the Colonies be at the same time repealed, and the British subjects on this side the water put in those respects on the same footing with those in Great Britain till the new Parliament, representing the whole, shall think it for the interest of the whole to re-enact some or all of them."

Needless to say, this proviso severely diminished the appeal to Parliament of Shirley's suggestion. What was the point of having colonies if not to be able to discriminate against them in trade, manufacture, or otherwise? Franklin knew this. Yet his stricture allowed him to explicate a larger argument: that the American colonists were and ought to be considered full members of the English nation. "I should hope too, that by such an union, the people of Great Britain and the people of the Colonies would learn to consider themselves, not as belonging to different communities with different interests, but to one community with one interest."

Franklin offered an analogy to the situation in which the colonies currently found themselves. At the eastern entrance to the Strait of Dover lay a line of shoals called the Goodwin Sands. Low tide exposed a stretch of the sands, lending the appearance that England's land area had grown.

> Could the Goodwin Sands be laid dry by banks, and land equal to a large country thereby gained to England, and presently filled with English inhabitants, would it be right to deprive such inhabitants

of the common privileges enjoyed by other Englishmen, the right of vending their produce in the same ports, or of making their own shoes, because a merchant or a shoemaker, living on the old land, might fancy it more for his advantage to trade or make shoes for them? Would this be right, even if the land were gained at the expence of the state? And would it not seem less right, if the charge and labour of gaining the additional territory had been borne by the settlers themselves?

The American colonies stood in an even stronger position than the hypothesized province, for unlike the imagined Goodwinites, the British Americans produced raw materials unavailable in England's latitude, and their distance across the sea served to strengthen Britain's shipping, essential to national defense.

The present habit of thinking of old England and New England as distinct diminished them both. "What imports it to the general state whether a merchant, a smith, or a hatter grow rich in *Old* or *New* England?" In either case the empire gained. Imperial laws ought to recognize this reality and reward effort wherever it occurred. "If, through increase of people, two smiths are wanted for one employed before, why may not the *new* smith be allowed to live and thrive in the *new Country*, as well as the *old* one in the *old*?" Britain must eventually realize the fundamental truth: "The strength and wealth of the parts is the strength and wealth of the whole."

⌒ **Franklin's** exchange with Governor Shirley followed a personal meeting between the two men. In the autumn of 1754 Franklin returned to Boston on a trip that combined public and private affairs. Abiah Franklin had died in May 1752 after some years of declining health. "I am very weeke and short bretht so that I cant set to rite much," she informed her son several months earlier, in her untutored manner. She was not one to complain, though, and was thankful for what was left to her. "I slepe well anits [a-nights] and my coff is better and I have a prity good stumak to my vettels."

News of her death came as no great surprise the following spring; and as in the case of Josiah seven years before, the news arrived too late for Benjamin to attend the funeral or do more than commiserate with his siblings. "I received yours with the affecting news of our dear good mother's death," he wrote Jane. "I thank you for your long continued care of her in her old age and sickness. Our distance made it impracticable for us to attend her, but you have supplied all. She has lived a good life, as well as a long one, and is happy."

After his own fashion Franklin sought to repay his familial debt to his sister and her husband, Edward Mecom. The couple had eleven children; for reasons not hard to fathom, Franklin took a special shine to the third, who was named after him. Benjamin Mecom possessed the same independent mind as his uncle, the same impatience with life close to kin, the same desire to get out of Boston. Franklin arranged for the lad to apprentice with James Parker, Franklin's New York printer-partner. "I am confident he will be kindly used there," Franklin assured the boy's mother, "and I shall hear from him every week." By way of admonition, the uncle added, "You will advise him to be very cheerful, and ready to do every thing he is bid, and endeavour to oblige every body, for that is the true way to get friends."

If Jane relayed the advice to Benny, it failed to make an impression. The apprenticeship with Parker yielded numerous complaints from both apprentice and master, complaints that usually intersected in the correspondence of Franklin. Whether Benny was more fractious than Franklin himself had been at the same stage of his career is impossible to tell from the distance of more than two hundred years; it was almost as hard for Franklin to tell from the distance of one hundred miles. Benny's mother heard her son's complaints and echoed them back to her brother; Parker related his side of the story directly.

Franklin found himself at something of a loss as to how to handle the matter. The best he could do was reassure Jane that her son's sufferings were exaggerated in the telling and really nothing out of the ordinary, while inquiring of Parker to determine whether such was indeed the case. His own visits to New York supplemented his inquiries of his partner.

"I am frequently at New York," he wrote Jane, exaggerating for soothing effect, "and I never saw him unprovided with what was good, decent, and sufficient." Benny had complained of being sent on petty errands. "No boys love it, but all must do it," his uncle said. Benny made a habit of staying out all night; Parker had good reason for reprimanding him. "If he was my own son, I should think his master did not do his duty by him, if he omitted it, for to be sure it is the high road to destruction." Benny had been beguiled by a privateer that brought rich prizes into port, prizes shared among the crew; like William Franklin, he determined to have done with dreary terrestrial existence and make for the open sea and the life of the licensed pirate. Parker had to pull him off, as Franklin pulled William off; now Franklin explained the attempted escape to the attempter's mother: "When boys see prizes brought in, and quantities of money shared among the men, and their gay living, it fills their heads with notions that half distract them and put them quite out of conceit with trades and the dull ways of getting money by working."

Having essentially said Benny was making up the stories of his poor treatment, Franklin offered his sister a comforting estimate of the boy. "I have a very good opinion of Benny in the main, and have great hopes of his becoming a worthy man, his faults being only such as are commonly incident to boys of his years, and he has many good qualities, for which I love him."

Franklin was willing to gamble on those good qualities when it became apparent that the apprenticeship to Parker would not work out. In 1748 Franklin had dispatched a journeyman to Antigua to establish a print shop there; shop and printer thrived until 1752, when a tropical fever carried him off. Franklin thought to solve two problems by relieving Parker of Benny and sending the young man to Antigua to fill the vacancy. Especially as the boy was not yet twenty, his mother was mildly appalled.

The uncle attempted to assuage her fears. "That island is reckoned one of the healthiest in the West Indies," he declared. "My late partner there enjoyed perfect health for four years, till he grew careless and got to sitting up late in taverns, which I have cautioned Benny to avoid." The opportunity trumped anything Benny would encounter closer to home. "He will find the business settled to his hand, a newspaper established, no other printing-house to interfere with him or beat down his prices, which are much higher than we get on the continent." Yet despite his assuring tone, Franklin had to grant that human provision would warrant only so much. "Having taken care to do what *appears to be for the best*, we must submit to God's Providence, which orders all things *really for the best*."

Perhaps God got distracted, or simply had other ideas regarding Benny. Independence suited the young man no better than apprenticeship, and he quickly found trouble in Antigua. He ran up debts to Franklin's friend William Strahan in London, failed by any reasonable measure of diligence, and nonetheless blamed his uncle for his problems. Even as Franklin decried such misbehavior, he accepted responsibility for at least part of it. "I fear I have been too forward in cracking the shell," he told Jane, "and producing the chick to the air before its time."

∽ **If nephew** Benny's course ran crooked, son William's was somewhat straighter, if not always less difficult. In Philadelphia, William adopted the pose of the demobilized war hero. "William is now 19 years of age, a tall proper youth, and much of a beau," Franklin had written Abiah in the spring of 1750. The beau was living off his father—to his stepmother's distress—and hoped to continue to do so. The father disabused him. "I have assured him that I intend to spend what little I have, my self, if it please God that I live long enough."

The friction between William and Deborah was no secret. Daniel Fisher, a clerk who worked for Franklin during the 1750s, kept a diary in which he recorded the stepmother's complaints.

> I have often seen pass to and from his father's apartment upon business (for he does not eat, drink or sleep in the house) without the least compliment between Mrs. Franklin and him or any sort of notice taken of each other, till one day, as I was sitting with her in the passage when the young gentleman came by, she exclaimed to me (he not hearing): "Mr. Fisher, there goes the greatest villain upon earth!" This greatly confounded and perplexed me, but did not hinder her from pursuing her invectives in the foulest terms I ever heard from a gentlewoman.

William read law with Joseph Galloway, the scion of a respected Philadelphia family and a man who would become one of Franklin's closest political allies before the American Revolution estranged them. When Franklin was elected to the Assembly in 1751, he got William appointed to the clerkship he was vacating.

He found the young man better work two years later. Since his appointment as Philadelphia postmaster in 1737, Franklin had moved in rather desultory fashion up the postal ranks, eventually becoming comptroller of the American posts. In 1751 he set his mind more determinedly to advancement. He wrote his English friend Peter Collinson that the deputy postmaster general of America, Elliott Benger of Virginia, who had been in poor health for some time, "is thought to be near his end." Franklin asked Collinson to use his influence to secure the position for him. "I would only add that as I have a respect for Mr. Benger, I should be glad the application were so managed as not to give him any offence, if he should recover." Benger did no such thing—although he took his time about dying—and two years later Franklin got the job, albeit in conjunction with William Hunter of Virginia.

Half the deputy postmaster position afforded Franklin the opportunity to improve mail service throughout the colonies, to increase his knowledge of conditions across America, and to engage the leading citizens of the different provinces. Eventually the job would earn him a fair income, but for the time being the investments required to put the American mails on an efficient footing ate up all profits and more.

The job also gave Franklin the ability to throw work to his son. Franklin was no stickler for disinterest in appointments to office; he was happy to keep within the family the perquisites of whatever positions he acquired. In this case he exercised his authority as deputy postmaster to appoint William postmaster of Philadelphia. A year later he named William continental comptroller.

Perhaps William now concluded that his father had something to offer; perhaps the young man had simply outgrown the annoyances of adolescence. Whatever the cause, the filial relationship warmed and ramified. William developed an interest in Franklin's experiments, contributing observations and hypotheses of his own. Significantly, it was William who served as the sole assistant of his father in the kite experiment. That the experiment led to international acclaim for Franklin only increased his son's respect.

For his part, Franklin could hope William was growing into a worthy manhood. A rebel himself in youth, Franklin could hardly hold William's earlier experiments—in life, not electricity—against him. But now the boy seemed to be finding himself. His father could only be gratified.

～ While William kept the accounts of the post office and read his law books, he dreamed of grander things. Grandest was an empire of western land. Like many others of his era—including George Washington—William caught a highly infectious disease during his journey to the Ohio Valley, a disease whose most significant symptom was a belief that fabulous wealth awaited whoever could win title to those boundless acres. William would spend years seeking such title. For now he dreamed.

Franklin would share his son's dream, if not the symptoms of virulent infection. Franklin would join William in speculating in western land, but in Franklin's case the western dream was less personal than imperial.

As his exchanges with William Shirley revealed, Franklin saw America as a potentially coequal part of the British empire, and the basis for American equality was land. In land lay the future of America; in American land lay the future of Britain.

Franklin addressed precisely this issue in what became one of the most influential essays he ever wrote. In 1751 he drafted "Observations concerning the Increase of Mankind, Peopling of Countries, &c." and circulated it to Peter Collinson and others. Collinson urged Franklin to publish the piece. "I wish, my Dear Friend, you'll oblige the ingenious part of mankind with a public view of your observations &c. on the increase of mankind," Collinson wrote. "I don't find anyone has hit it off so well." The draft was rough, however, and Franklin hoped to polish it before release to the "ingenious part" or anyone else. But politics, postmastering, and other interests intervened, and the polishing never took place. Finally, in 1754, Franklin consented to its publication as it stood, and the next year it was printed in Boston. It quickly crossed the Atlantic and was reproduced in London, Edinburgh, and Dublin. Economists Adam Smith and later Thomas Malthus, among many others, read it appreciatively.

Franklin's central idea was simple: that the increase of population depended on the availability of land. The critical element in reproductive rates was the age of marriage; couples who married young had more children than couples who married old. (Needless to say, Franklin's observation antedated convenient contraception.) The age of marriage in turn depended on the opportunities to establish economic independence. In Franklin's preindustrial day, economic independence for the many required access to land—of which America had an abundance relative to Europe. Europe was already filled with farmers; adding more required displacing some of those already there. America was filled with Indians, who subsisted by hunting, an occupation that resulted in a population far less dense, leaving ample room for farmers.

> Land being thus plenty in America, and so cheap that a labouring man that understands husbandry can in a short time save money enough to purchase a piece of new land sufficient for a plantation, whereon he may subsist a family; such are not afraid to marry, for if they even look far enough forward to consider how their children when grown up are to be provided for, they see that more land is to be had at rates equally easy, all circumstances considered.
>
> Hence marriages in America are more general, and more generally early, than in Europe. And if it is reckoned there that there is

but one marriage per annum among 100 persons, perhaps we may here reckon two; and if in Europe they have but 4 births to a marriage (many of their marriages being late), we may here reckon 8, of which if one half grow up, and our marriages are made, reckoning one with another, at 20 years of age, our people must at least be doubled every 20 years.

This was the part that caught the eye of Malthus—this and Franklin's assertion that "there is in short no bound to the prolific nature of plants or animals, but what is made by their crowding and interfering with each other's means of subsistence." From these (and contributions of his own, of course) Malthus extrapolated the theory of inevitable impoverishment that made him famous.

Adam Smith was taken by another part of Franklin's argument. In 1750 the British Parliament had bent to the demands of British manufacturers and prohibited the construction of ironworks in America; Franklin's essay was at least partly a response to this prohibition. He argued that despite the rapid increase in the American population, the vastness of the land available to these growing numbers would for generations dictate a dearness of labor compared to that in the old country. "The danger, therefore, of these colonies interfering with their Mother Country in trades that depend on labour, manufactures, &c. is too remote to require the attention of Great Britain." Far from weakening demand for manufactures of the home country, the growth of the colonies would strengthen it. "Therefore Britain should not restrain too much manufactures in her colonies. A wise and good mother will not do it. To distress is to weaken, and weakening the children weakens the whole family." Adam Smith, who made his name attacking the protectionist policies of British mercantilism—and who kept not one but two copies of Franklin's essay in his library—could not have put it better.

In an early indication that his views on slavery were changing, Franklin contended that the introduction of slaves could only diminish a nation. Slavery enabled whites to avoid labor, thereby undermining their health and rendering them "not so generally prolific." Slavery also sapped the moral health of the nation. Franklin at this point did not contend that trafficking in human souls was inherently immoral; rather he decried the bad example it set. "White children become proud, disgusted with labour, and being educated in idleness, are rendered unfit to get a living by industry." Franklin thought it significant that the northern colonies, having fewer slaves than the southern, multiplied their populations more rapidly.

The laws of population growth, as exhibited in America, promised a brilliant future for the colonies—a future whose brilliance need not dull in the slightest that of Britain.

> There are supposed to be now upwards of one million English souls in North America (though 'tis thought scarce 80,000 have been brought over sea), and yet there is perhaps not the one fewer in Britain, but rather many more, on account of the employment the colonies afford to manufacturers at home. This million doubling, suppose but once in 25 years, will in another century be more than the people of England, and the greatest number of Englishmen will be on this side the water. What an accession of power to the British Empire by sea as well as land! What increase of trade and navigation!

⌐ That the future of America, and with it of the British empire, depended on the availability of land was what made the contest with France so important. The defeat incurred by George Washington in 1754 inspired the British government to action; early the following year it dispatched an expedition of regular army officers and men to America to smite the French intruders and regain Britain's rightful hold on the Ohio. The commander of the expedition was Major General Edward Braddock of the Coldstream Guards. Braddock was sixty years old, had served occasionally as governor of Gibraltar, and hoped to cap his otherwise undistinguished military career with appointment as royal governor somewhere or other. Although fond of his pipe, his claret, and his mistresses, he liked to convey a stoic impression. "Braddock is very Iroquois in disposition," declared British diarist Horace Walpole. "He had a sister who, having gamed away all her little fortune at Bath, hanged herself with a truly English deliberation, leaving only a note upon the table with these lines: 'To die is landing on some silent shore,' etc. When Braddock was told of it, he only said, 'Poor Fanny! I always thought she would play till she would be forced to *tuck herself up.*' "

Braddock was not pleased at having to travel to a New World wilderness to win his governorship, but, as no other theater beckoned—other than the theaters of London, where he took in the performances of George Anne Bellamy, a famous actress who was one of his two current flames—away he must go. In leaving he demonstrated that some of Miss Bellamy's dramatic flair had rubbed off. "The General told me that he should never see me more," she recalled, "for he was going with a handful of men to conquer whole nations; and to do this they must cut their way through unknown woods. He produced a map of the country, saying at the same time: 'Dear Pop, we are sent like sacrifices to the altar.' "

The general conveyed a different impression to Franklin and others in America. Franklin encountered Braddock at Frederick, Maryland, having been sent there by the Pennsylvania Assembly, which wanted a personal assessment from one of their own of this officer come to rescue the colony from the French and the Indians. Rather than acknowledge his role as eye of Assembly, though, Franklin wore his postmaster's hat and averred his desire to facilitate the general's communications.

Braddock boasted he would make short work of his adversaries. "After taking Fort Duquesne," he told Franklin, "I am to proceed to Niagara; and having taken that, to Frontenac, if the season will allow time; and I suppose it will, for Duquesne can hardly delay me above three or four days; and then I see nothing that can obstruct my march to Niagara."

From William, and from his reading of recent history—including the experiences of George Washington—Franklin appreciated the peculiar difficulties attending frontier warfare. The Indians were masters of ambush; was the general taking this into account?

"These savages may indeed be a formidable enemy to your raw American militia," Braddock replied. "But upon the King's regular and disciplined troops, sir, it is impossible they should make any impression."

Only one thing worried the British general. The Americans, for whom he and his men would accomplish their heroics, were failing to do their part. "These Americans," he grumbled to an associate, "coaxed us over here to fight their battles and then, by God, they overcharge us for wagons and supplies and refuse to fight in their own quarrel." To Franklin he declared that the lack of cooperation, particularly in providing transport, could scuttle the expedition before it had well started.

Franklin could not deny that his own province was acting the miser in its defense; as before, the Quakers in the Assembly were blocking military appropriations. But he thought the people of Pennsylvania would be happy to hire out their wagons and horses to the Crown, and told Braddock as much.

"Then you, sir," Braddock answered, "who are a man of interest there, can probably procure them for us; and I beg you will undertake it."

Franklin accepted the invitation. He printed a broadside advertising for the use of 150 wagons and teams, and 1,500 horses, on attractive financial terms. In an accompanying letter Franklin assured the owners that "the service will be light and easy, for the Army will scarce march above 12 miles per day." He additionally assured his audience that he himself had no pecuniary interest in the matter. "I shall have only my labour for my pains." Patriotism should inspire those who found the financial incentives insufficient; to those indifferent to finances and patriotism both, Franklin closed with a caution: "If this method of obtaining the waggons and horses is not like to succeed, I am obliged to send word to the General in fourteen days; and I suppose Sir John St. Clair the Hussar, with a body of soldiers, will immediately enter the province for the purpose aforesaid, of which I shall be sorry to hear."

"I cannot but honour Franklin for the last clause of his advertisement," chuckled Braddock's military secretary upon reading Franklin's broadside. General St. Clair, Braddock's quartermaster, was not really a Hussar, one of those shock troops of the Habsburg Empire, but the uniform of his unit looked sufficiently similar to that of the Hungarian originals to unsettle the Pennsylvania Germans—people who knew how the Hussars acquired their unsavory reputation. St. Clair contributed to the effect by acting in the haughtiest manner imaginable. He refused to employ his soldiers in cutting roads through the forest, instead insisting that civilians do the work. He threatened fire and sword—he said he would burn their houses and kill their cattle—if they did not comply. If delays on the road prevented the defeat of the French, he would treat those responsible for the delay as a "parcel of traitors."

Franklin got his horses and wagons, but not before putting his own money at risk. Hussar memories notwithstanding, the canny farmers of the backcountry wanted to make sure they got paid for their animals and kit. They did not know Braddock, but they did know that the British government had been slow to pay in other circumstances; before they accepted Franklin's terms, they made him post personal bond for their property. This he loyally but nervously did.

Braddock, now provisioned for victory, rode off to accomplish it. Franklin returned to Philadelphia, where he encountered a confidence in Braddock's prospects he did not share. Some of his fellow citizens got up a subscription for fireworks to celebrate the certain victory. Franklin frowned and said there would be time enough for celebrating when the battle was won.

"What the devil!" said one of the sponsors. "You surely don't suppose that the fort will not be taken?"

"I don't know that it will not be taken," Franklin replied. "But I know that the events of war are subject to great uncertainty."

And so they were. Despite the train of wagons and horses Franklin had attracted (and was currently underwriting), Braddock found the going through the forest agonizingly slow. On the advice of Washington, who had rejoined the military as an aide to Braddock, the general divided the column, pushing ahead with the lighter and faster units and leaving the baggage train to follow.

On the morning of July 9, 1755, Lieutenant Colonel Thomas Gage (who twenty years later would get to know Washington in a quite different capacity) led a contingent of some 450 troops toward a broad meadow just a few miles south of Fort Duquesne. Because he failed to send an adequate number of scouts ahead, he moved forward largely blind.

Meanwhile a force of French and Indian soldiers was reconnoitering south from the fort. Somewhat to their surprise they encountered the British, and in the forest the battle commenced. Gage had no good idea how many enemy soldiers he faced; rather than thrust forward into the clearing ahead, he retreated. Braddock, behind, hearing the gunfire, ordered an advance. The retreating column and the advancing unit collided on the narrow road, clumping in confusion. As they did, the forest-savvy French commander split his force into two files that streamed through the underbrush past the British on both sides, then opened a withering fire upon the redcoats from the shadowed cover.

"I cannot describe the horrors of that scene," said a survivor. "No pen could do it. The yell of the Indians is fresh on my ear, and the terrific sound will haunt me till the hour of my dissolution." Washington, who had recovered from a violent fever just in time to ride into battle (albeit on a cushioned saddle), had two horses shot from under him and four bullets pierce his coat; miraculously he escaped injury.

Braddock was no less brave but much less lucky. The general lost four horses before being bowled off the fifth by a ball that penetrated his lung. He lived just long enough to appreciate the magnitude of the disaster: two-thirds of his 1,450 men killed or wounded. Among the officers the casualty rate was three-quarters.

In some instances the dead did better than the living. Prisoners taken by the French-friendly Indians were subjected to torture. One British prisoner, captured earlier, told of the return of the Indians to Fort Duquesne "with about a dozen prisoners, stripped naked, with their hands tied behind their backs, and their faces and part of their bodies blacked. These prisoners they burned to death on the bank of the Allegheny river, opposite to the fort. I stood on the fort wall until I beheld them begin to burn one of these men; they had him tied to a stake and kept touching him with firebrands, red-hot irons, &c., and he screamed in the most doleful manner; the Indians, in the mean time, yelling like infernal spirits."

11

The People's Colonel

1755–57

∽ Braddock's defeat on the Ohio sent Pennsylvania
into shock. Philadelphia got the bad news from
the fleeing British troops. Colonel Thomas Dunbar,
who inherited Braddock's command, panicked
at the thought of an enemy he could neither see nor
number; convinced that his whole force risked destruction,
he burned his baggage train and led his men in a rush
to Philadelphia, where he proposed to go into winter
quarters, although it was not yet August.

Dunbar's disappearance left the frontier defenseless. The French commander, Captain Jean Dumas, had, like Dunbar, inherited command from a superior killed in the recent battle, but unlike Dunbar he knew what to do with his unanticipated authority. He immediately launched a campaign of terror from the Ohio south and east into the hinterlands of Pennsylvania, Maryland and Virginia. His intent was to intimidate England's Indian allies into turning coat, and to drive the settlers of the English colonies back upon the Atlantic seaboard.

From Dumas's perspective at Fort Duquesne, the campaign went very well. Several months after its start he informed the French government, "I have succeeded in setting against the English all the tribes of this region who had been their most faithful allies." The policy was calculated and cruel. Referring to the tribes lately loyal to the English, Dumas boasted, "I have succeeded in making almost all of them attack the English, and if any of them resisted I have always managed to destroy them, so that I have put the Iroquois in fear of the Delawares and Shawnees unless they follow their example; and since the war-parties I have intercepted here have taken scalps and prisoners back to their towns, they find themselves engaged in the war, so to speak, in spite of themselves." With some exaggeration, Dumas continued, "I have succeeded in ruining the three adjacent provinces, Pennsylvania, Maryland, and Virginia, driving off the inhabitants, and totally destroying the settlements over a tract of country thirty leagues wide, reckoning from the line of Fort Cumberland." Six or seven war parties were in the field at once, each headed by a Frenchman. "Thus far, we have lost only two officers and a few soldiers; but the Indian villages are full of prisoners of every age and sex. The enemy has lost far more since the battle than on the day of his defeat."

From Franklin's perspective in Philadelphia, the French campaign seemed hardly less effective. The autumn of 1755 brought regular reports of the terror on the frontier. From Penn's Creek came a lurid tale of massacre and kidnapping: fourteen dead and scalped, eleven spirited away to God-knew-what fiendish fate. From Cumberland (later Fulton) County came reports that the Delaware chief Shingas—Shingas the Terrible, as he was now called—was leading his people against their former allies. "All burned to ashes," wrote a person who escaped the destruction of the community of Great Cove by Shingas and his warriors. "It is really very shocking to see an husband looking on while these Indians are chopping the head off the wife of his bosom, and the children's blood drank by these bloody and cruel savages."

That the terror was inflicted by recent allies made it all the more terrible. Franklin's friend John Bartram recounted his backcountry informants' assertion that "most of the Indians which are so cruel are such as was almost daily familiar at their houses: ate, drank & swore together, was even intimate play mates. And now without any provocation destroyeth all before them with fire, ball & tomahawk." Bartram described how even apparently secure houses were ravaged:

> If they attack a house that is pretty well manned, they creep up behind some fence or hedge or tree & shoot red hot iron slugs or punk into the roof & fires the house over their heads & if they run out they are sure to be shot at and most or all of them killed. If they come to a house where the most of the family is women & children they break into it, kills them all, plunders the house & burns it with the dead in it or if any escaped out they pursueth them & kills them.

The raiders crossed the Allegheny Mountains, then the Susquehanna River. A frontier offensive no longer, the French-inspired campaign endangered the oldest, most heavily settled parts of the province. Attacks near Reading prompted the German inhabitants of that town to threaten to occupy Philadelphia unless they received immediate support. "We must not be sacrificed," their ultimatum declared, "and are therefore determined to go down to Philadelphia with all that will follow us, and quarter ourselves on its inhabitants and await our fate with them." Getting no satisfaction, the Germans marched on the provincial capital, a thousand strong.

By this point the enemy was within a day's ride of Philadelphia. The greatest portion of the province had been lost to the French and their Indian allies, and more continued to be lost. "Almost all the women & children over Sasquehannah [the Susquehanna River] have left their habitations," wrote provincial secretary Richard Peters in November 1755, "and the roads are full of starved, naked, indigent multitudes."

⁓ With the populace on the run, Pennsylvania's government was paralyzed. During the last crisis of provincial security, in 1747, the failure of the government to fund defense had resulted largely from the pacifist scruples and residual influence of the Quaker party. Since then the Quakers had undergone something of a conversion experience, the result of two scares: one at the polls, where their opponents had mounted a vigorous campaign to oust them on grounds that they who would not defend the province should not govern the province, and the other in the west, from the French and the Indians. As this latter persisted and intensified, the Quakers conducted themselves as model citizens in regard to defense. "The Quakers have now shown that they can give and dispose of money for that purpose as freely as any people," Franklin remarked approvingly.

The present paralysis arose not from the Quakers but from the proprietors. The Penns adamantly refused to countenance any tax upon their lands in Pennsylvania, even for provincial defense; the Assembly refused to exempt them, especially for defense. During the summer and autumn of 1755, while the frontier burned and the settlers fled for their lives, the proprietors and the Assembly locked in legislative stalemate.

The agent of the proprietors was the current governor, Robert Morris, in office since the previous autumn. Franklin had known Morris as a public official in New Jersey; he encountered him again in New York, on Morris's route from England to Pennsylvania. As charming in his own way as Franklin, Morris asked Franklin whether he might expect a difficult time with the Assembly. Franklin responded, doubtless with the slight smile that accompanied those comments of his intended to be half jesting but half serious, that he need not expect any difficulty whatsoever as long as he avoided disputes with the Assembly.

"My dear friend," Morris answered, perhaps with a smile of his own, "how can you advise my avoiding disputes? You know I love disputing; it is one of my greatest pleasures. However, to show the regard I have for your counsel, I promise you I will if possible avoid them."

The problem was not Morris's disputatious temperament, although that hardly helped matters. The problem was the Penns' insistence that any candidate for governor promise, on pain of financial penalty, to veto any measure taxing the proprietary estates. Morris was particularly ill placed to refuse such a promise, or to break it once given; an impecunious sort, he needed every shilling of his salary (to pay, among other obligations, child support to his recent London landlady, a fetching widow who bore a son with a noticeable resemblance to the Pennsylvania governor).

While Morris defended the proprietors' interests, Franklin spoke for the people of Pennsylvania. As before, he sat on all the most important committees of the Assembly; even more than before, he drafted the most important documents to emerge from the Assembly. During the second half of 1755 the contest between the proprietors and the Assembly became a duel between Morris and Franklin.

In late July the Assembly received the stunning news of Braddock's defeat. The body quickly authorized the expenditure of £50,000 for provincial defense. To raise the money, the Assembly approved a property tax, applicable to all real and personal property within the province.

The governor received the tax bill in early August; he shortly returned it, unapproved, with suggestions for amendment that would exempt the proprietary estates.

Franklin drafted the Assembly's response, the gist of which was that taxing the proprietary estates, along with all the other estates in the province, was "perfectly equitable and just." Tactically trying to corner the governor, Franklin and his colleagues requested to know whether the governor's veto reflected his reasoned judgment or a previous commitment to the proprietors. If the former were the case, the Assembly would be pleased for the governor to elaborate his thinking; if the latter, it would only waste everyone's time to pursue this bill.

Morris defended his veto on its merits—thereby initiating a series of exchanges that were never particularly enlightening and grew less edifying with each round. Franklin singled out the governor for personal attack, branding him the enemy not only of provincial safety but of the cherished rights of Englishmen.

> How odious it must be to a sensible manly people, to find *him* who ought to be their father and protector, taking advantage of public calamity and distress, and their tenderness for their bleeding country, to force down their throats laws of imposition, abhorrent to common justice and common reason! Why will the Governor make himself the hateful instrument of reducing a free people to the abject state of vassalage; of depriving us of those liberties which have given reputation to our country throughout the world, and drawn inhabitants from the remotest parts of Europe to enjoy them?

Eventually the governor admitted that the terms of his commission prohibited his accepting any measure that taxed the proprietary estates. This prompted Franklin to take on the proprietors themselves. Morris had objected to Franklin's use of the word "vassalage" to describe the situation of the Pennsylvanians; Franklin answered that in fact their condition was worse than that of vassals. "Vassals must *follow* their lords to the wars in defence of their lands; our Lord Proprietary, though a subject like ourselves, would *send* us out to fight *for* him, while he keeps himself a thousand leagues remote from danger! Vassals fight at their lord's expence, but our lord would have us defend his estate at our own expence! This is not merely vassalage, it is worse than any vassalage we have heard of; it is something we have no adequate name for; it is even more slavish than slavery itself."

Within a short generation this language of slavery would characterize colonial complaints against the government of Britain itself. Franklin and the Pennsylvanians anticipated affairs by applying it to their proprietor.

Yet if Franklin was precocious, he was not foolish. Morris charged that the logical terminus of the Assembly's line of argument was democracy—a concept that in the mid-eighteenth century was commonly equated with anarchy. Franklin would grow more democratic with age, but at this point he refused Morris's bait. "We are not so absurd as to 'design a Democracy,' of which the Governor is pleased to accuse us," he wrote. If anyone, it was Morris who was bringing democracy closer, by his adamancy in defense of the proprietors. "Such a conduct in a Governor appears to us the most likely thing in the world to make people incline to a Democracy, who would otherwise never think of it."

Looking back on the fight with Morris, Franklin later conceded its intemperate nature. "Our answers as well as his messages were often tart, and sometimes indecently abusive. And as he knew I wrote for the Assembly, one might have imagined that when we met we could hardly avoid cutting throats."

Yet in the governor Franklin found a kindred temperament, if not a kindred intellect. Politics aside, Morris was as reasonable as Franklin. "He was so good-natured a man that no personal difference between him and me was occasioned by the contest, and we often dined together." At one of these dinners Morris remarked jokingly that he much admired the idea of Sancho Panza, the companion and foil of Cervantes's Don Quixote, who, when offered a government, requested that it be a government of Africans, as then, if he could not agree with his black subjects, he might sell them for slaves. A friend of Morris, seated next to Franklin, picked up the governor's theme (perhaps by previous arrangement). "Franklin," he queried, "why do you continue to side with these damned Quakers? Had you not better sell them? The Proprietor would give you a good price." Franklin responded, "The Governor has not yet blacked them enough." In his recollection Franklin went on to say of Morris (and of himself), "He had indeed laboured hard to blacken the Assembly in all his messages, but they wiped off his colouring as fast as he laid it on, and placed it in return thick upon his own face."

At the time, and privately, Franklin reckoned Morris "the rashest and most indiscreet Governor that I have known." This made him difficult to deal with, but might yet work to the advantage of the Assembly and the people. "He has 1000 little arts to provoke and irritate the people, but none to gain their good-will, esteem or confidence, without which public business must go on heavily, or not at all." Such being the case, Franklin thought, Morris would "do more mischief to the Proprietaries' interest than good, and make them more enemies than friends."

The only question was whether the province could hold out till then. "We are all in flames," Franklin told Peter Collinson.

⌐ Amid the flames of war the spark of something Franklin had not felt for years—or at least not acted on—flickered anew.

Catharine Ray was the daughter of Simon and Deborah Greene Ray of Block Island, in the colony of Rhode Island. Twenty-three years old at the time of Franklin's visit to Boston at the end of 1754, Katy Ray was staying with her sister Judith, who happened to be married to the stepson of Franklin's brother John. Franklin met Katy through that familial connection, and was immediately entranced by her beauty and charm. He may have been smitten equally by the mere fact of her youth, and the fact that she appeared quite taken by him.

There was nothing in Franklin's home life to push him toward a liaison with a woman the same age as his son. By all evidence Debbie suited him as well as ever; indeed he quoted to Katy the song he had composed about Debbie and his acceptance of her faults. Yet on certain days this acceptance must have seemed like resignation, and as his fame and horizons expanded, he must have wondered whether life held more for him. He was not the first traveler to feel the constraints of domesticity lessen with distance from home.

The circumstances of Franklin's introduction to Katy Ray are uncertain, but at some point it became apparent that he would be heading south for New York and Philadelphia about the same time she would depart in the same direction for her parents' Block Island home. Likely Franklin suggested they travel together; Judith, feeling responsible for her younger sister, must have been happy to accept this offer of a chaperone. He would accompany Katy as far as Westerly, Rhode Island, where another sister lived. From there he would take the road west to New York, while she would backtrack to where she could catch a boat to Block Island.

Precisely what transpired on that journey through the frozen New England countryside is impossible to re-create with confidence. The only record is found in a handful of letters exchanged between the two in the succeeding several months—and in the relationship that persisted between them for the next thirty years. Katy wrote first, shortly after her safe arrival at her parents' home. Her letter is lost—doubtless partly because Franklin did not desire it to fall into the hands of Debbie.

He answered with an alacrity commanded by no other correspondent during this busy time of his life. "Your kind letter of January 20 is but just come to hand, and I take this first opportunity of acknowledging the favour," he wrote. Evidently the two had stretched their journey beyond what was strictly necessary; only with real reluctance had Franklin—who extended his own journey even farther, to accompany her right to the Rhode Island shore—let her go. "I thought too much was hazarded when I saw you put off to sea in that very little skiff, tossed by every wave. But the call was strong and just, a sick parent. I stood on the shore and looked after you, till I could no longer distinguish you, even with my glass."

Franklin explained how he had tarried in New England, lingering on the road, soaking up memories of his childhood—"my earliest and most pleasant days"—and basking in the recognition that accompanied his recent accomplishments. "I almost forgot I had a home." New England revivified him; by contrast, when he reached New York he felt "like an old man who, having buried all he loved in this world, begins to think of heaven."

It was not New England alone that made Franklin feel young; it was Katy Ray. Apparently at some point on their journey he attempted to trade the role of chaperone for one more passionate; she rebuffed him—but with such gentleness and tact as to enamor him of her even more. "I write this during a N. East storm of snow, the greatest we have had this winter. Your favours [those expressed in her letter] come mixed with the snowy fleeces which are as pure as your virgin innocence—and as cold."

Katy's rebuff reminded Franklin that he was, by her standards, an old man. His hopes of something more than a kiss on the cheek would remain unrequited; her further favors would be bestowed on one much younger—and unattached. Referring again to that "cold" virgin innocence, he declared, "Let it warm towards some worthy young man, and may Heaven bless you with every kind of happiness."

Perhaps his hopes revived, perhaps he merely experienced confusion, when she responded with some of that warmth he thought was reserved for another. "Absence rather increases than lessens my affections," she said.

Franklin's quartermastering work for Braddock kept him away from home during the spring of 1755; consequently he was slow receiving her letters and responding to them. "My not getting one line from you in answer to 3 of my last letters . . ." she wrote in June, "gives me a vast deal of uneasiness and occasioned many tears." Franklin did not save these letters either; this, and Katy's own remarks in the surviving correspondence, suggest they contained comments inappropriate from a single woman to a married man. "Surely I have wrote too much and you are affronted with me," she said, "or have not received my letters in which I have said a thousand things that nothing should have tempted me to say to any body else, for I knew they would be safe with you." She must hear from him. "Tell me you are well and forgive me and love me one-thousandth part so well as I do you."

Their letters crossed in the mail. "You may write freely everything you think fit, without the least apprehension of any person's seeing your letters but myself," he said. "You have complimented me so much in those I have already received that I could not show them without being justly thought a vain coxcomb for doing so." He teased her for what she denied him. She had asked whether everybody loved him yet; he replied, "I must confess (but don't you be jealous) that many more people love me now than ever did before. For since I saw you, I have been enabled to do some services to the country and to the army, for which both have thanked and praised me, and say they love me. They *say so*, as you used to do, and if I were to ask any favours of them, would, perhaps, as readily refuse me. So that I find little real advantage in being beloved, but it pleases my humour."

Real advantage or no from Katy's love, he urged her to keep sending him letters. "The pleasure I receive from one of yours is more than you can have from two of mine. The small news, the domestic occurrences among our friends, the natural pictures you draw of persons, the sensible observations and reflections you make, and the easy chatty manner in which you express every thing, all contribute to heighten the pleasure; and the more, as they remind me of those hours and miles that we talked away so agreeably, even in a winter journey, a wrong road, and a soaking shower."

She had spoken of a long thread she spun. He answered, "I wish I had hold of one end of it, to pull you to me." Yet his wish was merely that, he knew. "You would break it rather than come."

⌐ In the contest between the Assembly and the proprietors, the proprietors yielded first, but in a manner initially unacceptable to the Assembly. In November, Governor Morris received word from London that the Penns were pleased to make a "free gift from us to the public" of £5,000, to be used for colonial defense but not to be construed in any way whatsoever as a tax payment or other concession to the unwarranted and irresponsible demands of the Assembly.

This news reached Philadelphia about the same time the Germans from Reading did; almost simultaneous with both came a report of a massacre at Tulpehoccon, which included the ghastly tale of Indians scalping children alive. A bitterly ironic plea accompanied the report: "The Assembly can see by this work how good and fine friends the Indians are to us. We hope their eyes will go open & their hearts tender to us, and the Governor's the same, if they are true subjects to our King George the Second, of Great Britain, or are willing to deliver us in the hands of these miserable creatures."

Under the circumstances Franklin and his allies in the Assembly decided that to allow the impasse with the proprietors to continue would be unconscionable. Without yielding the principle that the Assembly should determine which properties were taxed and at what level, they accepted the Penns' gift and approved a defense appropriations bill that exempted the proprietary estates.

Meanwhile the Assembly weighed a militia bill that would put the appropriated money to use. Almost without exception, substantive bills laid before the Assembly originated in committees; the militia bill was one of the exceptions, being directly proposed by Franklin. That such was the case indicated both the extreme danger to the province and the increasingly obvious ascendancy of Franklin within the Assembly. The militia envisioned by the bill was similar to that of Franklin's 1747 Association. Service would be voluntary, and the militiamen would elect their own officers. There was, however, one important difference between the militia of 1755 and the Association: The new version was organized under the auspices of the provincial government, rather than outside the government.

This last aspect might well have made the new plan more acceptable to the proprietors than the Association had been. Thomas Penn's complaint at that time, that the Association was extralegal and therefore potentially insurrectionary, no longer applied. But in fact this was thin comfort, for Franklin's success in gaining Assembly approval of a militia simply indicated that he had taken over the government—at any rate the popular part of it. Where once the Quakers had stood against a provincial armed force, now they stepped aside. Not even the governor—handpicked by Thomas Penn himself—could prevent Franklin's coup, for with the colony in flames, refugees on the roads, and the backcountry folk clamoring for protection, Morris was obliged to swallow his reservations and accept the militia bill.

He nearly gagged, as he related to Penn. Morris made clear that Franklin was the evil genius behind the recent developments. The governor described a meeting with representatives of the "back People" at the capital; he had explained that they long since would have had their protection if not for the recalcitrance of the legislature. They had been satisfied with his explanation, he told Penn, and proceeded to visit the Assembly.

> Upon this Franklin harangued them, telling them the Assembly had done every thing that was consistent with the liberties and privileges of the people, for which they, the House, were contending. Some of the people answered that they did not know that their liberties were invaded, but they were sure their lives and estates were, and while they [the Assembly] were contending, the country was bleeding, and therefore hoped they would dispute no longer but send the Governor such a bill as he could pass.
>
> His harangue had not, therefore, the effect he desired, and I suppose expected, for great pains had been taken by some of the members and all their numerous emissaries to sow sedition in the minds of these country people, who were, however, proof against all their lies.

Morris almost certainly exaggerated Franklin's "harangue." Franklin rarely addressed large groups, and then, by most evidence, without conspicuous success. But Franklin did lead the opposition to the proprietors on this issue as on others, and thereby singled himself out for criticism. In another letter Morris told Thomas Penn, "Since Mr. Franklin has put himself at the head of the Assembly they have gone to greater lengths than ever, and have not only discovered the warmth of their resentment against your family but are using every means in their power, even while their country is invaded, to wrest the Government out of your hands."

If Morris was happy to charge the current disarray to Franklin, Franklin preferred to split the blame between the governor and the proprietors. In a letter to Richard Partridge, the Assembly's agent to the British government, Franklin asserted, "If we cannot have a Governor of some discretion (for this gentleman is half a madman) fully empowered to do what may be necessary for the good of the province and the King's service, as emergencies may arise, this Government will be the worst on the continent." As for the Penns, Franklin declared that by their "sense-less refusal" of the initial defense bill and by their "mean selfish claim" to exemption from taxes, they had brought upon themselves "infinite dis-grace and the curses of all the continent."

⌒— The distrust and alarm the governor and proprietors felt toward Franklin escalated dramatically when the de facto leader of the Assembly donned the uniform of the soldier. In view of his experience organizing the Association and his central role in winning approval of the militia bill, Franklin naturally took charge of raising the troops the bill autho-rized. "We meet every day, Sundays not excepted," he informed an old friend, regarding the committee supervising provincial defense. When the governor and other allies of the Penns began circulating rumors that the militia was designed simply to glorify Franklin and perhaps allow him to seize the government, he published an imagined dialogue among some ordinary Pennsylvanians, explaining the bill, justifying its objectives, and countering its critics—all in plain, straightforward language. "I am no coward," says one, in a typical passage, "but hang me if I'll fight to save the Quakers." Answers his companion, "That is to say, you won't pump ship, because 'twill save the rats, as well as yourself."

In late November an enemy raiding party attacked the Moravian mis-sion of Gnadenhutten on the Lehigh River northwest of Bethlehem, a village some fifty miles north of Philadelphia. The viciousness of the at-tack and the continuing lack of provisions for defense had terrorized the inhabitants and threatened to depopulate the region. The governor and the Assembly, finally—and temporarily—working in harness, dispatched Franklin, former governor James Hamilton, and Joseph Fox, a Quaker assemblyman who would be disowned by his coreligionists for his activi-ties on behalf of their defense, to the northwest frontier. Fifty mounted militiamen and a small baggage train accompanied the commissioners. William Franklin, having reenlisted in the military and wearing the scarlet uniform of the king's grenadiers, rode beside his father, who at this point remained in mufti.

The purpose of the expedition was to organize frontier defense. The first step was simply to show up, thereby giving flesh-and-blood sub-stance to the recent legislative promise to secure the border. With luck the commissioners' appearance would rally the locals to their own and the colony's defense. Initial evidence indicated just such luck. Franklin had feared that the pacifist Moravians, who had a special Parliamentary exemption from military service, would refuse to take up arms; his first view of Bethlehem revealed an opposite intent. "I was surprised to find it in so good a posture of defence," he wrote. "The principal buildings were defended by a stockade. They had purchased a quantity of arms and ammunition from New York, and had even placed quantities of small paving stones between the windows of their high stone houses, for their women to throw down upon the heads of any Indians that should attempt to force into them." When Franklin expressed his surprise to the local bishop, the prelate explained that pacifism was not a principle of their faith but had been thought, at the time of the Parliamentary exemption, to be a tenet embraced by the members individually. The bishop said the members had amazed themselves by their alacrity to arms. Franklin remarked wryly, "It seems they were either deceived in themselves, or deceived the Parliament. But common sense aided by present danger will sometimes be too strong for whimsical opinions."

The situation elsewhere was less promising. The commissioners traveled from Bethlehem to Easton, at the eastern terminus of the Pennsylvania frontier (next door was the Delaware River, across which lay New Jersey). On Christmas Day, James Hamilton wrote to Governor Morris, "The people here are not very numerous and are besides very backward in entry into the service, though the encouragement is great, and one would think they would gladly embrace the opportunity of avenging themselves on the authors of their ruin." But they lacked the nerve to do so. "The terror that has seized them is so great, or their spirits so small, unless men come from other parts of the province I despair of getting such a number here as will be sufficient to garrison the block houses we proposed to build."

Franklin adopted the attitude that the building of a block house would go far toward bolstering those quavering souls. Hamilton at first had charge of the commission, although his inclusion at all seems to have represented as much an effort by Morris to keep watch on Franklin as a measure to strengthen the frontier. Hamilton had no sympathy whatever with Franklin's militia bill, describing it to Thomas Penn as "the quintessence of absurdity." In the field he got in the way, and before long Franklin elbowed him aside. By the end of December, Franklin was drafting orders like a career soldier. "You are immediately to raise and take into pay for one month a company of foot consisting of 24 men, to be employed as a garrison, guard and watch for the town of Easton," he wrote Major William Parsons. "You are to keep a constant regular watch with your company every night, 4 sentinels being placed at the outer ends of the four principal streets, and one near the guard room. . . . You are likewise once at least in every day to send out a scout to range some miles round the town, to examine all thickets and places capable of concealing parties of the enemy." A week later, following a dismaying new report from Gnadenhutten that enemy Indians had routed not merely isolated settlers, as in the recent past, but a well-armed company of militia, Governor Morris acknowledged the obvious and formally appointed Franklin military commander for that sector of the frontier, with complete authority over all aspects of the emergency.

On January 15 Franklin led a march across the Blue Mountains to Gnadenhutten. The winter weather was miserable, with the temperature just above freezing and a heavy rain that soaked the men and, more worryingly, their firearms. The Indians of that region were used to winter warfare and knew how to keep their powder and gunlocks dry; had Franklin's column been attacked on the march, the men would have had difficulty returning fire. Indeed, the one survivor of an earlier raid said his ten companions had been killed because the wetness had incapacitated their weapons.

The route of the march intensified the danger. One of Franklin's men, Thomas Lloyd, left a description of a particularly perilous stretch: "Hills like Alps on each side and a long narrow defile where the road scarcely admitted a single wagon at the bottom of it; a rapid creek with steep banks and bridge made of a single log situated so the Indians might with safety to themselves from the caverns in the rocks have cut us all off notwithstanding all human precaution."

The column arrived intact, only to witness what the unseen enemy was capable of. "All round appears nothing but one continued scene of horror and destruction," wrote Lloyd. "Where lately flourished a happy and peaceful village is now all silent and desolate, the houses burnt, the inhabitants butchered in the most shocking manner, their mangled bodies for want of funerals exposed to birds and beasts of prey and all kinds of mischief perpetrated that wanton cruelty can invent."

The first order of business was burying the dead; the second, commencing construction of a fort. Of necessity the men of that part of the country were adept at hewing wood; as important as the firearms Franklin's men brought were the seventy axes. Amid the danger and destruction Franklin indulged his scientific curiosity to time two men felling a tree (six minutes for a tree fourteen inches in diameter). Once the branches were removed, each pine trunk was cut into three pieces eighteen feet long. One end was pointed with the axes; the other was tipped into a trench three feet deep that served as the foundation of the stockade. Raised and secured, some 450 timbers made a fortress 150 yards in circumference. Carpenters constructed a platform several feet above the ground on the inside of the walls, from which the men might fire through loopholes at attackers. At one of the corners was mounted a small swivel gun. Franklin ordered a round fired to apprise any enemies within hearing that the English now had a cannon to defend themselves. From start to finish the construction required less than a week, despite downpours that recurrently halted the work.

Franklin's approach to military command was typical of his approach to social affairs generally. The furthest thing from a martinet, he preferred to appeal to his men's reason and self-interest. The chaplain of the company complained that the men were insufficiently attendant to prayers and his sermons; Franklin suggested a change in the rationing system. Each man, as part of the enlistment agreement, had been promised a gill (roughly four ounces) of rum a day. "It is perhaps below the dignity of your profession to act as steward of the rum," Franklin told the chaplain. "But if you were to deal it out, and only just after prayers, you would have them all about you." Attendance at prayers improved at once.

Upon completion of the stockade Franklin sent a scouting party into the forest about the fort; the rangers found that there had indeed been an audience for the warning shot—and apparently an audience for the entire construction process. On a wooded hill overlooking the fort Franklin's men discovered several holes dug in the dirt. At the bottom of these holes were the ashes of charcoal fires; in the grass at the edges of the holes were the imprints where the Indians had sat, their feet hanging down in the holes next to the smoldering (but nonsmoking) fires. Thus warm and invisible, the Indians had watched the fort go up. Presumably they had decamped to give notice of the construction to their comrades.

The fort at Gnadenhutten, named Fort Allen for William Allen, the chief justice of Pennsylvania and a longtime friend of Franklin, was one of three built under Franklin's command. The others—subsequently called Fort Norris for the speaker of the Assembly, and Fort Franklin—were fifteen miles to either side of Fort Allen along a southwest-to-northeast line that paralleled the mountains.

By themselves the forts did little to secure the frontier from Indian attack. Although they did provide a refuge for settlers in the event of further attacks, their primary purpose was psychological. The Indians of Pennsylvania and the neighboring provinces must have known long before this time that they would never be able to resume the ways of life that had sustained their ancestors prior to the arrival of the Europeans; in light of the conveniences consequent to European contact—guns, metal tools, and the like—it was doubtful that many of the present generation *wanted* to recapture their ancestors' less sophisticated lifestyle. In any case, the Europeans were here to stay. The only question was *which* Europeans the Indians would have to deal with. If the French drove out the English, the Indians would have to make peace with the French. During the last two years the French had indeed seemed about to drive the English into the sea. But if the English were determined to stay, then the Indians would have to accommodate themselves to the English. More than outposts for defense, Franklin's forts were a statement of imperial purpose.

⌒ **In time** of danger, capable military leaders capture the hearts of their countrymen. Franklin's part in rallying the Assembly and then leading the militia made him the hero of the hour in Pennsylvania. At the beginning of February 1756 he learned that Governor Morris was convening the Assembly; hoping to ensure that what he had accomplished in the backwoods of Northampton County not be lost in the back rooms of Philadelphia, Franklin relinquished operational command to Colonel William Clapham, a veteran of the Indian wars on the frontier, and, riding hard, covered the seventy-five miles from Fort Allen to the capital in two long days and a short night.

Yet only part of Franklin's hurry reflected his anxiety about the governor's aims. The rest revealed a desire to avoid what he considered excessive praise. As he prepared to return to Philadelphia, he heard that a large body of citizens intended to ride out and greet him and to escort him back to the capital. "To prevent this," Franklin explained to Peter Collinson, "I made a forced march, and got to town in the night, by which they were disappointed, and some a little chagrinned."

The chagrin and disapproval did not, however, prevent Franklin's being elected colonel of the Philadelphia regiment. Now it was Governor Morris who was chagrined. Although he had been forced to turn to Franklin in the hour of maximum danger, he did not wish to make Franklin's command official—both because he knew that the proprietors despised Franklin and because he himself distrusted him. Yet in light of the clear requirements of the militia bill, which he had signed, he had no alternative to accepting whom the militiamen chose. After two weeks of hoping for providential deliverance in one form or another, Morris grudgingly gave his approval.

Franklin shortly treated the city to a review of the troops. The ghost of William Penn must have groaned to hear the tramp of a thousand soldiers' boots across his city of brotherly love. The first company reached the reviewing stand, drew up, waited until the second company neared, then fired into the air and retreated in close order. The second company did the same, and so on. Four freshly painted cannon were hauled along the street by teams of powerfully built horses. Oboes ("haut-boys") and fifes filled the air with their martial melodies; just after them rode Franklin alone, master of all he surveyed. "So grand an appearance was never before seen in Pennsylvania," asserted the *Gazette*.

Franklin's triumph was not without minor amusements. As the troops marched past his house, they honored their colonel with thunderous volleys—"which shook down and broke several glasses of my electrical apparatus," Franklin noted wryly.

Governor Morris, and Thomas Penn at a distance, could only shudder at the swelling enthusiasm for their chief adversary. For a decade Penn had suspected Franklin of designs against the established government of the province. During most of that period Franklin had challenged the status quo by political means, but briefly in the days of the Association, and now again as colonel of the Philadelphia regiment, he appeared capable of leading a military revolt.

The appearance only intensified a few days later when Franklin set off for Virginia. This time he was wearing his postmaster's cap rather than his colonel's hat, but his men provided a send-off suited to a victorious general. "Twenty officers of my regiment with about 30 grenadiers presented themselves on horseback at my door just as I was going to mount, to accompany me to the ferry about 3 miles from town," Franklin told Collinson. "Till we got to the end of the street, which is about 200 yards, the grenadiers took it in their heads to ride with their swords drawn."

The show was hardly Franklin's idea; inwardly he groaned, knowing that it could "serve only to excite envy or malice." In fact it excited both. Provincial secretary Richard Peters wrote Penn describing Franklin's behavior as an "abomination" and declaring, "The city is in infinite distraction all owing to the officers of the militia puffed up and now solely directed by Colonel Franklin. . . . Matters are ten times worse in the city than ever and the Antiproprietary party will gain more ground than ever by means of the Colonel who continues to evidence a most implacable enmity against the Proprietors."

Thomas Penn was less alarmed than Peters, living much farther from the scene, but he was no less concerned. "I much wonder the Governor would appoint Mr. Franklin colonel," Penn told Peters. "He should never have any commission given to him till it is certain he has changed his sentiments." Penn decried Franklin's "republican principles" and asserted, "I have scarcely seen such an instance of baseness as in this of Franklin's."

Penn's criticism of Franklin must have reflected at least a little annoyance at himself for misjudging the man. Franklin almost certainly could not have received his appointment as deputy postmaster without Penn's approval, at least tacit. Doubtless the proprietor hoped that the appointment would purchase Franklin's cooperation on matters touching proprietary prerogatives. It was not an unreasonable hope. It had been borne out in Penn's gubernatorial appointments; applied generally, the principle was what held the empire together.

But it underestimated Franklin badly. Financially, Franklin did not need the job; this alone set him apart from most placemen. Indeed, he had yet to make a pound from the post. Penn had no real experience with civic-mindedness; that a person might assume a task for the good of his country and people was beyond him.

Before long, Penn would get to know Franklin personally and would come to appreciate the extent of his misjudgment of Franklin's motives. Meanwhile he sought to neutralize Franklin's influence. One method set fire against fire, figuratively. Franklin's current influence derived from his control of the provincial militia; Penn encouraged Governor Morris to create anti-Franklin military units. Either from want of imagination or from conscious irony, the governor's companies modeled their organization on Franklin's 1747 Association; they even appropriated the Association's name. Needless to say, the supporters of this new group cited public spirit and a desire to defend the province as their reasons for taking arms; almost as needless to say, their taking arms was interpreted—just as it was intended—as a riposte to Franklin's growing fame and influence.

It was not inconceivable that at some point the contest between Franklin's soldiers and the governor's would take direct, armed form; for now the clashes consisted of rival reviews in the streets of Philadelphia and nasty clashes in the newspapers of the city. Franklin scored the governor for dividing the province when he should have been uniting it. The governor's friends responded that Franklin's fame had gone to his head.

From experimenting with electricity, he now experimented with the welfare of the people. "To be convinced whether a shock of the electric fluid will kill rats or turkeys, must the experiment be made general on all the rats and turkeys on the face of the earth?"

∽ As the controversy raged, Franklin went about his business—which only incensed the proprietary party the more. When King George dispatched Lord Loudoun to America as commander in chief, following the belated formal declaration of war, Franklin traveled to New York to meet him. Loudoun apparently found Franklin's counsel useful, for he conferred with him repeatedly during the summer of 1756 on the state of frontier defense and the politics of provincial security. Franklin in turn developed a high regard for the new commander. "I have had the honour of several conferences with him on our American affairs," Franklin told William Strahan, "and am extremely pleased with him. I think there cannot be a fitter person for the service he is engaged in."

Meanwhile the proprietary campaign against Franklin continued. Thomas Penn tried to have Franklin stripped of his postmastership. When this failed—after Franklin defended himself to his postal superiors—Penn tried another approach. Franklin's Militia Act had challenged not merely proprietary control of Pennsylvania politics but some of the basic principles of imperial rule, among these the selection of officers. As Penn explained to Morris, "The militia is taken out of the hands of the Crown, and the appointment of officers given to the people, which can never be allowed."

Penn revealed Franklin's offense to the appropriate officers of the Crown, who, agreeing, canceled the Militia Act. This neat trick not only solved Penn's problem with the turbulent colonel but placed the proprietor in the comfortable and relatively unusual position of defending His Majesty's authority in North America.

Franklin viewed this latest development with equanimity. After half a century on earth he knew—better than most great men do—what he was good at and what not. He knew he was no soldier. He might organize frontier defense and command construction battalions, but he had no experience of combat and little inclination to acquire it. Franklin had met Colonel Washington of Virginia on the road; he could tell at once that Washington possessed far more of the martial spirit than he would ever have. At one point of maximum alarm, Governor Morris offered to make Franklin a general if he would lead a campaign to capture Fort Duquesne. Franklin rejected the offer. "I had not so good an opinion of my military abilities as he professed to have," he said later. Consequently he could not be too disappointed at Parliament's decision to terminate his military career.

Besides, he had something better than a military command. "The people happen to love me," he told Peter Collinson in November 1756. Franklin could put aside military authority, but his ego was not immune to popular acclaim. A warrior like Washington might find charm in the sound of bullets whistling overhead; Franklin was more beguiled by the sense of embodying the virtuous desires of ordinary people. This feeling of being virtue's agent was not new in Franklin's life. His earlier civic initiatives had afforded a taste of it. But only upon entering politics—upon placing himself before voters—had he felt it so directly. And it was this that allowed him to shrug off the attacks by the proprietors and their agents. Referring to a recent barrage, he told Collinson, "I am not much concerned at that, because if I have offended them *by acting right*, I can, whenever I please, remove their displeasure *by acting wrong*."

Franklin appreciated the possibility of self-delusion in such matters. He regularly examined his motives. For the present at least, regarding the struggle with the proprietors, he was satisfied. "I am persuaded that I do not oppose their views from pique, disappointment, or personal resentment, but, as I think, from a regard to the public good. I may be mistaken in what is that public good; but at least I mean well." The proprietors quite clearly did not. "I am sometimes ashamed for them, when I see them differing with their people for trifles, and instead of being adored, as they might be, like demi-gods, become the object of universal hatred and contempt."

Franklin never lost the conviction that virtue conferred right and ought to confer power. Yet neither did he lose the ability to question whether his view of virtue was the only accurate one. "Forgive your friend a little vanity," he asked Collinson, "as it's only between ourselves." The people loved him today, and concurred in his view of virtue, but they might change their minds tomorrow. "You are ready now to tell me that popular favour is a most uncertain thing. You are right. I blush at having valued myself so much upon it."

12

A Larger Stage

1757–58

℘ The people still loved him enough three months later to send him away. In January 1757 Franklin's fellows in the Assembly appointed him their agent to the government in England, to argue the Assembly's side in the dispute with the proprietors. Isaac Norris was also appointed, and initially Franklin deferred to Norris on grounds of the speaker's "long experience in our public affairs, and great knowledge and abilities." But Norris declined the appointment, pleading ill health, and Franklin protested no more. "Look out sharp," he wrote to William Strahan in London, "and if a fat old fellow should come to your printing house and request a little smouting [piecework], depend upon it, 'tis your affectionate friend and humble servant."

Franklin's removal to London in 1757 marked a turn in his life no less important than his move from Boston to Philadelphia thirty-four years earlier. Had he known he would live the rest of his life mostly abroad, he undoubtedly would have weighed his acceptance of the Assembly's appointment more carefully. The last three and a half decades had been good to him. Philadelphia in 1723 had received the runaway apprentice and given him a chance to make a career. Capitalizing on his chance, the young man achieved a combination of affluence and influence he could not have imagined on that rainy trek across New Jersey to his new home. His business thrived to where it ran itself (with the aid of David Hall), leaving him free to follow other interests. Of these, his scientific experiments had won him world renown and the esteem of the most distinguished natural philosophers of the age. His political accomplishments were less well known in the world at large but more appreciated locally. He was a great man in his adopted city: author of numerous improvements to civic life, facilitator of others. He was a force in his province: leader of the popular party, spokesman of the emerging middle class. He was a presence in America: deputy postmaster general (and, as such, one of a handful of officials with duties that crossed colonial lines), architect of a plan for union that captured the imagination of many of his fellow Americans (even if the provincial assemblies had yet to act on it).

In London, however, Franklin's reputation and accomplishments would count for little. The philosophers of the Royal Society could be expected to welcome him, but—as scientists often are—they were a circle unto themselves. Franklin's political achievements would merit him scant consideration, being the work of a mere provincial. And much of that consideration, certainly among the grandees of the realm, would be negative. Thomas Penn understood the situation better than Franklin did. The proprietor assured a worried Richard Peters that there was nothing to fear from "Mr. Franklin's republican schemes" upon the arrival of their originator. "Mr. Franklin's popularity is nothing here," wrote Penn. "He will be looked very coolly upon by great people. There are very few of any consequence that have heard of his electrical experiments, those matters being attended to by a particular set of people, many of whom of the greatest consequence I know well. But it is quite another sort of people who are to determine the dispute between us." Penn added confidently, "I do not care how soon he comes, and am no ways uneasy at the determination."

◦— In many respects the London to which Franklin returned in 1757 had not changed much from the London he left in 1726. The whores still haunted the hairdressers' shops. The ravings at Bedlam, the floggings at Bridewell, and the executions at Newgate attracted the same crowds. Bears and bulls fought as before at Hockley-in-the-Hole. The manners of theatergoers had not noticeably improved, nor the consumption of alcohol measurably diminished.

But in another respect London had changed dramatically, at least for Franklin. Political London—the London of Crown and court and Parliament—had been a world removed from the humble neighborhoods frequented by the stranded journeyman in the 1720s. Three decades later, political London was Franklin's primary destination, the milieu in which the Pennsylvania Assembly's agent would operate.

Political London's central landmark was Westminster, the home of Parliament. Once subordinate to the Crown, Parliament had established its primacy during the seventeenth century, in the Civil War and the Glorious Revolution. Even had there been no civil war or revolution, Parliament probably would have emerged supreme, for the simple reason that by the beginning of the eighteenth century, foreign policy—the sinkhole of British public finance—could no longer be conducted out of the monarch's own purse. Parliament had always been the provider of tax monies; the interminable conflict with France starting in the 1690s meant that tax monies were chronically necessary. Hence the importance of Parliament.

But Parliament was a legislative body; it had not yet developed an executive arm. The executive power remained with the Crown. In theory this power was *simply* executive: "the king in Parliament," in the era's formulation. Yet as any student of government knows, and any practitioner of government experiences, the line between legislation and execution is often fine and always subject to transgression. An eighteenth-century British monarch could never wield the power the Tudors took for granted in the sixteenth century, but he or she could still make a mark.

The size of the mark depended on the talents of the monarch. George I, king at the time of Franklin's 1723 arrival in London, was generally thought stupid. Stupidity, however, has rarely been a disqualification from kingship, and it did not disqualify George in the eyes of Parliament, which selected him over several other claimants with better pedigrees, to succeed Queen Anne in 1714. But George had other problems. He was a bad husband and a worse cuckold; after abandoning his wife's bed for the couches of his courtesans, he responded to *her* straying by (almost certainly) having her lover murdered and locking her up in a castle for the rest of her unhappy life. He subsequently divided his attentions between the Duchess of Kendal (as she became, after winning his favor), a thin woman of great tenacity, and the Countess of Darlington, whose contrast to the Duchess could hardly have been more striking. Horace Walpole gossiped:

> Lady Darlington, whom I saw at my mother's in my infancy, and whom I remember by being terrified at her enormous figure, was as corpulent and ample as the Duchess was long and emaciated. Two fierce black eyes, large and rolling beneath two lofty arched eyebrows, two acres of cheeks spread with crimson, an ocean of neck that overflowed and was not distinguished from the lower parts of her body, and no part restrained by stays—no wonder that a child dreaded such an ogress, and that the mob of London were highly diverted at the importation of so uncommon a seraglio!

George—a Hanoverian German by birth—never mastered English; during his reign French was the language of the British court. Nor did he master *the* English, whom he scorned as treacherous—a characterization many of his courtiers merited. So he amused himself with his mistresses and indulged his resentments against his slightly more gifted son.

The most obvious gift of the man who became George II was his wife, Princess Caroline. A beauty of an earthy sort, she entered a room like a ship breasting the waves of the sea. Her husband was infatuated with her charms, as were any number of other men; she used their infatuation against them (her husband called her *"Cette diablesse Madame la Princesse"*) even as she similarly deployed her considerable intelligence.

The favorite of Caroline was Robert Walpole, the brother of Horace and an unprepossessing man with short arms, short legs, long torso, and buttocks that received rather more airing in the English press of the day than comported with the dignity of one who essentially governed the country for two decades. Walpole is generally considered the first prime minister of England; his buttocks became an issue in cartoons that depicted members of Parliament kissing them in order to secure his favor. He came to power under George I; that he survived the accession of George II, whose feud with his father led at one point to the son's arrest at the baptism of *his* son, when monarch and the father of the baptized could not agree on a godfather, owed to Walpole's astute sense of balance and the good offices of Queen Caroline.

Walpole's policies embodied two principles: fiscal caution and the avoidance of war. The former reflected his (and England's) close scrape with disaster in the collapse of the South Sea bubble, but it did not prevent him from being pilloried for corruption. The reign of Sir Robert became known as the "Robinocracy," and the prime minister inspired a criminal character in John Gay's *Beggar's Opera*: "*Robin of Bagshot*, alias *Gorgon*, alias *Bluff Bob*, alias *Carbuncle*, alias *Bob Booty*." George II had his reservations about Walpole and the prime minister's associates, especially his brother Horace, the Duke of Newcastle, and Lord Townshend. A court insider described the king's reaction to the quartet: "He used always to speak of the first as a great rogue, of the second as a dirty buffoon, of the third as an impertinent fool, and of the fourth as a choleric blockhead."

Walpole's foreign policy brought England a generation of peace—the generation in which Franklin grew up. Yet peace did not satisfy the prime minister's increasing number of enemies, and after the death of Caroline in 1737 he could no longer resist the demand for revenge of the injury suffered by Captain Jenkins (of the missing ear). Walpole would have resigned then, but George II, for all his distrust of his prime minister, demanded that he stay on. In 1742 Parliament overruled the king and overthrew Walpole.

Yet his legacy remained. Had George II been a better Briton (he spoke English, but with a heavy German accent, and in other matters appeared to put the interests of his ancestral Hanover above those of his inherited kingdom), or had he simply been a more masterful monarch, he might have regained some of the power Walpole had acquired at Crown expense. But his gifts lay elsewhere—he had an uncanny memory for the minutiae of royal genealogy and military uniformage—and the primary result of his reign was the consolidation of Parliamentary control over the politics of the kingdom and the empire.

George II sat heavily, and after thirty years wearily, on his throne when Franklin arrived from America. Franklin was weary himself, although from a long journey rather than a long reign. After hurrying to New York from Philadelphia to catch the first government packet to England, he and William (who volunteered to accompany his father—and see the world) wound up waiting on Lord Loudoun, and waiting, and waiting. The general insisted that the ship not leave until he had completed his correspondence, but though he appeared to be scribbling industriously each time Franklin called on him, he never finished the letters. A week passed, then another, then a month, then two months. Franklin's initial positive impression of Loudoun dissolved into an estimate of terminal indecision. Not till June did the travelers get away.

Franklin made typical good use of his time on the voyage east. Besides suggesting experiments to increase the speed of sailing ships, he composed what became his most famous piece of writing. The approaching autumn would see the twenty-fifth edition of *Poor Richard's Almanack*; Franklin judged a quarter century sufficient for any philomath and prepared to send Richard Saunders into well-deserved retirement. But Saunders must go out, as he had come in, with a flourish. Franklin created a new character, Father Abraham, who, readers discovered, had been following the almanac faithfully these many years. "A plain clean old man, with white locks," in Saunders's description, Father Abraham was asked by passersby at a market what he thought of the present times. He responded with a soliloquy comprising the choicest of Poor Dick's pearls, drawn from the entire run of the almanacs. "We may make these times better if we bestir ourselves," he said.

> *Industry need not wish,* as Poor Richard says, and *he that lives upon hope will die fasting. There are no gains without pains;* then *help hands, for I have no lands,* or if I have, they are smartly taxed. And as Poor Richard likewise observes, *he that hath a trade hath an estate,* and *he that hath a calling hath an office of profit and honour.* . . . If we are industrious we shall never starve, for, as Poor Richard says, *at the working man's house hunger looks in, but dares not enter.* Nor will the bailiff and the constable enter, for *industry pays debts, while despair increaseth them,* says Poor Richard. What though you have found no treasure, nor has any rich relation left you a legacy, *diligence is the mother of good luck,* as Poor Richard says, and *God gives all things to industry.* Then *plough deep, while sluggards sleep, and you shall have corn to sell and to keep,* says Poor Dick.

The idea was clever enough, and the speech of Father Abraham was reprinted hundreds of times in English and at least fifteen other languages. Yet for all its popularity, the piece was not one of Franklin's best efforts. The "Poor Richard says" tag, while perhaps an apt marketing device, began to wear on readers' ears before old Abram stopped speaking. More to the point—again a literary point, rather than a commercial one—the speech missed much of the best of Richard Saunders. Poor Dick's irreverent wit and sly feistiness is suppressed here in favor of admonitions to industry, frugality, and other virtues attuned to material success. The title under which the piece was often published—*The Way to Wealth*—reflected this capitalist emphasis, almost certainly increasing sales but equally certainly coloring Franklin historically as a dour grinder. "Snuff-coloured little man!" sneered D. H. Lawrence more than a century and a half later. Recalling how, as a boy, he had been introduced to the wisdom of Poor Richard, Lawrence complained, "I haven't got over those Poor Richard tags yet. I still rankle with them. They are thorns in young flesh.... It has taken me many years to get out of that barbed wire enclosure Poor Richard rigged up." Concluded Lawrence of Franklin, "I admire him.... I do not like him."

At times on the voyage it appeared that Father Abraham might be buried at sea (which surely would have pleased Lawrence). The war with France raged as fiercely as ever, and though Franklin's vessel traveled in a convoy, its capture or destruction was a constant possibility. (This possibility doubtless inspired Franklin's experimental design for faster ships.) The enemy grew thicker near England; as the captain of Franklin's ship tried to evade them off Falmouth under cover of night, he nearly ran onto the rocks. Franklin was as shaken as the rest. "Were I a Roman Catholic," he wrote Deborah on reaching shore, "perhaps I should on this occasion vow to build a chapel to some saint; but as I am not, if I were to vow at all, it should be to build a *lighthouse*."

The Franklin party—consisting of Franklin, William, and two slaves: Peter and King—arrived in London in late July 1757. They took up residence with Mrs. Margaret Stevenson, who lived at 7 Craven Street, Strand. The apartment suited Franklin so well he remained there during his entire London stay. The location could hardly have been better, convenient to the government offices in Whitehall and the houses of Parliament in Westminster.

Nor could the company have been more congenial. Mrs. Stevenson was a widow of about Franklin's age. She had a bubbly good nature, she appreciated a joke, and, living as she did at the crossroads of English life, she afforded Franklin a street-level perspective on the high and powerful who passed her front door, as well as the low and put-upon who constituted the mass of London society. She also had a daughter, Mary, who quickly became as charmed with Franklin as her mother did. Franklin had left Debbie and Sally behind in Philadelphia; as his correspondence would reveal, he missed them. But Peggy and Polly Stevenson soon became at least partial substitutes.

Franklin received a still-warmer greeting from Peter Collinson, who, having corresponded with Franklin for ten years, was delighted finally to meet the American genius. Collinson hosted Franklin and William at his house outside the city, where he kept a noteworthy botanical collection. He escorted Franklin to the Royal Society and introduced him to various ingenious men about London, including the "Honest Whigs," a discussion group that soon filled the same social and intellectual niche in Franklin's life the Junto had filled in Philadelphia.

William Strahan had known Franklin—from a distance—even longer than Collinson had, and his admiration and affection were even greater. "I had for many years conceived a very high, and now find, a very just, opinion of Mr. Franklin," he wrote to Deborah Franklin. "But though the notion I had formed of him in my own mind, before I had the pleasure of seeing him, was, really as far as it went, just enough, I must confess it was very unequal to what I now know his singular merit deserves. . . . I never saw a man who was, in every respect, so perfectly agreeable to me. Some are amiable in one view, some in another, he in all."

Strahan so loved Franklin that from the outset he conspired to keep him in England forever. Strahan's letter to Debbie was only partly a paean to her husband; it was also a brief on behalf of her crossing the ocean to join him. Strahan described the slow pace of politics in the imperial capital and warned that it might be years before Franklin achieved the aim of his journey. Debbie should really consider coming over—with Sally, of course, who would benefit immensely from London. Franklin had mentioned that Debbie feared sea travel; Strahan reassured her that not a soul had been lost between Philadelphia and London in living memory. (He neglected to say that ships had gone down on other routes) His trump— he hoped—was an argument that must have seemed rather presumptuous from one Debbie had never met. Strahan asked her to ponder what a long separation from her husband might entail. "As I know the ladies here consider him in exactly the same light I do, upon my word I think you should come over with all convenient speed to look after your interest; not but that I think him as faithful to his Joan [he had heard Franklin's song] as any man breathing, but who knows what repeated and strong temptation may in time, and while he is at so great a distance from you, accomplish."

⌒ Some charming persons appeal to nearly everyone; friend and foe find their personalities irresistible, often to the foes' confusion and dismay. Franklin's charm was more selective. It worked upon those who shared his open, inquisitive, generous outlook on life. Strahan fell into this category, which was why he became so enamored of Franklin. Collinson was the same way, if less demonstrative about his affection.

But those who felt threatened by genius could find Franklin hard to abide. Franklin never flaunted his powers, but in middle age, with those powers at their height, he made less effort to disguise them than he had at times past. His fame as a philosopher preceded him, and he did not attempt to prove it unwarranted. He did not demand deference from others, but neither did he defer. The intellectually or emotionally insecure, those who insisted on measuring themselves against Franklin, could easily become jealous of one who mastered nearly everything to which he turned his mind. The politically insecure, those who possessed something Franklin might take away, could find his powers even more sinister.

Thomas Penn's animus toward Franklin reflected the proprietor's political insecurity; Lord Granville's unfriendliness may have manifested intellectual insecurity but more obviously followed from his insistence on deference that Franklin refused to yield. Shortly after reaching London, Franklin asked John Fothergill, a well-connected friend of Collinson's (and one of the Honest Whigs) for advice. Should he approach the British government with the Pennsylvania Assembly's dispute with the proprietors, or should he appeal to the proprietors? Fothergill advocated the latter. British politics was a maze; a man might enter and never get out. Better to settle the affair directly with the Penns if at all possible. Franklin prepared to follow Fothergill's advice, only to receive a summons from Lord Granville, the president of the Privy Council, the body of King George's closest advisers. Granville also happened to be Thomas Penn's brother-in-law.

The interview began unpromisingly. Granville delivered a pronunciamento on the misapprehensions of colonials regarding imperial politics. "You Americans have wrong ideas of the nature of your constitution," he said. "You contend that the King's instructions to his governors are not laws, and think yourselves at liberty to regard or disregard them at your own discretion. But those instructions are not like the pocket instructions given to a minister going abroad, for regulating his conduct in some trifling point of ceremony. They are first drawn up by judges learned in the laws; they are then considered, debated and perhaps amended in Council, after which they are signed by the King. They are then, so far as relates to you, the law of the land, for the King is the legislator of the colonies."

This was deeper water than Franklin had expected to encounter so soon, but, strong swimmer that he was, he struck out confidently. He declared that this was "new doctrine" to him. Under their charters, he explained, the colonies made their laws for themselves, in their assemblies. These laws were then presented to the king for his assent or veto. But once the king gave his assent, he could not repeal or alter the laws. And just as the assemblies could not make laws without his assent, neither could the king make laws for the colonies without the assemblies' assent.

Granville assured Franklin he was totally mistaken. Franklin declined to argue the matter further in this venue but remained convinced he was right. Yet he could not help being troubled by what Granville's position portended. "His Lordship's conversation having a little alarmed me as to what might be the sentiments of the Court concerning us, I wrote it down as soon as I returned to my lodgings. I recollected that about twenty years before [thirteen, actually] a clause in a bill brought to Parliament by the ministry had proposed to make the King's instructions laws in the colonies, but the clause was thrown out by the Commons, for which we adored them as our friends and friends of liberty." This sentiment would change when Parliament itself began encroaching on colonial liberties, but for now Franklin was happy to look to Parliament as a protector.

A few days after his meeting with Granville, Franklin called upon Thomas Penn. The proprietor was civil but evasive. His brother Richard was out of town; until Richard returned, there was nothing Thomas felt free to discuss. Franklin knew full well that for a decade Richard had left the affairs of Pennsylvania to his brother, but he saw little purpose in protest.

When Richard returned, Franklin visited the now-plural proprietors. As Franklin expected, Thomas spoke for their side. "The conversation at first consisted of mutual declarations of disposition to reasonable accommodation," Franklin remarked, adding, "But I suppose each party had its own ideas of what should be meant by *reasonable.*" This conversation indicated as much. Thomas Penn laid out the prerogatives of the proprietors as he interpreted them; Franklin forwarded the counterclaims of the Assembly. "We now appeared very wide, and so far from each other in our opinions as to discourage all hope of agreement," Franklin recalled later. Whether Penn was discouraged at the evident impasse, Franklin could not read; the proprietor suggested that Franklin put the position of the Assembly in writing and promised to consider the matter further.

Franklin thereupon repaired to his quarters in Craven Street. Forty-eight hours later he handed the Penns a paper entitled "Heads of Complaint," identifying the most important of the difficulties between the

Assembly and the proprietors. The first was the unreasonable restraints placed upon the Penns' appointee as governor (deputy governor to be precise; Thomas Penn himself was technically governor). Of late, Governor Morris had been replaced by Governor William Denny, a man who seemed reasonable enough but, like his predecessor, was bound by instructions that left no room for his own judgment. The result, in Franklin's words, was "great injury of His Majesty's service in time of war, and danger of the loss of the Colony."

The second complaint followed from the first, to wit, that the restrictions placed upon the governor infringed the right of the Assembly to raise supplies essential for the defense of the country. Indeed, the proprietors extorted assent from the Assembly to unwise and unconstitutional measures, under duress of emergency. "The Assembly, in time of war, are reduced to the necessity of either losing the country to the enemy, or giving up the liberties of the people and receiving law from the Proprietary."

Franklin's third and final complaint identified the most onerous of these extortions, specifically the exemption of the vast proprietary estates from taxation. The proprietors expected the people to defend proprietary property but refused to contribute their fair share. "This, to the Assembly and People of Pennsylvania, appears both unjust and cruel."

Franklin concluded his précis of grievance with a request that the proprietors consider the complaints and redress them in the "most speedy and effectual manner, that harmony may be restored between the several branches of the legislature, and the public service be hereafter readily and fully provided for."

෬— Almost immediately upon delivering his list to the Penns, Franklin fell sick. What at first seemed a cold ramified into the second noteworthy illness of Franklin's life, lasting two months. The cold symptoms subsided after several days but were replaced by those of some secondary infection, including a high fever and "great pain in my head, the top of which was very hot, and when the pain went off, very sore and tender." The bouts of pain persisted for twelve to thirty-six hours at a time, accompanied by occasional delirium. A physician bled Franklin from the back of the head, which relieved the pain temporarily. The doctor also prescribed a medicinal bark, administered both ground and brewed into a tea. "I took so much bark in various ways," Franklin informed Debbie, "that I began to abhor it." An emetic was recommended, which Franklin at first resisted from fear it would exacerbate his headache. Eventually he achieved equivalent results on his own. "I was seized one morning with a vomiting and purging, the latter of which continued the greater part of the day, and I believe was a kind of crisis to the distemper, carrying it clear off, for ever since I feel quite lightsome, and am every day gathering strength."

~ During his time of suffering the patient took some comfort from the belief that the proprietors were preparing their response to his catalog of complaints. In fact they were doing no such thing. Rather they were commencing a campaign of psychological attrition. They received Franklin's paper and simply held it, evidently convinced that either the emergency in Pennsylvania would pass or Franklin would weary of delay and go home.

The Penns' strategy followed the advice of their lawyer, an expert in the art of glacial litigation. Ferdinand John Paris had been counseling the proprietors since before Franklin's first visit to London; for most of that time he had charge of the Penns' endless (thus far) border dispute with Lord Baltimore of Maryland (which, after Paris's death diminished his obstructional abilities, ultimately yielded to the survey of Messrs. Mason and Dixon). Yet Paris was not simply patient; he was also nasty. Thomas Hutchinson considered him a solicitor of the "first rate," but one who possessed "a peculiar talent at slurring the characters of his antagonists."

Paris probably did not need any encouragement toward antipathy to Franklin; as the Penns' agent he considered it part of his job. (For a time Paris had been the Pennsylvania Assembly's agent, but the Assembly severed the relationship on discovering his preference for the Penns over the Pennsylvanians.) Whether or not he required the encouragement, he received it from Franklin's Philadelphia foe, former governor Morris. "Mr. Franklin will be in England exhibiting his complaints against the proprietors, as is thought and expected by many that sent him," Morris warned. "But I imagine his own schemes are very different from those of his employers [that is, the Assembly]. He is a sensible, artful man, very knowing in American affairs, and was his heart as sound as his head, few men would be fitter for public trust. But that is far from being the case. He has nothing in view but to serve himself, and however he may give another turn to what he says and does, yet you may be assured that is at the bottom and in the end will shew itself."

Franklin knew of Paris, and knew Paris knew of him. "He was a proud angry man, and as I had occasionally in the answers of the Assembly treated his papers with some severity, they being really weak in point of argument and haughty in expression, he had conceived a mortal enmity to me." Franklin did not improve Paris's opinion by refusing to meet with him, insisting instead on dealing with the proprietors directly or not at all.

Only gradually did Franklin realize that this attitude played into Paris's hands. The proprietors found one excuse after another for not being able to meet Franklin, leaving him no one to talk to. The months passed, and Pennsylvania's problems were no closer to being solved.

~ Yet Franklin was not without resources. Prevented from making his case to the proprietors, he argued it before the court of public opinion. During the late summer and autumn of 1757 London papers carried letters motivated, if not paid for, by the Penns, criticizing the Pennsylvanians for using their differences with the proprietors as an excuse not to defend themselves. Franklin denied the allegation directly, even as he employed it as an excuse to launch a broader campaign in the press against the proprietors.

In September *The Citizen* carried a long letter over the signature of William Franklin. William doubtless contributed to the letter; indeed he boasted of his role in the composition, at the same time explaining the logic: "For although it might not be so proper for my father to take notice of these aspersions, while the negotiation was on foot, there could be no reason why I, as an inhabitant of Pennsylvania, now on my travels in England, no ways concerned in conducting the negotiation, should not vindicate the honour and reputation of my country when I saw it so injuriously attacked." Yet quite clearly the inspiration behind the letter and the language in which it was written were Franklin's. The disguise almost certainly failed to fool Paris or the Penns, but they were not the audience. Whether or not ordinary readers, who *were* the audience, were fooled, Franklin preferred this thin disguise to none at all.

The essentials of Franklin's argument here differed little from those he had made in Pennsylvania and in letters to the governor and recently to the proprietors themselves; yet, appealing to his readers, he emphasized the consonance of interests between the people of Pennsylvania and the people of England. The proprietors had attempted to abrogate "the privileges long enjoyed by the people, and which they think they have a right to, not only as Pennsylvanians, but as Englishmen." Employing the famous formula of John Locke, Franklin expressed astonishment that during wartime, "when the utmost unanimity and dispatch is necessary to the preservation of life, liberty, and estate," the Penns should send a governor to America with instructions "as must inevitably produce endless dispute and delay, and prevent the assembly from effectually opposing the French upon any other condition than the giving up their rights as Englishmen."

Franklin's letter was reprinted from *The Citizen* to the *London Chronicle*, then repeated in *The Citizen* and picked up by the *Gentleman's Magazine*. At Franklin's urging it was subsequently included as an appendix in a book, *An Historical Review of the Constitution and Government of Pennsylvania*.

By the evidence of this editorial interest, Franklin's appeal to the rights of Englishmen touched a sympathetic chord. When *The Citizen* ran the letter the second time, the editors cited popular demand and asserted that the journal stood ready to defend the people "by exposing the artifices of those who would, in a remote land, overthrow the native rights and liberties of Englishmen."

~ Franklin relished a good fight in the press, but no more than he appreciated an ingenious experiment. His growing circle of friends included several whose tastes in science matched his own. John Pringle, a member of the Royal Society and the Honest Whigs, was a Scottish doctor well versed in contagious diseases and the sorts of infirmities encountered by soldiers in the field; he also dabbled in the use of electricity to alleviate paralysis. Franklin, upon hearing Pringle inform the Royal Society of recent discoveries in this last area, shared findings of his own, based on work he had done some years earlier in Pennsylvania. The patients had presented themselves to him, Franklin said, following reports in the papers of electrical cures in Europe. He had wired them to his electrical jars and sent shocks through the palsied limbs.

> The first thing observed was an immediate greater sensible warmth in the lame limbs that had received the stroke than in the others; and the next morning the patients usually related that they had in the night felt a pricking sensation in the flesh of the paralytic limbs, and would sometimes shew a number of small red

spots which they supposed were occasioned by those prickings.
The limbs too were found more capable of voluntary motion, and
seemed to receive strength; a man, for instance, who could not,
the first day, lift the lame hand from off his knee, would the next
day raise it four or five inches; the third day higher, and on the
fifth was able, but with a feeble languid motion, to take off his hat.

Needless to say, the patients were ecstatic, and Franklin was most encouraged. Unfortunately, the positive effects wore off.

I do not remember that I ever saw any amendment after the fifth
day; which the patients perceiving, and finding the shocks pretty
severe, they became discouraged, went home and in a short time
relapsed, so that I never knew any advantage from electricity in
palsies that was permanent. And how far the apparent temporary
advantage might arise from the exercise in the patients' journey
and coming daily to my house, or from the spirits given by the
hope of success, enabling them to exert more strength in moving
their limbs, I will not pretend to say.

Franklin had long been intrigued by the principle that would underlie
refrigeration, namely, the capacity of an evaporating liquid to absorb
heat. One hot summer day in 1750, when the thermometer in the shade
stood at 100 (of the degrees devised earlier in Franklin's life by the German instrument-maker Fahrenheit), he had observed how as long as he
wore a shirt wetted with his sweat, and sat in the breeze of an open window, he remained relatively cool; but when he changed his wet shirt for a
dry one, he grew noticeably warmer.

In the spring of 1758 he traveled from London to Cambridge, where
he collaborated with another physician-scientist and fellow of the Royal
Society, John Hadley. Franklin and Hadley took turns wetting the ball of a
thermometer with ether, which they then evaporated off the ball by
means of a bellows. With each round of wetting and evaporating, the
mercury dropped. Though the air in the room remained at 65 degrees, the
thermometer fell below the freezing point. Hadley and Franklin terminated the experiment when the thermometer read 7 degrees, or 25 degrees below freezing, and the ice on the ball was a quarter inch thick.
"From this experiment," Franklin concluded, "one may see the possibility
of freezing a man to death on a warm summer's day, if he were to stand in
a passage through which the wind blew briskly, and to be wet with ether."

This conclusion prompted other speculations. "May not this be a reason why our reapers in Pennsylvania, working in the open field, in the clear hot sunshine common in our harvest-time, find themselves well able to go through that labour, without being much incommoded by the heat, while they continue to sweat, by drinking of a thin evaporable liquor, water mixed with rum; but if the sweat stops, they drop, and sometimes die suddenly?" It was generally believed of Africans that they bore heat better than whites. "May there not be in negroes a quicker evaporation of the perspirable matter from their skins and lungs, which, by cooling them more, enables them to bear the sun's heat better than whites do?" Might not evaporation from leaves serve to cool trees, even in the summer sun? Might not evaporation from the earth's surface tend to mitigate summer temperatures?

Franklin's interest flattered his hosts at Cambridge, who invited him back for commencement in the summer of 1758. He was flattered in turn. "My vanity was not a little gratified by the particular regard shown me by the chancellor [the Duke of Newcastle] and vice chancellor of the university, and the heads of colleges," he reported to Deborah.

His vanity was gratified the more several months later when the University of St. Andrews awarded him an honorary doctorate of laws. "The ingenuous and worthy Benj. Franklin has not only been recommended to us for his knowledge of the law, the rectitude of his morals and sweetness of his life and conversation," the citation read, "but hath also by his ingenious inventions and successful experiments, with which he hath enriched the science of natural philosophy and more especially of electricity which heretofore was little known, acquired so much praise throughout the world as to deserve the greatest honours in the Republic of Letters." The governing body of the ancient university went on to declare that henceforth said Franklin should be addressed and treated by all as "the most Worthy Doctor." Neither in that era nor later were the recommendations of educators always followed, but this recommendation took, and Franklin thereafter was generally referred to as "Dr. Franklin."

With each honor that came his way, Franklin felt farther from home. The feeling evoked ambivalence, for while he missed his wife and daughter and the familiar sights of Philadelphia, the larger circles in which he now moved possessed an undeniable appeal.

Franklin acknowledged his ambivalence to Debbie. "You may think perhaps that I can find many amusements here to pass the time agree-able," he wrote in January 1758. " 'Tis true, the regard and friendship I meet with from persons of worth, and the conversation of ingenious men, give me no small pleasure. But at this time of life, domestic com-forts afford the most solid satisfaction, and my uneasiness at being ab-sent from my family, and longing desire to be with them, make me often sigh in the midst of cheerful company."

Certainly the first part of Franklin's statement—about the pleasure of the company he now kept—was true; undoubtedly the second part was true as well. Yet he could say no less, especially in a letter in which he informed his wife that "I shall hardly be able to return before this time twelve months." The work was slow, and he was determined to do it properly, which required "both time and patience."

Franklin appreciated Debbie's efforts to keep him abreast of events at home. "I thank you for sending me brother Johnny's journal," he wrote. "I hope he is well, and sister Read and the children. I am sorry to hear of Mr. Burt's death. . . . I am not much surprized at Green's behav-iour. He has not an honest principle, I fear. . . . I regret the loss of my friend Parsons. Death begins to make breaches in the little Junto of old friends that he had long forborne, and it must be expected he will now soon pick us all off one after another."

Similarly he sought to include Debbie in his life in London, at least vicariously. She had asked about his accommodations; he responded, "We have four rooms furnished, and every thing about us pretty genteel, but living here is in every respect very expensive. Billy is with me, and very serviceable. Peter has behaved very well. Goodies I now and then get a few; but roasting apples seldom. I wish you had sent me some." She had urged him to hire a coach to have on hand; he answered that he had done just that, to avoid foul weather and preserve appearances. "The hackney coaches at this end of town, where most people keep their own, are the worst in the whole city, miserable dirty broken shabby things, unfit to go into when dressed clean, and such as one would be ashamed to get out of at any gentleman's door." He had lamented the smoke from coal fires; she suggested burning wood. "It would answer no end," he ex-plained, "unless one could furnish all one's neighbours and the whole city with the same." Smoke was London's bane, and would become Franklin's while there. "The whole town is one great smoky house, and every street a chimney, the air full of floating sea-coal soot, and you never get a breath of what is pure, without riding some miles for it into the country."

He sent her presents, that she might enjoy the bounty of the metropolis even if she could not be there. "Bowl remarkable for the neatness of the figures," he wrote, in a partial inventory. "Four silver salt ladles, newest, but ugliest, fashion . . . six coarse diaper breakfast cloths: they are to spread on the tea table, for no body here breakfasts on the naked table . . . a little basket, a present from Mrs. Stevenson to Sally, and a pair of garters for you which were knit by the young lady her daughter, who favoured me with a pair of the same kind, the only ones I have been able to wear, as they need not be bound tight, the ridges in them preventing their slipping." He sent carpeting for the floor at home, blankets and bed linen, napkins, and "7 yards of printed cotton, blue ground, to make you a gown. I bought it by candlelight, and liked it then, but not so well afterwards; if you do not fancy it, send it as a present from me to Sister Jenny." Two sets of books and some sheet music were for Sally. A candle-extinguisher was "for spermaceti candles only." A large jug was for beer. "I fell in love with it at first sight, for I thought it looked like a fat jolly dame, clean and tidy, with a neat blue and white calico gown on, good natured and lovely, and put me in mind of—Somebody."

Franklin must have thought he knew his Debbie to be able to liken her to a beer jug, even if he declined the explicit reference at the last word. He also knew her well enough to recognize her reluctance to come over to England. William Strahan, with whom Franklin obviously discussed the matter, continued to urge her to join her husband. Writing to David Hall, Strahan said, "Tell her I am sorry she dreads the sea so much. . . . There are many ladies here that would make no objection to sailing twice as far after him."

Perhaps it was her dread of the deep that kept Deborah away. But something else was almost certainly involved as well. She had watched her husband grow over the years, from the promising but penniless journeyman she married in 1730 to a public figure honored by many of the greatest men and institutions of the British empire. Debbie was the same simple soul she had been at the start: a thrifty housewife, a good mother (if a sometimes testy stepmother), a competent business partner (who was now handling her husband's affairs in his absence). Philadelphia was not merely her home; it was her world. Franklin could move in another, larger world, and do so comfortably. Debbie could not, and she knew enough not to try.

13

Imperialist

1759–60

⁓ On the Plains of Abraham, high above the St. Lawrence
River, where the St. Charles River entered the larger stream
and formed a point on which the French had built the
fortress of Quebec, in the summer of 1759 the struggle for
North America drew to a climax. That it did so was the
work of one man more than any other.

William Pitt first won fame with a wicked tongue in the House of Commons. When George II put 16,000 troops from his native Hanover on the British payroll, Pitt denounced the move as reducing England to the status of "a province to a despicable electorate." Pitt characterized John Carteret, the courtier generally held responsible for the king's pro-German policy (and a man with a weakness for burgundy), as one who "seemed to have drunk of the potion described in poetic fictions, which makes men forget their country."

George did not appreciate having his favorites so described; still less did he like hearing his homeland called a "despicable electorate." But such was Pitt's strength in Commons that after the disappointments of first phase of the Seven Years' War (as Europe dubbed the struggle that began with Braddock's defeat in western Pennsylvania), the monarch decided he had no choice but to turn to the "Great Commoner." Pitt agreed; with typical egotism he asserted, "I am sure I can save the country and nobody else can."

What Pitt knew—besides the fact that he must be England's savior—was that salvation would be found not in Europe but overseas. The American colonies might occupy the frontier of the British empire, but they became the center of Pitt's strategy. He ordered an attack on Louisbourg, which succeeded in July 1758. He sent a new force against Fort Duquesne; this effort also succeeded. When the retreating French blew up the fort, the victorious British troops built a fort of their own and named it for Pitt.

But the hinge of Pitt's American strategy, and the fulcrum of empire for both Britain and France, was the assault on Quebec. Pitt's ministry gave the command to James Wolfe, a major general just thirty-three years old, who would lead a force of some 8,000 against the Canadian town. He would, that is, if he could get the men up the St. Lawrence from the sea. Admiral Charles Saunders had overall authority for transport, but the hazardous negotiation of the shallows and eddies of the vexing river fell to Captain James Cook. Although Cook's destiny awaited him in the Pacific, the French were plenty impressed at his work in the St. Lawrence. "The enemy have passed sixty ships of war where we dare not risk a vessel of a hundred tons by night and day," declared the suddenly worried Canadian governor, the Marquis de Vaudreuil.

Though reaching Quebec was half the battle, the other half was harder. The site of the city afforded its greatest protection, with the St. Lawrence on the east and south, the St. Charles on the north, and the third side of the triangle commanded by the Plains of Abraham, which in turn were protected from the St. Lawrence by an intimidating escarpment. The French commander, the Marquis de Montcalm, was so confident that the bluff could not be scaled that he did not bother to defend it.

Wolfe initially agreed with Montcalm's assessment. He landed his troops below the city and tried every trick he could conceive to lure Montcalm away from the city into an open fight. Montcalm refused to be drawn. Wolfe sent a detachment to capture Point Lévis across the St. Lawrence from the city, at a place where the stream abruptly narrowed from a mile and a half to three-quarters of a mile (this narrowing was what gave Quebec its name—an Algonquin word meaning "strait" or "narrow"). From Point Lévis, British cannon bombarded the city. Montcalm remained unmoved.

Yet if position favored Montcalm, time did not. Provisioning the city posed a growing problem. Obviously no supplies would be coming up the river, which was now covered with British warships. Should Saunders and Cook proceed upstream, they might well cut the French supply lines from the interior. For this reason Montcalm could not simply wait for winter's ice to freeze out his attackers.

So he tried fire instead. Torching seven of his own vessels, he cast them upon the current in the direction of the British squadron. All eyes on both sides of the river followed the floating infernos as they bore down on the attackers, but between the waywardness of the flow and the watchfulness of British boatmen who hooked the most threatening craft and pulled them aside, the incendiary ships drifted harmlessly away.

Weeks passed, then months. The British could not lure Montcalm from his redoubt. In frustration Wolfe sent rangers up and down the river to destroy whatever might give aid or comfort to the enemy. More than a thousand homes and farms were ravaged in the process, but Quebec remained untouched. One impetuous action by some British grenadiers against the French emplacements below the city produced—amid rain, thunder, mud and misfiring muskets—a sharp rebuke by the French. "Everything proves that the grand design of the English has failed," wrote Governor Vaudreuil.

Wolfe fell sick under the strain. Feverish, his high hopes from the spring fading as the frosts of autumn approached, the British general turned to his lieutenants for ideas. They urged a landing miles upriver from Quebec, beyond the cliffs; from there the city could be approached overland. Wolfe assented, and preparations for moving some 3,500 men fifteen miles upstream commenced.

But rain delayed the operation, in the process intensifying Wolfe's anxiety. He had a boat crew row him up and down the river, seeking something he had overlooked, some weakness in the enemy's defenses. Several days into September he found it: a narrow strip of land on a tiny cove directly below the heights of Abraham's plain. Reconnaissance suggested that an ascent might conceivably be accomplished via a steep, treacherous path. Artillery in any numbers was out of the question, but lightly burdened infantry might manage the climb.

Wolfe determined to try. With 1,800 men, in the dead of night on September 12, he floated silently down the river to the cove. Through deserters the British commander had learned that a French supply convoy was scheduled to arrive that night; in fact it had been canceled, but, as British luck would have it, the officer in charge failed to notify Quebec of the cancellation. When a French sentry, hearing the British boats in the darkness, called out, a French-speaking British captain convincingly responded, *"Vive le roi!"*

At four in the morning the lead boats landed. Wolfe and Lieutenant Colonel William Howe led an ascent by a select squadron up the steep side of the cliff; hand over hand, clinging to roots and rocks, they scaled the bluff to surprise the guards at the top of the winding path. Before being overpowered, the guards managed to send a message into the city, but by the time Montcalm could react, the rest of Wolfe's landing party of 4,500 had climbed the path.

This ascent was either a brilliant stroke or a stupid one, depending on what happened next. The French outnumbered the British and had the better position. If the redcoats got into trouble, the same steep slope that had been so difficult to surmount on the attack would be even more difficult in retreat—in confusion and under fire. For Wolfe and the British, on the Plains of Abraham it was triumph or die.

Wolfe did both. Montcalm, alarmed at the sudden appearance of his enemy where they were least expected, ordered an immediate attack. The French forces advanced bravely but in poor order; irregulars among the ranks fired from too far away to inflict much damage on the British. Wolfe meanwhile commanded his men to hold their fire. The French came closer, closer, closer—until at forty paces Wolfe gave the order. The British volley decimated the French line, which staggered and broke. Montcalm's troops fell back, fighting as they went. Wolfe, leading the pursuit from the front, took a ball in the wrist, then one in the groin, then one in the lung. Dying, he gave a final order to cut off the French retreat, before declaring, "Now, God be praised, I will die in peace."

Montcalm died no less heroically but considerably less happy.

Wounded in the retreat, the French general survived long enough to appreciate the extent of his failure. Those French troops that could leave
the city fled to the west; those that could not were captured and transported to France. The French fleur-de-lis was struck from the ramparts
of the citadel above the St. Lawrence; the British Union Jack went up in
its place. Canada was not yet British, but Quebec, the key to Canada, was.

∾— It was a glorious victory, and recognized as such, but, to the astonishment of Franklin and his fellow Americans, the victory looked likely
to be undone even before the glow of its doing diminished. The capture
of Louisbourg, Duquesne, and Quebec, combined with other victories in
America, as well as thrashings of the French in India and Europe and on
the high seas, augured an auspicious peace for Britain. But any peace with
France would be negotiated rather than dictated, partly because Britain's
triumphs at arms, stunning though they were, did not warrant dictation,
and partly because Britain's foreign policy was premised on a maintenance, rather than destruction, of the European balance of power.
Britain would have to live with France; it therefore behooved the British
to leave a France they could live with. The question for Britain's negotiators was how much of what the nation's armies had won in the field its
diplomats ought to retain at the bargaining table.

As after the previous round of fighting, the Americans discovered
that their interests counted for little in the thinking of Britain's leaders.
The news of the capture of Quebec had hardly reached London before
interested parties began talking of handing Canada back to the French.
British forces had captured Guadeloupe, the French sugar island in the
West Indies, during that same glorious season; on the assumption that
one or the other would have to be restored to France, influential voices in
England advocated keeping Guadeloupe and returning Canada.

Franklin accounted such a course the height of folly. Had the British
government learned nothing from this latest round of conflict with
France? Had a peace treaty that left France in control of Canada ever led
to anything but another war?

Franklin initially employed satire against the arguments for the return of Canada, thinking folly should be met with derision. He wrote a
letter to the *London Chronicle* adducing a list of absurdities arguing for return, among them that British commerce was already too great and could
not stand the increase certain to follow access to all of Canada; that a

surfeit of beaver pelts would drive down prices for the broad-brimmed hats favored by "that unmannerly sect, the Quakers"; that England ought soon to have another costly war in order to avoid the dangers of becoming too rich; that the French Indians might continue their scalping campaigns against the colonists and thus prevent the colonies from growing too strong; that the English tradition of fighting bravely but negotiating meekly should continue unbroken ("Otherwise we shall be inconsistent with ourselves").

Franklin's barbs glanced off, and the campaign for restoration of Canada gained strength. In light of the seriousness of the threat, Franklin himself grew more serious. In April 1760 he published a pamphlet with the sober title *The Interest of Great Britain Considered, with Regard to Her Colonies and the Acquisitions of Canada and Guadeloupe.* He left off his name, after the custom (his and the era's) of anonymity and in recognition that as the agent of Pennsylvania he might be accused of special pleading. Yet though he spoke as a loyal subject of King George, close reading suggested that anyone this conversant with circumstances on the North American frontier must be a colonial. And even a cursory reading indicated that the author possessed a powerful mind, one that might benefit Britain—or endanger Britain, if it came to that.

Advocates of returning Canada to France contended that imperial security in North America might be guaranteed by the judicious placement of well-provisioned forts and the control of key mountain passes. Such statements, Franklin asserted, betrayed an utter ignorance of frontier warfare. "Security will not be obtained by such forts, unless they were connected by a wall like that of China, from one end of our settlements to the other." As for the passes, "If the Indians, when at war, marched like the Europeans, with great armies, heavy cannon, baggage and carriages, the passes through which alone such armies could penetrate our country or receive their supplies, being secured, all might be sufficiently secure." But the reality was wildly different. "They go to war, as they call it, in small parties, from fifty men down to five. Their hunting life has made them acquainted with the whole country, and scarce any part of it is impracticable to such a party. They can travel through the woods even by night, and know how to conceal their tracks. They pass easily between your forts undiscovered." They required no convoys of provisions, instead living off the land. Nor was there any punishing them after the fact. "When they have surprised separately and murdered and scalped a dozen families, they are gone with inconceivable expedition through unknown ways, and 'tis very rare that pursuers have any chance of coming up with them." In short, as long as France held Canada, it would hold the English settlers in America hostage. And unless the British government was willing to abandon those settlers to a ghastly fate, it must be prepared to fight more wars like the last two.

Another argument for Guadeloupe over Canada marshaled the theories of the mercantilists, who as always decried the drain of cash from the home economy. In the two centuries since the first planting of sugarcane in the West Indies, the English had developed quite a sweet tooth; supporting their sucrose habit tipped the balance of payments in an adverse direction. Bringing Guadeloupe into the empire would alleviate the imbalance without forcing the British to forgo their sweets.

Against this argument Franklin employed what might have been called a neo-mercantilist argument. In the early days of the European empires, colonies had been seen as territories to exploit, and perhaps proselytize, but hardly to settle. For the Spanish, Portuguese, Dutch, and French, the original model of nonsettlement remained the rule, as it did for the British colonies in the tropics. But in North America the original population of religious dissenters and fortune-seekers had flourished, until the number of North Americans in the British empire equaled a substantial fraction of the population of Britain itself. And, for reasons Franklin had explained in his pamphlet on population growth—reasons he reiterated in summary here—the number of North Americans would continue to grow, perhaps one day surpassing the population of the home country.

This growing population, Franklin noted, provided an obvious clientele for the manufactures of England. In mercantilist terms of effect on the balance of trade, the export of manufactures to the colonies might be fully as beneficial as the import of sugar or tea. Moreover, while the trade in sugar had reached maturity—the islands were limited in size, and supported all the plantations they would ever be able to support—the North American trade would continue to grow, almost without limit. Citing the case of Pennsylvania, Franklin pointed out that exports to that province had multiplied by seventeen times in scarcely more than a generation. Such an extreme rate of increase might not continue, but the general trend certainly would. The trade with North America already eclipsed that with the West Indies; with each year the Indies would fall further into the shade.

Some in the contra-Canada camp used the growth of the North American colonies against them, contending that as they grew they would compete with the home country in manufactures. All the more reason for keeping Canada, replied Franklin, denying the conclusion even as he accepted the concern it reflected. What prevented the development of manufactures in the colonies was not legal prohibition but the cheapness of land. Again echoing his earlier pamphlet, he asserted, "All the penal and prohibitory laws that were ever thought on will not be sufficient to prevent manufactures in a country whose inhabitants surpass the number that can subsist by the husbandry of it." To return Canada to the French would bottle up the British population between the seaboard and the mountains, thereby producing, if not in this generation, then in the next or the next after that, precisely the situation British manufacturers wanted to prevent. To open up Canada to British settlement would have the opposite effect. "While there is land enough in America for our people, there can never be manufactures to any amount or value."

Some warned that without the French threat from Canada, the North Americans would become dangerously independent-minded. Franklin did not deny that Americans thought on their own. Such was no more than their heritage as Englishmen. But he dismissed any notion that they might become dangerous to Britain. Indeed, it was the colonies' very independent-mindedness that would prevent danger to London; the danger was entirely to themselves. "Their jealousy of each other is so great that however necessary an union of the colonies has long been, for their common defence and security against their enemies, and how sensible soever each colony has been of that necessity, yet they have never been able to effect such an union among themselves, nor even to agree in requesting the mother country to establish it for them." If the American colonies could not combine against a universally acknowledged foe, still less could they combine against their mother country. "An union amongst them for such a purpose is not merely improbable, it is impossible."

Though this last part of Franklin's argument was certainly convenient in the present context, there is no reason to doubt his sincerity in making it. As the author of the most promising unrealized plan of union, he understood full well the difficulty of creating a united colonial front. Yet he did not despair entirely, nor was he above suggesting a circumstance that lent an edge to his argument, if only indirectly.

> When I say such an union is impossible, I mean without the most grievous tyranny and oppression. People who have property in a country which they may lose, and privileges which they may endanger, are generally disposed to be quiet, and even to bear much, rather than hazard all. While the government is mild and just,

while important civil and religious rights are secure, such subjects will be dutiful and obedient. The waves do not rise, but when the winds blow.

∽ Franklin did not anticipate rising waves; still less did he hope for them. The *annus mirabilis* of British arms—the period from the recapture of Louisbourg through the conquest of Quebec—was also the season of Franklin's most intense attachment to the British empire. He took pride in Britain's prowess and pleasure at the thought that America was extending British influence across the New World.

A personal experience during the summer of 1758 reinforced his attachment to Britain. Following his second visit to Cambridge, he and William toured Northamptonshire, the Franklins' ancestral homeland. From his father and Uncle Benjamin, Franklin knew a little of his roots, but in his childhood and youth, when he heard their stories, where he was from meant far less to him than where he was going. A boy who abandoned the city of his birth could hardly be bothered with the village where his father was born. Yet as the road behind him grew longer, and the road before him presumably shorter, he paid more heed to his family's origins. That he was traveling in company with his own son simply augmented his desire to learn about the land and people from which both sprang.

They visited the village of Ecton, where his father, grandfather, great-grandfather, and generations of Franklins before them had lived. The rector of the parish showed them the church register, which recorded Franklin births, marriages, and deaths for two centuries—as far back as the book went. They met his cousin Mary Fisher, the daughter of Thomas Franklin, Josiah's eldest brother. "She seems to have been a very smart, sensible woman," though now "weak with age," Franklin told Deborah.

But it was Thomas Franklin whose story particularly struck his nephew. At the village church Franklin and William met the wife of the rector, who showed them around the churchyard and ordered a pail of water and a stiff brush, which Franklin's slave Peter used to scour the moss from the family headstones. While William copied the inscriptions on the stones, she acted as local historian.

She entertained and diverted us highly with stories of Thomas Franklin, Mrs. Fisher's father, who was a conveyancer, something of a lawyer, clerk of the county courts, and clerk to the archdeacon in his visitations; a very leading man in all county affairs, and much employed in public business. He set on foot a subscription for erecting chimes in their steeple, and completed it, and we heard them play. He found out an easy method of saving their village meadows from being drowned, as they used to be sometimes by the river, which method is still in being; but when first proposed, nobody could conceive how it could be; but however they said if Franklin says he knows how to do it, it will be done. His advice and opinion was sought for on all occasions, by all sorts of people, and he was looked upon, she said, by some, as something of a conjurer.

One envisions Franklin listening to this description, and with each new detail identifying more fully with his uncle. Part of Franklin's problems with his father had followed from the simple fact that he was more gifted and ambitious than Josiah; on many occasions he must have wondered—not literally, but emotionally—whether he was really his father's son. Now it all fell into place: whether or not his father's son, he was his uncle's nephew. The rootless boy who had abandoned Boston had grown fond of Philadelphia, but this was different. The roots here ran far deeper, providing a sense of familial continuity that spanned centuries.

Imagine, then, what Franklin felt when the rector's wife furnished the final detail: that Thomas Franklin had died on the very day of the very month, four years beforehand, that young Benjamin Franklin was born. William Franklin, like his father already struck by the similarity between his father's career and his great-uncle's, commented that had Thomas died four years later, those who knew the two might have supposed a transmigration of souls. As it was, Franklin could not forget the coincidence, and when he wrote his memoirs he mentioned it almost in the first breath.

◦— After a stop at Coventry the two Franklins traveled to Birmingham, where they sought out Deborah's relations. Numerous aunts, uncles, and cousins survived—indeed thrived. Of one cousin of Deborah's mother, Franklin wrote, "She is a very sensible, smart, old lady, reads a great deal and is well acquainted with books, and her conversation very agreeable, she seems to be the scholar of the family." Regarding a cousin of Deborah's own, Franklin said, "Mrs. Salt is a jolly, lively dame. Both

Billy and myself agree that she was extremely like you; her whole face has the same turn, and exactly the same little blue Birmingham eyes."

Without doubt Franklin felt an emotional connection to the country whence his parents came; perhaps, in describing Deborah's kin so warmly, he was trying to make her feel something similar. As subsequent comments would reveal, Franklin was starting to think of following William Strahan's advice and relocating permanently to England. Needless to say, doing so would require that Deborah join him.

Even as he grew closer to ancestral England, he felt the loosening of certain ties to America. Upon his return to London he received a letter from Hugh Roberts, the charter Juntoist, reporting that two other members, Stephen Potts and William Parsons, had died. The old club was not what it once had been, having drifted away from impartial public service into the eddies of provincial politics. In his honest moments Franklin might have faulted himself, at least in part, for the change: no one had become more embroiled in politics than himself, the Junto's founder. But whatever the reason, the club had lost some of its former appeal. And with the passing of two of its oldest members, it lost still more.

Besides reminding him how far he was from Philadelphia, the deaths of Potts and Parsons caused Franklin to reflect on human nature. "Odd characters, both of them," he told Roberts.

> Parsons, a wise man, often acted foolishly. Potts, a wit, that seldom acted wisely. If *enough* were the means to make a man happy, one had always the *means* of happiness without ever enjoying the *thing*; the other always had the *thing* without ever possessing the *means*. Parsons, even in his prosperity, always fretting! Potts, in the midst of his poverty, ever laughing! It seems, then, that happiness in this life rather depends on internals than externals; and that, besides the natural effects of wisdom and virtue, vice and folly, there is such a thing as being of a happy or an unhappy constitution.

∽ From what Franklin could tell, Thomas Penn was of an unhappy constitution. But then Franklin may not have been in the best position to judge, having almost nothing to do with Penn after their unproductive early meetings. An interview at the beginning of 1758 ended in a spectacular failure, alienating Penn beyond recall and casting doubts upon Franklin's fitness for his office as agent.

The meeting was occasioned by questions involving the Indian trade on the Pennsylvania frontier. Franklin faulted the proprietors for failing to regulate the trade—or, more precisely, for preventing the Assembly from instituting reforms that would rein in the rogue traders. As before, Franklin judged the abuses of the trade largely responsible for turning the Indians against the English; combined with the proprietors' past mistreatment of the Indians in land sales, these had made the present troubles on the frontier all but inevitable.

This ongoing quarrel provided the context for the January 1758 meeting; the immediate issue was the narrower question of whether the proprietors ought to be able to veto the appointments of commissioners chosen by the Assembly to treat with the Indians. Penn held that proprietary participation in selecting the commissioners was necessary to defend the interests of the proprietors and was fully authorized by the colony's charter. Franklin countered that a proprietary veto guaranteed that the commissioners were mere creatures of the proprietors. Franklin went on to espouse the view that the Pennsylvania Assembly was the equivalent in provincial matters to the British House of Commons in British and imperial matters. In support of this position he cited Thomas Penn's own father, William Penn, whose charter for Pennsylvania declared that the Assembly of Pennsylvania should have all the power and privileges of an assembly according to the rights of the freeborn subjects of England. Thomas Penn answered that this was more than his father was empowered to grant under the royal charter creating Pennsylvania and therefore had no validity. Franklin replied that if such was true, all the people who were drawn to Pennsylvania under the belief that they would have such privileges had been deceived, cheated, and betrayed. To which Penn responded that they should have looked out for themselves; the royal charter was no secret. If they were deceived, it was their own fault.

"That," wrote Franklin, referring to Penn's last remark, "he said with a kind of triumphing laughing insolence, such as a low jockey might do when a purchaser complained that he had cheated him in a horse." Franklin added, "I was astonished to see him thus meanly give up his father's character, and conceived that moment a more cordial and thorough contempt for him than I ever before felt for any man living—a contempt that I cannot express in words, but I believe my countenance expressed it strongly. And that his brother was looking at me, must have observed it. However, finding myself grow warm I made no other answer to this than that the poor people were no lawyers themselves and, confiding in his father, did not think it necessary to consult any."

If Franklin's countenance had not made his contempt for the proprietors plain, these very words did, for not long after they reached their intended audience—Isaac Norris—they found their way to friends of the proprietors in Pennsylvania. From there they were relayed back to Thomas Penn, who denounced Franklin's letter as "a most impudent paper and a vile misrepresentation of what passed." Penn asserted that it was as unsafe for the people of Pennsylvania as for the proprietors to claim privileges not warranted by the king's charter, and that it was only out of concern for the people that he had spoken as he had. He did "not exult at all on the occasion" and had given Franklin no just cause for offense—certainly no such offense as he had taken. "How Mr. Franklin looked I cannot tell," Penn added. "My brother says like a malicious V. [villain], as he always does." But patience had its limits. "From this time I will not have any conversation with him on any pretence."

Franklin was angry to learn that his enemies were reading his mail, but despite some second thoughts on language he stood by his judgment. "I still see nothing in the letter but what was proper for me to write, as you ought to be acquainted with every thing that is of importance to your affairs," he wrote to Joseph Galloway, who at this time was an important Franklin ally in the Assembly. "And it is of no small importance to know what sort of a man we have to deal with, and how base his principles. I might indeed have spared the comparison of Thomas to a *low jockey* who triumphed with insolence when a purchaser complained of being cheated in a horse, an expression the Dr. [Fothergill, who had told Franklin of Penn's feelings about the letter] particularly remarked as harsh and unguarded. I might have left his conduct and sentiments to your reflections, and contented myself with a bare recital of what passed; but indignation extorted it from me, and I cannot yet say that I repent much of it." If anything, Franklin took continued satisfaction. "It sticks in his liver, and e'en let him bear what he so well deserves." Poor Richard could have told Thomas Penn what to expect. "By obtaining copies of our private correspondence, he has added another instance confirming the old adage, that listeners seldom hear any good of themselves."

The bad feelings between Franklin and Thomas Penn certainly did nothing good for accommodation between the Assembly and the proprietors. In November 1758, after a delay of more than a year, the Penns finally delivered their response to Franklin's original complaints. Ferdinand Paris placed the burden of obstruction on Franklin's shoulders, although without deigning to name him; reaffirming his clients' commitment to "that harmony which they most sincerely desire," the Penns' lawyer lamented that the Assembly had not designated some "person of candour" as its representative to the discussions. Paris went on to assert that the members of the Assembly had not pointed out "clearly and distinctly any grievances they thought themselves under."

Franklin could dismiss the lack-of-candor charge as ad hominem flummery; the assertion that he had failed to delineate Pennsylvania's grievances rang hollow when the proprietors would not even respond to his general complaints. More troublesome was the crux of the proprietors' argument: "The Charter (when read in its own language) gives the power to make laws to the Proprietary." The role of the Assembly was to provide "advice and assent," but the initiative rested with the proprietors. This was just the opposite of the view of Franklin and the Assembly, who judged the initiative in lawmaking to reside in the people, with the proprietors reduced to the advise-and-assent role.

The personal animus between Franklin and the Penns continued to obscure this essential political difference. Bypassing Franklin, Thomas and Richard Penn wrote directly to the Pennsylvania Assembly charging Franklin with "disrespect," again aspersing his "candour," and asserting that fruitful relations between Assembly and proprietors necessitated "a very different representation." Franklin attacked the proprietors' response as of a piece with all of their actions. "I need not point out to you the studied obscurity and uncertainty of their answer, nor the mean chicanery of their whole proceeding," he wrote Isaac Norris. Franklin added, "Thus a final end is put to all farther negotiation between them and me."

Yet this hardly ended the struggle between the people of Pennsylvania and the proprietors. To Franklin it simply suggested a change of venue. Form required his offering to resign as the Assembly's agent. "The House will see that if they purpose to continue treating with the proprietors, it will be necessary to recall me and appoint another person or persons for that service, who are likely to be more acceptable or more pliant than I am, or, as the Proprietors express it, persons of candour."

But he advised against this, suggesting instead the radical alternative of replacing rule by the Penns with rule by the Crown. "If the House, grown at length sensible of the danger to the liberties of the people necessarily arising from such growing power and property in one family with such principles, shall think it expedient to have the government and property in different hands, and for that purpose shall desire that the Crown would take the province into its immediate care, I believe that point might without much difficulty be carried, and our privileges preserved." He added, "In that I think I could still do service."

Not many years would pass before Franklin's preference for Crown rule above propriety rule would appear hopelessly naïve. At the moment it reflected both his terminal contempt for Thomas Penn and his increasing enchantment with things British.

෴ That his son William shared his enchantment increased it the more. Before leaving Philadelphia, William had fallen in love. Elizabeth Graeme was the belle of the city—bright, vivacious, beautiful. Her father, Thomas Graeme, was wealthy and distinguished, a leading member of the proprietary party. This political connection bothered Franklin somewhat—and may have contributed to his invitation to William to accompany him to England. If so, the strategy worked, for merry London soon banished thoughts of Betsy. "The infinite variety of new objects, the continued noise and bustle in the streets, and the viewing such things as were esteemed most curious, engrossed all my attention," he wrote Betsy, by way of explaining why he had not written earlier.

Whether or not Franklin had intended the relationship to end this way, he did not mourn its demise. Yet at times he must have wished that William had remained faithful to his lover across the sea. Just as Franklin himself had done in his own youth, William began consorting with the "low women" of London. And just as Franklin had done, William fathered a son out of wedlock. William Temple Franklin was born about 1760. His mother was as lost to history as William Franklin's own mother.

A bastard child had not been convenient to Franklin three decades earlier, but he took it in. William made a different decision—perhaps from his own experience growing up a bastard and a stepchild. He put William Temple in a foster home and for some years disguised his connection to the boy. Franklin almost certainly felt inhibited from criticizing his son on this point; he paid the bills for his grandson and kept quiet.

Otherwise William's life went according to plan. He entered the Middle Temple shortly after arrival in London; by the end of the following year he had completed his law studies and put on the gown of the barrister. Franklin's pride in his son was matched by his appreciation of William's usefulness. No lawyer himself, and a failed judge, Franklin valued William's advice on the legal points of the dispute with the Penns.

∽ William joined his father on a journey to Scotland in the late summer and autumn of 1759. Edinburgh had asked to honor Franklin; upon arrival he was named a burgess and guild-brother of the city. Glasgow presented a similar award. St. Andrews bestowed the freedom of the burgh.

With continued repetition such notice would lose some of its appeal; for now each mark of esteem delighted him. Equally delightful were the friends Franklin made on this trip. Sir Alexander Dick and Lady Dick knew Franklin by reputation; on hearing of the Franklins' visit they invited father and son to stay with them at Prestonfield, their manor near Edinburgh. Sir Alexander, like several of Franklin's admirers, was a physician and more; at the time of Franklin's visit, he was president of Edinburgh's College of Physicians and a member of the Edinburgh Philosophical Society. He would help found the Royal Society of Edinburgh some years hence, but only after winning a gold medal for growing the best rhubarb in Britain.

Franklin charmed Sir Alexander and Lady Dick and the assorted guests they brought to meet the marvelous American. Franklin was in fine form, reciting one of his literary hoaxes, a blasphemous revision of the Bible, contending for religious toleration. The first verses of this chapter recounted how Abraham received a visitor, an old man bowed with age. Abraham offered him food and a place to sleep, only to be dismayed when the visitor failed to bless Abraham's God. Annoyed, Abraham queried why he did not.

7. And the man answered and said, I do not worship the God thou speakest of; neither do I call upon his name; for I have made to myself a God, which abideth always in mine house, and provideth me with all things.

8. And Abraham's zeal was kindled against the man; and he arose, and fell upon him, and drove him forth with blows into the wilderness.

9. And at midnight God called unto Abraham, saying, Abraham, where is thy stranger?

10. And Abraham answered and said, Lord, he would not worship thee; neither would he call upon thy name. Therefore have I driven him out from before my face into the wilderness.

11. And God said, Have I borne with him these hundred ninety and
    eight years, and nourished him, and clothed him, notwithstanding
    his rebellion against me, and couldst not thou, that art thyself a
    sinner, bear with him one night?

Lady Dick insisted that Franklin send her a copy of this "Parable
Against Persecution," as it came to be called; so also did Lord Kames, a
Scottish jurist who had a reputation as a hanging judge but otherwise was
a merry fellow. Franklin and William spent a few days with Kames and
his family. While William conversed with the young people of the household, Franklin and Kames rode about the neighborhood on horseback,
philosophizing about law, agriculture, mechanics, fish, religion, fireplaces,
population growth, and history.

Upon returning to London, Franklin wrote Kames regretting that he
and William had not had the company of the lord and his lady on the
long journey south. "We could have beguiled the way by discoursing
1000 things that now we may never have an opportunity of considering
together; for conversation warms the mind, enlivens the imagination, and
is continually starting fresh game that is immediately pursued and taken."

Retrieving a thread of their conversations, Franklin raised the critical
issue of Canada. "No one can rejoice more sincerely than I do on the reduction of Canada; and this, not merely as I am a colonist, but as I am a
Briton."

And not merely a Briton, but a British imperialist—one with a vision
grander than almost any found in Whitehall or Westminster.

> I have long been of opinion that the foundations of the future
> grandeur and stability of the British Empire lie in America; and
> though, like other foundations, they are low and little seen, they
> are nevertheless broad and strong enough to support the greatest
> political structure human wisdom ever yet erected.

For this reason Canada must be retained.

> If we keep it, all the country from the St. Lawrence to Mississippi
> will in another century be filled with British people. Britain itself
> will become vastly more populous by the immense increase of its
> commerce; the Atlantic Sea will be covered with your trading
> ships; and your naval power thence continually increasing, will ex-
> tend your influence round the whole globe, and awe the world!

Evidently Kames had not shared all of Franklin's grand vision, for Franklin terminated this part of his letter: "But I refrain, for I see you begin to think my notions extravagant, and look upon them as the ravings of a mad prophet."

Yet the prophet was not without honor in his own country—that country being the one he shared with Kames and Collinson and the dons of Cambridge and the guild-brothers of Edinburgh. The honors he had received and the friends he had made since arriving in Britain were enough to win any man; this recent trip to the north of the United Kingdom added further friendships to still more honors. Franklin wrote Kames, "The time we spent there was six weeks of the *densest* happiness I have met with in any part of my life. And the agreeable and instructive society we found there in such plenty has left so pleasing an impression on my memory that, did not strong connections draw me elsewhere, I believe Scotland would be the country I should choose to spend the remainder of my days in."

14

Briton

1760 – 62

o— British pride was in the air that season. Just months after
Franklin's declaration of "I am a Briton," a new monarch
was crowned in London, and in his first speech from the
throne declared, "I glory in the name of Briton."

o— Or it may have been "Britain" he gloried in the name of;
the homonyms were hard for listeners to distinguish. Yet the
point was the same: George III, unlike his Hanoverian
forebears, considered himself British before anything else—
just as Franklin did. Eventually Britain would prove too
small for the two of them together, but for now the blessed
isle seemed to bless them both.

George III's path to the throne was not an easy one. His grandfather, George II, ruled for forty years, to the vexation of his son and heir apparent, Frederick. During much of that time Frederick thought his father was clinging to life to spite him—as indeed he was, at least in part. British politics in the eighteenth century almost guaranteed conflict between a monarch and the next-in-line. The eldest son of the sovereign was both Prince of Wales and Duke of Cornwall, and as such commanded income and influence independent of the throne. This income and influence in turn attracted those who had personal or political reasons for opposing the government, and those thus attracted typically made a habit of whispering oppositionist, if not seditious, thoughts in the ear of the impatient heir.

To this institutional conflict George II and Frederick added the bad blood that characterized the house of Hanover. Queen Caroline evinced a hatred toward her son almost inconceivable in a mother. "My dear firstborn," she was reported to have said, "is the greatest ass, and the greatest liar, and the greatest canaille, and the greatest beast, in the whole world, and I most heartily wish he was out of it." In her final moments, when Frederick expressed a desire to see his mother, she refused, saying, "I shall have one comfort in having my eyes eternally closed—I shall never see that monster again." Frederick's father—whose experience with his own father foreshadowed that with his son—shared his wife's hatred and disdain for their son. "Bid him go about his business," George said in response to Frederick's plea for a last chance at reconciliation, "for his poor mother is not in a condition to see him act his false, whining, cringing tricks now, nor am I in a humour to bear his impertinence."

If Frederick thought that mourning for Caroline would shorten George's life, he was mistaken. It was Frederick who died first, nine years before his father, after catching a chill playing tennis in the rain. George's death, when it came, was in its own unexalted way similarly indicative of the hazards of ruling-class life. The rich diet of the rich in eighteenth-century England led to gout and other maladies, including constipation. On October 25, 1760, George II awakened at Kensington Palace to his usual cup of chocolate, after which he retired to the royal water closet for his morning effort. The effort proved too much for the royal blood vessels; a critical one burst and killed the king.

George III was twenty-two when his grandfather died, and, although he had been training since birth to take the throne, he was woefully unprepared. A princely youth is a sure recipe for arrested development—princes rarely encounter the reverses that constitute essential elements of the maturing process—yet young George's development was arrested even by royal standards. He was awkward socially, and emotionally dependent on John Stuart, the Earl of Bute. The merest accident had brought Bute to the attention of the royal family. One day in 1747 a downpour suspended a cricket match Frederick was attending (he had bad luck with weather and sports); while waiting for the storm to lift, the prince proposed a card game but discovered that his party was one man short. Bute was pressed into service, made a favorable impression, and was attached to the royal retinue. He became a lord of the bedchamber and later groom of the stole. He also became, upon Frederick's death, the mentor, father figure, and *beau idéal* of the new prince.

In George's eyes Bute was everything the young man could never be: intelligent, cultivated, handsome. Everything, that is, except king, which made the younger man's deficiencies the more distressing. A mild correction from Bute conjured the specter of rejection—deserved rejection. "If you should now resolve to set me adrift," the prince said, "I could not upbraid you, but on the contrary look on it as the natural consequence of my faults." When George fell in love for the first time he submitted that frightening emotion to Bute's approval. "I surrender my future into your hands," George wrote, "and will keep my thoughts even from the dear object of my love, grieve in silence, and never trouble you more with this unhappy tale; for if I must either lose my friend or my love, I will give up the latter, for I esteem your friendship above every earthly joy."

As it turned out, Bute disapproved, and the prince forgot the young lady and put on the stiff upper lip that proved his Britishness. "I am born for the happiness or misery of a great nation," he said, "and must consequently often act contrary to my passions." He thereupon asked for a list of those young ladies Bute deemed acceptable—"to save a great deal of trouble," given that "matrimony must sooner or later come to pass." When it did, Queen Charlotte dutifully bore her husband fifteen children. (Known, perhaps unfairly, for her lack of physical beauty as a young woman, Charlotte grew in the opinion of her husband's subjects, at least comparatively. Horace Walpole commented that as the queen aged, "her want of personal charms became, of course, less observable." Walpole mentioned this to her chamberlain, who agreed. "Yes," the chamberlain said, "I do think the *bloom* of her ugliness is going off.")

As a protégé of Frederick, Bute naturally imbibed the prince's distrust of George II and his ministers; as the protégé of Bute, George III imbibed the same distrust of the same men. "The conduct of this old K. makes me ashamed to be his grandson," the grandson said. William Pitt, then at the height of his wartime glory, was described by the young George as "the blackest of hearts" and "a true snake in the grass."

To some extent the young monarch was simply jealous of Pitt. At almost the moment when George III mounted the throne, the city of London dedicated a new bridge across the Thames as a monument to "the man who by the strength of his genius and steadfastness of his mind and a certain kind of happy contagion of his probity and spirit" had saved the empire. Needless to say, the authors of this encomium were not speaking of the new king, who for just such reasons felt obliged to demonstrate—to Pitt and everyone else—that he, George III, was king. "I am happy to think that I have at present the real love of my subjects," he wrote Bute, "and lay it down for certain that if I do not show them that I will not permit ministers to trample on me, that my subjects will in time come to esteem me unworthy of the Crown I wear."

Proving his fitness to rule became a preoccupation with George III, coloring his relations with his ministers and subsequently with his American subjects. Bute, warned by the Duke of Devonshire that as long as the war with France lasted, the new king could not dispense with Pitt, replied, "My Lord, I would not for the world the king should hear such language. He would not bear it for a moment." "Not bear it!" rejoined the amazed duke. "He must bear it! Every king must make use of human means to attain human ends, or his affairs will go to ruin."

But George would *not* bear it. In his first meeting with the ministers he emphasized the need to bring to a conclusion the present "bloody and expensive war"—Pitt's war, as all present, including Pitt, understood. Pitt resented this slap; he equally resented his eclipse by Bute. Within the year the Great Commoner resigned—so discouraged regarding his future as to risk his reputation as tribune of the people by accepting a peerage for his wife and a pension for himself. "Oh, that foolishest of great men, that sold his inestimable diamond for a paltry peerage and a pension," lamented one of his disappointed partisans.

⌒ **Franklin** observed the events surrounding the accession of George III with mixed emotions. As a proud Briton himself, he could not help applauding the new king's embrace of Britain. Yet neither could he help considering ominous the ouster of Pitt, the architect of the war policy that promised finally to secure the borders of Pennsylvania and the other colonies against French and Indian attack.

Franklin had further reason for paying attention to the politics of court and Parliament. Having resolved, upon the breakdown of his relations with the Penns, to seek the protection of the Crown, he had to approach the Crown—or rather the officers of the Crown responsible for the colonies. These included the members of the Board of Trade and the Privy Council.

Bureaucracies being what they are, and Pennsylvania being as far from the minds of most British bureaucrats as it was from British shores, simply scheduling a hearing took many months. Franklin employed the time to probe the weaker points of the proprietors' defense. He could not expect the Board of Trade to become exercised about who paid what taxes in Pennsylvania; such a provincial matter hardly touched high interests of state. But the board *might* pay attention to proprietary policies responsible for unrest among the Indians, for it was this unrest that had provoked the current war.

In this tactical maneuvering Franklin had a most unlikely ally. Tedyuscung was a chief of the Delawares, a man who had been a friend of the English, then an enemy (his raiders were responsible for at least some of the attacks Franklin had countered in Northampton County in 1755), then again a friend. Yet even in burying the hatchet, Tedyuscung complained of historic wrongs the English had done his people, beginning with the Walking Purchase of 1737. Franklin and his allies in the Assembly thereupon urged Tedyuscung to address his people's complaints to King George, who might protect them against the evil proprietors.

Upon arrival in London, Franklin took up Tedyuscung's petition, and, in an audaciously broad interpretation of representative government, made the Indians' case the Assembly's own. As had become his custom, Franklin contrasted the beneficent policy of William Penn with the "deceit and circumvention" of the great man's heirs. Franklin did not go quite so far as to blame the present Penns for the current war, but he cited, without contradiction, the Indians' assertion that land fraud had been a principal cause of what Franklin himself described as "the cruelest murders and most horrid devastation" suffered by the people of Pennsylvania. By now Franklin's letter likening Thomas Penn to a "low jockey" had reached the proprietor's eyes; Franklin could not resist sticking a finger in one of those eyes by declaring, in his petition presenting Tedyuscung's case, that the Walking Purchase exhibited "such arts of jockeyship" as to give the Indians the worst possible opinions of the English.

Franklin was not quite cynical in forwarding the Delawares' grievances, but he was certainly opportunistic. Having witnessed the bloody effects of bad Indian policy, Franklin was all for redressing wrongs. Yet without question he cared less for an old land dispute than for the continuing struggle with the proprietors. (He also realized that while Tedyuscung might be useful as a character witness against the Penns, the chief's own character could be impeached. Besides having made war against Britain, Tedyuscung shared the weakness for alcohol that afflicted so many of his people. He died when Iroquois enemies caught him comatose and burned his house down around him.)

∽ The Tedyuscung petition was a flanking maneuver; Franklin's central assault on the proprietors involved several laws passed by the Assembly and accepted by Governor Denny but rejected by the proprietors. The rejection put the Penns in the awkward position of overruling their appointed deputy; they defended this awkwardness by alleging that the Assembly had bribed the governor to ignore his instructions. The substance of the allegation, if not the proprietors' interpretation of it, was true enough. After years of frustration with governors financially bound to veto measures favored by a majority of Pennsylvanians, the Assembly awakened to the possibility of outbidding the proprietors. The Assembly voted to indemnify Denny against the Penns; in addition it awarded him £3,000 in appreciation of his courage. Predictably, the Penns judged this transaction unethical and unacceptable.

Whether it was unlawful was what they and Franklin spent most of 1760 arguing about. Franklin and his fellow agent, Robert Charles, hired a team of legal professionals to prepare and present their case; the Penns engaged their own lawyers. The Privy Council referred the dispute to the Board of Trade, which put the matter on the docket for late March or early April. But a scandalously exciting murder trial of a prominent member of the House of Lords (who was convicted and hanged) distracted the board and delayed the case. Then Thomas Penn lost a son to illness just before the boy's fourth birthday; this occasioned further delay. (If Franklin, remembering the death of his own Franky at four, felt sympathy for his foe, he concealed it well.)

When the board finally convened the hearings, the Penns' lawyer indignantly attacked the Assembly for its "almost rebellious declarations" against royal authority and its "other acts of avowed democracy." He repeated the charge against the Assembly of bribing the governor, and he chastised that body for taking advantage of the proprietors' good nature in allowing it to meet on a regular basis. He implied that he need not say—although he certainly did say—that the late measures levying taxes on the proprietors' holdings were unwarranted and illegal.

Franklin's legal strategist was Francis Eyre; his courtroom lawyers were William de Grey and Richard Jackson. De Grey denied that any bribery had taken place. The Assembly had indeed voted an allowance for the governor, but this hardly represented a quid pro quo; it was simply a reimbursement for the governor's expenses. De Grey disputed the charge of incipient democracy; no less authorities than officers of the king's army testified to the loyalty and meritorious conduct of the Assembly. The proprietors had no business appealing the statutes in question to the Crown, for their own agent—the governor—had signed them, making them, under the terms of the royal charter, the law of the colony.

The hearings lasted four days; the board's deliberations on what it had heard, three weeks. In late June 1760 the board delivered an opinion that said, at length, that the proprietors were basically right and Franklin wrong. On the critical issue of whether the proprietors were bound to accept a measure simply because their governor had done so, the board declared that this was "not only against the essential nature of all deputed power" but would tend to "establish an uniform system of collusion between the governor and the Assembly."

Disappointing as this verdict was to Franklin, it was merely advisory. The Privy Council, acting through its Committee for Plantation Affairs, would make the final determination.

Accordingly the arguments were repeated, in the Whitehall hearing room called the Cockpit, in late August. Perhaps Franklin's attorneys had learned from their earlier setback; perhaps the council committee felt freer to take a broadly political, rather than narrowly legal, view of the dispute. Whatever the cause, the council ruled more or less in favor of Franklin and the Assembly on the most important single measure, the bill that levied a tax on the proprietors' estates. Some of the most heated rhetoric of the proprietors' attorneys alleged that the Assembly intended to shift the burden of taxation from its constituents to the proprietors; Franklin's advocates denied this. While the charges and denials flew across the Cockpit, Franklin received a summons. As he told the story years later:

> Lord Mansfield, one of the Council, rose, and beckoning to me, took me into the clerks' chamber, while the lawyers were pleading, and asked me if I was really of opinion that no injury would be done the proprietary estate in the execution of the act. I said, Certainly. Then says he, You can have little objection to enter into an engagement to assure that point. I answered, None at all. He then called in Paris [actually, Henry Wilmot, Fernando Paris having died the previous winter], and after some discourse his lordship's proposition was accepted on both sides.

This compromise marked a signal victory for Franklin and the Assembly. The proprietors, after years of resisting, accepted the principle that their holdings might be taxed along with those of every other property holder in Pennsylvania. Whether they had actually *believed* their lawyers' arguments about being victimized by runaway democrats in Pennsylvania, only they knew; in any case the assurances Franklin agreed to promised they would not be so victimized. (As it happened, getting the Assembly to accept Franklin's assurances was another matter.)

On the larger question, however, Franklin lost. The very fact that the Privy Council consented to hear the case meant that it accepted the Penns' argument that Assembly approval and governor's signature did not a Pennsylvania law make. The proprietors had been forced to yield on the tax issue, but there was nothing to prevent their contesting any number of other measures in the future.

○— As Assembly agent, Franklin also found himself investment manager for the people of Pennsylvania. The Assembly authorized him to receive Pennsylvania's portion of £200,000 allotted by Parliament to reimburse the American colonies for expenses incurred during the war with France, and over Thomas Penn's objections—principled and personal—the Board of Trade approved.

To this point in his life Franklin's investments had consisted chiefly of printing partnerships and occasional real-estate purchases. The money involved had been quite modest—certainly nothing like the £30,000 he now commanded. For help in putting that sum to safe use, he turned to

John Rice, a stockbroker suggested by Franklin's friends, and a man whose record revealed a career of care and circumspection. Rice recommended the purchase of a variety of stocks chosen for their stability and long-term promise. By the end of the summer of 1761 Franklin had bought shares worth nearly £27,000.

An unfortunate combination of events soon soured the investment. The Assembly decided it needed the money at once, and in late 1761 directed Franklin to sell the stocks and reclaim the cash. "A more unlucky time could not have been pitched upon to draw money out of the stocks here," Franklin replied. The peace negotiation with France had broken down, Pitt had been forced from office, and the war had widened to include Spain. Wars are notorious for deranging stock markets; in this case the derangement hammered the issues Rice and Franklin had selected. "All imaginable care and pains was taken to sell our stocks to the best advantage," Franklin said, "but it could only be done by degrees and with difficulty, there being sometimes no buyers to be found." The bottom line was abysmal; in the space of months Franklin managed to lose almost £4,000 of the province's £27,000 investment.

Things could have been worse. As events shortly proved, John Rice was not the sober stock picker he seemed. Not long after Franklin closed Pennsylvania's accounts with the broker, Rice came up seriously short on some speculative issues. To cover his losses he forged documents granting him power of attorney and embezzled other people's money. His crimes coming to light, he fled for France. Perhaps he hoped the hostilities between Britain and France would protect him from extradition; perhaps they would have had they persisted. But Rice's crowning bad luck was the arrival of peace hard upon his landing in France. The French packed him back across the Channel, where the authorities jailed, tried, and hanged him.

 The bad end of John Rice reinforced Franklin's desire to proceed with a project long in the planning—"a little work for the benefit of youth," he explained to Lord Kames, "to be called *The Art of Virtue*." Franklin feared that the title sounded slightly pretentious, so he took some pains to delineate his intent.

Many people lead bad lives that would gladly lead good ones, but know not *how* to make the change. They have frequently *resolved* and *endeavoured* it; but in vain, because their endeavours have not been properly conducted. To exhort people to be good, to be just, to be temperate, &c. without *shewing* them *how* they shall *become* so, seems like the ineffectual charity mentioned by the Apostle, which consisted in saying to the hungry, the cold, and the naked, *be ye fed, be ye warmed, be ye clothed*, without shewing them how they should get food, fire, or clothing.

Most people naturally had some virtues, but none naturally had *all* the virtues. To secure those bestowed by nature, and to acquire those wanting, was the subject of an art.

It is as properly an art as painting, navigation, or architecture. If a man would become a painter, navigator, or architect, it is not enough that he is *advised* to be one, that he is *convinced* by the arguments of his adviser that it would be for his advantage to be one, and that he *resolves* to be one; but he must also be taught the principles of the art, be shewn all the methods of working, and how to acquire the *habits* of using properly all the instruments. And thus regularly and gradually he arrives by practice at some perfection in the art.

Franklin distinguished virtue from religion. Christians were exhorted to have faith in Christ as the means to achieving virtue; having spent his life among Christians, Franklin was by no means inclined to deny the possibility of this path to virtue. But that same life among Christians disinclined him to assert its inevitability. Besides, Christians—either nominal or practicing—were not the whole world.

All men cannot have faith in Christ; and many have it in so weak a degree that it does not produce the effect. Our *Art of Virtue* may therefore be of great service to those who have not faith, and come in aid of the weak faith of others. Such as are naturally well-disposed, and have been carefully educated, so that good habits have been early established, and bad ones prevented, have less need of this art; but all may be more or less benefited by it. It is, in short, to be adapted for universal use.

Franklin's *Art of Virtue* became his unfinished masterpiece. His friends encouraged him to put his project to paper. Kames had been thinking about something similar as applied to thinking; at the beginning of 1761 he published his *Introduction to the Art of Thinking*. Franklin was impressed. "I never saw more solid useful matter contained in so small a compass," he told the author. "A writer can hardly conceive the good he may be doing when engaged in works of this kind." He was speaking as much to himself as to Kames. "With these sentiments you will not doubt my being serious in the intention of finishing my Art of Virtue." He explained that the work had been under way for thirty years. "I have from time to time made and caused to be made experiments of the method, with success. The materials have been growing ever since; the form only is now to be given."

Yet the form was never given. Exactly what form Franklin had in mind cannot be known. In his autobiography, which he began writing ten years later, he included the tale of his attempt at moral perfection, with the charts recording his daily progress in each of thirteen virtues. Perhaps this provided the basis for his projected work. But perhaps not, considering the failure of that experiment.

A lifelong writer and a career publisher, Franklin almost never suffered from the perfectionism that prevents many would-be authors from committing themselves to print. Perhaps he suffered so in this case, thinking a work about perfection ought to be perfect. Perhaps perfectionism of a different sort crept into his thinking. He may have recalled that early failure to achieve perfect virtue and deemed presumptuous any attempt to instruct others in what he had not mastered. In the letter to Kames containing the outline of his project, Franklin concluded, "I imagine what I have now been writing will seem to savour of great presumption; I must therefore speedily finish my little piece and communicate the manuscript to you, that you may judge whether it is possible to make good such pretensions."

Kames never had the opportunity, for Franklin—perhaps judging on his own that it was impossible to make good his pretensions—never finished the work.

⌁ Yet if he could not direct the public at large to perfection, he did manage to provide guidance to a particular friend. Polly Stevenson, leaving her mother's Craven Street house to live with an elderly aunt in Essex, had proposed a correspondence touching matters of moral and natural philosophy. Franklin was happy to oblige. He sent her books to seed the conversation, urging her to write regarding "whatever occurs to you that you do not thoroughly apprehend, or that you clearly conceive and find pleasure in."

Polly proved an apt pupil, and inquisitive. Why did the tide in rivers rise first at the mouth? she asked. Franklin had remarked that sailors at sea did not catch cold from wet clothes, the way landsmen did; she wondered whether the salt in the water had something to do with it. Spring-water at a particular location seemed warmer after being pumped than it was at the spring itself; could Franklin explain?

On the last question Franklin remarked that he expected the pumping "to warm not so much the water pumped as the person pumping." He would not impugn Polly's observation, but, especially as he had never heard of nor encountered this phenomenon, he wished to verify its existence before trying to explain it. "This prudence of not attempting to give reasons before one is sure of facts," he said, "I learnt from one of your sex, who, as Selden [John Selden, jurist and Orientalist] tells us, being in company with some gentlemen that were viewing and considering something which they called a Chinese shoe, and disputing earnestly about the manner of wearing it, and how it could possibly be put on, put in her word, and said modestly, *Gentlemen, are you sure it is a shoe? Should not that be settled first?*"

On the other points he endeavored to instruct. He devoted many pages of correspondence and at least one detailed diagram to explain the theory of waves and tides. The causes of colds stumped him. "No one catches cold by bathing, and no clothes can be wetter than water itself. Why damp clothes should then occasion colds is a curious question, the discussion of which I reserve for a future letter, or some future conversation." (Eventually Franklin would decide that colds had nothing to do with wet clothes, or even wet bodies.)

The correspondence and their now-occasional conversations convinced Franklin that Polly was an unusual young woman. Apparently through her mother, he learned that she did not wish to wed; he jokingly asked, "Why will you, by the cultivation of your mind, make yourself still more amiable, and a more desirable companion for a man of understanding, when you are determined, as I hear, to live single? If we enter, as you propose, into *moral* as well as natural philosophy, I fancy, when I have fully established my authority as a tutor, I shall take upon me to lecture you a little on that chapter of duty."

Franklin was teasing Polly here, but his words were not without significance. Recognizing what an intelligent and thoughtful young woman she was, he naturally considered what sort of wife she would make some man. Scarcely a month later he wrote her, "The knowledge of nature may be ornamental, and it may be useful, but if to attain an eminence in that, we neglect the knowledge and practice of essential duties, we deserve reprehension. For there is no rank in natural knowledge of equal dignity and importance with that of being a good parent, a good child, a good husband, or wife, a good neighbour or friend, a good subject or citizen, that is, in short, a good Christian."

The more Franklin corresponded with Polly, the more he became convinced she would make some lucky man a fine wife. In fancy he might have wished he himself were twenty-five or thirty again and had met such a charmingly intelligent young woman. Polly, like Katy Ray and the numerous women to whom Franklin would become attached in subsequent years, could hardly have contrasted more sharply with Debbie, his old country Joan. He would never leave Debbie—not permanently, at any rate. But he could dream.

Franklin obviously was in no hurry to get home to Debbie. The Privy Council's decision of September 1760 fairly well concluded the business he had been sent to London to transact. Not till two years later—the end of August 1762—did he cast off from Portsmouth for Philadelphia. In the interim he found a few things to do to earn his keep as the Assembly's agent, such as overseeing the investment of Pennsylvania's funds. Yet this might easily have been left to Robert Charles, who could hardly have handled it worse than Franklin did.

For the most part Franklin continued to enjoy the life of the celebrity philosopher. Oxford University awarded him the degree of Doctor of Civil Law, holding a special convocation for the purpose. He met David Hume, the Scottish philosopher and historian who was completing the final volumes of his *History of England*, the work that would earn him a large income to accompany his already substantial reputation. Franklin and Hume talked philosophy, politics, and etymology; on the last subject Franklin lamented a deficiency of English compared to certain other languages.

I cannot but wish the usage of our tongue permitted making new words when we want them, by composition of old ones whose meanings are already well understood. The German allows of it, and it is a common practice with their writers. Many of our present English words were originally so made; and many of the Latin words. In point of clearness such compound words would have the advantage of any we can borrow from the ancient or from foreign languages. For instance, the word *inaccessible*, though long in use among us, is not yet, I dare say, so universally understood by our people as the word *uncomeatable* would immediately be, which we are not allowed to write.

Alexander Dick and Lord Kames consulted Franklin on the matter of internal combustion—to wit, fireplaces in their homes, and how to keep them from smoking. Franklin responded with customized suggestions for their particular circumstances. George Keith, the Earl of Marischal, wanted to know how to protect his house from lightning; Franklin responded with practical advice informed by his electrical theory.

This same Lord Marischal, in his capacity as governor of Neuchâtel, found himself required to adjudicate a theological dispute over the duration of damnation, namely, was time in hell apportioned according to the grievousness of sin, or did all sinners suffer eternally? Franklin, through David Hume, forwarded an anecdote appropriate to the matter:

> The Church [of England] people and the Puritans in a country town had once a bitter contention concerning the erecting of a Maypole, which the former desired and the latter opposed. Each party endeavoured to strengthen itself by obtaining the authority of the mayor, directing or forbidding a Maypole. He heard their altercation with great patience, and then gravely determined thus: You that are for having no Maypole shall have no Maypole; and you that are for having a Maypole shall have a Maypole. Get about your business and let me hear no more of this quarrel. So methinks Lord Marischal might say: You that are for no more damnation than is proportioned to your offences have my consent that it may be so; and you that are for being damned eternally, G-d eternally d—n you all, and let me hear no more of your disputes.

With other interlocutors Franklin examined other topics. Why were the oceans salty? Many naturalists said this was because the rivers and streams of the planet dissolved rock salt, such as that found in salt mines, and carried it downstream to the sea. "But this opinion takes it for granted that all water was originally fresh, of which we can have no proof," Franklin said. "I am inclined to a different opinion, and rather think all the water on this globe was originally salt, and that the fresh water we find in springs and rivers is the produce of distillation. As to the rock-salt found in mines, I conceive that instead of communicating its saltness to the sea, it is itself drawn from the sea, and that of course the sea is now fresher than it was originally." (On this matter Franklin was partly right and partly wrong. The salt in mines did indeed come from the sea, but the seas were—and are—getting saltier.) On a similar subject Franklin noted the presence of fossil fishes and seashells in highlands far from the sea. "Either the sea has been higher than it now is, and has fallen away from those high lands; or they have been lower than they are, and were lifted up out of the water to their present height, by some internal mighty force such as we still feel some remains of, when whole continents are moved by earthquakes."

Another force was less mighty but more frequent. Many years earlier Franklin had noted the seeming paradox that northeasterly storms were felt first in the southwest. (The occasion was a strong northeaster that obscured his view in Philadelphia of a lunar eclipse but left observers in Boston—who communicated the fact to him—several hours more of clear sky to see the event.) Although Franklin had since corroborated the phenomenon, he had never been able to explain it. Now he thought he could. He employed two analogies. "Suppose a long canal of water stopped at the end by a gate. The water is quite at rest till the gate is open, then it begins to move out through the gate; the water next the gate is first in motion, and moves towards the gate; the water next to that first water moves next, and so on successively, till the water at the head of the canal is in motion, which is last of all." In other words, lowered pressure at the end of the canal propagated up the canal to the head, opposite the motion of the water itself. "Again, suppose the air in a chamber at rest, no current through the room till you make a fire in the chimney. Immediately the air in the chimney, being rarefied by the fire, rises; the air next the chimney flows in to supply its place, moving toward the chimney; and, in consequence, the rest of the air successively, quite back to the door." This latter was the closer analogy to the actual phenomenon. "Thus to produce our North-East storms, I suppose some great heat and rarefaction of the air in or about the Gulf of Mexico; the air thence rising has its place supplied by the next more northern, cooler, and therefore denser and heavier air; that, being in motion, is followed by the next more northern air, &c &c. in a successive current, to which current our coast and inland ridge of mountains give the direction of North-East, as they lie N.E. and S.W."

Franklin's meteorological perspicacity—his explanation here was modern and accurate—was not matched in matters geographical. Like nearly all American and European natural philosophers of his era, Franklin was fascinated by the outstanding question of North American geography: Was there a water passage from the Atlantic Ocean to the Pacific? By all evidence no such passage existed in temperate latitudes. Yet the straits to the north of Canada remained unexplored, and might include the long-sought Northwest Passage. In the early 1750s Franklin himself had joined the search vicariously and financially, helping to sponsor two voyages of the ship *Argo* from Philadelphia to the vicinity of Hudson Bay.

That the *Argo* found nothing of note did not discourage Franklin, in part because he had what he took to be independent evidence that a passage did indeed exist. In 1708 a London journal had published a letter ascribed to a Bartholomew de Fonte, said to be an erstwhile admiral of New Spain and Peru and a present prince of Chile. The Fonte letter recounted a journey by water from the Pacific, in the latitude of the 53rd parallel, to Hudson Bay. It was a remarkable journey, and utterly fanciful.

But Franklin did not know it was fanciful; he thought the opposite. And at a moment when the British papers and members of Parliament were pondering whether to retain Canada, the prospect of a Northwest Passage just beyond the territory in question made that territory all the more valuable. Such a passage would enable British merchants and explorers to reach the Pacific without sailing near or through Spanish waters around South America; Britain's recent victories over France in the East Indies would become doubly valuable.

In the spring of 1762 Franklin was requested to comment on the Fonte account by John Pringle, who had connections to George III's favorite, Bute. Franklin proceeded to compose a detailed defense of the Fonte account. Perhaps because his own hoaxes were of a much higher literary quality than this one, the very lack of literary sophistication in the Fonte piece seemed evidence of its authenticity. "Entertainment does not appear to be aimed at in it," Franklin said. " 'Tis in short a mere dry account of facts, which, though all possible and probable, are none of them wonderful like the incidents of a novel."

Franklin adduced additional corroboration. The flora and fauna described by Fonte comported with those mentioned by other travelers. The skin-covered boats employed by the natives he said he saw exactly matched the boats Russian traders encountered in the far-northern Pacific. That the Spanish now disavowed the voyage hardly discredited Fonte's account; Spain had no desire to broadcast knowledge of a northern route to the Pacific—a route that could only imperil Spain's Pacific possessions. Nor did an evident discrepancy between sea level at the western end of Fonte's passage and at the eastern end (the eastern end appeared to be downstream from the western) disqualify the account, in Franklin's judgment; quite the contrary. "One would think no writer of a feigned voyage, who desired to have it received as true, would of choice invent and insert a circumstance so objectionable."

Though Franklin was fooled in this case, he had company. Other authorities shared his respect for the Fonte account, and not till many more years had passed was it proven to be a fake. His defense of the spurious story is notable not merely for showing that the most astute minds can be mistaken but for including his first mention of the Gulf Stream. Sailors, he said, had christened it thus, and knew whence and whither it flowed—from the Gulf of Mexico to the North Atlantic. But they did not know why. Franklin proposed a mechanism: a differential in height of sea level occasioned by the trade winds. Although this was only partly right, it pointed him in the right direction.

∾ What most amazed his friends about Franklin was his breadth, his competence in a daunting diversity of fields of human knowledge. A true polymath, he was at home with experts in electricity, meteorology, geology, linguistics, mathematics, literature, philosophy, and politics. That he became one of a relative handful of people in history to invent a popular musical instrument simply added to the luster of his reputation.

Franklin's genius generally consisted in observing commonplace phenomena and applying the principles behind them in a novel or peculiarly productive way. His "armonica" fit the pattern. Like any number of other bored dinner guests, Franklin had occasionally amused himself by rubbing a wetted finger over the rim of a wineglass, thereby evoking a musical tone. At the time of Franklin's arrival in London, a transplanted Irishman named Pockrich gave concerts playing glasses tuned to different notes by the different amounts of water in them. But his career was cut short by a fire in his room, which killed him and destroyed his apparatus. A friend of Franklin's and a fellow of the Royal Society, Edward Delaval, extended the experiments of Pockrich, contriving a set of glasses better tuned and easier to play.

"Being charmed with the sweetness of its tones, and the music he produced from it," Franklin explained, "I wished only to see the glasses disposed in a more convenient form." This letter was to Giambattista Beccaria, an Italian priest and electrician. Beccaria had inquired about Franklin's latest electrical work; Franklin responded that his research into electricity had lapsed for the present but that he had devised a curious musical instrument that might interest the good father.

Franklin described in considerable detail the construction of the instrument. His principal improvement was the elimination of the water and the rearrangement of the glasses. Franklin's glasses were actually hemispheres of increasing diameter, from three inches to nine. Thirty-seven in all, they achieved by their differing size—and careful grinding—three octaves' worth of tones, including semitones. The glasses were fitted onto an iron spindle, each one nesting partially inside the next; as the spindle turned, all the glasses did too. The spindle was mounted horizontally in a wooden case and attached to a flywheel, which in turn was attached to a foot pedal that powered the mechanism. The player sat in front of the case, spun the spindle with his foot, and drew wetted fingers across the rims of the turning glasses. "The advantages of this instrument," Franklin told Beccaria, "are that its tones are incomparably sweet beyond those of any other; that they may be swelled and softened at pleasure by stronger or weaker pressures of the finger, and continued to any length; and that the instrument, being once well tuned, never again wants tuning." Franklin added, "In honour of your musical language, I have borrowed from it the name of this instrument, calling it the Armonica."

Franklin did not exaggerate when he described the armonica's tones as "incomparably sweet." They had a haunting, ethereal quality, much like that which would characterize "New Age" music more than two hundred years later. Franklin quickly became adept at playing, and took to entertaining guests on the instrument. Others followed his lead. Marianne Davies, a singer who played flute and harpsichord—and who was another young woman charmed by Franklin—became proficient enough to offer public performances. For a time the armonica achieved a genuine vogue. Royal wedding vows were exchanged in Vienna to armonica accompaniment; some of the greatest composers of the eighteenth and early nineteenth centuries, including Mozart and Beethoven, wrote for Franklin's instrument.

Like most vogues, that for the armonica eventually passed. Certain performers, including Marianne Davies, were afflicted with a melancholia attributed to the plaintive tones of the instrument. More tellingly, the sound-producing mechanism did not generate sufficient power to fill the large halls that became home to modern stringed instruments, brass, woodwinds, and percussion. That it was glass, and subject to easy breakage, did not help either.

~ In the summer of 1761 Franklin visited continental Europe for the first time. France would have been the obvious destination, but the war was still on; consequently Franklin and William, accompanied by Richard Jackson, contented themselves with Holland and Flanders. "We saw all the principal cities and towns," William explained to his sister, Sally. The Roman Catholic cathedrals at Ghent, Bruges, and Antwerp impressed the travelers; less impressive but more curious were the convents. "We went and saw the nuns," William said, "but they being at their devotions we could have no conversation with them. Indeed they did not look very inviting but on the contrary appeared like cross old maids who had forsaken the world because the world had first forsaken them."

Franklin was treated with as much respect as on his triumphal tours of England and Scotland. At Leyden they were greeted by the pioneer electrician Pieter van Musschenbroek, the inventor of the Leyden electrical jar. The British ambassador at The Hague hosted a dinner for the Franklins with the diplomatic corps. At Amsterdam, Thomas Hope, one of the most powerful merchants in Europe, put a coach and driver at their disposal. At Brussels the brother-in-law of Austrian Empress Maria Theresa entertained them.

The Dutch were a cleanly people, fastidiously so—which made a certain national habit almost shocking in its incongruity. William was especially offended. "I don't recollect that I saw more than one Dutch man without a pipe in his mouth, and that was a fellow who had hung in chains so long that his head had dropped off," William wrote. "Their very children are taught smoking from the moment they leave sucking, and the method they take to teach them is to give them when they are cutting their teeth an old tobacco pipe which is smoked black and smooth to rub their gums with instead of coral. But what surprised me most of all was the seeing at one of the houses a man of ninety drag out his partner and dance a minuet smoking most solemnly a long pipe the whole time."

Franklin preferred to comment on another national practice, encountered in Flanders. Writing to Jared Ingersoll of Connecticut, where a rigid observance of the Sabbath was a matter of law, Franklin explained:

> When I travelled in Flanders I thought of your excessively strict observation of Sunday, and that a man could hardly travel on that day among you upon his lawful occasions, without hazard of punishment; while where I was, every one travelled, if he pleased, or diverted himself any other way. And in the afternoon both high and low went to the play or the opera, where there was plenty of singing, fiddling and dancing.
>
> I looked round for God's judgments, but saw no signs of them. The cities were well built and full of inhabitants; the markets were filled with plenty; the people well favoured and well clothed; the fields well tilled; the cattle fat and strong; the fences, houses and windows all in repair; and no Old Tenor [paper currency] anywhere in the country; which would almost make one suspect that the Deity is not so angry at that offence as a New England justice.

⌐ They arrived back in London just in time to see the coronation of George III. Franklin had made arrangements for himself and William to watch the procession of the great and good of the empire, the first such event in forty years. As it happened, however, William did not sit with his father but walked in the procession himself.

Precisely how he rated this honor is unclear; hardly more transparent is how William suddenly became one of the king's favorite, or at least most favored, Americans. In August 1762 the Crown announced the appointment of William Franklin as royal governor of New Jersey.

Deliberate secrecy cloaked the consideration leading to the appointment. One contemporary remarked that the affair was "transacted in so private a manner that not a tittle of it escaped until it was seen in the public papers." Part of the secrecy reflected the desire of William's supporters to keep the Penns in the dark lest they mobilize opposition. The last thing Pennsylvania's proprietors wanted was the proliferation of Franklins in positions of influence; at a minimum, the bestowal of such an honor on such a young and inexperienced person would be read as approbation of his father. Doubtless more important to the king and his close advisers was the turmoil through which the government was going during this period. The accession of George III, the ascendancy of Bute, the eclipse and resignation of Pitt—all left little room and less stomach for a fight over the governorship of New Jersey.

Not that New Jersey was worth much of a fight. As plums went, it was small and not especially sweet. The job paid little and included few nonsalary emoluments; George's first choice turned the offer down flat.

But William Franklin was looking for work. He had applied for a post as deputy secretary of Carolina and would have been happy with anything respectable in the Admiralty court or the customs service. He definitely would not say no to a provincial governorship.

Promising as the young man might be, he almost certainly received his appointment because of his connection to his famous father. Through John Pringle, Bute had become acquainted with Franklin. Bute required little insight to recognize Franklin's gifts, nor to determine that Franklin would make a better friend than an enemy. New Jersey was an inexpensive down payment on Franklin's goodwill.

William's appointment inspired him to pursue another goal: matrimony. Some while earlier his eye had fallen on Elizabeth Downes, the daughter of a Barbados planter whose family possessed money but lacked station. William now had station but scant money; the match seemed ideal.

Franklin endorsed both his son's appointment to governor and his marriage to Betsy Downes. "The lady is of so amiable a character that the latter gives me more pleasure than the former," he told Jane Mecom, "though I have no doubt but that he will make as good a governor as husband, for he has good principles and good dispositions, and I think is not deficient in good understanding."

⁓ Yet perhaps he was not quite so delighted as he let on. Franklin did not attend William's wedding, having departed for America some weeks before. Considering that he had put off and put off again going back to Pennsylvania, one might have expected he could wait a little longer to see his only son married. But he did not. Nor did he subsequently explain why not.

He may have decided, by the summer of 1762, that if he was ever to go home, he had to go now. Until the moment Franklin's ship weighed anchor, William Strahan tried to get him to stay—and nearly succeeded. Franklin told Strahan that it required his most resolute efforts to depart, "in opposition to your almost irresistible eloquence, secretly supported by my own treacherous inclinations." To Lord Kames he wrote from Portsmouth:

> I am now waiting here only for a wind to waft me to America, but cannot leave this happy island and my friends in it without extreme regret, though I am going to a country and a people that I love. I am going from the Old World to the new, and I fancy I feel like those who are leaving this world for the next: grief at the parting, fear of the passage, hope of the future.

If Franklin regretted going, still more did his friends and admirers regret his leaving. "I am very sorry that you intend soon to leave our hemisphere," said David Hume. "America has sent us many good things: gold, silver, sugar, tobacco, indigo &c. But you are the first philosopher, and indeed the first great man of letters for whom we are beholden to her. It is our own fault that we have not kept him; whence it appears that we do not agree with Solomon, that wisdom is above gold, for we take care never to send back an ounce of the latter which we once lay our fingers on."

William Strahan was still more regretful. He sent a letter to David Hall via Franklin, remarking, "This will be brought you by our worthy friend Dr. Franklin, whose face you should never again have seen on your side the water had I been able to prevail upon him to stay, or had my *power* been in any measure equal to my *inclination*." Strahan's letter to Hall afforded a glimpse at the man Strahan and many others in England, including Kames and Hume, considered one of the most remarkable personalities of their day.

> Though his talents and abilities in almost every branch of human science are singularly great and uncommon, and have added to the pleasure and knowledge of the greatest geniuses of this country, who all admire and love him, and lament his departure, yet he

knows as well how to condescend to those of inferior capacity, how to level himself for the time to the understandings of his company, and to enter without affectation into their amusements and chit-chat, that his whole acquaintance here are his affectionate friends.

As for myself, I never found a person in my whole life more thoroughly to my mind. As far as my knowledge or experience or sentiments of every kind could reach his more enlarged sagacity and conceptions, they exactly corresponded with his; or if I accidentally differed from him in any particular, he quickly and with great facility and good nature poured in such light upon the subject as immediately convinced me I was wrong.

Strahan mourned Franklin's departure as akin to an untimely death and cherished the hope that his friend would soon return to Britain. Yet if fate decreed otherwise, Strahan knew that Franklin would always be "an honour to his country and an ornament to human nature."

15

Rising in the West

1762–64

↷ Franklin left England as full-blooded a Briton
as he had ever been. By his own testimony he intended to
return, permanently. He wrote to Strahan just prior
to leaving, "I shall probably make but this one vibration
and settle here forever. Nothing will prevent it, if I can,
as I hope I can, prevail with Mrs. F. to accompany
me, especially if we have a peace."

Franklin's inquisitive mind craved stimulation, consistently gravitating toward whatever community of intellects asked the most intriguing questions; his expansive temperament sought souls that resonated with his own generosity and sense of virtue. In five years in England he had found more of both than in a lifetime in America. "Of all the enviable things England has," he told Polly Stevenson, "I envy most its people. Why should that petty island, which compared to America is but like a stepping stone in a brook, scarce enough of it above water to keep one's shoes dry; why, I say, should that little island enjoy in almost every neighbourhood more sensible, virtuous and elegant minds than we can collect in ranging 100 leagues of our vast forests?" He left such people reluctantly and, he trusted, temporarily.

◦— The voyage home—Franklin's fourth Atlantic passage—was slow but pleasant. The slowness reflected the wartime need to travel in a convoy, which, as convoys do, traveled at the rate of the slowest member. The pleasantness resulted from fair weather, agreeable company, and a delightful three-day stop at Madeira, located on the southern loop to the west, which carried the convoy close to Africa and out of the reach of the Gulf Stream. "It produces not only the fruits of the hot countries, such as oranges, lemons, plantains, bananas, &c. but those of the cold also, as apples, pears and peaches in great perfection," Franklin recorded. "The mountains are excessively high, and rise suddenly from the town, which affords the inhabitants a singular conveniency, that of getting soon out of its heat after they have done their business, and of ascending to what climate or degree of coolness they are pleased to choose, the sides of the mountains being filled with their country boxes at different heights." Grapes were in season at the time of Franklin's visit; he and his shipmates took on numerous bunches, which they hung from the ceiling of the ship's cabin and plucked for dessert after dinner for weeks afterward.

Franklin may have envied England its people, but he would have been churlish to complain of the welcome he received from the people of Pennsylvania. Rumors had arisen during his last year in England that he had fallen somewhat out of favor with his home folks; foremost of the rumormongers was the Reverend William Smith, recently arrived in London with what he retailed as the latest intelligence from the west. Franklin guessed that Smith was spinning stories, but he could not be sure. Now he was. "I arrived here well on the 1st ultimo," Franklin told

Richard Jackson at the beginning of December, "and had the pleasure to find all false that Dr. Smith had reported about the diminution of my friends. My house has been filled with a succession of them from morning to night almost ever since I landed to congratulate me on my return; and I never experienced greater cordiality among them."

If Philadelphians had not changed, Philadelphia had. "I find this city greatly increased in building," he told Jackson. "And they say it is so in numbers of inhabitants." On this last point he did not consider himself the best judge, for his perspective had changed. "To me the streets seem thinner of people, owing perhaps to my being so long accustomed to the bustling crowded streets of London."

The cost of living had greatly increased in the five years Franklin had been gone. "It is more than double in most articles, and in some 'tis treble." For decades Franklin had advocated an expanded currency as a spur to trade; lately the currency had expanded so much the horse had run right out from under the rider. Citing the £800,000 Parliament had spent in Pennsylvania during the war, as well as large paper issues by Pennsylvania and its neighbors, Franklin asserted, "This is such an overproportion of money to the demand for a medium of trade in these countries that it seems from plenty to have lost much of its value. Our tradesmen are grown as idle, and as extravagant in their demands when you would prevail on them to work, as so many Spaniards." Franklin wondered whether something similar might afflict England, now that it led the world in trading. "Your commerce is now become so profitable," he told Jackson, "and naturally brings so much gold and silver into the island, that if you had not now and then some expensive foreign war to draw it off, your country would, like ours, have a plethora in its veins, productive of the same sloth and the same feverish extravagance."

⌐ Franklin was hardly advocating war for the sake of the economy; this last remark was rather a relic from the arguments he had been making in England against an early halt to the war. By the end of 1762 such arguments were unnecessary, for the war was concluding, and to Britain's advantage. Spain had entered the conflict opportunistically late—but also foolishly so, for the revivified British navy soon descended on Cuba and isolated Havana. The city fell in October 1762. Franklin described the victory as "a conquest of the greatest importance." Yet Canada was more important, and Franklin feared that the earlier victory in the north would be frittered away. Pointing out the expense of the Havana campaign, in which thousands of British soldiers died of disease, he said that the success there would help Britain achieve favorable terms of peace—"if John Bull does not get drunk with victory, double his fists, and bid all the world kiss his a——e till he provokes them to drub him again into his senses."

John Bull sobered up shortly. In November his negotiators initialed preliminary articles of peace with France and Spain; the following February the treaty became definitive.

Having taken such a strenuous part in the debate over the terms of peace, Franklin naturally and anxiously awaited details of the accord. To his delight he learned that on the issue of compelling concern west of the Atlantic and north of the Caribbean, the British negotiators had held firm. Canada, won in war, would be British in peace. With Canada came the eastern half of Louisiana, between the Appalachian Mountains and the Mississippi, including the Ohio Valley. France would get back Martinique and Guadeloupe. Havana was returned to Spain, but Britain kept Florida.

Franklin greeted the settlement with enthusiasm. It was a "glorious peace," he said, "the most advantageous to Great Britain, in my opinion, of any our history has recorded." "Throughout this continent," he told William Strahan, "I find it universally approved and applauded." Franklin had been proud before of his Britishness; he was now nearly bursting. "The glory of Britain was never higher than at present."

Franklin was more than happy to include the new young king in his encomiums. Britain, he said, "never had a better prince." In his excitement Franklin went so far as to compare the prince of this peace to the Prince of Peace. Franklin's informants in London described certain mumblings against George III; whence the complaints?, he asked an English correspondent rhetorically.

> I can give but one answer. The King of the Universe, good as he is, is not cordially beloved and faithfully served by all his subjects. I wish I could say that half mankind, as much as they are obliged to him for his continual favours, were among the truly loyal. 'Tis a shame that the very goodness of a prince should be an encouragement to affronts. An answer now occurs to me, for that question of Robinson Crusoe's Man Friday, which I once thought unanswerable, *Why God no kill the Devil?* It is to be found in the Scottish proverb: *Ye'd do little for God an the Deel were dead.*

Franklin put the matter slightly differently to Strahan. "Grumblers there will always be among you, where power and places are worth striving for, and those who cannot obtain them are angry with all that stand in their way. Such would have clamoured against a ministry not their particular friends even if instead of Canada and Louisiana they had obtained a cession of the Kingdom of Heaven."

Franklin left the kingdom of heaven to the hereafter; he concentrated on empires of this earth. And he saw every reason to believe that the empire Britain had built would grow and prosper, especially on the western side of the Atlantic. "Here in America she has laid a broad and strong foundation on which to erect the most beneficial and certain commerce, with the greatness and stability of her empire." In his Canada pamphlet he had argued that Britain could return the sugar islands to France with impunity; the treaty, he believed, bore him out. "While we retain our superiority at sea, and are suffered to grow numerous and strong in North America, I cannot but look on the places left or restored to our enemies on this side the ocean as so many pledges for their good behaviour. Those places will hereafter be so much in our power that the more valuable they are to the possessors, the more cautious will they naturally be of giving us offence."

~ Franklin's imperial vision included himself. Since 1754 he had floated proposals for erecting new settlements beyond the mountains to the west. In that year, as part of the thinking that produced his Albany Plan of union, he advocated the establishment of two colonies between the Ohio River and the Great Lakes. Such colonies would appeal to the chronic land hunger of Americans (Franklin described the "many thousands of families that are ready to swarm, wanting more land"); at the same time they would forestall the French, subdue the Indians, and buffer the colonies of the seaboard from the turbulence of the frontier.

The war that broke out that summer prevented any action on Franklin's proposal, even as it underscored the advantages he described. During the nine years of the Seven Years' War, western settlement did not simply stop but was reversed; Americans at war's end were hungrier than ever for cheap land. The French were banished from Canada and the Ohio but not from beyond the Mississippi; British settlements on the eastern bank of that mighty river would help keep them beyond it. The Indians, though less troublesome in the absence of the French than in their presence, remained a potential source of friction; new settlements would encourage the aborigines to embrace an English fate.

And what would be good for the British empire might be very good for Franklin. Perhaps the rising price of nearly everything in Pennsylvania worried him; perhaps the life he led in England enhanced his tastes; perhaps the bug that bit almost everybody in America in position to be bitten found his soft spot—but for whatever reason, Franklin determined to speculate in western lands. While in England he had discussed a speculative scheme with John Sargent, a member of Parliament and a director of the Bank of England, and Sir Matthew Featherstone, a principal in the East India Company and also a presence in the Bank of England (and a fellow of Franklin's in the Royal Society). The idea was that Sargent and Featherstone would use their influence with those who counted in England and apply for a land grant; Franklin would stroke the egos that needed stroking in America. At the time Franklin left London, the scheme was afoot but not moving very fast. "I know not how that application goes on, or if it is like to succeed," he told Richard Jackson. Jackson by now had been elected to Commons himself; Franklin kindly offered to include him in the land deal. The offer reflected Franklin's generosity but also his estimate that recent reversals in British politics— in particular the resignation of Featherstone's sponsor, the Duke of Newcastle—had weakened the speculators politically. "I think it rather probable that it may fail," Franklin said of the project.

Simultaneously he found a second road west. In 1629 Charles I, in a fit of political magnanimity and geographic ignorance, had granted to Sir Robert Heath an enormous tract of land extending from the 31st parallel to the 36th and from the Atlantic Ocean to the South Sea (the Pacific). For various reasons Heath made nothing of his claim, which, by a series of deaths and purchases, passed to the sons of Daniel Coxe of New Jersey. The sons, Franklin's contemporaries, hoped to make good the original claim—or as much as was feasible after 150 years and the establishment of the Carolinas and Georgia on the old Heath claim.

The Coxe sons, William and Daniel, appealed to Franklin for help. They asked him to recommend someone in England to defend their claim or arrange for them to receive other territory in compensation for it. Cash compensation might be acceptable in lieu of land. They were prepared to offer the person thus engaged the option to purchase for £5,000 half of what they received.

Franklin agreed to help them find such a representative—for a fee of his own. He told the Coxe brothers he knew just their man: Richard Jack-

son. "I have assured them that no one was more capable, or would be better disposed to serve them, than yourself," Franklin wrote Jackson. Then
he recommended the brothers—and himself—to Jackson: "If this application of Messieurs Coxe should succeed, which, from its great equity may
I think be very reasonably expected, I would very willingly engage with
you and those gentlemen, and any others you may think proper to associate with you, and take a fifth of the half Messrs. Coxe offer in their letter
to you, upon the terms there mentioned; and shall use all my diligence and
all my interest in these colonies to promote a speedy settlement."

Franklin went on to suggest bringing John Pringle into the plan.
Franklin liked Pringle but especially valued Pringle's tie to Bute. In regis-
tering confidence that Jackson would know whom to approach, Franklin
said, "I would only request you to offer a share to my good friend Dr.
Pringle, as, if the affair succeeds it may be advantageous to him whom I
much desire to serve, and I have reason to think he has an interest that
may greatly facilitate the application."

Time was of the essence. Franklin sent Jackson a four-year-old article
from a New Jersey magazine promoting a scheme to settle a new colony
on the Ohio, and projecting the eager emigration thereto of ten thousand
families. This enthusiasm was in spite of expectations then that the
French would continue to control Canada. "Now that power is reduced,"
Franklin said, "we may suppose people are much more willing to go into
those countries. And in fact there appears every where an unaccountable
penchant in all our people to migrate westward." Within the week of writing these words, Franklin received reports of other settlement schemes.
He postscripted Jackson: "We must strike while the iron is hot."

〜 **Franklin's** closest partner in his land schemes would be his son,
William, who arrived from England with his bride in the dead of February 1763 after a stormy Atlantic crossing. William and Betsy stayed with
Franklin and Debbie and Sally for three days before William and Franklin
ventured over the frozen Delaware River to New Jersey. (Betsy waited for
warmer weather.) Father and son spent the first night at Trenton, the
next at New Brunswick. Several inquisitive gentlemen in sleighs met
the new governor on the road to Perth Amboy, the more eastern of the
province's twin capitals and the one in which William took his oath of
office. Despite the bad weather, the ceremony brought out the leading
figures of the province, who wished the new man well. Governor and

father proceeded to Princeton, where the president of the College of New Jersey congratulated the two together by commending the governor for his education "under the influence and direction of the very eminent Doctor Franklin."

The citizens of Burlington, New Jersey's other capital, were even more generous in their welcome than those of Perth Amboy—hoping to persuade the new governor to make his residence there. Bonfires burned far into the night; church bells rang; volleys of gunfire echoed along the frozen streets. And where would the governor be staying? the event's organizers asked. William declined to commit.

His father could not have been prouder. "I am just returned from a journey I made with him through his government," Franklin told William Strahan, "and had the pleasure of seeing him every where received with the utmost respect and even affection by all ranks of people. So that I have great hopes of his being now comfortably settled."

∽ Franklin had his own official duties to tend. During his absence in England he had kept his job as deputy postmaster general for North America. Holding office in absentia was nothing unusual in the British empire in those days, when governors and other officials often managed for years at a time never to visit the territories under their care. That Franklin had a fellow deputy postmaster, William Hunter of Virginia, and a competent comptroller, James Parker of New York (taking the post previously held by William Franklin), eased both the task of directing the mails from a distance and the portion of his conscience that needed easing. Yet his conscience was not so calm that he did not feel obliged to cultivate his superiors in London on a regular basis, and to worry at times that his falling-out with the Penns might cost him his post-office job.

Another element that assuaged his conscience was the fact that at the time he left Philadelphia for London—after holding the postmaster's position for four years—he still had not made any money at it. He and William Hunter had great hopes that their various improvements would pay for themselves and more, but until they did, the money came out of the postmasters' pockets. By Franklin's accounting, at the time he left for London the post office owed him and Hunter some £900.

Eventually the accounts improved, although not soon enough to yield full benefit to Hunter, who died in 1761. Franklin initially hoped Hunter would not be replaced—that the joint postmastership would become a sole occupancy. He reminded his superior, the Earl of Bessborough, that his commission specified that upon the death of either himself or Hunter, full powers would pass to the survivor. "Notwithstanding the decease of Mr. Hunter," he wrote, "there is properly no vacancy; unless you should think fit to make one by revoking that commission, which, when my long and faithful service of 24 years in the Post Office is considered, I hope will not be done." Franklin touted the improvements he and Hunter had made, hinted—not inaccurately—that they were mostly his doing, and expressed the desire that "now that in the course of things some additional advantage seems to be thrown in my way, I cannot but hope it will not be taken from me in favour of a stranger to the office."

His hopes were vain. The governor of Virginia, who had better connections than Franklin did, was not about to let this piece of patronage escape. In November 1761 Franklin learned that his new joint deputy postmaster would be John Foxcroft, lately secretary to the Virginia governor.

Franklin thereupon laid plans to meet with Foxcroft and review their partnership. The peace with France made the meeting more necessary, for upon war's end certain innovations became possible, others necessary. The necessary ones included the extension of Franklin and Foxcroft's territory to Canada; they were now responsible for delivery of the mail to Montreal, Quebec, and beyond. According to the rate schedule posted by Parliament, a single-sheet letter from New York to Montreal must be delivered for two shillings. (For comparison, a similar letter from Philadelphia to London, which benefited from the subsidies supporting the government packet ships, cost one shilling.) Whether Franklin and Foxcroft could make any money at those rates was one of the issues they had to discuss.

Another innovation was the commencement of night travel for postal riders. On certain central routes—from New York to Philadelphia, for example—this allowed an expeditiousness of delivery that would not be surpassed even two centuries later. A Philadelphia writer could post a letter for New York one day and receive a reply back the next.

Implementing these and other innovations required personal oversight; to this end Franklin embarked in the late spring of 1763 on a tour of his postal domain that lasted nearly five months. Foxcroft met him at Philadelphia; thence they traveled through New Jersey, where they were entertained by the governor. They spent several days in New York City before embarking for New England. Unusually hot weather convinced them to travel by water rather than overland, causing them to miss Connecticut on the way to Newport, Rhode Island. From there they took a coach to Boston, which became their base for journeys to nearby towns and villages.

Franklin joined post-office business to personal pleasure. Sally accompanied him most of the way; he was delighted to introduce her to her New England kin and them to her. Sally turned twenty in Boston; the trip also served as something of a coming-out for an eligible young woman.

In visiting with his sister Jane Mecom and reflecting on how few of their large family remained alive, Franklin doubtless reflected on his own mortality. Two unanticipated events of the trip made him feel more mortal than ever. In July in Rhode Island he managed to be pitched from the open chaise in which he was riding and to fall heavily on his right shoulder. Fortunately the house of Katy Ray, now Catharine Ray Greene, and her husband, William, was not far away, and he recuperated there. A month later he fell again, reinjured the shoulder, and was confined to bed and chair for much of his Boston visit—which for this reason persisted longer than expected. "I am not yet able to travel rough roads," he explained to Katy Greene in September, "and must lie by a while, as I can neither hold reins nor whip with my right hand till it grows stronger."

The lying-by lasted till October. Franklin, fifty-seven now and beginning to feel his age, healed slowly. Luckily Jane Mecom and her neighbors could tend to him—but this was a mixed blessing, as he alluded in a letter to her from Philadelphia following his eventual arrival back home. He explained that his shoulder still hurt (as it would for many more months) but was better than before. "I am otherwise very happy in being home, where I am allowed to know when I have eaten enough and drank enough, am warm enough, and sit in a place that I like, &c. and nobody pretends to know what I feel better than I do myself." Lest this gentle jibe give the wrong impression, he immediately added, "Don't imagine that I am a whit the less sensible of the kindness I experienced among my friends in New England. I am very thankful for it, and shall always retain a grateful remembrance of it."

⟳ "Now I am returned from my long journeys which have consumed the whole summer, I shall apply myself to such a settlement of all my affairs as will enable me to do what your friendship so warmly urges." Franklin was writing to Strahan, and what Strahan's friendship was urging was what it had been urging for years: for Franklin to relocate to London. "I have a great opinion of your wisdom . . ." Franklin said, "and am apt to think that what you seem so clear in, and are so earnest about, must be right; though I own that I sometimes suspect my love to England and my friends there seduces me a little, and makes my own middling reasons for going over appear very good ones. We shall see in a little time how things will turn out."

How things turned out depended in part on Debbie. As before, she adamantly resisted any transatlantic transplantation. She had been born in Philadelphia, had grown up in Philadelphia, intended to die in Philadelphia. Nothing Franklin said could change her mind.

Yet that did not quite resolve the issue. Over the years Franklin and Debbie had learned to get along without the physical presence of each other. Her letters to him in England have been lost, but from his responses she does not appear to have complained particularly at his absence. That he spent five years apart from her, and then another five months not long after his return, suggests that for all his sentimental attachment to home and hearth, the attachment did not run very deep.

Moreover, he had missed Sally as much as he had missed her mother, and now that Sally was of marriageable age, that tie to home grew more tenuous. By all odds Sally would be another man's responsibility before long. Her father would continue to care about her, but—as his relationship with his own parents had demonstrated—his was an affection able to sustain itself at a distance.

In 1763 Franklin contracted with a builder to construct a house for him and Debbie. Until this point in their married life the two had always lived in rented quarters; for the first time the Franklins would own the roof that sheltered them. William Franklin interpreted the hammering and sawing as evidence that his father had come home to stay. "My mother is so averse to going to sea," William told Strahan, "that I believe my father will never be induced to see England again. He is now building a house to live in himself."

As events would demonstrate, William was not the best judge of his father's mind (nor the father of the son's). William may have been right that Franklin aimed to settle into his new house forever; he may have been wrong. Like many another renter in inflationary times, Franklin may have decided for financial reasons that owning beat renting. He may also have had in mind that Debbie ought to have a house of her own even if—*especially* if—her husband did not always occupy it with her.

The most likely explanation of the discrepancy between Franklin's words and his actions is that he simply did not know what he was going to do. He loved England and longed to rejoin his friends there; he also loved Debbie, after his fashion, and Philadelphia. Nothing now forced

him to choose between the two sides of the Atlantic, and until something
did, he would not.

∽ **Meanwhile** he insisted on being apprised of events in London.
"I expected when I left England to have learnt in your letters the true
state of things from time to time among you, but you are silent and I am
in the dark," he chided Strahan. The papers carried reports of faction,
even sedition, in court and Parliament. What was the true story? "Think,
my dear friend, how much satisfaction 'tis in your power to give me, with
the loss only of half an hour in a month that you would otherwise spend
at cribbage."

"Not an hour have I spent on cribbage since you left us, nor shall it
cost me one till you return, which I hope you still *seriously* think of," answered Strahan. All the same, Franklin's friend devoted a long letter to
lamenting the sorry state of British politics. In the process he may have
undermined Franklin's inclination to return—a consequence that, anticipated, may have been a reason for Strahan's reticence.

Strahan interpreted events of which Franklin had read. The most
shocking of these events—shocking to conventional opinion, at any
rate—was the inexplicable emergence of one of the most scurrilous
characters—again the conventional judgment—to cross the stage of
British politics in the eighteenth century. John Wilkes was a well-educated,
uncommonly ugly man with a frightful squint who nonetheless, through
wicked wit and ribald humor, managed to charm persons of both sexes.
He himself liked to say it took him half an hour to "talk away his face"
with any woman, but then she was his. He may have overstated his
persuasiveness, but on the evidence of his conquests, not excessively.
Among his male acquaintances Edward Gibbon declared that Wilkes had
"inexhaustible spirits, infinite wit and humour, and a great deal of knowledge." Samuel Johnson said, "Jack has a great variety of talk, Jack is a
scholar, Jack is a gentleman." Johnson's biographer, James Boswell, asserted that Wilkes had "an elasticity of mind that nothing can crush."

Wilkes's private life was a scandal in an age and a city not easily scan-
dalized; reports regularly circulated of his participation, with a group
called the "Medmenham Monks" (alternatively the "Hell-fire Club"), in
orgies of the most obscene character in the ruins of the abbey at Medmenham. The order broke up when Wilkes released a baboon, dressed as
the devil, in the middle of a prayer to Satan by one of the members, who

went nearly insane upon seeing his prayer answered so swiftly and in the flesh.

Wilkes habitually skewered his critics with verbal thrusts, more than one of which were appropriated by subsequent sharp tongues. After Wilkes entered politics a constituent vowed he would vote for the devil over Wilkes. "Naturally," retorted Wilkes. "But if your friend is not standing, may I hope for your support?" The Earl of Sandwich predicted that Wilkes would die on the gallows or of venereal disease. "That depends, my lord," Wilkes replied, "on whether I embrace your principles or your mistress."

Wilkes entered Parliament in 1757 but made little splash until five years later, when he began publishing a paper called *The North Briton*. With the encouragement of William Pitt and others in opposition, Wilkes ridiculed Bute and the ministry he headed. The Paris peace treaty became a particular target. "It is certainly the peace of God for it passeth all understanding," Wilkes declared in the fifth issue of *The North Briton*. Bute could not abide the criticism, and retired from office in early 1763. (Lord Shelburne was not surprised, observing of Bute that despite being "proud, pompous, imposing," he was "the greatest political coward I ever knew.") Wilkes's triumph raised questions as to what he would do next. On a visit to Paris he was asked by Madame de Pompadour how far freedom of the press extended in England. "I do not know, madame," Wilkes replied. "But I am trying to find out."

He did, soon. Wilkes typically attacked by indirection, denying some low rumor about a minister but in the process publicizing it—if not simply creating it. He modified this approach in the forty-fifth issue of *The North Briton*, an issue of that journal that became as famous, or notorious, as any single publication in the history of English-language journalism. The occasion of Wilkes's latest blast was a speech from the throne proroguing Parliament in the wake of Bute's resignation. Wilkes took a large swipe at the king even as he disclaimed doing so. "The King's speech," he wrote, "has always been considered by the legislature, and by the public at large, as the speech of the Minister." The minister in question was the new premier, George Grenville, whom Wilkes accused of putting falsehoods in the mouth of the king. The speech asserted that the Paris treaty was honorable to the Crown and beneficial to the people; this was a lie, Wilkes alleged. The speech asserted that the peace was beneficial to Britain's allies; another lie, Wilkes asserted. The treaty had been ratified not on its merits but by bribery, Wilkes claimed. The chief culprit—Bute—had been forced from office, but the current ministers were no better: "tools of despotism and corruption." Summarizing, Wilkes registered indignation and wonder that "a prince of so many great and amiable qualities" could be persuaded "to give the sanction of his sacred name to the most odious measures, and to the most unjustified public declarations."

Whatever *The North Briton* Number 45 said about Grenville and the other ministers, it put George in the position of choosing between being a ventriloquist's dummy and a liar. The king felt no obligation to accept such a choice; instead he signed a general warrant (one that did not name a particular individual) for the arrest of those responsible for the publication of the noxious issue. The charge was seditious libel. The sweep yielded more than two score prisoners before Wilkes was apprehended. He was clapped in irons and tossed into the Tower of London.

But the arrests backfired. A judge freed Wilkes on grounds that his arrest violated his immunity as a member of Parliament. Juries threw out charges against the other prisoners. Wilkes and the others sued the ministers who signed the general warrant; Wilkes won £1,000, while several others received smaller amounts, and the use of general warrants was declared illegal.

But Wilkes's scrapes were far from over. Some years earlier he had collaborated on an obscene, blasphemous, and likely libelous parody of Pope's *Essay on Man*, entitled *Essay on Woman*. Through theft and bribery the authorities acquired copies of the proof sheets. These were read to Parliament, with some gusto, by Lord Sandwich, formerly a Wilkes ally but now a member of the government. ("Satan preaching against sin," remarked one listener of Sandwich's performance.) Wilkes's ouster from Parliament seemed certain, prosecution probable. Hoping to add injury to insult, a partisan of Bute's challenged Wilkes to a duel. Wilkes was considerably less skilled with pistol than pen; moreover, his challenger had been practicing. This was frowned upon among gentlemen, but few gentlemen were willing to include Wilkes among their number.

Yet the masses loved him. Mobs crowded the streets shouting "Wilkes and Liberty!"; the scrawled numeral "45" decorated walls across the city. Nor did enthusiasm diminish when Wilkes, assessing the weight of the forces arrayed against him, decamped from London on Christmas Eve of 1763 and fled to France. Three weeks later he was formally expelled from Commons; the following month a (specific) warrant was sworn out for his arrest. When he refused to return to England he was officially declared an outlaw. And thus was completed, according to the *Annual Register*, "the ruin of that unfortunate gentleman."

⌐ Events would reveal the gross prematurity of this judgment, but it was one Franklin shared. Writing at the time of Wilkes's expulsion from Parliament, Franklin told Richard Jackson he was "pleased to find a just resentment so general in your House against Mr. W.'s seditious conduct."

Gratified though he was at Wilkes's comeuppance, Franklin could hardly take comfort from other developments in British politics. Strahan, as promised, provided Franklin a firsthand view. Bute's fall, Strahan asserted, was richly deserved. "I am sorry to tell you that my countryman [both were Scots] has shewn himself altogether unequal to his high station. Never did a ministry, in our memory, discover so much weakness. They seem to have neither spirit, courage, sense, nor activity, and are a rope of sand." Pitt, the leader of the opposition, was no better. Citing recent insults the former prime minister had hurled against constituents who differed with him on the merits of the peace treaty, Strahan said, "Did you ever before hear of such an instance of arrogance?" Strahan went on to call Pitt "this imperious tribune of the people," a man "of whose honesty I entertain no good opinion, and whom I strongly suspect to be a secret abettor and fomentor of the present unreasonable discontents, and of that contempt with which the king and his government hath of late been treated."

Strahan saw little prospect of improvement. The "jaws of faction" were closing on the king, who was well meaning but "not possessed of any striking talents or any great degree of sagacity." Strahan closed gloomily: "In my mind the danger is greater than most people seem to apprehend."

Such a statement from the most ardent advocate of Franklin's relocation to England could not but call the project into question. "Surely you would not wish me to come and live among such people," Franklin said half jokingly. "You would rather remove hither, where we have no savages but those we expect to be such."

Yet Franklin hoped for better, as he usually did. "I think your madmen will ere long come to their senses, and when I come I shall find you generally wise and happy."

⌐ If Strahan spied danger in political corruption, Richard Jackson detected it in political reform. At the end of the war with France and

Spain the Grenville ministry undertook to reorganize the finances of the empire and reinstitute responsibility where profligacy had reigned. Government debt had reached record levels, largely from the cost of the war. Government spending, which included enormous sums devoted to debt service, was projected for 1764 at twice what it had been just twenty-five years earlier. Grenville, head of the Treasury as well as premier, scrutinized both sides of the ledger in seeking a solution to the country's financial problems; he would raise revenues even as he curtailed expenditures.

Revenues meant taxes. Inhabitants of Britain paid a discouraging diversity of taxes, of which the most important were property taxes, import taxes, and excise taxes. By the end of the war the British people bore about all the taxes they or their leaders thought they could stand; indeed, an excise on cider touched off demonstrations in Exeter and the burning of Bute in effigy.

If Britons in Britain could not be made to pay more, perhaps Britons across the sea could be. From the east side of the Atlantic the Americans looked like the chief winners of the war, which freed them from fear of the French. They were taxed lightly by British standards, and little of what they paid went to imperial purposes, broadly construed. It certainly occurred to Grenville and others contemplating new sources of revenue that the Americans, unlike those boisterous cider-makers in Exeter, could not vote for members of Parliament. This rendered new American taxes constitutionally suspect, in that a cardinal tenet of English constitutionalism insisted that taxes could be levied only by the representatives of those who would pay. But it made such taxes politically tempting. If the Americans complained, who would be listening?

As part of the Grenville program, Charles Townshend, the president of the Board of Trade, proposed a change in the duty on molasses imported into America from non-British sources—meaning, for the most part, the French and Spanish West Indies. For thirty years the tax had been six pence per gallon; Townshend recommended a reduction to two pence. This may have seemed like a gift to the Americans but decidedly was not. At six pence the duty had been widely evaded, via smuggling and bribery of customs officials; at two pence importers might actually pay it, for honesty would then become competitive with criminality. It would certainly be so if, as London threatened, it cracked down on bribery in the customs ranks and sent warships to patrol the coasts.

"I fear something relating to America will be done very much against my opinion," Jackson wrote Franklin regarding the molasses proposal. "But I shall endeavour to prevent it by all the means in my power both in the House and out of the House." The government and British molasses-makers were too strong to prevent some such change as Townshend proposed, but Jackson would try to mitigate the ill effects. "I shall only say that though I wish the duty on foreign molasses was but 1 *d.* I shall not oppose a duty of 2 *d.* a gallon."

In the event, Jackson's efforts were not simply unsuccessful but perhaps counterproductive. By the time the Townshend proposal became the Sugar Act of 1764, the duty on foreign molasses had been increased to three pence per gallon. The measure also levied a fee on foreign wine and certain luxury goods, including silk from the East Indies.

Franklin was phlegmatic about the change. He understood London's logic in lowering the molasses tax. "A moderate duty on foreign molasses may be collected, when a high one could not," he told Jackson. At the time he wrote, duties on tea and slaves were under consideration, along with those on molasses and wine; Franklin thought such taxes could benefit both the character and commerce of the empire. "A duty not only on tea but on all East India goods might perhaps not be amiss, as they are generally rather luxuries than necessaries, and many of your Manchester manufactures might well supply their places. The duty on Negroes I could wish large enough to obstruct their importation, as they everywhere prevent the increase of Whites."

Although an imprudent ministry and Parliament might get carried away with taxing the colonies, Franklin hoped for prudence—or, more specifically, an appreciation that the interests of the empire subsumed, but need not subordinate, those of the colonies. "If you lay such duties as may destroy our trade with the foreign colonies, I think you will greatly hurt your own interest as well as ours," he said. He elaborated: "I am not much alarmed about your schemes of raising money on us. You will take care for your own sakes not to lay greater burthens on us than we can bear; for you cannot hurt us without hurting your selves. All our profits center with you, and the more you take from us, the less we can lay out with you."

↶ As **neither** an importer of molasses nor a heavy consumer of the rum into which the molasses was made, Franklin fretted little over the Sugar Act. (He preferred milk punch, made with brandy.) But as a student of population growth, an expansive imperialist, and a promoter of settlement schemes, he remained intensely interested in the question of land.

Americans—including Franklin—interpreted the end of the war as the beginning of a new age of expansion, across the mountains and into the valleys of the Ohio and the Mississippi. Two other interested parties took a different view. The British government, having just finished a long and expensive war that began on the American frontier, had no desire to let the frontier trigger another such war. To be sure, the French were no longer as able to provoke unrest among the Indians as formerly, but the English (and Scottish and German) settlers had shown themselves sufficiently provocative on their own. The best way to minimize such provocations, it seemed to Grenville and his associates, was to insulate the Indians and the settlers from each other. To this end the government issued a proclamation in October 1763 placing the transmontane territories essentially off-limits to settlement.

The Proclamation of 1763 came too late to mollify the third party interested in the question of western lands—the party, in fact, most interested of all. If the defeat of the French augured peace and cheap land for the English, it did so at the expense of the Indians. As long as two imperial powers had vied for control of North America, the Indians had been able to play one against the other; now, with but one imperial power, the Indians were at that power's mercy. To what extent the Indians appreciated that London wished to protect them against the Americans is unclear; considering their experience of the last few decades they might have been forgiven for thinking all English acted alike. In any event, while the British government prepared the proclamation it would make regarding the American west, the Indians launched a war against the settlers.

Almost at once the war became associated with the name of Pontiac, an Ottawa chief of uncertain origins but undeniable ambition and charisma. Pontiac invoked the Great Spirit, as translated by a mystic called the Delaware Prophet, in calling for Indians to return to their traditional ways and drive out the invaders. One account (historically problematic, to be sure, in that it was fourth hand, quoting Pontiac quoting the Delaware Prophet quoting God) caught the gist of the message:

> Why do you suffer the white man to dwell among you? My children, you have forgotten the customs and traditions of your forefathers. Why do you not clothe yourselves in skins, as they did, and use the bows and arrows, and the stone-pointed lances, which they used? You have bought guns, knives, kettles, and blankets from the white men, until you can no longer do without them; and, what is worse, you have drunk the poison fire-water, which turns you into fools. Fling all these away; live as your wise fore-

fathers lived before you. And as for these English—these dogs dressed in red, who have come to rob you of your hunting grounds and drive away the game—you must lift the hatchet against them. Wipe them from the face of the earth. And then you will have my favor back again, and once more be happy and prosperous.

The message caught on. The fighting between British and French had hardly ended before fighting erupted between British and the Indians under Pontiac. During the spring and summer of 1763 Pontiac's forces swept through the region of the Ohio and the Great Lakes, capturing half a dozen British forts and besieging British garrisons at Detroit and Pittsburgh. The British commander for North America, General Jeffrey Amherst, was sufficiently alarmed to suggest employing biological warfare against Pontiac's soldiers, in the form of smallpox-laced blankets. Whether the local commander complied is unclear (like others in similar positions, Colonel Henry Bouquet feared that his own troops would succumb to the germ attack).

Reports of the new war in the west reached Franklin at New York on his postal journey in the summer of 1763. Amherst, aware of Franklin's experience with Indians, summoned him for an interview. Underestimating the seriousness of Pontiac's offensive, the British general judged it a vestige of the French war that would subside once word got out to the Indians that England was now the master of the continent.

Franklin did not deny this explanation but deemed it incomplete. The source of the trouble touched the fundamental relationship between Indians and whites, he said. "The Indians are disgusted that so little notice has lately been taken of them, and are particularly offended that rum is prohibited [not all the Indians followed the Prophet in forswearing alcohol], and powder dealt among them so sparingly. They have received no presents. And the plan of preventing war among them, and bringing them to live by agriculture, they resent as an attempt to make women of them, as they phrase it, it being the business of women only to cultivate the ground. Their men are all warriors."

Yet this interpretation did not prompt Franklin to advocate a more moderate policy toward the Indians, at least not under current circumstances. Indeed he recommended just the opposite. "We stooped too much in begging the last peace of them, which has made them vain and insolent. . . . We should never mention peace to them again till we have given them some severe blows and made them feel some ill consequences of breaking with us."

British troops belatedly delivered the blows Franklin spoke of. In August, Bouquet smote the Indians at the battle of Bushy Run and rescued Pittsburgh; three months later, Pontiac dropped the siege of Detroit. An uncertain peace settled upon the Pennsylvania hinterland.

Franklin worried that the peace, such as it was, came too soon. "I only fear they have not smarted enough to make them careful how they break with us again."

◦— Many of Franklin's Pennsylvania compatriots felt the same way. Some of them attempted, in the most brutal fashion, to make the peace more permanent.

If the Paris treaty had not seemed to promise an end to the warfare that had plagued the frontier for a generation, the Pontiac uprising might not have provoked the overreaction it did. But to settlers who looked for a respite from the terror and guerrilla warfare, the renewal of fighting came as a heartbreaking last straw. In December 1763 a band of armed frontiersmen from the town of Paxton, on the Susquehanna River, descended on a small community of Indians living on the proprietors' Conestoga Manor near Lancaster. Reports had indicated the presence of arms among Conestoga Indians; rumors suggested that an Indian implicated in recent raids was hiding there. The Paxtonites did not tarry long with questions; instead they massacred the six Indians unfortunate enough to be at home, and burned the village to the ground.

The other fourteen Indian members of the (very small) Conestoga community were thereupon taken into protective custody in Lancaster. Tragically for them, the custody afforded insufficient protection, and on December 27 the Paxton mob battered down the doors of the workhouse that provided their refuge, and murdered them all: men, women, and children.

The Lancaster County massacres shocked even those Pennsylvanians not especially sympathetic to the Indians; the shock intensified when the Paxton mob threatened to march on Philadelphia. Some weeks earlier a group of Indians living among the Moravians near Bethlehem had been accused of abetting the recent uprising. The Pennsylvania government encouraged these "Moravian Indians" to take refuge near the provincial capital. More than a hundred accepted the offer. The Paxtonites, hot with the lust of killing, vowed to dispatch all these Indians—and anyone who tried to prevent them.

As his earlier remarks revealed, Franklin shed no tears for warpath Indians, but this murder of innocents appalled him. And the threat the Paxton mob posed to government and order dismayed him almost beyond bearing. A man of reason, he saw reason being challenged by the darkest, bloodiest forces of unreason.

At first he took up pen. Near the end of January he wrote *A Narrative of the Late Massacres in Lancaster County, of a Number of Indians, Friends of This Province*. The pamphlet was quickly published and began circulating.

Franklin never wrote a more emotional piece. To some degree his lamentations were calculated, designed to impress on readers the terrible wrong inflicted not only on the unfortunate victims of the violence but on society itself. But without doubt the murders troubled him deeply. Much of his philosophy of life was based on the premise that human nature was, if not perfectible, at least improvable. That such savage acts could be perpetrated, with apparent impunity, in his own Pennsylvania, by his fellow Pennsylvanians, hit at the heart of this premise.

Franklin reminded readers that the Conestoga Indians were descendants of the Indians who welcomed the first settlers in Pennsylvania, with gifts of venison, corn, and skins. They had peaceably sold land to the settlers and moved to their present community, which had been guaranteed them by the proprietors. "There they have lived many years in friendship with their white neighbours, who loved them for their peaceable inoffensive behaviour."

Franklin identified the victims by name. One very old man, Shehaes, had known William Penn and had sat down to treaty with the original proprietor in 1701. Peggy was Shehaes's daughter: "She worked for her aged father, continuing to live with him, though married, and attended him with filial duty and tenderness." John was "another good old man." John Smith was "a valuable young man," Peggy's husband and father of their three-year-old child (whose name Franklin apparently did not know). Betty was "a harmless old woman." Her son Peter was "a likely young lad." Sally was "a truly good and an amiable woman" with no children of her own; but a relative had died, leaving a child, whom Sally had adopted "to bring up as her own, and performed toward it all the duties of an affectionate parent."

"The reader will observe," Franklin editorialized, "that many of their names are English. It is common with the Indians that have an affection for the English to give themselves, and their children, the names of such English persons as they particularly esteem."

The reader would also note how few the Indians were. "It has always been observed that Indians settled in the neighbourhood of white people do not increase, but diminish continually." At the time of the murders the tribe consisted of twenty souls altogether—by no stretch of the imagination a threat to anyone.

Franklin related the atrocities in heartrending detail. He told how fifty-seven mounted and heavily armed men had ridden down upon Conestoga Manor.

> They surrounded the small village of Indian huts, and at just break of day broke into them all at once. Only three men, two women, and a young boy were found at home, the rest being out among the neighbouring white people, some to sell the baskets, brooms and bowls they manufactured, and others on other occasions. These poor defenceless creatures were immediately fired upon, stabbed and hatcheted to death! The good Shehaes, among the rest, cut to pieces in his bed. All of them were scalped, and otherwise horribly mangled. Then their huts were set on fire, and most of them burnt down. When the troop, pleased with their own conduct and bravery, but enraged that any of the poor Indians had escaped the massacre, rode off.

Nearly all the white people in the neighborhood were shocked and outraged at this display of barbarism, Franklin explained. The magistrates of Lancaster County brought the other members of the tribe under official protection, and the governor of the province ordered a search for the perpetrators.

But the evildoers were undeterred.

> Those cruel men again assembled themselves, and hearing that the remaining fourteen Indians were in the work-house at Lancaster, they suddenly appeared in that town, on the 27th of December. Fifty of them, armed as before, dismounting, went directly to the work-house, and by violence broke open the door and entered, with the utmost fury in their countenances. When the poor wretches saw they had no protection nigh, nor could possibly escape, and being without the least weapon for defence, they divided into their little families, the children clinging to the parents. They fell on their knees, protested their innocence, declared their love to the English, and that, in their whole lives, they had never done them injury; and in this posture they all received the

hatchet! Women and little children—were every one inhumanly murdered!—in cold blood!

The murderers again rode off, again congratulating themselves on their valor. As yet they remained at large, defiant of human and divine authority. "But the wickedness cannot be covered," Franklin promised. "The guilt will lie on the whole land till justice is done on the murderers. THE BLOOD OF THE INNOCENT WILL CRY TO HEAVEN FOR VENGEANCE."

☙ Heaven gave no sign of listening, instead leaving the mortals involved to sort matters out themselves. Franklin's pamphlet struck some readers as melodramatic and factually suspect. How did he know what the Indians said and did in their last moments? The only surviving witnesses were the murderers, and they were not talking. Even so, the pamphlet galvanized opinion against the Paxtonites as they threatened to kill the Moravian Indians. "It would perhaps be vanity in me to imagine so slight a thing could have any extraordinary effect," Franklin told Richard Jackson. "But however that may be, there was a sudden and very remarkable change; and above 1000 of our citizens took arms to support the government in the protection of those poor wretches."

This spur-of-the-moment militia included many Quakers, which amazed Philadelphians who remembered when Friends categorically refused to bear arms. Yet by itself the rally to arms did not end the crisis. With the Paxton Boys, as they were called (doubly misleadingly, in that they were not boys nor all from Paxton), camped at Germantown, the provincial authorities hastened to devise means to keep them at bay. "You may judge what hurry and confusion we have been in for this week past," Franklin told Jackson. "I was up two nights running, all night, with our governor; and my rest so broken by alarms on the other nights that the whole week seems one confused space of time, without any distinction of days." During one alarm the governor ran to Franklin's house at midnight and set up temporary headquarters there. Franklin's suggestions became tantamount to orders. The governor sought to formalize this command by giving Franklin control of the militia, but he declined. "I chose to carry a musket and strengthen his authority."

Yet he did agree to lead a delegation to parley with the Paxton mob. Representatives of the latter listed their grievances, which went beyond what they saw as the harboring of Indian enemies, and included neglect by the provincial government of frontier security, and underrepresentation of the frontier counties in the Assembly. Franklin's delegation agreed to present the grievances to the Assembly and to allow a (carefully supervised) search of the Moravian Indians' camp for Indians involved in recent raids. As Franklin knew it would, all this took time; as he hoped, during that time the fury of the frontiersmen dissipated. They eventually returned to their homes.

It was a partial victory at best. Philadelphia was secure against insurrectionary violence, but the Paxton murderers remained at large.

Under the circumstances a partial victory would have to do. With a certain exhilarated satisfaction Franklin summarized events for John Fothergill in England: "Your old friend was a common soldier, a counsellor, a kind of dictator, an ambassador to the country mob, and on their returning home, *nobody*, again. All this has happened in a few weeks!"

~ The Paxton rising afforded an opportunity for Franklin to reflect on something novel he had recently encountered. In his *Narrative of the Late Massacres* he pointed out that the behavior of the murderers would have put to shame even those considered savages by most Pennsylvanians. He recounted a story he had read of a New Englander marooned on the Guinea coast amid raids by Dutch slavers. A crowd of angry locals wished to vent their anger on the New Englander, the only white man in reach, but another African, who had befriended him and taken him in, refused to let the would-be murderers approach. They must not kill a man that had done no harm, simply for being white, he said. This was wrong, and he would not allow it. They would have to kill him before they killed his guest. "The Negroes," Franklin concluded the story, "seeing his resolution, and convinced by his discourse that they were wrong, went away ashamed."

Franklin might have used this anecdote anyway, because it served his current purpose, but he almost certainly was encouraged to do so by an observation he had made just the previous month, which compelled him to reconsider his perceptions of the African race. Since the visit of George Whitefield to America in 1739, Franklin had supported the idea of Negro education, even as he continued to hold slaves. In this he assumed, with most members of his own race and era, that education might improve black children but could never make them the equal of whites.

A visit to a school run by the Reverend William Sturgeon in Philadelphia changed his mind. The students were bright, cooperative—and promising. As he explained to an English friend, also involved in Negro education:

> They appeared all to have made considerable progress in reading for the time they had respectively been in the school, and most of them answered readily and well the questions of the catechism. They behaved very orderly, and showed a proper respect and ready obedience to the mistress, and seemed very attentive to, and a good deal affected by, a serious exhortation with which Mr. Sturgeon concluded our visit.
>
> I was on the whole much pleased, and from what I then saw, have conceived a higher opinion of the natural capacities of the black race, than I had ever before entertained. Their apprehension seems as quick, their memory as strong, and their docility in every respect equal to that of white children.

Recollecting his audience, Franklin added, "You will wonder perhaps that I should ever doubt it, and I will not undertake to justify all my prejudices, nor to account for them."

Nor in this letter did Franklin undertake to justify that massive social prejudice, slavery, in which he still participated. But having concluded—almost alone among his generation—that blacks were innately equal to whites in matters of intelligence, he had started down the road that would compel him to conclude that slavery was indefensible.

⌐ **Under the guns** of the Paxton mob, Franklin had been willing to make common cause with the governor, but as the mob dispersed, the two men turned upon each other. John Penn was the grandson of William Penn and the nephew of Thomas Penn; like his grandfather he had incurred paternal wrath for youthful indiscretions, in his case a marriage to a young woman the Penn elders deemed below his (and their) station. Like his grandfather he returned to the fold—he sent his wife packing—and prepared to receive his inheritance: his father Richard's quarter of the proprietary rights to Pennsylvania. Thomas and Richard thought the boy would benefit from personal experience of his estate-to-be, and they put him on a ship for Philadelphia, where he served for three years as a member of the provincial council. In this capacity he joined Franklin at

Albany for the 1754 congress. He returned to England for several years before the bribing of William Denny convinced his father and uncle that the only way to guarantee the loyalty of their American deputy was to make him one of them. John Penn was named (lieutenant) governor of Pennsylvania in June 1763; he arrived in Philadelphia in October (to a rare earthquake that rattled the windows of the city and shook down the autumn leaves).

Franklin determined to give the young man—who was thirty-four on arrival—a fair hearing. The first meetings went well enough. "He is civil, and I endeavoured to fail in no point of respect," Franklin told Peter Collinson. "So I think we shall have no personal difference; at least I will give no occasion. For though I cordially dislike and despise the uncle, for demeaning himself so far as to back-bite and abuse me to friends and to strangers, as you well know he does, I shall keep that account open with him only."

Franklin was fooling himself if he thought John Penn would not take personally Franklin's attacks on Thomas Penn, which of course he did. By the spring of 1764 the governor was writing lurid letters home regarding the "rank abuse" of the proprietors and identifying Franklin as the "chief cause" of the troubles.

> It is observed by every body that while he was in England there was at least an appearance of peace and quietness, but since his return the old sparks are again blown up, and at present the flame rages with more violence than ever. I really believe there never will be any prospect of ease or happiness here, while that villain has the liberty of spreading about the poison of that inveterate malice and ill nature, which is so deeply implanted in his own black heart.

The occasion for the governor's comments was a renewal of Franklin's antiproprietary campaign. Franklin had returned from London convinced that Pennsylvania needed to break the proprietary shackles that kept it from becoming the country it might be; in the ebullience of his Britishness he embraced royal rule as the solution to the problems of the province. The Indian troubles and the Paxton uprising had distracted him from this objective even as they confirmed his conviction that Pennsylvania was nearly ungovernable under current arrangements. During the spring of 1764 he resumed the offensive.

The opening salvo was a series of resolutions that Franklin guided through the Assembly. This "necklace of resolves," as he called it, amounted to a twenty-six-part indictment of proprietary government. The proprietors were said to be merely owners of private property, without the least authority regarding legislation; therefore it was "high presumption" in them to interfere between the Crown and the people. Despite the affectionate regard and continuing generosity of the people, the proprietors were endeavoring to "diminish and annihilate" the people's rights. The Indian policy of the proprietors having rendered the inhabitants of the frontier "easy prey to the small skulking parties of the enemy," the proprietors—acting in a manner "dishonourable, unjust, tyrannical and inhuman"—exploited this danger "to extort privileges from the people, or enforce claims against them, with the knife of savages at their throat." The current victims of the proprietors were the people of Pennsylvania, but should the proprietors' interpretation of the provincial charter prevail, their powers would inevitably become "as dangerous to the prerogatives of the Crown as to the liberties of the people." In conclusion, "as all hope of any degree of happiness, under the proprietary government, is, in our opinion, now at an end," the Assembly resolved that power ought to be taken from the proprietors "and lodged where only it can be properly and safely lodged, in the hands of the Crown."

Such language, needless to say, did not endear Franklin to the proprietors or their man on the scene. John Penn called the resolves a "dirty piece of scurrility." A subsequent Franklin pamphlet entitled *Cool Thoughts on the Present Situation* fanned the flames, being anything but cool. The people of Pennsylvania, Franklin said, were in a "wretched situation." The government was weak and ineffectual. "Mobs assemble and kill (we scarce dare say *murder*) numbers of innocent people in cold blood, who were under the protection of the government." Proclamations against the violence were issued, but were treated "with the utmost indignity and contempt" by the killers. "They assemble again, and with arms in their hands, approach the capital. The Government truckles, condescends to cajole them, and drops all prosecution of their crimes; whilst honest citizens, threatened in their lives and fortunes, fly the province, as having no confidence in the public protection."

In making such an argument Franklin elided his own participation in the government he contemned; his entire purpose here was to cast obloquy on the status quo. The objective was nothing less than the destruction of that status quo: the replacement of proprietary government by royal government.

Though Franklin framed his case as one of the people against the proprietors, the situation was considerably more complicated, and as the annual elections of October 1764 approached, a bitter campaign developed. Franklin continued to assault the proprietors and their governor; the governor and his friends counterattacked with a vengeance. Among other asserted sins, Franklin was charged with desiring the governorship of Pennsylvania for himself, to be bestowed by the king in exchange for Franklin's help in converting Pennsylvania into a royal colony. Much was made of William Franklin's bastardy; Franklin was said to have mistreated the mother—the alleged Barbara—allowed her to starve, and dumped her body in an unmarked grave.

Franklin joked of his enemies, "God has blessed me with two or three, to keep me in order." They certainly tried—and they succeeded, temporarily. During the months before the election Franklin grew even more visible as the symbol of the antiproprietary cause when the Assembly unanimously elected him speaker of the house. Yet the visibility brought liability, for Franklin became the lightning rod (a term just now being used metaphorically) for all manner of complaints against the legislature and its antiproprietary majority.

The voting began at nine o'clock on the morning of October 1. Philadelphia had never witnessed the like. From morning till long past midnight the poll was crowded with voters, who stood in a line that ran far down the street. At three o'clock on the morning of October 2 the proprietary party called for a close, but Franklin and the antiproprietors insisted that the voting continue.

"O! fatal mistake," declared Charles Pettit, an eyewitness insider, who went on to explain the thinking of Franklin and his allies: "They had a reserve of the aged and lame, which could not come in &c., and some who needed no help: between 3 and 6 o'clock, about 200 voters." But the proprietary party meanwhile sent messengers to Germantown and other outlying neighborhoods aggrieved against the Assembly. The messengers roused several hundred voters, most of whom backed the proprietors.

This late vote doomed Franklin's candidacy. Running simultaneously for seats from the city of Philadelphia and Philadelphia County, Franklin lost the former by a small margin, the latter by a whisker—19 votes of nearly 31,000 cast.

16

Stamps and Statesmanship

1764–66

~ "Mr. Franklin died like a philosopher," Charles Pettit said. The Stoic himself attributed his defeat to his rivals' clever mistranslation of an earlier comment by him on Pennsylvania's Germans, in which he was said to have called them pigs. (He had spoken of the "Boers herding together"; this came out as "herd of boars.") "They carried (would you think it!) above 1000 Dutch from me," Franklin told Richard Jackson. Though hardly pleased at losing, Franklin could see the humor in his situation. "This is quite a laughing matter."

Laughing came easier when the Assembly, in an obvious slap at the Penns, reappointed Franklin agent to England. He should sail back east and petition for an end to proprietary rule. Franklin gladly obliged, and his departure turned into a raucous triumph. Three hundred supporters followed him from his home to the quay at Chester; cannons were fired in his honor and hurrahs shouted. An anthem was sung—"God Save the King," with lyrics adapted to the occasion, culminating in "Confound their politics/Frustrate such hypocrites/Franklin, on thee we fix/God save us all."

His reception in London, after a rough but fast winter crossing, was quieter but hardly less devoted. William Strahan greeted him with delight, determined that his friend not escape again. Mrs. Stevenson had held his rooms for him; he resumed residence on Craven Street as though he had never been gone. He surprised Polly Stevenson by writing her from her mother's own parlor; Polly responded with her usual warmth. Other old friends, he told Deborah, gave him a "most cordial welcome."

⌒ **Richard Jackson** had a political reason for being happy to see Franklin. George Grenville had lately proposed a new plan for taxing the American colonies; it involved stamps on various documents and papers. Jackson and some of his fellow agents for the American colonies—including Charles Garth, representing South Carolina—had objected to the stamp tax, but to no avail. Now Jackson enlisted Franklin, as a person recently arrived from America and consequently familiar with the mood there, to approach Grenville directly. Jared Ingersoll of Connecticut, another recent arrival, joined Jackson, Franklin, and Garth. Ingersoll later summarized the meeting.

> Mr. Grenville gave us a full hearing—told us he took no pleasure in giving the Americans so much uneasiness as he found he did— that it was the duty of his office to manage the revenue—that he really was made to believe that considering the whole of the circumstances of the Mother Country and the colonies, the latter could and ought to pay something, and that he knew of no better way than that now pursuing to lay such tax, but that if we could tell of a better he would adopt it.

Franklin and the others had reason to doubt Grenville's candor on this point. The Americans did not love taxes, but they chose to make their case on the question of *who* would levy the taxes: Parliament or the colonial assemblies? The Americans stood on the right of Englishmen to be taxed only by their own representatives—that is, their assemblies. Grenville and most members of Parliament, without disputing the principle of self-taxation, contended that the writ of Parliament ran to America, that the colonies *were* represented in Parliament, at least as well represented as many of the king's subjects living in Britain.

When Grenville had first floated the possibility of a stamp tax, Jackson and other agents argued that if revenue needed to be raised, the colonies ought to be allowed to raise it themselves. Grenville voiced vague support for this alternative but failed to provide the information necessary to apportion the tax burden fairly among the several colonies. In the meeting with Franklin and the others, Grenville again said he might listen to a proposal from the colonial assemblies; he asked if the agents "could agree upon the several proportions each colony should raise." At this late hour, and still lacking critical details, the agents were in no position to answer affirmatively. "We told him no," Ingersoll recorded—which, by most evidence, was what Grenville wanted to hear.

Yet Franklin would not leave the matter at that. Instead he proposed an alternative to Grenville's stamp scheme. Franklin's plan would raise the revenue Grenville needed; it would also solve a perennial problem for the colonies—and for that reason be far more palatable than a batch of new taxes. As part of Grenville's program for reorganizing imperial finances, Parliament recently had forbidden the colonies to issue paper currency. Presumably the ban was temporary, but in the meantime the colonial economies, already suffering from a postwar depression, might strangle.

Franklin proposed that Parliament authorize the issue of paper currency at interest. In effect this would be a stamp tax on paper money, but Franklin thought it would go down far better than a stamp tax on the sorts of items Grenville envisioned: licenses, deeds, indentures, leases, newspapers, almanacs, playing cards, dice. Grenville's list hit people unused to paying for those items, people often without much money. The appeal of Franklin's plan was that the people likely to avail themselves of the paper money—merchants, most obviously—were used to paying for money (in the form of interest) and had the wherewithal to do so. As Franklin explained his scheme, "It will operate as a general tax on the colonies, and yet not an unpleasing one, as he who actually pays the interest has an equivalent or more in the use of the principal." He added, "The rich, who handle most money, would in reality pay most of the tax."

It was an intriguing idea. It might have worked. If it had, it would have saved both Britain and America a great deal of trouble and ill will. Whether it would have materially altered the course of the next two decades is impossible to know.

But Grenville—"besotted with his stamp scheme," according to Franklin—refused to entertain it. Nor was Parliament interested. To some degree the very unpalatableness of the stamps in America became an argument for approving them. Charles Townshend, whom the Americans would learn to loathe, defended the principle of Parliamentary taxation of the colonies: "Will these Americans, children planted by our care, nourished up by our indulgence until they are grown to a degree of strength and opulence, and protected by our arms, will they grudge to contribute their mite to relieve us from the heavy weight of that burden which we lie under?"

A lonely few in Westminster challenged this version of imperial history. Isaac Barré, a veteran of the French and Indian War, rebuffed Townshend:

> They planted by *your* care? No! Your oppressions planted them in America. . . . They nourished by *your* indulgence? They grew by your neglect of them. . . . They protected by *your* arms? They have nobly taken up arms in your defence, have exerted a valour amidst their constant and laborious industry for the defence of a country whose frontier, while drenched in blood, its interior parts have yielded all its little savings to your emolument.

Barré's words drew cheers in America but moved Grenville not at all. The prime minister pushed the stamp bill through the necessary three readings; on February 27, 1765, it passed the House of Commons; on March 22 it received the royal assent.

∼ Franklin had done as much as any reasonable man in his position could to prevent Grenville's bill from becoming law; once it became law he did what any reasonable man in his position would have done to make the best of an unsatisfactory situation.

"I think it will affect the printers more than anybody," he told David Hall when passage appeared inevitable; "as a sterling halfpenny stamp on every half sheet of a newspaper, and two shillings sterling on every advertisement, will go near to knock up one half of both. There is also fourpence sterling on every almanac." Franklin could not do much about the almanacs, but he hoped to save Hall and himself some money on the newspapers. The *Pennsylvania Gazette* was printed on what technically was called a full sheet (although when folded and printed on both sides it yielded four pages). Certain London papers were printed on half-sheets, which despite their name yielded almost as much printed area (when folded twice into an eight-page paper) as the full sheets. Yet an American paper printed on the latter would pay but half the new tax of a paper made from the former. Aiming to outfox the taxman, Franklin ordered one hundred reams of the half-sheets from his friend and supplier Strahan, to be sent to Hall in Philadelphia.

He was too clever for his and Hall's good. As the Stamp Act took final shape, it mandated that newsprint receive its stamp in England. The fifty thousand sheets proved useless as sent, and had to be expensively returned. "I hope you will excuse what I did in good will, though it happened wrong," Franklin wrote Hall.

Another Franklin slip was less easily excused. In working to stop the stamp bill, Franklin found himself in an uncomfortable alliance with Thomas Penn, who likewise opposed new taxes on his colony. The alliance dissolved upon passage, however, not only because of the long-standing hostility between the two men but because Grenville, evidently appraising Franklin as the more significant of the two, awarded him the right to name the stamp commissioner for Pennsylvania. The post would not be the most lucrative in the colony, but it might earn its holder a neat supplement to an existing income.

Franklin put forward John Hughes, whom Grenville approved at once. Hughes was a Franklin friend from Philadelphia, a staunch ally in the fight against the proprietors. It was Hughes who had moved that Franklin be dispatched to England after his defeat at the polls in October 1764; Hughes continued to defend Franklin against the attacks of the proprietary party in Franklin's absence. The contest was more bitter than ever. Chief justice and ardent Penn man William Allen, judging Franklin a "grand incendiary . . . fully freighted with rancour and malice," lambasted him from behind a thin veil of anonymity. Franklin's friends responded with "tomahawk, scalping knife, chewed bullets, or any other barbarous weapons," in the metaphor of Penn foe Cadwalader Evans. John Hughes was in the thickest of the fight. Hughes challenged Allen to come out in the open, promising to pay £10 to the provincial hospital for every accusation against Franklin that could be proved true, if Allen would agree to pay £5 for every accusation shown false. Allen declined the challenge, allowing Hughes and the pro-Franklin forces to claim a "victory as complete as we could wish," in Evans's characterization. Franklin, appreciating his debt to Hughes, sought to repay it by having Grenville award Hughes the concession on the stamps.

This turned out to be no favor to Hughes, and it was one of the worst mistakes of Franklin's career. Franklin had a tendency to believe he knew best in most situations, and, brilliant and reasonable man that he was, he usually did. But he grievously misgauged the reaction to the Stamp Act. When news of the act's approval reached America, several colonies erupted in protest. The first outburst was rhetorical. In Williamsburg, Virginia, a twenty-nine-year-old lawyer named Patrick Henry stood up in the House of Burgesses—after a tenure there of less than two weeks—and declared the Stamp Act unconstitutional. As Englishmen, Henry said, Americans had the right to be taxed by none but their own elected representatives; as Englishmen they must resist this encroachment on their rights. Inflamed by his own eloquence, Henry uttered words to the effect that Caesar had met his Brutus and Charles I his Cromwell, and that George III might encounter someone similar among the Americans. At this the speaker of the house shouted treason and cut Henry off. Henry thereupon begged the House's pardon and swore his loyalty to the king—but then undercut his apology by explaining that he had been carried away by fear for his country's "dying liberty."

The apology was undercut further by a set of resolves Henry laid before the House. Four of these reiterated in comparatively innocuous terms the rights of Englishmen regarding taxes. The fifth was more straightforward, claiming for the Virginia assembly the "only sole and exclusive right and power" to tax Virginians, and asserting that any effort to vest this right and power elsewhere had a "manifest tendency to destroy British as well as American freedom."

Support for Henry's resolves was far from overwhelming. He introduced them only at the end of the legislative session, after most of the burgesses had gone home. The debate over the fifth resolve was, in Thomas Jefferson's recollection, "most bloody." Jefferson also recalled Peyton Randolph declaring afterward, "By God, I would have given five hundred guineas for a single vote!" Following the bloody debate all five resolves passed the house, but the fifth was rescinded after Henry departed in premature triumph.

Yet the point had been made, and during the following summer and autumn it was made again and again, and far more violently. In Boston the Stamp Act exacerbated tensions of long duration and deep bitterness; opponents of the act seized the occasion to take their fight to the streets. A group of artisans and shopkeepers initially calling themselves the Loyal Nine (a name soon changed to Sons of Liberty) met at a distillery on Hanover Square and, after fortifying their spirits, plotted a protest. Of late the historically competing North End and South End mobs had linked arms; the Sons of Liberty engaged the combined mob to attack the property of Andrew Oliver, the stamp commissioner for Massachusetts, and those connected to him.

On August 14 the mob hanged Oliver in effigy. The lieutenant governor, Thomas Hutchinson, who was Oliver's brother-in-law, took the insult both officially and personally and ordered the sheriff to remove the effigy. The sheriff prudently gathered intelligence regarding the mood of the mob before reporting back to Hutchinson that any effort to follow his orders would result in loss of life, probably starting with his and his deputies'.

As evening fell, the leader of the mob, Ebenezer MacIntosh, and his fellows cut down the effigy themselves and carried it about the town. They hooted at the office where the governor was meeting with his council, then marched to the waterfront, to Oliver's dock. Somewhat arbitrarily denominating a new building on the dock the "Stamp Office"— although no stamps had yet arrived from England—MacIntosh and crew demolished it. They proceeded to Oliver Street, where Oliver lived. While some amused themselves ripping the head of the Oliver effigy from the torso, others hurled rocks through the windows of the Oliver house. The rioters did not lack a certain sense of humor, as they demonstrated by "stamping" the stamp commissioner's effigy—with their boots. Then they burned it.

The mob began to hunt for Oliver himself. They broke through the barricaded doors of Oliver's house and searched each room—splintering furniture along the way. But the owner was not at home, and after a futile examination of nearby houses—in one of which Oliver in fact was hiding—they called off the hunt.

The experience persuaded Oliver to resign his post as stamp commissioner, which he did the next day; but the mob was not appeased. On August 26 the crowd mobilized once more and went on a rampage against houses owned by various government officials known or merely thought to favor the Stamp Act. Hardest hit was the mansion of Thomas

Hutchinson. The Hutchinson house was not only magnificent, it was sturdy—so sturdy that the mob needed all night to complete its destruction, and even then some brick walls and part of the roof remained. But everything else—doors, windows, wainscoting, wallpaper, china, silver, lamps, furniture, clothing, £900 cash—was shattered, burned, scattered, or stolen. Hutchinson escaped with his life, but perhaps not by much. He was dining with his family when word arrived that the mob was approaching; he vowed to defend his home against the intruders. Only when his daughter swore similar defiance, saying she would not leave if he would not, did he relent and retreat.

⌒ John Hughes anticipated like treatment in Philadelphia. In early September he wrote Franklin:

> You are now from letter to letter to suppose each may be the last that you will receive from your old friend, as the spirit or flame of rebellion is got to a high pitch amongst the North Americans; and it seems to me that a sort of frenzy or madness has got such hold of the people of all ranks that I fancy some lives will be lost before this fire is put out.

Four days later Hughes wrote again.

> Our clamours run very high, and I am told my house shall be pulled down and the stamps burnt. To which I give no other answer than that I will defend my house at the risque of my life.

Another four days later:

> Common report threatens my house this night, as there are bonfires and rejoicings for the change of ministry [for reasons unrelated to the Stamp Act, Grenville had resigned in favor of the Marquis of Rockingham]. . . . I for my part am well-armed with fire-arms, and am determined to stand a siege. If I live till tomorrow morning I shall give you a farther account.

Fortunately for Hughes, his friends rallied to his side in large numbers, and the storm passed. At five the next morning he wrote Franklin:

We are all yet in the land of the living, and our property safe. Thank God.

༈ **Franklin** himself had reason to thank God, for the same mob that threatened Hughes made angry noises about him. The house he had begun building before leaving for England was essentially complete—and suggested to suspicious or envious souls that its owner intended to fatten with his friend Hughes on the stamps the commissioner would sell to the oppressed Pennsylvania.

Samuel Wharton, a Philadelphia merchant and political ally of Franklin, described the night of maximum danger in a letter to Franklin: "In the evening, a large mob was collected at the coffee house and the party declared that your house, Mr. Hughes', Mr. Galloway's and mine should be leveled with the street, for that you had obtained the Stamp Act and we were warm advocates for the carrying it into execution."

Deborah Franklin heard of the danger. During all her husband's political contests she had remained on the sidelines, but she was not about to see her house pulled down. Friends and relatives warned her to leave the city and get out of harm's way; though she sent Sally to Burlington and William, she stubbornly stayed. She related the critical several hours to Franklin:

> Cousin [Josiah] Davenport came and told me that more than twenty people had told him it was his duty to be with me. I said I was pleased to receive civility from any body, so he stayed with me some time.
>
> Towards night I said he should fetch a gun or two as we had none. I sent to ask my brother to come and bring his gun. So we made one room into a magazine. I ordered some sort of defence upstairs such as I could manage myself.
>
> I said when I was advised to remove that I was very sure you had done nothing to hurt any body, nor I had not given any offence to any person at all. Nor would I be made uneasy by any body nor would I stir or show the least uneasiness. But if any one came to disturb me I would show a proper resentment and I should be very much affronted with any body.

Deborah's resolve encouraged Franklin's friends to come to her and his defense. Years earlier he had taught them to mobilize for good causes;

now they mobilized for his. Some of the more rambunctious, led by a group of artisans and mechanics calling themselves the White Oak Company, let it be known that if Franklin's house came down, so would the houses of those responsible. This sobered the plotters long enough for the authorities of the city to bring matters under control.

Franklin obviously did not learn about the events until weeks later. When he did, he could not help admiring his wife. "I honour much the spirit and courage you showed," he said, "and the prudent preparations you made in that time of danger. The woman deserves a good house that is determined to defend it."

◦— Although Franklin's house survived the Stamp Act rioting, his reputation remained in jeopardy. It did so partly because his enemies in Pennsylvania crafted lurid tales of how he had conspired to foist stamps upon the unsuspecting populace. Franklin's friends countered the slanders as best they could, but he and they realized there was only so much they could do. Of one critic, a leader of Philadelphia Presbyterians, who, not content with alleging stamp conspiracy, added other heinous actions, Franklin told Debbie, "I thank him he does not charge me (as they do their God) with having planned Adam's fall, and the damnation of mankind. It might be affirmed with equal truth and modesty."

Yet there was more to Franklin's predicament than unjust accusations. With the response to the Stamp Act, American politics commenced a remarkable change—a change Franklin had not anticipated and to which he was slow to react. Ironically, however, it built on work Franklin himself had done a decade earlier. Then he had tried to forge a collective identity among the British colonies in North America, and failed. Now just such a collective identity was taking shape in the resistance to the Stamp Act. Upon the initiative of the Massachusetts assembly, a congress was held in New York in October 1765. Nine colonies were represented, including Pennsylvania; the delegates produced a series of resolutions denying the right of Parliament to tax the colonies and urging repeal of the noxious measure.

Such petitioning was entirely within the English constitutional tradition; no one in Parliament could have much quarrel with it. But the insurrectionary spirit that drove the riots was another matter. And as that spirit took hold throughout the American colonies, it made the events of 1765 distinctive and portentous. This was what Franklin misunderstood.

He was not a violent man; he much preferred the politics of reason to the politics of passion.

So did Thomas Hutchinson, who felt the irony of the situation more immediately, and more painfully, than Franklin. Hutchinson wrote Franklin in November assessing the violence in the various colonies, and noting, from his own experience, that in Massachusetts all doubts of the legitimacy of the mob's opinions had been forcibly suppressed. "It is not safe there to advance any thing contrary to any popular opinions whatsoever," Hutchinson said. "Every body who used to have virtue enough to oppose them is now afraid of my fate." Briefly the violence in Boston had diminished, only to revive from example elsewhere. "The riots at New York have given fresh spirits to the rioters here." Pointing out that the opponents of the Stamp Act had seized Franklin's motto from 1754, "Join or Die," Hutchinson remarked, "When you and I were at Albany ten years ago we did not propose an union for such purposes as these."

~ The riots gave bite to demands by the opponents of the Stamp Act for a coordinated rejection of the stamps. As few souls dared incur the wrath of the mobs, and as the stamps were necessary for the conduct of most legal and commercial transactions, daily life was thrown into confusion. Joseph Galloway, writing from Philadelphia in late November, three weeks after the date on which the Stamp Act had been scheduled to take effect, informed Franklin of the situation:

> It is difficult to describe the distress to which these distracted and violent measures have subjected the people of this province and indeed all North America. Here are Stamp papers, but the mob will not suffer them to be used, and the public officers of justice and of trade, being under obligation of their oaths and liable to the penalties of the statute, will not proceed in their duties without them.
>
> A stop is put to our commerce, and our Courts of Justice is shut up. Our harbours are filled with vessels, but none of them, save those cleared out before the 2d. of November dare to move, because neither the Governor or Collector will clear them out, and if they would, the men of war threaten to seize them as forfeited for want of papers agreeable to the laws of trade.

Our debtors are selling off their effects before our eyes, and removing to another country, with innumerable other mischiefs brought on us by this fatal conduct, from which I can see no relief but from an immediate repeal of the Act.

However emotionally satisfying, the rejection of the stamps had little effect on Parliament, as it inflicted most of its injury on the colonies, whose influence with Parliament on this subject was demonstrably nil. Another mass action, one that hit closer to the homes of the honorable members, appeared more promising. Upon the passage of the Sugar Act the previous year, calls for an embargo against British imports arose here and there among the American colonies. But not until the Stamp Act galvanized opposition to Parliamentary taxation—and the stamp riots suggested a formidable mechanism for enforcing an embargo—did concerted nonimportation take hold. Just as the Stamp Act was to go into effect, some two hundred New York merchants pledged to have nothing to do with British imports. Philadelphia merchants followed suit, as did those of Boston.

Almost immediately nonimportation evoked the desired response. British merchants petitioned Parliament for repeal of the Stamp Act. For them the niceties of constitutionalism were irrelevant; what mattered were their vanishing sales. The point of empire was profit, and without sales there would be no profits.

꒲ Franklin had reckoned from the start that Parliament's weakness would be the ledgers of the British merchant class. And he believed that this weakness might be exploited by the practice of one of the virtues— frugality—that Poor Richard had long extolled. In a letter written after the Stamp Act passed but before the rioting began, Franklin repeated his counsel of patience, with an economic and moral addendum:

We might as well have hindered the sun's setting. That we could not do. But since 'tis down, my friend, and it may be long before it rises again, let us make as good a night of it as we can. We may still light candles. Frugality and industry will go a great way towards indemnifying us. Idleness and pride tax with a heavier hand than kings and Parliaments. If we can get rid of the former we may easily bear the latter.

As a moralist, Franklin found the violence of the stamp riots appalling, in the same way that the terrorism of the French and Indian War and the murderous rampage of the Paxton Boys were appalling. In such violence the better angels of human nature were held hostage to its basest devils.

As a politician, Franklin found the violence counterproductive. Parliament already considered the tax issue a matter of principle; the riots simply stiffened Parliament's resolve to impress its sovereignty on the people of the provinces.

Both aspects of Franklin's thinking informed a letter to John Hughes, written before Hughes faced the full blast of popular wrath. Franklin explained that he was doing all he could to cause repeal of the Stamp Act, but success was uncertain.

> If it continues, your undertaking to execute it may make you unpopular for a time, but your acting with coolness and steadiness, and with every circumstance in your power of favour to the people, will by degrees reconcile them. In the meantime, a firm loyalty to the Crown and faithful adherence to the government of this nation, which it is the safety as well as the honour of the colonies to be connected with, will always be the wisest course for you and I to take, whatever may be the madness of the populace or their blind leaders, who can only bring themselves and country into trouble, and draw on greater burthens by acts of rebellious tendency.

As word of the riots reached London, Franklin shuddered at their effect. "The disturbances in the colonies give me great concern," he wrote David Hall, "as I fear the event will be pernicious to America in general."

His concern caused him to redouble his efforts toward a compromise solution. A compromise, of course, was precisely what both the street rioters in America and the Parliamentary supremacists in England did *not* want. Yet Franklin hoped that reason, combined with the interests of moderate elements on both sides of the Atlantic, might yet make a compromise possible. In the second week of November he called upon Rockingham and Lord Dartmouth, the president of the Board of Trade.

A practical man speaking to practical men, Franklin explained that enforcing the Stamp Act would occasion more mischief than it was worth. Americans would be utterly alienated from Britain and would simply stop buying British goods. He acknowledged that the riots in America had freighted the problem with political peril for the Rockingham ministry; to repeal in the face of violence might be unacceptable. But the act could be suspended for a time, till the heat on both sides had dissipated a bit. Then a pretense could be found for quietly dropping it, without ever bringing the constitutional question to a head.

Franklin elaborated on the difficulties of enforcing the act upon an unwilling American populace. London might send armies, but the Americans would take every opportunity to encourage the soldiers to desert, which, given the high wages commanded by laborers and the ease of vanishing into the frontier, would be very tempting. A naval blockade could interdict commerce but would ruin Britain's trade.

Franklin recognized that suspension of the Stamp Act, even if followed by repeal, would be a stopgap. Eventually the question of Parliamentary sovereignty and colonial rights would have to be addressed. "I strongly recommended either a thorough union with America," Franklin told William afterward, "or that government here would proceed in the old method of requisition, by which I was confident more would be obtained in the way of voluntary grant than could probably be got by compulsory taxes laid by Parliament."

But to insist on a final decision at present could be disastrous. To do so would risk creating a deep-rooted aversion between the two countries and laying the foundation of "a future total separation."

⁓ At the start of 1766, a total separation was the last thing Franklin wanted. On his previous visit he had found Britain more congenial in many respects than Pennsylvania; in light of the abuse and threats of violence to which he and his had been subjected of late in Pennsylvania, Britain seemed more congenial still. Had Debbie been willing, he almost certainly would have relocated to London by now. But it seemed clear that Debbie would never be willing; a woman who armed herself against an angry mob to defend her home would not be talked out of it even by one as persuasive as her husband. This being so, separation between America and Britain would force Franklin to choose between wife and friends. He loved his wife; he loved them. He did not wish to have to choose.

Franklin spent January and February 1766 striving to mend the breach between Britain and America. It was a demanding business, in that the loudest voices on both sides of the Atlantic were trying to shout him down. Joseph Galloway wrote from Philadelphia describing "the violent temper of the Americans, which has been so worked up as to be ready even for rebellion itself." Galloway wanted to urge moderation by composing a pamphlet to that effect. "But the difficulty will be in getting it published, the printers on the [American] continent having combined together to print every thing inflammatory and nothing that is rational and cool. . . . The people are taught to believe the greatest absurdities, and their passions are excited to a degree of resentment against the Mother Country beyond all description."

On the other side of the water, the insisters on respect for the rule of law issued dire warnings to the Rockingham ministry against retreating in the face of illegal and unwarranted violence. "Can it be supposed that the colonists will ever submit to bear any share in those grievous burdens and taxes, with which we are loaded, when they find that the Government will not or dare not assert its own authority and power?" demanded one regular contributor to the published debate. "Have we not reason to expect that they will shake off all dependence and subjection, and neither suffer a limitation of their trade nor any duty to be imposed upon their commodities? Is not this want of spirit and resolution a direct encouragement of the mob to redress every imaginary grievance by force and violence?"

Franklin entered the fray in print and in person. He wrote several pieces for London journals defending American moderates against charges of guilt by association with the rioters, countering imputations of American niggardliness in matters touching imperial defense, pointing out that much of the tax burden Britons complained of got passed on to the Americans in the form of higher prices, and generally reminding readers of the essential unity of interest between colonies and mother country.

He also produced and circulated a political cartoon depicting to what end the Stamp Act and other such measures might lead. The picture was a bloody one, showing Britannia dismembered, her legs and arms lying about her as she leaned disconsolately against a globe. The lost limbs were labeled Virginia, Pennsylvania, New York, and New England; the motto declared *"Date Obolum Bellisario,"* or "Give a penny to Belisarius," referring to a Roman general who reduced the provinces to Rome's rule but was reduced himself to poverty in old age. Franklin had the cartoon printed on cards "on which I have lately wrote all my messages," he explained to David Hall. His sister Jane Mecom got one, along with a note: "The moral is, that the colonies might be ruined, but that Britain would thereby be maimed."

༛ His most telling testimony, however, came in an appearance before the House of Commons. For three days the House convened as a

committee of the whole to examine evidence relating to the Stamp Act,
its unfavorable reception in America, and the demands of both the
colonists and British merchants to have the measure repealed. The leading witness was Franklin.

As is often the case in such hearings, Franklin's appearance was not
entirely unorchestrated. The Rockingham ministry was looking for a way
to distance itself from what it considered the shortsighted, if not downright stupid, legacy of its predecessor. But it needed better reason than
the riots in Boston and New York and Philadelphia. Franklin—the august doctor, the celebrated philosopher and scientist, the astute observer
of politics and human character, the deft writer and discussant; in short,
the epitome of reason—fit the ministry's need admirably. Many of the
questions put to Franklin gave the impression of having been scripted—
an impression confirmed by Franklin's later remarks and writings.

Yet his appearance at Westminster was hardly a love-fest. By mid-
February 1766 the wailing of the British merchants made repeal of
the Stamp Act almost certain, but the terms of repeal—in particular,
whether it would be accompanied by a reaffirmation of Parliament's sovereignty over the American colonies, and what form such reaffirmation
might take—remained to be determined. Several of Franklin's question-
ers sought to undermine his answers by reading either more or less into
them than he intended.

A friend opened the questioning by asking what taxes the Americans
paid, of their own levying. "Many, and very heavy taxes," Franklin
replied. Asked to specify regarding Pennsylvania, Franklin continued,
"There are taxes on all estates real and personal; a poll tax; a tax on all offices, professions, trades, and businesses, according to their profits; an
excise on all wine, rum, and other spirits; and a duty of ten pounds per
head on all Negroes imported, with some other duties."

A second friend inquired of the feasibility of distributing the
stamps in the American colonies. Deputy Postmaster Franklin, speaking
with knowledge unexcelled of transport and communications in North
America, described grave difficulties. "The posts go only along the sea
coasts; they do not, except in a few instances, go back into the country;
and if they did, sending for stamps by post would occasion an expense of
postage amounting, in many cases, to much more than that of the stamps
themselves."

An adversary, a member of the late Grenville ministry, broke in to
ask bluntly whether the colonies could afford to pay the stamp duty.

Franklin replied equally bluntly. "In my opinion, there is not gold and silver enough in the colonies to pay the stamp duty for one year."

George Grenville himself queried whether Franklin thought that the Americans, protected by the British army and navy, should pay no part of the expense of maintaining those forces.

Franklin rejected the premise. The colonies, he said, had essentially defended themselves during the last war, raising 25,000 soldiers and spending millions of pounds.

Quite so, Grenville continued, but had not Parliament reimbursed the colonies for their expenses?

Franklin parried this as well. "We were only reimbursed what, in your opinion, we had advanced beyond our proportion, or beyond what might reasonably be expected from us; and it was a very small part of what we spent."

Franklin's friends put questions that allowed him to state his argument most succinctly. What was the temper of the Americans toward Great Britain before 1763?

"The best in the world," he answered. "They submitted willingly to the government of the Crown, and paid, in all their courts, obedience to acts of Parliament. Numerous as the people are in the several old provinces, they cost you nothing in forts, citadels, garrisons, or armies, to keep them in subjection. They were governed by this country at the expense only of a little pen, ink, and paper. They were led by a thread."

And what was the temper of the Americans now?

"Very much altered."

In what light had the Americans formerly viewed Parliament?

"As the great bulwark and security of their liberties and privileges." Arbitrary ministers might overstep, but as a body Parliament could always be counted on to redress grievances.

And did the Americans retain their respect for Parliament?

"No, it is greatly lessened."

A questioner probed the matter of taxes and duties. Had the Americans formerly objected to Parliament's authority on these subjects?

"I never heard any objection to the right of laying duties to regulate commerce; but a right to lay internal taxes was never supposed to be in Parliament, as we are not represented there."

After additional discussion of duties—which Franklin interchangeably called external taxes—and taxes proper, or internal taxes, a former minister under Grenville suggested that a tax was a tax. What was the difference?

"The difference is very great. An external tax is a duty laid on commodities imported; that duty is added to the first cost, and other charges on the commodity, and when it is offered to sale, makes a part of the price. If the people do not like it at that price, they refuse it; they are not obliged to pay it. But an internal tax is forced from the people without their consent, if not laid by their own representatives. The Stamp Act says we shall have no commerce, make no exchange of property with each other, neither purchase nor grant, nor recover debts; we shall neither marry nor make our wills unless we pay such and such sums, and thus it is intended to extort our money from us, or ruin us by the consequences of refusing to pay it."

A friend asked whether anything less than military force could compel the Americans to accept the stamps.

"I do not see how a military force can be applied to that purpose."

Why not? one of the Grenville men asked.

"Suppose a military force is sent into America. They will find nobody in arms. What are they then to do? They cannot force a man to take stamps who chooses to do without them. They will not find a rebellion; they may indeed make one."

⁓ By the testimony of those most interested, the effect of Franklin's appearance in Commons was electric. "The Marquis of Rockingham told a friend of mine a few days after, that he never knew truth make so great a progress in so very short a time," said William Strahan. "From that very day, the repeal was generally and absolutely determined, all that passed afterwards being only mere form." Strahan was never shy about heralding Franklin's triumphs, but even he thought his friend had outdone himself. "Happy man! In truth I almost envy him the inward pleasure, as well as the outward fame, he must derive from having it in his power to do his country such eminent and seasonable service."

Repeal had more fathers than Strahan conceded, but Franklin's performance was indeed inspired. The opponents of repeal could rouse indignation against the rabble who tore down Thomas Hutchinson's house and defied king and Parliament, but indignation dissolved in the sweet reason of Dr. Franklin. If that sweet reason included some tenuous reasoning—Franklin's distinction between internal and external taxes, for example, was more his own invention than a reflection of opinion in America—none present was placed to refute him. (When one unfriendly questioner tried to do so, Franklin rebuffed him with a clever riposte. This member suggested that the Americans might use the same arguments Franklin deployed against internal taxes to reject external taxes. "They never have hitherto," Franklin responded. "Many arguments have been lately used here to shew them that there is no difference, and that if you have no right to tax them internally, you have none to tax them externally, or make any other law to bind them. At present they do not reason so, but in time they may possibly be convinced by these arguments.")

To reasonableness he added just the right note of resolve. He was not defiant, not bellicose. He was simply reporting the state of the American mind and the American spirit. Here again he bent the truth to suit his purpose. He must have known, after all the violence of the summer and autumn in America, that a return to the status quo would not appease those who now had the bit in their teeth. But as with his posited distinction between internal and external taxes, he was willing to deal with the consequences of that interpretation later. For the present the goal was repeal of the Stamp Act.

The goal was achieved in March 1766, almost a year to the day after the act had received royal approval. To no one's great surprise, repeal was accompanied by a Declaratory Act, which asserted the right of Parliament to legislate for the colonies "in all cases whatsoever."

Equally unsurprising, this mixed outcome left a certain sour taste. Many in America remained unreconciled to Parliament's authority; many in Britain resented the Americans' ability to flout the law with impunity. The latter feeling gave rise to a demand that the colonies compensate the home government for the cost of stamping all that paper, which was never used.

Franklin registered a sardonic judgment on this demand. In an anonymous letter to a London journal he wrote that the affair put him in mind of a Frenchman who used to accost English visitors on the Pont-Neuf in Paris, with effusive compliments in his mouth and a red-hot poker in his hand.

"Pray Monsieur Anglais," says he, "Do me the favour to let me have the honour of thrusting this hot iron into your backside?"

"Zoons, what does the fellow mean! Begone with your iron, or I'll break your head!"

"Nay, Monsieur," replies he, "if you do not choose it, I do not insist upon it. But at least you will in justice have the goodness to pay me something for the heating of my iron."

17

Duties and Pleasures

1766–67

~ "My Dear Child," Franklin wrote Debbie a little later,

packing a box for shipment home:

As the Stamp Act is at length repealed, I am willing you should
have a new gown, which you may suppose I did not send sooner
as I knew you would not like to be finer than your neighbours, unless in a gown of your own spinning. Had the trade between the
two countries totally ceased, it was a comfort that I had once been
clothed from head to foot in woolen and linen of my wife's manufacture, that I never was prouder of any dress in my life, and that
she and her daughter might do it again if it was necessary.

Franklin described how he had told Parliament that the Americans could learn to make their own clothes before the ones they were wearing wore out. "And indeed if they all had as many old clothes as your old man has, that would not be very unlikely; for I think you and George reckoned when I was last at home, at least 20 pair of old breeches."

So Debbie got a bolt of satin and Sally a new negligee and petticoat, while ships traveling in the opposite direction carried cargo of another sort, namely congratulations for Franklin on a job well done. "The Assembly entertain the most grateful sense of the firmness and integrity with which you have served your country on this very important occasion—and will not be wanting in their demonstrations of it on your return," reported Joseph Galloway. The truly inveterate of Franklin's enemies, Galloway said, still slandered him, but counterproductively. "They are daily put to shame on that account."

Franklin could not but be pleased at the praise, yet he refused to overvalue it. If he was lionized now, he would be lambasted again. Two weeks after his session in Commons, but before reports of it reached America, he wrote to Jane Mecom, who herself had written to him complaining of his ill treatment at the hands of his enemies. "As to the reports you mention that are spread to my disadvantage, I give myself as little concern about them as possible," he said.

> I have often met with such treatment from people that I was all the while endeavouring to serve. At other times I have been extolled extravagantly when I have had little or no merit. These are the operations of nature. It sometimes is cloudy, it rains, it hails, again 'tis clear and pleasant, and the sun shines on us.
>
> Take one thing with another, and the world is a pretty good sort of world; and 'tis our duty to make the best of it and be thankful. One's true happiness depends more upon one's own judgement of one's self, on a consciousness of rectitude in action and intention, and in the approbation of those few who judge impartially, than upon the applause of the unthinking undiscerning multitude, who are apt to cry Hosanna today, and tomorrow, Crucify him.

Franklin had turned sixty during the fight for repeal; this personal milestone understandably occasioned reflection of the sort he shared with his sister, who had just lost her husband of many years. Some months earlier one of his oldest friends, Junto charter member Hugh

Roberts, had written with news of the club and how the political quarreling in Philadelphia had continued to divide the membership. Franklin expressed hope that the squabbles would not keep Roberts from the meetings. " 'Tis now perhaps one of the *oldest* clubs, as I think it was formerly one of the *best*, in the King's dominions; it wants but about two years of forty since it was established." Few men were so lucky as to belong to such a group. "We loved and still love one another; we are grown grey together and yet it is too early to part. Let us sit till the evening of life is spent; the last hours were always the most joyous. When we can stay no longer 'tis time enough then to bid each other good night, separate, and go quietly to bed."

And in what consisted that final sleep? Franklin's theology had changed over the years, from borderline atheism to rationalistic deism. At times in his later years he would approach Christianity. Throughout, however, Franklin's God remained as reasonable as Franklin himself. In Philadelphia before leaving for London this latest time, Franklin heard from his old friend, the evangelist George Whitefield. Franklin replied:

> Your frequently repeated wishes and prayers for my eternal as well as temporal happiness are very obliging. I can only thank you for them, and offer you mine in return. I have my self no doubts that I shall enjoy as much of both as is proper for me. That Being who gave me existence, and through almost threescore years has been continually showering his favours upon me, whose very chastisements have been blessings to me, can I doubt that he loves me? And if he loves me, can I doubt that he will go on to take care of me not only here but hereafter? This to some may seem presumption; to me it appears the best grounded hope: hope of the future, built on experience of the past.

And that Being looked after not only individual souls but their actions together. Franklin was the least sectarian person he knew, and he shuddered at the illegitimate intrusion of religion into politics. But he believed that right would eventually win out. "The malice of our adversaries I am well acquainted with," he reassured a friend and ally who had gone down to defeat in the 1764 Assembly election. "But hitherto it has been harmless, all their arrows shot against us have been like those that Rabelais speaks of which were headed with butter hardened in the sun. As long as I have known the world I have observed that wrong is always growing more wrong, till there is no bearing, and that right, however opposed, comes right at last."

⁓ Franklin passed another milestone during that same busy period. After eighteen years his printing partnership with David Hall came to its scheduled end. Franklin at sixty had no desire to extend it; Hall was happy to proceed in the printing business on his own. Before leaving for London, Franklin had given James Parker his power of attorney to settle the account with Hall; the report Parker filed revealed, among innumerable details, that Franklin had taken nearly £14,000 out of the business over the eighteen years, in the form chiefly of cash but including certain in-kind supplies and services. At the termination of the partnership, Franklin owed Hall slightly less than £1,000, by Hall's (and Parker's) reckoning.

This amount injected a slight element of friction at the close of what had been a productive and profitable relationship for both men. Franklin questioned some of the entries and totals in Parker's accounting, but his distance from Philadelphia postponed any final settlement.

Hall was willing to trust Franklin for the balance; somewhat more unsettling was what Hall interpreted to be Franklin's participation in a new printing venture just months after Franklin & Hall dissolved. Two of the prime movers behind the new partnership were Joseph Galloway and Thomas Wharton; the expressed purpose was the dissemination of the views of the antiproprietary party through a new paper called the *Pennsylvania Chronicle*. The partnership and purpose certainly suggested Franklin's participation, as did rumors that Franklin was putting money into the new venture. When it opened for business in a house owned by Franklin, the connection appeared confirmed.

Not surprisingly, Hall was miffed. He wrote Franklin relating what he knew of this upstart press, and what he was hearing about Franklin's taking a part. "This I will never allow myself to believe, having still, as I always had, the highest opinion of your honour," he declared, as if requesting reassurance. Hall reminded Franklin of the clause in their contract that forbade either to compete with the other. "Though you are not absolutely prohibited from being any farther concerned in the printing business in this place, yet so much is plainly implied." But Hall preferred not to rely on a contract; rather he appealed their long-standing friendship, a friendship "I shall always value and endeavour to deserve."

Franklin supplied the requested reassurance. He had no hand in the new printing business and told Hall so. "It was set on foot without my knowledge or participation, and the first notice I had of it was by reading the advertisement in your paper."

Yet he could not let Hall's interpretation of their own partnership agreement go uncontested. That agreement forbade competition *during the life* of the partnership but not beyond. There was reason for this. "I could not possibly foresee 18 years beforehand, that I should at the end of that term be so rich as to live without business. And if this did not happen, it would be obliging myself to the hard alternative of *starving* or *banishment*, since threescore is rather too late an age to think of going 'prentice to learn a new trade, and I have no other."

As matters currently stood, Franklin did not expect to reenter the printing trade. His office as deputy postmaster provided an income, as to a lesser extent did rents from his various properties. Certain debts were owed him, which he hoped to collect. Nor were his needs great: "I am not inclined to much expense." But things might change, and he could not bar himself his trade. "I am sure you would take no pleasure in seeing me ruined, or obliged at my time of life to quit my country, friends and connections to get my bread in a strange place."

◆— Franklin had other hopes for his retirement from the printing business. His speculative schemes in land moved forward—slowly, to be sure, and in a different direction than originally planned, but forward still. Although the Proclamation of 1763 ruled out the Ohio project for the time being, opportunities elsewhere beckoned. The British government appeared eager to make British the territories seized from France; to this end London granted real estate in Nova Scotia to speculators willing to develop the property and plant settlements. Richard Jackson alerted Franklin to this opportunity, and in the autumn of 1765 Franklin became one of twenty-three individuals, mostly Philadelphians, jointly awarded 200,000 acres on the St. John and Peticodiac rivers.

The land was not free. Legal and surveying costs had to be covered. Attempt was made to minimize the former by chartering the venture on October 31, 1765, the day before the Stamp Act, which decreed a tax on such transactions, was to take effect. (In light of the colonies' refusal of the stamps, and the later repeal of the act, what Franklin and his associates saved by their timeliness was not money but several months.) Regarding the surveying costs, Deborah six weeks later reported paying £53 to a young surveyor named Anthony Wayne (who would win renown as "Mad Anthony" Wayne of the Revolutionary War). "So you see that I am a real land jobber," Deborah remarked, in words that applied as well to her husband.

The grantees committed themselves to improving their lands—enclosing them, cultivating them, or finding others to do so—at the rate of one-third of the grant for each ten years elapsed. An annual quitrent eventually amounting to one farthing per acre would be owed the Crown, starting in five years. Should the grantees fail to meet these conditions, the land would revert to the Crown.

But should the grantees find settlers to whom to sell the land, they might expect to turn a profit. The most ambitious speculators in that era could hope to become very wealthy, from holdings in the hundreds of thousands or even millions of acres. Franklin, whose Nova Scotia tracts totaled some 11,500 acres, initially set his sights lower. Yet even he could hope to leave a legacy. "I tell Sally this is for grandchildren," Debbie said in the letter to Franklin about paying Anthony Wayne. "She seemed very well pleased."

Encouraged, Franklin applied for a grant on his own. Early in 1766 he requested 20,000 acres in Nova Scotia, to be selected where he or his agent thought best. His request bubbled slowly up through the British bureaucracy; in June 1767 the Privy Council awarded Franklin his prize, subject to conditions similar to those on the earlier grant.

Even as the second Nova Scotia request was moving forward, Franklin was working on a scheme far grander—one, moreover, in which he cooperated more closely than ever with his son. Perhaps because William sensed, after the tumultuous events surrounding the Stamp Act, that the tenure of a royal governor might be brief, he worked assiduously, almost obsessively, to gain a stake in unsettled lands. With some Philadelphia friends of his father's, the Indian agent George Croghan, and Sir William Johnson, the superintendent for Indian affairs in the northern part of the colonies, William organized a group called the Illinois Company to seek vast grants in the Illinois country beyond the Ohio River. Eventually the project grew to encompass the creation of a new colony in the west. William knew that such a venture required an agent in England; for this purpose he invited his father to join. Franklin did so with pleasure.

During the latter half of 1766 and most of 1767 father and son corresponded regularly; the most frequent object of discussion was the status of the Illinois project. "I have mentioned the Illinois affair to Lord Shelburne," Franklin wrote William in September 1766. Shelburne was secretary of state of the Southern Department of the American colonies and was considered supportive of western settlement. "His Lordship had read your plan for establishing a colony there, recommended by Sir William Johnson, and said it appeared to him to be a reasonable scheme." Two weeks later Franklin reported further progress: "I was again with Lord Shelburne a few days since, and said a good deal to him on the affair of the Illinois settlement. He was pleased to say he really approved of it." Yet Shelburne cautioned that during the current period of financial retrenchment, patience must be the watchword.

Franklin was patient—but not inactive. He enlisted the help of Richard Jackson, who, upon request from the ministry, delivered his opinion that the Illinois plan was "certainly well framed." Jackson added, "I have no doubt of its practicability or utility." Franklin kept at his task, until in August 1767 he was able to announce a major hurdle surmounted. He had again dined with Shelburne, who was accompanied in this case by the secretary of state for the Northern Department, Henry Conway. "The Secretaries appeared finally to be fully convinced," Franklin wrote William. The only remaining obstacle was the Board of Trade, which, the two secretaries suggested, ought to be brought round privately before the matter reached that body in official form.

The lobbying took a few months; in late October the Board of Trade summoned Franklin and Richard Jackson to answer certain questions. Apparently satisfied with what they heard, the members approved the plan.

And then, at the edge of success, the project encountered a new obstacle. The better to coordinate colonial policy, the imperial government melded the Northern and Southern departments into a single American Department; over this new office was placed Lord Hillsborough. Shelburne had been a friend of the Americans; Hillsborough proved just the opposite. He was skeptical of new projects and new expenses; he was also suspicious of most things American. The Illinois project came to a shuddering halt; the two Franklins' dream of western wealth danced beyond their reach.

⌁ The elevation of Hillsborough at just this moment was no accident, although the reason had nothing to do with the Franklins' land scheme. The British government had never been stable since the accession of George III, and it remained unstable—not least since George himself was less than a rock. The young king's infatuation with Bute had worn off the way infatuations do, but, as infatuations often do, it left traces of jealousy and suspicion, and not in the king alone. George Grenville might have become a powerful and long-tenured prime minister, but he could never put out of his mind that Bute had been George's first love. In 1765 the king fell seriously ill; though none knew it, these were the first symptoms of the hereditary disease—apparently porphyria—that would drive him mad. The malady prompted calls for the creation of a regency in the event the monarch was carried off or permanently incapacitated. Although George recovered, the regency bill passed, and in doing so provoked a row over the identity of the regent. George wanted to appoint his own; Grenville and the ministry wanted their man. When George won out, Grenville refused to accept defeat gracefully. He insisted on spiting the king, and demonstrating his power, by forcing the resignation of Bute's brother, whom George still favored, from an inconsequential office.

The king wept and gnashed his teeth. He struggled to free himself of Grenville but found no rescuer. "George the Third," jibed Horace Walpole, "is the true successor of George the Second, and inherits all his grandfather's humiliations." But the grandson had learned from those humiliations, and before long he found the alternative to Grenville he had been seeking. That this alternative and his friends were discovered at the racetrack at Ascot prompted another wag to declare that the new government was formed of "persons called from the *stud* to the *state*, and transformed miraculously out of jockeys into ministers." On the lead horse was the Marquis of Rockingham.

Yet Grenville had his revenge. Rockingham's first order of business was liquidating the Stamp Act fiasco Grenville had created, and he rallied what he trumpeted to George as "public opinion" behind repeal. The public in question did not include Grenville and his friends, as they demonstrated in cross-examining Franklin during his testimony before Commons; and although they failed to prevent repeal they weakened Rockingham. Subsequent Rockingham reforms—of the Sugar Act, for instance, which was revised to lower the molasses duty from three pence to one, while extending it to British molasses—pleased certain constituencies (Americans especially) but further alienated the Grenville crowd.

This alienation might not have unseated Rockingham had Rockingham not simultaneously alienated the king. George was unhappy with the repeal of the Stamp Act, preferring a stiffer line against the unruly Americans. Nor did he like Rockingham's appeal to the public, a strategy that promised to place the Crown in the shade of such rabble as were ruining the empire in America. Moreover, following his recovery from his illness, George was in a mood to place his own stamp, even if not Grenville's stamps, on imperial politics.

Between Grenville's enmity and George's envy, Rockingham was pushed aside. His successor seemed, at first glance, an odd choice. William Pitt had most recently distinguished himself by speaking out against the Stamp Act. "I rejoice that America has resisted," he proclaimed in Commons (in the very face of Grenville, a single seat away). "Three millions of people, so dead to all the feelings of liberty, as voluntarily to submit to be slaves, would have been fit instruments to make slaves of the rest." Americans rejoiced, in their turn, at Pitt's rejoicing; a statue to Pitt went up in New York. But this was hardly language to reassure a worried monarch confronting incipient rebellion.

All the same, Pitt proved the indispensable man now, as he had previously. He was as popular as Grenville was not, and George could hope that some of the Great Commoner's popularity would rub off on the Crown. Unfortunately for both, George offered Pitt an earldom, and Pitt accepted. Almost at once his popularity with the masses began to dissipate; how could an earl (of Chatham) be the Great Commoner? Popularity aside, Pitt's move from Commons to Lords was a tactical blunder, for it precluded control of the lower house, by now far and away the most important body in British politics. As if this were not enough, he fell badly ill, leaving day-to-day direction of government affairs in the hands of his associates, who showed even worse judgment and considerably less talent.

⟳ Franklin observed the ministerial minuets with a mixture of fascination and dismay. "The confusion among our Great Men still continues as great as ever," he told Joseph Galloway. "And a melancholy thing it is to consider, that instead of employing the present leisure of peace in such measures as might extend our commerce, pay off our debts, secure allies, and increase the strength and ability of the nation to support a future war, the whole time seems wasted in party contentions about power and profit, in court intrigues and cabals, and in abusing one another."

Also abused were the Americans. Franklin visited the House of Lords and heard the peers rant about the insubordinate wretches across the sea. "It gave me great uneasiness to find much resentment against the colonies in the disputants," he recorded. "The word *rebellion* was frequently used."

Franklin did what he could to avert the abuse. He frequented the pages of the London journals, writing under various noms de plume. As "A Friend to Both Countries" he characterized the current atmosphere and sought to deflate it.

> Every step is now taken to enrage us against America. Pamphlets and news papers fly about, and coffee-houses ring with lying reports of its being in rebellion. Force is called for. Fleets and troops should be sent. Those already there should be called in from the distant posts and quartered on the capital towns. The principal people should be brought here and hanged, &c. And why?
>
> Why! Do you ask why?
>
> Yes. I beg leave to ask why?
>
> Why they are going to throw off the government of *this country*, and set up for themselves.
>
> Pray how does that appear?
>
> Why, are they not all in arms?
>
> No. They are all in peace.
>
> Have they not refused to make the compensation to the sufferers by the late riots, that was required of them by government here?
>
> No. They have made ample satisfaction. Which, by the way, has not been done here to the sufferers by your own riots.
>
> Have they not burnt the custom-house?
>
> No. That story is an absolute invented lie, without the least foundation.

As "Benevolus," Franklin answered several allegations commonly laid against the Americans. The colonies were *not* settled at the expense of Parliament, he explained. "If we examine our records, the journals of Parliament, we shall not find that a farthing was ever granted for the settling any colonies before the last reign, and then only for Georgia and Nova Scotia, which are still of little value." The colonies had *not* received their constitutions from Parliament, but from the king. Consequently Parliament could not claim that the colonial assemblies were creatures of Parliament.

The colonies had *not* been constantly protected from the Indians at Parliament's expense. "They protected themselves at their own expence for near 150 years after the first settlement and never thought of applying to Parliament for any aid against the Indians." The last two wars were fought *not* for the colonies' protection, but for the protection of British trade. In the most recent case: "The colonies were in peace, and the settlers had not been attacked or molested in the least, till after the miscarriage of Braddock's expedition to the Ohio."

The colonies had *not* refused to contribute their share toward the war effort. The colonial contribution in men was "far beyond their proportion," in treasure an expense "ten times greater than the money returned to them." The colonies were *not* the great gainers from the latest war. In fact just the opposite. The new acquisitions of land went to the king, not the Americans; moreover, the new land available for settlement diminished (through oversupply) the value of existing holdings; finally, the colonies in prosecuting the war assumed a heavy burden of debt they would be years retiring. The colonies did *not* escape taxes. "There cannot be a greater mistake than this." The colonies paid taxes to support civil and military establishments, to fund the debt from the war, and to create various public works—roads, bridges, and the like—that were already built and paid for in Britain. As a proportion of property, taxes in America were greater than those in Britain.

Lastly, the colonies did *not* claim that Parliament had no authority over them. All acts of Parliament had been accepted as such by the colonies—"acts to raise money upon the colonies by internal taxes only and alone excepted." Put otherwise: "The colonies submit to pay all external taxes laid on them by way of duty on merchandises imported into their country, and never disputed the authority of Parliament to lay such duties."

⌐ Charles Townshend probably read this piece. If so, the new chancellor of the exchequer, and de facto prime minister in Chatham's illness, might have taken issue with parts of Franklin's argument. The king had indeed granted the colonial charters, but since then England had fought a civil war to vindicate the primacy of Parliament over the Crown. The colonies might have defended themselves for the first 150 years, but for the several years after that they were happy for Parliament's help. To imply that the Americans paid taxes comparable to Britons was simply ludicrous; Franklin's standard of comparison—property values—grossly distorted the true tax burden.

But what must have interested Townshend most was Franklin's reiteration that the Americans did not object to external taxes. Townshend had heard Franklin make this argument in Commons; likely he guessed that "Benevolus" was actually Franklin. Townshend may have accepted Franklin's characterization of the American mind, or he may simply have wished to see Franklin hoist by his own petard. In either case, Townshend drew up a schedule of external taxes—to which, by Franklin's reasoning, the Americans ought not to object. The Townshend taxes were import duties: on glass, lead, paint pigments, paper, and tea.

Even had the Townshend program consisted of nothing more than this, many Americans would have complained. By no means was Franklin's distinction between internal and external taxes universally shared. Yet Townshend went beyond imposing new duties. The revenues from the new duties were earmarked not simply for the defense of the colonies but for the administration of colonial government. The effect of this, as Townshend intended and the Americans immediately recognized, would be to free royal governors and other royal officials from the control of the local assemblies, which heretofore had paid their salaries—and might withhold their salaries at displeasure.

Another alarming measure involved the Quartering Act of 1765, which required the colonies to barrack British troops on the request of the British commander in America. General Gage had so requested of New York, which resisted the request, leading to minor violence between American civilians and British troops. Townshend proposed to punish the New Yorkers by suspending their assembly.

That such measures should emanate from a ministry nominally headed by a friend of America surprised some members of Parliament. But a widespread feeling that the rebellious colonials must be brought into line overrode such surprise, and during the summer of 1767 the Townshend program became law.

~ During this period, Franklin found himself distracted by an important personal matter. His only daughter determined to wed a man of dubious character and prospects.

Richard Bache was the brother of a New York merchant named Theophylact Bache, a native of Yorkshire who migrated to Manhattan in

1751 and took up business with his aunt's husband, a former mayor of New York. The uncle died, leaving Theophylact the business. This proved successful enough to attract Theophylact's brother over from Yorkshire but not successful enough to support both Baches in New York itself, at least not at the level to which they aspired. Richard Bache accordingly was dispatched to Philadelphia, by now the leading city in the colonies, to open a branch of the business.

Somewhere between Yorkshire and New York the family name, which had been pronounced "beach," became "baytch," and it was under this pronunciation that Richard Bache met Sally Franklin shortly after his arrival in Philadelphia. (The pronunciation apparently wobbled, however. Franklin said "beach" at least occasionally, to judge by the misspellings in his dictated letters.) Almost certainly Bache arrived in finer style than Sally's father had displayed to her mother some forty years earlier, if only because Richard Bache was twenty-eight to Franklin's seventeen and already established in his trade. But the result was the same, and before long, Sally and Richard Bache were speaking of marriage.

Until now Deborah had managed the affairs of the family with adeptness and aplomb in Franklin's absence. Rearing Sally had fallen largely upon her shoulders, certainly during the last ten years. But arranging—or approving, rather—her daughter's marriage was not a responsibility she wished to take on unassisted. As the daughter of Pennsylvania's most famous citizen, and the (half) sister of New Jersey's governor, Sally did not want for company. "Sally has friends all about," her mother explained. Yet this new "addition of her friends," as Deborah described Richard Bache to Franklin, was special—to Sally, at any rate. Debbie was not quite sure how to deal with him, and so opted for a friendly yet watchful approach. Better this than to try to keep them apart. "I think it would only drive her to see him somewhere else, which would give me much uneasiness." It was very difficult to know how to proceed. "I am obliged to be father and mother," she said, somewhat plaintively. She added, "I hope I act to your satisfaction. I do according to my best judgment."

Franklin was concerned to know the character and prospects of Sally's suitor. Yet he appreciated the handicap his absence from home placed him under in this regard, and he did not want his handicap to become his daughter's. In May 1767 he could not know when he would be returning to Philadelphia, so he referred the matter to the combined judgment of Deborah, who knew Sally best, and William, who was in a position to find out something about Richard Bache. "I would not occasion a delay of her happiness if you thought the match a proper one."

But he could not leave the matter at this—after all, Sally was his only daughter. "I know very little of the gentleman or his character, nor can I at this distance," he wrote Debbie just a month later. He worried that Bache might have developed a wrong impression.

> I hope his expectations are not great of any fortune to be had with our daughter before our death. I can only say, that if he proves a good husband to her, and a good son to me, he shall find me as good a father as I can be. But at present I suppose you would agree with me that we cannot do more than fit her out handsomely in clothes and furniture, not exceeding in the whole five hundred pounds of value. For the rest they must depend, as you and I did, on their own industry and care, as what remains in our hands will be barely sufficient for our support, and not enough for them when it comes to be divided at our decease.

Per Franklin's request—and doubtless from a fraternal feeling as well—William inquired of Bache's business. Bache himself confessed to some recent financial reverses that left him temporarily illiquid; this prompted William to investigate further. What he found occasioned grave worry. It seemed Sally was not the first woman Bache had wooed, nor even the first in Philadelphia. He had initially fallen for Margaret Ross, one of Sally's closest friends. But two untoward occurrences had prevented the consummation of the romance. The first was Bache's inability to prove his worthiness to John Ross, Margaret's father. Ross investigated Bache's finances and discovered they were substantially less sound than Bache made them out to be. As William Franklin learned secondhand, and described to Franklin, Ross declared not only "that Mr. B. had often attempted to deceive him about his circumstances, but that he was well convinced he was not, before this unlucky affair [the recent reverse to which Bache owned up] happened, worth any thing if all his debts were paid. In short, that he is a mere fortune hunter who wants to better his circumstances by marrying into a family that will support him."

William conceded that the nature of the evidence against Bache was such that one could not know exactly where the truth lay, but on their face things looked bad. "I think it evident that these bills have involved him in a load of debt greatly more than he is worth, and that if Sally marries him they must both be entirely dependent on you for subsistence." William closed with an admonition revealing his sense that he had touched delicate issues. "Do burn this," he told his father.

The second, and definitive, development that had prevented the marriage of Bache and Margaret Ross was the young lady's sudden death in August 1766. This not only released Bache from a relationship that seemed stalled, but threw him into Sally's arms, for according to subsequent family tradition, Sally received a deathbed request from Margaret Ross to take Margaret's lover as her own and marry him. Perhaps the romantic-tragic aspect of this request was too much for Sally; perhaps she simply found Bache as charming as Margaret had. In any case, she then fell for Bache (if she had not already), and determined to marry him.

Franklin was torn by the situation. He did not wish to prevent Sally's happiness, but neither did he want her to marry a ne'er-do-well. In May 1767 Bache wrote Franklin a detailed accounting and explanation of his financial affairs. Evidently he was persuasive, for Franklin wrote back: "I received yours of the 21st of May and am truly sorry to hear of your misfortune. It must however be a consolation to you that it cannot be imputed to any imprudence of your own."

Franklin went on to make Bache's misfortune a test of his devotion to Sally. Bache was young; through industry and good management he might in a few years recoup his loss.

> But in the mean time your own discretion will suggest to you how far it will be right to charge yourself with the expense of a family which if undertaken before you recover yourself, may forever prevent your emerging. I love my daughter perhaps as well as ever parent did a child, but I have told you before that my estate is small, scarce a sufficiency for the support of me and my wife, who are growing old and cannot now bustle for a living as we have done. . . .
>
> I am obliged to you for the regard and preference you express for my child and wish you all prosperity; but unless you can convince her friends of the probability of your being able to maintain her properly, I hope you will not persist in a proceeding that may be attended with ruinous consequences to you both.

This was hardly a blessing on the match, but neither was it a veto. Had Franklin been on hand, he might have taken a stronger stand. Yet from across the Atlantic he could not reasonably do so. Sally knew her mind, while her father did not quite know his—on this subject. Setting aside his misgivings, she went ahead with the marriage.

During this third stay in England, Franklin continued his practice of summer vacations away from London. However great the city might be in many respects, it took a toll on one's health. Whether the thick smoke and damp chill of winter were worse than the infectious diseases of summer was partly a matter of taste. The taste of government officials tended toward summer departures, which afforded another reason for Franklin's holidays: when the city cleared out, there was nothing for a colonial agent to do. Additionally, of course, a man of Franklin's wide interests thrived on new sights and experiences.

In the summer of 1766 he traveled to Germany with John Pringle. "Though I was not quite to say sick, I was often ailing last winter and through this spring," Franklin explained to Debbie. Pringle wanted to drink the waters at Bad Pyrmont, a spa in the neighborhood of George III's ancestral home. "I hope more from the air and exercise," Franklin said. They left London in mid-June; because Pringle was physician to Queen Charlotte and she was expecting a child in the early autumn, they had to be back before the end of August.

After a week's journey by road, channel packet, and again road, they arrived at Bad Pyrmont. For two weeks they took the waters there. Pringle had intended to stay longer, but either because the treatment effected its benefits sooner than expected or because it appeared unlikely to do so at all, Pringle decided to join Franklin on a tour of the north German countryside. "I found a very fine country," Franklin explained, "and seemingly not so much hurt by the late war as one might have expected, since it appears every where fully cultivated, notwithstanding the great loss it sustained in people." For the first time Franklin saw the source of all those Germans who had emigrated to Pennsylvania over the years. At the same time he discovered that America was not the only place they were going. "It should seem their numbers are inexhaustible, since the Empress of Russia is now inviting into her country such Germans as are willing to leave their own, and obtained no less than forty thousand of them last year."

In mid-July they visited the city of Hanover, where they examined the Royal Library and watched the noted German scientist Johann Friedrich Hartman conduct a series of electrical experiments. From Hanover they went south to Göttingen; both were inducted into the

Royal Academy. A professor at the University of Göttingen, Gottfried Achenwall, took the opportunity to query Franklin at length on past and current conditions in the British North American colonies. Franklin expatiated on American geography, on the founding of the colonies, on the growth of their populations, on Indian affairs, on the diverse modes of free and bound labor, on American relations with Britain. Not surprisingly the professor received an account of recent events that favored the colonies. In an afterword to his transcript of their conversation, Achenwall summarized the lesson: "Every colony respects its founders, if it is well treated. But if it feels injured and despised, it is alienated. Colonies are not sent out to be slaves, but as lawful equals to those who remain at home."

Franklin and Pringle traveled south to Frankfurt and Mainz, then north down the Rhine to Cologne and the Netherlands, whence they crossed the Channel back to England. They arrived in good time for Pringle to oversee the birth of a healthy Princess Charlotte. As for Franklin, in reporting to the Pennsylvania Assembly that he was back on the job, he pronounced himself "well and hearty, my journey having perfectly answered its intention."

∽ The following year Franklin repeated his Continental cure. Again he traveled with Pringle, who again had a couple of months free before he had to be back with the queen, who again was pregnant.

The trip started in late August. "I have stayed too long in London this summer, and now sensibly feel the want of my usual journey to preserve my health," Franklin wrote Debbie. The principal symptoms of his delay were two: a backful of rashes and boils that "made him very uneasy," according to Mrs. Stevenson, and a sour temper, doubtless an expression of that uneasiness. From London to Dover he found nothing good to say about the journey. "I was engaged in perpetual disputes with the innkeepers, hostlers and postillions," he told Polly Stevenson. He could not understand why every post chaise he and Pringle rode in had a hood or canopy so pitched as to make it nearly impossible for the passengers to see out—which, in Franklin's opinion, was the whole reason for traveling. When he tried to persuade his drivers to change the rigging, they explained that this would be impossible. The chaises were rigged for the safety and benefit of the horses; to change would kill the animals. Franklin thought this absurd and said so, to no avail. "They added other reasons that were no reasons at all, and made me, as upon a hundred other occasions, almost wish that mankind had never been endowed with a reasoning faculty, since they know so little how to make use of it and so often mislead themselves by it; and that they had been furnished with a good sensible instinct instead of it."

The crossing to the Continent offered further evidence of human folly. "We embarked for Calais with a number of passengers who had never been before at sea. They would previously make a hearty breakfast, because if the wind should fail, we might not get over till supper-time. Doubtless they thought that when they had paid for their breakfast they had a right to it, and that when they had swallowed it they were sure of it. But they had scarce been out half an hour before the sea laid claim to it, and they were obliged to deliver it up. So it seems there are uncertainties even beyond those between the cup and the lip."

Things improved in France, slightly. Describing the boatmen and porters on the two sides of the Channel, Franklin declared, "I know not which are most rapacious, the English or French; but the latter have, with their knavery, the most politeness."

The roads from Calais to Paris were as good as those in England, paved in many places with smooth stones and lined with rows of trees. "But then the poor peasants complained to us grievously, that they were obliged to work upon the roads full two months in the year without being paid for their labour. Whether this is truth, or whether, like Englishmen, they grumble cause or no cause, I have not yet been able fully to inform myself."

Franklin was struck by the different complexions he encountered: dark at Calais and Boulogne but much lighter at Abbeville. He suspected that the change might be due to the immigration of Dutch spinners and weavers some generations earlier; these people were naturally lighter, and their work kept them indoors, away from the sun. Whatever the cause of their fairness, they were hard workers. "Never was I in a place of greater industry, wheels and looms going in every house."

At Paris the complexion changed again, but for a reason more readily discerned. Franklin thought Polly Stevenson would be interested in the beauty secrets of French ladies, so he shared them in some detail. The use of rouge was most striking.

> I have not had the honour of being at any lady's toilette to see how it is laid on, but I fancy I can tell you how it is or may be done: Cut a hole of 3 inches diameter in a piece of paper, place it

on the side of your face in such a manner as that the top of the hole may be just under your eye; then with a brush dipped in the colour paint face and paper together, so when the paper is taken off there will remain a round patch of red exactly the form of the hole.

This is the mode, from the actresses on stage upwards through all ranks of ladies to the princesses of the blood.

The practice stopped just short of the queen, as Franklin could attest from personal observation. He and Pringle were invited to a *grand couvert*, where King Louis XV and Queen Marie supped in public. Franklin was favorably impressed. "Serenity, complacence and beauty" characterized the queen; as for the king: "He spoke to both of us very graciously and cheerfully, is a handsome man, has a very lively look, and appears younger than he is." (Louis, called the Well-Beloved, was fifty-seven.) Yet Franklin did not wish Polly to get the wrong impression. "I would not have you think me so much pleased with this King and Queen as to have a whit less regard than I used to have for ours. No Frenchman shall go beyond me in thinking my own King and Queen the very best in the world and the most amiable."

Versailles alone was worth the trouble and expense of the trip. "The range of building is immense; the garden front most magnificent, all of hewn stone; the number of statues, figures, urns, &c. in marble and bronze of exquisite workmanship is beyond conception." The cost of construction was estimated to Franklin at £80 million. Yet someone was stinting on maintenance. "The waterworks are out of repair, and so is a great part of the front next the town, looking with its shabby half brick walls and broken windows not much better than the houses in Durham Yard." The effect was odd, but French. "There is, in short, both at Versailles and Paris, a prodigious mixture of magnificence and negligence, with every kind of elegance except that of cleanliness and what we call *tidyness*."

Yet Franklin conceded the palm to Paris on two points of civic hygiene. The first had to do with the water supply, which was rendered "as pure as that of the best spring by filtering it through cisterns filled with sand." The second involved the streets, which "by constant sweeping are fit to walk in though there is no paved foot path." For that reason many well-dressed people did indeed walk in the streets, eschewing the coaches and chairs essential for unspattered travel in London.

Franklin found the French people to be the politest he had met. "It seems to be a point settled here universally that strangers are to be treated with respect; one has just the same deference shewn one here by being a stranger as in England by being a lady." At a customs house near Paris the officers were about to seize two dozen bottles of Bordeaux wine given to Franklin and Pringle at Boulogne. "But as soon as they found we were strangers, it was immediately remitted on that account." At the cathedral of Notre-Dame, where an immense crowd had gathered to see an exhibit dedicated to the recently deceased dauphiness, Franklin and Pringle initially despaired of getting in. "But the officer being told that we were strangers from England, he immediately admitted us, accompanied and showed us everything." Franklin asked himself and Polly, "Why don't we practice this urbanity to Frenchmen? Why should they be allowed to outdo us?"

The experience occasioned reflections on travel and life. "Travelling is one way of lengthening life, at least in appearance. It is but a fortnight since we left London, but the variety of scenes we have gone through makes it seem equal to six months living in one place." The present journey had wrought effects upon the traveler obvious at first glance.

Perhaps I have suffered a greater change to my own person than I could have done in six years at home. I had not been here six days before my tailor and peruquier had transformed me into a Frenchman. Only think what a figure I make in a little bag wig [which gathered the hair in a bag at the nape of the neck] and naked ears! They told me I was become 20 years younger, and looked very *galante*. So being in Paris where the mode is to be sacredly followed, I was once very near making love to my friend's wife.

Vacation once more produced its intended effect. The travelers wended back to London early in October, with Franklin revived in body and spirit. Three weeks later he wrote to Debbie, "I have been extremely hearty and well ever since my return from France, the complaints I had before I went on that tour being entirely dissipated, and fresh strength and activity, the effects of exercise and change of air, have taken their place."

18

Reason and Riot

1768–69

꒰— He needed the revival, for awaiting his return to
England was the worst flare-up of anti-American feeling
since the aftermath of the Stamp Act riots. To Franklin's
embarrassment, the Townshend duties—which were just
the kind of external taxes he said the Americans
preferred—were immediately rejected in America as
illegitimate. Boston called a town meeting that endorsed a
renewal of the nonimportation compact of the Stamp Act
crisis. Providence and Newport did the same. New York
merchants embargoed trade with Britain; New York artisans
embargoed business with merchants who failed to live up to
the merchandise embargo.

Although the American response lacked the violence of the Stamp Act period, it convinced many in England of the Americans' fundamental bad faith. The Townshend duties, in this view, were a generous effort by Parliament to keep peace within the empire; the American call for nonimportation was therefore an insult and an outrage. The London journals throbbed with denunciations of the rebellious ingrates across the water; demands that they be brought to heel rang through the taverns and clubs of the city.

Franklin again found himself in a difficult position. As during the Stamp Act crisis, many in America suspected him of toadying to Parliament. By his own words, had he not brought on these new duties? At the same time, many in England considered him a sly deceiver. Had he not said the Americans accepted the idea of external taxes? Why were they then rejecting these external taxes?

Out of self-defense as much as the defense of American interests, Franklin felt obliged to respond. Characteristically, he called for calm. "Instead of raving (with your correspondent of yesterday) against the Americans as 'diggers of pits for this country,' 'lunatics,' 'sworn enemies,' 'false,' 'ungrateful,' 'cut-throats,' &c. which is a treatment of customers that I doubt is not like to bring them back to our shop," he wrote to the editor of the London *Gazetteer*, "I would recommend to all writers on American affairs (however *hard* their *arguments* may be) *soft words*, civility, and good manners." The current differences with the colonies were not fatal, and might be bridged by reason and fairness. Intemperate words would only aggravate matters. "Railing and reviling can answer no good end; it may make the breach wider; it can never heal it." The raver Franklin referred to had adopted the name "Old England": Franklin signed himself "Old England in its Senses."

A more thorough piece appeared in the *London Chronicle*. "The waves never rise but when the winds blow," he quoted the proverb and himself, before essaying to smooth the waters by diminishing the gale. The source of the trouble, he said, was a basic misunderstanding; a recounting of the distant and recent past by "an impartial historian of American facts and opinions" would set things straight. Again writing anonymously, he explained that the colonies' traditional method of contributing to imperial upkeep was by grants, supplied in response to royal requisition. This method "left the King's subjects in those remote countries the pleasure of showing their zeal and loyalty, and of imagining that they recommended themselves to their Sovereign by the liberality of their voluntary grants." This practice, and the opinions it entailed, conformed to the

Americans' belief that their rights as Englishmen forbade their taxation by any assembly not of their choosing.

All was well, he continued, until an unnamed (but easily identified) minister determined to levy a stamp tax upon the Americans. The Americans naturally resented this imposition and resisted it, till Parliament wisely rescinded it. The rescission put the Americans in "high good humour," but the ousted ministers in England who had designed the Stamp Act were resentful and eager for revenge. The objection of New York to quartering the king's troops afforded a pretext for suspending the assembly there. This greatly alarmed all the people of America, who inferred that what was done to New York might be done to them.

Their alarm intensified from the concurrent introduction of a new set of taxes. The taxes themselves were less odious than the purposes for which they were designed, namely, to support governors, judges, and other royal officials, thereby freeing those officials from any dependence on the provinces in which they served. This was the critical point. The governors, judges, and the rest had no permanent interest in the colonies, typically being sent out from England for a few years, to return to England at the end of their service. Should they be relieved of even the necessity of looking to the provincial assemblies for their pay, there would be no influencing them in the least. Governors might well take to ignoring the assemblies entirely, perhaps not even calling them. "Thus the people will be deprived of their most essential rights."

The colonists had other complaints. At the insistence of a handful of self-interested British merchants, they had been deprived of the right to issue paper currency of their own. Equally selfish parties benefited from prohibitions against the Americans' producing nails, steel—even hats. "It is of no importance to the common welfare of the empire, whether a subject of the King's gets his living by hats on this side or that side of the water. Yet the hatters of England have prevailed to obtain an act in their own favour, restraining that manufacture in America, in order to oblige the Americans to send their beavers to England to be manufactured, and purchase back the hats, loaded with the charges of a double transportation." No less galling was the long-standing practice of allowing the prisons of Britain to dump their human refuse upon American shores. For decades England had been availing itself of this opportunity to export its rogues and villains; just recently Scotland won this dubious distinction.

How were the Americans to respond? Could they conclude other than to look out for themselves by the only means in their power? Contravening no law, they simply decided not to import goods from Britain, the better to conserve the gold and silver they needed as currency, to avoid the taxes they had no part in designing, to lighten the burden British monopolies regularly exacted from them, to prepare for the day when a reenlightened Parliament and Crown would constitutionally *request* support rather than unconstitutionally *extort* it. "For notwithstanding the reproaches thrown out against us in their public papers and pamphlets, notwithstanding we have been reviled in the senate as *rebels* and *traitors*, we are truly a loyal people. Scotland has had its rebellions, and England its plots against the present royal family; but America is untainted with those crimes; there is in it scarce a man, there is not a single native of our country, who is not firmly attached to his King by principle and by affection."

But something novel was expected: a loyalty to Parliament, a loyalty that extended to surrender of all Americans' property to a body in which there sat not a single member of America's choosing. This was not merely novel; it was unconstitutional, and it threatened mortal harm to the empire. "We were separated too far from Britain by the Ocean, but we were united to it by respect and love, so that we could at any time freely have spent our lives and little fortunes in its cause. But this unhappy new system of politics tends to dissolve those bands of union, and to sever us for ever."

The anonymous Franklin, posing as a devoted supporter of Parliament, disowned these views for himself. "No reasonable man in England can approve of such sentiments." They were, rather, "the wild ravings of the at present half distracted Americans." Yet British self-interest required taking them into account. "I sincerely wish, for the sake of the manufactures and commerce of Great Britain, and for the sake of the strength which a firm union with our growing colonies would give us, that these people had never been thus needlessly driven out of their senses."

~ Franklin's distancing himself from the views of the American malcontents was a tactic of propaganda, aimed to avoid throwing his readers on the defensive. But it was also an indication of an honest ambivalence. Even while writing regularly on relations between the British government and the American colonies, he was unsure quite what those relations were or ought to be.

To his surprise, he received an education in the matter from a man he had until lately vehemently opposed. John Dickinson was a near-contemporary of William Franklin, and for a time their career paths ran parallel. Dickinson read law in Philadelphia at about the same time William did; he finished his legal education at London's Middle Temple just before William. Both went into politics after a brief legal practice; each became a solid supporter of the status quo.

But where William's appointment as royal governor of New Jersey placed him in league with Franklin, Dickinson's election to the Pennsylvania Assembly put him opposite Franklin, for the status quo Dickinson supported was that of the province's proprietary government. That Dickinson was an ardent advocate and facile writer merely made him, in Franklin's opinion, the more dangerous. Consequently it was with some surprise that Franklin read a series of articles published by Dickinson in the *Pennsylvania Chronicle* starting in the winter of 1767–68, articles that comprised the most astute and incisive argument in print on the subject of relations between Britain and the American colonies.

Actually, the surprise came after the fact, for the "Letters from a Farmer in Pennsylvania" were published, like most of Franklin's own pieces during this period, anonymously. Lord Hillsborough initially guessed that Franklin himself was the author. "My Lord H. mentioned the Farmer's letters to me," Franklin wrote William, "said he had read them, that they were well written, and he believed he could guess who was the author, looking in my face at the same time as if he thought it was me." Franklin did not know who the author was, and did not discover Dickinson's identity until some months later. By then he had arranged the republication of the "Letters" as a pamphlet in London, to which he appended an appreciative preface.

Dickinson's letters denied the central argument Franklin had made in his testimony before Parliament, and again when writing as Benevolus: that a meaningful distinction existed between internal and external taxes. This was the wrong way to slice the taxing issue, Dickinson said. The distinction that mattered was between taxes designed for revenue and those designed for regulation. The latter were unavoidable in a mercantile empire and were constitutionally innocuous. The former, even if devised as external taxes upon imports, were illegitimate and insidious when levied, as the Townshend taxes were, without the consent of those required to pay them.

Dickinson's letters provided the theoretical justification for colonial opposition to the Townshend acts. Most colonists had concluded that the acts were mischievous or worse, but they had struggled to find constitutional grounds for this conclusion. Dickinson discovered what they were looking for.

Franklin thought so, although he was fairly certain the Farmer would not have the last word. The problem, Franklin told William, was that even Dickinson's distinction was philosophically suspect. Dickinson allowed Parliament the power to regulate the trade of the colonies but withheld the right to tax trade for revenue. Where did one draw the line between regulation and revenue? Was a sugar tax of one penny a tariff for regulation and a sugar tax of two pence a tariff for revenue? More important than where the line lay, who would draw it? "If Parliament is to be the judge, it seems to me that establishing such principles of distinction will amount to little."

The fundamental problem was that any effort to subdivide sovereignty was almost certainly doomed to fail. Either Parliament was sovereign over the American colonies or it was not.

> The more I have thought and read on the subject the more I find myself confirmed in my opinion that no middle doctrine can be well maintained, I mean not clearly with intelligible arguments. Something might be made of either of the extremes: that Parliament has a power to make *all laws* for us, or that it has a power to make *no laws* for us.

At this moment, in March 1768, Franklin reached what seemed the Rubicon of relations between Britain and the American colonies. Either Parliament was supreme in all areas pertaining to the provinces or it was supreme in none. "I think the arguments for the latter more numerous and weighty than those for the former," he told William.

Typically, however, Franklin declined to be dogmatic on this point, nor on the conclusions to which it logically led. If Parliament was supreme in nothing touching the colonies, then the colonies were perfectly justified—in theory—in resisting every effort by Parliament to legislate for them in any manner whatsoever. "Supposing that doctrine established, the colonies would then be so many separate states, only subject to the same King, as England and Scotland were before the Union." Whether a union like that between England and Scotland should be effected between the American colonies and England would be a matter for Americans and English to decide. Franklin, still the British imperialist, favored a transatlantic union. "Though particular parts might find particular disadvantages in it, they would find greater advantages in the security arising to every part from the increased strength of the whole." He realized, however, that the moment was not propitious. "Such union is not likely to take place while the nature of our present relation is so little understood on both sides the water, and sentiments concerning it remain so widely different."

Two years earlier Franklin had parried a hostile question in Parliament suggesting that Americans' denial of Parliament's right to tax would logically lead to a denial of Parliament's right to legislate; he had asserted that they did not so reason then but might be convinced if Parliament got pushy. He had spoken half humorously, in an effort to turn aside an uncomfortable query. But events were proving him right, against his own wishes. He had no desire to break up the British empire, but logic was leading in that direction. And emotion—the emotion of others, not yet himself—was encouraging logic.

༄— **Emotions** were running high in England during the spring of 1768 on subjects besides the colonies. John Wilkes was back from France, and back in the thick of popular and Parliamentary politics. Defying his outlawry, Wilkes stood for Parliament from the City of London. He lost badly, finishing last in a field of seven, but blamed it on his late arrival. Unabashed, he hied off to Middlesex, where a seat was open and a cooperative opponent of the government gave him land enough to qualify to stand. Middlesex, like much of England during this season, was in a ferment from rising prices and falling wages. Silk weavers were striking; sailors refused to set sail; coal heavers dropped their shovels and raised their fists. Wilkes became an instrument of the popular distress, and disgruntled individuals discovered that the old cry of "Wilkes and liberty!" transmuted easily to "Wilkes and the coal heavers forever!" and the like.

Wilkes won handily, and on election night mobs of his supporters marched howling on London. King George called out the troops but himself stayed indoors; the troops proved sadly insufficient to their assignment. The Wilkites smashed windows at the house of London's Lord Mayor, a known foe of their hero, and at houses of such other notables as Bute and Lord Egmont. The Duke of Northumberland was cowed into drinking Wilkes's health; the Austrian ambassador, whose entire offense consisted of being caught in a coach on a street the rowdies made their own, was hauled out, thrown to his knees, and had "45" scrawled across the soles of his shoes.

Wilkes let the entertainment run its course before declaring, the following evening, that as the authorities were obviously incapable of keeping the peace, he and his friends would do so. A committee was appointed to patrol the streets; the group had special instructions to steer unruly persons—themselves included—away from St. James's Palace, "that no insult or indecency might be offered to the King."

Wilkes's libel conviction still hung over his head, but the government was too terrified to arrest him. The ministers were certain this would simply loose the mob again. Although Wilkes offered to surrender peacefully, he was rebuffed by the Lord Chief Justice, who wanted nothing to do with him; Wilkes finally had to insist on his right as an Englishman to be arrested. With great reluctance, the sheriff accepted him into custody—only to see his reluctance corroborated when Wilkes's followers hijacked the vehicle carrying him, cut free the horses, and then, to the amazement of all, put themselves in the shafts and traces and pulled the vehicle forward. Coach and team rumbled along the Strand and past Temple Bar before halting for refreshments at the Three Tuns Tavern, where Wilkes thanked his friends for their support but excused himself to proceed to prison afoot.

Conditions grew only more unruly with Wilkes behind bars. Actually, the bars on his room at the prison in St. George's Fields were more notional than real: the prisoner entertained guests of both sexes, including a seemingly endless train of young women who found Wilkes even more fascinating as a convicted criminal than he had been as a mere rake. Admirers sent cases of wine, butts of ale, countless hams, pheasants, turtles; from Maryland (the cause of Wilkesian liberty resonated across the Atlantic) arrived forty-five hogsheads of tobacco, which contributed their share to the further fouling of London's atmosphere.

Outside the prison thousands demonstrated against Wilkes's confinement. On May 10 the crowd swelled to perhaps twenty thousand, shouting, gesticulating, threatening authorities and passersby alike. The nervous authorities attempted to disperse the mob, but as the justice was reading the Riot Act, a hurled stone struck him. He summoned the troops that had been standing nearby and set them upon the crowd. In the melee that followed, some half dozen civilians were killed and many more wounded. The "St. George's Fields Massacre," as it was immediately labeled, triggered additional violence across London and environs. Wilkes was one theme of the window-smashing and house-wrecking but not the only one. Unemployed artisans shouted for work; sailors swung staves for cheaper bread; coalers demanded better beer. The defiance of authority revealed a common opinion, expressed variously, that hanging was better than starving. The upper classes held their breath. "We are glad if we can keep our windows whole, or pass and repass unmolested," wrote Horace Walpole. "I call it reading history as one goes along the street. . . . I do not love to think what the second volume must be of a flourishing nation running riot."

Franklin watched with astonishment. "The scenes have been horrible," he wrote William in April.

> London was illuminated two nights running at the command of the mob for the success of Wilkes in the Middlesex election; the second night exceeded any thing of the kind ever seen here on the greatest occasions of rejoicing, as even the small cross streets, lanes, courts, and other out-of-the-way places were all in a blaze with lights, and the principal streets all night long, as the mobs went round again after two o'clock, and obliged people who had extinguished their candles to light them again. Those who refused had all their windows destroyed.

The damage done to property (and the cost of the candles) had been computed at £50,000; the cost to the morale of the law-abiding citizenry was still higher. " 'Tis really an extraordinary event," Franklin said, "to see an outlaw and exile, of bad personal character, not worth a farthing, come over from France, set himself up as candidate for the capital of the kingdom, miss his election only by being too late in his application, and immediately carrying it for the principal county." Wilkes's hoodlums had terrorized not only London but far out into the countryside. Franklin had been to Winchester, more than sixty miles from London, and seen their scrawled "45" and other evidence of their passage the entire way.

As the anarchy persisted, so did Franklin's astonishment. "This capital, the residence of the King, is now a daily scene of lawless riot and confusion," Franklin wrote in May.

> Mobs are patrolling the street at noon day, some knocking all down that will not roar for Wilkes and liberty; courts of justice

afraid to give judgment against him; coalheavers and porters pulling down the houses of coal merchants that refuse to give them more wages; sawyers destroying the new sawmills; sailors unrigging all the outbound ships, and suffering none to sail till merchants agree to raise their pay; watermen destroying private boats and threatening bridges; weavers entering houses by force, and destroying the work in the looms; soldiers firing among the mobs and killing men, women and children; which seems only to have produced an universal sullenness that looks like a great black cloud coming on, ready to burst in a general tempest.

Nothing remained to hold the chaos at bay. "All respect to law and government seems to be lost among the common people, who are moreover continually enflamed by seditious scribblers to trample on authority and every thing that used to keep them in order."

Wilkes symbolized a system beset by cynicism and corruption. Electioneering had become little but bribery and boozing. "There have been amazing contests all over the kingdom," Franklin recorded, "£20 or 30,000 of a side spent in several places, and inconceivable mischief done by debauching the people and making them idle, besides the immediate actual mischief done by drunken mad mobs to houses, windows, &c." No less discouraging than the fact of the corruption was the insouciance that informed it. " 'Tis thought that near two millions will be spent in this election. But those who understand figures and act upon computation say the Crown has two millions a year in places and pensions to dispose of, and 'tis well worth while to engage in such a seven years lottery though all that have tickets should not get prizes."

The entire spectacle appalled Franklin, and it called into question an objective toward which he had been working his whole political life. From the 1740s until now he had opposed Pennsylvania's proprietary government, contending that Pennsylvanians would be better off under direct Crown rule. But England was under the rule of the Crown, and this was the sorry state to which it had fallen. He wrote one of his allies in the fight for royal rule, "I have urged over and over the necessity of the change we desire; but this country itself being at present in a situation very little better, weakens our argument that a royal government would be better managed and safer to live under than that of a proprietary."

If not proprietary rule, and not royal rule, then what? Logic—the same logic that was pushing Franklin to deny Parliament's right to legislate for the colonies—indicated an answer. But it was an answer he was not ready to accept.

~ As bad as things were in Britain, Franklin feared they could get worse. Rumors swirled of the replacement of Shelburne as secretary of state by Grenville. Franklin had jousted personally with Grenville and felt the man's animosity toward Americans; and he knew that Americans wasted no love on the author of the Stamp Act. The prospect of Grenville's return chilled him. "If this should take place," Franklin wrote Joseph Galloway, "or if in any other shape he comes again into power, I fear his sentiments of the Americans and theirs of him, will occasion such clashings as may be attended with fatal consequences."

Franklin had hoped that the Parliamentary elections would render the future clear enough for him to return to Pennsylvania; during the spring of 1768 he repeatedly anticipated embarking in a few weeks. But this new possibility pulled him back from wharfside and left him ensconced in Craven Street. With the fate of America in the balance, it would be irresponsible to leave.

There was something else. Franklin was clever at playing the politics of the imperial capital, with his artful phrasing in Parliament and his veiled authorship of articles in the London journals; but the politicians he was playing against included some who were clever in their own right, and were not entirely inept at playing *him*. Upon the appointment of Hillsborough as secretary of state for America, rumors began swirling of a possible appointment for Franklin as Hillsborough's undersecretary. Franklin initially discounted the rumors. "It is a settled point here that I am too much of an American," he told William. But apparently the point was not as settled as Franklin suggested, for the rumors persisted for many months. Significantly, he did nothing to stifle them—as by a declaration that he did not want the job.

From the perspective of the ministry, a Franklin appointment made obvious sense. Franklin was clearly the most capable of the colonial agents, and governments are always on the lookout for capable people. More to the immediate point, Franklin aboard would be less dangerous than Franklin adrift. As a member of the government rather than an antagonist, he would be unable—because unwilling—to frustrate the government's designs, which would be *his* designs. It was one of the oldest practices of politics, because it was one of the most effective.

During much of 1768 various ministers dangled the possibility of appointment before Franklin. Under the circumstances existing between the colonies and the government this was a topic Franklin was reluctant to share with most correspondents; the one to whom he confided was his son, the recipient and continuing beneficiary of just such an appointment. In a letter of July, Franklin explained both his prospects and his predicament. Sometime earlier the secretary to the Treasury, Grey Cooper—"my fast friend," Franklin called him—had said that the Duke of Grafton had lately been speaking favorably of him. Grafton headed the Treasury; more important, following Townshend's sudden death, he had assumed the role of acting leader of the government, and heir apparent, in place of the still-ailing Chatham. Some question had been raised regarding Franklin's long residence in England, and whether this hindered his fulfillment of his duties as deputy postmaster. There were two ways to skin this cat, Grafton intimated to Cooper, in words intended for Franklin. Grafton had directed Cooper to tell Franklin—as Franklin retold the story to William—"that though my going to my post might remove the objection, yet if I chose rather to reside in England, my merit was such in his opinion as to entitle me to something better here, and it should not be his fault if I was not well provided for."

Franklin responded cagily. "I told Mr. Cooper that without having heard any exception had been taken to my residence here, I was really preparing to return home, and expected to be gone in a few weeks." But his trunk was not on the boat yet. He informed Cooper "that I was extremely sensible of the Duke's goodness in giving me this intimation and very thankful for his favourable disposition towards me; that having lived long in England, and contracted a friendship and affection for many persons here, it could not but be agreeable to me to remain among them some time longer, if not for the rest of my life." Moreover, "there was no nobleman to whom I could from sincere respect for his great abilities and amiable qualities so cordially attach myself, or to whom I should so willingly be obliged for the provision he mentioned, as to the Duke of Grafton, if his Grace should think I could, in any station where he might place me, be serviceable to him and to the public."

Cooper was delighted to hear this. He said he had hoped to keep Franklin in England and was pleased that Franklin was not averse to staying. Cooper suggested that Franklin call at the Treasury for a personal meeting with the duke.

Franklin did call, only to learn that the duke was out. Cooper instead ushered him to a meeting with Lord North, the chancellor of the exchequer. North was as complimentary as Grafton had been, and said he hoped the government could find some way to make it worth the doctor's while to remain in England. "I thanked his lordship, and said I should stay with pleasure if I could any ways be useful to government."

Cooper insisted that Franklin come to his country house at Richmond with him, where they dined and Franklin spent the night. Shortly thereafter Cooper introduced Franklin to other ministerial worthies, including Lord Sandwich, who had been a critic but was won over by Franklin's charm. "We parted very good friends," Franklin told William. Lord Clare, lately president of the Board of Trade, was another admirer. "He gave me a great deal of flummery, saying that though at my examination [before Commons] I answered some of his questions a little pertly, yet he liked me from that day, for the spirit I showed in defence of my country; and at parting, after we had drank a bottle and a half of claret each, he hugged and kissed me, protesting he never in his life met with a man he was so much in love with."

Since then nothing had come of these overtures. Franklin could not say whether Grafton had changed his mind about him, or whether some appointment impended. He had another meeting scheduled with Grafton at the Treasury in a few days. If a post were offered, he indicated to William, he would not turn it down. "I did not think fit to decline any favour so great a man expressed an inclination to do me, because at court if one shews an unwillingness to be obliged it is often construed as a mark of mental hostility, and one makes an enemy."

Yet there were limits on what a person could ethically accept. "If Mr. Grenville comes into power again in any department respecting America, I must refuse to accept of any thing that may seem to put me in his power, because I apprehend a breach between the two countries; and that refusal will give offence."

For this reason a person must not place excessive store in the future. "A turn of a die may make a great difference in our affairs. We may either be promoted, or discarded; one or the other seems likely soon to be the case, but 'tis hard to divine which."

⌒ As a young tradesman in America, Franklin had made much of the virtues of industry and frugality. Industry allowed the tradesman to employ each moment gainfully, frugality to husband the gains of industry.

Even the appearance of these virtues was important, for it won customers to the man so diligent in his craft and thrifty with his resources.

As a mature politician and philosopher, Franklin had less use for such bourgeois values. The governing classes in England were the leisured and comfortable classes, and a man who wished to make headway among them needed to fit in. Excessive industry was cause for suspicion, while frugality reflected poorly on one's accomplishments. The philosopher, of course, required leisure to think and read and write, and pleasant circumstances conduced to such intellectual endeavors.

Franklin never lived extravagantly, but the longer he stayed in London, the more attached he became to London's standards of living. His comfortable Craven Street apartment, his servants, his private coach, his annual travels, his socializing at clubs—all contributed to a life he learned to enjoy considerably.

Yet enough of those early values survived that when he discovered an indulgence that gave pleasure while costing nothing, or while allowing time for productive work, he took double delight. A French admirer had written with news of a novel method for treating smallpox, one that involved cold baths. Franklin answered that he had long heard cold baths touted as a tonic, but considered the shock to the system too violent.

> I have found it much more agreeable to my constitution to bathe in another element, I mean cold air. With this view I rise early almost every morning, and sit in my chamber without any clothes whatever, half an hour or an hour, according to the season, either reading or writing. This practice is not in the least painful, but on the contrary, agreeable; and if I return to bed afterwards, before I dress myself, as sometimes happens, I make a supplement to my night's rest, of one or two hours of the most pleasing sleep that can be imagined.

Air baths were free; another indulgence actually saved money—and trouble. "I reckon it among my felicities," Franklin told his Scottish friend Kames, "that I can set my own razor and shave myself perfectly well, in which I have a daily pleasure, and avoid the uneasiness one is otherwise obliged to suffer sometimes from dull razors and the dirty fingers or bad breath of a slovenly barber."

The naked philosopher pondered matters large and small, among them why shaving himself was such a pleasure. Franklin and Kames had been comparing notes on true happiness; Franklin summarized for them both: "I have long been of an opinion similar to that you express, and think happiness consists more in small conveniences or pleasures that occur every day, than in great pieces of good fortune that happen but seldom to a man in the course of his life."

Happiness was the subject of another correspondence. A young man asked Franklin's views on marriage—in particular, whether youth or age was more likely to contract connubial bliss. "From the matches that have fallen under my observation," Franklin replied, "I am rather inclined to think that early ones stand the best chance for happiness. The tempers and habits of young people are not yet become so stiff and uncomplying as when more advanced in life, they form more easily to each other, and thence many occasions of disgust are removed." To be sure, youth lacked experience. But this might be remedied by the advice of relatives and friends. Perhaps recalling his own oat-sowing days, he asserted that despite occasional reasons to delay entrance into the married state, it was best not to tarry. "In general, when Nature has rendered our bodies fit for it, the presumption is in Nature's favour, that she has not judged amiss in making us desire it."

Still other correspondence concerned a more literal plunge. "I cannot be of opinion with you that 'tis too late in life for you to learn to swim," he wrote an acquaintance who had accepted employment entailing frequent boat travel but feared for his life because he had never learned to swim. In a long letter that conjoined the physics of floating bodies, the psychology of desensitization to fear, and the pedagogy of new tricks to old dogs, Franklin laid out a concise program for basic drown-proofing. Yet this should be but the first step—for anyone. "Learn fairly to swim, as I wish all men were taught to do in their youth. They would, on many occurrences, be the safer for that skill, and on many more the happier, as freer from painful apprehensions of danger, to say nothing of the enjoyment in so delightful and wholesome an exercise."

A public-health issue of a different sort involved a mysterious medley of complaints from people in diverse locations and occupations. In his years as a practicing printer, Franklin had sometimes warmed his type pieces during cold weather to make them easier to handle, but at the end of days when he had done so he often noted a curious pain and stiffness in his hands. Inquiry of veteran typesetters revealed instances where regular practice of this kind had deprived persons of the use of their hands permanently. Something in the lead type, released upon heating, seemed toxic.

Franklin filed away this information, and learned to set cold type. He may or may not have recalled it in 1745 when he printed an article for Thomas Cadwalader entitled *Essay on the West India Dry Gripes*, but it certainly came to mind when he and John Pringle traveled to France the first time. The pair toured a hospital devoted to patients afflicted with the "dry belly ache," a gastrointestinal disorder associated with various occupations. Analyzing the list of patients, Franklin concluded that what the jobs had in common was chronic exposure to lead.

Not long back in London, Franklin received a letter from Cadwalader Evans, apparently a relative of Thomas Cadwalader. Evans noted that the symptoms of the dry gripes of the West Indies were similar to the symptoms of the dry bellyache of the British North American colonies and Britain. He also noted that although the climate and lifestyle of the British West Indies approximated that of the French West Indies, the latter exhibited nothing like the incidence of the malady in the former. Evans suggested a reason: while the inhabitants of the French Indies drank wine, the people of the British Indies drank rum—as did many people in the North American colonies and Britain. Rum, unlike wine, was distilled, and often the stills used a worm—or coil—made of lead.

Franklin replied that something similar had been observed in New England, and indeed the local authorities there had outlawed the use of lead in stills. He went on to say of the dry gripes, "I have long been of opinion that that distemper proceeds always from a metallic cause only, observing that it affects among tradesmen those that use lead, however different their trades, as glazers, type-founders, plumbers, potters, white lead-makers and painters."

The epidemiology and etiology of lead poisoning were ongoing interests for Franklin; likewise other of his scientific studies. He helped coordinate what amounted to an international effort to calculate the distance from the earth to the sun, an effort that involved observing the transit of Venus across the sun's face from different spots on earth and measuring the parallax. His electrical investigations took practical form when he advised the custodians of St. Paul's Cathedral in London on how to preserve Christopher Wren's masterwork from lightning bolts. A venture by William Franklin into farming prompted his father to delve into the latest thinking on scientific agriculture. The possibility of starting a British silk industry propelled him into the natural history of the silkworm and the mulberry tree.

He devised a new phonetic alphabet to regularize English spelling.

Polly Stevenson was his experimental subject in this endeavor. "Diir Pali," he wrote her—in a note that then introduced six invented letters (irreproducible without Franklin's special fonts) and numerous redefinitions of use and pronunciation. He conceded that convincing anyone else to employ the new alphabet would be difficult. But it was worth trying. English spelling was already so far from pronunciation as to make literacy difficult for native speakers, nearly impossible for foreigners. "If we go on as we have done a few centuries longer," he said (in translation), "our words will gradually cease to express sounds; they will only stand for things, as the written words do in the Chinese language."

Not content with editing man, Franklin marked up God. The Lord's Prayer, in Franklin's rendering, became:

> Heavenly Father, may all revere thee, and become thy dutiful children and faithful subjects. May thy laws be obeyed on Earth as perfectly as they are in Heaven. Provide for us this day as thou has hitherto daily done. Forgive us our trespasses, and enable us likewise to forgive those that offend us. Keep us out of temptation, and deliver us from evil.

Franklin glossed his revision with arguments literary, historical, and theological. "Heavenly Father" replaced "Our Father which art in heaven" because the former was "more concise, equally expressive, and better modern English." "Lead us not into temptation" gave way to "Keep us out of temptation" because the former reflected an outdated view of the relationship of God to man. "The Jews had a notion that God sometimes tempted, or directed or permitted the tempting of people. Thus it was said he tempted Pharoah; directed Satan to tempt Job; and a false prophet to tempt Ahab; &c. Under this persuasion it was natural for them to pray that he would not put them to such severe trials. We now suppose that temptation, so far as it is supernatural, comes from the Devil only." To blame God for temptation was unworthy of Him.

⁂ Among his other distractions, Franklin continued to pursue his land schemes. His modest success in Nova Scotia having whetted his appetite, he looked again to the far greater rewards to be anticipated in the Ohio and Mississippi valleys. Compared to cold Nova Scotia, the heartland of the continent was warm and welcoming; the one essential thing that prevented settlement there was the presence of Indian tribes unreconciled to the loss of their ancestral lands (or, in some cases, lands they had taken from other tribes' ancestors). This military barrier was what had prompted the legal barrier thrown up by the Proclamation of 1763; it seemed fair to assume that should the first be removed, the second would fall in turn. Indeed, the government in London had indicated a readiness to move the Proclamation Line west should a settlement be reached with the Indians.

Just such a settlement took tentative place in the autumn of 1768. At Fort Stanwix, on the New York frontier, governors William Johnson of New York and William Franklin of New Jersey met with some three thousand Indians to negotiate a treaty and the sale of lands to the English. The transaction was complicated—but very promising for William Franklin, who attended both as the representative of his province and as a personal empire-builder. He and some partners from New Jersey purchased 30,000 acres in Albany County, New York. With another group he acquired rights to a separate 100,000 acres. And he helped supervise the transfer of 1.8 million acres to a motley collection of hopefuls calling themselves the "Suffering Traders"—the principal suffering of whom consisted of so-far-disappointed dreams of vast wealth. The whole arrangement was tied to the treaty between the representatives of the Indians and the British Crown; approval of the treaty would signify approval of the land sales.

William Franklin knew just the man for help getting the treaty approved, and his father, shortly apprised of the details and invited to join in the prospective rewards, was more than happy to oblige. In the spring of 1769 Franklin met with two of the Suffering Traders (whose suffering seemed materially diminished by the Fort Stanwix deal) to plot political strategy. Franklin fully realized by now that nothing passed through the British government on its merits; what counted was friends. He advised the Traders to broaden their partnership to include individuals influential at court and in Parliament. With such sponsorship their project stood a chance of approval; without it, none.

Among those added to the list, the most prominent were Thomas and Richard Walpole, nephews of the great Robert Walpole; and Thomas Pitt, nephew of Chatham. In honor of the Walpoles, the bruited partnership became known as the Walpole Company colloquially, although officially it was denominated the Grand Ohio Company. Upon reconsideration of the politics and economics of the project, Franklin and the others proposed to petition the Crown for the right to purchase

2.4 million acres in the territory included under the terms of the Fort Stanwix treaty; the land would be divided into 60 shares of 40,000 acres each, which would be distributed among the participants or sold to additional partners.

Franklin took it upon himself to find those additional partners. He started at the top, or as close as seemed feasible. He approached Grey Cooper, Grafton's deputy at the Treasury, with an appeal to profit and posterity. "An application being about to be made for a grant of lands in the territory on the Ohio lately purchased of the Indians," Franklin wrote Cooper, "I cannot omit acquainting you with it and giving you my opinion that they will very soon be settled by people from the neighbouring provinces, and be of great advantage in a few years to the undertakers." Franklin had met Cooper's children. "I wish for their sakes you may incline to take this opportunity of making a considerable addition to their future fortunes." The expense would be a "trifle": £200 for 40,000 acres. He pressed to close the deal: "If therefore you will give me leave, I shall put your name down among us for a share."

⌒ **While Cooper** considered the offer, Franklin pondered his own posterity, for even as he wrote this letter he was awaiting his first legitimate grandchild. Franklin had grown accustomed to the marriage of Sally to Richard Bache—but slowly. For many months he refused to answer Bache's letters; when he finally got around to writing back he explained that in light of Bache's financial problems he had considered the marriage "very rash and precipitate." "I could not therefore but be dissatisfied with it, and displeased with you whom I looked upon as an instrument of bringing future unhappiness upon my child." In this frame of mind he had deliberately not written. "I could say nothing agreeable; I did not choose to write what I thought, being unwilling to give pain where I could not give pleasure." But his anger had subsided. "Time has made me easier." He now chose to be encouraged by reports of improving prospects in the Bache business and urged his son-in-law to industrious application, whereby past losses might be retrieved. "I can only add at present that my best wishes attend you, and that if you prove a good husband and son, you will find in me an affectionate father."

A happy marriage for his daughter mattered more to Franklin the older he got, for he suspected he would not live much longer. A letter to

Debbie written two weeks before his sixty-third birthday—a letter in which he expressed pleasure that Debbie found much to approve of in Bache—contained an assessment of Franklin's physical condition and his expectations regarding the future. He suffered a "touch of the gout" but otherwise was in good health. Yet he did not flatter himself that he would live to a great age. "I know that men of my bulk often fail suddenly; I know that according to the course of nature I cannot at most continue much longer, and that the living of even another day is uncertain. I therefore now form no scheme but such as are of immediate execution."

Yet grandchildren held out the prospect of immortality, after an earthly fashion. Franklin had one grandchild already, of course: William's son, Temple. What inheritance the child might claim was problematic; as yet even his father did not acknowledge him. Temple was six at the beginning of 1769, and that January, William suggested a roundabout way of bringing the boy into the family. Franklin talked of returning to America come spring; could he bring Temple along? "He might then take his proper name and be introduced as the son of a poor relation, for whom I stood godfather and intended to bring up as my own."

That situation would have to sort itself out; before it did, Sally brought into the world a grandchild the family could openly delight in. Even William, who might have been expected to have at least mildly mixed feelings about his half sister's child, registered pleasure in "my little nephew," as he wrote in introducing Benjamin Franklin Bache to his grandfather. "He is not so fat and lusty as some children at his time are, but he is altogether a pretty little fellow, and improves in his looks every day." The boy's grandmother told her husband, "Every body says he is much like you."

᠀— **Franklin** had to take Debbie's word on the subject. Although he constantly talked about returning home—especially in letters to her—he stayed in London. The marriage of his daughter did not bring him home, nor the arrival of his grandson.

Not even a serious illness in Debbie drew him back across the Atlantic. During the winter of 1768–69 Debbie suffered a stroke that slurred her speech and erased her memory. Although she recovered somewhat, in June 1769 a Philadelphia doctor friend, Thomas Bond,

wrote Franklin that "her constitution in general appears impaired." Bond
added, "These are bad symptoms in advanced life and augur danger of
further injury on the nervous system."

Debbie's affliction was evident in her letters to Franklin. Spelling and
punctuation had always given her trouble, but now the very meaning of
her sentences strayed and circled back upon itself. In her words on the
pages before him, Franklin could trace her decline.

Yet he did not go home. In fairness, there was nothing he could have
done at home to alleviate her condition. She would get better, God willing, or she would not, God unwilling. It was out of human hands.

All the same, had he been looking for a reason to leave London, this
was more than he needed. His allies in the Pennsylvania Assembly would
have understood, as would his friends in England. No one would have
accused him of abandoning his post.

∽ But he was not looking for a reason to go home; he was looking
for reasons to stay. And he did not have to look far. He hoped to win approval of the land schemes he and William had been pushing; success
was hardly assured, but it appeared more likely than ever. Yet success was
a delicate flower that required constant cultivation, especially in the demanding environment of political London; to leave now would jeopar-
dize years of work and dreams. The possibility of a choice appointment
to government remained a tantalizing possibility. Franklin eschewed ambition, but for the runaway from Boston to culminate his career in a distinguished position in the imperial capital would be most satisfying. As
Poor Richard might have said, plums don't fall far from the tree; for
Franklin to depart London would eliminate any chance of his catching one.

Both the land scheme and the possibility of an appointment depended on the larger and overriding issue of the day—overriding at least
for a colonial agent. The elections in England had temporarily eclipsed
the question of the nature and fate of relations between the American
colonies and the motherland. But the new Parliament would soon be sitting, and it would certainly take up the colonial question.

As before, Franklin did what he could to influence Parliament's
thinking. He wrote letters to London papers urging conciliation and
warning against the opposite. In one such letter he recalled the revolt of
the United Provinces of the Netherlands against Spanish rule, a conflict

that lasted eighty years and ruined the Spanish empire. British soldiers might justly judge themselves braver and more competent than their Spanish counterparts, Franklin conceded (again anonymously), but a war against America would place them in unusually unfavorable circumstances. "It is well known that America is a country full of forests, mountains, &c. That in such a country a small irregular force can give abundance of trouble to a regular one that is much greater." In the late war against France, Canada held out for five years against 25,000 British regulars and a like number of American troops. Canada, now British, was far from the strongest of the fifteen American colonies; a war against all fifteen, with those colonial troops now in opposition, would take—by Franklin's half-spurious, half-serious arithmetic—fifteen times as long, or seventy-five years.

In another published piece he vigorously disavowed an intention often imputed to the Americans: to gain independence. "Allow me to tell you that you are *certainly* mistaken," he replied to a journal's letter-writer who had described the colonies as harboring advocates of independence, "and that there is not a single wish in the colonies to be free from subjection to their amiable sovereign, the King of Great Britain." This contribution was only slightly pseudonymous, as anyone who thought twice about the name of the author, "Francis Lynn," might have recognized.

In another instance he posed as a Frenchman. France was in the process of subduing a rebellion in Corsica and was coming under considerable criticism in England for doing so. "You English consider us French as enemies to liberty," Franklin covertly wrote. "How easy it is for men to see the faults of others while blind to their own." Corsicans had never enriched France by their labor and commerce, had never fought side by side with Frenchmen in war, had never loved and honored France, were not the very children of France. "But all this your American colonists have been and are to you! Yet at this very moment, while you are abusing us for attempting to reduce the Corsicans, you yourselves are about to make slaves of a much greater number of those British Americans." What did the British know about liberty? "All the liberty you seem to value is the liberty of abusing your superiors, and of tyrannizing over those below you."

Franklin supplemented his public—if often disguised—campaign with private letters devoted to preventing the situation in America from escalating beyond control. Boston seemed the likeliest location of trouble. In October 1768, British troops had been landed at Boston to suppress incipient sedition, which Governor Francis Bernard detected in the

Massachusetts assembly, in the streets of the city, and in the writings of Samuel Adams and others. Franklin feared the worst. "I am under continued apprehensions that we may have bad news from America," he wrote to George Whitefield. "The sending soldiers to Boston always appeared to me a dangerous step; they could do no good, they might occasion mischief." The colonists considered themselves injured and oppressed; the soldiers were as insolent as young men under arms usually were. "I cannot but fear the consequences of bringing them together. It seems like setting up a smith's forge in a magazine of gunpowder."

(In this letter to the great evangelist, Franklin continued their theological debate of thirty years. "I *see* with you that our affairs are not well managed by our rulers here below; I wish I could *believe* with you that they are well attended to by those above." But he could not. "I rather suspect, from certain circumstances, that though the general government of the universe is well administered, our particular little affairs are perhaps below notice, and left to take the chance of human prudence or imprudence, as either may happen to be uppermost.")

After the new Parliament met and failed to repeal the Townshend acts, refusing even to entertain American petitions against them, Franklin wrote to friends in Boston, pleading patience. From his youth he knew the sort of roughnecks who roamed from the North End to the South End and back; they must not be given their heads. Rather Boston—and the other colonies—should stick to their peaceful nonimportation agreements as the antidote to the Townshend acts. Parliament appeared fixed in its determination not to repeal the acts. "I hope my country-folks will remain as fixed in their resolutions of industry and frugality till those acts are repealed," Franklin wrote Samuel Cooper, a Boston minister who subsequently circulated Franklin's views. Parliament underestimated the Americans, Franklin said. "They flatter themselves that you cannot long subsist without their manufactures; they believe that you have not virtue enough to persist in such agreements; they imagine the colonies will differ among themselves, deceive and desert one another, and quietly one after the other submit to the yoke and return to the use of British fineries." Franklin said he had told his British acquaintances otherwise; he hoped his American friends would not prove him wrong.

Franklin laid the blame directly, and exclusively, at the door of Parliament. The people of Britain were not at fault, being of "a noble and generous nature." "We have many, very many friends among them," Franklin told Cooper. Still less was King George responsible for America's woes. "I can scarcely conceive a King of better disposition, of more exemplary virtues, or more truly desirous of promoting the welfare of all his subjects." Parliament was quite another matter. "Though I might excuse that which made the acts [that is, the previous Parliament] as being surprised and misled into the measure, I know not how to excuse this, which under the fullest conviction of its being a wrong one, resolves to continue it." Even American opponents of the Townshend acts diplomatically referred to the "wisdom and justice" of Parliament; Franklin remarked, "If this new Parliament had really been *wise* it would not have refused even to read a petition against the Acts; and if it had been *just* it would have repealed them and refunded the money."

Nor could Franklin honestly hope for much better. Though sentiment existed in Parliament for repeal—out of mercantile self-interest, as after the Stamp Act, rather than any love for the Americans—the government could not muster the will or energy to move. On this point Franklin had to agree with Grenville, who from the opposite vantage point likened the present ministry to two inexperienced sailors. The pair found themselves up in the round top, knowing nothing of what they were supposed to be about, so they simply pretended to keep busy. "What are you doing there, Jack?" cried the boatswain (in Franklin's retelling of Grenville's story). "Nothing," replied Jack. "And, pray, what are you about, Tom?" the boatswain asked the other. "I," answered Tom, "am helping him."

With such in charge, the future was clouded at best. "It is very uncertain as yet what turn American affairs will take here," Franklin told William in October 1769. "The friends of both countries wish a reconciliation; the enemies of either endeavour to widen the breach. God knows how it will end."

19

The Rift Widens

1770–71

∽ In March 1770 the spark from the forge Franklin
had spoken of hit the gunpowder of the magazine.

∽ Boston's winter had everyone in the city on edge. The
cold white blanket that covered the streets and the Common
had long lost the charm of first snowfall; the icicles that
hung from each eave and had once seemed picturesque now
simply threatened the crania of passersby. Yet such was true
every winter; what made this winter worse was that to the
insults of nature were added those of Parliament. Boston
was a town under siege. British soldiers patrolled the
streets; British warships were anchored in the harbor.
The soldiers had little to do, and less money to do it with;
to supplement both deficiencies they sought casual work.

This annoyed unskilled Bostonians who themselves wanted work and needed it more than the soldiers did. Both groups were young, male, physically inclined, and prone to spend what little cash they did command drinking rum in the town's taverns. To some, brawling was the intended climax of an evening out; to others simply a satisfactory alternative when loose women were in short supply—as they usually were to men short of money.

Had the young bucks been left to themselves, the brawling might have produced broken heads, the odd bitten ear, and little more, but upon their rowdy shoulders was placed the burden of the escalating imperial conflict. The most vocal elements of Boston's popular political class—Sam Adams, James Otis, and the Sons of Liberty—seized every opportunity to attack the Parliament that had sent the young men in red uniforms to keep such as Adams, Otis, and the Sons in line. Boston papers related, and in some cases created, lurid stories of insults and atrocities inflicted upon the innocent people of the city by the mercenaries camped in their midst. Townsmen tried to sap said mercenaries' morale by enticing them to desertion, which the British officers combated by floggings and, in one exemplary instance, execution.

The tension turned Boston upon itself. A merchant accused of violating the nonimportation pact was branded an enemy of the people; a shouting crowd of young men and boys put up a sign—IMPORTER—outside his shop. A neighbor, Ebenezer Richardson, came to his friend's defense and tore down the sign. The crowd turned on Richardson, who himself labored under the radicals' suspicion (one of them called him "the most abandoned wretch in America"). Richardson was cornered in his house; a radical challenged him, above the tumult: "Come out, you damn son of a bitch. I'll have your heart out, your liver out!" Rocks through Richardson's windows punctuated the challenge.

Richardson had seen what happened to Thomas Hutchinson's house, and though his was hardly so elegant, it was home, and he aimed to defend it. He emerged with a shotgun; when the crowd continued to taunt and threaten, he unleashed a load of swan shot. A boy of eleven named Christopher Seider was killed by the discharge; another lad was wounded. This sobered some in the crowd but inflamed others; while Richardson paused to reload, the latter group engulfed him and might well have torn him limb from limb had not one of their number, a well known Son of Liberty, insisted that he receive a trial before being executed.

Richardson was a Bostonian, not a British soldier, but the killing of the Seider boy was blamed upon the British policies the soldiers represented. And the boy's funeral became an occasion for display of popular fury at the condition of servitude to which Parliament appeared bent on subjecting Boston. For the next two weeks tempers in the taverns and on the streets grew shorter. A patriot ropemaker provoked a fight by asking a soldier if he wanted work; when the soldier said he did, the hemp man told him what he might do: "Clean my shithouse."

On the night of March 5 a feisty apprentice mocked a British officer on King Street. A British private named Hugh White, who happened to be standing nearby, struck the apprentice for his insolence. The young man shouted for help, which appeared as if from nowhere. In the middle distance, church bells began ringing, as they did for a fire. Hundreds of men and women answered the call—but suspiciously armed. "It is very odd to come to put out a fire with sticks and bludgeons," an observer remarked.

As the crowd surged, the captain of the British guard mobilized his men to rescue Private White. Muskets at the ready, with bayonets fixed, the small company thrust its way through the shouting throng to White. But the crowd closed in behind, and instead of one hostage it now held nine. Curses, oaths, snowballs, and chunks of jagged ice rained down upon the soldiers; in the semi-glow of moonlight (Boston's byways lacked streetlamps) the soldiers credibly feared for their lives. The crowd bayed for blood—at times not seeming to care whose. "Damn you, you sons of bitches, fire!" taunted one radical. "You can't kill us all!"

An especially vicious frozen missile struck another private, Hugh Montgomery. The young man staggered, slipped, and went down. In response—on orders or otherwise: the question became the focus of bitter and ultimately unresolved controversy—soldiers fired. At point-blank range the balls could only be lethal. Three of the crowd were killed at once; two more died later; half a dozen were wounded but survived.

"Horrid Massacre" was how Sam Adams styled the affair. "Bloody Massacre" was the headline of the Paul Revere print that soon began circulating. "Boston Massacre" was the message that echoed down the American seaboard, and across the Atlantic to where Franklin was expecting word of some such tragedy.

～ "Those detestable murderers," Franklin called the soldiers. Although anticipated, the violence at Boston still came as a shock. The killings demonstrated more graphically than anything yet the stakes in the struggle between the American colonies and the British government. The contest was about constitutionalism, but it was also about people's lives—and their deaths.

Until 1770 Franklin had often chosen to blur the issues between America and Britain, hoping reasonableness might soften reason and allow both sides to live with a solution imperfect on strictly logical grounds. The Boston Massacre and the events surrounding it forced him to focus, to think very carefully about what an acceptable ultimate outcome might be. Ironically—and figuratively—they also drove him back to Boston, the city he had fled in his own personal rebellion half a century earlier.

Ironies abounded that season. On the very day of the Boston Massacre, a new prime minister in London (Chatham having finally resigned due to his illness) laid before Parliament a bill repealing nearly all the Townshend duties. As Rockingham had done after the Stamp Act, Lord North distanced himself from what he considered the failed policies of his predecessors; but, also like Rockingham, he had to take account of the sentiment in Parliament that could not abide capitulation to the colonists. Rockingham had appeased the Grenvillites with the Declaratory Act; North employed the device of lifting all the Townshend taxes but one—the tax on tea. In a separate but related decision, the Quartering Act was allowed to expire.

Getting the news of this change of course across the Atlantic took several weeks; by the time Boston learned that Parliament had backed most of the way down, the hot anger over the killings had hardened into cold hatred of Parliament and all its works. What many Bostonians noticed was not the taxes that were repealed but the tax that remained, not the olive branch the new ministry was holding out but the club that branch could quickly become.

In the month between the creation of the North ministry and the decision for partial repeal, Franklin had done his best to discredit such a half measure, hoping to steel the resolve of the repealers to be through with the duties entirely. "The Grenvillenians, who have done all this mischief, would terrify us (in case of a repeal) with the apprehensions of imaginary future demands from the Americans," he wrote in the *Gazetteer*, over the signature "Another Merchant." This was silly; the Americans wanted nothing more than to have restored the rights they enjoyed "before these new-fangled projects took place." The idea of partial repeal brought to mind a story:

A collector on the King's highway, who had rifled the passengers in a stage coach, desirous to shew his great civility, returned to one a family seal, to another a dear friend's mourning ring, which encouraged a third to ask a watch that had been his grandmother's?

"Zounds," says he, "have you no conscience? Presently you will all expect your money again! A pack of unreasonable dogs and b——s; I have a great mind to blow your brains out."

Such was the proper pose when complete repeal remained possible, yet it was more than a pose, for Franklin continued to hold it after partial repeal occurred. In late March, Franklin had not yet heard of the killings at Boston, but the debate over repeal had convinced him that if the colonies held firm they might complete the job they had started. North and his supporters would have been happy to have dumped the Townshend duties completely, Franklin inferred. Yet a faction surrounding the Duke of Bedford resisted any such thing. "This party never speak of us but with evident malice," Franklin related to a Philadelphia friend, Charles Thomson. "Rebels and traitors are the best names they can afford us, and I believe they only wish for a colourable pretence and occasion of ordering the soldiers to make a massacre among us."

By themselves the Bedfordites lacked the power to block repeal; what had briefly tipped the balance to their side were reports from America that the nonimportation pacts were fragmenting. Since then, however, the merchants of Britain had received material proof that nonimportation was alive and well. A ship had sailed all the way from Bristol to Boston with nails and glass, items thought to be of utmost necessity in America; finding no buyers for its cargo, it had sailed all the way back, to the serious financial embarrassment of its owners. Ten merchant captains from New York had held their vessels in harbor in England, hoping for repeal; on learning that the tea tax would remain, they sailed off, bearing only ballast. British manufacturers lost ten cargoes in the bargain.

"The tone of the manufacturers begins to change," Franklin reported, "and there is no doubt that if we are steady and persevere in our resolutions, these people will soon begin a clamour that much pains has hitherto been used to stifle." Nonimportation was working; it must not be abandoned. "In short, it appears to me that if we do not now persist in this measure till it has had its full effect, it can never again be used on any future occasion with the least prospect of success; and that if we do persist another year, we shall never afterwards have occasion to use it."

In a letter to Joseph Galloway, Franklin amplified his argument. "I am assured that the manufacturers cannot another year be kept quiet by all the artifices of our adversaries, as they begin now seriously to feel the effects of their late credulity." He elaborated his earlier contention that the self-denial of nonimportation would strengthen American virtue, to Americans' lasting benefit.

> This stoppage in the trade, if it should continue longer, will have this good effect among us, to assist several new manufactures in striking root so as afterwards to support themselves in a flourishing condition. Great sums of money too, for our produce, will come into the country and remain there to the improvement of our estates and increase of their value; so that though a few traders may be hurt at present, not having English goods in such quantities as heretofore to sell, yet in a little time those who cannot turn to other businesses will have their shops and stores replenished with our own commodities; while their customers, grown richer by industry and frugality, though they do not buy so much, will be enabled to make better pay for what they do buy.

For decades, since long before the current controversy over taxes and duties, the American colonies had been economically dependent on English merchants due to the buying habits of the colonists. They would remain dependent long after the repeal of the last Townshend duty, unless those buying habits changed. The current crisis was a challenge, but equally an opportunity—for Americans to take control of their fate.

Americans must seize the opportunity, for it might not return. The recent scandalous events in England presaged more, and worse. "The public affairs of this nation are at present in great disorder," Franklin told Galloway. "Parties run very high, and have abused each other so thoroughly that there is not now left an unbespattered character in the kingdom of any note or importance; and they have so exposed one another's roguery and rapacity that the respect for superiors, trust in Parliament, and regard to Government, is among the generality of the people totally lost."

◦— For many months Franklin had labored under a cloud in the minds of observers on both sides of the Atlantic. Radicals in America observed his continuance as deputy postmaster and assumed he therefore was a creature of the ministers who could have snatched that office away. As father of the royal governor of New Jersey he incurred additional doubts. On the other hand, proponents in England (and, less numerously and vocally, in America) of Parliamentary supremacy read or heard of his testimony to Parliament, encountered his views personally, or divined his authorship (which was no deep secret in any event) of numerous pieces defending the American colonies, and concluded that he was one of the radicals himself, or close to it.

Franklin recognized the betwixt-and-betweenness of his predicament. "Being born and bred in one of the countries, and having lived long, and made many agreeable connections of friendship in the other, I wish all prosperity to both," he remarked in a letter printed, with his authentic name, in the *Gentleman's Magazine*. But despite his best efforts he was making little headway in bringing the two countries together. "I do not find that I have gained any point in either country, except that of rendering myself suspected by my impartiality: in England of being too much an American, and in America of being too much an Englishman."

The Boston Massacre, the fight for repeal of the Townshend duties, and Franklin's stout endorsement of continued nonimportation cleared up much of the confusion surrounding where he stood. Those parties in America rejecting Parliamentary authority over the colonies embraced him happily. Joseph Galloway wrote from Philadelphia with congratulations for what had been accomplished and assurances regarding what remained. "I am much obliged to you for the state of American affairs on your side the water," said Galloway, speaking for his allies in the Assembly as well. "The Ministry are much mistaken in imagining that there will ever be an union either of affections or interest between Great Britain and America until justice is done to the latter and there is a full restoration of its liberties."

The reaction in Boston was still more striking. From the passage of the Stamp Act until almost the present, Franklin's friends in that hotbed of protest had had to apologize for or explain away his search for a middle ground. Jane Mecom regularly wrote wondering whether the unflattering things her neighbors were saying about her brother could possibly be true.

But now, with his ringing endorsement of continued nonimportation, he became something of a hero. His letter to Charles Thomson in Philadelphia, in which he had essentially accused the Bedford group of provoking the Boston Massacre, was quickly forwarded to Boston and published there, placing him in the ranks of the most radical.

Sam Adams thereupon drafted a letter, signed by other members of a committee of the town meeting, appealing to Franklin as one of "our friends on your side the water" to help ensure that the true circumstances of the late crime at Boston not be muddied by the enemies of American liberty. Shortly thereafter the Massachusetts House of Representatives voted to make Franklin that body's agent in England. The resolution offering him the post registered considerable confidence in his abilities and bona fides, describing the House as "entirely relying on his vigilance and the exertion of his utmost endeavours to support the constitutional rights of this House and of the Province." A following letter, signed by House speaker Thomas Cushing, explained that the House "greatly confided" in Franklin's abilities and asserted assuredly that "your own acquaintance with this Province, and your well known warm attachment to it, will lead you to exert all your powers in its defence."

⌒ **Franklin** appreciated that accepting the Massachusetts offer would render him still more suspect in the eyes of many in England. In the months after the Boston Massacre, and as his support for continued nonimportation echoed back across the Atlantic to London, his position in the post office came under regular attack. He resented the attacks, both because they impugned his performance as postmaster and because they revealed (to him, if not to his attackers) an unconstitutional animus to the rights of Americans.

"I have enemies, as every public man has," he explained to Postmaster General Lord Le Despencer, his superior, by way of attempting to neutralize those enemies. "They would be glad to see me deprived of my office; and there are others who would like to have it." Yet they should not be suffered to do so. Besides the money—£300 per year, which if lost "would make a very serious difference in my annual income"—there were principles involved. "I rose to that office gradually through a long service of now almost forty years, have by my industry and management greatly improved it, and have ever acted in it with fidelity to the satisfaction of all my superiors." Moreover, a British subject should be able to speak his mind on public matters. "I hope my political opinions, or my dislike of the late measures with America (which I own I think very injudicious) expressed in my letters to that country, or the advice I gave to adhere to their resolutions till the whole Act was repealed, without extending their demands any farther, will not be thought a good reason for turning me out."

Franklin persuaded Le Despencer not to sack him; whatever the postmaster general's opinion of Franklin's politics, he appreciated the efficiencies Franklin had brought to the delivery of the mail, and he knew Franklin could not easily be replaced. This did not silence Franklin's critics, however; they simply modified their tactics and opened a campaign to force him to resign.

"In this they are not likely to succeed, I being deficient in that Christian virtue of resignation," he told Jane Mecom. "If they would have my office, they must take it." He went on to summarize a philosophy of public service that forever became attached to his name. "I have heard of some great man, whose rule it was with regard to offices, *Never to ask for them,* and *never to refuse them.* To which I have always added in my own practice, *Never to resign them.*"

◈─ The Massachusetts agency cost him more trouble than he could have imagined. In the first place, as he learned only after the fact, his appointment was by no means unanimous. Sam Adams still suspected him of closet Anglophilia; Adams and James Otis had sponsored instead the candidacy of Arthur Lee, a physician currently studying law in London. Although Speaker Cushing and a majority of the House of Representatives voted for Franklin, Adams and Otis won approval of Lee as an alternate in case Franklin declined the agency or was otherwise unavailable.

More vexing was the opposition of Lord Hillsborough. When Hillsborough had assumed the new post of secretary of state for (all) the American colonies, Franklin at first expressed guarded optimism. "I do not think this nobleman in general an enemy to America," he told Galloway. Six months later, in July 1768, Franklin added, "His inclinations are rather favourable towards us (so far as he thinks consistent with what he supposes to be the unquestionable rights of Britain)."

But that qualification proved critical. Hillsborough brooked nothing that hinted of sedition or even obstruction of the smooth administering of the colonies. He had ordered the Massachusetts House of Representatives to rescind its appeal to the other colonies for common action against the Townshend acts, and when Adams and the others refused, he sent the troops ashore in Boston.

In matters relating to Franklin personally, Hillsborough had proved something of a puzzle. Like Grafton he early dropped hints of an appointment for Franklin as undersecretary, but these came to no more than Grafton's had (or would). He opposed the land schemes of the Franklins and their partners until a critical hearing in December 1769, when he suddenly told them that far from asking too much, they were asking far too little. Surprised, Franklin and the others redrew their maps of the Ohio Valley and, instead of asking for 2.4 million acres, requested 20 million. But rather than back this new proposal, Hillsborough let it disappear into the maw of the British bureaucracy, leading Franklin to surmise that Hillsborough had lent his weight to the project the better to sink it.

At the beginning of 1771 the Hillsborough puzzle acquired a new piece. Franklin visited Hillsborough's house for what he thought would be a routine presentation of his credentials as the agent for the Massachusetts House of Representatives. At first he was put off and told to try later, but as his coach drove away, the porter called out, saying that his lordship could see him after all. Franklin entered the secretary's quarters, only to encounter Governor Francis Bernard of Massachusetts, the most outspoken critic of the Massachusetts House, and various other gentlemen. Franklin settled into a chair for what he assumed would be a substantial wait. But after just minutes Hillsborough's assistant summoned Franklin ahead of the others.

"I was pleased with this ready admission and preference (having sometimes waited 3 or 4 hours for my turn)," Franklin recorded; "and being pleased, I could more readily put on the open cheerful countenance that my friends advised me to wear."

Hillsborough initially reciprocated the cheer. He had been dressing to go to court, he said, but on learning that Franklin had arrived, desired to see him at once.

Franklin thanked the secretary and explained that he would not delay him. He merely wished to inform him of his recent appointment by the Massachusetts House, and to say that he hoped to be of service to the public in this capacity.

Hillsborough did not let him finish this sentence. With what Franklin identified as "something between a smile and a sneer," he interjected, "I must set you right there, Mr. Franklin. You are not agent."

"Why, my lord?" responded Franklin.

"You are not appointed."

"I do not understand your lordship. I have the appointment in my pocket."

"You are mistaken. I have later and better advices. I have a letter from [Lieutenant] Governor Hutchinson. He would not give his assent to the bill."

"There was no bill, my lord. It is a vote of the House."

"There was a bill presented to the Governor, for the purpose of appointing you, and another, one Dr. Lee, I think he is called, to which the Governor refused his assent."

"I cannot understand this, my lord. I think there must be some mistake in it. Is your lordship quite sure that you have such a letter?"

"I will convince you of it directly." Hillsborough rang a bell. "Mr. Pownall will come in and satisfy you."

"It is not necessary that I should now detain your lordship from dressing. You are going to court. I will wait on your lordship another time."

"No, stay. He will come in immediately." Hillsborough motioned to a servant. "Tell Mr. Pownall I want him."

Pownall arrived. Hillsborough addressed him: "Have you not at hand Governor Hutchinson's letter mentioning his refusing his assent to the bill for appointing Dr. Franklin agent?"

Pownall answered, "My lord?"

Hillsborough: "Is there not such a letter?"

Pownall: "No, my lord."

Hillsborough was annoyed at being shown wrong, but he was more annoyed at the Massachusetts House for presuming to appoint an agent without the concurrence of the governor. This, of course, was common practice; Franklin's appointment from Pennsylvania had not, needless to say, elicited the approval of the Penns' governor. But as part of the overall effort to tighten the administration of the colonies, Hillsborough was determined to put an end to it.

"The House of Representatives has no right to appoint an agent," he told Franklin angrily. "We shall take no notice of any agents but such as are appointed by acts of assembly to which the governor gives his assent. We have had confusion enough already."

Franklin challenged this novelty. "I cannot conceive, my lord, why the consent of the *governor* should be thought necessary to the appointment of an agent for the *people*. It seems to me that—"

Hillsborough's visage assumed what appeared to Franklin "a mixed look of anger and contempt." He snapped, "I shall not enter into a dispute with *you*, sir, upon this subject."

Franklin persisted. "I beg your lordship's pardon. I do not presume to dispute with your lordship"—though of course both men realized this was precisely what he was doing. "I would only say that it seems to me that every body of men, who cannot appear in person where business relating to them may be transacted, should have a right to appear by an agent. The concurrence of the governor does not seem to me necessary. It is the business of the people that is to be done. He [the Governor] is not one of them; he is himself an agent."

"Whose agent is he?" demanded Hillsborough.

"The king's, my lord."

Hillsborough dismissed this. "Besides," he added, "this proceeding is directly contrary to express instructions."

"I did not know there had been such instructions. I am not concerned in any offence against them."

"Yes, your offering such a paper [the copy of the House vote, which Franklin had handed Hillsborough upon entering] to be entered is an offence against them. No such appointment shall be entered."

Hillsborough then launched into a diatribe. "When I came into the administration of American affairs, I found them in great disorder. By *my firmness* they are now something mended; and while I have the honour to hold the seals, I shall continue the same conduct, the same *firmness*. I think my duty to the master I serve and to the government of this nation require it of me. If that conduct is not approved, they may take my office from me when they please. I shall make 'em a bow, and thank 'em. I shall resign with pleasure. That gentleman knows it"—here he pointed to Pownall. "But while I continue in it, I shall resolutely persevere in the same firmness."

Franklin recorded that at this point Hillsborough was "turning pale in his discourse, as if he was angry at something or somebody besides the agent, and of more importance."

By Franklin's telling, the agent had the last word. "I beg your lordship's pardon for taking up so much of your time. It is, I believe, of no great importance whether the appointment is acknowledged or not, for I have not the least conception that an agent can *at present* be of any use, to any of the colonies. I shall therefore give your lordship no farther trouble."

⌒ "I have since heard that his lordship took great offence at some of my last words, which he calls extremely rude and abusive," Franklin confided to Samuel Cooper three weeks later. "He assured a friend of mine, they were equivalent to telling him to his face that the colonies could expect neither favour nor justice during his administration. I find he did not mistake me."

Franklin rarely let emotion displace reasonableness, but after three years of trying to make Hillsborough and the rest of the ministry see reason in relations with the colonies, he had had his fill; and after the secretary of state declared that he would have nothing to do with Franklin, Franklin reciprocated. He had grown accustomed to mediocrities in positions of power, but this particular mediocrity at this particular moment was more than he could stand. "His character is conceit, wrongheadedness, obstinacy and passion," he told Cooper. "Those who would speak most favourably of him allow all this; they only add that he is an honest man, and means well. If that be true, as perhaps it may, I wish him a better place, where only honesty and well-meaning are required, and where his other qualities can do no harm."

Perhaps on reflection Franklin considered that by alienating Hillsborough he was jeopardizing the interests of those he was representing (which by now included Georgia and New Jersey as well as Pennsylvania and Massachusetts). Yet Hillsborough had already taken great umbrage at Franklin's writings on behalf of the colonies; there was really little to lose. In any event, Franklin was willing to pay the cost of his actions. "Whatever the consequences of his displeasure, putting all my offences together, I must bear them as well as I can." Yet not everything was bleak. "One encouragement I have: the knowledge that he is not a whit better liked by his colleagues in the Ministry than he is by me, that he cannot probably continue where he is much longer, and that he can scarce be succeeded by anybody who will not like me the better for his having been at variance with me."

~ Siding with Boston lost Franklin any lingering leverage with Hillsborough; it also forced him to hone his thinking on the nature of relations between Britain and America. Not long after leaving his stormy session with the secretary of state, Franklin received a letter from a committee of correspondence of the Massachusetts House, consisting of Thomas Cushing, Sam Adams, John Hancock, and John Adams. This letter laid out current conditions in the colonies and the present state of opinion there. The colonies, the committee said, "are justly tenacious of their constitutional and natural rights, and will never willingly part with them." Nor could it be to the advantage of the British nation to steal them. "Great Britain can lose nothing that she ought to retain, by restoring the colonies to the state they were in before the passing the obnoxious Stamp-Act, and we are persuaded that if that is done they will no further contend."

Franklin drew reassurance from this comparatively moderate statement and believed it might form the basis for reconciliation. "The doctrine of the right of Parliament to lay taxes on America is now almost generally given up here," he replied to Cushing and the others, "and one seldom meets in conversation any who continue to assert it."

If Franklin was speaking of the English public at large, he may have been right; if of the influential factions in Parliament, he overspoke—as his own letters had already revealed and as events would soon demonstrate. Yet he wished to make clear to the Boston men the position of those in England he considered the likeliest to seek reconciliation. "We ought to be contented, they say, with a forbearance of any attempt hereafter to exercise such a right; and this they would have us rely on as a certainty." Not simply Parliamentary prestige but British dignity was at stake. The colonists could hardly expect the British government to honor demands that would subject it "to the contempt of all Europe." In other words, if Americans could live with the *reality* of the status quo ante the Stamp Act ("Hints are also given that the duties now subsisting may be gradually withdrawn"), Parliament would settle for the *principle* underlying the Declaratory Act.

Even as he delineated this rationale, Franklin was not sure how far to trust it. Status quos had a way of congealing around whatever was not challenged. Regarding the duties said to be on the verge of repeal, such repeal could be assured only by continued pressure from America. "If by time we become so accustomed to these as to pay them without discontent, no minister will afterwards think of taking them off, but rather be encouraged to add others." Franklin was far from advocating violence, but determination was indispensable. "I hope the colony assemblies will show, by frequently repeated resolves, that they know their rights, and do not lose sight of them."

Obviously this counsel undercut the conciliatory scenario he sketched; at the same time it revealed Franklin's increasing conviction that America was fundamentally distinct, and essentially independent of England. His conversation with Hillsborough had underscored the ministry's view that the colonies were creatures of Parliament; only on this reasoning ought the ministry, acting through the colonial governors, to have any voice in the selection of the colonial agents.

By contrast, Franklin saw the agents almost as ambassadors, sent by the people of America to the British government. A correct understanding of the nature of the colonies vis-à-vis Britain would yield this conclusion as a corollary. "When they come to be considered in the light of *distinct states*, as I conceive they really are, possibly their agents may be treated with more respect, and considered more as public ministers."

This was strong punch, which could hardly fail to provoke a fight with Britain if quaffed straight; in the months after his argument with Hillsborough, as his anger subsided, Franklin began to dilute it. Even after the repeal of most of the Townshend duties, the Massachusetts House protested the Crown's policy of paying royal officials in America. Franklin understood the argument against the policy, having made it himself, but he was fairly certain most people in England did not, or did not credit the argument if they understood it. "It is looked on as a strange thing here to object to the King's paying his own servants sent among us to do his business; and they say we should seem to have much more reason of complaint if it were required of us to pay them." Indeed, because the American complaint on this count seemed so counterintuitive, many in England suspected the Americans of attempting to suborn the king's servants and subvert his rule. Franklin advised against mounting a major campaign against this issue; better to protest it politely on occasion and continue to shun British imports.

Although Franklin's anger had abated, his opinion of Hillsborough had not improved, and this low opinion was another reason for counseling restraint. The secretary of state for America was "proud, supercilious, extremely conceited (moderate as they are) of his political knowledge and abilities, fond of every one that can stoop to flatter him, and inimical to all that dare tell him disagreeable truths." Hillsborough's deficiencies were recognized by many in Britain; he could not long retain his office. Wisdom therefore cautioned against actions that might provoke other, more reasonable, souls to join the secretary in his "settled malice against the colonies, particularly ours [in this case, Massachusetts]."

Franklin gave greater credence than before to arguments from British honor. The latter half of 1770 had produced a crisis with Spain over the Falkland Islands; for months war impended. Such a war might well reopen the long struggle against France, with all that that struggle entailed. Although the war scare had considerably diminished by early 1771, it reminded Franklin of one reason he had been a British imperialist: that in the cruel world of nations, safety often resided in numbers. Accordingly he urged the Massachusetts men to consider "whether it will not be prudent for us to indulge the Mother Country in this concern for her own honour, so far as may be consistent with the preservation of our essential rights, especially as that honour may in some cases be of importance to the general welfare."

He perceived two possible outcomes should the colonies push to a test of British authority. "If we are not found equal, that authority will by the event be more strongly established." Needless to say, this would not conduce to the welfare of America. But neither, necessarily, would the other outcome. "If we should prove superior, yet by the division the general strength of the British nation must be greatly diminished."

Although Franklin refrained from offering explicit advice to Massachusetts, his inclination was clear. He suggested that it would "be better gradually to wear off the assumed authority of Parliament over America" than to mount a direct challenge. Moreover, Americans should remember that Parliament was not the entire British government. "I wish to see a steady dutiful attachment to the King and his family maintained among us."

Predictably, Franklin's espousal of moderation failed to satisfy those holding more radical views. Arthur Lee disputed Franklin's politics; he apparently also resented Franklin's appointment as Massachusetts agent ahead of himself. From whatever amalgam of politics and pique, Lee launched a one-man campaign to discredit Franklin and undermine his influence.

Sam Adams presumably required little convincing, but Lee provided plenty. "I have read lately in your papers an assurance from Dr. Franklin that all designs against the charter of the colony are laid aside," Lee wrote Adams from London. "This is just what I expected of him, and if it be true, the Dr. is not the dupe but the instrument of Lord Hillsborough's treachery." On sudden second thought, Lee dismissed the notion of Franklin as dupe, for "notorious as he [Hillsborough] is for ill faith and fraud, his duplicity would not impose on one possessed of half Dr. F.'s sagacity." Whatever Franklin might write to the House of Representatives, his interests—and therefore his intentions—lay elsewhere. "The possession of a profitable office at will, the having a son in a high post at pleasure, the grand purpose of his residence here being to effect a change in the government of Pennsylvania, for which administration must be cultivated and courted, are circumstances which, joined with the temporising conduct he has always held in American affairs, preclude every rational hope that in an open contest between an oppressive administration and a free people, Dr. F. can be a faithful advocate for the latter." Calling Franklin a "false friend," Lee said he himself would gladly serve as Massachusetts's agent for nothing "rather than you and America, at a time like this, should be betrayed by a man who, it is hardly in the nature of things to suppose, can be faithful to his trust."

Doubtless Lee intended to damage Franklin with this letter. If so, he was disappointed. Adams, intentionally or otherwise, allowed an unsigned copy of the letter to reach Thomas Cushing, Franklin's sponsor in the Massachusetts House. Cushing showed the letter to Samuel Cooper, who, on the basis of conversation with Cushing and others, assured his friend, "It will make no impression to your disadvantage, while it shows the baseness of its author."

 By this period Franklin's summer travel had become a fixed habit, the closest thing to a religious practice in a man who observed no sectarian rituals. He was convinced that his annual escape from the smoke and congestion of London, combined with the stimulation of seeing new places, people, and things, was what kept him in the surprisingly good health he enjoyed for a sexagenarian. "I imagine I should have fallen to pieces long since but for that practice," he told Joseph Galloway.

In 1771 his vacation was more extended than usual and came in multiple installments. At the end of May he toured the north of England, where the industrial revolution was well under way. The high point of the trip was a boat ride on a canal that crossed a river via an aqueduct, so that to travelers below, the canal boat appeared to be plying the sky. The low point—relative to topography—occurred on this same canal, at a place where it penetrated the earth far into a coal mine, from which that essential fuel was dug and loaded into canal boats and hauled to Manchester. Franklin saw an ironworks near Rotherham, which impressed him with the ingenuity of its design. "It appeared particularly odd," wrote Jonathan Williams, one of Franklin's fellow travelers, "to see a small river of liquid iron running from the furnace into the reservoir and from thence carried in ladles like hot broth." At Derby they toured a silk works, of which Franklin, who was still promoting the production of silk in America, took special notice. A single powered shaft drove, via pulleys and belts, scores of smaller shafts, which culminated in thousands of reels. Much of the process was tended by children "of about 5 or 7 years old," according to Williams. At Birmingham they saw the famous metalworks of Matthew Boulton. Seven hundred persons, including women and children, fabricated all manner of products, from farthing buttons to hundred-guinea ornaments. The noise, the pace of the process, and the sheer audacity of the undertaking were overwhelming. "It is almost impossible for the strongest memory to retain it," wrote Williams.

Franklin's next respite was more restful but also more productive. Jonathan Shipley was an Anglican bishop of the absentee sort: his see was in Wales, but he spent nearly all his time in London or at his country home at Twyford. He was a great admirer of Franklin and invited the American to visit Twyford. Franklin accepted with pleasure—the more so for the company of Mrs. Shipley and the couple's five daughters. Perhaps their mere presence, or their inquiries about what life was like when *he* was a child, recalled to mind his early years; in any event it was at Twyford that summer that he began writing his memoirs. Although taking the form of a (very long) letter to William, it was obviously intended for publication, for Franklin wrote on large folio sheets, leaving one vertical half of each page blank for subsequent interpolations (which in fact he later provided). By subsequent tradition, he wrote during the day, then read his draftwork to the Shipley family in the evening.

He charmed them all, and they him. Kitty, the youngest, rode with him back to London, where she attended school. On the way they discussed suitable husbands for her sisters (a country squire for one, a merchant for another, a duke and an earl for the third and fourth). For Kitty herself? he asked. An old general, she said. "Hadn't you better take him while he's a young officer, and let him grow old upon your hands?" asked Franklin (as he related the conversation to Kitty's mother). "No, that won't do," she replied. "He must be an old man of 70 or 80, and take me when I am about 30. And then you know I may be a rich young widow."

For a final fling that summer of 1771, Franklin joined Richard Jackson for a tour of Ireland and Scotland. The condition of Ireland, which also stood in a colonial position to Britain, had long intrigued Franklin, and his interest only grew with the constitutional controversy between Britain and America. In theory Ireland provided an alternative model for American relations with Britain. Franklin, the essential empiricist, wished to measure theory against practice. He devised a set of questions to direct his observations. "Can the farmers find a ready market and a good living price for the produce of their lands? Or do they raise less than they might do, if the demand was greater and the price better? . . . Is Ireland much in debt to England or any foreign country for goods or merchandise consumed in it? . . . Is Ireland in general in a state of progressive improvement, or the contrary?"

The answers shocked him. "Ireland itself is a fine country," he noted to Thomas Cushing, speaking of the land and climate; "and Dublin a magnificent city." But that was as far as his compliments went. "The appearances of general extreme poverty among the lower people are amazing. They live in wretched hovels of mud and straw, are clothed in rags, and subsist chiefly on potatoes. Our New England farmers of the poorest sort, in regard to the enjoyment of all the comforts of life, are princes when compared to them."

Why was this so? Not, apparently, because of some deficiency in the people (as the English liked to say); rather the arrangements of society prevented the improvement of the Irish people.

> Such is the effect of the discouragements of industry, the nonresidence not only of pensioners but of many original landlords who lease their lands in gross to undertakers that rack the tenants, and fleece them skin and all, to make estates to themselves, while the first rents, as well as most of the pensions, are spent out of the country.
>
> An English gentleman there said to me, that by what he had heard of the good grazing in North America, and by what he saw of the plenty of flaxseed imported in Ireland from thence, he could not understand why we did not rival Ireland in the beef and butter trade to the West Indies, and share with it in its linen trade. But he was satisfied when I told him, that I supposed the reason might be, *Our people eat beef and butter every day, and wear shirts themselves.*

Conditions among the common people of Scotland were hardly better. Franklin and Jackson crossed over from Ireland during a lull between two hurricanes; the human devastation they saw in Scotland made hurricanes appear almost benign by contrast. And together with what Franklin had lately observed of the manufacturing regions of England, it confirmed his conviction of the superiority of the American mode of social organization.

I thought often of the happiness of New England, where every man is a freeholder, has a vote in public affairs, lives in a tidy warm house, has plenty of good food and fuel, with whole clothes from head to foot, the manufactory perhaps of his own family. Long may they continue in this situation!

But if they should ever envy the *trade* of these countries, I can put them in a way to obtain a share of it. Let them with three-fourths of the people of Ireland live the year round on potatoes and butter milk, without shirts, then may their merchants export beef, butter and linen. Let them with the generality of the common people of Scotland go barefoot, then may they make large exports in shoes and stockings. And if they will be content to wear rags like the spinners and weavers of England, they may make cloths and stuffs for all parts of the world.

Farther, if my countrymen should ever wish for the honour of having among them a gentry enormously wealthy, let them sell their farms and pay racked rents; the scale of the landlords will rise as that of the tenants is depressed, who will soon become poor, tattered, dirty, and abject in spirit.

Had I never been in the American colonies, but was to form my judgment of civil society by what I have lately seen, I should never advise a nation of savages to admit of civilisation. For I assure you, that in the possession and enjoyment of the various comforts of life, compared to these people every Indian is a gentleman; and the effect of this kind of civil society seems only to be the depressing multitudes below the savage state that a few may be raised above it.

If Franklin's observation of common life reinforced his patriotic feelings about America, so did his conversations with the better-off sort. The Irish parliament made a habit of allowing visiting members of the English parliament to sit among the Irish members; they accorded a similar privilege to Franklin as a distinguished representative of the American assemblies, reasoning that the American assemblies *were* English parliaments. "I esteemed it a mark of respect for our country," he wrote Thomas Cushing. Franklin compared experiences with Irishmen who chafed under British rule as he and his American friends did. "They are all on the American side," he informed Joseph Galloway.

In Edinburgh he stayed with David Hume, "in an elegant house in the new part of the city," according to a visitor from Rhode Island, Henry Marchant. Franklin was in usual fine form. "We had a good dish of tete-a-tete," Marchant remarked. "The Doctor was pleased to open very freely and to enter minutely into many matters—interesting as well as entertaining." Hume could be prickly, as Franklin would discover, but on this visit host and guest enjoyed each other's company. "The good wishes of all your Brother Philosophers in this place attend you heartily and sincerely," Hume wrote Franklin afterward.

The encounter with Hume was a pleasure; another encounter was a puzzle. In Dublin, Franklin and Jackson chanced to meet Lord Hillsborough. Franklin expected a snub or worse from his foe, but received quite the opposite. "He was extremely civil," Franklin related to William, "wonderfully so to me whom he had not long before abused to Mr. Strahan as a factious turbulent fellow, always in mischief, a republican, enemy to the king's service, and what not." Hillsborough engaged Franklin and Jackson in frank conversation and insisted they visit him at Hillsborough (the lord's home).

"In my own mind I was determined not to go that way," Franklin said. But the vagaries of travel made the town unavoidable, and so the man.

As soon as his Lordship knew we were arrived at the inn he sent a message over for us to come to his house. There we were detained by 1000 civilities from Tuesday to Sunday. He seemed extremely solicitous to give me and America through me a good opinion of him. In our first conversations he expressed himself as a good Irishman, censuring the English government for its narrowness with regard to Ireland, in restraining its commerce, manufactures, &c., and when I applied his observations to America, he agreed immediately that it was wrong to restrain our manufactures, that the subjects in every part of the King's dominions had a natural right to make the best use they could of the production of their country. . . .

His attentions to me in every circumstance of accommodation and entertainment were very particular, putting his own cloak about my shoulders when I went out, that I might not take cold, placing his eldest son, Lord Kilwarling, in his phaeton with me, to drive me 40 miles round the country, to see the manufactures, seats, &c., and when we took leave, requesting that I would let him see me often in London, &c., &c.

Franklin wondered at Hillsborough's hospitality and apparent change of heart, clear back to London. "Does not all this seem extraordinary to you?" he wrote William from Craven Street.

20

To Kick a Little

1772–73

∾ By the early 1770s Franklin was by far the most famous
American in the world, and arguably the most illustrious
subject of George III. His electrical papers, first published
in London in 1751 as *Experiments and Observations on
Electricity*, were now in their fourth edition; translations
circulated across the European continent. The Marquis
de Condorcet, one of France's leading mathematical and
literary lights, wrote to *"mon cher et illustre confrère"*
to strike up a correspondence that lasted for years.
Giambattista Beccaria of Turin, by now a regular

correspondent, declared, "To you it is given to enlighten human minds with the true principles of the electric science, to reassure them by your conductors against the terrors of thunder, and"—referring to Franklin's armonica—"to sweeten their senses with a most touching and suave music." The German philosopher Immanuel Kant dubbed Franklin the "modern Prometheus."

In 1772 Franklin was notified of his election as an *associé étranger* of the French Royal Academy of Sciences, one of only eight foreigners so honored. He was speaking no less accurately than politely when he answered, "A place among your foreign members is justly esteemed by all Europe the greatest honour a man can arrive at in the Republic of Letters."

The following year his fame widened further. A Paris physician named Jacques Barbeu-Dubourg, himself something of a scientific celebrity, with membership in royal academies and societies across Europe, had for some time been translating Franklin's papers into French. In 1773 these appeared as the *Oeuvres de M. Franklin* in two volumes. Dubourg was delighted to report to the author that the edition was being received *"avec une sorte de passion favorable."*

"Learned and ingenious foreigners that come to England almost all make a point of visiting me," Franklin matter-of-factly wrote William in the summer of 1772. "Several of the foreign ambassadors have assiduously cultivated my acquaintance. . . . The King too has lately been heard to speak of me with great regard."

⌒ Franklin continued to give his admirers cause for admiration. The most superficial knowledge of chemistry and electricity revealed that gunpowder and lightning made bad companions; in 1769 an enormous explosion in Italy followed a lightning strike upon a powder magazine at Brescia, in which a thousand persons perished and much of the town was leveled. The disaster made the London papers and alerted the keepers of the Crown's munitions to the potential for similar peril at home. Fortunately, they noted, the world's leading expert on lightning resided in Craven Street; ignoring the questions that surrounded Franklin's politics, they invited him to join a commission devoted to diminishing—eliminating, if possible—the danger from aerial electricity to the large new magazine at Purfleet on the Thames. The appointment involved Franklin in an ongoing debate regarding the optimal shape for lightning rods—pointed (Franklin's view) or blunt. Franklin's arguments won in the end, and by the autumn of 1773 the king's gunpowder nestled quietly beneath pointed rods—from where, but two years hence, it was loaded onto ships hostilely bound for America.

While preserving England from death by explosion, Franklin also strove to keep the English free from coughing themselves to pieces. At least since his early correspondence with Polly Stevenson he had been curious as to what caused colds. He was convinced to a moral and medical certainty that the conventional notion betrayed by the malady's very name—that one caught cold by being cold—was quite mistaken. "Travelling in our severe winters, I have suffered cold sometimes to an extremity only short of freezing, but this did not make me *catch cold,*" he asserted to Benjamin Rush, a Philadelphia friend and noted physician. Nor did moisture have much to do with the matter. "I have been in the river every evening two or three hours for a fortnight together, when one would suppose I might imbibe enough of it to *take cold* if humidity could give it; but no such effect followed. Boys never get cold [that is, catch cold] by swimming. Nor are people at sea, or who live at Bermudas, or St. Helena, where the air must be ever moist, from the dashing and breaking of waves against their rocks on all sides, more subject to colds than those who inhabit part of a continent where the air is driest."

So what *was* the cause? "People often catch cold from one another when shut up together in small close rooms, coaches, &c. and when sitting near and conversing so as to breathe in each other's transpiration." Additional agents were bedclothes and other items that caught and somehow preserved "that kind of putridity which infects us."

If close quarters contributed to colds, fresh air guarded against them—especially if the fresh air came in the course of outdoor exercise. Franklin was an early and ardent advocate of regular vigorous exercise. In a day when exercise for the upper classes often meant riding in a coach or sitting on a horse, Franklin devised a graduated—and remarkably modern—scale of physiological effort. William had written of a recent indisposition; his father told him to engage in exercise, which was "of the greatest importance to prevent diseases." Franklin elaborated:

> In considering the different kinds of exercise, I have thought that the *quantum* of each is to be judged of, not by time or distance, but by the degree of warmth it produces in the body. Thus when I observe if I am cold when I get into a carriage in a morning, I may ride all day without being warmed by it; that if on horse back my

feet are cold, I may ride some hours before they become warm; but if I am ever so cold on foot, I cannot walk an hour briskly without glowing from head to foot by the quickened circulation.

I have been ready to say (using round numbers without regard to exactness, but merely to mark a great difference) that there is more exercise in *one* mile's riding on horseback, than in *five* in a coach; and more in *one* mile's walking on foot, than in *five* on horseback; to which I may add, that there is more in walking *one* mile up and down stairs, than in *five* on a level floor.

The two latter exercises may be had within doors, when the weather discourages going abroad [this of course defeated the fresh-air purpose of being outdoors, but some days were simply too nasty for that]. And the last may be had when one is pinched for time, as containing a great quantity of exercise in a handful of minutes. The dumb bell is another exercise of the latter compendious kind; by the use of it I have in forty swings quickened my pulse from 60 to 100 beats in a minute, counted by a second watch. And I suppose the warmth generally increases with quickness of pulse.

If Franklin's study of exercise was strikingly modern, his observations in another area were almost ancient. Pliny had described how sailors soothed the angry sea by spreading oil on the waves; Franklin, in hours stolen from his apprenticeship to his brother James, had read Pliny's account and wondered if it were truly so. Not till his voyage to England in 1757 had he managed to investigate the phenomenon. Then, observing that the wakes of two ships were remarkably smooth compared to the dozens of others in the convoy, he inquired of one of the old salts, who told him, with an air of disdain for such landlubbing ignorance, that the cooks in the two vessels must have dumped greasy water through the scuppers, which in turn greased the sides of the ships and thereby smoothed the waves.

Since then Franklin had pondered the subject further, collecting anecdotal evidence, devising conjectures, and considering how they might be tested. In time opportunity arose, in the form of a windy day on the pond of the common at Clapham, east of Lancaster, during his tour of northern England. "I fetched out a cruet of oil, and dropt a little of it on the water," he wrote. "I saw it spread with surprising swiftness upon the surface." But the sheen had scant effect in stilling the wind-driven waves, for he had oiled the water on the leeward side of the pond, where the wind drove the oil back onto the bank. "I then went to the windward side, where they [the waves] began to form; and there the oil, though not more than a tea spoonful, produced an instant calm, over a space several yards square, which spread amazingly, and extended itself gradually till it reached the lee side, making all that quarter of the pond, perhaps half an acre, as smooth as a looking glass."

Delighted and intrigued, Franklin determined to exploit every chance to investigate further. He placed a small quantity of oil in the upper hollow joint of a bamboo cane he carried when walking or riding in the country; at each opportunity he spilled the oil on ponds and streams and observed the effects. Gradually he conceived a quite ambitious experiment, one to quell not merely the ripples on a pond but the breakers on the open sea.

A captain in the Royal Navy, stationed at Portsmouth, heard of Franklin's design and invited him to come test it. Accordingly, on a day in October 1772 when the wind was blowing toward the shore, a crew was sent out in a longboat beyond the breakers, there to pour oil from a large stone bottle onto the water. A team of observers was specially chosen to observe the waves and determine whether they diminished after application of the oil.

"The experiment had not in the main the success we wished, for no material difference was observed in the height or force of the surf upon the shore," Franklin explained to an interested friend. Yet the oil did smooth the water somewhat behind the longboat, rendering the surface there largely immune to roughening by the brisk wind.

And in this Franklin saw both the cause for the present failure and the reason for success on smaller bodies of water. Waves on water, he said, resulted from friction between windy air and the surface of the water. Oil acted as a lubricant between air and water, diminishing the friction and the wave-raising power of the wind. On a pond, the entire surface might be covered with oil, entirely depriving the wind of its purchase and allowing a complete stilling. On the ocean, needless to say, any such comprehensive covering was out of the question; the waves that broke on the shore acquired their momentum long before encountering the oil from the longboat.

"It may be of use to relate the circumstances even of an experiment that does not succeed, since they may give hints of amendment in future trials," Franklin remarked. He went on to suggest just such amendment. "If we had begun our operations at a greater distance [from shore], the effect might have been more sensible. And perhaps we did not pour oil in sufficient quantity. Future experiments may determine this."

‹— Franklin's simultaneous experiments in pouring oil of the metaphorical sort on politically troubled waters were even less successful, and for a similar reason: the waves were originating beyond his reach.

Much of the turbulence was transatlantic. On their face, the affairs of the colonies were more placid than for some years. Franklin's advocacy of continued nonimportation failed to persuade most American merchants, who decided to accept the partial victory of the partial repeal of the Townshend duties and retreat to a partial embargo—of tea, the still-dutied item. Boston held out longer for nonimportation than New York and Philadelphia, but finally Boston too abandoned the beyond-tea embargo. By then the furor over the Boston Massacre had quieted as well, partly because Governor Hutchinson nodded to prudence and withdrew the British troops from the city proper to island quarters in the harbor, and partly because the soldiers involved in the shooting were brought to trial. If Captain Preston and the others were initially nervous that their defense was directed by the well-known patriot John Adams, they could not complain at the verdict: Preston and six of his men were acquitted of all charges; the remaining two were found guilty of manslaughter rather than murder and were released with a brand on the hand. "There seems now to be a pause in politics," Samuel Cooper wrote Franklin on the first day of 1771.

But a pause was not a halt, and beneath the surface calm, deep trouble impended. On the fundamental issue of constitutional relations, the Americans and the British were further apart than ever. Parliament claimed the right to legislate in all matters for the Americans; the American assemblies denied that right, with increasing fervor. At the moment Parliamentary rule rode lightly on American shoulders; but for the tax on tea they were choosing not to drink, the colonists hardly noticed. Yet the Declaratory Act remained on the statute books, and while it did it threatened to be the rock on which the empire would break.

Other sources of trouble were closer to Franklin's current residence but hardly more within his reach. After Hillsborough's unexpected hospitality in Ireland, Franklin decided to test the secretary's good faith. "When I had been a little while returned to London," he informed

William, "I waited on him to thank him for his civilities in Ireland, and to discourse with him on a Georgia affair." It was as though the Irish interlude had never happened. "The porter told me he was not at home. I left my card, went another time, and received the same answer, though I knew he was at home, a friend of mine being with him. After intermissions of a week each, I made two more visits, and received the same answer." The last occasion was a levee day, when a row of carriages lined the lane by Hillsborough's door. "My coachman driving up, alighted and was opening the coach door, when the porter, seeing me, came out, and surlily chid my coachman for opening the door before he had enquired whether my lord was at home; and then turning to me, said, 'My lord is not at home.' " Franklin concluded that whatever had motivated the secretary's superficial kindness in Ireland had already failed. "As Lord Hillsborough in fact got nothing out of me, I should rather suppose he threw me away as an orange that would yield no juice, and therefore not worth more squeezing."

Yet it was Hillsborough who was thrown away, not many months later. And though Franklin was hardly responsible, those who *were* responsible were allies of Franklin, which afforded Franklin fleeting satisfaction and Hillsborough lasting distress.

Unfortunately—to Franklin's way of thinking—the issue that brought Hillsborough down was not the central one of constitutionalism but the peripheral one of land. Since falling out with Hillsborough in 1770, Franklin had retreated to the rear of efforts by the Walpole Company to win its western bonanza. Franklin had always been a small player in this large game; his value to the bigger bettors was the influence he wielded among those who could make the project or break it. By alienating Hillsborough he lost what influence he possessed; discretion dictated he step back.

Yet Hillsborough himself was alienating many people, as Franklin saw, and this group included some who took a growing interest in the Walpole Company. The prospective Ohio grandees infiltrated the government by the tested means of offering shares to ministers and friends of ministers. Hillsborough still opposed the scheme, but he was outmaneuvered, and when the Walpole-friendly Privy Council overruled Hillsborough's Board of Trade and approved the land grant, the secretary of state (and president of the board) resigned.

"At length we have got rid of Lord Hillsborough," Franklin reported to William. Franklin conceded that the Walpole question was the proximate cause of the secretary's downfall, but the ultimate cause was Hillsborough's lack of friends, and excess of enemies, among his fellow ministers. Nor did his troubles stop there. "The King too was tired of him, and of his administration, which had weakened the affection and respect of the colonies for a royal government"—here Franklin could not resist a little self-congratulation, adding, "with which (I may say to you) I used proper means from time to time that his Majesty should have due information and convincing proofs."

After Hillsborough anyone would have been an improvement. Lord Dartmouth certainly seemed so. The new secretary of state indicated that he much admired Franklin, and at an early levee made a special point of greeting Franklin ahead of a crowd of others. He said nothing about Franklin's not having the approval of the Massachusetts governor but treated him like any fully accredited agent. "I hope business is getting into better train," Franklin told Thomas Cushing.

Better—but still not good. In November 1772 Franklin presented Dartmouth a petition from Massachusetts complaining at the Crown's paying the salary of the Massachusetts governor. A few days later Dartmouth summoned Franklin to discuss the matter. In tones Franklin found reasonable and ultimately persuasive, the secretary of state explained that the present was a poor season for forwarding such a petition. The king would be offended. He might turn it over to his lawyers; if he did, they would deliver an adverse opinion. If he handed it to Parliament, that body almost certainly would censure the province—which in turn would produce more unrest there. Dartmouth professed great goodwill for New England and said he did not wish the first act of his administration to be one that led to unavoidable dissatisfaction there. When Franklin interjected that it would be a dangerous thing for the government to deny the people the right of petition, Dartmouth responded that Franklin misunderstood. As a government minister he was not refusing the Massachusetts petition, and if Franklin insisted, he would receive it. But as a friend of America he hoped Franklin would reconsider whether he really wished to insist just now. Perhaps he could consult once more with the Massachusetts House. After all, since the petition was initially ordered, there had been a change in the administration in London. The responsible thing would be to confirm that the Massachusetts body still desired to go forward.

"Upon the whole I thought it best not to disoblige him in the beginning of his administration," Franklin told Thomas Cushing, by way of explaining why in fact he was not going forward at once with the petition. The House ought to reconsider the matter and re-advise. "If after deliberation they should send me fresh orders, I shall immediately obey them." The petition might well gain weight from the mere reconsideration. Sounding somewhat unsure of himself, Franklin added, "I hope my conduct will not be disapproved."

~ Franklin's uncertainty probably reflected an understanding that his conduct *would* be disapproved, at least by such skeptics as Sam Adams and James Otis. From the start they had suspected him of being too easy on the ministry, and here he was meekly following Dartmouth's lead. Quite likely a desire to show he was no minister's tool contributed to the most fateful misstep of his career—fateful for both himself and the British empire.

"There has lately fallen into my hands part of a correspondence that I have reason to believe laid the foundation of most if not all our present grievances." This was Franklin writing to Cushing, in the same letter breaking the news that he was delaying the petition. Franklin declined to say *how* the correspondence fell into his hands, and in fact he never did say, to Cushing or to anyone else who recorded the information for posterity. The pilferage of mail was hardly unheard of; Franklin had some reason to think his own letters to America were being opened. One might have guessed that his many years as postmaster would have inspired a deep respect for the confidentiality of the mails; on the other hand, as Poor Richard and any number of other aphorists knew, familiarity breeds contempt. Moreover, the pragmatist in Franklin was never one to set airy principle above practical effect; if a peek beneath someone else's seal could effect a reconciliation between the colonies and Britain, the sin would be venial and easily forgiven.

The correspondence in question consisted of several letters by various authors written between 1767 and 1769. The most important authors were Thomas Hutchinson and his brother-in-law, Andrew Oliver. The offices of the two men—Massachusetts governor and lieutenant governor, respectively—were what gave the letters such interest, for the opinions expressed were no more inflammatory than many others emanating from Massachusetts at this time, and the authors' views on constitutional relations between that colony and Britain paralleled the conventional wisdom of officials of the British government—among whom, of course, they numbered themselves. Yet at the same time they spoke as Massachusetts men, which of course they also were and were so understood in England to be. This was what galled Franklin, and doubtless what moved him to forward the letters to Cushing.

The gist of the letters was that the troubles in America reflected no broad disaffection but simply the political perversions of a minority. The most damning passage—damning in the eyes of American patriots—was one written by Hutchinson in January 1769 outlining the measures he judged necessary to restore order and respect for government in Massachusetts.

> There must be an abridgment of what are called English liberties. I relieve myself by considering that in a remove from the state of nature to the most perfect state of government there must be a great restraint of natural liberty. I doubt whether it is possible to project a system of government in which a colony 3000 miles distant from the parent state shall enjoy all the liberty of the parent state. I am certain I have never yet seen the projection. I wish the good of the colony when I wish to see some further restraint of liberty rather than the connexion with the parent state should be broken; for I am sure such a breach must prove the ruin of the colony.

In forwarding the letters to Cushing, Franklin still sought reconciliation. He hoped to show that the oppressive policies lately pursued by the British government were the result of evil counsel from an identifiable source—namely Hutchinson and Oliver—and not the consequence of a general conspiracy in England against American liberty. The malicious influence of the two men could be countered and neutralized, and the situation corrected.

Franklin understood the delicacy of what he was doing, and when he passed the correspondence to Cushing, he included a proviso: "I have engaged that it shall not be printed, nor any copies taken of the whole or any part of it; but I am allowed and desired to let it be seen by some men of worth in the province for their satisfaction only." He expected the letters back after "some months in your possession"; presumably he would return them to his source.

Franklin did not deal in stolen goods without compunction. But Hutchinson and Oliver had crossed the line. For years they had been "bartering away the liberties of their native country for posts"—it was not lost on Franklin, nor did he want it lost on Cushing and the others in Massachusetts, that Hutchinson and Oliver had gained their present positions *after* these letters reached Britain. As part of the bargain the two received increases in their salaries and pensions, "for which the money is to be squeezed from the people." The people naturally resisted; to suppress the resistance, and preserve their ill-gotten gains, Hutchinson and Oliver summoned British troops, conjuring "imaginary rebellions" and "exciting jealousies in the Crown, and provoking it to wrath against a great part of its faithful subjects." In sum, the malign pair had shown themselves "mere time-servers, seeking their own private emolument through any quantity of public mischief; betrayers of the interest, not of their native country only, but of the Government they pretend to serve, and of whole English Empire."

So angry was Franklin that he wanted the world to know of the duplicity of the governor and lieutenant governor. "I therefore wish I was at liberty to make the letters public." But his source insisted he not. "I can only allow them to be seen by yourself," he told Cushing, "by the other gentlemen of the Committee of Correspondence, by Messrs. Bowdoin and Pitts, of the Council, and Drs. Chauncey, Cooper and Winthrop, with a few such other gentlemen as you may think fit to show them to."

Franklin was no innocent in the political arts. He understood how valuable the letters of Hutchinson and Oliver would be to their many opponents in the Massachusetts House, a group that included those Franklin named. He must have expected that the letters would find the light of New England day even if his own promise precluded their publication in old England. By his own statement, he would have published them himself had he been free. Indeed, Cushing might easily have read Franklin's statement as implicit permission to publish.

Apparently Cushing did not, for the speaker treated the letters circumspectly. Others, however, felt less constrained. It may have been John Hancock who laid the letters before the House; it certainly was Sam Adams who read them to the members. Shortly thereafter the House ordered the letters printed for members' use. Soon they were available in pamphlet form and in installments in the *Massachusetts Spy*. Copies quickly found their way all over the colony.

→ In Franklin's correspondence and apparently in his feelings during this period occurred a curious reversion. The boy who at seventeen had eagerly shaken the dust of Boston from his shoes found himself at sixty-seven reidentifying with the city of his birth. Had Franklin reflected on the matter he might have detected an underlying consistency, for the rebel who left Boston for its being too conservative now returned to Boston when the city itself grew rebellious. For the first twenty years of his political life Franklin had fought the powers that be in Pennsylvania; now that the contest with Parliament had superseded the struggle with the Penns, he transferred his emotional loyalties to the liveliest fight going, between Boston and London.

Yet Philadelphia continued to exercise a hold. Various people and events recalled what tied him to his adopted city. In late 1771 Franklin finally met Richard Bache, who was visiting his parents at Preston. Bache experienced more than the usual trepidation of the son-in-law upon encountering his wife's father, for the father in this case was not merely a world-famous figure but also a stern sire who had left no doubt as to his opposition to the marriage. Yet Debbie had been working on Franklin, as had Mrs. Stevenson and Polly (now Polly Stevenson Hewson). They might have suggested, or Bache perhaps reckoned on his own, that he would make his best appearance among friends and family; from this followed an invitation to Franklin during his northern tour to stop at the Bache family home in Yorkshire. Richard Bache joined them there.

His sigh of relief was audible clear back to Philadelphia. "I can now, with great satisfaction, tell you that he received me with open arms and with a degree of affection that I did not expect to be made sensible of at our first meeting," Bache wrote Debbie.

The younger man accompanied the elder on the return to London. During the journey Franklin grew to like Bache. "His behaviour here has been very agreeable to me," Franklin told Debbie. He also gave Bache some advice, which he—Franklin—shared with Sally in a letter. "I advised him to settle down to business in Philadelphia where he will always be close to you." This might have seemed odd coming from a husband who had spent less than two years of the last fifteen on the same continent with his own wife, but perhaps no odder than an additional pearl—from the king's postmaster of thirty-five years—about eschewing public office. "I am of opinion that almost any profession a man has been educated in is preferable to an office held at pleasure, as rendering him more independent, more a freeman less subject to the caprices of superiors." In this letter he urged Sally and her husband to be industrious and frugal; that way whatever he and Debbie bequeathed them "may be a pretty addition, though of itself far from sufficient to maintain and bring up a family." As a foretaste, however, of that pretty addition, and perhaps recalling how peace treaties with the Indians were always sealed with gifts, he told Sally he had given Bache £200, "with which I wish you good luck."

If Bache's visit reminded Franklin of home, so did his encounters with his godson, Polly Hewson's little boy William. Franklin had never seen Sally's son Benjamin Franklin Bache, now nearly four years old; what he knew he got by letter from her and her mother. His imagination supplied the rest as he watched Billy Hewson grow. "In return for your history of your *Grandson*," he wrote Debbie, "I must give you a little of the history of my *Godson*. He is now 21 months old, very strong and healthy, begins to speak a little, and even to sing. He was with us a few days last week, grew fond of me, and would not be contented to sit down to breakfast without coming to call *Pa*, rejoicing when he had got me into my place. . . . It makes me long to be at home to play with Ben."

Thoughts of Ben recalled another child. Across the ocean and across the years, Franklin still thought of his second son, dead now thirty-six years and buried in Philadelphia. "All who have seen my grandson agree with you in their accounts of his being an uncommonly fine boy," he told his sister Jane, "which bring often afresh to my mind the idea of my son Franky." This was the letter in which the still-grieving father declared his lost child to be a boy "whom I have seldom seen equaled in every thing, and whom to this day I cannot think of without a sigh."

Another grandson was nearer to hand, even if his circumstances were problematic. Temple Franklin, now twelve, spent most months at a school in Kent operated by a brother-in-law of William Strahan. The precise relation of Temple to his father and grandfather remained publicly obscure, but Franklin brought him to London for holidays and attended to him much as he attended to Billy Hewson. "He improves continually," Franklin informed Temple's father, "and more and more engages the regard of all that are acquainted with him, by his pleasing, sensible, manly behaviour."

If cover were needed for Temple, some was supplied by Sarah Franklin, granddaughter of Franklin's cousin Thomas. Hoping to expand upon the opportunities available to a young woman in the English countryside, Sally came to London to live with Franklin. In exchange she helped look after the needs of her older relative, who no longer kept a servant man. "She is nimble-footed and willing to run of errands and wait upon me," Franklin told Debbie. Unfortunately for him, her venture to the city had proved successful, and she was to be married. "I shall miss her."

Observing youth, Franklin pondered age. On January 6, 1773, he wrote Debbie, "I still feel some regard for this Sixth of January, as my old nominal birth-day, though the change of style has carried the real day forward to the 17th, when I shall be, if I live till then, 67 years of age. It seems but t'other day since you and I were ranked among the boys and girls, so swiftly does time fly!"

∽ Thoughts of home warred in Franklin's heart against the continuing attractions of England. For all his distaste of recent English politics, London still offered much to a man of the world. The famous scientists and philosophers who called on him in London would never find their way to Philadelphia. His closest current friends all lived in England; with each passing year more old friends from Philadelphia passed on. A decade and a half after he had really made Philadelphia home, Franklin found London more familiar and comfortable, in many respects, than the city of the Quakers.

Torn between his old and present homes, Franklin applied a method of decision-making he had developed over time. He explained the method in a letter to Joseph Priestley, the scientist who had done much to spread Franklin's fame even while winning a first-rate reputation of his own. Priestley had received an offer from Lord Shelburne to be his librarian; the offer appealed on grounds of pay, prestige, and patronage. But Priestley was happy with his current life in Leeds, which afforded him both personal satisfaction and scientific opportunity. What should he do? he asked Franklin.

"I cannot, for want of sufficient premises, advise you *what* to determine," Franklin replied. "But if you please I will tell you *how*." The reason hard choices were hard, he said, was that persons facing such decisions typically considered arguments on opposite sides serially—first the pros, then the cons—and as a result vacillated from one side to the other.

> To get over this, my way is to divide half a sheet of paper by a line into two columns, writing over the one *Pro*, and over the other *Con*. Then during three or four days' consideration I put down under the different heads short hints of the different motives that

at different times occur to me for or against the measure. When I have thus got them all together in one view, I endeavour to estimate their respective weights; and where I find two, one on each side, that seem equal, I strike them both out. If I find a reason *pro* equal to some two reasons *con*, I strike out the three. If I judge some two reasons *con* equal to some three reasons *pro*, I strike out the five; and thus proceeding I find at length where the balance lies.

Franklin did not pretend to mathematical precision in this method; reasons on one side never exactly canceled reasons on the other. "Yet when each is thus considered separately and comparatively, and the whole lies before me, I think I can judge better, and am less likely to make a rash step; and in fact I have found great advantage from this kind of equation, in what might be called *Moral* or *Prudential Algebra*."

Franklin applied his prudential algebra to the question of returning to America. In one column he listed the reasons to stay in England; in the other, to go home. The former included his political work, his various philosophical projects, and the Ohio land scheme. The latter involved the settlement of certain accounts and the attractions of retirement. Thus reckoned, the reasons to stay prevailed.

⌐ Although the omens were not auspicious, Franklin retained hope that the contest between Massachusetts, the most forward of the American colonies, and the British government could be worked out. Dartmouth continued to express goodwill, which was much more than could be said for his predecessor. And Dartmouth might bring his colleagues around.

The key, Franklin believed, was time. He explained to Thomas Cushing, "Our great security lies, I think, in our growing strength both in wealth and numbers, that creates an increasing ability of assisting this nation in its wars, which will make us more respectable, our friendship more valued, and our enmity feared. Thence it will soon be thought proper to treat us, not with justice only, but with kindness; and thence we may expect in a few years a total change of measures with regard to us." Needless to say, the Americans must maintain their sturdy spirit in order to effect this appreciation in English minds. But sturdiness need not imply belligerence, which in fact would disrupt the process. "In confidence of this coming change in our favour, I think our prudence is meanwhile to be quiet, only holding up our rights and claims on all occasions, in resolutions, memorials, and remonstrances, but bearing patiently the little present notice that is taken of them. They will all have their weight in time, and that time is at no great distance."

Perhaps Franklin's years provided the patience that informed this advice; perhaps it simply reflected a temperament long willing for progress to arrive incrementally. Not everyone possessed Franklin's patience. The Massachusetts House itched to have matters out with Parliament. Thomas Cushing, hardly the most radical member, asserted that the petition to the Crown that Franklin had postponed delivering represented "the sentiments of nine tenths of the people." Referring to the previous autumn, when he had reiterated the grievances of the colony, Cushing added, "I apprehended it was high time the controversy was settled and thought *that* was as good a time as any, and that any further delay would render it more difficult. . . . I foresaw a storm arising and the breach widening. It is in vain for administration to flatter themselves that the people will rest quiet, when they find the ministry are depriving them of their charter by piece meal and there is not a year passes without one essential clause or another's being rendered null and void." In no uncertain terms Cushing instructed Franklin as the agent of the House to put the petition before Dartmouth. For good measure the House had passed a second petition, expanding the complaints about Parliamentary usurpation; Franklin was to deliver this as well.

⌐ **Franklin** followed instructions. To no one's surprise—certainly not his—the petitions raised tempers in Parliament. But the anger over the petitions was lost in the uproar surrounding the publication of the Hutchinson-Oliver letters.

"They have had great effect; they make deep impressions wherever they are known," a delighted Samuel Cooper reported to Franklin from Boston. "They strip the mask from the authors who under the profession of friendship to their country have been endeavouring to build up themselves and their families upon its ruins. They and their adherents are shocked and dismayed. The confidence reposed in them by many is annihilated; and Administration must soon see the necessity of putting the provincial power of the Crown into other hands."

But the administration saw no such necessity. If anything, the publication of the Hutchinson letters confirmed the government in its belief that the Americans were ingrates and scoundrels. Nor did the official opinion improve when the Massachusetts House formally responded to the Hutchinson letters by petitioning for the recall of Hutchinson and Oliver.

In his dealings with the government Franklin strove to place the most favorable light on this latest petition. "I have the pleasure of hearing from that province by my late letters," he informed Dartmouth, "that a sincere disposition prevails in the people there to be on good terms with the Mother Country; that the Assembly have declared their desire only to be put into the situation they were in before the Stamp Act; they aim at no novelties. And it is said that having lately discovered, as they think, the authors of their grievances to be some of their own people, their resentment against Britain is thence much abated."

This was a brave front—although it would have been braver, if perhaps less a front, had Franklin acknowledged his part in the printing of these private letters. But he saw no good that could come from doing so, and much harm. He still considered himself a conciliator, one of the few voices of calm reason in a time when the shouts of passion threatened to make conciliation impossible. Let the deed speak for itself.

◦— **Franklin** was a conciliator, but he was also a propagandist. During the summer and autumn of 1773 he wrote regularly for the London papers; two pieces from the period became two of his most famous short works. One was cast in the form of a dispatch from Danzig containing an edict of the king of Prussia, Frederick II. This edict informed the inhabitants of Britain that henceforth they would be subject to a variety of taxes and other impositions, payable to and enforced by Prussia. The asserted justification for these measures was the historic fact that Germans in distant times past had settled in the island of Britain, thereby planting what Frederick was pleased to denominate his German colonies. Moreover, Prussia had fought to defend Britain against France in the late war, a boon for which Prussia had not received adequate compensation. The taxes to be levied, on imports to Britain and exports therefrom, would afford Prussia just such compensation. Various restraints on British trade would benefit Prussian merchants and manufacturers. The edict additionally decreed the transport of German felons to Britain *"for the Better Peopling of that country."* Lest the inhabitants of Britain conceive this order as unreasonable, Frederick pointed out that he had modeled his edict on several statutes—he obligingly listed them—that the monarchs and Parliament of Britain had enacted toward their own colonies in America and Ireland.

The entire article, until the very end, was written in all apparent seriousness. Only in the last paragraph, a comment by the unnamed person communicating the edict from Danzig, did Franklin tip his hand.

> Some take this edict to be merely one of the King's *jeux d'esprit*. Others suppose it is serious, and that he means a quarrel with England. But all here think the assertion it concludes with, "that these regulations are copied from Acts of the English Parliament respecting their colonies," a very injurious one; it being impossible to believe that a people distinguished for their love of liberty, a nation so wise, so liberal in its sentiments, so just and equitable towards its neighbours, should, from mean and injudicious views of petty immediate profit, treat its own children in a manner so arbitrary and tyrannical!

Upon publication of this piece Franklin had the pleasure of watching readers swallow the bait before realizing they had been hooked. "I was down at Lord Le Despencer's when the post brought in that day's papers," he wrote William. Several gentlemen were present, including Paul Whitehead, a satirist of some note (and a former associate of John Wilkes).

> He had them in another room, and we were chatting in the breakfast parlour, when he came running in to us, out of breath, with the paper in his hand. Here! says he, here's the news for ye! *Here's the king of Prussia, claiming a right to this kingdom!* All stared, and I as much as any body; and he went on to read it. When he had read two or three paragraphs, a gentleman present said, *Damn his impudence. I dare say we shall hear by next post he is upon his march with one hundred thousand men to back this.* Whitehead, who is very shrewd, soon after began to smoke it, and looking in my face said, *I'll be hanged if this is not some of your American jokes upon us.*

Franklin's other noteworthy piece that autumn was more straightforwardly satire. The title—"Rules by Which a Great Empire May Be Reduced to a Small One"—put readers on notice that something was amiss.

An ancient sage (Themistocles, as it happened) had once formulated a set of rules by which a small city might be enlarged into a great one; the current author—who labeled himself "a modern Simpleton" and signed himself "Q.E.D."—essayed the reverse.

"In the first place, Gentlemen, you are to consider that a great empire, like a great cake, is most easily diminished at the edges. Turn your attention therefore first to your remotest provinces, that as you get rid of them, the next may follow in order."

Second, in order that such separation remain possible, special care should be taken that the provinces not be incorporated into the Mother Country, that they not enjoy the same rights and privileges, but that they be subject to laws more severe, and not of their own enacting.

Third, should said provinces acquire strength of trade or fleet, strength that enabled them to assist the Mother Country in wartime, this must be forgotten by the Mother Country, or treated as an affront. Should the colonists acquire the spirit of liberty, nurtured in the principles of the Mother Country's own revolution, this must be stamped out. "For such principles, after a revolution is thoroughly established, are of *no more use*; they are even *odious and abominable*."

Fourth, however peaceable the provinces, and however inclined to bear grievances patiently, "you are to suppose them always inclined to revolt, and treat them accordingly." Troops should be quartered among them, troops who by their insolence might provoke them, and by their bullets and bayonets suppress them. "By this means, like a husband who uses his wife ill from suspicion, you may in time convert your suspicions into realities."

There were several more principles along similar lines. Some mirrored policies already in place; others projected from present policies. The colonists, after loyally supporting the Mother Country in war, should be burdened with taxes and treated with contempt. "Nothing can have a better effect in producing the alienation proposed, for though many can forgive injuries, none ever forgave contempt." If news arrived of general dissatisfaction in the colonies, such news must be disbelieved. "Suppose all their complaints to be invented and promoted by a few factious demagogues, whom if you could catch and hang, all would be quiet. Catch and hang a few of them accordingly; and the blood of the martyrs shall work miracles in favour of your purpose."

By the time all these rules were put into effect in the colonies, the outcome would be guaranteed. "You will that day, if you have not done it sooner, get rid of the trouble of governing them, and all the plagues attending their commerce and connection from thenceforth and for ever."

⌒ **Not long after** these pieces appeared, Franklin received a letter from his sister Jane, expressing her hope that he might be the instrument of restoring harmony between America and Britain. He replied that he would be very happy to see such harmony restored, whoever was the instrument. He went on to say that his strategy for seeking harmony had changed. "I had used all the smooth words I could muster, and I grew tired of meekness when I saw it without effect. Of late therefore I have been saucy." Referring to his two recent sallies in the press, he explained:

> I have held up a looking-glass in which some ministers may see their ugly faces, and the nation its injustice. Those papers have been much taken notice of. Many are pleased with them, and a few very angry, who I am told will make me feel their resentment, which I must bear as well as I can, and shall bear the better if any public good is done, whatever the consequence to myself.
>
> In my own private concerns with mankind, I have observed that to kick a little when under imposition has a good effect. A little sturdiness when superiors are much in the wrong sometimes occasions consideration. And there is truth in the old saying, that *if you make yourself a sheep, the wolves will eat you.*

21

The Cockpit

1774–75

∿ The wolves were after more than sheep.

They wanted Franklin. And they got him.

In the spring of 1773, while Thomas Cushing

and Sam Adams were considering how to make most

effective use of the Hutchinson letters, Parliament revised

the last remnant of the Townshend duties. At one time

Franklin had hoped for repeal of the duty on tea, but the

abandonment of nonimportation removed what pressure

Parliament felt on the subject, and Americans settled back

into their routine of an afternoon cup of tea, sometimes

smuggled from Holland but often brought from Britain,

with the three pence duty legally and openly paid.

Yet Parliament, with the clumsiness that had become characteristic of its American policy, managed to revive the rebellious spirit. In May 1773 it passed a Tea Act that, while leaving the American duty on tea unchanged, rebated other duties paid by the East India Company and allowed that company to market its tea directly to the American colonies, rather than through middlemen. Little effort was made to cloak the fact that this constituted a favor to the well-connected but abysmally run East India Company, nor to disguise the great advantage it gave the company over the American merchants who hitherto had bought tea at auction in England. Those merchants, who had little quarrel with Parliament once the bulk of the Townshend duties had been lifted, now confronted the looming specter of monopoly crushing them beneath its greedy heel.

Patriots in Philadelphia and New York were quicker than those in Boston to respond to the new threat, partly because of Boston's distraction with the Hutchinson letters. But once Boston mobilized, it soon seized the lead against what the Bostonians accounted this latest manifestation of a British conspiracy upon American liberty. Sam Adams and allies insisted that the agents, or consignees, of the East India Company abandon their positions; when the consignees hesitated, the Sons of Liberty attacked the warehouse and home of one of them.

The controversy came to a head with the arrival in late November 1773 of the *Dartmouth*, the first of the ships bearing the East India Company's tea. A standoff ensued between the Sons and the consignees. Adams whipped up enthusiasm for the former by calling a series of mass meetings; several thousand persons from the city and suburbs attended, shouting defiance at the East India Company, at Parliament, and at Governor Hutchinson, who was attempting to have the tea landed and who happened to be the father of two of the consignees.

On the evening of December 16 the largest meeting yet brought perhaps eight thousand people to Boston's Old South Church. At a signal from Adams a group of about fifty men thinly disguised as Indians stormed the wharf where the *Dartmouth* lay, moored next to its recently arrived sister ships, the *Eleanor* and the *Beaver*, which also carried tea. Quite evidently the band of raiders included some longshoremen, for they knew the business of unloading a ship. They brought the casks of tea from hold to deck, opened them, and dumped the leaves out upon the bay. It was a long night's work, for by morning some 90,000 pounds of tea, worth £10,000, had been consigned to the waves. For weeks leaves washed ashore all about the area. Nothing else aboard the ships was damaged; a single padlock, broken by mistake, was replaced.

❧ **The Boston Tea Party** could hardly have happened at a more awkward time for Franklin. While the news of this most recent outburst was crossing the Atlantic, Franklin became linked to Massachusetts in the minds of ministers and others in England as never before, and the linkage did him no credit.

Upon the printing in Boston of the Hutchinson letters, Franklin initially hoped to keep clear of the affair. "I am glad my name has not been heard on the occasion," he told Thomas Cushing. "And as I do not see it could be of any use to the public, I now wish it may continue unknown." Yet he added, realistically, "I hardly expect it."

To his surprise his secret held for several months. As in all good scandals, secrecy inflamed public interest; the London papers verily quivered with intimations, accusations, rejoinders, and denials regarding who had lifted the papers. Matters grew serious in early December when William Whately, the brother of the now-deceased original recipient of the letters, Thomas Whately, essentially charged John Temple, a minor government official born in America and known to sympathize with the Americans, with having stolen the letters. Temple challenged Whately to a duel; in Hyde Park they slashed at each other ineptly with swords till Whately's wounds caused him to retire.

Franklin might have kept quiet even after this, but Whately's partisans circulated stories that John Temple had not fought fair—which caused Temple to declare the feud still open. A second duel impended.

Franklin thereupon spoke up. In late December he wrote a signed letter to the *London Chronicle* declaring Whately and Temple at once "totally ignorant and innocent" of the events over which they fought, and asserting forthrightly, "I alone am the person who obtained and transmitted to Boston the letters in question." He was equally forthright in justifying his action. "They were not in the nature of *private letters between friends*"—as had been stated by those condemning the dissemination. "They were written by public officers to persons in public station, on public affairs, and intended to procure public measures; they were therefore handed to other public persons who might be influenced by them to produce those measures. Their tendency was to incense the Mother Country against her colonies, and by the steps recommended, to widen the breach, which they effected." The principal caution expressed by the letters' authors with regard to privacy was to keep their contents from the agents of the colonies, who might try to return the letters, or copies thereof, to America. "That apprehension was, it seems, well founded; for the first agent who laid his hands on them thought it his duty to transmit them to his constituents."

Franklin's statement was as much polemic as explanation. He was not alone responsible for lifting the letters; someone, whom he still and henceforth declined to name, handed the letters to him. Nor were the letters quite the public communications he indicated. To be sure, the individuals involved held public office, but these were not official reports or correspondence drafted under public compulsion. By Franklin's argument all his letters to and from William should have been open to general perusal. (In fact some of those letters apparently *were* being opened, but Franklin hardly approved the practice.)

If any in England expected repentance, they certainly did not get it. Franklin's assertiveness condemned him the more in the eyes of those who considered Boston a nest of sedition and judged all who spoke for Boston abettors of rebellion. Until now Franklin—the famous Franklin, scientist and philosopher feted throughout the civilized world—had been above effective reproach. His admission of responsibility for transmitting the purloined letters afforded his foes the opening they had long sought.

The initial skirmish took place on January 11, 1774. The Privy Council summoned Franklin to a hearing on the petition of the Massachusetts House to remove Hutchinson from office. No one, least of all Franklin, expected that the council was seriously considering dismissing Hutchinson; the question involved the manner of the council's rejecting the petition—and its treatment of the agent delivering the petition. Franklin had reason to suspect trouble, if not a trap, for not until the late afternoon prior to the hearing did he learn that the opposition would be bringing legal counsel. Nor was the opposition counsel just any London lawyer, but Alexander Wedderburn, the solicitor general and a man with a reputation for putting courtroom invective to the service of personal and political ambition. He held his current position not from any philosophical affinity with the North administration but because North determined that it was better to have Wedderburn on the side of the government spewing out, than on the side of the opposition spewing in.

Franklin had hoped to argue for Hutchinson's dismissal on political grounds; the appearance of Wedderburn indicated that the government intended to mount a legal—and personal—counteroffensive. Moreover, the target of the counteroffensive would not be Massachusetts but

Franklin. Wedderburn's opening statement in response to the petition—"address"—of the Massachusetts House set the tone: "The address mentions certain papers. I would wish to be informed what are those papers."

Wedderburn, and everyone else at the hearing, knew what the papers were, but he wanted to hear the admission from Franklin's mouth.

"They are the letters of Mr. Hutchinson and Mr. Oliver," Franklin replied.

The Lord President of the Privy Council, Earl Gower, inquired if Franklin had brought the letters.

Franklin answered that he had not. He did *not* say that the originals were in America, where he had sent them; that too was common knowledge. "But here are attested copies."

"Do you not mean to found a charge upon them?" the Lord President insisted. "If you do, you must produce the letters."

Franklin now implicitly conceded the present location of the letters. "These copies are attested by several gentlemen at Boston, and a notary public."

Wedderburn interposed himself, with a show of magnanimity. "My Lords, we shall not take advantage of any imperfection in the proof. We admit that the letters are Mr. Hutchinson's and Mr. Oliver's handwriting." He appended a hook, however, saying that the government's side was "reserving to ourselves the right of inquiring how they were obtained."

That side clearly had Franklin outmanned at this hearing, having informed him too late for him to secure legal counsel of his own. He objected that lawyers were really unnecessary. The case for removing Hutchinson and Oliver rested on the undeniable fact that they had forfeited the confidence of the people of the province they were charged with governing. Did the Crown desire to retain such men in office? And was this not a matter their lordships were perfectly capable of deciding on their own, without the intrusion of attorneys?

The government rejoined that attorneys were indeed necessary. The agent for Hutchinson and Oliver, Israel Mauduit, said he lacked personal knowledge of Massachusetts politics. Moreover, he lacked Franklin's gifts. "I well know Dr. Franklin's great abilities, and wish to put the defense of my friends more upon a parity with the attack. He will not therefore wonder that I choose to appear before your Lordships with the assistance of counsel."

The court—that is, the Privy Council—agreed to allow the lawyers. Franklin could employ them or dispense with them, as he chose.

Franklin strongly considered waiving the right to counsel. He said he had intended simply to lay the pertinent documents before their lordships; these spoke for themselves. But wishing to give the Massachusetts House every possible chance to make its case, he decided to summon legal reinforcements. "I shall desire to have counsel," he said.

The Lord President asked how long he would require to engage counsel and prepare.

"Three weeks," Franklin replied.

∼ Had Franklin waived counsel, or had he asked for one week rather than three, what happened next might have gone differently. As it was, the interim between the first and second Privy Council hearings brought news of the Boston Tea Party. For years Franklin had been urging Thomas Cushing, and through Cushing the rest of Massachusetts, to refrain from violence and the destruction of property. Just possibly public opinion in London might come round to America's view of liberty and English rights—if that view were pressed peacefully and through legitimate channels. If Americans resorted to violence, however, their enemies in England would be able to say they were rebels one and all. Put otherwise, Thomas Hutchinson would be seen not as a betrayer of liberty but as a defender of the order on which liberty must be based.

And Franklin would be perceived not as a defender of liberty but as a betrayer of confidences. The campaign to cast him so began before the second hearing. Anonymous correspondents to the London journals hurled insults at the American agent, implying that if he were not directly culpable in this latest assault on property and order, his mark was figuratively all over the floating tea. That his days as deputy postmaster were numbered was taken as foregone. He even heard rumors that the authorities were on their way to arrest him, seize his papers, and throw him into Newgate prison.

By the time he arrived at the Cockpit on January 29, the ostensible reason for the hearing had almost been forgotten. Meetings of the Privy Council often evoked indifferent attendance, even from the lords themselves; but on this day the council chairs were filled. The Lord President of the council, Earl Gower, presided; thirty-four other eminences sat on either side of him. These included Lord North, the prime minister; Lord Dartmouth, the American secretary; Lord Hillsborough, Franklin's foe of long standing; the Archbishop of Canterbury; the Bishop of London;

the Lord Chief Justice of Common Pleas; the Duke of Queensberry; the Earls of Sandwich, Suffolk, and Rochford; Viscount Townshend (brother of the deceased author of the Townshend duties); Sir Jeffrey Amherst; and a score more. None present could recall a fuller meeting of the council. Nearly all were eager—the other few were anxious—to see what Solicitor General Wedderburn did with the estimable Dr. Franklin. The sole friendly visage among the group belonged to Lord Le Despencer.

On the rest of the main floor of the large hall, and in the gallery that ran around the room above the floor, scores of men and women crowded close to witness the highlight of the political season. Edmund Burke was there; also Jeremy Bentham and General Thomas Gage. Joseph Priestley managed to shadow Burke into the hall. Edward Bancroft, whom Franklin did not yet know, slipped in with that mysterious ease that characterized all his actions.

As the crowd waited for the hearing to begin, the air of expectancy intensified. It was like no other hearing most in attendance had ever witnessed; it seemed closer to a trial of a notorious murderer or one of the blood sports that so delighted the English masses. Franklin himself compared it to a "bull-baiting," with him as the bull, chained to a post at the center of the arena.

The hearing began with a reading of the Massachusetts petition and supporting documents, including the Hutchinson-Oliver letters. Then John Dunning, a barrister Franklin had engaged on behalf of the Massachusetts House, reiterated Franklin's previous point that the matter at hand was political, not legal, and that a judicial proceeding was hardly called for. Unfortunately for Franklin and Massachusetts, Dunning suffered from an illness of the lungs, which weakened his voice considerably, rendering it nearly inaudible and therefore unintelligible to the audience and most of the lords.

Before Dunning had a chance to finish his argument, Solicitor General Wedderburn leaped to his feet and seized the floor. He summarized the history of the Massachusetts colony from the Stamp Act riots to the present, paying special attention to the depredations of the Boston mob upon the current governor, Mr. Hutchinson. Listeners presumably expected him to connect this review to the issue at hand—or perhaps they expected otherwise, in light of the roasting said to be readied for Franklin.

If the latter, they were not disappointed, for the solicitor general suddenly launched into a tirade against Franklin that filled nearly an hour. Precisely what he said is difficult to reconstruct in all particulars; his language was too foul or libelous for even the scandalmongers of Grub Street. One person present called Wedderburn an "unmannered railer" who employed the "coarsest language," unleashed "all the licenced scurrility of the Bar," and decorated his diatribe with "the choicest flowers of Billingsgate." Another auditor, friendly to Franklin, recorded, "I had the grievous mortification to hear Mr. Wedderburn wandering from the proper question before their Lordships, pour forth such a torrent of virulent abuse on Dr. Franklin as never before took place within the compass of my knowledge of judicial proceedings, his reproaches appearing to me incompatible with the principles of law, truth, justice, propriety, and humanity." Edmund Burke characterized Wedderburn's "furious Philippic" as transcending "all bounds and measures."

Those words of Wedderburn that *did* see print were indeed furious. Franklin was called "the first mover and prime conductor" of the conspiracy by the Massachusetts House against the honor and integrity of two fine servants of the king. "Having by the help of his own special confidants and party leaders first made the Assembly *his* agents in carrying on his own secret designs, he now appears before your Lordships to give the finishing stroke to the work of his own hands."

The correspondence adduced by Franklin and his cabal to defame the governor and lieutenant governor in fact condemned Franklin himself, Wedderburn declared.

The letters could not have come to Dr. Franklin by fair means. The writers did not give them to him; nor yet did the deceased correspondent, who from our intimacy would otherwise have told me of it. Nothing then will acquit Dr. Franklin of the charge of obtaining them by fraudulent or corrupt means, for the most malignant of purposes, unless he stole them, from the person who stole them. This argument is irrefragable.

I hope, my Lords, you will mark and brand the man, for the honour of this country, or Europe, and of mankind. Private correspondence has hitherto been held sacred, in times of the greatest party rage, not only in politics but religion. He has forfeited all the respect of societies and of men. Into what companies will he hereafter go with an unembarrassed face, or the honest intrepidity of virtue? Men will watch him with a jealous eye; they will hide their papers from him, and lock up their escritoires. He will henceforth esteem it a libel to be called *a man of letters: homo trium litterarum.*

This last line brought roars of laughter from the lords and many of the gallery. All could appreciate the play on the English phrase; those who recalled their classics understood the reference to Plautus: *"Tun, trium litterarum homo me vituperas? fur."* ("Do you find fault with me? You, a man of three letters—thief!")

From wit Wedderburn returned to invective.

He not only took away the letters from one brother, but he kept himself concealed till he nearly occasioned the murder of the other. It is impossible to read his account [the one in which Franklin had owned up to his role in the publication of the letters], expressive of the coolest and most deliberate malice, without horror. Amidst these tragical events, of one person nearly murdered, of another answerable for the issue, of a worthy governor hurt in his dearest interests, the fate of America in suspense—here is a man who with the utmost insensibility of remorse, stands up and avows himself the author of all. I can compare it only to Zanga in Dr. Young's *Revenge:*

> *Know then 'twas—I.*
> *I forged the letter, I disposed the picture;*
> *I hated, I despised, and I destroy.*

I ask, my Lords, whether the revengeful temper attributed, by poetic fiction only, to the bloody African, is not surpassed by the coolness and apathy [that is, lack of emotion] of the wily American.

Wedderburn dissected and held up to gory scorn Franklin's published argument that the letters somehow belonged in the public domain because they were written from public men to another public man on public issues. No, these were private missives, "as sacred and as precious to gentlemen of integrity as their family plate or jewels are." Franklin had added the argument that the letters were intended to influence public policy. "Is this crime of so heinous a nature as to put Mr. Whately's friends out of the common protection? And to give Dr. Franklin a right to hang them up to party rage, and to expose them, for what he knew, to the danger of having their houses a second time pulled down by popular fury?" Franklin had cited the fact that Hutchinson and Oliver desired to keep their letters secret as evidence that they had much to hide. "But if the desiring of secrecy be the proof, and the measure of guilt, what then are we to think of Dr. Franklin's case, whose whole conduct in this affair has been secret and mysterious, and who through the whole course of it has discovered the utmost solicitude to keep it so?"

Wedderburn reiterated the argument made by the government (and by Hutchinson and Oliver) that the unrest in America was not the work of ordinary people—"these innocent, well-meaning farmers, which compose the bulk of the Assembly," Wedderburn said—but of self-serving conspirators, of whom Franklin was the "first mover and prime conductor" (Wedderburn liked this phrase enough to repeat it), the "actor and secret spring," and the "inventor and first planner."

> My Lords, we are perpetually told of men's incensing the mother country against the colonies, of which I have never known a single instance. But we hear nothing of the vast variety of arts which have been made use of to incense the colonies against the mother country. And in all these arts no one I fear has been a more successful proficient than the very man who now stands forth as Mr. Hutchinson's accuser. My Lords, as he has been pleased in his own letter to avow this accusation, I shall now return the charge, and shew to your Lordships who it is that is the true incendiary, and who is the great abettor of that faction at Boston which, in the form of a Committee of Correspondence, have been inflaming the whole province against his Majesty's government.

Wedderburn linked Franklin to Sam Adams, and Adams to the effort to forge a united front against Parliament by the circulation of "an inflammatory letter sounding an alarm of a plan of despotism, with which the Administration and the Parliament intended to enslave them, and threatened them with certain and inevitable destruction." This letter was accompanied by a pamphlet designed to incite the ordinary people still further. "It told them a hundred rights of which they never had heard before, and a hundred grievances which they never before had felt." Franklin and Adams did their work well; the townships of Massachusetts responded as if on cue, with resolves like none ever seen. "They are full of the most extravagant absurdities, such as the most enthusiastic rants of the wildest of my countrymen in Charles the Second's days cannot equal." Not least of the absurdities was the treasonous assertion of desire to call in foreign powers to rectify imagined injuries perpetrated by Parliament against the people of New England. "These are the lessons taught in Dr. Franklin's school of politics."

What was the purpose of the conspirators in attacking Governor Hutchinson? "To establish their power, and make all future governors bow to their authority. They wish to erect themselves into a tyranny greater than the Roman; to be able, sitting in their own secret cabal, to dictate for the Assembly, and send away their *verbosa et grandis epistola*, and get even a *virtuous* Governor dragged from his seat, and made the sport of a Boston mob." The destructive capacities of Boston mobs were most lately revealed in the destruction of the tea cargoes of the three British vessels lying peacefully in Boston's harbor.

For Franklin the prize was more specific: the governorship for himself. Wedderburn conceded that their lordships might find this hard to believe. "But nothing, surely, but a too eager attention to an ambition of this sort could have betrayed a wise man into such a conduct as we have now seen." Wedderburn offered no real evidence on this point; their lordships would have to judge for themselves. But they should surely keep the possibility in mind in weighing the issue at hand. "I hope that Mr. Hutchinson will not meet with the less countenance from your Lordships for *his rival*'s being his accuser. Nor will your Lordships, I trust, from what you have heard, advise the having Mr. Hutchinson replaced, in order to make room for Dr. Franklin as a successor."

◦— Through all of this Franklin remained silent. The audience, including many of the lords, laughed and cheered at the solicitor's slashing assault on Franklin's behavior and character, but the object of the day's entertainment stood before his accuser betraying not the slightest emotion. "The Doctor was dressed in a full dress suit of spotted Manchester velvet," Edward Bancroft recalled, "and stood *conspicuously erect*, without the smallest movement of any part of his body. The muscles of his face had been previously composed, so as to afford a placid tranquil expression of countenance, and he did not suffer the slightest alteration of it to appear during the continuance of the speech in which he was so harshly and improperly treated." He appeared, Bancroft said, "as if his features had been made of *wood*."

Franklin maintained his stoic silence after Wedderburn ended his tirade. Understanding the nature of the proceeding, he refused to rebut the solicitor or to answer his questions. John Dunning, his counsel, started to reply to Wedderburn but, unable to speak above a croaking whisper, had to stop. Franklin made no effort to speak for him—that is, for himself. He preferred not to dignify Wedderburn's diatribe with a response, confident that honest men would appreciate the unfairness of the situation into which he had been thrust. At present honest men seemed in short supply; the Privy Council sneeringly rejected the Massachusetts petition as baseless and intended only "for the seditious purpose of keeping up a spirit of clamour and discontent." The Lord President thereupon adjourned the session.

The government shortly added the expected sanction. Within forty-eight hours of his session in the Cockpit, Franklin received notice of his dismissal as deputy postmaster. Although anticipated, this move struck Franklin as both unfair to one who had built the American post from nothing to an efficient and profitable operation, and symptomatic of the wicked folly of a government that would cut off its nose to spite its face.

The entire business outraged Franklin. He normally made it a point of pride to keep his emotions clear of his pen; he almost always composed himself before composing. But more than two weeks after his encounter with Wedderburn and the Privy Council, he told Thomas Cushing bluntly, "I am very angry." His anger was both personal and political. Of the former he declined to speak, even to Cushing, lest his remarks "should be thought the effects of resentment and a desire of exasperating." But he went on, "What I feel on my own account is half lost"—but only *half* lost—"in what I feel for the public. When I see that all petitions and complaints of grievances are so odious to government that even the mere pipe which conveys them becomes obnoxious, I am at a loss to know how peace and union is to be maintained or restored between the different parts of the empire. Grievances cannot be redressed unless they are known; and they cannot be known but through complaints and petitions. If these are deemed affronts, and the messengers punished as offenders, who will henceforth send petitions? And who will deliver them?" Wise governments encouraged the airing of grievances, even those that were lightly founded. Foolish governments did the opposite—to their peril. "Where complaining is a crime, hope becomes despair."

◠ **And Franklin,** treated as a criminal for complaining, had reached the point of despair. There was nothing for honest Americans in the empire but illegitimate insult and unwarranted condemnation. Franklin wrote William with information and advice:

> This line is just to acquaint you that I am well, and that my office of Deputy-Postmaster is taken from me.
>
> As there is no prospect of your being ever promoted to a better government [that is, a more lucrative governorship], and that you hold has never defrayed its expenses, I wish you were settled in your farm. 'Tis an honester and a more honourable because a more independent employment.
>
> You will hear from others the treatment I have received. I leave you to your own reflections and determinations upon it.

William might well have read this as encouragement to resign his post; Franklin might well have intended it so. Two weeks later Franklin wrote to Richard Bache, who evidently had hoped to use his father-in-law's connections to gain employment for himself. Franklin said that those connections now no longer existed, and hence no possibility of a post-office job. He added, "As things are, I would not wish to see you concerned in it. For I conceive that the dismissing me merely for not being corrupted by the office to betray the interests of my country will make it some disgrace among us to hold such an office."

Yet if resigning had been his message to William, he soon amended it. Not that he considered service under the Crown any more honorable than in the immediate aftermath of his Cockpit ordeal; he simply reverted to his previous philosophy of never resigning. William had been weighing a move from Burlington to Perth Amboy; Franklin told him to go slow incurring the expense of such a move, as the future of his governorship was in jeopardy. Some reports suggested that William would simply be dismissed, while others hinted at a more indirect approach by their mutual foes. "They may expect that your resentment of their treatment of me may induce you to resign, and save them the shame of depriving you whom they ought to promote." Franklin went on, "But this I would not advise you to do. Let them take your place if they want it, though in truth I think it scarce worth your keeping. . . . One may make something of an injury, nothing of a resignation."

For himself, he thought he had already made something of his injury. He wrote to Jane Mecom, whose own money problems disposed her to worry about her brother in his loss of income, telling her not to be troubled. "You and I have almost finished the journey of life. We are now but a little way from home, and have enough in our pockets to pay the post chaises." As for the principle involved, it was plainer than ever, to honest men if not to his enemies. "Intending to disgrace me, they have rather done me honour. No failure of duty in my office is alleged against me; such a fault I should have been ashamed of. But I am too much attached to the interests of America, and an opposer of the measures of Administration. The displacing me is therefore a testimony of my being uncorrupted."

The more he reflected on his situation, the more he understood the heart of the matter. To his partner in the American post office, John Foxcroft, he explained his dismissal in a sentence: "I am too much of an American."

～ As philosophical as he could be with relatives and friends, Franklin remained irate at those who were forcing this choice between America and Britain. They displayed their folly by word and deed, and though, as he told Cushing, he might have suffered their folly for his own sake, that folly was rending the empire. No man of public feeling could keep silent.

In the London papers he struck back with scorn. "The admirers of Dr. Franklin in England are much shocked at Mr. Wedderburn's calling him a thief," he wrote in the *Public Advertiser*, over a signature no one present at the Cockpit hearing, or familiar with Wedderburn's by-now-famous assault, could mistake: *Homo Trium Litterarum*. "But perhaps they will be less surprised at this circumstance when they are informed that his greatest admirers on the Continent agree in entertaining the same idea of him." As evidence Franklin enclosed a poetical epigraph from Dubourg's recently published *Oeuvres de M. Franklin*. "It will even be seen that foreigners represent him as much more impudent and audacious in his thefts than the English orator (though he was under no restraint from a regard to truth)." Franklin reproduced the stanza in French, then helpfully supplied a translation:

> *To steal from Heaven its sacred fire he taught,*
> *The Arts to thrive in savage climes he brought.*
> *In the New World the first of men esteemed;*
> *Among the Greeks a god he had been deemed.*

It was unlike Franklin to boast of his fame, particularly in such transparent manner, but after the abuse he had received from the Privy Council, he allowed himself this riposte. Who did these people think they were dealing with? What had Wedderburn, of these cribbed classical allusions, ever done besides extort office from his betters—or men who would have been his betters had they not lowered themselves to his level?

In American papers he spoke at greater length. The *Boston Gazette* carried his unsigned account of the proceedings at the Cockpit. He explained how the counsel for the Massachusetts House had begun its presentation with propriety and decency, whereupon the solicitor general "totally departed from the question and was permitted to wander into a new case, the accusation of the person who merely delivered the petition." The lords of the Privy Council disgraced themselves by their toleration of—indeed their conniving in—this astonishing performance. "Not a single lord checked and recalled this orator to the business before them; but on the contrary (a very few excepted) they seemed to enjoy highly the entertainment and frequently burst out into loud applause."

To what purpose this ad hominem attack? To wound Dr. Franklin's character, and to distract attention from the issue at hand. As to the former design, the shaft missed its mark. "His character is not so vulnerable as they imagined." As to the latter:

> Even supposing he had *infamously* obtained the letters, would that have altered the nature of them, their tendency and design? Would that have made them innocent? How weak and ridiculous is this?
>
> The truth is, the Doctor came by the letters *honourably*; his intention in sending them was *virtuous*: to lessen the breach between Britain and the colonies, by showing that the injuries complained of by *one* of them did not proceed from the *other*, but from *traitors among themselves*. The *treason* thus discovered, the *conspirators* were complained of. The agent is suffered to be abused by a *solicitor*; the complaint *called*—I had like to have said *judged*—false, vexatious, scandalous; and the complainers factious and seditious.

The pain we feel on Dr. Franklin's account is lost in what we feel for America and for Britain.

The government had followed this shameful affair by dismissing Dr. Franklin from his position with the post office. Such action was discreditable in itself; it was even more pernicious in its prospect. Appointments to the post office—a service essential to all who lived in the colonies—were being held hostage to adherence to the policies of whatever ministry happened to hold power. Moreover, at a time when committees of correspondence in the several colonies were attempting to coordinate opposition to oppression, the very mails communicating those attempts were subject to surveillance by government placemen. *"Behold Americans where matters are driving!"*

⌒ Where they were driving was hard against Boston and the liberty of Massachusetts. The Boston Tea Party had excited great wrath in England, a substantial portion of which had broken upon the head of Franklin. But more remained. King George, heretofore in the background on colonial issues, took a direct interest in the insurrectionary activity across the water. He called in General Gage—fresh from seeing Franklin being pilloried—for advice. The British commander-in-chief for America was esteemed an expert on the colonies; he urged vigorous measures. "He says they will be lions whilst we are lambs," George recorded. "But if we take the resolute part, they will be very meek." Lord North, hardly a truculent sort, concurred. "We are not entering into a dispute between internal and external taxes," the prime minister declared, "not between taxes laid for the purpose of revenues and taxes laid for the regulation of trade, not between representation and taxation, or legislation and taxation; but we are now to dispute the question whether we have, or have not, any authority in that country." He added, "If they deny authority in one instance, it goes to all; we must control them or submit to them."

Parliament agreed. It immediately passed the Boston Port Act, which closed the port of Boston to overseas trade (with tightly controlled exceptions for food and fuel). The closure would remain in force until the king decided to lift it, a decision that could not come before the East India Company had been compensated for its tea. Although the act threatened Massachusetts with economic strangulation—as Franklin, who had grown up in sight and sound of all those ships in Boston's harbor, appreciated full well—it might have been worse, given the mood in London. Even Isaac Barré, who had opposed the Stamp Act and was generally thought a friend of America, offered his "hearty affirmative" for the port closure. Likening the protesters to wayward children, he told Parliament, "Boston ought to be punished."

Whether the acts that followed were more or less moderate depended on one's point of view. The Massachusetts Government Act suspended the charter of the colony and granted the Crown much greater control over its affairs. The Administration of Justice Act allowed royal officials charged with certain crimes to be tried in England. The Quartering Act required private householders to take in troops upon the order of the British commanding officer. The Quebec Act—not a direct response to the Boston Tea Party but passed in the same atmosphere of disregard for American sensibilities—established a London-dominated civil government for Canada and extended the boundaries of Canada to the Ohio River, effectively vetoing claims of several of the existing colonies to the region.

The five measures together were called the "Intolerable Acts" in America, for after everything else of the previous decade, they seemed more than the Americans could bear. Even before the last of the laws was enacted, committees of correspondence in the colonies were writing furiously, dispatching messages up and down the Atlantic Coast, calling on the assemblies and people of the separate provinces to join forces against this latest usurpation. The Intolerable Acts fell most heavily on Massachusetts, of course, but what Parliament and the Crown could do to Massachusetts, they could do to the other colonies.

Virginia thought so; the House of Burgesses there, led by Patrick Henry, Richard Henry Lee, and Thomas Jefferson, declared that Boston was suffering a "hostile invasion." In a touch doubtless appreciated in Puritan Boston, the Virginia assembly denominated June 1, 1774, as a "day of fasting, humiliation, and prayer, devoutly to implore the divine interposition for averting the heavy calamity which threatens the destruction to our civil rights, and the evils of civil war."

During the weeks that followed, one colony after another selected delegates to a continental convention. In some cases the regular assemblies did the choosing; where royal governors attempted to derail the process by dissolving the assemblies, extraordinary bodies supplied the names. Pennsylvania offered to host the convention; September was set for the time, and Philadelphia for the place.

∾ Franklin half expected to be home in time for the gathering. His two hours in the Cockpit erased what thoughts remained of retiring to England. He still had friends in Britain; he hoped he always would. But that part of imperial politics he had been able to put aside as superficial— the place-mongering, partisanship, sheer personal nastiness—he now saw as the central theme of London life. What had appealed about England was its intellectual openness, the opportunities it afforded to share ideas with men (and the occasional woman, such as Polly Stevenson) of curiosity, ingenuity, and a willingness to challenge received wisdom. But there was nothing open about a system determined to stifle the most fundamental liberties of a large portion of its people simply because they lived across the ocean.

Franklin was no stranger to political abuse; the proprietary party in Pennsylvania had circulated slanders petty and grand against him for years. But until now—and this had been one aspect of England's appeal—those kinds of criticisms had gained little currency in London. The Penns muttered against him, of course, and Lord Hillsborough. But for the most part the British were courteous and respectful, even admiring.

No longer. In the London papers he was assailed as "this old snake" and "the old veteran of mischief." He was called a "traitor," "old Doubleface," a "grand incendiary," the "living emblem of iniquity in grey hairs." His living quarters became "Judas's office in Craven Street"; in that place were conceived and hatched his "vindictive subtlety, watchfulness, and politician tricks." To his face—Franklin was in the gallery— Lord Sandwich castigated him before the House of Lords as "one of the bitterest and most mischievous enemies" Britain had ever known.

Franklin took the slanders for what they were worth. "You know that in England there is every day in almost every paper some abuse on public persons of all parties," he wrote an Austrian acquaintance. "The King himself does not always escape; and the populace, who are used to it, love to have a good character cut up now and then for their entertainment." He comforted himself that his friends were able to pierce the propaganda against him. "I do not find that I have lost a single friend on the occasion. All have visited me repeatedly with affectionate assurances of their unalterable respect and affection."

In fact things were not so simple. Franklin's friends were indeed willing to give him the benefit of the doubt—but they did have their doubts. Joseph Priestley's were fewer than most others'; he stood by Franklin, literally, in his hour of distress. Priestley described the denouement of the Cockpit scene:

> Dr. Franklin, in going out, took me by the hand, in a manner that indicated some feeling. I soon followed him, and going through the anteroom, saw Mr. Wedderburn there, surrounded with a circle of his friends and admirers. Being known to him, he stepped forwards as if to speak to me; but I turned aside, and made what haste I could out of the place.

The next morning Priestley ate breakfast with Franklin and heard his friend's reaction to events of the previous day. "He said he had never been so sensible of the power of a good conscience; for that if he had not considered the thing for which he had been so much insulted, as one of the best actions of his life, and what he should certainly do again in the same circumstances, he could not have supported it."

David Hume was not present for Wedderburn's performance, but he heard all about the Hutchinson affair. He wanted to believe the best of Franklin yet found it difficult. He wrote William Strahan:

> I hope you can tell me something in justification, at least in alleviation, of Dr. Franklin's conduct. The factious part he has all along acted must be given up by his best friends. But I flatter myself there is nothing treacherous or unfair in his conduct; though his silence with regard to the method by which he came by these letters leaves room for all sorts of malignant surmizes. What a pity, that a man of his merit should have fallen into such unhappy circumstances!

Hume added an anecdote he thought applicable to the case of Franklin and America. Hume had been visiting the Earl of Bathurst, whose son was currently Lord Chancellor. Discussion turned to America, and the authority formerly exercised over the colonies.

> I observed to them that nations, as well as individuals, had their different ages, which challenged a different treatment. For instance, My Lord, I said to the old Peer, you have sometimes, no

doubt, given your son a whipping; and I doubt not but it was well merited and did him much good. Yet you will not think it proper at present to employ the birch. The colonies are no longer in their infancy. But yet I say to you, they are still in their nonage, and Dr. Franklin wishes to emancipate them too soon from their mother country.

John Pringle defended Franklin against Hume's aspersions. "I think your notion of his being naturally of a factious disposition unjust," he wrote Hume. Yet the physician did not defend everything his erstwhile traveling partner had done. "I do not dispute his being carried by zeal for his country, and for the better serving those who employed him, to do things which cannot be easily justified." Pringle considered himself one of Franklin's closer friends; he was struck that during the whole Hutchinson affair Franklin had not uttered a single word to him on the subject. Pringle thought this confidentiality a fault, one that had led to the current imbroglio. "He could have advised with no mortal of common sense and common delicacy but who must have dissuaded him from availing himself in that manner of a private correspondence between two friends, much less transmitting of those letters."

Having said this, Pringle again defended Franklin's motives. "I must do him the justice to say that as long as there was any prospect (at least in his eyes) of accommodation, he laboured to bring it about; and that if his advice had been taken, all this mischief would have been prevented, and England and her colonies had been again on the best terms possible." Hume had registered a belief that the Americans had been searching for a pretext for rebellion against the mother country; Pringle disputed this, especially as it applied to Franklin. "I can witness for our friend that, for the first seven years he was amongst us, I never heard a word intimating any thing else than a perfect satisfaction in the happiness the colonies enjoyed in the state they were in. And this sentiment continued with him and them until the unlucky act of Mr. Grenville [that is, the Stamp Act]."

Horace Walpole, a rather more distant observer, concurred that Franklin had been badly treated. Describing Wedderburn's speech as "most bitter and abusive," yet "much admired" by those present, Walpole continued, "The Ministry determined to turn Franklin out of his place of postmaster of America, which could but incense him and drive him (a man of vast abilities) on farther hostilities, and recommend him as a martyr to the Bostonians." (The editor of Walpole's journal subsequently appended his own comment on the Cockpit scene, calling it "a capital one in giving date to the American war.")

Edmund Burke shook his head at the fatuity of the entire affair. And as it became clear that the mind-set of Wedderburn characterized that of the government, Burke observed, "A great empire and little minds go ill together."

"Your popularity in this country, whatever it may be on the other side, is greatly beyond whatever it was," William wrote his father from America. Popular evidence certainly indicated as much. Indignant crowds carried effigies of Wedderburn and Hutchinson through the streets of Philadelphia; the tag on the Wedderburn figure read, "Such horrid monsters are a disgrace to human nature, and justly merit our utmost detestation and the gallows, to which they are assigned, and then burnt by ELECTRIC FIRE."

Franklin was gratified at the support, but he was more interested in what it was leading to. "I rejoice to find that the whole Continent have so justly, wisely, and unanimously taken up our cause as their own," he told Thomas Cushing as the Continental Congress gathered in Philadelphia. Even now Franklin hoped history might be rescued from those who would foolishly wreck the empire. "I have been taking pains among them to show the mischief that must arise to the whole from a dismembering of the empire, which all the measures of the present mad Administration have a tendency to accomplish." The Philadelphia meeting was what kept him in London. "Much depends on the proceedings of the Congress. All sides are enquiring when an account of them may be expected. And I am advised by no means to leave England till they arrive." Those advising him not to leave gave him cause for optimism, which he passed along to Cushing. Referring to the resolutions expected from the Congress, he predicted, "Their unanimity and firmness will have great weight here, and probably unhorse the present wild riders."

If he allowed himself some small hope, it came not at the expense of his determination. Indeed, his views hardened with the passing months. In the immediate aftermath of the Boston Tea Party he had argued for compensation to the East India Company as a magnanimous gesture, but now that the British government was insisting, he changed his mind and counseled withholding that satisfaction. To a Boston merchant (who happened to be married to Franklin's niece) he urged steadfastness: "If you should ever tamely submit to the yoke prepared for you, you cannot conceive how much you will be despised here, even by those who are endeavouring to impose it on you. Your very children and grandchildren will curse your memories for entailing disgrace upon them and theirs, and making them ashamed to own their country."

He suffered no illusions as to the stakes of the game. If the British government failed to respond to reason, war was a real possibility, if not indeed a likelihood. General Gage had replaced Thomas Hutchinson as governor of Massachusetts; the military grip was tightening. "I am in perpetual anxiety lest the mad measure of mixing soldiers among a people whose minds are in such a state of irritation may be attended with some sudden mischief," Franklin told Cushing. "For an accidental quarrel, a personal insult, an imprudent order, an insolent execution of even a prudent one, or 20 other things, may produce a tumult, unforeseen, and therefore impossible to be prevented, in which such a carnage may ensue as to make a breach that can never afterwards be healed."

His own personal welfare was in jeopardy. "My situation here is thought by many to be a little hazardous," he said, "for that if by some accident the troops and people of N[ew] E[ngland] should come to blows I should probably be taken up, the ministerial people here affecting every where to represent me as the cause of all the misunderstanding." Friends advised his departure. But he would accept the risk, and stay till the outcome of the Continental Congress was known.

≈ In fact he stayed longer. There was nothing new in Franklin's lingering in London; he had been doing that for nearly two decades. But this time he really wanted to leave. He would have, but for an unusual chess match with an unexpected outcome.

In November 1774 Franklin heard from one of his fellows in the Royal Society that a certain distinguished lady, the sister of Lord Howe, had taken a fancy to the notion of playing chess with the famous Dr. Franklin. Though the good doctor was celebrated throughout Europe for his keen mind and quick imagination, she believed she could beat him. Would he accept the challenge?

Franklin replied that he was far out of practice, not having played the game regularly for many years. But in light of the honor the lady did him in issuing the challenge, he would accept.

Splendid, said the go-between. Dr. Franklin should call on the lady at earliest convenience. No further introduction was required.

Franklin made plans to visit Mrs. Howe (who had married a cousin, also named Howe, thus keeping the name in the family). But feeling rather awkward about presenting himself on her doorstep, he put off the match. Only after the mutual acquaintance reiterated the invitation and escorted Franklin to her door did the contest take place.

It proved a very agreeable affair. They played a few games; from modesty or otherwise, Franklin did not record who won. He enjoyed himself; she, herself. They arranged to meet again.

At the second session they played again, with as much pleasure as before. Then Mrs. Howe directed the conversation to a mathematical problem she had been considering. Franklin, impressed, pursued the matter.

The lady changed the subject once more. "What is to be done with this dispute between Britain and the colonies?" she asked (in Franklin's reconstruction of the conversation). "I hope we are not to have civil war. They should kiss and be friends." She said she had long believed the government ought to employ the distinguished doctor to settle the quarrel. "I am sure nobody could do it so well. Don't you think the thing is practicable?"

"Undoubtedly, madam," Franklin responded, "if the parties are disposed to reconciliation. For the two countries have really no clashing interest to differ about. It is rather a matter of punctilio, which two or three reasonable people might settle in half an hour. I thank you for the good opinion you are pleased to express of me; but the ministers will never think of employing me in that good work. They choose rather to abuse me."

Mrs. Howe agreed with this last comment. "They have behaved shamefully to you. And indeed some of them are now ashamed of it themselves."

At the time, Franklin considered these remarks simply accidental conversation and thought no more of it. On his next visit, however, the relationship acquired a new wrinkle. The day happened to be Christmas; Mrs. Howe happened to be joined by her brother, who was most interested in making Dr. Franklin's acquaintance. Lord Howe followed his sister in regretting the disgraceful treatment Franklin had suffered at the hands of the government. Yet in light of the alarming situation with regard to America, Howe hoped personal resentments might be put aside in the interest of attempting reconciliation.

Franklin responded that, whatever the injuries he personally had suffered, those done his country were so much greater as to put the other in shadow. "Besides," he said, "it is a fixed rule with me not to mix my private affairs with those of the public. I could join with my personal enemy in serving the public, or, when it was for its interest, with the public in serving that enemy." He would be happy to explore the prospect of reconciliation, but the prospect appeared quite slim. The government seemed as set as ever on the course that had led to all the troubles. Until that changed, there was little to discuss.

Franklin expected this to dampen his lordship's interest, but it did not. Howe hinted at discontent in the government; some of the ministers were in fact quite favorably disposed to any reasonable settlement that would allow saving the government's dignity. He requested Franklin to prepare a document delineating terms to which the colonies might be disposed to agree. He added that under other circumstances he would be delighted to call on the doctor at his home in Craven Street or to have the doctor come to his house, but such open meetings might inspire speculation, which could be only detrimental to discussion. They probably ought to continue to meet at Mrs. Howe's, where the chess matches could provide cover.

Agreeing, Franklin determined to test the waters of conciliation himself. Some months earlier he had spoken with Lord Chatham, who as William Pitt had been more responsible than any other man for creating the current empire. Not surprisingly, the earl was distressed to see his successors bent on frittering it away. The Continental Congress was about to meet; Chatham requested Franklin apprise him as soon as he learned what the Congress accomplished.

The news had arrived just before Franklin's surprise meeting with Lord Howe. The Americans were as steadfast and united as Franklin had hoped. The Congress condemned the Intolerable Acts and the assorted other encroachments by Parliament on the rights of Americans, reasserted the exclusive authority of the colonial legislatures to make laws for the colonies, and revived nonimportation. At the same time, however, the Congress reiterated American allegiance to the Crown.

Franklin took the news to Chatham the day after Christmas. "He received me with an affectionate kind of respect that from so great a man was extremely engaging. But the opinion he expressed of the Congress was still more so. They had acted, he said, with so much temper, moderation and wisdom that he thought it the most honourable assembly of statesmen since those of the ancient Greeks and Romans in the most virtuous times." Chatham inquired of Franklin whether the colonies would support the resolutions of the Congress. Franklin said they would—which answer increased the earl's respect for America even further. "He expressed a great regard and warm affection for that country, with hearty wishes for their prosperity; and that Government here might soon come to see its mistakes and rectify them."

Franklin could not help being encouraged. Chatham's opposition to government policies was no secret, but after a season of merely grumbling in his den, the old lion indicated he might roar once more. And so he did, after making a point of honoring Franklin by escorting him on his arm into the House of Lords. This created a stir, for none had known of the communications between the American and the earl. On that day Chatham moved that General Gage withdraw his troops from Boston as a gesture of goodwill and a first step toward reconciliation. "I was quite charmed with Lord Chatham's speech in support of his motion," Franklin recorded. "He impressed me with the highest idea of him as a great and most able statesman." Others joined Chatham, speaking ably on behalf of reason and moderation.

Unfortunately, however, the lords as a group were unreceptive. "All availed no more than the whistling of the winds," Franklin observed. The motion was defeated.

Yet Chatham did not give up, nor did Lord Howe. During January and February of 1775 Franklin met regularly with them, and with a number of other peers. He advised them in word and writing what America required to feel secure in its rights and how far America would defend those rights against continued usurpation. His interlocutors had somehow gained the impression he was in a position to bargain for the colonies, that if *he* could be persuaded to make a concession on this point or that, a deal might be struck. Howe in particular hinted that the Crown would be most grateful of any help Franklin could provide, and could be counted on to render material proof of its gratitude.

Diplomatically but firmly Franklin rejected the very idea. "My Lord," he said, "I shall deem it a great honour to be in any shape joined with your lordship in so good a work. But if you hope service from any influence I may be supposed to have, drop all thoughts of procuring me any previous favour from ministers. My accepting them would destroy the very influence you propose to make use of; they would be considered as so many bribes to betray the interest of my country."

Gradually Franklin realized that the men he was talking to, for all their distinction, lacked the power to pull the British government back from the brink. A telling moment occurred in a subsequent session of the House of Lords. Chatham, after extended discussion with Franklin—including one meeting at Franklin's Craven Street residence, which caught the eye of the neighbors and the attention of political London—presented a comprehensive plan for settling the troubles. Dartmouth, representing the government, treated the proposal courteously, saying it deserved serious consideration. Franklin, again in the gallery, described what happened next.

> Lord Sandwich arose, and in a petulant vehement speech opposed its being received at all, and gave his opinion that it ought to be immediately rejected with the contempt it deserved. That he could never believe it the production of any British peer. That it appeared to him rather the work of some American; and turning his face towards me, who was leaning on the bar, said he fancied he had in his eye the person who drew it up, one of the bitterest and most mischievous enemies this country had ever known.

Chatham came to Franklin's defense, and his own. He said he resented the insinuation that any bill he presented was another man's work, but if he were prime minister he would deem it no disgrace—indeed quite the opposite—to rely on one so distinguished in the eyes of all Europe as Dr. Franklin.

Chatham's motion failed miserably, even Dartmouth changing his initial neutrality to opposition. Franklin concluded that no hope remained. A final visit to the House of Lords sealed the verdict. Lord Camden, one of those with whom he had discussed a possible settlement, spoke favorably of the Americans. As with Chatham, he was hooted down. Franklin recorded:

> I was much disgusted from the ministerial side by many base reflections on American courage, religion, understanding, &c., in which we were treated with the utmost contempt, as the lowest of mankind, and almost of a different species from the English of Britain; but particularly the American honesty was abused by some of the Lords, who asserted that we were all knaves and wanted only by this dispute to avoid paying our debts; that if we had any sense of equity or justice we should offer payment of the tea &c.

Franklin by this time had already made plans to leave for America. As a parting gesture he gave vent to his anger in a memorial he drafted to

Dartmouth. Far from owing Britain anything for the tea, he declared, Massachusetts was owed by Britain for the damage incurred as a result of the British blockade. "I, the underwritten, do therefore, as their agent, in behalf of my Country and the said town of Boston, protest against the continuance of the said blockade. And I do hereby solemnly demand satisfaction for the accumulated injury done them beyond the value of the India Company's tea destroyed."

Aside from the fact that he had no instructions from Massachusetts to make this demand, Franklin realized on second thought that such a piece of impertinence might simply confirm the ministers in their collective misjudgment. He decided to consult his friend (and land-seeking ally) Thomas Walpole. "He looked at it and me several times alternately," Franklin recorded, "as if he apprehended me a little out of my senses." Franklin asked Walpole to take the letter to Lord Camden and see what *he* thought. Camden agreed that Franklin must not deliver it. Walpole returned to Franklin's lodgings to warn him in writing and in person that delivery would be interpreted as a "national affront" that might produce "dangerous consequences to your person." Franklin reluctantly acceded, and dropped the matter.

22

Rebel

1775–76

◦— When Franklin left London at the vernal equinox
of 1775 he believed he would never return. For most of
eighteen years London had been his home; he knew
London now better than he knew Philadelphia. But the
London he left by coach to catch the Pennsylvania packet at
Portsmouth was not the London he had known just a few
years earlier. Corruption had always troubled its politics, yet
corruption now overwhelmed all else. The placemen, the
toadies, the cynics had triumphed; honest seekers after the
welfare of the empire as a whole had no place. For eighteen
years he had resisted returning to America, for the last
eleven successfully; he resisted no more.

What he was returning to he could only guess. When he had left America in 1757 he was fifty-one, in the prime of his adult life. Now he was sixty-nine, an old man by anyone's reckoning. Few of his contemporaries survived; for a decade or more his associates had been primarily of a younger generation.

The latest, and most poignant, reminder of mortality was the death of Deborah. After her stroke six years earlier she had never been the same. He could read in her letters that she was slipping from this earthly sphere. If it pained him he did not say—neither in letters nor in comments recorded by friends. Nor did he mention feeling guilty at having essentially abandoned her in her old age. "Her death was no more than might reasonably be expected after the paralytic stroke she received some time ago, which greatly affected her memory and understanding," William wrote on Christmas Eve 1774, conveying the sad news. "She told me, when I took leave of her on my removal to Amboy [several months earlier] that she never expected to see you unless you returned this winter, for she was sure she should not live till next summer." When Franklin read this, did it hurt more to know that Debbie felt this way, or that she had not told him? "I heartily wish you had happened to have come over in the fall, as I think her disappointment in that respect preyed a good deal on her spirits," William concluded. Did Franklin need his son—who was not even *her* son—to tell him this?

If he felt any regrets about Deborah, he could comfort himself that she was now beyond whatever pain he might have caused her. William was another matter. The atrocious treatment Franklin received from the British government appeared not to have moved William at all. He had not protested; if anything, his relocation to Amboy, against his father's advice, indicated a decision to make his future with Britain, whatever happened. The governor appeared a more dutiful servant to his king than son to his father. Did Franklin feel betrayed? Again, he did not say. But he had to sense that he and William were near a parting of the ways. Having just lost his wife, he was about to lose his son. Perhaps at this time, certainly at others, he must have reflected that however competent he might be at other aspects of human life, he fell short when it came to family.

Yet all was not lost in this regard. If he started to feel regretful during his westerly voyage that spring, he had only to look across the deck to where young Temple was conversing with the sailors or throwing a line over the side, for his spirits to revive. The lad was fifteen—bright, capable, curious. Franklin could not help seeing himself in the boy, or seeing William as he had been at that age, or seeing what Franky might have been. Then he would sigh, but the sigh would include a breath of hope.

~ The line Temple was tossing over the side had one of his grandfather's instruments attached to the end. Franklin spent much of the voyage recording the final failure of his efforts at imperial reconciliation, but between pages he made what he described to Joseph Priestley as "a valuable philosophical discovery" regarding the Gulf Stream, which remained almost as mysterious as on his first Atlantic crossing in 1724. He and Temple took regular measurements of the water through which their ship was sailing. The changes were striking as they entered the stream; the water was as much as nineteen Fahrenheit degrees warmer than water to the side. It also had a different color, Franklin thought, and did not sparkle at night the way water outside the stream did. And it carried what the sailors called "gulf weed."

Though he learned much about the Gulf Stream, he did not yet understand its mechanism nor its actual consequences. The question that prompted his investigations in the first place was the venerable one of why ships sailing from America to England made better time than ships sailing the reverse route. At this point he speculated that it had to do with the excess angular momentum of bodies (including ships) farther from the earth's axis of rotation. Simple geometry revealed that a ship at latitude 40 degrees traveled 120 miles per hour faster about the earth's axis than a ship at 50 degrees. "This motion in a ship and cargo is of great force; and if she could be lifted up suddenly from the harbour in which she lay quiet, and set down instantly in the latitude of the port she was bound to, though in a calm, that force contained in her would make her run a great way at a prodigious rate. This force must be lost gradually in her voyage, by gradual impulse against the water, and probably thence shorten the voyage."

This explanation was inadequate, as Franklin himself subsequently recognized. But it was no less ingenious for its inadequacy, and it demonstrated that whatever else his disillusionment with imperial politics accomplished, it did not dampen his interest in the world around him.

~ Franklin's arrival in America in early May was treated throughout the colonies as an event of great moment. A broadside posted on the streets of New York relayed a letter from Philadelphia:

Yesterday evening Dr. Franklin arrived here from London in six weeks, which he left the 20th of March, which has given great joy to this town. He says we have no favours to expect from the Ministry; nothing but submission will satisfy them. They expect little or no opposition will be made to their troops. . . . Dr. Franklin is highly pleased to find us arming and preparing for the worst events. He thinks nothing else can save us from the most abject slavery and destruction; at the same time encourages us to believe a spirited opposition will be the means of our salvation.

This was a fair summary of Franklin's feeling, although it presupposed some critical knowledge Franklin did not possess until reaching American waters. On April 19 the war he had feared for many months began in earnest.

It did so for the reasons that were fully apparent in Franklin's final weeks in England. The British government was determined to have matters out with the Americans. "The die is now cast," George III declared. "The colonies must either submit or triumph." Shortly thereafter the monarch made his point more forcefully: "The New England governments are in a state of rebellion. Blows must decide whether they are to be subject to this country or independent."

On April 14 Governor Gage in Boston received orders from London to preempt the increasing strength of the Massachusetts militia. These "minutemen" and their slower comrades were training regularly, caching arms and ammunition, and growing more dangerous by the day. Though Dartmouth, the author of Gage's latest instructions, was not advocating war per se, he was entirely prepared for it—and preferred that it come on the government's terms and timing rather than those of the rebels. "It will surely be better that the conflict should be brought on, upon such ground, than in a riper state of rebellion."

During the next four days Gage prepared a preemptive strike. Informers indicated that the militia had stockpiled weapons at Concord, twenty miles from Boston. Gathering his grenadiers and light infantrymen, he devised a plan for an operation to be launched in the dead of night with strictest secrecy. The strike force would embark by boat for Cambridge, whence they would march overland to Concord.

But the rebels had spies too. Paul Revere arranged a simple signal scheme: one lantern in the steeple of the North Church meant a march by land, over the neck of the peninsula and around Back Bay; two lanterns meant a shortcut across the water. Almost before the British troops mustered on the Common for their rowboat ride to Cambridge, Revere had two lanterns hung in the church tower and splashed off in a boat of his own to Charlestown, where he mounted and tore away toward Concord. He dodged a British patrol that had orders to intercept messengers—especially any riding breathlessly through the night. At Lexington he roused Sam Adams and John Hancock, who expected to be arrested whenever Gage's soldiers could catch them. With other riders he resumed his journey to Concord. But he never reached that destination. Stopped by another British patrol, he was dehorsed and detained. (Later he was released to walk home.)

The alarm was abroad, however, and the minutemen mobilized. When the British reached Lexington at sunup, some seventy soldiers had arrayed themselves on the green at the side of the Concord road. The commander of the British force ordered the Americans to disarm and disperse. Counting red coats and concluding that in a skirmish they would be beaten, the Americans began to walk away—taking their guns with them. The British commander repeated his order for them to drop weapons; this time his tone was more insulting. Someone fired—an American, according to the British; a Briton, by the Americans. The shot triggered a volley by the British, then another, then a charge with bayonets. In five minutes the British had routed the Americans, who lost eight dead and ten wounded. One British soldier was nicked in the leg.

In high spirits the soldiers in the scarlet coats and the white breeches set off for Concord. By now all chance of surprise had evaporated; the drums beat the British march and the fifes pierced in the morning air. At Concord they encountered a larger group of militia—the Concord company plus several from the surrounding villages. For a few hours the two sides postured, marching and countermarching, not knowing whether this was war, peace, or something in between. The British began searching houses for guns, balls, and powder, finding little but provoking little resistance. Only when the courthouse and a smithy caught fire did the militiamen react strongly. "Will you let them burn the town?" demanded one of the American officers. To prevent it a group of the Americans began shooting at the British.

The British troops had no more experience than the Americans—the last war having ended a dozen years earlier, and these being young men. As it became clear the Americans were serious about resisting, the British fell back. They retreated down the road to Concord, with the Americans close behind. The rest of the day was a nightmare for the British; all the way to Boston they encountered snipers hiding behind the trees and rock walls at the side of the road, and were harassed at their rear by the advancing militiamen. Only after sunset did they reach the safety of the city. A tally of the losses showed some 270 killed or wounded. The American losses were a little over a third as many.

By the measure of men lost and mission unaccomplished, the British foray was a disaster. The Americans had reason to feel proud, and many did. But at the same time the reality of war was sobering. Jane Mecom wrote her brother with a personal account. In his last letter Franklin had told her to keep up her courage, as the current stormy weather could not last forever; she now replied:

> I believe you did not then imagine the storm would have arisen so high as for the General [Gage] to have sent out a party to creep out in the night and slaughter our dear brethren for endeavouring to defend our own property. But God appeared for us and drove them back with much greater loss than they are willing to own. Their countenances as well as the confession of many of them shew they were much mistaken in the people they had to deal with, but the distress it has occasioned is past my description. The horror the town was in when the battle approached within hearing, expecting they would proceed quite in to town, the commotion the town was in after the battle ceased by the parties coming in, bringing in their wounded men, caused such an agitation of mind I believe none had much sleep. Since which we could have no quiet, as we understood our brethren without were determined to dispossess the town of the [British] regulars; and the General shutting up the town, not letting any pass out, but threw such great difficulties as were almost insupportable.

In other words, it was war, with all the terrors, trials, and uncertainties war entailed. For her part, Jane Mecom fled the city; she informed her brother she was taking refuge with his old friend Catherine Ray Greene and her husband, William, in Warwick, Rhode Island.

Even as it drove Jane Mecom from her home, the fighting at Boston drew members of the Continental Congress back to Philadelphia. When last they met, the danger had been prospective; now it was actual. Then they had protested and petitioned; now they had to prosecute a war.

For this reason the man awaited most expectantly was not Franklin—whose appearance, in any event, took nearly all the delegates by surprise—but George Washington. The veteran soldier had attended the first Congress the previous year but been overshadowed by his Virginia colleagues Peyton Randolph, who was elected president, and Patrick Henry and Richard Henry Lee, who stirred the delegates with their speeches. Washington seemed no more than "a tolerable speaker" to Silas Deane of Connecticut. He himself accounted his role in the Congress as that of "attentive observer and witness."

The outbreak of fighting changed everything. Of speakers the new Congress had many; of military leaders it had but one. He packed his uniform when he left Mount Vernon for Philadelphia on May 4. Riding in his own chariot, he drew the cheers of Virginians and then Marylanders as he made his way north; six miles outside Philadelphia he was met by a boisterous brigade of five hundred horsemen. At the edge of the city several hundred more militia—mounted and foot—joined the cavalcade; a military band fell in step and played martial airs the rest of the way to the State House.

"We have a very full Congress," Washington reported home, "and I flatter myself that great unanimity will prevail." It did on one subject: the selection of a commanding general. "Colonel Washington appears at Congress in uniform," John Adams wrote his wife Abigail, "and by his great experience and abilities in military matters is of much service to us." (Adams added, with the envy and ambition that characterized his whole career, "Oh, that I were a soldier. I will be! I am reading military books.") Briefly the delegates considered other individuals for the command. But Artemas Ward of Massachusetts, the most likely alternate, lacked Washington's moral and military stature; Charles Lee (a professional soldier and resident Virginian who himself might have been a candidate but for his English birth) dismissed Ward as "a fat old gentleman who had been a popular churchwarden." Consequently in mid-June the Congress voted without dissent to confer the command upon Washington. He becomingly professed himself unequal to the task. "However," he continued, "as the Congress desire it, I will enter upon the momentous duty, exert every power I possess in their service, and for support of the glorious cause."

⌒ Franklin was one of those voting for Washington. Under other circumstances his fellow Pennsylvanians might have allowed him a well-deserved retirement upon his return. Franklin himself was looking forward to such when he left London. But the onset of war altered this as so much else. When the *Pennsylvania Packet* landed at the foot of Market Street on May 5, the delegates to the Continental Congress were already converging on Philadelphia. The Pennsylvania Assembly did not grant Franklin even twenty-four hours before electing him a delegate to the Congress. Who knew better than Franklin the mind of the ministry in London? Who better to advise the Congress on what to expect from Parliament?

Matters did not work out quite as expected. Franklin was weary from the voyage and needed time to readjust to a city he hardly knew. America had grown as rapidly as he had predicted it would; Philadelphia led the growth. The city was filled with new buildings and new faces. As he rode from the river the two blocks up Market Street—to the house Debbie had lived in these last ten years but that was new to him—he must have marveled at what a different place it was from the city that had first greeted him half a century before. At times he had felt old in London; here in Philadelphia he felt absolutely ancient.

And all the more ancient when the Congress convened at the State House. The building was the same one where he had so often sat while in the Assembly, but the generation of men filling the chairs was decidedly different. Franklin was easily the oldest man present, a full twenty or thirty years older than the moving spirits of the body. George Washington was forty-three; his fellow Virginians Patrick Henry and Thomas Jefferson were thirty-eight and thirty-two respectively. John Adams was thirty-nine; John Hancock, also of Massachusetts, thirty-eight.

The young men of the Congress exhibited the impatience of youth. "A frenzy of revenge seems to have seized all ranks of people," Jefferson observed as the delegates gathered in Philadelphia; and if the frenzy diminished slightly as the magnitude of the task before the Congress became apparent, audacity remained the predominant attitude.

Franklin disappointed some of those who knew him only by reputation—a group that encompassed nearly the entire membership. He struck no lightning bolts of rhetoric, preferring to sit silent while others orated. Washington cut a far more impressive figure in his soldier's uniform than Franklin in his philosopher's coat. The visitors from out of town—again, nearly the entire body—took dinner together in taverns and spent nights about town; Franklin retired to his own house when the Congress recessed, passing evenings with Sally and Richard Bache and his grandchildren. ("The youngest boy is the strongest and stoutest child of his age that I have ever seen," he boasted to Jane Mecom, regarding two-year-old William Bache. "He seems an infant Hercules.")

Franklin's diffidence struck some as suspicious. William Bradford, the son of Franklin's old printing rival, currently publisher of the *Pennsylvania Journal*, and like many another journalist an avid consumer of gossip, complained to James Madison (not a delegate to the Congress but at twenty-four already active in Virginia politics), "I have but little to tell you of the Congress; they keep their proceedings so secret that scarce any thing transpires but what they think proper to publish in the papers." Yet all was not lost to one who kept his ear to the keyhole. "I can however (inter nos) inform you that they begin to entertain a great suspicion that Dr. Franklin came rather as a spy than as a friend, & that he means to discover our weak side and make his peace with the minister by discovering it to him." Bradford could not vouch for the veracity of the report, which might sound implausible on its face. "But the times are so remarkable for strange events," he reasoned, "that improbability is almost become an argument for their truth."

The source of the rumors was Richard Henry Lee, the Virginia delegate who was also the elder brother of Arthur Lee. Obviously Arthur had been sharing his own suspicions (and jealousies) of Franklin; probably he had told Richard Henry to keep watch on the crafty old man. Perhaps the elder Lee had been poisoning other Virginia minds against Franklin; James Madison for one was entirely willing to credit Bradford's gossip. "If he were the man he formerly was, and has even of late pretended to be," Madison said of Franklin, "his conduct in Philadelphia on this critical occasion could have left no room for surmise or distrust. He certainly would have been both a faithful informer and an active member of the Congress. His behaviour would have been explicit and his zeal warm and conspicuous." (Madison possessed a brilliant legal mind but also a penchant for assuming the worst of others. Before maligning Franklin he had castigated Washington as one of a class of tidewater gentry that demonstrated "a pusillanimity little comporting with their professions or the name of Virginian.")

Franklin doubtless heard the rumors. As on other occasions he let silence supply his answer, and as on most other occasions it sufficed. "Hath any thing further been whispered relative to the conduct of Dr. Franklin?" queried the conspiratorially minded Madison after a dearth of additional dirt. Bradford could only disappoint. "The suspicions against

Dr. Franklin have died away," Bradford reported. "Whatever was his design at coming over here, I believe he has now chosen his side, and favours our cause."

John Adams put the matter more positively. Franklin's initial diffidence had reflected respect for the Congress and a desire to avoid claiming special wisdom for himself, Adams said. Of late Franklin had displayed "a disposition entirely American." Indeed, far from favoring Britain, he was Britain's bitterest foe. "He does not hesitate at our boldest measures, but rather seems to think us too irresolute and backward."

◇— What silenced the skeptics was their gradual realization that on the subject of resistance to British tyranny, none was more determined than Franklin. He took no pleasure in the present war—"which the youngest of us may not see the end of," he said. "But, as Britain has begun to use force, it seems absolutely necessary that we should be prepared to repel force by force, which I think, united, we are well able to do."

Franklin was still angry over his own and America's treatment by the British government, and his anger grew with accumulating evidence of British perfidy. Late June brought news of the Battle of Bunker Hill, in which British troops torched parts of Charlestown, outside of Boston. "She has begun to burn our seaport towns," he wrote Joseph Priestley, "secure, I suppose, that we shall never be able to return the outrage in kind." To Jonathan Shipley he complained of London's diplomacy. "All Europe is conjured not to sell us arms or ammunition, that we may be found defenceless, and more easily murdered." Eminent British figures, Franklin said, were advocating attempts "to excite the domestic slaves you have sold us to cut their masters' throats." Others urged "hiring the Indian savages to assassinate our planters in the back-settlements." "This is making war like nations who never had been friends, and never wish to be such while the world stands."

No one in Britain was closer to Franklin than Bishop Shipley; it pained Franklin to write as he did, but he felt he had reason—reason shared by his countrymen. "You see I am warm; and if a temper naturally cool and phlegmatic can, in old age, which often cools the warmest, be thus heated, you will judge by that of the general temper here, which is now little short of madness."

The clearest evidence of Franklin's anger—rage is hardly too strong a word—was a letter he wrote to William Strahan. The letter, to Franklin's oldest friend in England, was jarringly direct.

> Mr. Strahan,
>
> You are a member of Parliament, and one of that majority which has doomed my country to destruction. You have begun to burn our towns, and murder our people. Look upon your hands! They are stained with the blood of your relations! You and I were long friends; you are now my enemy, and I am yours.

Franklin never sent this letter; his anger, though powerful, did not carry him away. Yet the fact of its writing indicated the emotional separation he felt from England—and it suggested, with everything else, that political separation could not be far behind. "Words and arguments are now of no use," he said in a letter he did send to Strahan. "All tends to a separation." To Joseph Priestley he explained the circumstances surrounding what came to be called the "Olive Branch petition." "It has been with difficulty that we have carried another humble petition to the Crown, to give Britain one more chance, one opportunity more of recovering the friendship of the colonies, which however I think she has not sense enough to embrace." Anticipating the rejection that indeed occurred, he closed, "And so I conclude she has lost them forever."

A full year before the Congress declared officially in favor of independence, Franklin had come to believe that independence was inevitable. Now he began working to make it a reality. None but the most obtuse could conceive American independence absent some form of intercolonial union; in July 1775 Franklin proposed a plan for just such a union. In spirit these "Articles of Confederation" drew on the plan of union he had presented at Albany in 1754, but what then would have been a federation within the British empire now foreshadowed an independent state. The purpose of the confederation was the colonies' "common defence against their enemies" and "the security of their liberties and properties, the safety of their persons and families, and their mutual and general welfare." The congress of the confederation would be empowered to declare war and negotiate peace, enter into alliances, settle disputes among the separate colonies, create new colonies, arrange treaties with the Indian tribes, establish a post office, and administer or otherwise regulate a general currency. Representation in the congress would be proportional to population; executive power would be vested in an "executive council" whose members would serve staggered three-year terms. The congress would have the power to propose amendments to the articles of confederation; these would take effect on adoption by a majority of the colonies.

Franklin appreciated that all this was considerably more than many of the delegates to the Continental Congress were willing to accept. To allay their fears he appended a clause contemplating the dissolution of the confederation upon Britain's restoration of the rights and privileges of the American colonies, the withdrawal of all British troops from America, and the receipt of compensation for damages to Boston's commerce and Charlestown's structures and for the expense to the colonies of "this unjust war." How much this actually allayed the fears of the timid must be doubted; by all proclamation and policy Britain evinced that it would never accept such conditions. Failing acceptance, "this Confederation is to be perpetual."

Even with the escape clause Franklin's confederation was too forward, as he certainly realized. He contented himself with reading his articles to a committee of the whole Congress. He made no motion that required a vote or even a formal record of his proposal; his purpose was to set the delegates thinking about the kind of union that would be necessary to fight and win a war and to carry America into the peace beyond. In this he certainly succeeded, and when the time proved riper, his proposal became the starting point for the Articles of Confederation the Congress and the states finally adopted.

Other actions by Franklin bore fruit immediately. It was lost on none of the delegates, on none of the committees of correspondence of the several colonies, or for that matter on the British government, that the resistance to British usurpation could not have congealed as it had without an efficient postal service. Needless to say, British postal officials would be loath to deliver letters for practicing rebels; already the mails were being regularly opened. And already the colonial governments were making separate provisions for delivery. As one, the delegates to the Congress concluded that the obvious person to organize this alternative service was the man who had made the system run so well under the British. On July 26 the Congress unanimously elected Franklin postmaster general for the American colonies.

Even as he engaged the subordinates necessary to make the American post office a reality (true to nepotic form, he appointed Richard Bache his secretary and comptroller), Franklin received another appointment freighted with no less importance, albeit considerably less publicity. In September he was named to the "secret committee" of the Congress; this group bore primary responsibility for obtaining the weapons necessary to wage the war. Franklin's experience provisioning General Braddock's army at the outset of the French and Indian War stood him well in this endeavor, as did his repeated raising of militia to defend Philadelphia, and his construction of forts on the Pennsylvania frontier. But the job was immense, being hardly less than creating an army from scratch—or, what was worse, from a motley collection of militias jealous of their rights and confirmed in their ignorance.

∼ Franklin felt the immensity of the task on a visit to General Washington's headquarters. Following his appointment to the command of what was optimistically styled the "Continental Army," Washington traveled to Boston to take charge of the mostly Massachusetts force besieging the British there. He required a few weeks to assess his soldiers and reconnoiter the position; molding the militia into a real army took considerably longer. This necessitated the creation of an officer corps that knew its business and could teach the troops. But the troops did not want to learn, considering themselves above discipline and, in many cases, intending to leave the ranks when their brief terms of enlistment expired. To make bad worse, winter was fast descending on an army ill equipped even for a New England autumn. Washington appealed to the Congress for help; without it, he warned, the army would disintegrate.

The Congress did what congresses do: it appointed a committee to investigate. Franklin headed the committee; joining him were Thomas Lynch of South Carolina and Benjamin Harrison of Virginia. In October the three traveled to Washington's headquarters at Cambridge. For seven days they met with Washington and his staff in an effort to forge a policy that would meet the needs of the military moment without abridging the political liberties for which the war was being fought. Discipline was a central issue. The group authorized the death penalty for mutiny and incitement thereto. Drunken officers should be drummed out of the army with infamy. Sentries caught asleep should receive not less than twenty lashes nor more than thirty-nine. An officer absent without leave should be fined one month's pay for the first offense and cashiered for the second; an enlisted man should be confined and placed on bread and water for seven days for the first such offense and suffer similar confinement, with loss of a week's pay, for the second.

The group considered rations—to wit, what the Congress could afford and the men tolerate. They decided on a pound of beef or salt fish or three-quarters of a pound of pork per man per day; a pound of bread or flour; a pint of milk; a quart of spruce beer or cider (or 9 gallons of molasses per company—of somewhat fewer than a hundred men—per week, for making rum); a half-pint of rice or one pint of cornmeal per man per week; 24 pounds of soft soap or 8 pounds of hard soap per company per week; and 3 pounds of candles per company per week. Additional provisions—vegetables, beans and peas, extra milk—might be purchased by the troops at regulated prices.

Standards were established for the men's arms. The several colonies should set their gunsmiths to work fabricating firelocks with barrels three-quarters of an inch in bore and 44 inches in length, with bayonets 18 inches in the blade. For additional arms the colonies should "import all that can be procured."

The size of the army should be increased to 20,000 (the overly precise figure was 20,372). It should consist of regiments of 728 men (including officers), with each regiment divided into eight companies consisting of one captain, two lieutenants, one ensign, four sergeants, four corporals, two drums or fifes, and 76 privates. Some in the Congress, complaining of cost, advocated reducing the pay of the troops. Washington and his staff, and Franklin and his committee, agreed unanimously that lowering pay "would be attended with dangerous consequences." It should remain at 40 shillings per month.

Provisions for privateers were made, along with procedures for disposing of their prizes. General Washington should arrange for the sale of vessels and cargoes captured by warships outfitted at the expense of the Congress; the proceeds would support the war effort.

Many other matters were decided, but on a critical question of strategy the soldiers and civilians agreed to consult the Congress. Washington and his war council had determined that a frontal attack on the British forces in Boston was impractical before winter; he now requested guidance as to whether an artillery bombardment of British positions and troops in the city was appropriate. He could probably compel a withdrawal, but not without destroying the town. What should he do?

Franklin and the other committee members agreed, as they stated in their report, that this was "a matter of too much consequence to be determined by them"; therefore they referred it back to the Congress. In sending them off, Washington made another appeal for money: "The General then requested that the Committee would represent to the Congress the necessity of having money constantly and regularly sent."

Franklin had heard the dire reports from Washington and others of the army's troubles; having seen the soldiers and spoken to the officers, he thought the reports overblown. "Here is a fine healthy army," he wrote Richard Bache, "wanting nothing but some improvement in its officers, which is daily making."

As for the expense of the war, he was similarly optimistic. What was necessary could well be borne.

> Though I am for the most prudent parsimony of the public treasury, I am not terrified by the expence of this war, should it continue ever so long. A little more frugality, or a little more industry in individuals will with ease defray it. Suppose it [costs] £100,000 a month, or £1,200,000 a year. If 500,000 families will each spend a shilling a week less, or earn a shilling a week more; or if they will spend 6 pence a week less and earn 6 pence a week more, they may pay the whole sum without otherwise feeling it. Forbearing to drink tea saves three fourths of the money; and 500,000 women doing each threepence worth of spinning or knitting in a week will pay the rest. (How much more then may be done by the superior frugality and industry of the men?)
>
> I wish nevertheless most earnestly for peace, this war being a truly unnatural and mischievous one; but we have nothing to expect from submission but slavery and contempt.

In another letter Franklin examined the cost question from the British side and came to the same conclusion. He and Joseph Priestley had a mutual friend, Richard Price, a man of mathematical (among other) interests; Franklin sent Priestley a message to forward. "Tell our good friend Dr. Price, who sometimes has doubts and despondencies about our firmness, that America is determined and unanimous, a very few tories and placemen excepted, who will probably soon export themselves." Franklin then suggested a simple calculation. "Britain, at the expence of three millions, has killed 150 Yankees this campaign, which is £20,000 a head; and at Bunker's Hill she gained a mile of ground, half of which she lost again by our taking post on Ploughed Hill. During the same time 60,000 children have been born in America. From these data his mathematical head will easily calculate the time and expence necessary to kill us all, and conquer our whole territory."

~ While Washington maintained the siege of Boston (permission to bombard the city was withheld), another American force drove north to Canada. As it had for the French before them, Canada currently enabled the British to conceive a strike at the American interior, raising the possibility that New England might be cut off, via New York and the Hudson River, from the lower colonies. The American invasion of Canada was designed to deny that province to the British; if the Canadians could be persuaded to join the other colonies in opposition to Britain, all the better.

The invasion was a two-pronged affair. Philip Schuyler pushed up from Fort Ticonderoga along Lake Champlain to Fort St. John; after sickness disabled him he turned the command over to Richard Montgomery, who captured Montreal before driving down the St. Lawrence toward Quebec. Meanwhile Benedict Arnold led an appallingly arduous march across Maine, losing nearly half his men to cold, hunger, sickness, exhaustion, and discouragement before meeting up with Montgomery below the walls of Quebec. At dawn on the last day of 1775 the combined American force attempted to repeat Wolfe's feat of seizing the fortress. The assault was a fiasco, with Montgomery (like Wolfe in this respect at least) dying in the battle. A seriously wounded Arnold watched the American force break itself on the British defenses; in a howling blizzard the Americans—those who avoided death or capture—had all they could do to retreat beyond range of the defenders' guns. Snug behind their walls, the British let them freeze while both sides awaited the spring thaw, which would certainly bring British reinforcements up the river, and possibly American reinforcements overland.

Naturally the Continental Congress desired to know whether to send such reinforcements, especially in light of the other demands on American resources. In March 1776 the Congress appointed a commission to travel to Canada to investigate. The commissioners were Franklin, Samuel Chase of Maryland, and Charles Carroll, another Marylander, who was not a delegate to the Congress but who had been educated in France and was a prominent Catholic. Carroll was also the cousin of John Carroll, an even more prominent Catholic and a priest, who was persuaded to accompany the commission; the two Carrolls, the Congress thought, might have some influence with the largely Catholic, formerly French, Canadians.

The British government learned of the mission almost as soon as it began. None other than William Franklin informed Lord Germain, the new secretary for America and the man overseeing the American war, of his father's movements, company, and purpose. "I have just heard," the governor wrote on March 28, "that two of the delegates (Dr. Franklin and Mr. Chase) have passed through Woodbridge this morning in their way to Canada, accompanied by a Mr. Carroll, a Roman Catholic gentleman of great estate in Maryland, and a Romish priest or two. It is suggested that their principal business is to prevail on the Canadians to enter into the confederacy with the other colonies and to send delegates to the Continental Congress." William added a pleasant note: "It is likewise reported that a great number of the continental troops have returned to Albany, not being able to cross the lakes, several soldiers, carriages, etc. having fallen in and some lives lost by the breaking of the ice."

Franklin encountered the problems of the ice, as well as others felt acutely by a man of seventy. His trip up the Hudson–Lake George–Lake Champlain corridor was all he could manage. "I begin to apprehend that I have undertaken a fatigue that at my time of life may prove too much for me," he wrote Josiah Quincy while waiting at Saratoga for the ice to clear. "So I sit down to write to a few friends by way of farewell."

Yet Franklin's time had not come, and in fact he held up better in certain instances than his traveling companions. At St. Johns they spent two nights sleeping on the floor of a house that had been wrecked by fighting; while Charles Carroll complained of his aching back, Franklin amused the party with stories from his long personal history.

At Montreal they met with General Arnold, still hobbling and now directing the siege of Quebec from a distance. Arnold's was a personality that blew hot and cold; after a long winter the cold won out regarding Canada. From Arnold and others the commission learned of the discouraging prospects for American forces along the St. Lawrence. Part of the problem was military, reflecting the difficulties of supporting an invasion so far from home. But the larger part was political. American forces were living off the land—which was to say off the labor of the locals. Sometimes the American officers simply took what they needed; sometimes they promised to pay. The latter instances blurred into the former when the officers, lacking money from the south, failed to fulfill their promises. On May 1 Franklin and the others urged the Congress to apply the "utmost dispatch" in supplying Arnold with money—£20,000 would make a fair start. "Otherwise it will be impossible to continue the war in this country, or to expect the continuance of our interest with the people here, who begin to consider the Congress as bankrupt and their cause as desperate." In its charge to the commission the Congress had instructed the commissioners to propose a union of Canada with the other colonies; Franklin thought such an offer unwise under present circumstances. "Till the arrival of money, it seems improper to propose the federal union of this province with the others, as the few friends we have here will scarce venture to exert themselves in promoting it till they see our credit recovered and a sufficient army arrived to secure the possession of the country."

A week of additional discussions underscored this argument. Apparently the creditors of the American forces had been led to believe that the commissioners were bringing money; they were sorely disappointed to learn otherwise. The American Congress had become contemptible in Canadian eyes; with British ships even now on the way to lift the siege of Quebec, attachment to the Americans would have been nothing less than folly. "We have daily intimations of plots hatching and insurrections intended for expelling us on the first news of the arrival of a British army," Franklin wrote for himself and the others. "Your commissioners themselves are in a critical and most irksome situation, pestered hourly with demands great and small that they cannot answer, in a place where our cause has a majority of enemies, the garrison weak, and a greater would, without money, increase our difficulties." A single conclusion was possible: "If money cannot be had to support your army here with honour, so as to be respected instead of hated by the people, we repeat it as our firm and unanimous opinion that it is better immediately to withdraw it."

Unbeknownst to Franklin, American forces were already putting his advice into effect. At the beginning of May the freshly arrived American commander at Quebec, John Thomas, decided to drop the ragged siege there. Slowness in carrying out the decision, however, enabled the long-awaited British reinforcements to turn an orderly retreat into an ignominious rout. Thomas succumbed to smallpox, his successor mounted an unsuccessful counterattack, and by mid-July the Americans had been driven all the way back to Ticonderoga.

     Amid the bad news from the north came good news—or at least big news—from Philadelphia. For some months opinion in the colonies, and in the Congress, had been inching toward the conclusion Franklin had reached the previous summer: that independence was inevitable. To some extent this reasoning reflected the iron logic of battle; the longer Americans fought against the British, the less likely they were to desire reconciliation with the British. But even the inevitable requires explanation, often justification, of which none was more compelling than that provided by Thomas Paine.

Franklin knew Paine. Indeed Franklin was largely responsible for Paine's presence in Philadelphia. One of Franklin's fellows in the Royal Society had introduced young Paine to Franklin in London, and although Paine's career to date consisted chiefly of failure—at corsetmaking, schoolteaching, shopkeeping, tax-collecting—he was a self-taught seeker of practical knowledge in a variety of fields, with an obvious irreverence toward British authority. In other words, he was a young man of the sort Franklin might wish to encourage. This Franklin did. When Paine in 1774 indicated a desire to emigrate to America, Franklin supplied a letter of introduction to Richard Bache. Franklin described Paine to his son-in-law as "an ingenious, worthy young man," and requested a favor: "If you can put him in a way of obtaining employment as a clerk, or assistant tutor in a school, or assistant surveyor (all of which I think him very capable), so that he may procure a subsistence at least, till he can make acquaintance and obtain a knowledge of the country, you will do well and much oblige your affectionate father."

Franklin's letter was almost literally a lifesaver. On the voyage over, Paine took fearfully sick; he remained at death's portal when the ship docked in Philadelphia. "Dr. Kearsley of this place attended the ship upon her arrival," Paine wrote Franklin from America, "and when he understood that I was on your recommendation he provided a lodging for me and sent two of his men with a chaise to bring me on shore, for I could not at that time turn in my bed without help." Slowly Paine recovered, and as he did so he benefited still more from Franklin's good offices. "Your countenancing me has obtained me many friends and much reputation." Several gentlemen requested that he tutor their sons; a printer, Robert Aitken, enlisted his help producing a new magazine.

This latter connection had momentous implications for Paine and for America. Aitken's journal afforded the budding journalist scope to sharpen his now-discovered gift for political argumentation; in the course of the next year the *Pennsylvania Magazine* ran articles by Paine against slavery and in favor of various vital causes.

None was so vital as that of American independence, which in late

1775 inspired Paine to write perhaps the most inspired political pamphlet in American history. *Common Sense* appeared in January 1776; at two shillings for forty-seven pages it soon sold more than a hundred thousand copies. "I offer nothing more than simple facts, plain arguments, and common sense," Paine declared in asserting that continued connection with Britain made no more sense than perpetual childhood for a grown adult, that no continent should be forever governed by an island, that attachment to Britain would inevitably draw America into Europe's wars, and, finally, that "a government of our own is our natural right."

Common Sense produced a "great impression" among the delegates to the Continental Congress, Franklin said. In doing so it tilted the field of debate decidedly toward independence. One by one those advocating additional efforts toward reconciliation changed their minds; one by one the provincial assemblies instructed their delegates to consider formal separation. On June 7 Richard Henry Lee offered a motion declaring "that these United Colonies are, and of right ought to be, free and independent states, that they are absolved from all allegiance to the British Crown, and that all political connection between them and the State of Great Britain is, and ought to be, totally dissolved." The motion encountered some residual resistance, which prompted a decision to delay a final vote until the first of July. Meanwhile the Congress created a committee to draft a declaration justifying the decision for independence, should the Congress so decide. Appointed to the committee were John Adams, Thomas Jefferson, Roger Sherman of Connecticut, Robert Livingston of New York, and Franklin.

Franklin had little to do with the first drafting of the document, which the committee left to Jefferson, partly because of his known felicity of phrasing ("You can write ten times better than I," John Adams recalled telling Jefferson), partly because Jefferson was a Virginian (and hence would add geographic balance to a conflict provoked by New England), partly because none on the committee appreciated what a momentous document this would be, and partly because Franklin was happy to leave the task to another. He would explain this last point to Jefferson presently; for now his physical condition afforded sufficient excuse. "I am just recovering from a severe fit of the gout, which has kept me from Congress and company almost ever since you left us," Franklin wrote on June 21 to Washington, who had departed Philadelphia on June 4 after a series of meetings with delegates. Besides gout and fatigue, Franklin suffered from an assortment of rashes, boils, and related lesions that reflected both the strain of the Canada trip and the inability of travelers to keep as clean as at home. Franklin had tried to avoid two other chronic problems of travelers—bedbugs and lice—by carrying his own bedding; whether he succeeded is unclear. But June was, altogether, a miserable month for him.

So Jefferson retired to the second-story parlor of the house of a young German mason named Graff, and on his lap-desk drafted the declaration. When he had something he liked he sent it the short distance to Franklin's house. "Will Doctor Franklin be so good as to peruse it and suggest such alterations as his more enlarged view of the subject will dictate?" he requested in a covering note.

After decades as a writer and editor, Franklin knew good prose when he read it. He treated Jefferson's draft gently. Jefferson's phrase "reduce them to arbitrary power," referring to what the British were trying to do to the Americans, was strengthened to "reduce them under absolute despotism." "Amount of their salaries"—referring to what King George was trying to seize as a lever against colonial judges—was made more specific: "the amount and payment of their salaries." "Taking away our charters, and altering fundamentally the forms of our governments" was elaborated: "taking away our charters, abolishing our most valuable laws, and altering fundamentally the forms of our governments." "Answered by repeated injury" was sharpened: "answered only by repeated injury." "To invade and deluge us in blood" was toned down: "to invade and destroy us."

The Congress handled Jefferson's draft more harshly. Clause after sentence was struck, leaving Jefferson aghast. Franklin consoled him with what became one of his most famous stories. "I was sitting by Dr. Franklin, who perceived that I was not insensible to these mutilations," Jefferson recalled.

"I have made it a rule," said he, "whenever in my power, to avoid becoming the draughtsman of papers to be reviewed by a public body. I took my lesson from an incident which I will relate to you. When I was a journeyman printer, one of my companions, an apprentice hatter, having served out his time, was about to open shop for himself. His first concern was to have a handsome signboard, with a proper inscription. He composed it in these words, 'John Thompson, Hatter, makes and sells hats for ready money,' with a figure of a hat subjoined. But he thought he would submit it to his friends for their amendments. The first he showed it to thought the word 'Hatter' tautologous, because followed by the words 'makes hats,' which showed he was a hatter. It was struck out. The next observed that the word 'makes' might as well be omitted, because his customers would not care who made the hats. If good and to their mind, they would buy them, by whomsoever made. He struck it out. A third said he thought the words 'for ready money' were useless, as it was not the custom of the place to sell on credit. Every one who purchased expected to pay. They were parted with, and the inscription now stood, 'John Thompson sells hats.' 'Sells hats!' says his next friend. 'Why, nobody will expect you to give them away. What then is the use of that word?' It was stricken out, and 'hats' followed it, the rather as there was one painted on the board. So the inscription was reduced ultimately to 'John Thompson,' with the figure of a hat subjoined."

Another—briefer—statement attributed to Franklin may not actually have passed his lips (it was not recorded until many years later), but it certainly expressed his feeling. John Hancock, as president of the Congress, advocated that the body make the vote on the Declaration unanimous. "There must be no pulling different ways," Hancock said. "We must all hang together." To which Franklin reportedly rejoined, "Yes, we must indeed all hang together, or most assuredly we shall all hang separately."

⌐ **Franklin** had hardly put his signature to the Declaration of Independence before he went to work on a new constitution for Pennsylvania. Doubtless he was struck by the fact that the goal of his first mission to England—the end of proprietary rule in Pennsylvania—was finally achieved only by ending English rule in all the American colonies. In 1757 he had seen King George as the protector of the people against the Penns; in 1776 the people had to protect themselves, and against George even more than against the Penns.

Shortly after his return from London, Franklin had been elected by the Assembly to be president of its Committee of Public Safety. For a few months he tended assiduously to the committee's affairs, but his mission to Massachusetts and his other work for the Continental Congress cut into the time he could devote to the Pennsylvania committee, and in February 1776 he resigned.

This did not prevent his supporters in Philadelphia from electing him to a convention called in the summer of 1776 to write a new constitution for the state of Pennsylvania. The Declaration had dissolved the connections between the colonies and Britain and presumably nullified their colonial charters; the new states now set to work, with various degrees of dispatch, writing new charters. Pennsylvania's convention met on July 15, and on the following day it unanimously selected Franklin as its president.

For the next two months he alternated between the Congress and the convention—which conveniently met in the same building, the State House. As president of the convention he presided rather than participated directly; the heavy drafting he left to others. He did express strong support for perhaps the most distinctive feature of the constitution that emerged: the unicameral legislature. A legislature with two houses was like a wagon with two teams, he said. Where some conservatives took this idea as reassurance—that each team would check the other and prevent the people from running off with the government—Franklin saw equal likelihood that they would negate each other's effort and thereby prevent the people from enacting needed measures, in much the way the Penns had prevented the Assembly from acting on the people's behalf. In supporting a single house, Franklin manifested his faith in the people to govern themselves.

⌒ **This same** faith informed his principal contribution to a renewed debate in the Congress over articles of confederation for the United States as a whole. A central sticking point involved representation, specifically whether representatives would be apportioned by states, on the one hand, or by population (or wealth, its rough equivalent), on the other. Franklin urged the latter, on grounds of both equity and practicality. He was not quite a democrat, in the sense of thinking every person had a right to an equal voice in government. But he predicted that a confederation that countenanced gross disproportions in shared burdens between citizens of different states would not last. "Let the smaller colonies give equal money and men," he said, "and then have an equal vote. But if they have an equal vote without bearing equal burdens, a confederation upon such iniquitous principles will never last long."

Franklin lost this argument—and lived long enough to see his prediction prove true, when the confederation based on the one-state, one-vote principle came undone. On a related question he looked similarly to the future. If representation were not to be by states but by population or wealth, how should slaves be measured? By numbers, as people, or value, as property? The issue became moot at this time with the choice of representation by states, but in the discussion the question arose whether a state with many slaves was stronger than a state with few slaves, in the way that a state with many sheep or cattle was stronger than a state with few such livestock. Supporters of slavery, likening slaves to sheep, explicitly or implicitly judged slaves a net addition to states' strength.

Franklin disagreed tersely. "Slaves rather weaken than strengthen the state," he said, "and there is therefore some difference between them and sheep. Sheep will never make insurrections."

☙ Franklin had to break off constitution-making to tend to the hostilities at hand. Eighteen months earlier, when Lord Howe had consulted with Franklin on a plan for reconciliation, the British government had displayed no interest; now, after a year of fighting, Howe—an admiral as well as a lord, and currently the commander-in-chief for America—was on his way from London with an offer of peace. Franklin had been his American contact then; Franklin became his American contact again. Two weeks after Congress approved the Declaration of Independence, Franklin received a letter from his erstwhile interlocutor. "My Worthy Friend," began the letter, which proceeded to express Howe's earnest wish for "the reestablishment of lasting peace and union with the colonies." As means to this end, Howe informed Franklin and the Congress, he and his fellow peace commissioner— his brother, General William Howe—were authorized to offer amnesty to all Americans who renewed their allegiance to the Crown, to suspend hostilities against those colonies evincing a desire for peace, and to reward those persons who assisted in the restoration of order.

Franklin turned Howe's letter over to John Hancock and asked the Congress president that it be read to the body. After this was done, the Congress authorized Franklin to respond. He did so in a manner that left no doubt whatsoever that Howe had come a long way to no purpose. Nor did Howe have any difficulty discerning the anger that still burned in Franklin. "Directing pardons to be offered the colonies, who are the very parties injured," Franklin wrote, "expresses indeed that opinion of our ignorance, baseness and insensibility which your uninformed and proud nation has long been pleased to entertain of us; but it can have no other effect than that of increasing our resentment." The Declaration's litany of British crimes had not yet reached the king; Franklin supplied a short summary. "It is impossible we should think of submission to a government that has with the most wanton barbarity and cruelty burnt our defenceless towns in the midst of winter, excited the savages to massacre our farmers, and our slaves to murder their masters, and is even now bringing foreign mercenaries to deluge our settlements with blood." If Americans could never forgive such injuries, neither could they realistically expect the British to forgive the assertion of American rights. "And this must impel you, were we again under your government, to endeavour breaking our spirit by the severest tyranny, and obstructing by every means in your power our growing strength and prosperity." Franklin could describe what Britain needed to do to restore peace, but he would be wasting his time. "I know too well her abounding pride and deficient wisdom to believe she will ever take such salutary measures. Her fondness for conquest as a warlike nation, her lust of dominion as an ambitious one, and her thirst for a gainful monopoly as a commercial one (none of them legitimate causes of war), will all join to hide from her eyes every view of her true interests."

Franklin considered Howe a personal friend, and in this letter he got personal.

Long did I endeavour with unfeigned and unwearied zeal to preserve from breaking that fine and noble China vase, the British empire. For I knew that being once broken, the separate parts could not retain even their share of the strength or value that existed in the whole, and that a perfect re-union of those parts could scarce even be hoped for. Your Lordship may possibly remember the tears of joy that wet my cheek when, at your good sister's in London, you once gave me expectations that a reconciliation might soon take place. I had the misfortune to find those expectations disappointed, and to be treated as the cause of the mischief I was labouring to prevent.

Franklin averred his respect for Howe as a gentleman, but even gentlemen had to take responsibility for their actions. The present war against America was unwise and unjust.

> And I am persuaded cool, dispassionate posterity will condemn to infamy those who advised it, and that even success will not save from some degree of dishonour those who voluntarily engaged to conduct it. I know your great motive in coming hither was the hope of being instrumental in a reconciliation; and I believe when you find *that* impossible on any terms given you to propose, you will relinquish so odious a command and return to a more honourable private station.

Howe apparently was shocked by the vehemence of Franklin's letter. "I watched his countenance, and observed him often to express marks of surprise," recorded the emissary who delivered the letter. "When he had finished reading it, he said his old friend had expressed himself very warmly." The emissary—an officer from Washington's headquarters, through which Franklin's reply reached Howe—inquired whether there was a response. "He declined, saying the doctor had grown too warm, and if he expressed his sentiments fully to him, he should only give him pain, which he wished to avoid."

Eventually Howe did reply, first by letter to Franklin directly, then by a lately captured American officer, John Sullivan. Since the winter of 1775–76 the main theater of the war had shifted from New England to New York. In March the British evacuated Boston; General Howe pulled all his troops (and some thousand Loyalists) back to Halifax. Three months later he redeployed to the mouth of the Hudson River, landing at Staten Island on the same day the draft of the Declaration of Independence was laid before the Congress. Shortly thereafter Admiral Howe arrived with a large fleet and many more troops.

Washington had anticipated the redirection of British forces and marched his army south. But he was outnumbered and, after General Howe moved 20,000 troops east to Long Island, outflanked. In sharp fighting the British inflicted a major defeat on the Americans; only a skillful nighttime crossing of the East River to Manhattan averted the wholesale destruction of the American army.

Admiral Howe judged the aftermath of the battle of Long Island propitious for a parley. He paroled General Sullivan, the senior American prisoner, to Philadelphia to apprise the Congress of his sincere desire to terminate the conflict before it went further. Under the circumstances of the Long Island defeat, the Congress could not but listen; at the same time it resisted appearing in the role of supplicant. After some debate it appointed a committee, consisting of Franklin, John Adams, and Edward Rutledge of South Carolina, to visit the admiral and hear him out. If nothing else, Howe's acceptance of the credentials of the committee would confer a legitimacy upon the Congress the British government had heretofore refused to give.

Accordingly, Franklin set out from Philadelphia again. The roads and inns were crowded with soldiers and other travelers; this part of the country was not yet at war but obviously expected to be. John Adams, recuperating from an illness, recorded the first night.

At Brunswick, but one bed could be procured for Dr. Franklin and me, in a chamber little larger than the bed, without a chimney and with only one small window. The window was open, and I who was an invalid and afraid of the air in the night, shut it close.

"Oh!" says Franklin. "Don't shut the window. We shall be suffocated."

I answered I was afraid of the evening air.

Dr. Franklin replied, "The air within this chamber will soon be, and indeed is now, worse than that without doors. Come! Open the window and come to bed, and I will convince you. I believe you are not acquainted with my theory of colds."

Opening the window and leaping into bed, I said I had read his letters to Dr. Cooper in which he had advanced that nobody ever got a cold by going into a cold church, or any other cold air. But the theory was so little consistent with my experience that I thought it a paradox. However I had so much curiosity to hear his reasons that I would run the risque of a cold.

The Doctor then began an harangue, upon air and cold and respiration and perspiration, with which I was so much amused that I soon fell asleep, and left him and his philosophy together. But I believe they were equally sound and insensible, within a few minutes after me, for the last words I heard were pronounced as if he was more than half asleep.

The next day they arrived at Amboy, opposite Staten Island. Howe sent over a barge with an officer who had instructions to remain there, as a hostage for the return of the commissioners. Franklin and the others declined the offer, taking the officer back with them and thereby placing themselves as hostages to Howe's honor.

Howe appreciated this vote of confidence, although his men did not. "We walked up to the house between lines of guards of grenadiers, looking as fierce as ten furies," Adams wrote, "and making all the grimaces and gestures and motions of their muskets with bayonets fixed." The admiral did the best he could under trying circumstances. "The house had been the habitation of military guards, and was as dirty as a stable. But his Lordship had prepared a large handsome room, by spreading a carpet of moss and green sprigs from bushes and shrubs in the neighbourhood, till he had made it not only wholesome but romantically elegant, and he entertained us with good claret, good bread, cold ham, tongues and mutton."

Six months earlier Howe's efforts might have succeeded. Howe explained the terms of his commission from the king, and asserted that these afforded an ample basis for peace. "I also gave them to understand," the admiral reported to Lord Germain afterward, "that His Majesty was graciously disposed to a revision of such of his royal instructions as might have laid too much restraint upon their legislation, and to concur in a revisal of any of the plantation laws by which the colonists might be aggrieved."

If this offer meant what it appeared to mean, it amounted to everything Franklin and most other Americans had been saying for years was all they wanted: a return to the status quo as it existed before 1765. But the offer came too late. The colonies were no longer colonies but independent states. "The three gentlemen were very explicit in their opinions that the associated colonies would not accede to any peace or alliance but as free and independent states," Howe recorded.

This essentially ended the conversation. Yet Howe was a gentleman, and a friend of Franklin, and he would not simply turn away his guests. As he had told Franklin in England, now he explained to the others that he felt great affection for America, not least on account of the generosity of Massachusetts in paying to erect a statue in Westminster Abbey of his elder brother, who had been killed in the war with France. He said he felt for America as for a brother, and if America should fall he would lament it like the loss of a brother.

"Dr. Franklin," Adams recorded, "with an easy air and a collected countenance, a bow, a smile and all that naivetee which sometimes appeared in his conversation and is often observed in his writings, replied, 'My Lord, we will do our utmost endeavours to save your Lordship that mortification.'"

23

Salvation in Paris

1776 – 78

∽ Before the meeting with the American commissioners adjourned, Howe remarked, "I suppose you will endeavour to give us employment in Europe."

∽ This was precisely what Franklin was endeavoring to do. From the start of the war Franklin and other American leaders had recognized that their success might well hinge on the attitude of other European countries, especially France, toward the conflict. Four times in the last eighty years France had fought against Britain; a fifth time might free America from London's grasp.

In November 1775 the Congress appointed Franklin to a Committee of Secret Correspondence. His fellow committeemen were John Dickinson, Benjamin Harrison, John Jay, and Thomas Johnson; their job was to seek foreign support for the war. "It would be agreeable to Congress to know the disposition of the foreign powers towards us," Franklin wrote on behalf of the committee to Arthur Lee in London. "We need not add that great circumspection and impenetrable secrecy are necessary." The same day Franklin wrote in his own voice to the son of the Spanish King Charles. The infante, a noted classicist, had sent Franklin a copy of his translation of Sallust; Franklin took the opportunity to thank the prince for the gift. He apologized that he had nothing comparable to return. "Perhaps, however," he went on, "the proceedings of our American Congress, just published, may be a subject of some curiosity at your court. I therefore take the liberty of sending your Highness a copy, with some other papers which contain accounts of the success wherewith Providence has lately favoured us. Therein your wise politicians may contemplate the first efforts of a rising state, which seems likely soon to act a part of some importance on the stage of human affairs, and furnish materials for a future Sallust."

This was a bold statement seven months before the Declaration of Independence, but hardly bolder than Franklin's concurrent actions. During the same week Franklin and the Committee of Secret Correspondence met covertly—by night, in the Philadelphia Carpenters' Hall rather than the State House—with one Monsieur Bonvouloir, young aristocrat sent from the French court to spy out the American situation. Franklin and the others asked whether France was well disposed toward the colonies and whether she might sell them needed arms and ammunition. Bonvouloir, without avowing any formal connection to the French government, suggested that indeed his country wished the Americans well, and that weapons might be made available.

Concurrently Franklin, as a member of the Secret Committee (he could have been forgiven for confusing his secret committees), conducted negotiations with two French merchants who were not agents of King Louis but intimated they were. This pair hoped to profit from the Americans' predicament by selling them the matériel they needed. The Secret Committee supplied them a list of the Continental Army's requirements and sent them on their way, hoping for the best.

Not long thereafter the Committee of Secret Correspondence decided to act more forthrightly. Franklin approached Silas Deane, a former colleague on the Secret Committee who had lost his place there when the Connecticut assembly, for reasons best known to itself, refused to return him to Congress after the end of 1775. Since then he had donned the frock coat of the merchant, which seemed to Franklin appropriate apparel for an American agent. "On your arrival in France, you will for some time be engaged in the business of providing goods for the Indian trade," Franklin explained, after Deane agreed to serve the Congress in a new capacity. "This will give good countenance to your appearing in the character of a merchant, which we wish you continually to retain among the French in general, it being probable that the court of France may not like it should be known publicly that any agent from the Colonies is in that country." In addition Deane would carry letters from Franklin to some of Franklin's French friends; this would appear perfectly legitimate even as it allowed the envoy to contact influential people in Paris. "You will find in M. Dubourg [Franklin's French editor] a man prudent, faithful, secret, intelligent in affairs, and capable of giving you very sage advice."

But Dubourg would chiefly be a conduit to the key personage in French foreign affairs, the foreign minister Comte de Vergennes. At the earliest possible moment Deane should apply for an audience with Vergennes—"acquainting him that you are in France upon business of the American Congress, in the character of a merchant, having something to communicate to him that may be mutually beneficial to France and the North American colonies." Most pressing was the need of the colonies for arms and ammunition. Deane should point out to Vergennes that France was the first country to which the colonies were making application and "that if we should, as there is a great appearance we shall, come to a total separation from Britain, France would be looked upon as the power whose friendship it would be fittest for us to obtain and cultivate." Britain had benefited handsomely from the commerce of the American colonies; France might inherit that benefit in the likely event of American independence.

Franklin specified what the colonies required: "clothing and arms for twenty-five thousand men, with a suitable quantity of ammunition, and one hundred field pieces." Ideally the French government would provide the colonies sufficient credit to purchase these items, with repayment to come from Franco-American trade. Less ideal, but acceptable, would be for the French government to allow Deane to arrange private financing. Once purchased, the items "would make a cargo which it might be well to secure by a convoy of two or three ships of war."

This was asking much, as Franklin knew. But there was more. Should

Vergennes appear sympathetic, Deane ought to inquire "whether, if the Colonies should be forced to form themselves into an independent state, France would probably acknowledge them as such, receive their ambassadors, enter into any treaty or alliance with them?"

The premise in this question was the sticker. France was willing to grant the Americans a modest amount of money simply for the nuisance they caused Britain; in May 1776 Louis approved an appropriation of 1 million livres. But this amount, while numerically impressive, would not keep the Continental Army in boots and bullets long. France refused to plunge deeper until the Americans proved their willingness and ability to see their task to its end.

The willingness came with the Declaration of Independence, which was a document written for foreign readers as much as for Americans. The ability was more problematic. The collapse of the Americans' Canadian offensive, followed by Washington's defeat on Long Island, left the French and other Europeans with grave doubts the Americans would last another season of fighting.

The Americans were caught in a cruel trap. They could not win without French backing, but they could not gain French backing without showing they could win. The Congress, desperate, directed Franklin to Paris.

His purpose was the same as that of Deane (who would join him, and Arthur Lee, on a three-man diplomatic commission): to obtain arms and an alliance. The former would be paid for with promises, the latter extorted with threats. Just two weeks earlier Franklin had informed Lord Howe that reunion with Britain was beyond consideration. Now he was authorized to threaten just such a reunion, to spur France to prevent it. "It will be proper for you," read his instructions, "to press for the immediate and explicit declaration of France in our favour, upon a suggestion that a reunion with Great Britain may be the consequence of a delay."

⌒ For a man of seventy, suffering from gout and assorted lesser afflictions, to leave his home in the middle of a war, to cross a wintry sea patrolled by enemy warships whose commanders could be counted on to know him even if they knew nary another American face, was no small undertaking. John Adams declined nomination to Franklin's commission; Thomas Jefferson rebuffed election. Yet Franklin had made his decision that America must be free, and he was determined to pay whatever cost his country required. "I have only a few years to live," he told Benjamin Rush, "and I am resolved to devote them to the work that my fellow citizens deem proper for me; or speaking as old-clothes dealers do of a remnant of goods, 'You shall have me for what you please.'"

Crossing the Atlantic with the old man were his two grandsons, Temple Franklin and Benny Bache. Temple's presence reflected a family tragedy, the final estrangement between Franklin and William. Since his arrival back from London in May 1775, Franklin had seen his son but a handful of times. The first meeting, the one that set the tone for the others, occurred at Joseph Galloway's estate in Bucks County, outside Philadelphia. Long Franklin's ally against the Pennsylvania proprietors, Galloway had drifted away on the quarrel with Britain—or perhaps Franklin had drifted from Galloway. Galloway tried to span the gap between the colonies and England by proposing a plan of imperial union; though initially heard with respect, the plan was later shouted down in the rising clamor for independence, and the author was targeted for death threats. One grim morning he woke to find a noose on his doorstep. William Franklin of course was persona non grata anywhere near the Congress; as the prime representative of the Crown in New Jersey, he was feeling increasingly isolated even in his own province.

Distance had divided Franklin and William for ten years; now politics did so. William was loath to raise political issues, hoping to preserve the personal relationship even if their former political partnership was beyond rescue. But Galloway felt no filial compunctions, and as the Madeira was passed around, tongues and tempers loosened in all corners of this triangle. William and Galloway described the intolerance of the colonial radicals, their abuse of moderates like themselves, their insistence on having their way even at the cost of violence to their fellow provincials and of the destruction of the empire. Franklin had not experienced the excesses his son and his former ally described, having been out of the country since before the trouble began; he knew them only by hearsay, and then often from the pens and mouths of informers he distrusted, such as Thomas Hutchinson. For Franklin the corruption and self-interest that counted was the corruption and self-interest of London, which he doubtless described in some detail to Galloway and William this night. None of the three recorded their conversation, but it would have been odd if Franklin had not got around to his session in the Cockpit with Wedderburn and the lords of the Privy Council.

Perhaps Franklin had hoped to persuade his son in person, as he had not been able to persuade him by letters, to abandon the Crown in favor of the people. The conversation at Galloway's disabused him of any such idea. When he had last seen his son, William was thirty-four, hardly more than a boy in his father's eyes, and new in his post as governor. Now William was middle-aged and the longest-serving royal governor in North America. Away from his father he had grown into a man of his own, as convinced of the correctness of his principles as his father was of *his* principles, and as stubborn in defending them. The apple had fallen close to the tree in regard of character, if not of politics.

Franklin and William met once more, in November 1775. Franklin was returning from Massachusetts and his meeting with General Washington; accompanying him was Jane Mecom, a refugee from the British forces occupying her hometown. As they passed through Perth Amboy they visited William's three-story mansion, which his aunt accounted "very magnificent." But Franklin was uncomfortable there; such elegance, complete with gilt-framed portraits of King George and Queen Charlotte in the great parlor on the first floor, seemed to exemplify what the colonists were fighting against. Besides, he was the bearer of critical intelligence regarding the Continental Army; he must have guessed that William would feel compelled to pass along, in the letters he wrote regularly to London, any information his father let drop.

It was just such letters that sealed William's fate. In January 1776 the Continental Congress ordered the disarming of all potential threats to the patriot cause. William Alexander, the leader of the local militia and a former friend but now bitter enemy of William Franklin's, interpreted the order as authorizing the interception of the mail of royal officials, including the governor. Alexander snatched a parcel labeled "Secret and Confidential" and addressed to Lord Dartmouth, and forwarded it to the Congress in Philadelphia. For good measure he placed the governor under house arrest.

After some months' deliberation—during which William managed to smuggle out additional letters, including the one to Lord Germain about his father's mission to Canada—the case came to trial. By now the Congress was on the verge of declaring independence, and the separate colonies were forming new governments of their own. The provincial assembly of New Jersey declared William Franklin a "virulent enemy to this country, and a person that may prove dangerous." It requested the Congress to remove him from New Jersey. The Congress, having examined the governor's letters and determined that they contained intelligence damaging to the American cause, approved the request. In late June 1776 it ordered William sent to Connecticut, there to be placed under the authority of Governor Jonathan Trumbull.

Franklin lifted no finger on behalf of his son. He did send sixty dollars to William's wife, Elizabeth, who was utterly distraught by this turn of events. Betsy had feared for her husband's life at the time of his arrest, and still worried about his health. Her own health was poor, with asthma a chronic affliction. None of her own family were anywhere near. She could not join her husband in his Connecticut exile lest his enemies—or plain criminals—loot the house in Perth Amboy.

"I will not distress you by enumerating all my afflictions," she wrote Franklin in August 1776, "but allow me, Dear Sir, to mention that it is greatly in your power to relieve them. Suppose that Mr. Franklin would sign a parole not dishonourable to himself, and satisfactory to Governor Trumbull; why may he not be permitted to return into this province and to his family? . . . Consider, my Dear and Honoured Sir, that I am now pleading the cause of your son, and my Beloved Husband. If I have said or done anything wrong I beg to be forgiven."

Franklin may have been inclined to forgive Betsy, but he would not forgive William. Steeling his heart, he left him to his fate.

⌒ Worse, he stole William's son. Temple had carried the sixty dollars to his stepmother (who at some point had been apprised, as Temple himself had been, that Temple was William's son, rather than godson), and seeing her plight, decided to stay. Not long thereafter he proposed visiting his father in Connecticut and wrote Franklin for approval. The ostensible reason for the visit was to deliver a letter from his stepmother to his father; almost certainly he wished to see and talk to his father, whom he hardly knew.

"I have considered the matter, and cannot approve of your taking such a journey at this time, especially alone, for many reasons which I have not had time to write," Franklin replied. Two which he *did* write were that Mrs. Franklin could perfectly well get a letter to Temple's father in care of Governor Trumbull, and that Temple needed to return to Philadelphia to resume his studies at the college there. "This is the time of life in which you are to lay the foundations of your future improvement, and of your importance among men. If this season is neglected, it will be like cutting off the spring from the year."

Temple chose not to defy his grandfather for his father and step-mother, and he returned to Philadelphia—just in time to leave with Franklin for France. Whether Franklin explained how this comported with his professed desire that Temple continue his studies is unclear; if he did, he probably denominated it an education in public affairs. Temple would be his amanuensis and companion. The lad would go where Franklin went and meet whom Franklin met. He would also encounter the risks—from angry waves and angry men-of-war—his grandfather encountered. It would indeed be an education in public affairs, and doubtless an exciting one.

Benny Bache also accompanied his grandfather. Sally and Richard's boy would not stay with Franklin and Temple in Paris but would be sent to school somewhere creditable and convenient—and safer than the rebel capital in wartime. At seven Benny could understand only part of what was happening around him, but he too must have considered it the most exciting time of his young life.

⌒ The passage from America to France was "short but rough," in Franklin's contemporary account. His ship, the *Reprisal*, had been hastily pressed into the service of the fledgling United States navy, and though it was fast enough to capture two British merchantmen en route, it was hardly suited to the comfort of passengers. It pitched violently for nearly the whole of the thirty-day run, allowing Franklin hardly a night's—or day's—decent rest. The food was poor; he had to rely on salt beef because the chickens served were too tough for his teeth. His boils and rashes returned. In short, he told his daughter and son-in-law later, the voyage "almost demolished me."

To avoid the English Channel and the British vessels therein, the *Reprisal* made for the south coast of the Breton peninsula. Easterly winds hindered an ascent of the Loire to Nantes; rather than spend another night aboard the bucking vessel, Franklin packed himself, Temple, and Benny into a fishing boat that deposited them at Auray. A carriage was sent for—the village had none—to carry them to Nantes.

At Nantes, Franklin was recognized, but his purposes he kept to himself. "I have acquainted no one here with this commission, continuing incognito as to my public character," he wrote Silas Deane. He needed to sound out the French government before lowering his mask. Yet his silence simply fueled speculation. The learned doctor was traveling with his two grandsons; were they defecting from the American cause? Money appeared to be no object in his accommodations or conveyance; had he absconded with the American treasury?

In that impoverished neighborhood not even the carte blanche of the Congress could eliminate the discomforts and hazards of travel. "The carriage was a miserable one," Franklin wrote of one stretch of the journey, "with tired horses, the evening dark, scarce a traveller but ourselves on the road; and to make it more *comfortable*, the driver stopped near a wood we were to pass through, to tell us that a gang of eighteen robbers infested that wood, who but two weeks ago had robbed and murdered some travelers on that very spot."

Yet there were compensations. Tired and uncomfortable as he was, Franklin observed the countryside and its denizens with care. "On the road yesterday we met six or seven country-women, in company, on horseback and astride; they were all of fair white and red complexions, but one among them was the fairest woman I ever beheld."

Franklin's arrival in Paris was a personal triumph. "The celebrated Franklin arrived at Paris the 21st of December and has fixed the eyes of every one upon his slightest proceeding," recorded one French diarist. Another stated, "Doctor Franklin, arrived a little since from the English colonies, is mightily run after, much feted by the savants. He has a most pleasing expression, very little hair, and a fur cap which he keeps constantly on his head." This observer was pleased to note additionally: "Our *esprits forts* have adroitly sounded him as regards his religion, and they believe that they have discovered that he is a believer in their own— that is to say, that he has none at all." Some claimed Franklin as a Frenchman; the name "Franquelin," they pointed out, was common in Picardy. Others were content that he was part of the classical—if not mythological—heritage of Western civilization. "He was not given the title *Monsieur*; he was addressed simply as Doctor Franklin, as one would have addressed Plato or Socrates," said one who so addressed him. "If it is true that Prometheus was only a man, may one not believe that he was a natural philosopher like Franklin?" Poems were written to honor the American sage, the great philosopher of liberty. "It is the mode today," observed a Franklin-watcher in the French capital just three weeks after his arrival, "for everybody to have an engraving of M. Franklin over the mantelpiece."

Well they might have. Franklin offered something to almost everyone in France. He was a philosopher to the liberal *philosophes*, an ardent foe of Britain (by now it was clear he was not selling America out) to the conservatives who hungered for revenge against perfidious Albion, a wit to the habitués of the salons, a prophet of profits to the makers of weapons and outfitters of privateers.

~ He was also a bit of a puzzle to King Louis's foreign minister. Vergennes had a grand design for French policy, namely the restoration of French *grandeur*, so badly tarnished in the last war. Upon appointment in 1774 he had begun a buildup of French armed strength, of which the centerpiece would be a navy the fighting equal to Britain's. On current, necessarily secret, estimates, the buildup would reach fruition sometime in 1778.

The outbreak of the American war presented an opportunity and a problem. The opportunity was the obvious one: to capitalize on Britain's current discomfiture and distraction. The problem was less obvious (to those unaware of the foreign minister's timetable) but no less real: whether to accelerate war plans in order to exploit England's troubles, or to stick with the plan. How *much* help would the Americans be in a war? How *real* was the prospect of their reconciliation with Britain, or their defeat? Vergennes needed to know.

He did not get much out of Franklin—but then neither did Franklin get much out of him. Upon Franklin's arrival in Paris, where he was joined by Deane and Lee, the three applied for an interview with Vergennes. The foreign minister declined a formal meeting at Versailles in favor of a secret session in Paris, intended to take the measure of the Americans, Franklin especially, rather than to determine policy. "Intelligent, but very circumspect," was how the foreign minister characterized Franklin, adding, "This did not surprise me."

Franklin spoke for the group, and for the American Congress. He indicated his country's interest in a treaty with France (and, for good measure, with Spain). When Vergennes nodded noncommittally, Franklin promised a memorandum on the current state of American affairs. The foreign minister indicated he would read such a memorandum with great interest.

Franklin spent the last days of 1776 drafting the memo, which he delivered to Vergennes at Versailles early in January. Franklin's message mixed promises with threats.

As other princes of Europe are lending or hiring their troops to Britain against America, it is apprehended that France may, if she thinks fit, afford our Independent States the same kind of aid, without giving England just cause of complaint. But if England should on that account declare war, we conceive that by the united force of France, Spain and America, she will lose all her possessions in the West Indies, much the greatest part of that commerce that has rendered her so opulent, and be reduced to that state of weakness and humiliation she has by her perfidy, her insolence, and her cruelty both in the East and West so justly merited.

On the other hand, without French assistance, especially at sea, America might be forced to terminate the war.

While the English are masters of the American seas and can, without fear of interruption, transport with such ease their army from one part of our extensive coast to another, and we can only meet them by land marches, we may possibly, unless some powerful aid is given us, or some strong diversion made in our favour, be so harassed and put to such immense expense as that finally our people will find themselves reduced to the necessity of ending the war by an accommodation.

France and Spain must seize the moment to link arms with America. Franklin summarized and concluded:

North America now offers to France and Spain her amity and commerce. She is also ready to guarantee in the firmest manner to those nations all their present possessions in the West Indies, as well as those they shall acquire from the enemy in a war that may be consequential of such assistance as she requests. The interest of the three nations is the same. The opportunity of cementing them, and of securing all the advantages of that commerce, which in time will be immense, now presents itself. If neglected, it may never again return. We cannot help suggesting that a considerable delay may be attended with fatal consequences.

Vergennes was not to be moved by mere rhetoric. During the next few months he kept Franklin and the other Americans at arm's length. Their requests for interviews were diverted to his assistants, their very existence hardly acknowledged by the French court. Their request for a treaty was rebuffed, as was their application for such formal and undeniable assistance as a loan of ships of the French line. Clearly the government was not ready to embrace the American cause openly—for fear "of giving umbrage to England," Franklin explained to the Committee of Secret Correspondence.

Yet privately Vergennes facilitated the American war effort. The ports of France were opened to American vessels for the selling of American goods and the buying of French. Arrangements were made for the purchase of five thousand hogsheads of American tobacco by the Farmers General, a consortium of bankers and merchants closely connected to the government, which besides collecting taxes for the king ran the state's tobacco monopoly. The Farmers General would advance 1 million livres in payment; further sums would follow commencement of delivery of the tobacco. The government itself provided a grant of 2 million livres, to be paid in four quarterly installments.

On the whole Franklin found cause for optimism, as he usually did. The delay in winning an alliance with France simply meant France would be stronger when the alliance did come, as Franklin was certain it ultimately would—by either a positive act on France's part or a British declaration of war against France for assisting the Americans. And the French would bring Spain—"with which they mean to act in perfect unanimity," Franklin remarked. "Their fleet is nearly ready," he said of the French, "and will be much superior to the English, when joined with that of Spain, which is preparing with all diligence. The tone of the Court accordingly rises; and it is said that a few days since, when the British ambassador intimated to the minister, that if the Americans were permitted to continue drawing supplies of arms &c. from this kingdom, the peace could not last much longer, he was firmly answered, Nous ne desirons pas la guerre, et nous ne le craignons pas. We neither desire war, nor fear it." Franklin was not willing to predict a date for the onset of hostilities; this might be a matter of chance. But it could not be far off. "When all are ready for it, a small matter may suddenly bring it on; and it is the universal opinion that the peace cannot continue another year. Every nation in Europe wishes to see Britain humbled, having all in their turns been offended by her insolence."

America's star was on the rise. "All Europe is for us. Our Articles of Confederation, being by our means translated and published here, have given an appearance of consistence and firmness to the American states and Government, that begins to make them considerable. The separate constitutions of the several states are also translating and publishing here, which afford abundance of speculation to the politicians of Europe."

On this point Franklin was speaking more of popular opinion than of the views of the courts of the Continent—which on principle looked askance at republicanism. His meaning became clear as he described what victory would yield. "It is a very general opinion that if we succeed in establishing our liberties, we shall as soon as peace is restored receive an immense addition of numbers and wealth from Europe, by the families who will come over to participate our privileges and bring their estates with them." This made the American cause all the more worthy.

> Tyranny is so generally established in the rest of the world that the prospect of an asylum in America for those who love liberty gives general joy, and our cause is esteemed the cause of all mankind. Slaves naturally become base as well as wretched. We are fighting for the dignity and happiness of human nature. Glorious it is for the Americans to be called by Providence to this post of honour. Cursed and detested will everyone be that deserts or betrays it.

∼ The great goal of Franklin's French mission was an alliance with Louis's regime, but achieving that goal required keeping the United States afloat till the Bourbon monarch came round. Money was a constant problem, despite the grants and advances Vergennes arranged. Franklin knew something about financing a war from the last conflict with France, but the war against Britain ate through money faster than he or anyone else in America had imagined. For internal consumption the Congress could levy taxes and print money, both of which it did. Yet neither addressed the need for foreign exchange—the coin of the realms where Americans hoped to buy the muskets, cannons, ships, and other items they could not produce themselves in the quantities they needed. For these they had to pay in promises, which went at a severe discount after disasters like Long Island, or in trade goods the French, Spanish, and other foreigners wanted to buy. The tobacco deal marked a start, but it soon suffered from the same ailment that afflicted the rest of the trade from America: British men-of-war, which stopped up American ports and scoured the shipping lanes to Europe. Vessels got through now and again, compensating their captains for their audacity, but not frequently enough to keep the new republic in the livres it required.

An alternative was resort to privateers, the licensed pirates on whom the English had relied since the days of Francis Drake. The privateers preyed on the maritime trade of Britain, thereby depriving London of revenues; more positively (from the American perspective), the privateers' prizes might be sold on the open foreign market for the hard currency America desperately required.

The problem was that the market for prizes was not as open as Franklin and the other Americans wished. France was the obvious place to sell the captured cargoes and vessels, and France was where they were first disposed of. Lambert Wickes, the captain of the *Reprisal*, the bucking brig that brought Franklin over from Philadelphia, sold his two prizes to French purchasers willing to wink at the falsified papers that were to the privateers' practice what Continental dollars were to the fiscal practice of the American Congress. But the British were not so tolerant. They warned Vergennes that conspiracy in piracy might lead to belligerency. Vergennes initially told Franklin that American privateers in French ports must leave with their prizes at once, but upon being informed that the vessels in question required repairs, and that to turn them out would simply turn them over to the British, the foreign minister relented. They might stay—indeed they *must* stay—pending further notice.

Although Franklin was willing to abide by Vergennes's cease-and-desist order, the privateers themselves—for whom privateering was often as much a moneymaking venture as an exercise in patriotism—were not. Gustavus Conyngham was released from French custody at Dunkirk on the assurances of the American commissioners that he and his cutter *Revenge* would sail directly to America and engage in no activities hostile to Britain save self-defense. The captain blithely ignored written orders and set about picking off British merchantmen. To make matters worse, he allowed one of his prizes to be recaptured by the British, and the prize crew (the sailors from Conyngham's ship detailed to sail the captured vessel in place of the now-confined original crew) turned out to be mostly *Frenchmen*.

The fault was not all Conyngham's. Evidently the captain had received an oral message from one William Carmichael, a courier from Franklin and the commission, that countermanded his written orders. Carmichael evidently considered Franklin too timid and desired to force the French into the war. Whether or not Conyngham suspected Carmichael of free-lancing, the captain was happy to resume his predation.

Vergennes had no interest in *which* Americans were to blame; the fact that French sailors had been captured in what the British interpreted as piracy provoked a diplomatic crisis. A special envoy from King George arrived at Versailles threatening war against France. Vergennes and Louis took the matter most seriously, with the former warning the French ambassador in London that hostilities could begin at any time and the latter holding French ships in port. Louis also ordered American privateers and prizes out of French harbors, repaired or not. Vergennes refused to deal further with Franklin or the other American commissioners.

~ Franklin understood that Vergennes's displeasure was as much for Britain's benefit as America's, and he assumed that once the war scare passed, the displeasure would dissipate.

Other problems were less tractable. The American commissioners had charge of purchasing weapons and other war matériel for Washington's army, and though funding these purchases was a constant challenge, there was no lack of interest on the part of French and other European merchants and manufacturers in America's business. Yet precisely because of the uncertainty of getting paid, those expressing the interest were often of the enterprising—not to say shady—sort.

One of the more curious characters Franklin encountered was Pierre Augustin Caron de Beaumarchais, a Frenchman with background and interests almost as varied as Franklin's. The son of a watchmaker, Beaumarchais had developed a modest reputation as an inventor; his creativity found other outlets in music and drama. His popular play *Le Barbier de Séville* was still on the boards when Franklin arrived in Paris; he would proceed to write *Le Mariage de Figaro*. Meanwhile the playwright moved on to drama of another sort, namely the revolution unfolding in America. He became entranced with the American version of *liberté* and determined that France must midwife its birth. He urged Vergennes to back the American rebels and offered to act as secret agent supplying the support. When Louis approved the project, Beaumarchais created a front firm, Roderigue Hortalez & Co., to disguise the government's role. A substantial amount of French (and Spanish) money flowed through Beaumarchais's hands, winding up as weapons and other matériel in America.

Precisely what Beaumarchais was going to get out of the arrangement was unclear. The Americans resisted repaying him, on the reasoning that the money was intended for *them*, not for him. Whatever his emotional attachment to the American cause, he apparently expected some profit for his pains. It was his bad luck to attach himself to Silas Deane, who himself came under suspicion for profiteering (and eventually came under more than suspicion when he abandoned the American cause). Beaumarchais also antagonized Franklin's old friend Dubourg, who hoped to corner the French market for American supplies himself, and Jacques Donatien Leray de Chaumont, an intimate of Vergennes who became Franklin's host. Franklin, recognizing the cloud over Beaumarchais, kept his distance from this ingenious fellow with whom, under different circumstances, he must have found much in common.

Others were less easily put off. A small army of young men—and some not so young—besieged Franklin, seeking commissions in the American army. After nearly a decade and a half of boring peace, the warrior class of the Continent wanted work. A Swiss officer who had served with the Dutch wished to become a lieutenant colonel under General Washington, despite never having risen higher than lieutenant for the Dutch. A veteran of ten years in the French army, writing from Spain, where nothing was brewing, thought he should be a regimental quartermaster. A student from Lyons declared that the time had come for him to accomplish something grand; he would start by killing redcoats in America. An aristocrat from Orléans explained that his forty-two years in the French army had taught him how an army of 25,000 could defeat a host ten times as large; he would be honored to share this secret with General Washington. A German student wrote from Jena declaring candidly that his family could no longer fund his education; he would fight for his daily bread. A Dutch surgeon sought to expand his knowledge of physical trauma in the only place where bodies were being blown apart on a regular basis. A British subject who had been outlawed from England after fighting with the French in Corsica declared his desire to fight with the Americans against those who had treated him so shabbily. The abbess of St.-Michel de Doullens offered the nephew of one of the nuns, a lad of eighteen who, bless his heart, wanted to support his eleven brothers and sisters as a soldier with the Americans. A mother from Châtellerault with sons to spare forwarded three for the front. A Paris matron explained that a young male relation had been serving with the royal guard of Spain but found King Carlos's incessant hunting exhausting; he wished to rest up against the British.

There were a few diamonds amid the dross. "Count Pulaski of Poland, an officer famous throughout Europe for his bravery and conduct in defence of the liberties of his country against the three invading powers of Russia, Austria and Prussia will have the honour of delivering this into your Excellency's hands," Franklin wrote Washington in May 1777, sending along the man who would organize the Continental cavalry. A few months later he recommended "the Baron de Steuben, lately a Lieutenant General in the King of Prussia's service"—and shortly to impress Prussian discipline on Washington's troops (at which point the fact that he had been only a captain, rather than a lieutenant general as represented to Franklin, was forgiven). In another letter Franklin endorsed "the Marquis de la Fayette, a young nobleman of great expectations and exceedingly beloved here." Fulfilling those expectations, Lafayette became just as beloved in America.

Such as these Franklin could recommend forthrightly. In other cases he either ignored the entreaties or wrote something innocuous. "The bearer, Monsr. Dorcet, is extremely desirous of entering in the American service, and goes over at his own expense, contrary to my advice," Franklin wrote Washington regarding one worthy whose sponsors had to be appeased. Franklin assured Washington he had not given the gentleman in question "the smallest expectation" of a commission. Yet the man insisted on a recommendation, and Franklin obliged, after a fashion. Reiterating that the gentleman refused to be dissuaded, Franklin wrote, "This at least shows a zeal for our cause that merits some regard."

Even such backhanded compliments became too much for Washington. "Our corps being already formed and fully officered," the general wrote Franklin from Continental Army headquarters, "the number of foreign gentlemen already commissioned and continually arriving with fresh applications throw such obstacles in the way of any future appointments that every new arrival is only a source of embarrassment to Congress and myself and of disappointment and chagrin to the gentlemen who come over." Speaking candidly, Washington admitted mistakes in the past that had continuing consequences. "The error we at first fell into of prodigally bestowing rank upon foreigners without examining properly their pretensions, having led us to confer high ranks upon those who had none or of a very inferior degree in their own country, it now happens that those who have really good pretensions, who are men of character, abilities and rank will not be contented unless they are introduced into some of the highest stations of the army." This was impossible, as Franklin surely appreciated. Washington acknowledged the need to maintain the goodwill of influential Frenchmen, but, please, no more officer candidates.

Yet at Franklin's end the throngs only grew. "These applications are my perpetual torment," Franklin wrote Dubourg in the autumn of 1777. "You can have no conception how I am harassed. All my friends are sought out and teased to tease me; great officers of all ranks in all departments, ladies great and small, besides professed solicitors, worry me from morning to night. The noise of every coach now that enters my court terrifies me. I am afraid to accept an invitation to dine abroad, being almost sure of meeting with some officer, or officer's friend, who as soon as I am put into good humour by a glass or two of champagne begins his attack upon me. Luckily I do not often in my sleep dream myself in these vexatious situations, or I should be afraid of what are now my only hours of comfort." Dubourg had asked just such a favor for a friend; Franklin concluded his tale of woe with a supplication: "If therefore you have the least remaining kindness for me, if you would not help to drive me out of France, for God's sake, my dear friend, let this your 23rd application be the last."

Franklin would have admitted in this case that he was exaggerating for effect; despite the crush of requests he never lost his sense of humor. In a moment of respite he composed a reference for all occasions.

> Sir:
>
> The bearer of this who is going to America presses me to give him a letter of recommendation, though I know nothing of him, not even his name. This may seem extraordinary, but I assure you it is not uncommon here. Sometimes indeed one unknown person brings me another equally unknown, to recommend him; and sometimes they recommend one another! As to this gentleman, I must refer you to himself for his character and merits, with which he is certainly better acquainted than I can possibly be.

⌒ **What America** needed was not men but money. By the autumn of 1777 the situation was dire. The Congress had authorized the purchase of war supplies for the American army and the construction of warships for the American navy; now that the bills were coming due the commissioners discovered they lacked the funds to pay the suppliers and the builders. In September, Franklin, Deane, and Lee made a new appeal to the goodwill and self-interest of the French and Spanish courts.

"The Commissioners find themselves extremely embarrassed by their engagements," they explained in a memorandum drafted by Franklin for Vergennes and the Spanish ambassador. But worse than the embarrassment to themselves was the injury to their country's credit and cause. They briefly reviewed the events that had brought things to such a pass. Efforts to borrow money from European bankers foundered on the reluctance of the bankers to lend to America while its future hung in the balance. Ships carrying cargoes from America were lost to the British blockade. France's refusal to countenance the sale of American prizes curtailed the revenues America had derived therefrom. The Spanish court had lately stopped furnishing funds, for reasons unexplained.

Under the circumstances, Franklin and his fellow commissioners thought they should remind the French and Spanish governments what their countries would gain by an American victory. France and Spain would secure access to the American market, which would strengthen them; at the same time Britain's loss of its monopoly of the American trade would weaken the British, to the additional advantage of France and Spain. Lest the French and Spanish governments get the wrong impression—which was to say, the right impression—the commissioners quickly added, "They offer these advantages, not as putting them to sale for a price, but as ties of the friendship they wish to cultivate with these kingdoms."

In fact the commissioners did put a price on American actions—an entire list of prices. Eighty thousand blankets cost 56,000 livres. Eighty thousand shirts cost 32,000 livres. One hundred tons of powder cost 200,000 livres. One hundred tons of saltpeter cost 110,000 livres. Eight ships of the line came to 7,730,000 livres. The French and Spanish governments could see for themselves what it cost to continue the war.

As previously, Franklin and the others strove to seem confident even as they warned that without assistance the American cause might collapse. Rumors were circulating of an accommodation that would allow Britain once more to claim the American commerce for itself. The commissioners denied such rumors vigorously. "They can assure your Excellencies that they have no account of any treaty on foot in America for any accommodation; nor do they believe there is any. Nor have any propositions been made by them to the Court of England." If this sounded like protesting too much, it was intended to. "The Commissioners are firmly of opinion that nothing will induce the Congress to accommodate on the terms of an exclusive commerce with Britain but the despair of obtaining effectual aid and support from Europe."

Vergennes had been willing to see the Americans sweat, especially after all the trouble they had caused with their privateers, but he was not willing to see them expire. He promised enough cash to keep them going a while longer, and he hinted that France would take care of construction costs for their frigates. He also said to forget about paying Beaumarchais's company (which corroborated the American belief that the playwright was a profiteer). Yet all this was done under cover; as before, France remained officially aloof.

"We are scarce allowed to know that they give us any aids at all," Franklin reported to the Congress at the end of November 1777. "But we are left to imagine, if we please, that the cannon, arms &c. which we have received and sent are the effects of private benevolence and generosity." An open alliance was still the goal, yet the phlegmatic Franklin noted an advantage in its absence: "It leaves America the glory of working out her deliverance by her own virtue and bravery."

∾ At that particular moment such a prediction required a leap of faith. After the British victory on Long Island, General Howe chased Washington off Manhattan Island, across the Hudson River and New Jersey, and across the Delaware River into Pennsylvania. Washington assumed that the British objective was Philadelphia; he began destroying boats to keep the Delaware between Howe and the American capital. "We have prevented them from crossing," Washington wrote on December 17, "but how long we shall be able to do it, God only knows."

What God knew—and Washington learned, to his relief—was that Howe in fact was not driving for Philadelphia. The British commander had decided to spend the winter in New York, with isolated garrisons—manned in several instances by Hessian troops—posted at various towns between there and the Delaware.

Washington, desperate for a victory that would restore at least a little morale and thereby diminish the desertions that made the collapse of his army a frightening possibility, took advantage of the isolation of a Hessian unit at Trenton. Recrossing the ice-clogged Delaware during a storm of rain and snow on Christmas night, Washington struck the hungover

Trenton garrison at dawn the next day. The Hessian commander was hardly awake before an American bullet felled him; his confused subordinates surrendered by the hundreds. It was a brilliant victory, accomplished with negligible American losses.

Washington's hopes of following up with an assault on the British magazine at New Brunswick melted before the rapid arrival of reinforcements from New York under General Cornwallis, but the triumph at Trenton guaranteed that the Continental Army would survive the winter. The Congress returned to Philadelphia, whence it had fled on the rumors of Howe's advance; there it received Franklin's optimistic report, which afforded additional reason for hope.

Unfortunately, by the time that report arrived, General Howe was in the process of preparing to evict the Congress once more. Coordinating with his brother's ships, the British commander loaded 18,000 troops into transports and vanished into the Atlantic. The land-bound Washington, and the equally terrestrial Congress, could only guess where he had gone. "Not a word yet from Howe's fleet," John Adams wrote his wife on August 20. "The most general suspicion now is that it is gone to Charlestown S.C. But it is a wild supposition. It may be right, however, for Howe is a wild general."

It was wrong. Howe turned up not in South Carolina but in Maryland, at the head of the Chesapeake Bay. Quite evidently he intended to take Philadelphia from the rear. Washington hurried southwest to cut him off, and although he slowed the British advance at Brandywine Creek, Howe ground steadily forward. In mid-September the Congress once more fled, this time into the Pennsylvania hinterland; shortly thereafter Howe occupied the capital.

The loss of Philadelphia was a serious blow, but for most of the summer the really threatening news came from the north. General John Burgoyne had spent the winter in England, galloping with the king in Hyde Park, gallivanting with the ladies about London, and gabbing about how he would win the war with a thrust from Canada down to New York City. The government decided to give him his head and several thousand troops, with which, upon his return to Quebec, he set out for Lake Champlain.

All went well for Burgoyne at first. He reached Fort Ticonderoga at the head of the long lake by the beginning of July; within the week that strong spot was his. He pursued the American forces south, toward the Hudson, certain that victory was in his grasp. Once on the Hudson he would float magnificently down to Manhattan, thereby slicing the American colonies in two. Surrender would follow shortly, and probably an earldom for the man who forced it.

Amid his daydreams Burgoyne found time to draft a proclamation to the peoples still resisting the inevitable. "In consciousness of Christianity, my Royal Master's clemency and the honour of soldiership," he called on Americans to return to the British fold. If they did, all would be well. If not, "I have but to give stretch to the Indian forces under my direction, and they amount to thousands, to overtake the hardened enemies of Great Britain and America. . . . The messengers of justice and of wrath await them in the field, and devastation, famine and every concomitant horror that a reluctant but indispensable prosecution of military duty must occasion, will bar the way to their return."

The Presbyterians and other dissenters of New England did not take kindly to the preachments of an Anglican general, but what really infuriated them was Burgoyne's threat to unleash the Indians. In that wilderness district the memories of the French and Indian War still burned, and Burgoyne's boast made them burn the more.

To capitalize on the combustion, Washington replaced General Philip Schuyler, a stodgy Dutch patroon distrustful of the democratic tendencies of the New England militia, with Horatio Gates, an old shoe who openly admired the rank and file. Between Burgoyne and Gates, American recruitment swelled, and the farther the former got from his Canadian base, the larger the latter's army grew.

Franklin, the veteran of wilderness warfare, had predicted years past that the forests would swallow any force Britain was foolish enough to send against America; Burgoyne made the philosopher a seer. South of Ticonderoga, Burgoyne and his men found themselves slowed by narrow roads unsuited to the passage of armies and artillery, soaked by rushing streams rendered more difficult by the Americans' destruction of bridges, blocked by massive trees felled by American axes, weakened by short rations getting shorter by the week, and chilled by the deepening autumn. Unable to advance, unwilling to retreat, Burgoyne floundered. When the Americans repulsed a relief column coming up the Hudson and scattered another approaching from the west, the British were trapped. The final battle near Saratoga featured the mercurial American Benedict Arnold, who had recently been relieved of his command but now led by sheer ambition and bravery, hurling his men again and again upon the British lines, which staggered and broke.

The battle finished Burgoyne. Negotiating terms of surrender took several days; upon completion they erased the danger from the north, the threat to the integrity of the colonies, and most of the smugness with which Britain had entered the war.

◆— "When all are ready for it, a small matter may suddenly bring it on," Franklin had said regarding French entry into the war. The American victory at Saratoga was more than a small thing, and by the time news of the triumph reached Europe, all were ready.

The first report took Franklin by surprise, a mere five days after he had concluded that America might have to win her deliverance by her own virtue and bravery. An American messenger was said to have landed at Nantes with a dispatch from the front; in the late morning of December 4 this young man, Jonathan Loring Austin, galloped into the courtyard of Franklin's residence. "Sir, *is* Philadelphia taken?" demanded Franklin, his mind on the danger to the American capital—and his home.

"Yes, sir," replied Austin, whereupon Franklin wrung his hands and turned to go back inside.

"But, sir, I have greater news than that," the breathless courier continued. *"General Burgoyne and his whole army are prisoners of war!"*

This changed everything, of course. At once Franklin circulated the welcome news among the influentials of Paris and Versailles, with a gloss highlighting Gates's accomplishment and minimizing Howe's. The version that went to Vergennes described "the total reduction of the force under General Burgoyne" and the difficulties confronting Howe. At the time of the courier's departure from America, "General Gates was about to send reinforcements to General Washington, who was near Philadelphia with his army. General Howe was in possession of that city, but having no communication with his fleet, it was hoped he would soon be reduced to submit to the same terms with Burgoyne, whose capitulation we enclose."

Perhaps Franklin believed that Howe's end was near; certainly he judged it politic to appear so. When an acquaintance commiserated upon hearing of the loss of America's capital, Franklin replied, "You mistake the matter. Instead of *Howe* taking *Philadelphia, Philadelphia* has taken *Howe.*"

Before the future could prove him wrong—as it did, soon enough—Franklin moved to exploit the recent past. In this he received encouragement from Vergennes. The foreign minister sent his secretary, Conrad Alexandre Gérard, to Franklin's apartment. As Arthur Lee recorded the conversation, "He said as there now appeared no doubt of the ability and resolution of the states to maintain their independency, he could assure them it was wished they would reassume their former proposition of an alliance, or any new one they might have, and that it could be done none too soon."

The French had reason for haste. The British, alarmed at the prospect of an alliance between America and France, were scurrying to prevent it. To Paris came envoys informal and official to meet with Franklin and determine whether the Americans might settle their dispute with Britain without involving the French. Sir Philip Gibbes resumed an earlier conversation (of February 1777) in which Franklin had hinted— according to Gibbes's recounting—that an Anglo-American confederation for war and peace ("to make peace and war as one state") and for trade might follow Britain's recognition of American independence. If accurately reported, it was merely a suggestion, of which nothing came, as Britain was in no mood to grant independence. Eleven months later, independence was a de facto reality, and Britain's mood had changed. But so had America's. Franklin told Gibbes it would cost Britain more now to end the conflict. But he refused to say how much more. "America is ready to make peace. If Great Britain desires to make peace, let her propose the terms to the Commissioners here." At the same time he warned Gibbes that whatever Britain offered would be communicated to the French government. America, he said, was new at treaty-making and wished to employ the experience of its French friends.

Needless to say, this was not what London intended. "I am sorry, I much lament, sir," Gibbes replied, "that your engagements with France oblige you to submit to her the terms of a peace between Great Britain and America."

"Do not mistake me," Franklin rejoined. "I did not say we should *submit* them to France. I said, distrusting ourselves, we should *consult* France." Yet any British offer had better be good. "Terms that come voluntarily, and shew generosity, will do honour to Great Britain and may engage the confidence of America."

Gibbes had nothing to offer, but Franklin's next visitor did. Paul Wentworth was a British spy who came straight from the office of William Eden, the head of British intelligence. "I called on 72 yesterday," Wentworth reported to Eden, employing the code for Franklin (which Eden interlined for posterity upon receiving the letter). "We remained together two hours before 51 [Silas Deane] joined us, when the conversation ceased." In the course of the conversation Wentworth introduced a letter from Eden. "I said if he would pledge his honour to me that he would not, on any account whatever, now or hereafter mention the substance or any part of a letter I wished to show him, I would read him one, which induced me to come to 144 [Paris]. He agreed, and I read the first and second pages, ending in unqualified 107 [independence]." Franklin listened carefully. "He said it was a very interesting, sensible letter," Wentworth reported. "Pity it did not come a little sooner."

Wentworth had not said whom the letter was from. Franklin wanted to know. Wentworth declined to identify Eden, beyond indicating that the author was someone with the ear of the king.

This was not good enough for Franklin. In the small talk before Wentworth got to the letter, Franklin had explained how unsatisfactory had been previous informal efforts at reconciliation; he mentioned specifically Lord Howe's attempt during his—Franklin's—final months in England. The only result of such efforts then was lost time; the result now would be lost lives. Franklin thereupon lectured Wentworth on British barbarities in the cruel and unjust war against America.

Wentworth tried to return Franklin to the point of his visit, but Franklin refused. "I never knew him so excentric," Wentworth reported to Eden. "Nobody says less generally and keeps a point more closely in view; but he was diffuse and unmethodical today." Gradually the spy caught on to Franklin's game. "I must conclude he was involved in engagements which bound him too closely to attend to any propositions."

As indeed he was. Those engagements gained impetus from Franklin's talks with Gibbes and Wentworth, of which he allowed Vergennes to learn, without revealing details. Vergennes's eagerness for an alliance, now that the time had come—and now that Britain seriously sought to prevent it—was evident in the foreign minister's characterization of the negotiations as "lively and long"; for in fact the talks took less than three comparatively uncontentious weeks.

The result was a pair of accords: a treaty of amity and commerce, granting each country unbettered access to the markets of the other; and a treaty of alliance, pledging French support for American independence and American support for France in the event of an Anglo-French war.

24

Bonhomme Richard

1778–79

〜 Such difficulties as did arise in negotiating the treaties came less from differences with the French than from differences among the American negotiators. Indeed it was fortunate the United States and France pledged themselves to mutual amity when they did, for little such sentiment existed among the American commissioners, and its absence increasingly undermined Franklin's effectiveness.

Silas Deane was the occasion of the friction, but Arthur Lee was the cause. Deane's ambiguous position as commissioner and entrepreneur, combined with his friendship for the equally ambiguous Beaumarchais, convinced Lee that Deane and his fellow profit-seekers had their own interests, rather than those of the United States, closest to heart. "Let me whisper to you that I have reason to suspect there is jobbing both with you and with us," Lee confided to Sam Adams, who was always happy to spot conspiracy and did not like Deane's politics besides. "The public concerns and the public money are perhaps sacrificed to private purposes." Congress should insist on separating the commissioners from the commerce of the war. To his brother, Richard Henry Lee, Arthur Lee was more specific. "If in the arrangement of things I could be continued here, and Mr. D. removed to some other place, it would be pleasing to me, and disconcert effectually their wicked measures."

Lee's distrust of Franklin was more diffuse but of longer standing. From their days in London he still resented Franklin's primacy with the Massachusetts House of Representatives. At that time he had suspected Franklin of collusion with the British; now he thought Franklin too cozy with the French. The fact that Franklin frequently sided with Deane against Lee on the three-man commission convinced Lee that Franklin must be colluding with Deane and probably Beaumarchais.

Lee's style was not to accuse openly but to insinuate; not to adduce evidence but to accumulate slights. He was constantly complaining of being bypassed by Franklin and Deane; when Deane, during Lee's absence, moved into an apartment next to Franklin's, one that Lee himself had coveted, Lee read perfidy into proximity.

Lee's sniping drove Franklin to distraction. By the spring of 1778, after another complaint by Lee that he was being left out, Franklin could stand it no longer. "It is true I have omitted answering some of your letters," he wrote.

> I do not like to answer angry letters. I hate disputes. I am old, cannot have long to live, have much to do and no time for altercation. If I have often received and borne your magisterial snubbings and rebukes without reply, ascribe it to the right causes, my concern for the honour and success of our mission, which would be hurt by our quarrelling; my love of peace; my respect for your good qualities; and my pity for your sick mind, which is forever tormenting itself with its jealousies, suspicions and fancies that others mean you ill, wrong you or fail in respect for you. If you do

not cure your self of this temper, it will end in insanity, of which it is the symptomatic forerunner, as I have seen in several instances. God preserve you from so terrible an evil; and for his sake pray suffer me to live in quiet.

As he had a few years earlier with his angry letter to William Strahan, Franklin held this draft till his temper cooled, and ultimately decided against sending it. Fate—and the Congress—had thrown him together with Lee; until fate and Congress changed their minds, he would make the best of the situation.

As it happened, even as Franklin was filing this unsent letter, a new commissioner was making his way from Nantes to Paris. Franklin wished that Lee were the one being replaced; instead it was Deane, the victim of Lee's slanders and his own carelessness at accounting, which made Lee's accusations plausible. (Deane could take some ironic solace in the knowledge that when it came to carelessness he was no match for Lee, who on a mission to Prussia allowed his personal papers to be stolen by an agent of the British.)

The new man was John Adams, who had decided that being a commissioner of the United States in France was not beneath him after all. Adams was a Puritan at heart, and as touchy in his own way as Arthur Lee. His opinion of Franklin reflected both aspects of his personality. "That he was a great genius, a great wit, a great humourist and a great satirist, and great politician is certain," Adams wrote later. "That he was a great philosopher, a great moralist and a great statesman is more questionable."

Part of Adams's objection was that Franklin got all the credit. "On Dr. F. the eyes of all Europe are fixed, as the most important character in American affairs in Europe," he recorded contemporaneously. "Neither L. [Lee] nor myself are looked upon of much consequence." At first Adams did not particularly question this state of affairs. "The attention of the Court seems most to F., and no wonder. His long and great reputation, to which L.'s and mine are in their infancy, are enough to account for this."

Yet the more time he spent in France the more it annoyed him. His mood did not improve from constantly having to explain to curious French men and women that he was not the "famous Adams"—Sam Adams. He preserved sufficient sense of humor to remark afterward, "No body went so far in France or England as to say I was the infamous Adams"; but not enough to keep from grumbling, "It was a settled point at Paris and in the English news papers that I was not the famous Adams, and therefore the consequence was settled absolutely and unalterably that I was a man of whom no body had ever heard before, a perfect cypher, a man who did not understand a word of French—awkward in his figure—awkward in his dress—no abilities—a perfect bigot—and fanatic."

In the summer of 1779 the obscure Adams fell into conversation with a French gentleman, a "Mr. M.," who remarked that in France foreign ambassadors were free to hold religious services in their own way. "But Mr. Franklin never had any," the Frenchman said, with evident surprise.

"No, said I, laughing," Adams recorded in his diary, "because Mr. F. had no—I was going to say, what I did not say, and will not say here. I stopped short and laughed."

"No, said Mr. M., Mr. F. adores only great nature, which has interested a great many people of both sexes in his favour."

"Yes, said I, laughing, all the atheists, deists and libertines, as well as the philosophers and ladies are in his train—another Voltaire and Hume."

"Yes, said Mr. M., he is celebrated as the great philosopher and the great legislator of America."

"He is, said I, a great philosopher, but as a legislator of America he has done very little. It is universally believed in France, England and all Europe that his electric wand has accomplished all this revolution, but nothing is more groundless. He has done very little. It is believed that he made all the American constitutions, and their confederation. But he made neither. He did not even make the constitution of Pennsylvania, bad as it is."

Adams could never forgive Franklin for receiving too much credit for events. He held a similar grudge against Washington, and in the last year of Franklin's life complained to Benjamin Rush, "The history of our Revolution will be one continued lie from one end to the other. The essence of the whole will be *that Dr. Franklin's electrical rod smote the Earth and out sprung General Washington. That Franklin electrified him with his rod, and thence forward these two conducted all the policy, negotiations, legislatures and war.*"

The acid of Adams's envy continued to corrode his impression of Franklin; all the same, the sketch he drew of Franklin in his autobiography caught a substantial measure of truth, and what it missed revealed much about a man whom chance—and that Congress again—teamed with Franklin during some critical episodes of American history. Adams was unsparing.

> The life of Dr. Franklin was a scene of continual dissipation. I could never obtain the favour of his company in a morning before breakfast, which would have been the most convenient time to read over the letters and papers, deliberate on their contents, and decide upon the substance of the answers. It was late when he breakfasted, and as soon as breakfast was over, a crowd of carriages came to his levee, or if you like the term better, his lodgings, with all sorts of people; some philosophers, academicians and economists; some of his small tribe of humble friends in the literary way whom he employed to translate some of his ancient compositions, such as his Bonhomme Richard [Poor Richard] and for what I know his Polly Baker &c.; but by far the greater part were women and children, come to have the honour to see the great Franklin, and to have the pleasure of telling stories about his simplicity, his bald head and scattering straight hairs, among their acquaintances.
>
>   These visitors occupied all the time, commonly, till it was time to dress to go to dinner. He was invited to dine abroad every day and never declined unless we had invited company to dine with us. I was always invited with him, till I found it necessary to send apologies, that I might have some time to study the French language and do the business of the mission. Mr. Franklin kept a horn book always in his pocket in which he minuted all his invitations to dinner, and Mr. Lee said it was the only thing in which he was punctual.

Here Adams interjected that he often required days to get Franklin to supply something as simple as a signature to a paper he—Adams—had drafted. Franklin's social schedule was too full for mere commission business.

> He went according to his invitation to his dinner and after that went sometimes to the play, sometimes to the philosophers, but most commonly to visit those ladies who were complaisant enough to depart from the custom of France so far as to procure sets of tea gear, as it is called, and make tea for him. . . . After tea

the evening was spent in hearing the ladies sing and play upon their piano fortes and other instruments of music, and in various games as cards, chess, backgammon &c. &c. Mr. Franklin I believe however never played at any thing but chess or checquers.

In these agreeable and important occupations and amusements the afternoon and evening was spent, and he came home at all hours from nine to twelve o'clock at night. This course of life contributed to his pleasure and I believe to his health and longevity. He was now between seventy and eighty [seventy-two when Adams arrived], and I had so much respect and compassion for his age that I should have been happy to have done all the business, or rather all the drudgery, if I could have been favoured with a few moments in a day to receive his advice concerning the manner in which it ought to be done. But this condescension was not attainable.

∽ If Adams could not enjoy the pleasures of Paris, Franklin certainly could. After a brief sojourn in the Hôtel d'Hambourg, in the rue de l'Université, he moved to the village of Passy, just outside the city, on the way to Versailles. Passy was a comparatively rustic retreat from the crowds, smells, and noises of the capital; a ten-minute carriage ride transported the well-to-do and well connected to the villas and châteaux they had tucked among the wooded hills and vineyards overlooking the Seine. Franklin's landlord was both well-to-do and well connected—the latter on account of the former. The humble but ambitious Jacques Donatien Leray of Nantes had made a fortune in the India trade, and with his pile had purchased the Loire château of Chaumont, which came with the "de Chaumont" suffix he added to his name. As a nouveau riche, Chaumont worked harder at his responsibilities than the true aristocrats; while they glided smugly toward the doom of the *ancien régime*, Chaumont improved his properties, winning support of the peasants that would save him from the guillotine. Government officials appreciated his gifts—both those nature bestowed on him and those he bestowed on them—and awarded him assorted honors and appointments. Vergennes found his Anglophobia a useful asset in plotting France's revenge against the English.

It was probably Vergennes who suggested that Chaumont invite Franklin to stay at the Hôtel de Valentinois, the elegant property Chaumont had recently purchased at Passy. Chaumont gallantly refused to accept rent from the American commissioner, saying they could settle the bill once the United States confirmed its independence. If this arrangement placed Franklin under a certain obligation to one of France's leading merchants (of whom a Paris paper said, "He would grasp, if he could, the commerce of the thirteen united colonies for himself alone"), Franklin did not mind—even if Arthur Lee and John Adams *did*. (Adams tut-tutted at "the magnificence of the place, and tried to discover how much it was costing the American people. Failing, he wrote, "It was universally expected to be enormously high.")

Chaumont did not simply shelter Franklin but promoted him avidly. He arranged for the famous sculptor, Giovanni Battista Nini, whom he had lured from Italy to the Loire, to produce a series of medallions memorializing Franklin's stay in France. One version showed the subject in a fur cap, with the simple inscription, "B. Franklin, Américain." Another lacked the cap but contained the motto already popularized by Turgot, *Eripuit Coelum Fulmen Septrumque Tyrannis* ("He snatched the lightning from heaven and the scepter from tyrants"). Chaumont persuaded the royal portraitist, Joseph Siffrède Duplessis, to paint Franklin in both oil and pastel.

Chaumont introduced Franklin to his family, and also to the neighbors at Passy—the crowd Adams found so "dissipated." Madame Chaumont was a Franklin favorite from the start; so too the daughter of the lord of the manor of Passy, a young lady commonly called the Mademoiselle de Passy. Even John Adams noticed her; she was, he said, "one of the most beautiful young ladies I ever saw in France." Franklin noticed too, as Adams could not resist recording. "Mr. Franklin, who at the age of seventy had neither lost his love of beauty nor his taste for it, called Mademoiselle de Passy his favourite and his flame and his love and his mistress, which flattered the family and did not displease the young lady." Madame Chaumont observed the interplay between seventy and seventeen, and when the mademoiselle was married off to the Marquis de Tonnerre, she punned, "Alas! All the rods of Mr. Franklin could not prevent the lightning [*tonnerre*] from falling on Mademoiselle de Passy."

Franklin's flirtations survived this fall, not least because they had numerous other objects. Madame Chaumont had a sister, Madame Foucault, who found Franklin charming. Temple Franklin, visiting the Chaumonts in the Loire, wrote his grandfather, "All the family send their love to you, and the beautiful Madame Foucault accompanies hers with an English kiss." This presumably signified an actual touching of lips, rather than the neck-pecking the French ladies preferred, so as not to ruin their rouge. Franklin replied, "My best respects to Madame de Chaumont and my love to the rest of the family. Thanks to Madame Foucault for her kindness in sending me the kiss. It was grown cold by the way. I hope for a warm one when we meet." Whether or not Franklin received his warm English kiss on that next occasion, his thoughts of Madame Foucault were kept warm by a friend, Monsieur Brillon, who subsequently wrote from "Paris, across the street from Madame Foucault": "By Jove, what a splendid sight to be across the street from! We saw her yesterday. She is marvelously plump once again"—evidently she had previously lost weight—"and has just acquired new curves. Very round curves, very white."

⌐ **Monsieur Brillon** could laugh with Franklin about eyeing Madame Foucault partly because he was unaware that Franklin was eyeing Madame Brillon. And one reason for his unawareness was that he himself was busy chasing, and catching, the governess of his children. John Adams described the ménage.

> Madame Brillon was one of the most beautiful women in France, a great mistress of music, as were her two little daughters. The dinner was luxury, as usual in that country. A large cake was brought in, with three flags flying. On one of them, "Pride subdued"; on another, "Haec dies, in qua fit Congressus, exultemus et potemus in ea."
>
> Mr. Brillon was a rough kind of country squire. His lady all softness, sweetness and politeness. I saw a woman in company, as a companion of Madame Brillon, who dined with her and was considered as one of the family. She was very plain and clumsy. When I afterwards learned both from Dr. Franklin and his grandson, and from many other persons, that this woman was the *amie* of Mr. Brillon, and that Madame Brillon consoled herself by the *amitié* of Mr. Le Vailliant [Le Veillard], I was astonished that these people could live together in such apparent friendship and indeed without cutting each other's throats. But I did not know the world. I soon saw and heard so much of these things in other families and among almost all the great people of the kingdom that I found it was a thing of course.

Franklin, observing the same mores, determined to make himself at home. His pursuit of Madame Brillon commenced with a conversation on theology and the afterlife. She, a devout Catholic, was mildly shocked at his deism. He suggested, perhaps suggestively, that she take charge of his soul. She responded in like vein. "You were kind enough yesterday, my dear brother, to entrust me with your conversion," she wrote. "I will not be stern, I know my penitent's weak spot, I shall tolerate it! As long as he loves God, America, and me above all things, I absolve him of all his sins, present, past, and future; and I promise him Paradise where I shall lead him along a path strewn with roses."

She listed the cardinal sins, and absolved him of the first six. The seventh—lust—was not so easy to dispose of. "All great men are tainted with it; it is called their weakness," she said. "You have loved, my dear brother; you have been kind and lovable; you have been loved in return! What is so damnable about that? Go on doing great things and loving pretty women—provided that, pretty and lovable though they may be, you never lose sight of my principle: always love God, America, and me above all."

Franklin thanked his confessor for her leniency, remarking particularly that it covered sins yet to be committed. To her litany of the cardinal sins he riposted the Ten Commandments, although he said he had been taught that there were really twelve. "The first was: *Increase and multiply*, and replenish the earth. The twelfth is: A new commandment I give unto you, *that ye love one another*. It seems to me that they are a little misplaced, and that the last should have been the first." Yet he had never made any difficulty on that point. "I was always willing to obey them both whenever I had an opportunity." He wondered whether some bargain might be struck. "Pray tell me, my dear Casuist, whether my keeping religiously these two commandments, though not in the Decalogue, may not be accepted in compensation for my breaking so often one of the ten, I mean that which forbids coveting my neighbor's wife, and which I confess I break constantly, God forgive me, as often as I see or think of my lovely confessor. And I am afraid I should never be able to repent of the sin, even if I had the full possession of her." He added another argument. "I will mention the opinion of a certain Father of the Church, which I find myself willing to adopt, though I am not sure it is orthodox. It is this, that the most effectual way to get rid of a certain temptation is, as often as it returns, to comply with and satisfy it."

Madame Brillon saw she was losing ground in theology. She appealed to natural law. "Let us start from where we are. You are a man, I am a woman, and while we might think along the same lines, we must speak and act differently. Perhaps there is no great harm in a man having desires and yielding to them; a woman may have desires, but she must not yield." Switching back to the commandments, she reminded Franklin she was married. "My friendship, and a touch of vanity, perhaps, prompt me strongly to pardon you; but I dare not decide the question without consulting that neighbour whose wife you covet; because he is a far better casuist than I am. And then, too, as Poor Richard would say, 'In weighty matters, two heads are better than one.'"

Though denying herself to Franklin—or at least such of herself as the lover in him desired—Madame Brillon complained when he turned his attentions elsewhere.

> The dangerous system you are forever trying to demonstrate, my dear papa—that the friendship a man has for women can be divided *ad infinitum*—this is something I shall never put up with. My heart, while capable of great love, has chosen few objects on which to bestow it. It has chosen them well; you are at the head of the list. When you scatter your friendship, as you have done, my friendship does not diminish, but from now on I shall try to be somewhat sterner toward your faults.

He refused to repent. "You renounce and exclude arbitrarily every thing corporal from our amour, except such a merely civil embrace now and then as you would permit to a country cousin. What is there then remaining that I may not afford to others without a diminution of what belongs to you?" He compared his affection toward women to her playing on the pianoforte: several people might enjoy it without any being cheated from the others' partaking.

Switching metaphors, he employed a figure of speech that could have been interpreted doubly, and—given his care with words—was almost certainly intended to be. "My poor little boy, whom you ought methinks to have cherished, instead of being fat and jolly like those in your elegant drawings, is meagre and starved almost to death for want of the substantial nourishment which you his mother inhumanly deny him!"

Adopting yet another analogy, he likened their sparring to war, and proposed a preliminary peace treaty.

Art. 1.   There shall be eternal peace, friendship and love between Madame B. and Mr. F.

Art. 2.   In order to maintain the same inviolably, Made. B. on her part stipulates and agrees that Mr. F. shall come to her whenever she sends for him.

Art. 3.   That he shall stay with her as long as she pleases.

A few more concessions on his part, then:

Art. 8.   That when he is with her he will do what he pleases.

Art. 9.   And that he will love any other woman as far as he finds her amiable.

Let me know what you think of these preliminaries. To me they seem to express the true meaning and intention of each party more plainly than most treaties. I shall insist pretty strongly on the eighth article, though without much hope of your consent to it. And on the ninth also, though I despair of ever finding another woman that I could love with equal tenderness.

On another day he offered still another analogy. She had said she loved him more than he loved her. He responded:

Judge, by a comparison I am going to make, which of us two loves the most. If I say to a friend: "I need your horses to take a journey, lend them to me," and he replies: "I should be very glad to oblige you, but I fear that they will be ruined by this journey and cannot bring myself to lend them to anyone," must I not conclude that the man loves his horses more than he loves me? And if, in the same case, I should willingly risk my horses by lending them to him, is it not clear that I love him more than my horses, and also more than he loves me? You know that I am ready to sacrifice my beautiful, big horses.

Madame Brillon managed to resist this offer of Franklin's "beautiful, big horses," but she did grant him permission to drive them elsewhere. He was an Epicurean, she said, while she, a married woman, must remain a Platonist. "Platonism may not be the gayest sect, but it is a convenient defence for the fair sex. Hence, the lady, who finds it congenial, advises the gentleman to fatten up his favorite at other tables than hers, which will always offer too meagre a diet for his greedy appetites."

Finally Franklin got the message. Perhaps he tired of the game;

perhaps he suspected that even in Paris it might appear foolish for a man of seventy-two to be chasing after a woman less than half his age. Certainly the question of age colored a letter he sent her in the autumn of 1778, in which he essentially agreed to her platonic terms. Some weeks before, Franklin had spent a day with her (and others) at Moulin-Joli, the estate of a mutual friend, situated on the Seine a short distance from Paris. The visit occurred at a time when mayflies were hatching. The French called the species *Éphémère* for the very short life span of the individuals; to Franklin the insects supplied a metaphor for human lives as well.

"You remember, my dear friend," he wrote Madame Brillon, "that when we lately spent that happy day in the delightful garden and sweet society of the *Moulin-Joli*, I stopped a little in one of our walks, and stayed some time behind the company. We had been shown numberless skeletons of a kind of little fly, called an Ephemere, all whose successive generations we were told were bred and expired within the day. I happened to see a living company of them on a leaf, who appeared to be engaged in conversation. You know I understand all the inferior animal tongues; my too great application to the study of them is the best excuse I can give for the little progress I have made in your charming language." He went on to explain how the younger insects were speaking three or four at a time, which made it difficult for him to understand. Fortunately the youngsters were not the only ones around. "I turned from them to an old greyheaded one, who was single on another leaf, and talking to himself. Being amused with his soliloquy, I have put it down in writing."

It was, says he, the opinion of learned philosophers of our race, who lived and flourished long before my time, that this vast world, the *Moulin-Joli*, could not itself subsist more than 18 hours; and I think there was some foundation for that opinion, since by the apparent motion of the great Luminary that gives life to all nature, and which in my time has evidently declined considerably towards the ocean at the end of our Earth, it must then finish its course, be extinguished in the waters that surround us, and leave the world in cold and darkness, necessarily producing universal death and destruction.

I have lived seven of those hours, a great age, being no less than 420 minutes of time. How very few of us continue so long! I have seen generations born, flourish, and expire. My present friends are the children and grandchildren of the friends of my youth, who are now, alas, no more! And I must soon follow them, for by the course of nature, though still in health, I cannot expect to live above 7 or 8 minutes longer.

What now avails all my toil and labour in amassing honey-dew on this leaf, which I cannot live to enjoy! What the political struggles I have been engaged in for the good of my compatriots, inhabitants of this bush, or my philosophical studies for the benefit of our race in general! For in politics, *what can laws do without morals?* Our present race of Ephemeres will in a course of minutes become corrupt like those of other and older bushes, and consequently as wretched. And in philosophy, how small our progress! Alas, *art is long, and life short!*

My friends would comfort me with the idea of a name they say I shall leave behind me, and they tell me I have *lived long enough, to nature and to glory.* But what will fame be to an Ephemere who no longer exists? And what will become of all history, in the 18th hour, when the world itself, even the whole *Moulin-Joli*, shall come to its end, and be buried in universal ruin?

To me, after all my eager pursuits, no solid pleasures now remain, but the reflections of a long life spent in meaning well, the sensible conversation of a few good Lady Ephemeres, and now and then a kind smile and a tune from the ever amiable *Brillante*.

At his age Franklin may not really have expected to catch the swift Brillante, but he seems to have had higher hopes regarding another woman—who shocked John Adams even more than Madame Brillon did. Madame Helvétius was a wealthy widow who made a great show of lamenting her departed husband. "That she might not be, however, entirely without the society of gentlemen," Adams recorded, "there were three or four handsome abbes who daily visited the house, and one at least resided there." Such personal confessors were customary among families of distinction, Adams discovered, although he could not help observing that they seemed to have as much power to commit sins as to pardon them. "Oh Mores! I said to myself. What absurdities, inconsistencies, distractions and horrors would these manners introduce into our republican governments in America. No kind of republican government can ever exist with such national manners as these. Cavete Americani."

Franklin fit right in, which simply reinforced Adams's disgust at the libertine life his fellow commissioner was leading. Yet such was Adams's eventual mastery of the diplomatic arts that after leaving Paris he wrote Franklin asking him to convey his compliments to Madame Helvétius— and Madame Brillon—"ladies for whose characters I have a very great respect."

Adams's wife, Abigail, labored under no such constraints. Mrs. Adams supplied a fuller, but no more flattering, picture of Madame Helvétius.

> She entered the room with a careless, jaunty air; upon seeing ladies who were strangers to her, she bawled out, "Ah, mon Dieu, where is Franklin? Why did you not tell me there were ladies here?" You must suppose her speaking all this in French. "How I look!" said she, taking hold of a chemise made of tiffany, which she had on over a blue lute-string, and which looked as much upon the decay as her beauty, for she was once a handsome woman; her hair was frizzled; over it she had a small straw hat, with a dirty gauze half-handkerchief round it, and a bit of dirtier gauze, than ever my maids wore, was bowed on behind. She had a black gauze scarf thrown over her shoulders. She ran out of the room; when she returned, the Doctor entered at one door, she at the other; upon which she ran forward to him, caught him by the hand, "Helas! Franklin"; then gave him a double kiss, one upon each cheek, and another upon his forehead. When we went into the room to dine, she was placed between the Doctor and Mr. Adams. She carried on the chief of the conversation at dinner, frequently locking her hand into the Doctor's, and sometimes spreading her arms upon the backs of both the gentlemen's chairs, then throwing her arm carelessly upon the Doctor's neck.
>
> I should have been greatly astonished at this conduct, if the good Doctor had not told me that in this lady I should see a genuine Frenchwoman, wholly free from affectation or stiffness of behavior, and one of the best women in the world. For this I must take the Doctor's word; but I should have set her down for a very bad one, although sixty years of age, and a widow. I own I was highly disgusted, and never wish for an acquaintance with any ladies of this cast.
>
> After dinner she threw herself upon a settee, where she showed more than her feet. She had a little lap-dog, who was, next

to the Doctor, her favorite, and whom she kissed. This is one of the Doctor's most intimate friends, with whom he dines once every week, and she with him.

Madame Helvétius, born Anne-Catherine de Ligniville d'Autricourt, belonged to an aristocratic but straitened family of Lorraine; as the tenth of twenty children she lacked the dowry required for a match to a man of equivalent social rank. So she was placed in a convent where, all supposed, she would spend her life in prayer and contemplation. But even that prim prospect failed when the pension that supported her ran out. Luckily an aunt took pity and brought her to Paris, where her genteel poverty found a mate in a man of means but insufficient (in his eyes) station—one of the group of Farmers General that would subsidize the American Revolution. Monsieur Helvétius established his wife at Auteuil, not far from Passy, attracted an assortment of intellectuals and artists, and died. Madame Helvétius, in her late fifties on Franklin's appearance, currently maintained the salon.

Franklin was first drawn by the company. The economist and finance minister Turgot was a regular; in fact, Turgot had once wooed the lady but failed to pass the means test. Yet still he hovered about, hoping for a second chance now that she had all the money she needed. Diderot and d'Alembert took time from their *Encyclopédie*; Condorcet dropped by for the Tuesday dinners that commenced at two and lasted long into the night. David Hume occasionally found his way from Edinburgh. The writer Fontenelle, well into his nineties, captured the spirit of the gatherings with the witticism, uttered upon catching the casual hostess in one of her not uncommon states of undress: "Oh, to be seventy again!"

Franklin found intellectual pleasure in "l'académie d'Auteuil"; he sought pleasure of another sort in "Notre Dame d'Auteuil," as he called Madame Helvétius. "If Notre Dame is pleased to spend her days with Franklin, he would be just as pleased to spend his nights with her," he wrote. "And since he has already given her so many of his days, although he has so few left to give, she seems very ungrateful in never giving him one of her nights, which keep passing as a pure loss, without making anyone happy except Poupon [her cat]."

With Madame Brillon, whose husband was still very much alive—and a Franklin friend as well—Franklin could hope only for a liaison. With Madame Helvétius he hoped for something more permanent. Or perhaps his proposals were merely foreplay. In one letter he described his disappointment at her canceling an engagement, and the impatience with which he awaited his next meeting with her. "He will be there early, to watch her enter, with that grace and dignity which have charmed him," he wrote. "He even plans to capture her there and keep her to himself for life."

In a variation of the "Ephemere" letter he sent Madame Brillon (one wonders if the two women were comparing notes), he assumed the role of spokesman for the flies who lived in his apartment at Passy. The flies sent their respects to Madame Helvétius, who had taken pity on the untidy Doctor Franklin and ordered his apartment swept. This scattered the spiders that had preyed on the flies. "Since that time we have lived happily, and have enjoyed the beneficence of the said bonhomme F. without fear. There remains only one thing for us to wish in order to assure the stability of our fortune; permit us to say it, 'Bizz, izzz ouizz a ouizzzz izzzzzzz, etc.' It is to see both of you forming at last but one ménage."

Madame Helvétius deflected Franklin's entreaties with the memory of her husband. Franklin concocted another approach.

> Saddened by your barbarous resolution, stated so positively last night, to remain single the rest of your life, in honour of your dear husband, I went home, fell on my bed, believing myself dead, and found myself in the Elysian Fields.
>
> I was asked if I had a wish to see some important persons.
>
> "Take me to the philosophers."
>
> "There are two who reside quite near here, in this garden. They are very good neighbours and very good friends of each other."
>
> "Who are they?"
>
> "Socrates and H. [Madame Helvétius's late husband]."
>
> "I have prodigious esteem for both of them, but let me see H. first, for I understand some French and not a word of Greek."
>
> He received me with great courtesy, having known me by reputation, he said, for some time. He asked me a thousand questions on war, and on the present state of religion, of liberty, and of the government in France.
>
> "But you are not enquiring at all about your dear friend Madame H.; yet she is excessively in love with you, and I was with her but an hour ago."
>
> "Ah," said he, "you are bringing back to my mind my former felicity. But one must forget, in order to be happy in this place. For

several of the first years, I thought of nobody but her. Well, now I am consoled. I have taken another wife. One as similar to her as I could find. She is not, to be sure, quite as beautiful, but she has just as much common sense, a little more wisdom, and she loves me infinitely. Her continuous endeavour is to please me; and she has gone out right now to search for the best nectar and ambrosia to regale me with tonight. Stay with me and you shall see her."

"I notice," said I, "that your former friend is more faithful than you, for several matches have been offered her, and she has turned them all down. I confess that I, for one, loved her madly; but she was harsh towards me and rejected me absolutely for the love of you."

"I pity you," said he, "for your misfortunes, for she is truly a good and lovely woman, and most amiable. But Abbé de la R. and Abbé M., aren't they any more in her home, now and then?"

"Yes, of course; for she has not lost a single of your friends."

"Now, if you had won over Abbé M. (with coffee and cream) [this was a standing joke], and got him to plead your cause, you might have met with success, for he is as subtle a debater as Duns Scotus or St. Thomas; he puts his arguments in such good order that they become almost irresistible. Or, better still, if you had convinced Abbé de la R. (by the gift of some fine edition of an old classic) [this second priest was a bibliophile] to argue against you, for I have always observed that when he advises something she has a strong tendency to do the exact opposite."

As he was saying this, the new Madame H. came in with the nectar. I recognized her instantly as Madame F., my former American friend [that is, Deborah Franklin]. I claimed her.

But she said coldly, "I have been a good wife to you for forty-nine years and four months, almost half a century. Be content with that. I have formed a new connection here, that will last for eternity."

Grieved by this rebuke from my Euridyce, I resolved there and then to abandon those ungrateful shadows, and to come back to this good world, to see the sun again, and you. Here I am! Let us avenge ourselves!

❦— Franklin had no more success with Madame Helvétius than with Madame Brillon. Whether his pursuit of other women in Paris had a different outcome is impossible to know. Certainly he achieved a reputation there as a great lover of women, and considering the determination with which he wooed Madames Brillon and Helvétius, any failure would hardly have been for lack of trying. And considering the mores of French society at the time, he could hardly have wanted for willing partners.

On the other hand, Franklin appreciated the degree to which he was playing a role. John and Abigail Adams might be shocked at how the senior American commissioner was taking French liberties when he should have been promoting American liberty, but he understood that in doing the one he was doing the other. America was asking France to fight a war on America's behalf (and France's, to be sure), and even under monarchs wars require popular support. For the French, Franklin embodied America. If the French wanted to attribute the Articles of Confederation and all the state constitutions to him, he was not the one to correct them. (John Adams was more than happy to assume this chore.) If they saw in the septuagenarian gallant a reflection of what they hoped to be at his age—a lover of life, in all its glorious ramifications—that could only redound to America's benefit.

Franklin's cause was popular in France but not uniformly so. King Louis had let himself be persuaded to adopt an anti-British policy, but as the descendant of Louis XIV, the Sun King, he had little love for an America whose present revolution challenged the very principle of monarchical legitimacy. Shortly after Franklin and his fellow commissioners exchanged signatures with Vergennes on the two treaties, Louis received the American trio at court. A decade earlier Franklin had been an honored guest at an elegant ceremony hosted by Louis's grandfather; the present reception displayed no such protocol. Arthur Lee wrote of the current king: "He had his hair undressed, hanging down on his shoulders, no appearance of preparation to receive us, nor any ceremony in doing it." But another eyewitness—interestingly, a French aristocrat—read the reception differently.

The King, who had been in prayer, stopped and assumed a noble posture. M. de Vergennes introduced M. Franklin, M. Deane and

M. Lee, and two other Americans. The King spoke first, with more care and graciousness than I have ever heard him speak. He said: "Firmly assure Congress of my friendship. I hope this will be for the good of the two nations." M. Franklin, very nobly, thanked him in the name of America, and said: "Your Majesty may count on the gratitude of Congress and its faithful observance of the pledges it now takes."

Gracious or not, the king made little subsequent effort to hide his distaste for the republicans from across the water. According to a well-placed source, he presented one of Franklin's female admirers—a countess who, Louis thought, should have known better—a chamber pot with Franklin's face gazing up from the bottom.

Louis may have understood—or only sensed—the full threat Franklin represented to the *ancien régime*. Others were at least as prescient. "Franklin wore a russet velvet coat, white stockings, his hair hanging loose, his spectacles on his nose, and a white hat under his arm," Madame du Deffand wrote of the royal reception of the commissioners. "Is that white hat a symbol of liberty?" Apparently it was, and within weeks it began to have an effect. France's recognition of the American confederation caused Britain to withdraw its ambassador, who besides representing King George was an old friend of Madame du Deffand. "I most sincerely curse that American negotiator, le Seigneur Franklin," she wrote.

~ The suspicions Franklin aroused were only increased by his association with one of the most prominent subversive organizations in the French capital. The Masonic Lodge of the Nine Sisters had been the brainchild of the late husband of Madame Helvétius. Named for the muses of the arts and sciences, the lodge deliberately embraced philosophers of all disciplines; among its members were some of the freest-thinkers in the realm. This, and the secrecy the lodge shared with all Masonic affiliates, rendered it suspect in the eyes of the keepers of the status quo. Franklin was aware of these suspicions, and as senior American commissioner he took them into consideration. But as a longtime Mason, a lover of all nine sisters, and an incorrigible free-thinker, he could not decline membership. He was inducted during the spring of 1778 as the 106th member.

He came in the door just behind the most famous French subversive of the age. Voltaire had been skewering orthodoxies of various sorts for decades, making him persona non grata with the monarchs of France and Prussia, to name two in particular. At Franklin's arrival in 1776 Voltaire had been exiled from Paris for a quarter century. Yet as he felt the life flowing out of his bony frame—whether retarded or accelerated by the fifty cups of coffee he was said to drink each day, no one knew— he insisted on returning to the capital.

Franklin met him shortly thereafter. The rendezvous provoked considerable comment, not least among persons who disliked both the patriarch of the Enlightenment and the republican from America. Franklin brought along Benny Bache and, according to most accounts, asked Voltaire's blessing on the boy. In Voltaire's version, "When I gave the benediction to the grandson of the illustrious and wise Franklin, the man of all America most to be respected, I pronounced only the words: God and Liberty. All who were present shed tears of tenderness." Another version had him calling Benny "my child" and adding, after "God and Liberty," that "this is the only appropriate benediction for the grandson of M. Franklin." Yet an unfriendly Paris paper reported differently, asserting that Franklin, "by a base, indecent and puerile adulation, and, according to certain fanatics, by a derisive impiety, asked Voltaire to give his benediction to the child. The philosopher, playing out the scene no less thoroughly than the doctor, got up, placed his hands on the head of the little innocent, and pronounced with emphasis these three words, 'God, Liberty, and Tolerance.'"

Another meeting between Franklin and Voltaire was more public and, indeed, more staged. In late April the two attended a session of the French Academy of Sciences. "There presently arose a general cry that Monsieur Voltaire and Monsieur Franklin should be introduced to each other," John Adams wrote, in his typically jaundiced voice.

> This was done and they bowed and spoke to each other. This was no satisfaction. There must be something more. Neither of our Philosophers seemed to divine what was wished or expected. They however took each other by the hand. But this was not enough. The clamour continued, until the explanation came out, "Il faut s'embrasser, a la francoise." The two aged actors upon this great theater of philosophy and frivolity then embraced each other by hugging one another in their arms and kissing each

other's cheeks, and then the tumult subsided. And the cry immediately spread through the whole kingdom and I suppose over all Europe: Qu'il etoit charmant. Oh! il etoit enchantant, de voir Solon et Sophocle embrassans. How charming it was! Oh, it was enchanting to see Solon and Sophocles embracing!

It must indeed have been a sight—the full-fleshed Franklin, a veritable oak of robustness next to the frail, pale, obviously dying Voltaire. In fact Voltaire expired within the month, and created one last uproar in passing. A career anticleric, he waved the priests away from his deathbed, which raised difficulties as to where he should be buried and how remembered. He barely beat a bishop's interdict into the ground, and when the Academy feted his memory, the prelates were outraged.

The Lodge of the Nine Sisters added to the outrage when it conducted a memorial ceremony. Franklin attended, either from respect for the deceased or because he did not recognize how much it would annoy Louis. (Several of his French friends, including Diderot, d'Alembert, and Condorcet, thought better and stayed away.) The service took place in a hall dressed in black, lit by candles. Admirers delivered one eulogy after another. Lest the meaning of the life be lost, the poet Roucher read parts of a forthcoming work that slashed the clergy in true Voltairean fashion. The philosopher's niece—allowed in under a special waiving of the rules against women—presented the lodge a bust of her uncle by Houdon. A large painting of the apotheosis of Voltaire was unveiled. Franklin had just received a Masonic crown; he laid it at the foot of the ascending philosopher. The company adjourned to a banquet room, where Roucher then read a verse honoring Franklin, which elicited an ovation for the sage who yet lived.

The entire affair evoked the wrath of the Church and of the government. The Nine Sisters Lodge nearly lost its Masonic charter, and its current head, or *Vénérable*, received a harsh reprimand. The controversy subsided only when Franklin, by maneuverings revealed solely to Sisters, was selected *Vénérable* in May 1779. His prestige helped shield the lodge, as did his understanding that an American envoy ought not make himself (any more) odious to his host monarch. That he counted the chief of Paris police, the man charged with enforcing any edicts against the lodge, as a personal friend did not hurt either.

From the mysterious first appearance of Silence Dogood in the *New England Courant* when he was fifteen, Franklin had never gone long without seeing his thoughts in print. The foreignness of the French language initially deterred him from continuing the custom in Paris, as did the constraints of his position as American commissioner. Yet if the presses of others were problematic, he would have his own. Sometime during his first year at Passy he set up a printing press. Soon followed a foundry, where he cast his own type. He hired help, and before long was back in his old business.

But this business was really a hobby, and although the press produced the official forms the commission required, it also printed light literature composed by the printmaster. Most noteworthy of this genre were small pieces he called "bagatelles." *The Ephemera*, his reflection to Madame Brillon on the swift passage of time was one; likewise the letters to Madame Helvétius on the flies that inhabited his house, and on the Elysian Fields. To Madame Brillon he addressed the story of his childhood whistle and how he had paid too much for it.

Madame Brillon was also the inspiration for perhaps the most famous of the bagatelles, *Dialogue Between the Gout and M. Franklin*. She had been chiding him for the excesses beneath his chronic condition; he initially retorted that not excess but deficiency was to blame. "When I was a young man and enjoyed more of the favours of the fair sex than I do at present, I had no gout. Hence, if the ladies of Passy had shown more of that Christian charity that I have so often recommended to you in vain, I should not be suffering from the gout right now." He expanded this argument in a bagatelle composed amid an excruciating recurrence of his malady that kept him awake for nights and days at a time.

The dialogue commences with Franklin moaning on his bed. "My God! What have I done to deserve these cruel sufferings?" he wails.

The Gout, cast as a disembodied feminine voice, replies, "You have eaten too much, drunk too much, and too much indulged your legs in their indolence."

"Who is it that speaks to me?" the feverish Franklin asks in wonder.

"It is I myself, the Gout."

"My enemy in person!"

"Not your enemy."

Franklin insists that it *must* be his enemy; the Gout explains that if any enemy is involved in the matter, it is Franklin himself.

Franklin defends himself, saying that people know him as neither glutton nor tippler.

"People judge as they please," the Gout replies. "But I know well that what is not too much to drink nor too much to eat for a man who takes a reasonable amount of exercise, is too much for a man who takes scarcely any."

"I take—ow! ow!—as much exercise—ow!—as I can, Madame Gout. You are acquainted with my sedentary existence, and it seems to me that accordingly you could, Madame Gout, spare me a little, considering that it is not entirely my fault."

"Not at all. Your rhetoric and your politeness are equally lost. Your excuse is worth nothing. If your position is sedentary, your amusements, your recreation, should be active. You should go promenading on foot or on horseback; or if you are pressed for time, play billiards." The Gout upbraids Franklin in terms that sound surprisingly modern even two centuries later—yet at the same time characteristically Franklin.

> Let us examine your course of life. While the mornings are long, and you have leisure to go abroad, what do you do? Why, instead of gaining an appetite for breakfast by salutary exercise, you amuse yourself with books, pamphlets or newspapers, which commonly are not worth the reading. Yet you eat an inordinate breakfast: four dishes of tea with cream, and one or two buttered toasts with slices of hung beef, which I fancy are not things the most easily digested.
>
> Immediately afterwards you sit down to write at your desk, or converse with persons who apply to you on business. Thus the time passes till one, without any kind of bodily exercise. . . .
>
> What is your practice after dinner? Walking in the beautiful gardens of those friends with whom you have dined would be the choice of men of sense; yours is to be fixed down to chess, where you are found engaged for two or three hours! This is your perpetual recreation, which is the least eligible of any for a sedentary man.

One school of medical thought in Franklin's day contended that attacks of gout signified the body's efforts to cleanse itself of ill humors built up through want of exercise and other unhealthy habits. The Gout subscribed to this view, and reprimanded Franklin for being not merely foolish but ungrateful. If not for the gout, Franklin would have been visited by palsy, dropsy, or apoplexy—"one or other of which would have done for you long ago." She stabs him again.

"Pray, Madame, a truce with your corrections!" he cries in distress.

"No, sir, no—I will not abate a particle of what is so much for your good."

He pleads that he *does* take exercise—in his carriage.

"That, of all imaginable exercises, is the most slight and insignificant." Showing herself remarkably well versed in his theories, she throws back at him his argument about the efficiency of exercise being linked to the degree of heat produced. Why, even his female companions get more exercise than he. "Behold your fair friend at Auteuil, a lady who received from bounteous nature more really useful science than half a dozen such pretenders to philosophy as you have been able to extract from all your books." (This was a reminder to Madame Brillon that she had a rival.) "When she honours you with a visit, it is on foot. She walks all hours of the day, and leaves indolence and its concomitant maladies to be endured by her horses. In this you see at once the preservative of her health and personal charms. But when you go to Auteuil you must have your carriage, though it is no farther from Passy to Auteuil than from Auteuil to Passy."

Franklin complains that this reasoning grows tiresome to one so afflicted as he.

"I stand corrected," says the Gout. "I will be silent and continue my office. Take that! And that!"

He writhes and moans again.

She scolds him for ignoring the repeated invitations of "the charming lady" of the Brillon household to walk at evening through the gardens, up the steps and down. "You philosophers are sages in your maxims, and fools in your conduct." She stings him once more.

What should I do with my carriage, if not ride in it?, he asks, flinching.

"Burn it if you choose." Or better yet, send it to transport the poor old peasants of Passy home from the vineyards at night. "This is an act that will be good for your soul; and at the same time, after your visit to the Brillons, if you return on foot, that will be good for your body." Another jab.

"Oh! Oh! For Heaven's sake, leave me! And I promise faithfully never more to play at chess, but to take exercise daily, and live temperately."

"I know you too well. You promise fair, but after a few months of good health, you will return to your old habits. Your fine promises will be forgotten like the forms of the last year's clouds. Let us then finish the account, and I will go. But I leave you with an assurance of visiting you again at a proper time and place, for my object is your good, and you are sensible now that I am your *real friend.*"

Franklin's literary reputation had long preceded him to Paris—although in some cases the reality outreached the reputation. One such instance led to the discovery of the true identity of Polly Baker. Franklin and Silas Deane one day were remarking the numerous mistakes in Abbé Raynal's *Histoire des deux Indes*, when the author himself happened in the door. Franklin was diplomatic enough to drop the subject, but Deane was not. "The Doctor and myself, Abbé, were just speaking of the errors of fact into which you have been led in your history."

"Oh, no, sir," the abbé replied. "That is impossible. I took the greatest care not to insert a single fact for which I had not the most unquestionable authority."

"Why, there is the story of Polly Baker," Deane said, "and the eloquent apology you have put into her mouth when brought before a court of Massachusetts to suffer punishment under a law which you cite, for having had a bastard. I know there never was such a law in Massachusetts."

"Be assured you are mistaken, and that that is a true story. I do not immediately recollect indeed the particular information on which I quote it, but I am certain that I had for it unquestionable authority."

Franklin's diplomatic discretion failed him at this point. Laughing aloud, he said, "I will tell you, Abbé, the origin of that story. When I was a printer and editor of a newspaper, we were sometimes slack of news, and to amuse our customers I used to fill up our vacant columns with anecdotes and fables, and fancies of my own. This of Polly Baker is a story of my making on one of these occasions."

The abbé listened with horror quickly hidden by aplomb. "Oh, very well, Doctor," he declared. "I had rather relate your stories than other men's truths."

Raynal himself refuted his own certitude in another instance. Conventional philosophical wisdom in Europe held that the races of men and animals degenerated in the New World, becoming smaller and less fit. The abbé was convinced of this, and at a dinner party hosted by Franklin at Passy held forth at length on the subject. Franklin had designed his guest list to include as many Americans as French; while Raynal ran on, Franklin noticed something interesting about the seating arrangement and comparative statures of the two nationalities represented.

"Come, Monsieur l'Abbé," he said, "let us try this question by the fact before us. We are here one half Americans and one half French, and it happens that the Americans have placed themselves on one side of the table, and our French friends are on the other. Let both parties rise, and we will see which side nature has degenerated."

Thomas Jefferson, who heard this story from Franklin, and who knew several of the guests (and who, moreover, was as determined to refute this alleged New World degeneracy as Raynal was to confirm it), explained the rest. "It happened that his American guests were Carmichael, Harmer, Humphreys, and others of the finest stature and form; while those on the other side were remarkably diminutive, and the Abbé himself particularly was a mere shrimp."

To the initial surprise of his French guests, Franklin typically deferred to others in conversation. This reticence reflected both his temperament and his incomplete mastery of the French language, acquired initially from books and self-study. "If you Frenchmen would only talk no more than four at a time, I might understand you, and would not come out of an interesting party without knowing what they were talking about," he explained to a friend. Not surprisingly, the relative rarity of his spoken *mots* made them the more precious.

One that was long remembered came from a chess match between Franklin and the elderly Duchess of Bourbon. Inexpert, she illegally placed her king in check. Franklin, in the spirit of rule-breaking, captured it. She, knowing enough to realize that this was not permitted, declared that in France "we do not take kings."

With a sly smile he responded, "We do in America."

25

Minister Plenipotentiary

1779–81

〜 The Holy Roman Emperor Joseph II was traveling incognito in France during this period, and frequented the same salons as Franklin. Watching Franklin's chess game with the Duchess of Bourbon, he was asked why he did not share the general enthusiasm for America.

"I am a king by trade," he replied.

George III felt the same way, although most nights he had little more reason to lose sleep over the Americans' activities than the Holy Roman emperor did. Even after the American victory at Saratoga the war went poorly for the rebels. An American defeat at Germantown left British forces in control of Philadelphia, and efforts to keep the British fleet from reaching and reinforcing the city failed after an imaginative scheme for sinking the British vessels misfired. David Bushnell had tinkered with an underwater boat—"Bushnell's turtle," it was called—that would torpedo the enemy below the waterline; when this encountered technical difficulties, Bushnell switched to floating bombs. He stuffed kegs with explosives and surreptitiously drifted them down the river toward the British fleet. Most missed, and the scheme was discovered when a bargeman lifted one of the kegs from the water, setting it off and killing himself and several companions. Although no British ships were destroyed, the very thought of bobbing ruin put the British on edge. Soldiers were arrayed along the riverbank to fire at suspicious objects in the water; by one account, just as the scare was abating, a farmer's wife accidentally dropped a keg of cheese in the river, sparking a renewed alert and another outpouring of lead into the water.

As General Howe wintered in Philadelphia, warmed by his mistress and assisted in the governance of the city by Franklin's old friend and ally Joseph Galloway, Washington and the American army froze on the windy hillsides of Valley Forge. They arrived worn from their failed campaign against Howe, and they grew wearier from the effort to construct winter quarters from the ground up. In dark huts fourteen feet by sixteen they shivered and went hungry. The entire commissary when the winter began consisted of twenty-five barrels of flour—this for 11,000 officers and men. "Firecake"—a leavenless pancake cooked over campfire—and water was the sole fare. "What have you for your dinner, boys?," an army surgeon recalled the officers asking. "Nothing but firecake and water, sir." "What is your supper, lads?" "Firecake and water, sir." "What have you got for breakfast?" "Firecake and water, sir." The surgeon, in charge of maintaining the army's health on this meager regime, cursed those responsible. "The Lord send that our Commissary of Purchases may live on firecake and water till their glutted guts are turned to pasteboard."

Feeding the army was far from the only challenge Washington faced. Clothing the men was just as hard. "We have, by a field return this day made," he reported to Congress on December 23, "no less than 2898 men now in camp unfit for duty because they are bare foot and otherwise naked." Lack of blankets forced the men to spend nights crowded around fires "instead of taking comfortable rest in a natural way." Washington normally bore hardship stoically, but the trials of his men forced him to speak his mind about those state legislatures that postured bravely but failed to provide what the troops needed. "It is a much easier and less distressing thing to draw remonstrances in a comfortable room by a good fire side than to occupy a cold bleak hill and sleep under frost and snow without clothes or blankets." Unless some decided change took place, "this army must inevitably be reduced to one or other of these three things: Starve, dissolve, or disperse in order to obtain subsistence."

Washington opted for the last. Foraging parties were drawn from those with shoes and trousers and the strength to stand. The pickings were slim in that part of Pennsylvania, which was crowded with refugees—including both the Congress and the Bache family. So the parties were sent to other parts of the state, and into New Jersey, Delaware, and Maryland. Despite the urgings of the Congress, Washington hesitated to seize what he required, lest the people turn against the revolutionary cause. Some of his subordinates were less fastidious, arguing that in the case of New Jersey and Delaware, at any rate, those states were infested with Loyalists who would not have supported the revolutionary cause even if it came with kid gloves and cash.

In camp, Washington attempted to maintain morale by keeping the men busy. Baron von Steuben arrived with his letter from Franklin and commenced drilling the troops. He lacked English beyond the basics, but his prestige as an officer in the army of Frederick the Great counted for much where military professionals were few. Discipline improved, and with it the mood in camp. (Certain cultural problems would persist, however. "Believe me, dear Baron, that the task I had to perform was not an easy one," Steuben later explained to the Prussian ambassador in Paris. "My good republicans [that is, the Americans] wanted everything in the English style; our great and good allies [the French] everything according to the French *mode*; and when I presented a plate of *sauerkraut* dressed in the Prussian style, they all wanted to throw it out of the window. Nevertheless, by the force of proving by *Goddams* that my cookery was the best, I overcame the prejudices of the former; but the second liked me as little in the forests of America as they did on the plains of Rossbach.")

For all the hardship, Washington and the army survived the winter at Valley Forge—partly because by the standards of old-timers in that country, the winter of 1777–78 was relatively mild. The arrival of spring brought additional good news: that France had embraced the American cause. The effect of the alliance was felt most immediately when the

British, under Howe's replacement Henry Clinton, evacuated Philadelphia for New York, the better to fend off the expected French attack.

The first American cavalry unit entered Philadelphia fifteen minutes after the last British troops departed, and on a rising tide of American morale Washington's forces harried Clinton's across New Jersey. Washington was tempted to strike directly at the long, straggling British line, but after an engagement at Monmouth was mishandled (leading to the court-martial and conviction of Charles Lee), Washington was reduced to watching the British make their escape across the Hudson estuary to New York.

Had he delayed them just another week the war might have been materially shortened. On July 11 a French fleet of sixteen warships—which could have contested Clinton's crossing of the Hudson—arrived off Sandy Hook. As it was, the fleet admiral, the Comte d'Estaing, was content to hover outside New York harbor, prevented from attacking the city by shallow water and the British guns that guarded the entrance. Meanwhile Washington crossed the Hudson upstream from the city and settled in at White Plains to keep Clinton from escaping by land.

↶ With the capital clear, the Congress returned to Philadelphia and voted to terminate the American commission in Paris. Three heads had been better than one in negotiating treaties, the legislators thought, but now that Louis's government had recognized the United States, diplomatic precedent indicated representation by a single minister plenipotentiary. And where a certain skepticism, even suspicion, was called for in negotiators driving hard for a bargain, an expansive friendliness ought to guide the actions of an ambassador to a wartime ally. Franklin was the obvious choice, and the Congress made it.

Franklin delivered his letter of appointment to "Our Great Faithful & Beloved Friend and Ally," as the Congress styled Louis, in February 1779. The letter requested his majesty to accept Franklin's credentials and "to give entire credit to every thing which he shall deliver on our part."

In fact Louis would have been wise to discount one of Franklin's first messages. The Congress had instructed Franklin to ask the king for a French expeditionary force against Halifax and Quebec; Franklin unilaterally added British-occupied Rhode Island to the target list. In time Washington would accept the necessity of inviting French troops onto the soil of the United States, but for the moment the memories of frontier service against the French were too strong. Though the American commander wanted French forces to harass Britain, he preferred they do it elsewhere than from American soil. Fortunately for Franklin, Louis was not ready to send soldiers across the Atlantic, and the request languished, sparing Franklin substantial embarrassment.

At seventy-three Franklin was an unlikely one to be swept away by zest for battle; the inspiration of his indiscretion may have been a young man nearly fifty-two years his junior. Lafayette was back in France after a brilliant beginning in America. Armed with Franklin's letter of recommendation; with a desire to avenge his father, a colonel of grenadiers killed in the Seven Years' War; with a passion for *la gloire*; and, not least important, with a large independent income, he had convinced the Congress to make him a major general—at the tender age of nineteen. He immediately fell in love with Washington ("the God-like American hero" was how he described him to Franklin). Washington reciprocated by taking the boy general under his wing, almost as the son he never had. Lafayette was bloodied in his first battle, which endeared him to his men, and he shared their hardships at Valley Forge, which endeared him still more. A daring midwinter "irruption into Canada" by Lafayette and a handful of men foundered before launch, leaving Lafayette impatient for action. "Dear general," he wrote Washington, "I know very well that you will do everything to procure me the only thing I am ambitious of—glory." His ambition was satisfied slightly at the battle of Monmouth in June 1778, in which he performed with conspicuous bravery but incomplete success.

France's entry into the war brought tears of joy and a request to return to his homeland to prepare the troops he was certain must be marching toward the docks already. The Congress consented; yet lest the courageous general forget his adopted country it voted to award him a special sword, which Franklin would present in France after it was fashioned. A minor problem arose on the return voyage when the crew—consisting largely of British prisoners and deserters—mutinied. But Lafayette unsheathed his regular sword and cowed the mutineers.

A problem of a different sort arose on arrival in Paris, when he was reminded that his service in America had violated a direct order of the king (given before the alliance with the United States). To his chagrin, the young marquis was placed under house arrest. His detention postponed a meeting he had requested with Franklin, to whom he carried a letter from Washington extolling his "zeal, military ardour and talents."

Louis let Lafayette stew for a week before issuing a royal pardon. But he insisted that Lafayette come to court to apologize in person. This pro-voked additional bit-champing. "In our kingly countries we have a foolish law called *Etiquette* that any one, though a sensible man, must absolutely follow," Lafayette complained to Franklin. His enthusiastic reception at court momentarily alleviated his impatience. Even Marie Antoinette, who had laughed at his awkwardness on the dance floor and his inability to hold his liquor, joined the acclaim. The ladies of the court vied for his favors.

Yet he must return to soldiering. After Monmouth but before leaving for France, Lafayette had participated in a botched attempt to break the British hold on Newport, Rhode Island. Mortified by this failure, he ached to make it right. Lafayette was the courier who brought Franklin's commission as minister plenipotentiary and his instructions from the Congress about asking France for help attacking Halifax and Quebec; he may have intimated that an attack on Rhode Island was an oral adden-dum to the written instructions—perhaps too sensitive to commit to paper. Franklin should have been shrewd enough to know the difference, but he may simply have been moved by the young hero's obvious devo-tion to the American cause.

When the expedition to America was delayed, Lafayette proposed something more audacious: a strike at England itself. Louis's tentative ap-proval set him aquiver. "My blood is boiling in my veins," he declared. In another letter, to Admiral d'Estaing, Lafayette warned, "If you undertake an attack on England and land troops and I am not there with you, I shall hang myself!"

Franklin would not have put his own feelings the same way, but he shared the broad sentiment, and he endorsed the expedition with enthu-siasm. "I admire much the activity of your genius, and the strong desire you have of being continually employed against the common enemy," Franklin wrote Lafayette. "It is certain that the coasts of England and Scotland are extremely open and defenceless. There are also many rich towns near the sea, which 4 or 5000 men, landing unexpectedly, might easily surprise and destroy, or exact from them a heavy contribution, tak-ing a part in ready money and hostages for the rest." Bristol, for example, ought to be worth 48 million livres, Liverpool the same, Bath 12 mil-lion, Lancaster 6 million. If the raiding parties included cavalry, all the better. "It would spread terror to much greater distances, and the whole would occasion movements and marches of troops that must put the enemy to prodigious expence and harass them exceedingly."

Franklin did not presume to judge the military merits of one strategy over another. But if history was any guide, the very audacity of the endeavor augured well for it. "In war, attempts thought to be impossible do often for that very reason become possible and practicable, because nobody expects them and no precautions are taken to guard against them." Franklin concluded with an appeal he knew Lafayette could not resist: "Those are the kind of undertakings of which the success affords the most glory."

⌒— In this same letter Franklin noted that "much will depend on a prudent and brave sea commander who knows the coasts." He had just the man in mind, although some wondered if "prudent" was the appropriate word. John Paul Jones had been born simply John Paul, the son of the gardener of a Scottish squire. Young John left home and went to sea at the age of twelve—about the same age Franklin thought of doing so from Boston. By nineteen he had visited Virginia, studied navigation, and advanced to first mate aboard a slaver making the notorious Middle Passage from Africa to America. Before long he had a command of his own, a Dumfries merchantman to the West Indies. Paul proved a taskmaster who brooked no dereliction; he flogged crewmen with gusto and some regularity. One day at Tobago he flogged the ship's carpenter more severely than usual, and the man died. The carpenter's father brought charges of murder against Paul, who was jailed. Eventually he persuaded others aboard the ship to affirm his innocence, and the charges were dropped, although a cloud of suspicion continued to hover about his head. In 1773, while commanding another ship, his crew challenged his authority, and in a scuffle the leader of the challenge was killed by Paul's sword. Paul testified he was merely defending himself, but this time the witnesses were hostile, and he judged flight the better part of valor. A few weeks later he was in Virginia with a new surname: Jones.

During the next two years he discovered neither another ship nor work ashore. Yet the misfortunes of the British empire promised an end to his own, and when war broke out with Britain he sided with the Americans. He hurried to Philadelphia and received a commission as a lieutenant, upgraded to captain once the Congress acquired a few more ships. Commanding the *Providence* and then the *Ranger*, he won a reputation as the scourge of British shipping. In one especially daring raid he swooped down upon the Scottish coast with the aim of taking hostage the Earl of Selkirk, to be traded for American prisoners. But the earl was out, and Jones's crew satisfied themselves with stealing the family silver—which Jones subsequently purchased from them and returned to its owner.

The entry of France into the war allowed, and required, Jones to co-ordinate his actions with those of the French. As an American officer he reported to Franklin, the ranking representative of the United States government, but in the common interests of the alliance—and because Franklin was a self-admitted novice in naval matters—the minister plenipotentiary followed the lead of the French navy minister, Antoine Sartine. It was Sartine who prepared the invasion of England, and Franklin who urged the impetuous Jones to cooperate. "The Marquis de Lafayette will be with you soon," Franklin wrote.

> It has been observed that joint expeditions of land and sea forces often miscarry, through jealousies and misunderstanding between the officers of the different corps. This must happen when there are little minds actuated more by personal views of profit or honour to themselves than by the warm and sincere desire of good to their country. Knowing you both as I do, and your just manner of thinking on these occasions, I am confident nothing of the kind can happen between you, and that it is unnecessary for me to recommend to either of you that condescension, mutual good-will and harmony, which contribute so much to success in such undertakings.

Of course, if it really *had* been unnecessary, Franklin would not have written. In fact Franklin knew that Jones was touchy on matters of rank and precedence. Franklin felt compelled to remind Captain Jones that General Lafayette outranked him and therefore would command the ground forces. "But the command of the ships will be entirely in you, in which I am persuaded that what ever authority his rank might in strictness give him, he will not have the least desire to interfere with you." Because the operation joined not simply land and sea forces but American and French, "a cool prudent conduct in the chiefs is therefore the more necessary." Jones need not fear. "There is honour enough to be got for both of you if the expedition is conducted with a prudent unanimity."

Franklin followed this exhortation with Jones's formal instructions. Captain Jones was to accept the French forces Lafayette brought him and conduct them where the marquis requested. Once the troops were landed, Jones was to assist them "by all means in your power." He must stay close: "You are during the expedition never to depart from the troops so as not to be able to protect them or to secure their retreat in case of a repulse." Englishmen captured should be treated with care. "As many of your officers and people have lately escaped from English prisons either in Europe or America, you are to be particularly attentive to their conduct toward the prisoners which the fortune of war may throw in your hands, lest the resentment of the more than barbarous usage by the English in many places towards the Americans should occasion a retaliation, and an imitation of what ought rather to be detested and avoided for the sake of humanity and for the honour of our country." Similar sentiments should inform the captain's conduct in other areas. "Although the English have wantonly burnt many defenceless towns in America, you are not to follow this example, unless where a reasonable ransom is refused, in which case your own generous feelings as well as this instruction will induce you to give timely notice of your intention that sick and ancient persons, women and children may be first removed."

Jones replied that Franklin could count on him. "Your liberal and noble-minded instructions would make a coward brave. You have called up every sentiment of public virtue in my breast, and it shall be my pride and ambition in the strict pursuit of your instructions to deserve success."

Jones, who closed his letter rather fulsomely, even for that gushy era ("I am and shall be to the end of my life, with the most affectionate esteem and respect, Honoured and dear Sir, your most obliged friend and most obedient very humble servant"), seems to have been sincere. He took the ship Sartine provided him, the *Duras*, and rechristened it the *Bonhomme Richard*.

And it was in the *Bonhomme Richard* that Jones made himself an immortal of the waves. Logistics and politics scuttled the invasion of England, leaving Jones to put to sea against the British navy. In September 1779 he locked up in a death struggle against the *Serapis*, a much larger, more heavily armed vessel. Two of Jones's biggest guns exploded in the faces of their gunners at the start of the fight, while the eighteen-pounders of the *Serapis* battered the *Bonhomme Richard*. The captain of the British vessel, convinced he had won, shouted to Jones, offering him the chance to strike his colors. Jones replied defiantly, "No! I'll sink, but I'm damned if I'll strike!" (This was remembered much later by one witness as, "I have not yet begun to fight!" and so transmitted to posterity.)

Realizing that survival required closing with the *Serapis*, Jones rammed his bow into her stern, fastening the two vessels together, starboard to starboard, muzzle to muzzle. While the British guns blasted holes in the *Bonhomme Richard*, Jones's American and French crew climbed the rigging and rained down musket fire and grenades upon the British. One grenade landed in the magazine of the *Serapis*, causing a huge explosion. As the hull of the *Bonhomme Richard* filled with water, the decks of the *Serapis* filled with blood. "The scene was dreadful beyond the reach of language," Jones reported to Franklin. "A person must have been an eyewitness to form a just idea of the tremendous scenes of carnage, wreck and ruin which every where appeared. Humanity cannot but recoil and lament that war should be capable of producing such fatal consequences."

Some of Jones's men thought so too, and implored him to strike the colors before the ship sank and they all died. He ignored their pleas and urged them to redouble their efforts, leading by the example of manning a gun himself. Finally the nerve of the British commander broke. The *Serapis* was Jones's—which was a good thing, since the mortally wounded *Bonhomme Richard* went to a watery grave.

~ Franklin exulted at the news of the victory. "For some days after the arrival of your express," he wrote Jones, "scarce any thing was talked of at Paris and Versailles but your cool conduct and persevering bravery during that terrible conflict."

Glorious as it was, Jones's victory hardly won the war, nor did it much ease the financial strain America—and Franklin—faced. Jones, hoping to capitalize on the good feeling at the French court, asked Franklin to request the money he needed to refit his ship. "I must acquaint you that there is not the least probability of obtaining it," Franklin replied, "and therefore I cannot ask it." Jones did not want merely to fix what was broken but to improve the sea- and battle-worthiness of his vessel by sheathing the hull in copper. "It is totally out of the question," Franklin said. "I am not authorized to do it, if I had the money; and I have not the money for it, if I had orders." Jones was far from the only one calling on Franklin for funds, but he was the latest; as a result he received more than his share of Franklin's frustration. "For God's sake, be sparing, unless you mean to make me a bankrupt."

The alliance with France brought French resources into the conflict on America's side but did not place them at America's disposal. After four years of fighting, the credit of the United States was nearly nil. The

Congress continued to finesse the problem at home—imperfectly, to be sure—by issuing more and more currency. Troops and other creditors of the government could accept the Continental dollars or nothing at all. Franklin, the optimist, perceived a silver lining in the disastrous depreciation of the currency. "Though an evil to particulars, there is some advantage to the public in the depreciation, as large nominal values are more easily paid in taxes."

Foreign governments and individuals were under no compulsion to accept American paper. Indeed they marveled at the Americans' system of financing the war. "The whole is a mystery even to the politicians," Franklin said: "how we have been able to continue a war four years without money, and how we could pay with paper that had no previously fixed fund appropriated specifically to redeem it." Franklin himself sometimes marveled. "This currency as we manage it is a wonderful machine. It performs its office when we issue it; it pays and clothes troops, and provides victuals and ammunition; and when we are obliged to issue a quantity excessive, it pays itself off by depreciation."

At times Franklin felt that Americans' hearts were not really in the struggle—at least as it related to finances. "The extravagant luxury of our country in the midst of all its distresses is to me amazing," he wrote John Jay, president of the Congress. "When the difficulties are so great to find remittances to pay for the arms and ammunition necessary for our defence, I am astonished and vexed to find, upon enquiry, that much the greatest part of the Congress interest-bills come to pay for tea, and a great part of the remainder is ordered to be laid out in gewgaws and superfluities." This was a scandal for America—not to mention a pain for him. "It makes me grudge the trouble of examining, entering and accepting them, which indeed takes a great deal of time."

Franklin chastised his own daughter, Sally, for her part in this national extravagance.

> When I began to read your account of the high prices of goods— a pair of gloves seven dollars, a yard of common gauze twenty-four dollars, and that it now required a fortune to maintain a family in a very plain way—I expected you would conclude with telling me that every body as well as yourself was grown frugal and industrious. And I could scarce believe my eyes in reading forward that there never was so much dressing and pleasure going on, and that you yourself wanted black pins and feathers from France, to appear, I suppose, in the mode!

He refused to indulge her. "If you wear your cambric ruffles as I do, and take care not to mend the holes, they will come in time to be lace; and feathers, my dear girl, may be had in America from every cock's tail."

Sally responded with more than a touch of hurt. She explained she had simply wanted to look presentable when visiting General and Mrs. Washington and the elected officials of the government. "Though I never loved dress so much as to wish to be particularly fine, yet I will never go out when I cannot appear so as to do credit to my family and husband." Perhaps her father did not appreciate what it meant to be driven from home by an enemy army, and how it made her long for her old, settled life. "This winter approaches with so many horrors that I shall not want any thing to go abroad in, if I can be comfortable at home. My spirits, which I have kept up during my being drove about from place to place much better than most people I met with, have been lowered by nothing but the depreciation of the money, which has been amazing lately. So home will be the place for me this winter, as I cannot get a common winter cloak and hat but just under two hundred pounds."

⌐ There was other worrisome news from Philadelphia. Sally's husband, Richard, reported that Franklin's foe Arthur Lee was up to his old machinations. Lee sent the Congress a long memorial asserting that behind Franklin's smooth façade and tremendous popularity he was serving America poorly and was slandering Lee himself besides. Lee described Franklin as a "great politician, at least in the European estimate of that character." With affected sorrow he added, "Would to God he were in the truest sense of the word the greatest politician in Europe! Would to God he were the firmest patriot of the age, and that his talents had been employed with half that assiduity in promoting the cause of his country that his wiles have been in weaving little plots, sowing pernicious dissensions, countenancing and covering the most corrupt and selfish use of all the opportunities which his station furnished!"

Franklin was hardly happy to hear this, but he was beyond wasting energy on Lee. He had never done Lee the slightest injury, he told Bache, nor given any just cause for offense. But a good reputation and popular approval were more than the small minds of Lee and his allies could bear. He would not answer their charges unless the Congress specifically instructed him to do so. "I take no other revenge of such enemies than to let them remain in the miserable situation in which their malignant natures have placed them, by endeavouring to support an estimable character; and thus by continuing the reputation the world has hitherto indulged me with, I shall continue them in their present state of damnation."

Yet there was one part of the campaign against him he could not easily ignore. His critics complained that his employment of Temple amounted to nepotism, and demanded Temple's removal. The allegation was accurate enough (and in keeping with Franklin's fixed habit of employing relatives). This may have been why he rejected it so vociferously. Far from being censured, he told Bache, he should be congratulated. "Methinks it is rather some merit that I have rescued a young man from the danger of being a Tory and fixed him in honest republican Whig principles." Besides, Temple was showing real character and ability and promised in time to be of genuine service to his country.

There was more than this to Franklin's defense of Temple—something much more personal. "It is enough that I have lost my *son*; would they add my *grandson*! An old man of 70, I undertook a winter voyage at the command of the Congress, and for the public service, with no other attendant to take care of me. I am continued here in a foreign country, where, if I am sick, his filial attention comforts me, and, if I die, I have a child to close my eyes and take care of my remains."

Franklin knew that Richard and Sally would be even more interested in hearing of his other grandson. "Ben, if I should live long enough to want it, is like to be another comfort to me," he explained. The younger boy had started at boarding school near Passy, but his grandfather had lately sent him to Geneva. "I intend him for a Presbyterian as well as a republican."

⌒ **One reason** Franklin begrudged his daughter luxuries like pins and feathers was that he heard daily of Americans who lacked even necessaries. Franklin regularly received letters regarding the plight of American prisoners of war held in England. Typically these were sailors captured from American privateers; routinely they were tossed into prison and treated as common felons—and worse, as traitors and pirates.

At times during the eighteenth century, war could be a gentlemanly endeavor. Captured officers were regularly paroled—that is, sent home upon their promise to engage no longer in hostilities. Such had been the fate of General Burgoyne after Saratoga. Soldiers of the rank and file were often exchanged for their counterparts from the other side.

But the British government refused to accord such courtesies to captured Americans. London contended they were not belligerents but rebels. To an early application from Franklin regarding treatment of prisoners, the British ambassador in Paris, Lord Stormont, responded curtly, "The King's ambassador receives no letters from rebels, unless they come to implore his Majesty's mercy."

Such might have finished Franklin's hopes for ameliorating the prisoners' plight, if not for the assistance he gained from others in Britain. The Parliamentary opposition to the North ministry seized on the suspension of habeas corpus, as it related to the American prisoners, and attacked the government for hypocritically undermining essential English institutions in the name of defending them. English prisons were a scandal in the best of times, and though conditions there pricked few consciences regarding regular felons, the harsh treatment accorded the Americans elicited letters to editors and other forms of low-grade protest.

To publicize the prisoners' plight, Franklin sent a special envoy, John Thornton, to England to visit the prisons that held the Americans. Thornton had to bribe his way past the sentries; he did so with money supplied by Franklin. He reported prisoners half naked, constantly hungry, and, in dozens of cases, confined for weeks at a time to the "black holes," cramped, windowless dungeons where "the air doth not only become foul, but the stench sometimes insupportable."

Thornton's report supplied Franklin the basis for initiating a regular program of prisoner relief. English prisoners in those days were required to contribute to the cost of their detention, and while this might be difficult for those from poor families, it was nearly impossible for Americans with families thousands of miles away—families that were often ignorant of the whereabouts of their kin (or even whether the kin were still alive). Franklin diverted monies that might have gone to purchase weapons for Washington's army, creating a fund from which prisoners could draw some eighteen pence per week.

This was a temporary expedient; his larger goal was the release of the prisoners. Until 1779 he had little leverage to apply against the prison doors, lacking much meaningful to trade. But the raids of John Paul Jones, who shared Franklin's concern for the imprisoned Americans, netted hundreds of British sailors. Franklin wrote David Hartley, a member of Parliament who had served as a mediator when Franklin was working with Lord Howe in London before the outbreak of war, and suggested a swap.

The British government, although inclined to respond, did so diffidently. Each man to be released had to receive a pardon for his treason from the king, which took time. During this time recruiters for the Royal Navy attempted to persuade the Americans to defect, painting a grim picture of America's prospects generally and a dire one of theirs personally in the event they were captured again. But finally the exchanges began. One hundred Americans were sent to France, and one hundred Britons returned to Britain. Franklin was encouraged. "This is to continue till all are exchanged," he assured the Congress.

It did not continue nearly that long. The British government, apparently believing that the Americans lost more from having seamen detained than Britain did, threw additional hurdles in the way of the exchanges. It refused to trade Americans for British captured by French vessels or captured in America. After Franklin ran out of qualifying British prisoners, the exchanges clanked to a halt.

So Franklin adopted other—unsanctioned—methods. Escape from English prisons was hardly impossible, especially for Americans who spoke the language and looked like the locals. Sometimes all it took was money to bribe the guards. One successful escapee described how, after "oiling the sentry's conscience," he simply strolled out of prison in a cleric's garb. Franklin funded such ruses, often after the fact.

He also reimbursed sympathizers who helped the escapees get to France. Thomas Digges, a Maryland merchant living in London, frequently took in the fugitives—and frequently wrote Franklin for money. "I cannot describe to you the trouble I have with these people," Digges declared. "And the expence is so heavy on me at times that even with my curtailed and economic mode of living I am put to extreme difficulties. It is not trifles that will do for men who come naked by dozens and half dozens, and it is harder still to turn one's back upon them."

Such was just how Franklin felt, and why he spent the time he did on relatively small numbers of people. Those who solicited his aid discovered he had a soft place in his heart for those in distress. When that distress involved matters of the heart, his own heart was softer still. A young captain named John Lock, who claimed to be an American, was taken from a British vessel by a French ship and imprisoned at Nantes. His fiancée, a fair young Frenchwoman, visited Passy and poured out her feelings. Franklin comforted her and promised to write to French naval minister Sartine. "By the letters that have passed between this Captain and the lady," Franklin explained, "and by her earnestness in her solicitations, I perceive they are passionate lovers, and cannot but wish the obstacles to her union removed, and that there were a great many more matches made between the two nations, as I fancy they will agree better together in bed than they do in ships."

In this case Franklin's sympathies outran his judgment. The damsel's lament was genuine—but woefully ill informed. Her lover was not an American after all, but British. This discrepancy grieved her less than it embarrassed Franklin; what upset *her* was the fact that her handsome captain was already married.

Franklin's face reddened in another instance as well—but from anger more than embarrassment. Although Thomas Digges for a time did honest service on behalf of American escapees, that time terminated well before Franklin's funding did. In 1781 Digges disappeared with £400 Franklin had forwarded for prisoner relief. Franklin could hardly contain himself.

> He that robs the rich even of a single guinea is a villain; but what is he who can break his sacred trust by robbing a poor man and a prisoner of eighteen pence given charitably for his relief, and repeat that crime as often as there are weeks in a winter, and multiply it by robbing as many poor men every week as make up the number of 600? We have no name in our language for such atrocious wickedness. If such a fellow is not damned, it is not worth while to keep a Devil.

≈ **Franklin's** correspondence with David Hartley involved more than prisoner exchanges. A skeptic regarding the war, Hartley continued the pacifying efforts he had begun with Franklin in London in 1775. Hartley communicated confidentially with Lord North, who authorized Hartley to sound Franklin out. The terms offered were not insignificant, starting with what Hartley characterized—certainly with North's approval—as "a tacit cession of independence to America." For now the acknowledgment of independence must remain tacit; Parliament *did* have its pride. But the bridge from tacit to formal was plausible: a suspension of hostilities for a period of from five to seven years, during which time, presumably, minds as subtle as Franklin's ought to be able to find the language to satisfy all parties. The one real hitch for the Americans was Britain's insistence that they abandon their alliance with France.

Hartley made a compelling case for the plan. He quoted Franklin (circa 1775) back to Franklin: "A little time given for cooling might have excellent effects." He pointed out that the proposal committed no one to anything permanent. Should the transition from tacit to formal independence fail, "We can but fight it out at last. War never comes too late." Yet even then something would have been gained—namely, five years of peace. "Peace is a *bonum in se*, whereas the most favourable events of war are but relatively lesser evils." Besides, he could not believe that war would resume once halted. "If the flames of war could be but once extinguished, does not the Atlantic Ocean contain cold water enough to prevent their bursting out again?"

Hartley acknowledged that America's French connection complicated things. Yet Franklin ought to consider carefully the French interest in the affair. Doubtless the *French* did. "There is a certain point, to France, beyond which their work would fail and recoil upon themselves: If they were to drive the British ministry totally to abandon the American war, it would become totally a French war." For now the French alliance might serve America, but not forever—and perhaps not to the point of American independence.

Hartley did not ask Franklin for any commitment, which he supposed Franklin was not, by himself, in any position to give. He asked only for some encouraging sign. And let it come soon. "Peace *now* is better than peace a twelve-month hence, at least by all the lives that may be lost in the mean while and by all the accumulated miseries that may intervene by that delay."

Franklin refused to oblige. This was a better offer, because more authoritative, than the vague hints brought by Paul Wentworth a year earlier. The alliance with France was serving its purpose. Yet the offer was not good enough. Franklin assured Hartley that he remained as devoted to peace as ever. "But this is merely on motives of general humanity, to obviate the evils men devilishly inflict on men in time of war, and to lessen as much as possible the similarity of Earth and Hell." Britain had brought the war upon itself by bringing it on America, and America was not going to abandon the fight on some indefinite promises. The war would continue "till England shall be reduced to that perfect impotence of mischief which alone can prevail with her to let other nations enjoy peace, liberty and safety."

With equal adamance Franklin rejected abandonment of the treaties with France. America owed France a debt of gratitude and justice for taking America's part in time of need. The American alliance with France reflected a general appreciation of this fact; for this reason the alliance would last. "Though it did not exist, an honest American would cut off his right hand rather than sign an agreement with England contrary to the spirit of it."

Reconciliation had once been possible, but no longer. Reminding Hartley of the story of Roger Bacon's mythical brazen head, which held the secret of building a wall around England to defend against invaders but was ignored till too late, Franklin declared that the British government was now in the same situation. "It might have erected a wall of brass round England if such a measure had been adopted when Friar Bacon's brazen head cried out, 'Time is!' But the wisdom of it was not seen till after the fatal cry of 'Time's past!'"

≻ Franklin's defiant mood was easier to maintain in 1779 than it would be for some time thereafter. That spring Spain joined the war. Although the Congress failed to win an alliance, much money, or even recognition of American independence from the court of King Carlos, the fact that Britain now had another fleet to contend with buoyed American hopes.

But things began to go wrong again. Admiral d'Estaing grew tired of guarding General Clinton at New York and sailed away, whereupon Clinton escaped by sea for the American south, to exploit Loyalist sympathies there. He landed in the Carolinas at the beginning of 1780, laying siege to Charleston, the only real city of the entire region. In May, Charleston surrendered, along with an American army of 5,000 and four ships. Morale among the Americans in the neighborhood drooped badly; many availed themselves of Clinton's offer of amnesty in exchange for allegiance to King George. In August, British General Cornwallis routed American troops at Camden, South Carolina, raising the prospect of unraveling the American confederation from the bottom up.

In September even worse news arrived from the north. One of the American heroes of the war had turned coat. Benedict Arnold felt ill treated by the Congress, which jumped several junior officers over him in promotion, and he felt betrayed by the alliance with France, which married America to a bunch of murdering papists (Arnold had fought in the French and Indian War, and although he rejected the rigid Puritanism of his Connecticut youth, he drew the line well short of Rome). He also felt short of cash, having married—after the death of his first wife, while he was fighting the British in 1775—the belle of Philadelphia society (the crowd into which Sarah Bache despaired of fitting without lace and feathers from Paris). Britain offered a remedy for his resentments and his debts, and in the summer of 1779 he began selling secrets to General Clinton. Included was vital information on troop movements and the operations of the French fleet. The following year he obtained command of West Point on the Hudson—"a post in which I can render the most essential services," he informed John André, his British contact. Arnold offered to deliver West Point to Clinton, but the plot was discovered when André was captured with incriminating documents. Arnold fled downriver on a British warship, leaving André to the noose, and Mrs. Arnold, who apparently knew of his treachery and may have assisted in it, to fend for herself. At New York City he was greeted with congratulations and a commission as brigadier general in the British army.

The blow to the patriot cause was profound. "Arnold's baseness and treachery is astonishing!" Franklin declared upon hearing the news.

Nor was that the end of the evil tidings. The winter of 1779–80 had been even worse than the trial at Valley Forge, provoking a springtime mutiny after six weeks of one-eighth rations. In the winter of 1780–81 the mutiny came in January—followed by another three weeks later, and yet another in May. Amid the distress, Franklin received letters from Lafayette and Washington lamenting the lack of basic necessities. "We are naked, shockingly naked, and worse off on that respect than we have ever been," Lafayette wrote. "No cloth to be got. No money. . . . You have no idea of the shocking situation the Army is in." The marquis implored Franklin—"for God's sake, dear Friend"—to find something, anything, for his men to wear.

Washington was less emotional, but his words were the more ominous for that. "I doubt not you are so fully informed by Congress of our political and military state that it would be superfluous to trouble you with any thing relating to either," he told Franklin—before continuing, "If I were to speak on topics of the kind it would be to shew that our present situation makes one of two things essential to us: a peace, or the most vigorous aid of our allies, particularly in the article of money."

Peace or money—after nearly six years of war it had come to that. Washington was not the only one thinking peace; the Congress had appointed John Adams to pursue precisely the kind of cues Franklin had rejected from David Hartley. So far Adams had nothing to show for his efforts, but if the strains on the army continued to increase, he might be forced to find something.

Franklin, believing that a permanent peace would follow only upon a crushing British defeat, opted for the other horn of Washington's dilemma. He appealed once more to Vergennes for money. Franklin had kept the French court apprised of the British overtures lest Louis learn to doubt America's good faith, and also lest Louis forget that America had other suitors; now Franklin prefaced his appeal with a protestation of his country's continued devotion to the common cause. Speaking for the Congress, he declared that it was "the unalterable resolution of the United States to maintain their liberties and independence, and inviolably to adhere to the alliance at every hazard and in every event." Moreover, the misfortunes lately encountered by American arms, far from dampening American ardor, had redoubled it. This said, certain facts were undeniable. He cited the letter he had received from Lafayette about the troops' want of clothing; he quoted Washington about needing either peace or money.

"I am grown old," he explained to Vergennes. His gout had been plaguing him again; he could not say how long he would hold his current office. "I therefore take this occasion to express my opinion to your Excellency that the present conjuncture is critical; that there is some danger lest the Congress should lose its influence over the people if it is found unable to procure the aids that are wanted; and that the whole system of the new Government in America may thereby be shaken." The next several months might determine the fate of America for generations. "If the English are suffered once to recover that country, such an opportunity of effectual separation as the present may not occur again in the course of ages." And on the fate of America hung the fate of Europe. "The possession of those fertile and extensive regions and that vast sea coast will afford them [the British] so broad a basis for future greatness by the rapid growth of their commerce, and breed of seaman and soldier, as will enable them to become the terror of Europe, and to exercise with impunity that insolence which is so natural to their nation, and which will increase enormously with the increase of their power."

Was this what France wanted? It was not what America wanted. But it was what America—and France—would get if French aid failed. "In the present conjuncture, we can rely on France alone."

Franklin asked Vergennes for 25 million livres. He eventually received a promise of 6 million—and a lecture on the difficulty Louis himself was having raising money for France's campaigns. Vergennes also hinted that France was considering a negotiated settlement.

~ It was a most trying period. While Louis pondered his latest plea for money, Franklin wrote to John Adams, then in Holland similarly trying to raise funds. Franklin said he had made his most forceful presentation to the French court, and could only wait. "I have, however, two of the Christian graces: faith and hope. But my faith is only that of which the Apostle speaks, the evidence of things not seen. For in truth I do not see at present how so many bills drawn at random on our ministers in France, Spain and Holland are to be paid, nor that any thing but omnipotent necessity can excuse the imprudence of it." Franklin for one was willing to bow to that omnipotent necessity. "I think the bills drawn upon us by the Congress ought at all risques to be accepted." He would use his best endeavors to scrape together funds to pay the bills as they came due. "And if those endeavours fail, I shall be ready to break, run away, or go to prison with you, as it shall please God."

Franklin was half-joking; at his age he was in no position to break and run. Other days—when his gout, which had been gnawing his toes most of the winter, bit with particular energy—a half joke was more than he could manage. "I have passed my 75th year," he wrote to the Congress, "and I find that the long and severe fit of the gout which I had the last winter has shaken me exceedingly, and I am yet far from having recovered the bodily strength I before enjoyed. I do not know that my mental faculties are impaired; perhaps I shall be the last to discover that. But I am sensible of a great diminution in my activity, a quality I think particularly necessary in your minister for this court. I am afraid therefore that your affairs may some time or other suffer by my deficiency."

Since middle age he had maintained his health by summer vacations; but these he had not been able to take since the war started. Business barred other concessions to advancing years that might have made his existence more bearable.

His time had come. "I have been engaged in public affairs, and enjoyed public confidence in some shape or other during the long term of fifty years, an honour sufficient to satisfy any reasonable ambition, and I have no other left but that of repose, which I hope the Congress will grant me by sending some person to supply my place."

Though his tone belied his words, Franklin disclaimed any doubt regarding the ultimate success of what he called "the glorious cause." But he said the members of the Congress should not expect to see him soon after his replacement arrived. "As I cannot at present undergo the fatigues of a sea voyage, the last having been almost too much for me, and would not again expose myself to the hazard of capture and imprisonment in this time of war, I purpose to remain here at least till the peace, perhaps it may be for the remainder of my life."

He asked one thing of the Congress beyond relief from his duties—one favor to which he thought his service entitled him.

It is that they will be pleased to take under their protection my grandson William Temple Franklin. I have educated him from his infancy, and brought him over with an intention of placing him where he might be qualified for the profession of the law. But the constant occasion I had for his service as a private secretary during the time of the commissioners, and more extensively since their departure, has induced me to keep him always with me.

Without the boy, he could not have managed his work as minister. But the lad had lost so much time in his law studies that he could never recover. Yet he had shown himself adept in foreign affairs, demonstrating sagacity and judgment, a facility in the French language, and a general knowledge of how a minister's office ought to be conducted. One day he would make the Congress a fine minister. "In the mean time, if they shall think fit to employ him as a secretary to their minister at any European court, I am persuaded they will have reason to be satisfied with his conduct, and I shall be thankful for his appointment as a favour to me."

↶ Franklin's gloom persisted into summer. In July 1781 he learned that the Congress had appointed Robert Morris superintendent of American finances. Franklin knew the successful merchant from Philadelphia; they had served together on the Pennsylvania Council of Safety, on the Secret Committee of the Continental Congress, and on the Committee of Secret Correspondence. It was fair to say that Morris had few secrets from Franklin, and these did not include the large profits Morris made—if not at the public expense, then at least from the public treasury. But Morris's profits were no secret from anyone. "He has vast designs in the mercantile way," John Adams remarked. "And no doubt pursues mercantile ends, which are always gain." Yet, speaking of Morris's service in the Congress, Adams added, "He is an excellent member of our body." Morris himself acknowledged his intention to serve self and country at once. "I shall continue to discharge my duty faithfully to the public, and pursue my private fortune by all such honourable and fair means as the times will admit of." Tom Paine attacked Morris in the press for growing fat at a time when Continental troops were growing gaunt. But in the desperation of the winter of 1780–81, Congress suppressed such scruples as some of its members had and handed American finances to Morris, appreciating that while the signature of the president of the Congress meant nothing to the money men, the signature of Morris meant a great deal.

Franklin greeted Morris's appointment with pleasure. "From your intelligence, integrity, and abilities, there is reason to hope every advantage that the public can possibly receive from such an office," he wrote Morris. Yet he warned Morris what he had got himself into—and in doing so transparently revealed an aspect of his own feelings about the nature of public service. "The business you have undertaken is of so complex a nature, and must engross so much of your time and attention as necessarily to injure your private interests; and the public is often niggardly, even of its thanks, while you are sure of being censured by malevolent critics and bug-writers, who will abuse you while you are serving them, and wound your character in nameless pamphlets, thereby resembling those little dirty stinking insects that attack us only in the dark, disturb our repose, molesting and wounding us while our sweat and blood are contributing to their subsistence."

~ **Morris** indeed suffered the sort of abuse Franklin forecast, even as his efforts allowed Washington's army to fight another season. This by itself was a victory, and in keeping with Washington's overall strategy. Despite his continuing worries about money and mutinies, Washington's aim was straightforward: to keep fighting. The longer the rebellion lasted, the less British taxpayers liked it. So far the North ministry had managed to quell the stirrings of revolt in Parliament; how much longer it would be able to do so was an open question.

As Parliament grew impatient, so did Britain's commanders in America. British victories in the south were singly satisfying but added up to nothing. American irregulars prevented a consolidation of British control, leaving Clinton and Cornwallis to conclude that they had overrated the Crown's popularity in that region. Cornwallis, commanding the south after Clinton's return to New York, refused to spend the rest of his career in America. "I am quite tired of marching about the country in quest of adventure," he wrote. "If we mean an offensive war in America, we must abandon New York, and bring our whole force into Virginia. We then have a stake to fight for, and a successful battle may give us America."

With Clinton's approval, Cornwallis headed north, daring Washington to come out and fight. For several weeks Washington declined the dare. The British general swept into Virginia, driving Lafayette from Richmond; but still Washington held back. Cornwallis scattered Steuben's forces; Washington did not move. Cornwallis dispersed the Virginia legislature at Charlottesville, missing the capture of Governor Jefferson at Monticello by a mere ten minutes. Washington remained aloof.

Washington's patience paid off, albeit in an unexpected direction. In August he received word that the long-awaited French fleet under Admiral de Grasse was coming—but not to New York. The French commander had departed the West Indies with twenty-nine warships and 3,000 troops and was bound for the Chesapeake. At once Washington changed plans. He decided to leave Clinton to the comforts of Manhattan, and finally to accept Cornwallis's challenge. For the whole war Washington had fought an enemy who could take to the waves when backed to the beach; the presence of Grasse would erase that disadvantage. "The moment is critical," Washington reported to Congress, "the opportunity precious, the prospects most happily favourable."

Immediately he wrote Lafayette, who became as excited as Washington. "Should a French fleet now come in Hampton Roads," Lafayette predicted, "the British army would, I think, be ours." Washington ordered Lafayette to get south of Cornwallis and prevent at all costs his slipping back into Carolina.

Washington then began preparing his own troops for a dash south. A master of logistics and preparation, he personally mapped the march and tended to every imaginable matter of provisioning and transport. Clinton's spies saw signs of motion in Washington's camp, but the American general spread disinformation indicating that he was simply circling south to assault New York from Staten Island. He sent crews to repair roads and bridges on the Jersey banks of the Hudson. He even constructed a large oven to supply bread to the fictitious attackers. Not till too late did Clinton realize that the object of the preparations was not his army but Cornwallis's.

By the time Washington passed through Philadelphia his destination was plain, but by then the cork was in the bottle. Grasse reached the mouth of the Chesapeake at the end of August, and although contrary winds and his own cautiousness prevented an attack on Cornwallis's rear, the French presence precluded a British naval rescue of Cornwallis.

After the excitement of preparation and marching, the siege of Yorktown, where Cornwallis made his stand, went slowly. Washington wondered what his counterpart was thinking. "Lord Cornwallis's conduct," he remarked in the second week of October, "has hitherto been passive beyond conception. He either has not the means of defence, or he intends to reserve his strength until we approach very near him."

The answer was a bit of both. By night Americans constructed emplacements within cannon shot of the British lines; by day the emplacements came under British fire—until they were completed and could return the fire, eventually silencing the British guns. The work was capriciously dangerous. A lieutenant colonel of the Virginia militia, St. George Tucker, recorded in his diary for October 6, "A man was killed by a cannon ball a day or two past without any visible wound. He was lying with his knapsack under his head which was knocked away by the ball, without touching his head."

On the British side the situation was worse. Cornwallis went underground to escape the bombardment; others took their pounding at the surface. "An immense number of Negroes have died in the most miserable manner," wrote Tucker, after interrogating a refugee from the siege. Desperate work with bayonets accompanied occasional assaults on British redoubts, but mostly the American and French artillery wore the defenders gradually down. American spirits rose accordingly. "Our shot and shell went over our heads in a continual blaze the whole night," wrote an American soldier. "The sight was beautifully tremendous." British spirits traced an inverse arc. "Our provisions are now nearly exhausted and our ammunition totally," read the entry in one British officer's journal for October 16.

Cornwallis was not the man to fight to the death, nor Virginia the place for him to do so. By October 17, when a hundred American and French guns maintained an unceasing barrage, he had had enough. The sheer noise made surrender difficult. Cornwallis put a drummer on the parapet to signal intent to parley, but no one on the American side could hear him. "He might have beat away till doomsday," remarked an American officer. But the white handkerchief attracted attention, and the guns fell silent. The next day the surrender was formalized.

It was exactly four years since the other great American victory of the war, at Saratoga. Heaven itself seemed to endorse the end of the fighting. St. George Tucker described the hours after the surrender:

> A solemn stillness prevailed. The night was remarkably clear and the sky decorated with ten thousand stars. Numberless meteors gleaming through the atmosphere afforded a pleasing resemblance to the bombs which had exhibited a noble firework the night before, but happily divested of all their horror.

The next day the British troops marched out of the fortress. For nearly two miles American troops lined one side of the road, French troops the other. The British band played "Welcome, Brother Debtor" and other tunes, including "When the King Enjoys His Own Again." With a different set of words, the latter was called "The World Turned Upside Down," and it was by this title that Americans remembered it.

26

Blessed Work

1781–82

~ "My God! All is over," moaned Lord North on hearing
the news. Whether he meant the war or his ministry was
not immediately clear; before long any distinction was
moot. Even as King George prayed heaven "to guide me
so to act that posterity may not lay the downfall of this
once respectable empire at my door," the opposition
in Parliament was preparing to lay it at North's. America
was not the only issue causing complaints against
the ministry, but it was the one the complainers could
coalesce about. When a motion for abandonment of the
American cause came within one vote of passage, North
took this as his cue to resign after twelve years in office.
Conventional wisdom was that "Lord North's war"
would follow him off the stage.

It did, but not without effort—much of it Franklin's. The final phase of the conflict took him by surprise. "I wish most heartily with you that this cursed war was at an end," Franklin wrote to one of the British friends with whom he still corresponded, just before news of Yorktown arrived. "But I despair of seeing it finished in my time. Your thirsty nation has not yet drank enough of our blood."

It was with something less than despair, but hardly happiness, that Franklin learned he would have responsibility for bringing the war to an end. The Congress refused his request to retire, instead appointing him to a commission to negotiate a peace. He accepted the appointment from a sense of duty. "I have never known a peace made, even the most advantageous," he told John Adams, one of his fellow peace commissioners, "that was not censured as inadequate, and the makers condemned as injudicious or corrupt. *Blessed are the peace makers* is, I suppose, to be understood in the other world, for in this they are frequently *cursed*. Being as yet rather too much attached to this world, I had therefore no ambition to be concerned in fabricating this peace." All the same, he assured Adams, he deemed it an honor to serve with him in so important a business, and would work to the best of his ability.

The Congress named three peace commissioners besides Franklin and Adams. Thomas Jefferson never joined the group, remaining in America. Henry Laurens was an equally unhelpful choice, having been captured by the British on the Atlantic and currently residing in the Tower of London. John Jay was the fifth member; he, Franklin, and Adams did the bulk of the work.

For the first several months, however, Franklin was the only one of the three in Paris, where the serious talking took place. Adams was in Holland—which had entered the war against Britain, but refused alliance with the United States—trying to pry some guilders out of the Dutch burghers. (Holland's profit-minded approach to diplomacy moved Franklin to remark, "Some writer, I forget who, says that Holland is no longer a *nation* but a *great shop*; and I begin to think it has no other principles or sentiments but those of a shopkeeper.") John Jay was in Madrid having comparable bad luck with the Spanish, who likewise had declared war on Britain but likewise spurned the Americans. (Franklin urged Jay to hold firm against Spain's efforts to take advantage of America's distress, especially regarding the Mississippi. "Poor as we are," he said, "yet as I know we shall be rich, I would rather agree with them to buy at a great price the whole of their right on the Mississippi than sell a drop of its waters. A neighbour might as well ask me to sell my street door.")

The instructions from the Congress to the peace commissioners stipulated two nonnegotiable conditions: acknowledgment of America's independence and the continuation of the treaty with France. The rest was left to the discretion of the commissioners. At the time the instructions were drafted—June 1781—Americans could hardly hope for more. But the victory at Yorktown improved America's prospects, and Franklin intended to exercise his discretion to the utmost.

Yet even as Washington reinforced Franklin's bargaining position, Arthur Lee sapped it. Lee had not wanted Franklin to have anything to do with peace talks, and contended that his appointment as commissioner came only "by the absolute order of France"—as communicated by the French minister in Philadelphia, the Chevalier de la Luzerne. "At this very time, Congress had the fullest evidence and conviction that Dr. Franklin was both a dishonest and incapable man," Lee asserted. Several members of the Congress had registered concern at the terms of Franklin's commission, with its instruction to cling to France. "He, good man," Lee continued sarcastically, "felt no qualms at such a commission, no sense of dishonour or injury to his country. On the contrary, he expressed the utmost alacrity in accepting it, and I believe most cordially, since it puts him in the way of receiving money, which is the God of his idolatry." As to what this meant for America, "The yoke is riveted upon us. . . . The French therefore are to make peace for us."

Lee's libels were an extreme version of a sentiment widely shared: that Franklin was unduly partial to France. John Adams thought so. As an early anti-British radical, Adams was hardly an apologist for Britain. "They hate us, universally from the Throne to the footstool," he said, "and would annihilate us, if in their power." Yet Adams was equally skeptical of the French. In Adams's worldview, nations had no friends, only interests. French interests had motivated the alliance with America; French interests—rather than any attachment to republican values, for instance—would continue to motivate French policy after the war. And *American* interests dictated creating a certain distance from France now that the war was nearly over. Adams's skepticism was no secret. "He tells me himself," Franklin reported to Congress, "that America has been too free in expressions of gratitude to France; that she is more obliged to us than we to her; and that we should shew spirit in our applications."

John Jay felt similarly. He believed that Vergennes was deliberately delaying the negotiations, from a desire to extend American dependence on France. "It was evident the Count did not wish to see our independence acknowledged by Britain until they had made all their uses of us,"

Jay told Robert Livingston, the American foreign secretary, after an interview with Vergennes. Jay saw no reason to share his insight with the French. "We ought not to let France know that we have such ideas; while they think us free from suspicion they will be more open, and we should make no other use of this discovery than to put us on our guard."

Franklin had long since stopped answering criticism directed at his person, and he probably would have let the allegations of Francophilia pass had they not threatened what he considered to be essential American interests. "Your enemies industriously publish that your age and indolence have unabled you for your station," Robert Morris wrote; "that a sense of obligation to France seals your lips when you should ask their aid; and that (whatever your friends may say to the contrary) both your connections and influence at Court are extremely feeble." Morris said he related this information as a friend, but he added that many in Congress believed the allegations. Moreover, those who censured Franklin were the ones most vocal in their censure of France.

Franklin responded that he was "extremely sorry" to hear the railing against France, as it tended to hurt "the good understanding" that had existed between the governments of France and the United States. "There seems to be a party with you that wish to destroy it. If they could succeed, they would do us irreparable injury." The help of France had been crucial to America's success at arms, and it remained crucial to America's success at diplomacy. "It is our firm connection with France that gives us weight with England, and respect throughout Europe. If we were to break our faith with this nation, on whatever pretence, England would again trample on us, and every other nation despise us." Franklin acknowledged the prudence of allowing the British to hope for a reconciliation with their former colonies, but America's polestar must be Paris. "The true political interest of America consists in observing and fulfilling, with the greatest exactitude, the engagements of our alliance with France."

∼ The negotiations began in earnest with the arrival of Richard Oswald in France in April 1782. Oswald was the representative of the new ministry in London, which was headed by Lord Rockingham and included Charles James Fox as foreign minister and Lord Shelburne as secretary of state for home and colonial affairs. Oswald impressed all who knew him with his honesty and fair-mindedness. Henry Laurens—

writing from his London cell—called him "a gentleman of the strictest candour and integrity." Vergennes asserted, "He is a wise man who seems not to have even the idea of intrigues. Rich himself, devoid of ambition, he has yielded to his friendship for Lord Shelburne in coming here, and he does not claim other recompense than the glory of rendering a useful service to his homeland and to humanity."

Franklin was initially more guarded in his judgment. He granted that Oswald *appeared* "wise and honest," but he questioned the purpose of his mission. The fact that Oswald proposed to talk to him alone—apart from Vergennes—indicated a desire to separate America from France. Such a separation Franklin refused to allow. "I let him know that America would not treat but in concert with France," Franklin recorded in his journal of the negotiations.

Oswald did not dispute this. But he would never have received his present appointment had he been so easily dissuaded. "I told the Doctor I made no doubt that was the case," Oswald wrote. "Yet I could not see but it was in the power of the commissioners of the colonies, by meeting and consulting together, to smooth the way to an equitable settlement of general negotiation, by framing some particular points separately regarding Great Britain." This would be no more than an efficient use of time.

There *was* more, however. Oswald suggested that once the issue of American independence was settled, reconciliation between the two branches of the English-speaking people could take place quickly; it ought not be delayed by issues concerning only the French. Britain had its pride, and if the French confused British weariness for war in America with unwillingness to defend British interests against French encroachment, they would rue their error—and so would the Americans, if they tied themselves to France. "In case France should make demands too humiliating for England to submit to, the spirit of the nation would be roused, unanimity would prevail, and resources would not be wanting."

Franklin begged to differ. The issue of independence was *already* settled, he said. It had never been in question in American minds since 1776; and if Britain was slow to acknowledge the obvious, that was the problem of the king and Parliament. Britain said it desired *reconciliation*. "It is a sweet word." But it meant more than mere peace and required more than a termination of hostilities. For six years Britain had waged a cruel and unjust war upon America; not surprisingly, Americans harbored a great deal of resentment against Britain. Would his countrymen demand reparation for property destroyed by British troops? For homes and villages burned by Britain's Indian allies? Franklin did not presume to say. "But would it not be better for England to offer it? Nothing would have a greater tendency to conciliate, and much of the future commerce and returning intercourse between the two countries may depend on the reconciliation. Would not the advantage of reconciliation by such means be greater than the expence?"

What might be fair reparation? Franklin answered his own query: Canada. Britain could hardly get more from Canada in furs and other items of export than it cost her to defend and govern the province. Americans could make far better use of it. Franklin appreciated that Britain might not wish to give up Canada at the insistence of the United States; he acknowledged the role pride played in human affairs. But why not *offer* Canada without being asked, as a token of Britain's sincerity regarding reconciliation? Such an offer would have "an excellent effect" in America. It would settle the issue of reparations—and at the same time provide, through Canadian land sales, the means by which the Loyalists might be indemnified for loss of their estates.

If Oswald was surprised at the audacity of Franklin's opening offer, he diplomatically cloaked his feelings. He congratulated Franklin on the forthrightness of his statement, and the two agreed that Oswald ought to relay the message personally to Shelburne in London. Franklin had written out his position in advance; Oswald, explaining that his own paraphrase could not do justice to Franklin's own wording, asked to take Franklin's paper with him. He assured the author it would be returned safely. Franklin, though reminding Oswald that the American commission comprised others besides himself, and that these would have to be consulted before any decisions could be made, at length agreed.

Franklin's initial skepticism of Oswald had vanished. "We parted exceeding good friends," he recorded. To Shelburne he declared, "I desire no other channel of communication between us than that of Mr. Oswald, which I think your Lordship has chosen with much judgment." Franklin hoped that the secretary of state, replying through Oswald, would be as frank and serious as he himself had tried to be. "If he is enabled, when he returns hither, to communicate more fully your Lordship's mind on the principal points to be settled, I think it may contribute much to the blessed work our hearts are engaged in."

⌒ Blessed the work may have been, but complicated. Oswald returned in the first week of May with the news that Shelburne had read

Franklin's proposal with real interest. Oswald relayed that Shelburne had evinced surprise that a reparation was even under consideration, and he wondered if the Americans were going to demand it. Franklin, of course, had not said they would; and now Oswald tried to ensure that they would *not*. Speaking confidentially, he said—and subsequently repeated—that he thought the question of Canada would be settled to the Americans' satisfaction at the end of the negotiations. But if they brought it up at the beginning it might snarl the talks irreparably.

Franklin was not sure what to make of this. Was Oswald speaking for Shelburne or simply for himself? "On the whole," he wrote in his journal, "I was able to draw so little from Mr. Oswald on the sentiments of Lord Shelburne, who had mentioned him as entrusted with the communication of them, that I could not but wonder at his being sent again to me."

Franklin's wonder increased upon the arrival of a second envoy. The new man was young—only twenty-seven—and just recently elected to Parliament. But he was obviously well connected, for he was the son of Franklin's nemesis, George Grenville. And he was well tutored, in that his instructions from Charles Fox indicated precisely how he was to conduct himself. Thomas Grenville was to determine whether the diplomatic distance between Franklin and Vergennes remained as small as it appeared to Oswald, and to do everything in his power to increase it. In secret instructions to young Grenville, Fox explained:

> After having seen Mons. de Vergennes you will go to Dr. Franklin, to whom you will hold the same language as to the former, and as far as his country is concerned there can be no difficulty in shewing him that there is no longer any subject of dispute and that if unhappily this treaty should break off his countrymen will be engaged in a war in which they can have no interest whatever either immediate or remote. It will be very material that, during your stay at Paris, and in the various opportunities you may have of conversing with this gentleman, you should endeavour to discover whether, if the treaty should break off or be found impracticable on account of points in which America has no concern, there may not in that case be a prospect of a separate peace between G. Britain and America, which after such an event must be so evidently for the mutual interests of both countries.

Grenville's first efforts in this direction failed. Franklin ushered him to a meeting with Vergennes; when Grenville proposed that Britain formally acknowledge American independence in exchange for a return to the territorial status quo ante bellum, Vergennes smiled. The offer of independence amounted to nothing, he said. "America does not ask it of you. There is Mr. Franklin; he will answer you as to that point."

Franklin obliged. "We do not consider ourselves as under any necessity of bargaining for a thing that is our own," he said, "which we have bought at the expense of much blood and treasure, and which we are in the possession of."

Britain would have to do better, Vergennes continued. And as for a return to the status quo, had Britain been thus contented after the last war? That war had started over minor disputes regarding the Ohio and Nova Scotia; it ended with Britain taking Canada, Louisiana, and Florida, not to mention her gains in the East Indies. A country that gambled on war, Vergennes suggested, must accept its losses.

Grenville answered that France had provoked the present war by encouraging the Americans to revolt. "On which the Count de Vergennes grew a little warm," Franklin recorded, "and declared, firmly, that the breach was made, and our independence declared, long before we received the least encouragement from France; and he defied the world to give the smallest proof of the contrary. 'There sits,' said he, 'Mr. Franklin, who knows the fact, and can contradict me if I do not speak the truth.'"

This was cleverly worded. Vergennes did not ask Franklin to vouch for his statement with a positive assertion, which would have required Franklin to lie. In fact France *had* encouraged the American revolt, secretly supplying money long before the Declaration of Independence. Franklin, as a member of the Committee of Secret Correspondence, knew this perfectly well. Vergennes, as the moving spirit behind the money, knew he knew. Grenville may have known too, from British spies in America or France. On the other hand, as young and new to the game as Grenville was, he may *not* have known it. In any event, he did not call Vergennes's bluff.

Vergennes suspected there must be more to Grenville's mission than this initial unacceptable offer. France had entered the war not simply for America's sake; it expected to regain some of what it had lost the last time out. And, having done so, it was not about to give those gains back. Surely Grenville—and his superiors—realized this. Noting Grenville's antecedents, Vergennes wrote to the French ambassador in Spain, "He belongs to an important family which is connected by interest with the present ministry, and it is not very likely that the latter would intend him for a role so dull and so little analogous to his birth and his condition as that of coming to amuse and delude us."

Amusing, deluding, or otherwise, Grenville pursued Franklin back to Passy. Following Fox's instructions, he pointed out that America had accomplished its goal of independence, and he contended that America therefore had no reason to continue fighting. For the Americans to cling too closely to France would be to risk reopening the war for reasons that had nothing to do with American interests.

Franklin replied with a small lecture on debt and gratitude.

A, a stranger to B, sees him about to be imprisoned for a debt by a merciless creditor. He lends him the sum necessary to preserve his liberty. B then becomes the debtor of A and, after some time, repays the money. Has he then discharged the obligation? No. He has discharged the money debt, but the obligation remains, and he is a debtor for the kindness of A, in lending him the sum so seasonably. If B should afterwards find A in the same circumstances that he, B, had been in when A lent him the money, he may then discharge this obligation or debt of kindness, *in part*, by lending him an equal sum. *In part*, and not *wholly*, because when A lent B the money there had been no prior benefit received to induce him to it. And therefore if A should a second time need the same assistance, B, if in his power, is in duty bound to afford it to him.

Grenville rejoined that Americans would carry gratitude very far to apply this personal calculus to politics among nations. France, he pointed out, was the party that benefited by America's separation from Britain, as that separation materially weakened Britain and comparatively strengthened France.

Franklin responded that he was so strongly impressed by the kind assistance France afforded America in her time of trial, and by the generous and noble manner in which it was given, without the French exacting a single privilege in return, that he never entertained reasons to lessen the American obligation to France. He added that he did not doubt that his countrymen were all of the same sentiment.

"Thus he gained nothing of the point he came to push," Franklin recorded of Grenville. "We parted, however, in good humour."

In many respects the peace negotiations resembled a game of chess, a pastime of which Franklin was famously fond. The tale of his chess match with a friend in Madame Brillon's bathroom, which went on for hours while she watched from her tub, was a favorite around Paris. (Later tellings often elided that French tubs in those days had wooden covers, which shielded the bather's body from view.) His penchant for bending the rules when occasion indicated—as with the Duchess of Bourbon—was esteemed a charming foible. When one opponent, a Frenchman, checked his king, Franklin illegally ignored the check and moved another piece. Called on the violation, Franklin declared, "I see he is in check, but I shall not defend him. If he was a good king, like yours, he would deserve the protection of his subjects; but he is a tyrant and has cost them already more than he is worth. Take him, if you please. I can do without him, and will fight out the rest of the battle *en républicain*."

On another occasion he and one of the abbés who lived with Madame Helvétius were playing a game far into the night when the last candle sputtered down. The abbé assumed that the game would end. "My dear abbé," said Franklin, "it is impossible for two men such as us to stop merely because of lack of light." The abbé recalled where some candles were stored, and proposed to fetch them, even in the dark. "Go, then," Franklin encouraged, "and may the goddess of the night protect you in your adventurous course." In the abbé's absence, even as the candle flickered its last, Franklin rearranged the pieces to guarantee himself the victory. The abbé returned with the candles, lit one, and registered dismay at his hopeless position. Franklin chuckled and said, "The goddess of night has just answered my prayers and has sent one of Mercury's agents here to aid me while you were gone."

Franklin added to his chess lore with a written reflection on the subject. *The Morals of Chess,* printed on his Passy press, was more serious than some of the other bagatelles, but hardly ponderous. "Life is a kind of chess," he explained, "in which we have often points to gain, and competitors and adversaries to contend with, and in which there is a vast variety of good and evil events that are, in some degree, the effects of prudence or the want of it." In playing chess a person could learn foresight. "If I move this piece, what will be the advantages of my new situation? What use can my adversary make of it to annoy me?" Likewise circumspection, "which surveys the whole chessboard, or scene of action, the relations of the several pieces and situations, the dangers they are respectively exposed to." Also caution, in that once a piece was touched, that piece must be moved, and once a piece was set down, there it must stand. "If you have incautiously put yourself into a bad and dangerous position, you cannot obtain your enemy's leave to withdraw your troops and place them more securely; but you must abide all the consequences of your rashness."

Players must exercise good sportsmanship. "You must not, when you have gained a victory, use any triumphing or insulting expression, nor show too much pleasure; but endeavour to console your adversary, and make him less dissatisfied with himself by every kind and civil expression." Finally, players must remember that the best victory was not over the opponent but over oneself. A player might point out where the other slipped and graciously suggest a more effective move. "You may indeed happen to lose the game to your opponent, but you will win what is better: his esteem, his respect, and his affection, together with the silent approbation and good will of impartial spectators."

British negotiators in France certainly saw this essay. How Richard Oswald and Thomas Grenville interpreted it is hard to know. Was the army of Cornwallis a chess piece placed rashly and the British government the player that had to abide the consequences of the rashness? Who was the victor to whom magnanimity in triumph was recommended? Whose esteem was being sought? Franklin left them to guess.

⌒ **British** officials saw much more from Franklin's pen than his bagetelles. As a civil conflict the Revolutionary War was fertile soil for secret agents. The differences of language and culture that typically separate countries at war did not exist; patriots and loyalists looked alike, sounded alike, dressed alike. And—despite the nomenclature applied to the opposing parties—questions of patriotism and loyalty were often clouded. A Frenchman selling secrets to England during the Seven Years' War, for example, could be expected to have to wrestle harder with his conscience than an American cleaving to King George during the Revolutionary War. There is no evidence, and little reason to believe, that William Franklin's conscience was any less clear than his father's.

The elder Franklin was a prime target for British espionage. As minister to France he was the hinge of the alliance upon which the conflict turned; as peace commissioner (especially until the arrival of John

Adams and John Jay) he was the person who knew, or would determine, how far America could be pushed at the peace table. It would pay the British government greatly to learn this vital information.

And the British government in turn would pay to acquire this information. London found its man in Edward Bancroft. Nearly forty years Franklin's junior, Bancroft had been born in humble circumstances in Westfield, Massachusetts. When the boy was two his father died, in a pigsty of an epileptic seizure. His stepfather owned a tavern in which young Edward grew up; such schooling as he received was largely makeshift and self-administered. (Significantly, part of the formal portion came at the tutelage of Silas Deane.) Bancroft taught himself chemistry; his aptitude for the science was revealed in a path-breaking book on the chemistry of color and in a patent that promised to ruin the market for Carolina indigo. He also apprenticed to a doctor, eventually becoming a charter member of the Medical Society of London. Meanwhile he found time to sojourn in South America, a journey that provided the material for a natural history of Guiana and its peoples.

Bancroft's travels terminated, for the time being, in London, where, as a bright and inquisitive American transplant, he fell in with Franklin, who took to him at once. Franklin recommended Bancroft to the editor of the *Monthly Review*, in which Bancroft reported on American politics. Franklin introduced Bancroft to friends Pringle, Priestley, and others. Franklin successfully sponsored Bancroft for election to the Royal Society. Franklin even brought Bancroft in on the scheme to win a charter for the colony on the Ohio. Bancroft was present at Franklin's inquisition in the Cockpit and was one of the few persons who defended Franklin in the London papers in the matter of the Hutchinson letters.

This last activity may have been what cemented Franklin's friendship for Bancroft and inclined him to trust Bancroft with sensitive information regarding American affairs. When the Committee of Secret Correspondence appointed Silas Deane its agent in Europe, Franklin drafted instructions directing Deane to Bancroft. "From him you may obtain a good deal of information of what is now going forward in England," Franklin wrote, cautioning Deane to be as circumspect as Franklin was sure Bancroft would be.

Bancroft was circumspect, all right, but not in the manner Franklin anticipated. Bancroft was one of that middling group that saw little to choose between the colonies and the mother country in their escalating quarrel, and when the quarrel became a war he determined that whichever side won, he would too. Perhaps it was his association with Deane that alerted him to the prospect of profiting from the war; perhaps the provincial in the great city simply developed expensive tastes. But in either case, even while he was furnishing information to Deane—and after Franklin and Lee joined Deane in France, to the three commissioners together—about affairs in England, he supplied intelligence to the British ministry about the doings of the American commissioners. He later claimed that the role of the double agent was "as repugnant to my feelings as it had been to my original intentions," but the stipends he received from both sides evidently assuaged his distaste. The British paid better, for while Franklin supplied him only a secretary's salary, the British added a premium for the risk he was running; he ultimately received £1,000 per annum, with a promise of a permanent pension of £500.

In a postwar memorandum to the British government, Bancroft described his activities.

> I went to Paris, and during the first year, resided in the same house with Dr. Franklin, Mr. Deane etc., and regularly informed this Government of every transaction of the American Commissioners; of every step and vessel taken to supply the revolted colonies with artillery, arms etc.; of every part of their intercourse with the French and other European courts; of the powers and instructions given by Congress to the Commissioners; and of their correspondence with the Secret Committees etc.

When the Franco-American treaties were signed, Bancroft sped the news to London. When Admiral d'Estaing left Toulon with the French fleet, bound for America, London learned through Bancroft. After Yorktown, as Franklin and the other American peace commissioners devised strategy for dealing with the French and the British, the attentive Bancroft sent back reports that supplemented those of Oswald and Grenville.

Bancroft delivered his information by various means. Because Franklin and the other Americans thought he was spying for *them*, they did not begrudge his frequent visits to England, where he communicated directly with government officials. While in Paris he sometimes met with Paul Wentworth, Franklin's interlocutor and Britain's European spymaster. On other occasions he left messages in a sealed bottle secreted in the hollow of a tree on the south side of the Tuileries.

The British were pleased with Bancroft's work. They raised his stipend; as the peace negotiations neared a close, one of Bancroft's

British handlers called him "a valuable treasure to government" both as a source of intelligence regarding the Americans and as an indirect and unacknowledged means of influencing the American negotiating position.

For this reason the British ignored the fact that Bancroft had a third employer he served at least as diligently as he did the Americans and the British: himself. The value of various issues on the London stock exchange rose and fell, often sharply, on news from the battle front. Bancroft was uniquely placed to anticipate such news, and he used it to his advantage. Learning early of the travails of Burgoyne in the forests of New York in the autumn of 1777, he wrote to a speculator friend who evidently bet on a drastic drop in share prices, which duly followed. Although Bancroft did not volunteer information about his profits, Wentworth noted he had grown suddenly rich.

Arthur Lee suspected Bancroft of disloyalty to the American cause, but Franklin did not (perhaps partly because the paranoid Lee *did*). Franklin blithely confided in Bancroft information that doubtless damaged the American cause. Yet the damage could not have been especially great, for Franklin adopted a characteristic attitude regarding the possibility of espionage. Early in his stay at Paris he received a letter from an Englishwoman once resident in Philadelphia, now living in France. She apparently shared his politics, for she warned him against those who did not. "You are surrounded *with Spies*, who watch your every movement, who you visit, and by whom you are visited," she wrote. "Of the latter there are who pretend to be friends to the cause of your country but *that* is a mere pretence." She said her own security prevented her from being more explicit. "But of the truth of what I inform you, you may strictly rely."

Franklin responded diplomatically—and philosophically—to her advice.

> As it is impossible to discover in every case the falsity of pretended friends who would know our affairs; and more so to prevent being watched by spies, when interested people may think proper to place them for that purpose, I have long observed one rule which prevents any inconveniences from such practices.
>
> It is simply this: to be concerned in no affairs that I should blush to have made public, and to do nothing but what spies may see and welcome. When a man's actions are just and honourable, the more they are known, the more his reputation is increased and established. If I was sure, therefore, that my *valet de place* was a spy,

as he probably is, I think I should probably not discharge him for that, if in other respects I liked him.

Franklin remarked elsewhere that when rascals proliferated, honest men might prosper. "If the rascals knew the advantage of virtue, they would become honest men out of rascality." For himself, speaking the truth served admirably. "That is my only cunning."

⁓ Although Bancroft was an inadvertent link to London, others were deliberate. Even during the worst of the war Franklin had not severed all ties to England. He exchanged letters, of course, with David Hartley regarding prisoners and peace prospects. He communicated occasionally with William Strahan—a communication strained by the political rift that separated these erstwhile intimate friends.

In 1781 Franklin resumed a correspondence with Edmund Burke that had been briefly interrupted. Burke wrote in this instance on behalf of his friend General Burgoyne, who had been paroled to England after Saratoga but subsequently had his parole revoked. The general was liable to be returned to America. Burke did not deny that Burgoyne had prosecuted the war vigorously and capably. But in doing so, he said, the general had simply been following the king's directives and the soldier's code. Acknowledging the irregular character of his request, Burke nonetheless asked that Franklin intercede. "If I were not fully persuaded of your liberal and manly way of thinking," he wrote, "I should not presume, in the hostile situation in which I stand, to make an application to you. But in this piece of experimental philosophy, I run no risque of offending you. I apply, not to the Ambassador of America, but to Doctor Franklin the Philosopher; my friend; and the lover of his species."

Franklin answered in like tone. "Since the foolish part of mankind will make wars from time to time with each other, not having sense enough otherwise to settle their differences, it certainly becomes the wiser part, who cannot prevent those wars, to alleviate as much as possible the calamities attending them." As it happened, Franklin had just received authorization from the Congress to offer Burgoyne's freedom in exchange for that of Henry Laurens. Lacking formal relations with the appropriate ministers in London, Franklin forwarded the offer to Burke. "If you can find any means of negotiating this business, I am sure the restoring another worthy man to his family and friends will be an addition to your pleasure."

Unfortunately for Burgoyne—and Laurens—the ministry in London was not ready for the swap. "Difficulties remain," Burke replied in February 1782. But the growing Parliamentary opposition to the war gave Burke, a leader of that opposition, hope that the prisoner issue might soon become moot. "I trust it will lead to a speedy peace between the two branches of the English nation, perhaps to a general peace; and that our happiness may be an introduction to that of the world at large."

Other Franklin connections to England were unrelated to the war. Benjamin Vaughan was a young admirer and casual acquaintance; in 1779 he published in London a collection of Franklin's works. On the title page he violated British usage, if not British law, in identifying Franklin as the minister at the court of Paris of "the United States of America." Vaughan lamented England's folly in letting Franklin—and America—slip away. "Can Englishmen read these things [that is, Franklin's works], and not sigh at recollecting that the country which could produce their author was once without controversy *their own!*"

Franklin kept loose touch with the Royal Society. He sent the group an occasional paper and read their transactions. In the summer of 1782 he took time from the peace negotiations to reply to a letter from the president of the society. "Be assured that I long earnestly for a return of those peaceful times when I could sit down in sweet society with my English philosophical friends," Franklin wrote. The memory of those days filled him with delight. "Much more happy should I be thus employed in your most desirable company than in that of all the grandees of the earth projecting plans of mischief, however necessary they may be supposed for obtaining greater good." In this letter Franklin allowed himself a fond hope. "If proper means are used to produce, not only a peace, but what is much more interesting, a thorough reconciliation, a few years may heal the wounds that have been made in our happiness, and produce a degree of prosperity of which at present we can hardly form a conception."

⌑ Franklin's sentiments were not always so elevated. His press at Passy may have produced humorous and moral essays, but it also produced propaganda, occasionally of the most virulent and scurrilous sort. In the spring of 1782 Franklin began circulating a "Supplement to the

Boston *Independent Chronicle.*" Complete with local notices and advertisements, the publication carried readers straight to the streets of the Massachusetts capital.

But what really got their attention was a letter from Albany, written by a captain of militia named Gerrish. The alert officer related his interception of a shipment from the Seneca Indians to the British governor of Canada. "The possession of this booty first gave us pleasure," Gerrish wrote, "but we were struck with horror to find among the packages 8 large ones, containing SCALPS of our unhappy country-folks." There were hundreds of the grisly items, inventoried in a bizarre missive from the chief of the Senecas to the Canadian governor (helpfully transcribed by a British trader).

No. 1. Containing 43 scalps of Congress soldiers, killed in different skirmishes. . . . Also 62 of farmers killed in their houses . . . a black circle all around to denote their being killed in the night. . . .

No. 2. Containing 98 of farmers killed in their houses . . . great white circle and sun to show they were surprised in the daytime, a little red foot to show they stood upon their defence and died fighting for their lives and families.

No. 3. Containing 97 of farmers . . . killed in their fields. . . .

No. 4. Containing 102 of farmers . . . 18 marked with a little yellow flame to denote their being of prisoners burnt alive, after being scalped, their nails pulled out by the roots, and other torments. . . .

No. 5. Containing 88 scalps of women, hair long . . . 17 others very grey . . . knocked down dead or had their brains beat out.

No. 6. Containing 193 boys' scalps, of various ages . . . bullet-marks, knife, hatchet or club, as their deaths happened.

No. 7. 211 girls' scalps, big and little. . . .

No. 8. This package is a mixture of all the varieties above-mentioned, to the number of 122. . . . 29 little infants' scalps of various sizes . . . ripped out of their mothers' bellies.

As if this all were not shocking enough, the Seneca chief urged the governor to forward the tribute to London. "We wish you to send these scalps over the water to the great king, that he may regard them and be refreshed; and that he may see our faithfulness in destroying his enemies and be convinced that his presents have not been made to ungrateful people."

The whole business was absolutely appalling—and utterly false. There was no such shipment, and no such message for King George.

Yet Franklin, the author of the hoax, defended it as grounded in the reality of the warfare the Indians waged at Britain's behest. "The *form* may perhaps not be genuine," he admitted to a French friend, to whom he sent copies for distribution. "But the *substance* is truth; the number of people of all kinds and ages murdered by them being known to exceed that of the invoice. Make any use of them you may think proper to shame your Anglomanes, but do not let it be known through what hands they come."

◦— Franklin's propaganda may have changed a few minds but, coming this late in a long war, probably not many. It certainly did not change the positions of his counterparts in the peace negotiations.

Such a change required a substantive shift in the balance of military power—which, as matters transpired, took place in the spring of 1782. Following the allied victory at Yorktown, one who made it possible, the formerly cautious but now overconfident Grasse, sailed south to the West Indies, where he suffered a devastating defeat. In the Battle of the Saintes the admiral himself was captured, and the British gained what Charles Fox called, without excessive braggadocio, "the most important and decisive victory that has happened during the war."

Meanwhile, the Spanish effort to recapture Gibraltar stalled. Spain had entered the war hoping to win various prizes from the British, but the one that obsessed the Spanish was the monolith that guarded the passage from the Atlantic to the Mediterranean. Though ownership of the great rock had strategic implications, to Spain it was mostly a matter of pride. Unfortunately, Spanish pride had availed little so far against British cannons and the tunnels that shielded them.

In the summer of 1782 the Spanish mounted what promised to be their final offensive—however it turned out. Novel floating batteries were built to carry Spanish guns to sea; Spanish ships were massed in support. John Adams wrote from Holland that the Spanish ambassador there "trembled for the news we should have from Gibraltar." Well he might have, Adams thought, saying he himself had "no expectation at all" of a Spanish victory. "The earnest zeal of Spain to obtain that impenetrable Rock, what has it not cost the House of Bourbon this war? And what is the importance of it? A mere point of honour! A trophy of insolence to England and of humiliation to Spain!"

Adams's apprehensions proved out; the attack failed. This left France in an awkward position. Louis had promised to fight on Spain's side till the British were evicted from Gibraltar, yet on current trends that might take years—or generations. How long must France wait for this quixotic quest to succeed?

Vergennes had to consider something else. The Americans were tied to France directly, by the Franco-American treaty, but they were tied to Spain indirectly, by the Franco-Spanish treaty. There was no love lost between Spain and America, and if Vergennes clung to Spain too closely too long, the Americans might cut themselves loose of France— Franklin's protestations of friendship to the contrary notwithstanding.

A final factor complicated things further. Russia had sat out the war, more or less, behind the protection of its "league of armed neutrality." While Britain and France fought each other, Catherine the Great prepared to gobble up the Crimea. Vergennes, knowing the czarina's appetite, earnestly desired to keep her from this next meal. But doing so required the cooperation of the British. Needless to say, as long as Britain and France were fighting in the Atlantic, cooperation in the Black Sea would be problematic.

In short, by the autumn of 1782 Vergennes had concluded that time was no longer on France's side. Within limits, the sooner the present war drew to an end, the better.

As the shape of these events came into view, Vergennes shifted his position on the idea of separate negotiations. With feigned magnanimity he told Franklin the French court was resisting British efforts to deal with the Americans through France. "They want to treat with us for you, but this the king will not agree to. He thinks it not consistent with the dignity of your state. You will treat for yourselves; and every one of the powers at war with England will make its own treaty. All that is necessary for our common security is that the treaties go hand in hand, and are signed on the same day."

The British, perhaps alerted by Bancroft, responded at once to the new state of affairs. Richard Oswald, with what seemed to Franklin "an air of great simplicity and honesty," explained the dire financial straits into which Britain had fallen during the present war. "Our enemies may now do what they please with us," he confided. "They have the ball at their foot." Only Franklin, as representative of America, could extricate

England from its predicament. Indeed, Oswald said, it was perhaps the case that no single man ever possessed the power to do so much good as Franklin possessed at this moment.

Oswald assured Franklin that Shelburne shared this view, and showed him a letter from Shelburne saying as much. Oswald went on to say that he—Oswald—had told the ministers in London that however much they might seek Dr. Franklin's assistance, they must not ask him to do anything unsuitable to his character or inconsistent with his duty to his country. "I did not ask him the particular occasion of his saying this," Franklin recorded, "but thought it looked a little as if something inconsistent with my duty had been talked of or proposed."

That something Franklin inferred from a memorandum Oswald showed him, written by Shelburne and mentioning "a final settlement of things between Great Britain and America, which Dr. Franklin very properly says requires to be treated in a very different manner from the peace between Great Britain and France, who have always been at enmity with each other." In other words, a separate peace with the Americans was at the top of London's list.

Franklin did not reject the British overture, but neither did he accept it at face value. Nor did he conceal it from Vergennes. The two diplomats discussed Britain's efforts to drive them apart, and agreed on the prudence of their keeping together. Franklin—either from an honest suspicion of Britain's bona fides or from a desire to assure Vergennes of *America's* good faith—suggested that the British strategy of peacemaking might conceal a desire to conclude treaties with all parties, the better to isolate one to make war on after the treaties were signed. Egregiously exceeding his instructions, Franklin recommended that the four countries at war with Britain ought to enter into a new treaty, pledging all to the defense of each in the event of just such an English subterfuge. Vergennes concurred, noncommittally.

Following this nod to allied solidarity, Franklin pressed toward a settlement with Britain. He took pains to ensure that the British government acknowledge the independence of the United States *prior* to the commencement of formal negotiations, lest London try to count this as a concession compelling something of similar weight from the Americans. On this point Franklin demonstrated an ability to split hairs with the sharpest bargainers.

In early July he got down to particulars. He supplied Oswald with two lists. The first comprised matters he described as "necessary" to a peace treaty; the second, elements "advisable." Heading the necessary list was independence—"full and complete in every sense." An immediate corollary of independence was the evacuation of all British troops from American soil. Next was a definitive determination of the boundaries of the American states and of the British colonies of Canada. Related to this was the retreat of the boundaries of Canada to what they had been before the Quebec Act of 1774. Finally, Britain must recognize the rights of Americans to fish on the banks off Newfoundland, as they had for centuries. Franklin explained that these items were nonnegotiable, and he spent little time discussing them.

The advisable list—"such as he would as a friend recommend to be offered by England," was how Oswald paraphrased Franklin to Shelburne—required greater explanation. It started with a reparation payment to Americans ruined by the burning of towns and the destruction of farms. Franklin suggested £500,000 or £600,000 as a reasonable figure. "I was struck at this," Oswald recorded, and he indicated as much to Franklin. Franklin answered that it sounded like a large sum but in fact would be money well spent. "It would conciliate the resentment of a multitude of poor sufferers who could have no other remedy, and who without some relief would keep up a spirit of secret revenge and animosity for a long time to come against Great Britain."

Second of the advisables was a public acknowledgment by Britain of its error in distressing America so. "A few words of that kind would do more good than people could imagine," Franklin said.

Third was a free-trade compact between Britain and America. American ships should have the same privileges in British ports as British ships; British ships should trade in American ports as equals with American ships.

Fourth and finally, Britain should cede Canada to the United States. In British hands Canada would become the bone of contention in Anglo-American relations it had long been in Anglo-French relations. Better to bar such quarrels by transferring Canada to the United States at once.

It was not lost on Oswald that Franklin's position here was firmer than it had been in April. At that time Franklin had been vague on the boundaries of Canada and suggested using proceeds from the sale of Canadian land to compensate the Loyalists. Now he was adamant that Canada did not stretch south of the Great Lakes—which meant, in effect, that the western boundary of the United States must be the

Mississippi River. And he offered nothing to the Loyalists beyond a vague statement that the commissioners might recommend recompense to the separate states.

Oswald delivered Franklin's terms to Shelburne, who, following the unexpected death by influenza of Rockingham, was suddenly prime minister. (The same influenza gripped John Jay, recently arrived in Paris from Spain but now incapacitated by illness.) Shelburne therefore spoke with enhanced authority when he indicated general acceptance of Franklin's necessary terms. If the Americans could be persuaded to drop Franklin's advisable articles, Shelburne said, the treaty might be "speedily concluded."

In fact it was concluded, for the most part on Franklin's necessary terms, but not as speedily as Shelburne or Franklin hoped. John Jay recovered sufficiently to register suspicion that things were moving *too* quickly (why were the British suddenly so accommodating?). Jay insisted on stronger guarantees of American independence in the language of Oswald's commission. Without informing Franklin he sent an envoy to London to insist on a new commission, which Shelburne, still eager to move the talks along, granted.

Jay was no more trusting of the French. "This Court chooses to postpone an acknowledgment of our independence by Britain, to the conclusion of a general peace," he wrote Congress president Robert Livingston, "in order to keep us under their direction until not only their and our objects are attained, but also until Spain shall be gratified in her demands." Candor compelled him to a further comment: "I ought to add that Doctor Franklin does not see the conduct of this Court in the light I do, and that he believes they mean nothing in their proceedings but what is friendly, fair and honourable."

Franklin was disinclined to argue the matter. The same lifestyle that had given him gout now inflicted a kidney stone that bloodied his urine and made travel, even from Passy to Versailles, most painful. For several weeks Jay took the lead in the negotiations; Franklin, persuaded that nothing important was at stake in Jay's bustling about, gave the younger man his head.

The arrival of John Adams from Holland at the end of October complicated matters further. Whether Adams was more distrustful of France or of Franklin was hard to say; to him they seemed the same. By contrast, Jay seemed to Adams to be exhibiting a salutary "firmness and independence" toward France. "Between two as subtle spirits as any in this world, the one malicious [Franklin], the other I think honest [Jay], I shall have a delicate, a nice, a critical part to act," Adams told his diary. "Franklin's cunning will be to divide us. To this end he will provoke, he will insinuate, he will intrigue, he will maneuvre." Adams did not hide his preference for Jay over Franklin. After a conversation with Franklin, he recorded, "I told him without reserve my opinion of the policy of this Court, and of the principles, wisdom and firmness with which Mr. Jay had conducted the negotiation in his [Franklin's] sickness and my absence, and that I was determined to support Mr. Jay to the utmost of my power in the pursuit of the same system."

If Adams expected a fight, Franklin disappointed him. Having received the approval of Vergennes himself to talk separately with the British, he declined to dispute with Jay and Adams when they proposed to do just that, despite instructions from the Congress to the contrary. More to the point, he understood how close the principal parties were to a settlement. After a long war, if there would be quibbling, he would leave it to his fellow commissioners.

The quibbling lasted a month. At the end of November the Americans and British reached a settlement both sides could accept. It included all of Franklin's necessary conditions, as well as a guarantee of American navigational rights on the Mississippi. (Whether Spain would honor the guarantee where the river cut through Spanish territory remained unanswered.) In exchange the Americans agreed to recognize debts owed British merchants from before the war and to recommend to the states fair treatment of the Loyalists.

The settlement was only preliminary, not to take effect without a general settlement among all the warring parties. But that was merely a matter of time. For the United States the Paris pact marked an eminently satisfactory outcome to a conflict that had often threatened to end in disaster. The independence of the United States was now recognized by the world; American territory reached from the Atlantic to the Mississippi. In other words, America's present was safe and its future assured.

Best of all, the bloodshed and destruction were over. This prospect, more than anything else, was what inclined Franklin not to argue for the last advantage from either Britain or France. He could congratulate himself and his fellow commissioners for what they had accomplished at Paris, and he could applaud his fellow Americans for what they had won on the battlefield. But he remained utterly unconvinced of the efficacy of war as a general endeavor. If anything, the conflict just concluding reinforced his opposite feeling. Some months earlier he had received a letter from his old friend Jonathan Shipley hoping that the peace talks might soon bear fruit. Franklin seconded the hope, coining a motto that would forever be associated with his name. "After much occasion to consider the folly and mischiefs of a state of warfare," Franklin wrote, "and the little or no advantage obtained even by those nations who have conducted it with the most success, I have been apt to think that there has never been, nor ever will be, any such thing as a *good* war, or a *bad* peace."

27

Savant

1783–85

~ In March 1783 Franklin wrote Shipley again.
By this time the other belligerents had called an armistice,
and Franklin looked forward to a definitive conclusion to
the conflict between Shipley's country and his.

Let us now forgive and forget. Let each country seek its advancement in its own internal advantages of arts and agriculture, not in retarding or preventing the prosperity of the other. America will, with God's blessing, become a great and happy country; and England, if she has at length gained wisdom, will have gained something more valuable, and more essential to her prosperity, than all she has lost.

Yet Franklin doubted England really *had* learned anything from the war. Her "great disease," he said, was the large number and emoluments of her political offices; her downfall the "avarice and passion" these aroused in her public officials. "They hurry men headlong into factions and contentions, destructive of all good government." As long as riches attached to office, Britain would suffer. "Your Parliament will be a stormy sea, and your public councils confounded by private interests."

For Franklin the essence of the American Revolution was not simply self-rule for the former colonies, necessary though that was. The essence of the Revolution was the triumph of virtue over vice. In the years before the Revolution he had watched corruption permeate British politics; on that fateful morning in the Cockpit he had felt corruption's foul breath. He knew himself to be the most reluctant of revolutionaries, an ardent Briton driven from the arms of the mother country only by a deep, personal disillusionment. Others of the Revolutionary generation subscribed to the notion of America's peculiar virtue, but for few did it have the personal meaning it had for Franklin, because few had been so disillusioned.

The emotional counterpart to Franklin's disillusionment with Britain was his investment of hope in America. For Franklin the Revolution *had* to be about more than self-rule, for self-rule was, at bottom, simply another form of office-seeking. On the other hand, if the Revolution was about virtue, and the application of virtue to politics, then the struggle became transcendent. "Our Revolution is an important event for the advantage of mankind in general," he wrote his English friend Richard Price. Mankind already showed evidence of following the American lead. The summer of 1783 brought murmurings of anti-British rebellion in Ireland; Franklin credited "the contemplation of our successful struggle" as a central element in the resistance. He went on to reflect with satisfaction "that liberty, which some years since appeared in danger of extinction, is now regaining the ground she had lost; that arbitrary governments are likely to become more mild and reasonable, and to expire by degrees."

The patriot in Franklin might have been willing to accept American virtue on its face, but the philosopher demanded explanation. Franklin knew Americans—and Britons—well enough to recognize that on human merits there was little to distinguish the one people from the other. After chiding William Strahan for Britain's faults, he declared, "My dear friend, do not imagine that I am vain enough to ascribe our success to any superiority in any of these points." So what *did* account for the

American victory, if not the virtue of Americans? The virtue of that for which Americans fought. "If it had not been for the justice of our cause, and the consequent interposition of Providence, in which we had faith, we must have been ruined." With half a smile, one imagines, Franklin suggested that it was enough to drive a man to religion. "If I had ever before been an atheist, I should now have been convinced of the being and government of a Deity!"

∂— Franklin's interpretation of the Revolution as the victory of virtue made him worry at news that American virtue might be slipping. Robert Morris wrote of difficulty getting the states to pay their shares of national obligations. "The remissness of our people in paying taxes is highly blamable," Franklin replied; "the unwillingness to pay them is still more so." Franklin knew what the victory had cost in terms of American commitments, not least because he had been the one making most of those commitments. He hated to see Americans trying to disavow them. When tax resisters justified their opposition on grounds that the government was taking money out of their pockets, he countered that they were fundamentally mistaken. "Money, justly due from the people, is their creditors' money, and no longer the money of the people, who, if they withhold it, should be compelled to pay."

For one subsequently cited as an apostle of capitalist virtues, Franklin took a strikingly socialistic view of property. "All property, indeed, except the savage's temporary cabin, his bow, his match-coat, and other little acquisitions absolutely necessary for his subsistence, seems to me to be the creature of public convention," he wrote. Laws and customs made accumulation of property possible; the public therefore had the right to regulate the quantity and use of property. "All the property that is necessary to a man for the conservation of the individual and the propagation of the species is his natural right, which none can justly deprive him of; but all property superfluous to such purposes is the property of the public, who by their laws have created it, and who may therefore by other laws dispose of it whenever the welfare of the public shall demand such disposition." Needless to say, this was hardly a universal opinion among a people who had fought a war over taxes. But Franklin was unmoved. "He that does not like civil society on these terms, let him retire and live among savages."

When Samuel Cooper wrote from Boston that the Massachusetts

legislature had consented to pay up, Franklin replied with congratulations—and scorn for those states that remained in arrears. The latter put Franklin in mind of the improvident Quaker who pleaded poverty in not repaying the principal on a debt and conscience in not paying interest. His creditor damned him for a rogue, saying, "You tell me it is against your principle to pay interest, and it being against your interest to pay the principal, I perceive you do not intend to pay me either one or t'other."

Virtue in paying America's debts would have tangible benefits; a failure of virtue would exact material costs. In May 1784, following the final ratification of the peace treaty, Franklin wrote Charles Thomson, the secretary of Congress, that "the great and hazardous enterprise we have been engaged in is, God be praised, happily completed, an event I hardly expected I should live to see." Though the war had been hard, peace would quickly restore the country—assuming Americans kept their faith. If they failed in this regard, the vultures of the world, starting with the British, would be waiting. "If we do not convince the world that we are a nation to be depended on for fidelity in treaties, if we appear negligent in paying our debts, and ungrateful to those who have served and befriended us, our reputation, and all the strength it is capable of procuring, will be lost, and fresh attacks upon us will be encouraged."

~ An obvious and easy form of virtue was frugality. Beneficial in itself, it would help Americans pay their debts and redeem their foreign promises. In his letter to Thomson, Franklin warned against America's being "enervated and impoverished by luxury," and he lauded frugality as practical patriotism.

This was an old argument from Franklin. At seventy-eight years of age, he might have been thought to have little new to say on the subject. Yet such was his subtlety and flexibility of mind, and such his skepticism even of his own long-held opinions, that in the middle of speaking for frugality he was willing to find virtue in its opposite. Benjamin Vaughan, his English editor, had inquired if Franklin knew a remedy for the American penchant for luxury, on which Vaughan had heard travelers remark disapprovingly. Franklin replied that he knew of no such remedy, then added that the problem was much exaggerated, and in any event might not be a problem at all. "Is not the hope of being one day able to purchase and enjoy luxuries a great spur to labour and industry? May not luxury, therefore, produce more than it consumes?" Even the clearest cases of squandering resources might not be so clear after all. "A vain, silly fellow builds a fine house, furnishes it richly, lives in it expensively, and in a few years ruins himself. But the masons, carpenters, smiths and other honest tradesmen have been by his employ assisted in maintaining and raising their families; the farmer has been paid for his labour and encouraged; and the estate is now in better hands."

Franklin told a story from his own experience to illustrate the point. Decades ago the skipper of a Cape May shallop had done Franklin and Deborah a favor for which he refused payment. Deborah knew he had a daughter, and bought a cap for the girl. Three years later the captain, accompanied by a farmer friend, visited the Franklins. The captain said his daughter liked her cap very much. "But it proved a dear cap to our congregation," he added.

"How so?" inquired Franklin.

"When my daughter appeared with it at meeting, it was so much admired that all the girls resolved to get such caps from Philadelphia; and my wife and I computed that the whole could not have cost less than a hundred pounds."

The farmer broke in. "But you do not tell all the story. I think the cap was nevertheless an advantage to us, for it was the first thing that put our girls upon knitting worsted mittens for sale at Philadelphia, that they might have wherewithal to buy caps and ribbons. And you know that industry has continued, and is likely to continue and increase to a much greater value, and answer better purposes."

To which Franklin added, in his letter to Vaughan, "Upon the whole, I was more reconciled to this little piece of luxury, since not only the girls were made happier by having fine caps, but the Philadelphians by the supply of warm mittens."

~ Speculation on economics complemented Franklin's musings on other matters. For a decade his political and diplomatic labors had largely kept him from philosophy, but the conclusion of the peace talks allowed a return to his true intellectual passion. In 1784 he sent a paper to the Literary and Philosophical Society of Manchester, entitled "Meteorological Imaginations and Conjectures," which showed that his ability to reason from everyday observation to important insight about the natural world had not diminished. "There seems to be a region high in the air over all countries, where it is always winter, where frost exists continually," he wrote. The evidence? Hail, which fell even during the warmest months and occasionally acquired impressive dimensions. "How immensely cold must be the original particle of hail which forms the future hailstone, since it is capable of communicating sufficient cold, if I may so speak, to freeze all the mass of vapour condensed round it, and form a lump of perhaps six or eight ounces in weight!"

The winter of 1783–84 had been the coldest in many years. Franklin linked it to a "dry fog" that had been observed throughout the Northern Hemisphere the previous summer—which, he conjectured, was no fog at all but smoke from the Hecla volcano in Iceland, spread by the prevailing winds. Whatever its source, this persistent pall had diminished the solar energy reaching the earth, to such a degree that when concentrated by a burning (or magnifying) glass, the sun's rays that summer scarcely kindled brown paper. The surface of the earth consequently never acquired the heat that typically moderates winter weather, Franklin explained; hence the bitter season that followed.

This surprisingly modern account of the weather was followed by an even more ambitious explanation of phenomena physicists would still be puzzling over two centuries later. "Universal space, as far as we know of it, seems to be filled with a subtle fluid, whose motion, or vibration, is called light," Franklin wrote in a letter read to the American Philosophical Society. The vibrations of light—sunlight, for example—heated objects on which the light fell by causing the particles of those objects to vibrate in turn. Franklin used the word "fire" to denote a combination of electromagnetic, kinetic, and chemical energy—a combination about which he was rather vague (and, in fact, confused). He was not sure whether this "fire" was something material or immaterial (although in this he unknowingly anticipated the Einsteinian equivalence of mass and energy). But he hit on a fundamental law of conservation of mass-energy. "Thus, if fire be an original element, or kind of matter, its quantity is fixed and permanent in the world. We cannot destroy any part of it, or make addition to it; we can only separate it from that which confines it, and so set it at liberty, as when we put wood in a situation to be burnt; or transfer it from one solid to another, as when we make lime by burning stone, a part of the fire dislodged from the wood being left in the stone."

As always he mixed practical matters with the theoretical. Michel Guillaume Jean de Crèvecoeur, the author (under the pseudonym J. Hector St. John) of the *Letters from an American Farmer*, wrote for advice on the establishment of a packet service between France and America.

Franklin offered suggestions on the number of vessels necessary to maintain monthly service (five: four in regular service, one for backup), and on design. He had read of Chinese boats whose interiors were divided into separate watertight sections, and he urged Crèvecoeur to construct his boats similarly. "In which case if a leak should happen in one apartment, that only would be affected by it, and the others would be free; so that the ship would not be so subject as others to founder and sink at sea. This being known would be a great encouragement to passengers." With his letter he enclosed a map of the Atlantic Ocean showing the Gulf Stream as charted by himself and others.

In a concession to advancing age Franklin had taken to using two sets of eyeglasses, one for close work, the other to see things at a distance. This was never convenient, but Franklin found it particularly irksome in traveling, when he would shift his gaze from a book or paper he was reading to a distant object he wished to observe. After considering the matter for some time, he directed his optician to take one pair of each of his spectacles and cut the lenses in half horizontally. Two each of these half-lenses were then fitted together in a single set of wire frames, with the farsighted halves on top and the nearsighted on the bottom. "By this means," he explained, "as I wear my spectacles constantly, I have only to move my eyes up or down, as I want to see distinctly far or near, the proper glasses being always ready." The invention brought an unexpected bonus. "This I find more particularly convenient since my being in France, the glasses that serve me best at table to see what I eat, not being the best to see the faces of those on the other side of the table who speak to me; and when one's ears are not well accustomed to the sounds of a language, a sight of the movements in the features of him that speaks helps to explain; so that I understand French better by the help of my spectacles."

What Franklin called his "double spectacles" (others would call them "bifocals") assisted his observation of the most celebrated invention of the last two decades of the eighteenth century. For millennia men and women had watched clouds waft across the sky, many wondering what held those mountains of vapor aloft. In the early 1780s the Montgolfier brothers, sons of the famous papermaker Peter Montgolfier of Annonay, attempted to duplicate nature's feat by capturing a cloud in a light bag, which was then carried aloft. Their cloud consisted not of water vapor but of smoke from burning straw, yet it served the purpose, carrying the brothers' paper bag high into the air. Tickled, they graduated to larger bags, or balloons, sewn of linen or silk impregnated with a sealant, and experimented with other forms of lift, including "inflammable air," or hydrogen.

Ballooning became an overnight sensation. The summer of 1783 saw numerous variants of the basic concept; these drew large crowds in Paris. Franklin recorded an August launch.

> Not less than five thousand people were assembled to see the experiment, the Champ de Mars being surrounded by multitudes, and vast numbers on the opposite side of the river. At five o'clock notice was given to the spectators, by the firing of two cannon, that the cord was about to be cut. And presently the globe was seen to rise, and that as fast as a body of twelve feet diameter, with a force of only thirty-nine pounds, could be supposed to move the resisting air out of its way. There was some wind, but not very strong. A little rain had wet it, so that it shone and made an agreeable appearance. It diminished in apparent magnitude as it rose, till it entered the clouds, when it seemed to me scarce bigger than an orange, and soon after became invisible, the clouds concealing it.

The crowd went home well pleased; the balloon eventually landed in a field outside a village whose inhabitants, uninformed of the science involved, mistook the luminous globe for a monster and attacked it with stones, scythes and knives, rending it irreparably.

Weeks later another balloon went up from Versailles. Hot air lifted this one; suspended beneath the sack was a basket holding a sheep, a duck, and a rooster. The unwitting aeronauts survived their flight in fine health (a wing wound to the rooster was attributed to a prelaunch kick from the sheep).

If animals could fly, so could humans. On December 1 Franklin joined thousands of others to witness the momentous event. As he recorded:

> All Paris was out, either about the Tuileries, on the quays and bridges, in the fields, the streets, at the windows, or on the tops of houses, besides the inhabitants of all the towns and villages of the environs. Never before was a philosophical experiment so magnificently attended.

Some guns were fired to give notice that the departure of the great balloon was near, and a small one was discharged, which went to an amazing height, there being but little wind to make it deviate from its perpendicular course, and at length sight of it was lost.

Means were used, I am told, to prevent the great balloon's rising so high as might endanger its bursting. Several bags of sand were taken on board before the cord that held it down was cut, and the whole weight being then too much to be lifted, such a quantity was discharged as to permit its rising slowly. . . .

Between one and two o'clock, all eyes were gratified with seeing it rise majestically from among the trees, and ascend gradually above the buildings, a most beautiful spectacle. When it was about two hundred feet high, the brave adventurers held out and waved a little white pennant, on both sides their car, to salute the spectators, who returned loud claps of applause. . . .

When it arrived at its height, which I suppose might be three or four hundred toises [fathoms], it appeared to have only horizontal motion. I had a pocket-glass, with which I followed it, till I lost sight, first of the men, then of the car, and when I last saw the balloon, it appeared no bigger than a walnut.

The commencement of flight carried humanity into what Franklin predicted would be "a new epoch." Public expectations were readily raised—and as easily dashed. A Dutch admirer of Franklin, Jan Ingenhousz, wrote for specifics, with a mind toward launching balloons himself. Franklin included a warning with the information. "It is a serious thing to draw out from their affairs all the inhabitants of a great city and its environs, and a disappointment makes them angry. At Bordeaux lately a person pretended to send up a balloon, and received money from many people, but not being able to make it rise, the populace were so exasperated that they pulled down his house and had like to have killed him." (Franklin's grandson Benjamin Bache, now thirteen and on leave from studies in Switzerland, recorded something similar in Paris after a balloon caught fire and failed to ascend. "The people were furious and threw themselves upon the balloon, and tore it in pieces, each one carrying off a sample, some large enough to make a mattress; and I believe the authors would have been subjected to the same fate if they had not been escorted by a detachment of French guards.") When skeptics derided the new invention as a mere toy, of no practical use, Franklin uttered a *mot* that quickly circulated throughout Europe. What good was a balloon? demanded one critic. "What good is a newborn baby?" Franklin replied.

As one recently responsible for making war and peace, Franklin was intrigued by the possibility that balloons might become instruments of the former—and thereby of the latter. Seventeen decades before the development of the theory of nuclear deterrence, Franklin identified its essence in the discovery of balloon flight. "Convincing sovereigns of the folly of wars may perhaps be one effect . . ." he wrote, "since it will be impracticable for the most potent of them to guard his dominions. Five thousand balloons, capable of raising two men each, could not cost more than five ships of the line, and where is the prince who can afford so to cover his country with troops for its defence as that ten thousand men descending from the clouds might not in many places do an infinite deal of mischief before a force could be brought together to repel them?"

⌒ **Even more** amazing than flying was "animal magnetism." Franklin was indirectly responsible for this strangest enthusiasm of prerevolutionary Paris, somewhat to his chagrin. Its principal author, Friedrich Anton Mesmer, had studied medicine at Vienna during the period when Franklin's electrical experiments were becoming known on the European continent. Like many of Franklin's readers from the Poor Richard days, Mesmer believed in astrology; having learned from Franklin how lighting carried celestial energy to earth, he easily concluded that electricity provided an invisible but pervasive fluid that linked the stars to human lives. Unfortunately for both his scientific theory and his medical practice, electricity was unpleasant to patients, sometimes violently so. But Mesmer was resourceful, and substituting magnetism for electricity as the invisible transmitter, he developed a flourishing practice stroking patients with magnets. In time he dispensed with the magnets, relying simply on his own powers of persuasion to release the therapeutic effects of "animal magnetism."

Mesmer arrived in Paris about a year after Franklin did, and to the dismay of the medical establishment he quickly cultivated a large and devoted following. The king's brother, the queen, and such other notables as Lafayette flocked to his group-therapy sessions, which featured hypnosis, apparitions, and messages from beyond the horizon of the quotidian world; typically the groups dissolved into mass hysteria, to the shrieking delight of all present. Wealthy older women and attractive younger ones were particularly susceptible to the spells of the handsome Austrian—a fact not lost on their husbands and fathers.

Mesmer's success infuriated the French medical establishment, which denied him a license and sought means to banish him. The government stayed out of the doctors' spat until Mesmer created a joint stock company to promote his teachings, and raised a subscription of more than 300,000 livres. This moved the animal magnetism debate from the court of science to that of fraud.

In March 1784 King Louis appointed a committee of the Paris faculty of medicine to investigate; the distinguished members included Joseph Ignace Guillotin, who would add a word to several languages by his advocacy of the use of a swift and thereby comparatively humane decapitation machine. The doctors decided they needed help from the Academy of Sciences, whereupon Louis added five members, including the great chemist Lavoisier—who would meet his end at the device endorsed by Dr. Guillotin—and the eminent American, Dr. Franklin.

Franklin had met Mesmer before, in the company of Madame Brillon. Mesmer employed Franklin's armonica for background music during his séances, and Franklin naturally took an interest. He and Madame Brillon quickly determined that though Mesmer knew little about electricity or magnetism, he played the armonica passably. In her response to one of Franklin's descriptions of an afterlife in which he and she would consummate their love, Madame Brillon remarked, "In heaven, M. Mesmer will content himself with playing the armonica and will not bother us with his electrical fluid!"

Franklin did not altogether deny the efficacy of Mesmer's techniques, though he questioned the Austrian's explanation. The human body was a marvelous mechanism, Franklin told a person who had asked his opinion of Mesmer, and all the more marvelous for being connected to the human mind.

> There being so many disorders which cure themselves, and such a disposition in mankind to deceive themselves and one another on these occasions, and living long having given me frequent opportunity of seeing certain remedies cried up as curing every thing, and yet soon after totally laid aside as useless, I cannot but fear that the expectation of great advantage from this new method of treating diseases will prove a delusion.

That delusion may, however, and in some cases, be of use

while it lasts. There are in every great rich city a number of persons who are never in health, because they are fond of medicines and always taking them, whereby they derange the natural functions and hurt their constitutions. If these people can be persuaded to forbear their drugs in expectation of being cured by only the physician's finger or an iron rod pointing at them, they may possibly find good effects, though they mistake the cause.

The royal investigation commenced in the spring of 1784. It was complicated by Mesmer's refusal to participate. He left the demonstration of his techniques to a disciple, Dr. Charles Deslon, but cleverly distanced himself from Deslon, saying the doctor had borrowed his ideas yet lacked a full understanding of them. In other words, if the commission believed Deslon, he—Mesmer—would be vindicated; if Deslon fell, Mesmerism would still stand.

Franklin's kidney stone prevented his leaving Passy, so Deslon and the commission came to him. The Mesmeric cure was applied to several patients with maladies ranging from asthma to tumors. The results were ambiguous at best. In one of the more dramatic moments of the experiment, Deslon purportedly magnetized an apricot tree in Franklin's garden. A blindfolded twelve-year-old boy was then led to four unmagnetized trees, which he embraced, one after the other, to determine the magnetism they contained. At the first tree he sweated and coughed. At the second he said he felt dizzy and his head hurt. At the third his head hurt more and he reported feeling the magnetism growing (although he was in fact moving farther from the test tree). At the fourth tree he fainted, which terminated the experiment.

Franklin and the commissioners filed their report, with his name heading the list of signatures. A public version was hurried into print, and twenty thousand copies were snatched up. The report declared the claims of animal magnetism unproven; such mitigation of symptoms as appeared were due to the customary causes of self-delusion and ordinary remission.

A second version of the report was read to the Academy of Sciences but otherwise kept confidential. It addressed the moral—which was to say, sexual—dangers to women of the Mesmer approach. "Touch them in one point, and you touch them everywhere," it noted suggestively and most disapprovingly. By all means, the practice of animal magnetism must be discouraged.

The Franklin report did just that. A contemporary engraving showed Franklin and his colleagues delivering a copy of their report; the document radiated a magnetic force of its own that overturned Mesmer's apparatus, to the discomfiture of his patients, including one half-dressed and blindfolded woman. Mesmer and Deslon were shown fleeing the scene, the former on a broomstick, the latter on a winged donkey.

Yet Franklin was not so sure what he and the commission had accomplished. "The report is published and makes a great deal of talk," he wrote Temple. "Every body agrees it is well written, but many wonder at the force of imagination described in it, as occasioning convulsions &c., and some fear that consequences may be drawn from it by infidels to weaken our faith in some of the miracles of the New Testament. . . . Some think it will put an end to Mesmerism. But there is a wonderful deal of credulity in the world, and deceptions as absurd have supported themselves for ages."

↜ **Franklin** preferred philosophy, but diplomacy insisted. As ranking American minister in Europe, he carried the burden of counseling emigrants to the new nation on what to expect. And a burden it was. "I am pestered continually," he wrote Charles Thomson, "with numbers of letters from people in different parts of Europe who would go to settle in America but who manifest very extravagant expectations, such as I can by no means encourage, and who appear otherwise to be very improper persons." To save himself trouble Franklin composed and printed a pamphlet entitled *Information to Those Who Would Remove to America.* The pamphlet's nominal purpose was to correct common misconceptions about America; it also served as a confession by Franklin as to what America stood for.

First among the misconceptions was that Americans were rich but ignorant, able, and willing to shower wealth upon Europeans with the slightest ingenuity. Second was the belief that with so many new governments and so few families of standing, the thirteen states must have hundreds of offices available to well-born Europeans willing to cross the water. Third was the notion that the new governments bestowed land gratis on strangers, complete with livestock, tools, and slaves. "These are all wild imaginings," Franklin declared, "and those who go to America with expectations founded upon them will surely find themselves disappointed."

What was the reality? "Though there are in that country few people so miserable as the poor of Europe, there are also very few that in

Europe would be called rich. It is rather a happy mediocrity that prevails." Americans were far from ignorant; their country supported nine colleges or universities and numerous academies. The several states did employ many people, but those employed often served at personal sacrifice. "It is a rule established in some of the states that no office should be so profitable as to make it desirable."

Birth counted for next to nothing in America. "People do not enquire, concerning a stranger, *What is he?* But *What can he do?* If he has any useful art, he is welcome; and if he exercises it and behaves well, he will be respected by all that know him; but a mere man of quality, who on that account wants to live upon the public by some office or salary, will be despised and disregarded." This practical outlook colored every aspect of American life. "The people have a saying, that God Almighty is himself a mechanic, the greatest in the universe; and he is respected more for the variety, ingenuity and utility of his handiworks than for the antiquity of his family."

The only encouragement offered to strangers was what derived from liberty and good laws. Who came without a fortune must work to eat. "America is the land of labour, and by no means what the English call *Lubberland*, and the French *Pays de Cocagne*, where the streets are said to be paved with half-peck loaves, the houses tiled with pancakes, and where the fowls fly about already roasted, crying, *Come eat me!*"

Who, then, *should* travel to America? "Hearty young labouring men, who understand the husbandry of corn and cattle. . . . Artisans of all the necessary and useful kinds. . . . Persons of moderate fortunes and capitals, who having a number of children to provide for, are desirous of bringing them up to industry." Such people would find opportunities for material improvement unequaled in Europe.

They would find something else as well. America was a land where virtue grew among the corn. "Industry and constant employment are great preservatives of the morals and virtue of a nation. Hence bad examples to youth are more rare in America, which must be a comfortable consideration to parents." Comforting too was the encouragement American liberty and tolerance afforded to real religion. "Atheism is unknown there, infidelity rare and secret, so that persons may live to a great age in that country without having their piety shocked by meeting with either an atheist or an infidel. And the Divine Being seems to have manifested his approbation of the mutual forbearance and kindness with which the different sects treat each other, by the remarkable prosperity with which he has been pleased to favour the whole country."

⁓ **Loose ends** remained from the war. They entangled Franklin, who was still trying to resign, and they threatened to entangle the United States. The peace treaty had not even been initialed when Vergennes complained that the Americans had deceived and disappointed him. Yes, he had accepted that they might negotiate with the English separately from France, but he had no idea they would actually conclude a separate settlement. "I am rather at a loss, sir, to explain your conduct," the self-possessed foreign minister declared to Franklin, in what for him amounted to outrage. "You have concluded your preliminary articles without informing us, although the instructions of Congress stipulate that you do nothing without the participation of the King." Appealing to Franklin's personal honor, Vergennes complimented even as he complained. "You are wise and discreet, sir; you understand the proprieties; you have fulfilled your duties all your life. Do you think you are satisfying those that connect you to the King? I do not wish to carry these reflections further; I commit them to your integrity."

Franklin essayed to mollify his host. He explained that by sending the preliminary agreement to America, he and his fellow commissioners were merely informing their masters of a work in progress. The British, no doubt, would send the news across the Atlantic to *their* officers. "It was certainly very incumbent on us to give Congress as early an account as possible of our proceedings, who must think it extremely strange to hear of them by other means without a line from us."

Besides, the French government in fact had little cause for complaint. "Nothing has been agreed to in the preliminaries contrary to the interests of France, and no peace is to take place between us and England till you have concluded yours." Franklin granted that the American commissioners had erred in a minor matter of form in not consulting the French court before signing the preliminary articles. "But as this was not from want of respect for the King, whom we all love and honour, we hope it may be excused, and the great work which has hitherto been so happily conducted, is so nearly brought to perfection, and is so glorious to his reign, will not be ruined by a single indiscretion of ours." Already the British fancied they were causing a rift in the alliance. "I hope this little misunderstanding will therefore be kept a perfect secret, and that they will find themselves totally mistaken."

It was too late for that. Franklin wrote to Vergennes on December 17;

by December 19 London had the news from Edward Bancroft. British officials delighted at what one called Vergennes's "storm of indignation" against Franklin, and they gleefully anticipated a falling-out between America and France, which could only benefit Britain.

Yet Vergennes had no intention of letting such a thing happen. Fully aware of British ambitions regarding the Americans, he was content to let Franklin know that King Louis was not pleased; then he allowed the American back into His Majesty's good graces.

Which was precisely what Franklin had expected—as Vergennes doubtless realized. The two wily diplomats understood each other, and appreciated each other. Vergennes told the French ambassador in Philadelphia, Anne-César Luzerne, how all ended well at a recent interview with Franklin. "It passed very amiably for both of us. He assured me that the intention of his principals was not to take the least action at any time that might detract from the fidelity which they owed to their engagements and which, in spite of the necessity and the expediency of peace, they would renounce rather than neglect the obligations they have to the King and the gratitude they owe him."

Franklin's handling of Vergennes paid additional dividends when the foreign minister agreed to lend the United States more money. Better than Adams or Jay, Franklin understood that though the fighting was over, the American government needed money almost as much as ever. Its debts were daunting, and with the war's focusing effect on the national psyche largely dissipated, the states would be even less likely than before to pay their shares. If Congress expected France to keep furnishing funds, it behooved American representatives to be considerate of French interests.

Franklin's current application was for 20 million livres. Vergennes had professed to be aghast at its size. "That sum far exceeds all the proportions under consideration," he said. Yet at this late hour France was not inclined to see the United States fail. Louis approved a new loan of 6 million livres, of which 600,000 would be delivered to Franklin at once for dispatch to America.

The approval of the aid did not mean that Franklin had heard the last of Louis's annoyance. If nothing else, the French court intended to use the Americans' indiscretion as a bargaining chip against them. Vergennes initially directed Ambassador Luzerne to remonstrate to Congress about the deception perpetrated by the American commissioners; after Franklin's soothing letter and visit the foreign minister sent a new letter exonerating the commissioners. But Luzerne showed the first letter to the American foreign secretary, Robert Livingston, while verbally communicating the second—thereby reminding the Americans of their sins even while pardoning them. In a conversation with several members of Congress, Luzerne made clear (in the words of one member, James Madison) "that the King had been surprised and displeased and that he said he did not think he had such allies to deal with." When one of the members asked whether Louis was going to file a formal complaint against Franklin and the other commissioners, Luzerne's associate, François Barbé de Marbois, answered "that great powers never *complained* but that they *felt and remembered.*"

~ Had he been twenty years younger, Franklin might have summoned enthusiasm for this subtle game of nations. But probably not, even then; his was not a personality that reveled in intrigue and artful maneuvering. (It was perhaps significant in this regard that for all his affinity for chess, he never became very good at the game.)

Besides, he was tired. His gout and his stone—"the gout and gravel," he called them—made it impossible for him to travel with comfort, sometimes to travel at all. "I cannot bear a carriage on pavement," he wrote. The annual vacations that for years had guarded his health were out of the question. Entertainments that had enlivened his existence—a grand dinner he hosted on the second anniversary of the Declaration of Independence (the first anniversary since the alliance with France); a "salon" the following year, where his visage was celebrated in painting, in engraving, and in sculpture ("My face is almost as well known as that of the Moon," he commented to Jane Mecom); the afternoons at Auteuil; the summer days at Moulin-Joli; the meetings of Masons at the Lodge of the Nine Sisters; the pursuit of his women friends—all were things of the past. The memory was pleasant, but repetition almost unthinkable. "Repose is now my only ambition," he wrote in the spring of 1784.

Repose and retirement. This last comment was to John Jay and his wife, recently returned to America, where Jay would become foreign secretary. "Mr. Jay was so kind as to offer his friendly services to me in America," Franklin reminded. "He will oblige me by endeavouring to forward my discharge from this employment."

What would Franklin do on retirement? He thought seriously of staying in France. By the time his discharge arrived, he might be in no condition to return to America. "I may then be too old and feeble to bear the voyage." Besides, France held much for him, and America less and less. "I am here among a people that love and respect me, a most amiable nation to live with; and perhaps I may conclude to die among them; for my friends in America are dying off, one after another, and I have been so long abroad that I should now be almost a stranger in my own country."

Death held no terror for Franklin. To his friend George Whately he explained the principle of his bifocals and said they made his failing eyes almost as useful as ever. He went on, "If all the other defects and infirmities were as easily and cheaply remedied, it would be worth while for my friends to live a good deal longer; but I look upon death to be as necessary to our constitution as sleep. We shall rise refreshed in the morning."

❧ Some mornings he *still* rose refreshed. When he did, a measure of the old energy returned. And it was augmented by a new partner in diplomacy. The prospect of continued service with John Adams had been one reason Franklin was so eager to retire. In a transparent reference to Adams, Franklin wrote Robert Morris, "I hope the ravings of a certain mischievous madman here against France and its ministers, which I hear every day, will not be regarded in America." To Henry Laurens, the long-absent American commissioner, Franklin wrote saying he wished Laurens could come to Paris. "Mr. Jay will probably be gone, and I shall be left alone, or with Mr. A., and I can have no favourable opinion of what may be the offspring of a coalition between my ignorance and his positiveness."

Franklin received better than Laurens; in August 1784 the other missing commissioner, Thomas Jefferson, arrived. The contrast between Adams and Jefferson could hardly have been greater. Adams was jealous of Franklin (and of every other successful person he met); Jefferson easily accepted Franklin's status as the greatest American of all. Adams embodied the prudishness of New England; Jefferson lived the tolerance of Virginia. Adams cared little for philosophy or speculation; Jefferson was a philosopher and scientist second among Americans only to Franklin. Adams distrusted France and inclined toward England; Jefferson felt just the opposite.

The arrival of this kindred spirit lifted Franklin's own. Had he been more mobile he would have escorted Jefferson about Paris and to the court at Versailles; as it was, Jefferson met those of Franklin's friends who called at Passy. Jefferson's admiration for Franklin grew; the younger man later called the elder "the ornament of our country, and I may say, of the world." When the Congress, after finally allowing Franklin to retire, named Jefferson the American minister to France, and he was introduced around Paris as the one who replaced Franklin, he liked to interject that though he might succeed Dr. Franklin, no one could replace him.

⌐ In his final months in Paris, Franklin oversaw negotiation of treaties with various countries; one, with Prussia, contained an article he thought should be generalized. In the event of war between them, the United States and Prussia would forgo the use of privateers. Although privateers had played a critical role for America in the late war, with Franklin urging the privateers on, he disliked this form of licensed lawlessness. Privateers were nothing better than pirates, and to allow—indeed encourage—their depredations was to foster disrespect for law and order. "Justice is as strictly due between neighbour nations as between neighbour citizens," he wrote to Benjamin Vaughan, with the intention that his letter be published (it was). "A highwayman is as much a robber when he plunders in a gang as when single; and a nation that makes an unjust war is only a *great gang*." Needless to say, Franklin believed that America's defensive war against Britain had been just; it was this that excused America's resort to privateers. But every war entailed injustice on one side or the other, and Franklin judged that the greater justice dictated abolition of this evil practice.

He appreciated that America would be giving up more than other countries by such a ban. The rich trade routes of the European powers to the West Indies ran right by American shores, making the merchant vessels of those powers tempting targets for American craft. But privateering under any flag was a heinous business, starting with theft and ending with murder. "It is high time, for the sake of humanity, that a stop be put to this enormity." He and his fellow commissioners were trying to include antiprivateering clauses in all their treaties. "This will be a happy improvement in the law of nations. The humane and the just cannot but wish general success to the proposition."

Franklin's opposition to privateering suggested that he thought America would be involved in war rarely if ever; otherwise he would not so lightly have bargained away a potentially important American advantage. Indeed, a true son of the Enlightenment, he believed that wars would become less frequent—if national leaders employed their reason rather than their passions. To a correspondent who registered disapproval of war on grounds of its inhumanity, he agreed, then added that war was not simply inhumane but foolish. "I think it wrong in point of human prudence, for whatever advantage one nation would obtain from another, whether it be part of their territory, the liberty of commerce with them, free passage on their river, &c., it would be much cheaper to purchase such advantage with ready money, than to pay the expense of acquiring it by war." An army was a "devouring monster" that had to be fed, clothed, housed, and otherwise tended to; beyond the cost of the army itself were "all the knavish charges of the numerous tribe of contractors." If statesmen were better at arithmetic, wars would be far fewer. England might have purchased Canada from France for much less than England paid to fight the war that won that province. Similarly London was penny wise and pound foolish in its treatment of the American colonies. If Parliament had humored the Americans in their resistance to taxes, the British government might have got more through voluntary grants and contributions than her stamps and duties would ever have yielded. "Sensible people will give a bucket or two of water to a dry pump, that they may afterwards get from it all they have occasion for. Her ministry were deficient in that little point of common sense, and so they spent one hundred millions of her money, and, after all, lost what they had contended for."

⌐ War and its avoidance were serious matters. The approaching end of Franklin's public life encouraged such serious reflection. Yet the creator of Silence Dogood was older than the philosopher-diplomat, and must have his jokes.

In a short piece written for one of the Paris journals, Franklin reflected on the nocturnal habits of French high society, and recounted an astonishing discovery he had made. He had spent a March evening in company discussing the recent invention of a lamp by M. Quinquet; all present admired the lamp but wondered whether it did not burn oil excessively. The cost of lighting, everyone agreed, was outrageous, and must not be increased.

I went home, and to bed, three or four hours after midnight, with my head full of the subject. An accidental sudden noise waked me about six in the morning, when I was surprised to find my room filled with light; and I imagined at first that a number of those lamps had been brought into it; but, rubbing my eyes, I perceived the light came in at the windows. I got up and looked out to see what might be the occasion of it, when I saw the sun just rising above the horizon, from whence he poured his rays plentifully into my chamber, my domestic having negligently omitted, the preceding evening, to close the shutters.

Subsequent investigation revealed that this remarkable phenomenon occurred every morning, and in summer (here an almanac was consulted) still earlier. "Your readers, who with me have never seen any signs of sunshine before noon, and seldom regard the astronomical part of the almanac, will be as much astonished as I was, when they hear of his rising so early, and especially when I assure them *that he gives light as soon as he rises.*"

Savants with whom this finding had been shared refused to accept it. "One, indeed, who is a learned natural philosopher, has assured me that I must be mistaken as to the circumstance of the light coming into my room; for it being well known, as he says, that there could be no light abroad at that hour, it follows that none could enter from without; and that, of consequence, my windows, being accidentally left open, instead of letting in the light, had only served to let out the darkness."

Yet additional experiments confirmed the truth that Paris lay in broad daylight for several hours before noon. This prompted certain deep, and most useful, reflections. "I considered that if I had not been awakened so early in the morning, I should have slept six hours longer by the light of the sun, and in exchange have lived six hours the following night by candle-light." The latter being much dearer than the former, an elementary (if somewhat tedious) calculation revealed that the hundred thousand families of Paris might save more than 96 million livres every year by the simple device of rising with the sun.

For the great benefit of this discovery, thus freely communicated and bestowed by me upon the public, I demand neither place, pension, exclusive privilege, nor any other reward whatever. I expect only to have the honour of it.

And yet I know there are little, envious minds who will, as usual deny me this, and say that my invention was known to the ancients, and perhaps they may bring passages out of the old books in proof of it. I will not dispute with these people that the ancients knew not the sun would rise at certain hours; they possibly had, as we have, almanacs that predicted it; but it does not follow thence that they knew *he gave light as soon as he rose.*

This is what I claim as my discovery. If the ancients knew it, it might have been long since forgotten; for it certainly was unknown to the moderns, at least to the Parisians; which to prove, I need use but one plain simple argument. They are as well instructed, judicious, and prudent a people as exist anywhere in the world, all professing, like myself, to be lovers of economy; and, from the many heavy taxes required from them by the necessities of the state, have surely an abundant reason to be economical. I say it is impossible that so sensible a people, under such circumstances, should have lived so long by the smoky, unwholesome, and enormously expensive light of candles, if they had really known that they might have had as much pure light of the sun for nothing.

28

Home

1785–86

〜 Another bagatelle had a decidedly darker theme.
It involved a lion, king of the beasts, who numbered
among his subjects a body of faithful dogs, devoted to his
person and government, and through whose assistance
he had greatly extended his dominions. The lion,
however, influenced by evil counselors, took an aversion to
the dogs, condemned them unheard, and ordered his tigers,
leopards, and panthers to attack and destroy them.

The brave dogs, dismayed at their master's change of heart, reluctantly defended themselves—but not without internal dissent. "A few among them, of a mongrel race, derived from a mixture with wolves and foxes, corrupted by royal promises of great rewards, deserted the honest dogs and joined their enemies."

After a sore struggle the dogs fought off the tigers, leopards, and panthers. In their victory they refused to suffer the return of the mongrels—who thereupon applied to the lion to fulfill the promises he had made. The wolves and the foxes supported their appeal and urged that every loyal subject of the lion should be taxed to that end.

Only the horse, with a boldness and freedom that became the nobility of his nature, spoke against the mongrels and the wolves and foxes. The lion, he said, had been misled by bad ministers to war unjustly on his faithful subjects. Royal promises, when made to encourage subjects to act for the public good, should indeed be honored; but if made to encourage betrayal and mutual destruction, they were wicked and void from the beginning. "If you enable the King to reward those fratricides, you will establish a precedent that may justify a future tyrant to make like promises; and every example of such an unnatural brute rewarded will give them additional weight." Horses and bulls, as well as dogs, might thus be divided against their own kind, and civil wars produced at pleasure. All would be so weakened that neither liberty nor safety would survive, and nothing would remain but abject submission to a despot, "who may devour us as he pleases."

At the time Franklin wrote this fable, the British Parliament was complaining at the Americans' failure to compensate the Loyalists for their losses. The piece was written for a British audience; Franklin's point was that the Loyalists did not deserve compensation—certainly not from the Americans, nor even from the British king or Parliament.

In some respects Franklin was a magnanimous victor. He repaired relations with old friends in England, resuming correspondence where the war had broken it off. But on the subject of the Loyalists he never relented. Indeed, he went so far as to deny they deserved the label they adopted. "The name *loyalist* was improperly assumed by these people," he wrote a British friend. "*Royalists* they may perhaps be called. But the true loyalists were the people of America, against whom they acted." Eventually Franklin acknowledged that if Parliament wished to compensate the Loyalists, it might do so. But his reasoning revealed his continuing bitterness. "Even a hired assassin has a right to his pay from his employer."

Perhaps as consequence, perhaps as cause—probably as both—

Franklin's feelings toward the Loyalists as a group were closely connected to his feelings toward William. In August 1784, after a hiatus of several years, he received a letter from his son. William had been released from custody in a prisoner exchange in 1778, and after four years among his fellow refugees in the vicinity of New York he sailed for London. There he took up the cause of the American Loyalists, becoming one of the wolves and foxes of his father's fable—not to mention already being one of the foremost mongrels. For several months after the conclusion of the war neither father nor son made any move to contact the other, the former out of hurt and anger, the latter out of pride.

Finally the son took the step. Assuming that his father would be leaving France for America soon, and probably taking Temple with him, William averred his desire to "revive that affectionate intercourse and connexion which till the commencement of the late troubles had been the pride and happiness of my life." He conceded that his actions during the war had disappointed his father. Yet an honorable man did what he must. "I uniformly acted from a strong sense of what I conceived my duty to my King and regard to my country." At this late hour he would not apologize. "If I have been mistaken, I cannot help it. It is an error of judgment that the maturest reflection I am capable of cannot rectify, and I verily believe that were the same circumstances to occur tomorrow, my conduct would be exactly similar to what it was heretofore." All this was history, however. He hoped to resume the relationship as it had been before the war.

"Dear Son," Franklin replied. "I received your letter of the 22d past, and am glad to find that you desire to revive the affectionate intercourse that formerly existed between us. It will be very agreeable to me."

Yet not really. "Let us now forgive and forget," Franklin had said to Jonathan Shipley. But with William he could neither forgive nor forget.

> Nothing has ever hurt me so much and affected me with such keen sensations as to find myself deserted in my old age by my only son; and not only deserted, but to find him taking up arms against me, in a cause wherein my good fame, fortune and life were all at stake.
>
> You conceived, you say, that your duty to your King and regard for your country required this. I ought not to blame you for differing in sentiment with me in public affairs. We are men, all subject to errors. Our opinions are not in our own power; they are formed and governed much by circumstances that are often as

inexplicable as they are irresistible. Your situation was such that few would have censured your remaining neuter, *though there are natural duties which precede political ones, and cannot be extinguished by them.*

Franklin underlined these last words, which went to the heart of the issue—and to the heart of Franklin himself. Friends—even close friends like William Strahan—Franklin could forgive for their political differences with him on the issue of allegiance to the Crown; family he could not. He insisted that William's loyalty to his father come before his loyalty to his king.

Logic did not compel Franklin to frame the question this way. He did not accuse Loyalists as a group of waging war on him personally—of "taking up arms against me." But he so accused William. He seems not to have considered that William might have leveled an analogous accusation against *him*. After all, Franklin was the rebel of the two. Perhaps Franklin felt a son owed more to his father in this regard than the father owed the son. Yet if such was his conception of filial relations, he certainly had showed no evidence of it in his dealings with his own father, whom he disregarded whenever interest bade him.

All his life Franklin had sought respect. His search had been stunningly successful by the standards of most mortals. No man on earth was more broadly respected than Benjamin Franklin. Even the British government, whose conspicuous disrespect had made him one of the most formidable enemies the Crown ever faced, had come round, as Shelburne made abundantly clear during the peace talks.

But William refused to accord him the respect he demanded. William was not allowed to discover his own mind and honor his own convictions. To disagree with his father was, on this critical issue, to disrespect him.

It was not Franklin's finest hour. And he knew it. "This is a disagreeable subject," he wrote William. "I drop it." He promised to try to bury the past "as well as we can," but his tone left William little room for hope.

⌒ **Neither** did the sole meeting between the two. In May 1785 Franklin received the message he had long been awaiting. "You are permitted to return to America as soon as convenient," wrote John Jay on behalf of the Congress. Franklin's French friends urged him to stay. "They press me much to remain in France," he told Sally and Richard Bache, "and three of them have offered me an asylum in their habitations. They tell me I am here among a people who universally esteem and love me; that my friends at home are diminished by death in my absence; that I may there meet with envy and its consequent enmity which here I am perfectly free from; this supposing I live to complete the voyage, but of that they doubt."

Franklin himself had some questions on that score. He was not sure he could find a ship that would not kill him crossing the ocean. Remembering his latest journey from America, before his stone started plaguing him, he declared, "I must be better stowed now, or I shall not be able to hold out the voyage." The pain that accompanied the least journey on land made him dubious. But ultimately the desire "of spending the little remainder of life with my family" determined him to see if he could bear the motion of a ship. "If not, I must get them to set me on shore somewhere in the Channel, and content myself to die in Europe."

He bade *au revoir* to Vergennes, who regretted his departure. "This minister has won the King's esteem," Vergennes remarked to one of his subordinates. "And I personally have the greatest confidence in his principles and in his integrity. The United States will never have a more zealous and more useful servant than Mr. Franklin."

Franklin reciprocated the respect. "I think your minister, who is so expert in composing quarrels and preventing wars, the great blessing of this age," he told a French friend. "The Devil must send us three or four heroes before he can get as much slaughter of mankind done as that one man has prevented."

Finding a suitable ship required some weeks, and it was July before Franklin set out. "When he left Passy," Jefferson recorded, "it seemed as if the village had lost its patriarch." He had intended to float down the Seine on a barge, but a dry summer made navigation difficult. Instead the queen offered her royal litter, which was carried by two large mules— "who walk very easy," Franklin was relieved to note. (King Louis's gesture was a portrait of himself, framed in four hundred diamonds.) Several of Franklin's friends accompanied him; count, colonel, and cardinal hosted him on his journey to the sea. Delegations from towns and villages en route greeted him; the Academy of Rouen presented him with a magic square said to represent his name in numbers. ("I have perused it since," he wrote, "but do not comprehend it.")

A letter awaited him at Havre. The leave-taking had been hardest for the women Franklin loved, and who loved him. Madame Brillon could not bear to see him go. "My heart was so heavy yesterday when I left you," she wrote, "that I feared, for you and for myself, another such moment which would have only added to my misery without further proving the tender, unchanging love I have devoted to you forever. . . . If it ever pleases you to remember the woman who loved you the most, think of me. Farewell, my heart was not meant to be separated from yours, but it shall not be. You shall find it near yours; speak to it and it shall answer you."

Madame Brillon's letter he read in his litter (with the aid of his double spectacles); the one that caught him at the coast was from Madame Helvétius.

> I cannot get accustomed to the idea that you have left us, my dear friend; that you are no longer in Passy, that I shall never see you again. I can picture you in your litter, further from us at every step, already lost to me and to your friends who loved you so much and regret you so. I fear you are in pain, that the road will tire you and make you more uncomfortable.
>
> If such is the case, come back, my dear friend; come back to us. My little retreat will be the better for your presence; you will like it because of the friendship you will find here and the care we will take of you. You will make our life happier; we shall contribute to your happiness.

To his surprise, the journey was quite tolerable. The mules earned their oats keeping him comfortable; he wrote Madame Helvétius that his strength was improving. He must go on, though his heart resisted. "We shall stay here a few days, waiting for our luggage, and then we shall leave France, the country that *I love the most* in the world. And there I shall leave my dear Helvetia. She may be happy yet. I am not sure that I shall be happy in America, but I must go back. I feel sometimes that things are badly arranged in this world when I consider that people so well matched to be happy together are forced to separate." He closed as gallantly as ever: "I will not tell you of my love. For one would say that there is nothing remarkable or praiseworthy about it, since every body loves you. I only hope that you will always love me some."

From Havre the Franklin party—consisting of himself, Temple, Benny, and Franklin's nephew Jonathan Williams—traversed the Channel to Southampton, to catch a British ship. (Belatedly the French navy minister declared, "Had I been informed of it sooner, I should have proposed to the king to order a frigate to convey you to your own country in a manner suitable to the known importance of the services you have been engaged in." Franklin accepted the minister's apologies.)

The Channel boat encountered stiff headwinds and contrary seas. For nearly two full days the craft pitched and the passengers moaned—all but Franklin, the one aboard who did not get sick. "I feel very well," he wrote Madame Helvétius from Southampton—adding a last "I shall always love you."

Several of his surviving English friends came to see him. Jonathan Shipley and family put up at the Star tavern with the Franklin party; it was probably Shipley who introduced Franklin to one of the local attractions. "I went at noon to bathe in Martin's salt-water bath," Franklin wrote, "and, floating on my back, fell asleep, and slept near an hour by my watch, without sinking or turning! a thing I never did before, and should hardly have thought possible. Water is the easiest bed that can be."

Less pleasant was his meeting with William. The younger man still hoped for a reconciliation. He knew he would never see his father again, for age would claim the old man long before America would forgive the son. If they were ever to recapture some of the intimacy they had shared for many years, they would have to do so now.

The presence of Temple raised the emotional stakes for both men. Temple was the surrogate son Franklin had claimed after his own son abandoned him, and he did not want to give him up. Politics aside, he probably felt he had a better claim to Temple than William did, having raised Temple, educated him, and brought him to the beginning of a career. William doubtless regretted not having acknowledged Temple earlier, but he nonetheless must have felt that Franklin had stolen what was the natural right of all parents: the affection of a child. Franklin had grudgingly allowed Temple to visit William in London the previous summer. "I trust that you will prudently avoid introducing him to company that it may be improper for him to be seen with," Franklin wrote William, in what could only have been interpreted as a condescending tone. And he chafed as long as Temple was away, urging him to write by every post and making plain that, at least in his view, Temple answered to him rather than to William.

The meeting of the three generations occurred under inauspicious circumstances. Franklin's guests were coming and going; at the Star the three had scarce time and less privacy for the sort of soul-searching a genuine reunion required. Doubtless Franklin preferred it this way. Scars had formed over the wounds he felt at what he considered his son's betrayal; better not to reopen them.

Besides, there was business to transact. William had property in New Jersey and New York that was doing him no good; he decided to sell it to Temple. Franklin underwrote the transaction, applying toward the price various debts William owed him and authorizing William to seek payment from the British government of debts owed Franklin (William could keep half of any amount recovered; the other half would go to Sally). For the balance of 48,000 livres on the sale price, Franklin wrote to a banker friend in Paris for a loan.

William found the encounter acutely distressing. His hopes for reconciliation were dashed, his ties to his homeland severed. Shortly after Franklin and Temple sailed away, William wrote disconsolately that "my fate has thrown me on a different side of the globe."

Franklin kept his feelings to himself, as he generally did on this most painful part of his life. He turned from William to Shipley and other friends. On July 27 the group went aboard the ship that would take the travelers to America. "The captain entertains us at supper," Franklin recorded in his journal. "The company stay all night."

Yet the company did not stay all night. After Franklin retired, Shipley and the others slipped to shore. "We all left your ship with a heavy heart," Shipley's daughter wrote Franklin later. "But the taking leave was a scene we wished to save you as well as ourselves."

In the night the wind freshened, and the captain weighed anchor on the ebb tide. When Franklin awoke, the ship was miles at sea.

~ He had worried that the voyage would kill him; instead it restored him. A single stormy day interrupted an otherwise smooth passage. Since a visit by Polly Hewson to Passy the previous winter, he had been gently trying to persuade her to move to America with her children (her husband having died); he booked a cabin large enough to accommodate the whole group. When she chose to remain in England, he was left with more room than he could fill.

For years his friends had implored him to complete his memoirs. First the war got in the way, then the peace negotiations, then the fact that he had lost the part already written. It was among papers he left in the care of Joseph Galloway upon departing America in 1776. Although Galloway espoused the British cause, he certainly would have respected

Franklin's papers, but amid the confusion of the British occupation of Philadelphia his house was raided and its contents, including Franklin's papers, scattered. Consequently, when Franklin had sat down at Passy to continue his tale, he had no record of what he had already written and few materials with which to go forward. He found the work difficult and unsatisfactory. When friends persisted in urging him to tell his story, he put them off by intimating he would take up pen once more during the leisure of his voyage home.

He did take up pen, but not in the service of history. His memoirs had begun as a letter to William; perhaps the pain of this final parting from his son put him off the task. For whatever reason, he devoted his time at sea to his philosophical pursuits. He renewed his investigations of the Gulf Stream, with Jonathan Williams serving as assistant this time. He devised an ingenious method of measuring the temperature of the water at different depths. He corked an empty bottle and tied it to a leaded rope, letting out twenty fathoms, then drawing it back up. The cork remained in place and the bottle empty. Then he threw it back over the side and let it out thirty-five fathoms before drawing it up. This time, the pressure of the water at depth having pushed the cork into the bottle, the bottle was full of water from that depth. By Franklin's thermometer the difference between the temperature at the surface and the temperature below was as much as twelve degrees. In other words, the Gulf Stream was a river of warm water flowing over the colder body of the ocean. Franklin drew the characteristically practical conclusion that "the thermometer may be a useful instrument to a navigator." A captain sailing north should seek warm water, which would indicate a current moving from south to north; a captain sailing south should hunt for cold.

Other observations involved the safety of ocean travel. He reiterated his recommendation to build watertight bulkheads belowdecks, after the Chinese fashion. Recalling having read of the proas of the Polynesian islanders, which employed outriggers to resist oversetting, he wondered whether the same effect might be achieved by making double-hulled ships with spars between the hulls (a later generation would call such vessels catamarans). He remembered seeing "islands of ice" (icebergs) off Newfoundland on earlier voyages and advocated lookouts to avoid them. He noted that though these and other safety measures might make sense to landlubbers, they would probably be resisted by sailors. "Our seafaring people are brave, despise danger, and reject such precautions of safety, being cowards only in one sense, that of *fearing* to be *thought afraid*." Appealing over their heads, as it were, he pointed out that safety measures would reduce insurance rates and command a premium from passengers less careless with their lives than the sailors.

During the voyage Franklin also returned to his much earlier theme of efficient combustion. Recalling the trouble the smoke of London had occasioned him, he described an improved stove, one designed to burn the soft coal so coughingly common in England and to consume all its own smoke. In a separate essay he addressed the causes and cures of smoky chimneys. For all the honors he had received for his electrical work and other scientific speculations, he never forgot that upon such humble issues as access to heat was a happy society constructed. "In traveling I have observed that in those parts where the inhabitants can have neither wood nor coal nor turf but at excessive prices, the working people live in miserable hovels, are ragged, and have nothing comfortable about them. But when fuel is cheap (or where they have the art of managing it to advantage) they are well furnished with necessaries and have decent habitations."

On the forty-eighth day out, Franklin awoke to learn that the vessel had passed Cape May and entered the estuary of the Delaware. They ascended to Newcastle before the wind died and the tide turned, and they anchored for the night. "With the flood in the morning," Franklin recorded, "came a light breeze, which brought us above Gloucester Point, in full view of dear Philadelphia! when we again cast anchor to wait for the health officer, who, having made his visit, and finding no sickness, gave us leave to land. My son-in-law came with a boat for us; we landed at Market Street wharf, where we were received by a crowd of people with huzzas, and accompanied with acclamations quite to my door. Found my family well. God be praised and thanked for all his mercies!"

∾ The war had been hard on Philadelphia, but the peace was almost harder. The march of armies through the streets, the arrival of refugees, the flight of refugees, the occupation by the British, the evacuation by the British, the sundry other insults of war had left William Penn's "green country town" battered and worn. Visitors remarked the peeling paint and broken windows. Houses and public buildings that had sheltered soldiers and horses stank of the waste of both species. Light rains made rock-strewn quagmires of streets where tight cobbles had formerly defied the heaviest downpours.

But at least the war had been good for business. Bakers, butchers, tailors, printers, and purveyors of all manner of necessities and luxuries had supplied the contending armies in turn (and in some cases simultaneously). The same crew had fed, housed, entertained, and otherwise supplied the members of the Congress and their assorted supplicants and dependents.

The Congress was the first to go when the war ended, departing even before all the soldiers left. In June 1783 some three hundred troops of the Pennsylvania Line surrounded the State House and demanded assurances of Congress they would receive their back pay before being mustered out. The leadership of the Congress, incensed at this mutinous behavior, insisted that the Pennsylvania government discipline the rebellious troops. The Pennsylvania Executive Council respectfully demurred. The troops announced a twenty-minute deadline for the hostage Congress to redress their grievances. Some congressmen, noting the jugs being passed around among the rebels, feared for their lives; several others guessed that the liquor would distract the mutineers. Summoning all their dignity, these latter lawmakers marched straight out through the siege line to safety, whereupon the soldiers returned to their barracks.

Shortly thereafter the president of the Congress, Elias Boudinot, summoned the members to abandon this seat of sedition for the safer neighborhood of Princeton, New Jersey. The stated reason for the move was the refusal of the Pennsylvania government to take appropriate measures against the revolt. Additional reasons, which may have counted for more among many members, were the high cost of living and related distractions of Philadelphia. Even before the mutiny one member reported that it was "generally agreed that Congress should remove to a place of less expense, less avocation and less influence than are to be expected in a commercial and opulent city."

The pullout of Congress combined with the end of the war to derange business. The shortages of wartime had driven prices up; the surpluses of peacetime drove them back down. Determining whether they fell further than they had risen was complicated by the currency gyrations the Congress had fostered by its penchant for papering over its fiscal problems with flimsy money.

Philadelphia's—and Pennsylvania's—problems were aggravated by politics that made the old tiffs between the proprietary and antiproprietary parties appear almost genteel. The Revolution had solved the problem with the Penns, the one that had consumed so much of Franklin's political career, by placing them definitively on the wrong side of history.

Richard Penn, the last proprietary governor, had been commissioned by the Continental Congress to carry the Olive Branch petition of 1775 to King George; upon its rejection Penn calculated that safety lay on the eastern side of the Atlantic, and stayed in England. The new state constitution adopted the following year—over the drafting of which Franklin had presided—wrote the proprietors out of Pennsylvania politics; it meanwhile wrote in an entire class of voters heretofore excluded. Essentially all tax-paying adult males could now vote to elect members to the unicameral legislature Franklin favored. Annual elections guaranteed that the legislature would remain close to the people, as did term limits preventing members from serving more than four years out of any seven. An oath to uphold the people's interest was required of officeholders. A bill of rights protected the people from overreaching government.

In the flush of independence a populist government seemed just the thing for Pennsylvania, but before long, doubts began to surface. The constitution drew support among the artisans of Philadelphia (the people occupying Franklin's old niche), but its real backers were the farmers in the western part of the state (the heirs of the Paxton mob he had confronted on behalf of the Assembly). Evincing skepticism were members of the old proprietary party (whom Franklin had opposed), but also men who through their own efforts had attained a measure of wealth (men like Franklin). In time the two groups formed factions, with the former calling themselves Constitutionalists, the latter Republicans.

Franklin's arrival coincided with a raucous election campaign between the two groups. Consequently the effusive welcome he received reflected not simply gratitude for past accomplishments but hope for future support. Pennsylvanians—like Americans generally—were not yet reconciled to the existence of political parties: more or less permanent groupings with predictably clashing interests. They cherished a belief that parties were an artifact of English corruption; having done with England, America would be free of parties. In Pennsylvania, Constitutionalists and Republicans alike looked to Franklin to soothe factional passions and heal the growing rift in society.

He had hardly landed before the leaders of both parties came calling. A delegation of Constitutionalists remembered fondly his role in writing the constitution, and nominated him for a place on the Executive Council. The Republicans, applauding his unexampled efforts on behalf of independence, and more recently of peace, nominated him too.

The dual nominations assured his election to the Executive Council, which proceeded to choose him as its head. When the Assembly met a week later, it joined forces with the Council to elect Franklin president of Pennsylvania. The vote was nearly unanimous, only one ballot besides Franklin's own not naming him.

This turn of events surprised Franklin as much as it gratified him. Thomas Paine had written welcoming Franklin home; Franklin replied, "The ease and rest you wish me to enjoy for the remainder of my days is certainly what is most proper for me, what I long wished for, and what I proposed to myself in resigning my late employment. But it is what I am not likely to obtain." He recounted how the leaders of the two parties had approached him to reunify the people of Pennsylvania. "I had not sufficient firmness to refuse their request."

After all the slanders his reputation had suffered in his absence, it was nice to know that his work was appreciated. "The people, when one serves them faithfully and steadily, are not ungrateful," he wrote an English acquaintance. To Jonathan Williams he confessed, "Old as I am, I am not yet grown insensible with respect to reputation." At the same time, he guessed that by his accepting the new office, his reputation must suffer. "I apprehend they expect too much of me."

⌒ As the excitement of his homecoming wore off, so did the effect of that excitement on his health. Fresh from the boat he had written to John and Mrs. Jay of his delight at the revivifying effects of his journey. "I am now so well as to think it possible that I may once more have the pleasure of seeing you both perhaps at New York. I imagine that on the sandy road between Burlington and Amboy I could bear an easy coach, and the rest is water." During the next few months, however, his ailments returned, and the stone, especially, kept him close to home. Early in 1786 an acquaintance offered to sell him a farm just eight miles outside of Philadelphia; Franklin declined, saying he could not visit the estate if he owned it. "The stone does not permit me to ride either on horseback or in a wheel carriage."

Yet if he could not travel, he could enjoy the quiet satisfaction of life among family and his few surviving old friends. He met with the Union Fire Club, now approaching the half-century mark of its existence. Only four of the founding members were still alive, and they had not answered alarms for years. Yet Franklin gamely promised to have his bucket and kit ready for the next meeting. The American Philosophical Society welcomed him back; it would be honored, its editorial board averred, to print in its *Transactions* the pieces he had written at sea.

But home was what supplied the deepest personal satisfaction. "I am now in the bosom of my family," he wrote the Jays, "and find four new little prattlers who cling about the knees of their Grandpapa and afford me great pleasure." Jonathan Shipley, who had opened *his* home and family to Franklin, inquired of his friend's domestic circumstances. "They are at present as happy as I could wish them," Franklin replied. "I am surrounded by my offspring, a dutiful and affectionate daughter in my house, with six grandchildren, the eldest of which [Benny] you have seen, who is now at a College in the next street, finishing the learned part of his education; the others promising, both for parts and good dispositions. What their conduct may be when they grow up and enter the important scenes of life, I shall not live to *see*, and I cannot *foresee*. I therefore enjoy among them the present hour, and leave the future to Providence."

The proximity of his daughter and her children doubtless reminded Franklin of his two sons who were missing. He did not speak directly of William and Franky, but they almost certainly influenced his remarks to Jonathan Shipley about family life.

> He that raises a large family does, indeed, while he lives to observe them, *stand*, as Watts says, *a broader mark for sorrow;* but then he stands a broader mark for pleasure too. When we launch our little fleet of barques into the ocean, bound to different ports, we hope for each a prosperous voyage; but contrary winds, hidden shoals, storms, and enemies come in for a share in the disposition of events; and though these occasion a mixture of disappointment, yet, considering the risque where we can make no insurance, we should think our selves happy if some return with success.

Family was a form of immortality, but perhaps not the only form. Franklin explained to Shipley that though he fared as well as he had any right to expect at his age, he could not live much longer. "The course of nature must soon put a period to my present mode of existence." What would come after? Franklin was intrigued to find out. "Having seen during a long life a good deal of this world, I feel a growing curiosity to be acquainted with some other." He hoped not to be disappointed; rather, with "filial confidence," he resigned his spirit to "that great and good Parent of mankind who created it, and who has so graciously protected and prospered me from my birth to the present hour."

George Whately had remarked on what remained at the end of a long life, and had sent an epitaph written by Pope, which included a line scoffing at worldly praise: "He ne'er cared a pin/What they said or may say of the mortal within." Franklin was skeptical. "It is so natural to wish to be spoken well of, whether alive or dead, that I imagine he could not be quite exempt from that desire; and that he at least wished to be thought a wit, or he would not have given himself the trouble of writing so good an epitaph to leave behind him."

For himself, Franklin said, he preferred the sentiment of a traditional drinking song entitled "The Old Man's Wish," which in successive verses asked for a warm house in a country town, an easy horse, good books, ingenious and cheerful companions, pudding on Sundays, stout ale, and a bottle of burgundy. Each verse ended:

> *May I govern my passions with an absolute sway,*
> *Grow wiser and better as my strength wears away,*
> *Without gout or stone, by a gentle decay.*

"But what signifies our wishing?" Franklin asked. "Things happen, after all, as they will happen. I have sung that *Wishing Song* a thousand times when I was young, and now find, at fourscore, that the three contraries have befallen me, being subject to the gout and the stone, and being not yet master of all my passions—like the proud girl in my country who wished and resolved not to marry a parson, nor a Presbyterian, nor an Irishman, and at length found herself married to an Irish Presbyterian parson."

At times Franklin approached a belief in reincarnation. Observing the "great frugality" of nature, which the Deity had designed so as to ensure that nothing once created was lost, Franklin supposed that something similar applied to souls. "When I see nothing annihilated, and not even a drop of water wasted, I cannot suspect the annihilation of souls, or believe that he will suffer the daily waste of millions of minds ready made that now exist, and put himself to the continual trouble of making new ones." Franklin included his own soul in this conservation scheme. "Thus finding myself to exist in the world, I believe I shall, in some shape or other, always exist; and with all the inconveniences human life is liable to, I shall not object to a new edition of mine; hoping, however, that the *errata* of the last may be corrected."

Franklin did not share this unorthodox view with everyone—and he counseled others to exercise similar caution. An author unidentified in the surviving correspondence, but quite possibly Thomas Paine, sent Franklin a manuscript challenging the basis of organized religion; Franklin told him not to publish. "Though your reasonings are subtle, and may prevail with some readers, you will not succeed so as to change the general sentiments of mankind on that subject, and the consequence of printing this piece will be a great deal of odium drawn upon yourself, mischief to you, and no benefit to others. He that spits against the wind, spits in his own face." Even if the manuscript succeeded in its purpose, what good would come? The author might be able to live a virtuous life without the aid of religion, but not everyone was so blessed. "Think how great a proportion of mankind consists of weak and ignorant men and women, and of inexperienced and inconsiderate youth of both sexes, who have need of the motives of religion to restrain them from vice, to support their virtue, and retain them in the practice of it till it becomes *habitual*." Usually a model of tact, Franklin now chose bluntness. "Burn this piece before it is seen by any other person, whereby you will save yourself a great deal of mortification from the enemies it may raise against you, and perhaps a good deal of regret and repentance. If men are so wicked as we now see them *with religion*, what would they be *if without it?*" (If the author of the manuscript *was* Paine, Franklin's warning had some effect: Paine did not publish *The Age of Reason* for several years—to a reception very much like that Franklin forecast.)

Other advice was more positive. The young Noah Webster was busy formulating the declaration of lexicographical independence that would make his name synonymous with American dictionaries; on a visit to Philadelphia he shared his thoughts with Franklin, who resurrected his own ideas on a phonetic alphabet. The exchange fired Webster's enthusiasm. "I am encouraged by the prospect of rendering my country some service, to proceed in my design of refining the language and improving our general system of education," he wrote George Washington. "Dr. Franklin has extended my views to a very simple plan of reducing the language to perfect regularity." Though the "perfect regularity" of Franklin's phonetic scheme ultimately proved too radical for Webster, enough of the spirit of Franklin remained for Webster to dedicate his pioneering *Dissertations on the English Language* to Franklin.

⌐ **During** his first several months back from France, Franklin spent more time than he wished tending to details that remained from his diplomatic mission. One detail seemed more than a detail to his critics, for it involved a missing million livres. Because of the irregular nature of French aid to the United States prior to the treaties of 1778—through the likes of Beaumarchais and the Farmers General—records of the transactions were incomplete and contradictory. Certain receipts from King Louis, signed by Franklin, registered grants to America of 3 million livres, but only 2 million appeared on the deposit accounts of the American government in its French bank. "I wonder how I came to sign the contract acknowledging three millions of gift, when in reality there was only two," Franklin wrote Ferdinand Grand, America's banker in Paris. "I most earnestly request of you to get this matter explained, that I may stand clear before I die, lest some enemy should afterwards accuse me of having received a million not accounted for."

Unfortunately for Franklin's peace of mind, Grand could not find the money either. Franklin guessed that the records had been buried for a reason. "I conjecture it must be money advanced for our use to M. de Beaumarchais," he informed Congress, "and that it is a *mystère du cabinet*, which perhaps should not be further enquired into." The whole business had been delicate for the French government, and evidently remained delicate. "It may well be supposed that if the Court furnished him with the means of supplying us, they may not be willing to furnish authentic proofs of such a transaction so early in our dispute with Britain."

Franklin's conjecture eventually proved correct. But the evidence—in the form of a receipt from Beaumarchais for the million—did not surface until after Franklin's death, and in the meantime it complicated his efforts to settle his own account with Congress. An auditor engaged by Congress determined that Franklin was owed some 7,500 livres for his services in France. But between the continuing hostility of the Lee faction, which seized upon the missing money as evidence that Franklin had filled his own pocket, and the general tardiness of Congress in paying all its creditors, his balance remained unpaid.

He had better luck with Georgia. When that colony had engaged him to serve as its agent in London before the war, it promised him £100 per year. But the money was never paid, and with everything else that occurred in the interim, he had never pursued the debt. Now he reminded the appropriate officials of the state of Georgia, who responded by offering him land, of which they had much, in lieu of cash, of which they had little. Georgia had awarded a handsome tract to Admiral d'Estaing, who had been severely wounded fighting for Savannah; Franklin wrote to d'Estaing describing his own settlement with Georgia: "The Assembly of that state has granted me 3,000 acres of their land to be located wherever I can find any vacant. I wish much that it might be near yours, for you contrived to make your neighbourhood so agreeable to me at Passy that I could wish to be your neighbour everywhere."

Franklin did not worry excessively about his finances, partly because he did not expect to live long and partly because his fortunes had survived the war better than he had expected. "My own estate I find more than tripled in value since the Revolution," he wrote Ferdinand Grand. This figure was misleading, in that the war had inflated prices across the economy. In this same letter Franklin explained that the high price of labor was causing him to defer some building plans he had devised. All the same, he had resources sufficient to maintain him even in the more comfortable style to which he had grown accustomed in France.

~ In time he grew used to the higher cost of labor, and he determined to build. He tore down three old houses on lots he owned on Market Street and prepared to replace them with new ones. But before the construction commenced, a neighbor disputed a lot line, and litigation delayed the work. Because Franklin had already engaged the workmen and was obligated for their wages, he set them to building an addition to his own house, now too small for himself, Sally, Richard, and the grandchildren. "I propose to have in it a long room for my library and instruments, with two good bedchambers and two garrets," he explained to Jane Mecom. "The library is to be even with the floor of my best old chamber, and the story under it will for the present be employed only to hold wood, but may be made into rooms hereafter." He granted that this might not be the wisest use of resources. "I hardly know how to justify building a library at an age that will so soon oblige me to quit it." But he aimed to indulge himself. "We are apt to forget that we are grown old, and building is an amusement."

It was also a business. By the beginning of 1787, Philadelphia had pulled itself out of the postwar slump, and rising rents promised profits to landlords. Repeating himself to Ferdinand Grand that building was "an old man's amusement," Franklin added, "The advantage is for his posterity. Since my coming home, the market is extended before my ground next the street, and the high rents such a situation must afford have been one of my inducements."

Not for years had the entrepreneur in Franklin been heard from; now he returned. Franklin replaced the three decrepit houses on Market Street at the front of his lot with two large, fine ones, each twenty-four feet wide by forty-five feet deep, and three stories tall, besides the garrets. An arched passage between the two allowed access to Franklin's own house in back. Elsewhere in the neighborhood he built three other houses. "The affairs in dealing with so many workmen and furnishers of materials," he wrote a French friend in April 1787, "such as brick-layers, carpenters, stone-cutters, painters, glaziers, lime-burners, timber-merchants, copper-smiths, carters, labourers, etc., etc., have added not a little to the fatiguing business I have gone through in the last year." But on the whole he enjoyed the work, which, as he said to Jane Mecom, made him forget he was grown old.

~ The fatiguing business he referred to was that of Pennsylvania politics. In May 1786 Benjamin Rush dined with Franklin. "He appeared as cheerful and gay as a young man of five-and-twenty," Rush wrote, "but his conversation was full of the wisdom and experience of mellow old age. He has destroyed party rage in our state, or to borrow an allusion from one of his discoveries, his presence and advice, like oil upon trou-bled waters, have composed the contending waves of faction which for so many years agitated the State of Pennsylvania."

Rush was always generous to Franklin, who just weeks before had felt obliged to request that Rush omit an effusive encomium to Franklin he intended to employ as a dedication to a new book. And his descrip-tion of Franklin's calming effect on Pennsylvania politics may have been more apt than he intended. The surface was indeed smoothed—sufficiently that Franklin was reelected president in the autumn of 1786, this time unanimously (except, again, for his own vote).

Yet beneath the surface, deep currents still drove Pennsylvania poli-tics. Some reflected the old divisions within the province; others were pe-culiar to independent statehood. The latter category included the Bank of North America, a brainchild of Robert Morris, and in the eyes of the better-off classes, including most Pennsylvania Republicans, a necessary force for stability and progress in society. To the Constitutionalists, on the other hand, the Bank of North America—and in particular its existence as a corporation of unlimited duration—represented a threat to liberty and the very meaning of the Revolution. "The accumulation of enormous wealth in the hands of a society who claim perpetual duration," wrote one Constitutionalist, referring to the bank, "will necessarily produce a degree of influence and power which can not be entrusted in the hands of any set of men whatsoever without endangering the public safety."

Throughout the 1780s the Constitutionalists employed every opportunity to curtail the activities of the bank. In 1786 they succeeded in repealing its state charter. That the bank continued to operate under charters it had obtained from other states simply confirmed the Constitutionalist judgment that it was a hydra-headed monster ready to devour the people. Meanwhile the Republicans mounted a counterattack. When Robert Morris became head of the party, Benjamin Rush—a central figure in the adoption of the 1776 constitution but lately put off by the radicalism of the Constitutionalists—recorded hopefully, "It is expected that the charter of the Bank of North America will be restored."

A second bone of contention was closer to Franklin's heart, if perhaps further from his wallet. The College of Philadelphia, which had evolved out of Franklin's Academy, gradually grew away from its egalitarian roots, so that by the start of the Revolutionary era it was often seen as a nest of aristocracy and Anglicanism. When the provost and several of the trustees exhibited Tory tendencies—remaining in the city during the British occupation, for example—the state Assembly seized the institution. It threw out the administration and trustees, renamed the college the University of the State of Pennsylvania, and put it on the public dole.

But the provost and trustees waged a rearguard action. They alleged abrogation of legitimate property rights and, when the state failed to provide adequate funding, fiscal mismanagement. Restoration of the college became a central issue for Republicans; defense of egalitarianism in education remained a rallying cry for Constitutionalists.

◆— **Franklin** did his best to remain above the fray. Partly from pride of authorship, he held to the basic principles of the 1776 constitution:

the legislature of one house, the annual elections, the executive responsibility in the hands of a council (headed by a *primus inter pares* president—currently himself) rather than a single strong governor. In this regard he was a Constitutionalist. At the same time, he shared the philosophical and economic conservatism of many Republicans. He quietly backed recharter of the Bank of North America as good for business (this goal was accomplished in 1787). Ambivalent as he was, and appreciating the motives of those who voted for him as a symbol of unity, he avoided controversy. Indeed, he avoided most meetings of the Executive Council, attending the daily sessions about once a week.

Instead he made the rounds of his construction sites, querying here, nudging there. Workers on his own house, removing materials from the roof, discovered something that gave him satisfaction. Years earlier, while he was gone, the house had received a terrible blow from lightning. The neighbors, who saw the strike, ran to the house to inquire of the condition of the inhabitants and to put out the fire they believed must have been kindled. But there was no fire, and all inside were well, if rather dazed by the loud sound. Franklin now discovered why, as he explained to an Italian scientist who had sent him his latest work on lightning rods, electrical conductors, and the like. "The conductor was taken down to be removed, when I found that the copper point which had been nine inches long, and in its thickest part about one third of an inch in diameter, had been almost all melted down and blown away, very little of it remaining attached to the iron rod. So that at length the invention has been of some use to the inventor."

Yet the inventor did not intend to rely on copper and iron exclusively. The construction gave him scope to indulge his long interest in fire prevention. "I lament the loss your town has suffered this year by fire," he wrote Jane Mecom after hearing of Boston's latest blaze. "I sometimes think men do not act like reasonable creatures when they build for themselves combustible dwellings in which they are every day obliged to use fire. In my new dwellings I have taken a few precautions, not generally used: to wit, none of the wooden work of one room communicates with the wooden work of any other room; and all the floors, and even the steps of the stairs, are plastered close to the boards, besides the plastering on the laths under the joists. There are also trap-doors to go out upon the roofs, that one may go out and wet the shingles in case of a neighbouring fire."

One of the buildings on Market Street was intended for a print shop for Benny Bache, after he finished at the college. Almost certainly the young man joined his grandfather in supervising the work there; doubtless they discussed the prospects for a new printer in the city, assessing the strengths and weaknesses of the competition. Perhaps they spoke of the paper young Ben would publish.

From a distance Franklin observed his eldest grandson. Temple spent most weeks in New Jersey on his father's old farm; Franklin wrote with encouragement and advice. Ever the practical educator, Franklin apparently suggested that Temple apply gypsum to a meadow, in a pattern shaping the words, "This field has been plastered." When the grass of the letters grew lusher and taller than the rest of the meadow, passersby received a lesson in agronomy.

But it soon became apparent that Temple's heart was not in the soil. Franklin wrote Lafayette that his grandson "amuses himself with cultivating his lands." Franklin felt a bit guilty at having raised Temple to public office, the more since Congress had shown no inclination to honor the grandfather's request to find a post for the young man. Besides, the older Franklin got, the more he—the lifelong city dweller—came to view agriculture as the wellspring of virtue. "I wish he would make a serious business of it, and renounce all thoughts of public employment," Franklin wrote Lafayette, "for I think agriculture the most honourable, because the most independent, of all professions." But youth would have its way. "I believe he hankers a little after Paris, or some of the other polished cities of Europe."

When the work on his own house was complete, Franklin outfitted the new rooms to his pleasure. The library had shelves that ranged from floor to ceiling. Less agile than in years past, he invented a mechanical arm for pulling books from high shelves without resort to stools or ladders. In another room he installed an unusual shoe-shaped copper tub, in which he took long hot baths to ease his stone. "He sits in the heel," reported a guest, "and his legs go under the vamp; on the instep he has a place to fix his book; and here he sits and enjoys himself." (This guest had both a low opinion of Pennsylvania politics and a droll sense of humor. Referring to Franklin's selection as head of the Executive Council, he said, "His accepting the office is a sure sign of senility. But would it not be a capital subject for an historical painting—the Doctor placed at the head of the Council Board in his bathing slipper?")

Franklin reckoned himself blessed. "I have found my family here in health, good circumstances, and well respected by their fellow citizens," he reported to Polly Hewson. The companions of his youth were almost all departed, but he enjoyed the company of their children and grand-children. "I have public business enough to preserve me from *ennui*, and private amusement besides in conversation, books, my garden, and crib-bage." He played cards with friends for amusement. Occasionally he felt a twinge of compunction when he reflected on his idleness. "But another reflection comes to relieve me, whispering: 'You know that the soul is im-mortal; why then should you be such a niggard of a little time, when you have a whole eternity before you?' So, being easily convinced, and, like other reasonable creatures, satisfied with a small reason when it is in favour of doing what I have a mind to, I shuffle the cards again, and begin another game."

29

Sunrise at Dusk

1786–87

᠆ In correspondence with British friends, Franklin took
pains to defend America against reports of post-
Revolutionary troubles. Many Britons, for reasons not
difficult to fathom, liked to read that their wayward cousins
had cause to rue their waywardness, and consequently their
papers often carried such stories. Franklin regularly rebutted
these tales. "Your newspapers, to please honest *John Bull*,
paint our situation here in frightful colours, as if we were
very miserable since we broke our connexion with him," he
wrote in the autumn of 1786, in one letter of many like it.
"But I will give you some remarks by which you may form
your own judgment. Our husbandmen, who are the bulk of
the nation, have had plentiful crops; their produce sells at
high prices and for ready, hard money—wheat, for instance,

for 8 s. and 8 s. 6 d. per bushel. Our working people are all employed and get high wages, are well fed and well clad." Philadelphia was growing; smaller towns were springing up in every part of the state. "The laws govern, justice is well administered, and property as secure as in any country on the globe. Our wilderness lands are daily buying up by new settlers, and our settlements extend rapidly to the westward." European goods were never cheaper, with the British monopoly broken. Franklin spoke of Pennsylvania from personal observation; as to the other states, "When I read in all the papers of the extravagant rejoicings every 4th of July, the day on which was signed the Declaration of Independence, I am convinced that none of them are discontented with the Revolution."

To French friends, who were more sympathetic to the American Revolution, Franklin was more candid. "That there should be faults in our first sketches or plans of government is not surprising," he said. "Rather, considering the times and the circumstances under which they were formed, it is surprising that the faults are so few." To a pair of priests he had known in Passy, he explained, "Our public affairs go on as well as can be reasonably expected after so great an overturning. We have had some disorders in different parts of the country, but we arrange them as they arise, and are daily mending and improving, so that I have no doubt but all will come right in time." He added significantly, and in keeping with many earlier comments, that all depended on the American character. "Only a virtuous people are capable of freedom."

⌐ Almost no one in America disputed Franklin's assertion that freedom required virtue, but by this time many were questioning whether America possessed that requirement. The war had not even ended when unsettling tendencies surfaced. In March 1783 a group of disgruntled officers at Washington's camp at Newburgh, New York, threatened to use military force to compel Congress to award them back pay and pensions. A shadowy group of conspirators within Congress itself vaguely encouraged the officers, hoping to employ their discontent to pry power from the states, which were the source of the inability of Congress to pay the soldiers.

George Washington shared the frustration of his subordinates, as he had demonstrated on many occasions. But he would brook no hint of military coercion of the civil authorities. He summoned the officers to a meeting and told them to abandon their plans. "How inconsistent with the rules of propriety!" he declared. "How unmilitary! And how subversive of all order and discipline!" Washington decried the "blackest designs" and "most insidious purposes" behind the cabal. To act against the government of the United States—the government for which everyone present had endured such hardship and danger—would "cast a shade over that glory which has been so justly acquired, and tarnish the reputation of an army which is celebrated through all Europe for its fortitude and patriotism." Urging his men to put aside every thought of disloyalty, he predicted (and implicitly ordered), "You will, by the dignity of your conduct, afford occasion for posterity to say, when speaking of the glorious example you have exhibited to mankind, 'had this day been wanting, the world had never seen the last stage of perfection to which human nature is capable of attaining.' " Washington rarely addressed his officers as a group, but he showed himself to be a natural at it. He closed by producing a letter from a member of Congress sympathetic to the army's plight; as he began to read it, he stopped and pulled his glasses from his pocket. "Gentlemen," he explained, "you will permit me to put on my spectacles, for I have not only grown gray, but almost blind, in the service of my country." None present could resist their leader; as one later recalled, Washington's performance "drew tears from many of the officers."

Although the Newburgh conspiracy dissipated, certain of the sentiments behind it—particularly the notion that military officers possessed greater virtue than civilian officials—persisted. The officer corps of the Continental Army created something called the Society of the Cincinnati, a hereditary order that would honor the service its founding members provided during the war. Washington initially considered the society innocuous enough to accept its presidency, but many outsiders feared that such an organization would attempt to influence the political process.

Franklin scorned what he called this "order of hereditary knights." It insulted the American people, who had registered both legal and emotional opposition to the conferral of titles and ranks of nobility. Besides, like all schemes of hereditary honors, it put things just backward. "Honour, worthily obtained (as for example that of our officers) is in its nature a *personal* thing, and incommunicable to any but those who had some share in obtaining it." If honor had to be assigned to families, it ought to be handed *up* to parents rather than down to children. The parents of a person who did good deeds might logically share some credit for the good deeds of their child, in that they were responsible for the child's education and overall rearing; but the children of the one who did good deeds could not share any such credit. Besides, even granting the principle of descending honor, the mathematics of procreation rendered its application absurd. "A man's son, for instance, is but half of his family, the other half belonging to the family of his wife. His son, too, marrying into another family, his share in the grandson is but a fourth." And so on, till by the eighth or tenth generation, and allowing for "a reasonable estimation of the number of rogues and fools and royalists and scoundrels and prostitutes that are mixed with," the contribution of the original Cincinnatus was diluted beyond recognition.

Another argument against the Cincinnati was more whimsical. The group had adopted the bald eagle as an avian emblem; Franklin objected.

> He is a bird of bad moral character; he does not get his living honestly. You may have seen him perched on some dead tree, near the river where, too lazy to fish for himself, he watches the labour of the fishing hawk; and when that diligent bird has at length taken a fish, and is bearing it to his nest for the support of his mate and young ones, the bald eagle pursues him and takes it from him. With all this injustice he is never in good case; but, like those among men who live by sharping and robbing, he is generally poor, and often very lousy. Besides, he is a rank coward; the little kingbird, not bigger than a sparrow, attacks him boldly and drives him out of the district. He is therefore by no means a proper emblem for the brave and honest Cincinnati, who have driven all the King-birds from our country.

Better if the Cincinnati had adopted the turkey, a more honest bird and a genuine American. "He is, though a little vain and silly, it is true, but not the worse emblem for that, a bird of courage, and would not hesitate to attack a grenadier of the British Guards who should presume to invade his farm yard with a *red* coat on."

๑ **Many shared** Franklin's view of the Cincinnati, if not of the turkey; and after Washington, reconsidering, resigned, the order fizzled. Yet in other respects American society showed additional hangover effects from its wartime militarization. The siege of the State House in Philadelphia that prompted the flight of Congress to Princeton was one indication of a lingering propensity to violence. Another, more disturbing illustration emerged in Massachusetts. The disruption of trade consequent to the war had injured the entire state. With the British West Indies off-limits to American merchantmen, departures from the wharves Franklin wandered about as a boy had diminished drastically. Shipbuilding sagged for the same and related reasons. Yet the troubles of the state hit farmers the hardest, and western farmers hardest of all. The same sound-money interests that had joined Thomas Hutchinson in opposing paper currency thirty years earlier opposed paper now, and in addition endorsed an accelerated payoff of the state's war debts. The vehicle for the redemption was the land tax, which fell most heavily on farmers, and which now rose by more than half. Meanwhile prices for agricultural commodities—commodities that formerly went to the West Indies but now went begging—plunged. Between rising taxes and falling prices, farmers felt peculiarly victimized.

Their first appeal was to the state legislature. They cried for paper money to stimulate the economy, boost prices, and ease their debts. Failing that, they demanded stay laws to prevent seizure of property for nonpayment of debts. The lower house of the state legislature—the chamber more attuned to popular sentiment—responded to the farmers' appeal, but the money men of Boston blocked the bills in the upper house. The machinery of the courts ground into motion, mandating foreclosures and auctions of land, farm tools, houses, even furniture and clothes of the luckless debtors.

One such unfortunate was Daniel Shays, a thirty-nine-year-old veteran of the war, a former captain. Shays recalled how he and his fellows had refused to let London harry them into bankruptcy, and he saw no reason Boston should do what London had been prevented from doing. He rallied hundreds of men of like experience; by the end of August 1786 Shays's band was a thousand strong. The insurgents forcibly redefined justice in Northampton County, closing the courts and preventing prosecutions of debtors. Echoes of the Stamp Act resistance and the Boston Tea Party rolled from the valley of the Connecticut to the foothills of the Berkshires.

This time, however, respectable opinion opposed the insurgents. A Springfield merchant called the Shays crowd "a party of madmen." A commercial colleague from Attleboro decried the "fury and madness of the people." A Southampton creditor declared, "Monarchy is better than the tyranny of this mob." Massachusetts Governor James Bowdoin warned that the uprising was fraught with the "most fatal and pernicious consequences," potentially including "universal riot, anarchy, and confusion, which would probably terminate in absolute despotism." In the name of the ideals of the Revolution—"of lives, liberty and property"—but with rather more emphasis on property than on liberty, Bowdoin dispatched the militia to suppress the rebels.

Shays and his battle-hardened fellows refused to be intimidated, not least because many militiamen refused to obey the governor's order. During the autumn of 1786 the ranks of the rebels swelled, and they threatened to seize a federal arsenal at Springfield. Bowdoin sent more troops, and a suddenly alarmed Congress authorized General Henry Knox to raise a small federal army against the rebels.

The nation watched in horror as Massachusetts, the cradle of American liberty, the most patriotic of all the colonies, dissolved into civil war. George Washington, observing the disorders from the distance of Mount Vernon, was appalled. "Good God!" he wrote Knox. "Who besides a Tory could have foreseen or a Briton predicted them!" Americans had prided themselves on a national character superior to that of Britain. The current events gave the lie to this claim. "Notwithstanding the boasted virtue of America, we are far gone in every thing ignoble and bad." For the present, Massachusetts approached anarchy alone; but it might have company soon. "There are combustibles in every state," Washington said, "which a spark may set fire to."

To many Americans, Shays's rebellion revealed the need for a more energetic national government. Although the federal forces under Knox in fact played little role in eventually subduing the insurgency, the uprising demonstrated the vulnerability of the state governments to pressure by armed minorities. From classical times the argument against republicanism was that it degenerated into democracy—government not simply in the name of the people but by the people themselves. And democracy degenerated into anarchy, because the people were not fit to govern themselves. In Massachusetts the name of anarchy was Daniel Shays, and the lesson Shays taught was that if American republicanism did not take preventive measures soon, it might be lost.

Other embarrassments to republicanism amplified the feeling. Three years after the Paris treaty the British had still not evacuated their forts in the northwest, claiming that the Americans had not fulfilled their commitments regarding prewar debts and treatment of the Loyalists. That the claim was accurate hardly mitigated the affront to the United States—debt issues were not insignificant, but territorial questions touched the heart of national sovereignty. Meanwhile the Spanish were intriguing on America's southwestern frontier, to what end none could say, but certainly to no good. At the same time the states were intriguing against one another in matters of trade and navigation, deranging markets and destroying commerce. Finally, the states were more reluctant than ever to pay their share of the expenses of the national government, which threatened to grind to a halt.

In September 1786 advocates of a stronger central government summoned the similarly minded to Annapolis. The harmonization of trade rules was the stated agenda; the unspoken aim was broader. Disappointingly for James Madison, Alexander Hamilton, and the other organizers, only five states sent delegates; cleverly, the organizers doubled their bets by adjourning in favor of a more ambitious conference to convene at Philadelphia the following May. The job of delegates, according to the formal charge from Congress, would be the formulation of such amendments to the Articles of Confederation as would "render the federal constitution adequate to the exigencies of Government & the preservation of the Union."

Who would answer the summons was a matter of doubt during the next several months. Congress gave its approval, but hesitantly. Such enthusiasm as existed was almost balanced by skepticism. Madison, the prime mover of the project, did not know what to anticipate. "It seems probable that a meeting will take place, and that it will be a pretty full one," he wrote at the end of February 1787. "What the issue of it will be is among the other arcana of futurity and nearly as inscrutable as any of them. In general I find men of reflection much less sanguine as to a new than despondent as to the present system." Yet something had to be done. "The present system neither has nor deserves advocates, and if some very strong props are not applied will quickly tumble to the ground."

᎓— Franklin had lived much longer than Madison—much longer, in fact, than all but a handful of the other delegates to the constitutional convention. And he adopted a much less alarmist view of the future. He referred to Shays's rebellion as merely the work of "some disorderly people," and declared—this to a French friend, to whom he spoke candidly—"The rest of the states go on pretty well, except some dissensions in Rhode Island and Maryland respecting paper money."

Yet if he did not think doom at the door, Franklin heard its rumblings in the distance. Briefing Jefferson, still in France, he wrote that from what he knew of the delegates, they seemed to be men of prudence and ability. "I hope good from their meeting." But the risks were great. "If it does not do good it must do harm, as it will show that we have not wisdom enough among us to govern ourselves, and will strengthen the opinion of some political writers that popular governments cannot long support themselves."

Anticipating the convention, Franklin organized a group called the Society for Political Inquiries, which met weekly in the library of his new home. Philadelphians made up the active membership, but the group enrolled various outside luminaries as honorary members. Among these was Washington, who was thought to be favorably disposed to constitutional revision yet was also known to be reluctant to take a leading role. The former general cherished his exalted reputation and was correspondingly hesitant to involve himself in any divisive venture. At the same time, however, he hardly desired the undoing of the cause to which he had devoted eight years of his life. Nor did he wish to appear derelict in his duty. Franklin was among those telling Washington that duty called him to Philadelphia. "Your presence will be of the greatest importance to the success of the measure," Franklin wrote. Washington allowed himself to be persuaded.

Washington's arrival in Philadelphia prompted a civic celebration the likes of which had not been seen since the end of the war. A cadre of his old officers rode out to greet him; the party crossed the Schuylkill on a floating bridge built by the British but abandoned intact at the evacuation of the city and since maintained by the locals. Church bells pealed as the hero passed; the leading citizens vied for his favor. Robert and Mrs. Morris won the prize of housing him, in their mansion on Market Street just east of Sixth. If the Morris house was any evidence, the financier's interests were thriving; besides a hothouse (for winter enjoyment), the compound boasted an icehouse (especially appreciated during the sweltering weeks of the convention) and a stable for twelve horses. (Yet, not content with a standard of living unsurpassed "by any commercial voluptuary of London," in the words of a French visitor, Morris subsequently speculated in western lands and lost all. He spent three years in a debtors' prison within wailing distance of his former mansion.)

On arrival Washington paid his respects to Franklin; the next day the general returned for dinner. The other delegates followed suit. Franklin's new dining room seated twenty-four; he now probably wished it bigger, for everyone insisted on seeing the man who was at once America's resident sage and, as Pennsylvania president, the convention's ex officio host. On Friday, May 18, he wrote a London brewer who had sent him a cask of porter, "We have here at present what the French call *une assemblée des notables*, a convention composed of some of the principal people from the several states of our confederation. They did me the honour of dining with me last Wednesday, when the cask was broached, and its contents met with the most cordial reception and universal approbation."

On this festive note the convention commenced its sober business. Only two men were even contemplated for president of the convention: Franklin and Washington. Franklin deferred to Washington, perhaps partly from concern that his health would not stand the wear of daily sessions, but at least equally from knowledge that the project would have the greatest chance of success under the aegis of the eminent general. (Washington's distance above mere mortals was already legendary. Several delegates were discussing this phenomenon when Franklin's Pennsylvania colleague, Gouverneur Morris, a hearty good fellow, suggested it was all in their minds. Alexander Hamilton challenged Morris: "If you will, at the next reception evenings, gently slap him on the shoulder and say, 'My dear General, how happy I am to see you look so well!' a supper and wine shall be provided for you and a dozen of your friends." Morris accepted the challenge and did what Hamilton demanded. Washington immediately removed Morris's hand from his shoulder, stepped away, and fixed Morris with an angry frown until the trespasser retreated in confusion. Hamilton paid up, yet at the dinner Morris declared, "I have won the bet, but paid dearly for it, and nothing could induce me to repeat it.")

Franklin was right to worry about his ability to attend all the sessions. His mode of travel these days—to the limited extent he *did* travel—was via sedan chair, a seat mounted between two poles, which he had brought from France. Four prisoners from the Walnut Street jail hoisted the chair on their shoulders, and, if they walked slowly, Franklin's stone did not pain him too much. Although the seat was covered, with glass windows, it was not really suited to foul weather, and when heavy rain doused the opening day of the convention, Franklin was forced to stay home. He had been planning to nominate Washington for convention president himself; instead the nomination was put forward by the Pennsylvania delegation. The gesture was appreciated all the same. "The nomination came with particular grace from Pennsylvania," recorded James Madison, "as Doctor Franklin alone could have been thought of as a competitor."

Before the convention most of the delegates knew Franklin only by reputation. His long absence from America rendered him something of a mystery; most wondered whether he would live up to all the good things said of him—or down to the few bad things. William Pierce of Georgia was one of the handful of delegates who recorded his impression:

> Dr. Franklin is well known to be the greatest philosopher of the present age; all the operations of nature he seems to understand, the very heavens obey him, and the clouds yield up their lightning to be imprisoned in his rod.
>
> But what claim he has to be a politician, posterity must determine. It is certain that he does not shine much in public council. He is no speaker, nor does he seem to let politics engage his attention.
>
> He is, however, a most extraordinary man, and tells a story in a style more engaging than anything I ever heard. Let his biographer finish his character. He is 82 [actually 81] years old, and possesses an activity of mind equal to a youth of 25 years of age.

Franklin would have been the first to agree he was no orator, and in a gathering of fifty-five politicians, most of whom prided themselves on their forensic skills, he was content to let others carry the oratorical burden.

In fact he allowed others to carry even the burden of *his* statements. Very early the intentions of the organizers of the convention became evident: not merely to revise the Articles of Confederation but to draft an entirely new charter. The Virginians—especially Madison and Edmund Randolph—had been busy, and on the third day Randolph revealed a comprehensive plan for a national government. The centerpiece of the Virginia plan was a powerful legislature of two houses, one house elected by the people, the other chosen by the popular house from nominations forwarded by the states. The legislature would name the executive and the judiciary, and it would possess a veto over state laws infringing its prerogatives.

Franklin had preferred a unicameral legislature for Pennsylvania, and he preferred it for America. He preferred an executive council, again on the Pennsylvania model, over a single president. But his first speech addressed another issue: how the executive was to be paid. Apologizing for the fact that his memory was not what it had been, he explained that he had written out his remarks. Franklin's Pennsylvania colleague James Wilson offered to read them, and Franklin accepted.

Franklin proposed that the executive, whether singular or plural, receive no compensation beyond expenses. "There are two passions which have a powerful influence on the affairs of men," he asserted. "These are ambition and avarice: the love of power, and the love of money. Separately, each of these has great force in prompting men to action; but when united in view of the same object, they have in many minds the most violent effects. Place before the eyes of such men a post of *honour* that shall at the same time be a place of *profit*, and they will move heaven and earth to obtain it."

Franklin spoke from his experience of British politics, where precisely the dynamics he described had rendered British policies self-destructive—as the very existence of the United States demonstrated. Merely limiting the salaries of government officials would not prevent the evils Franklin foresaw. "Though we may set out in the beginning with moderate salaries, we shall find that such will not be of long continuance. Reasons will never be wanting for proposed augmentations. And there will always be a party for giving more to the rulers."

The essential issue was not the cost in money of supporting the executive but the cost in liberty of introducing money so directly into politics. "There is scarce a king in a hundred who would not, if he could, follow the example of Pharaoh: get first all the people's money, then all their lands, and then make them and their children servants forever." Franklin anticipated the obvious objection to this statement: that no one was proposing a king for America. (Alexander Hamilton would get around to that later.) "I know it. But there is a natural inclination in mankind to kingly government. It sometimes relieves them from aristocratic domination. They had rather have one tyrant than five hundred. It gives more of the appearance of equality among citizens, and that they like. I am apprehensive, therefore—perhaps too apprehensive—that the government of these states may in future times end in a monarchy. But this catastrophe I think may be long delayed if in our proposed system we do not sow the seeds of contention, faction and tumult by making our posts of honour, places of profit."

Some would call his proposal utopian, Franklin conceded; men must be paid for their labors. Yet he begged to differ, and he cited evidence. In English counties the office of high sheriff yielded no profit to its holder;

on the contrary, the office cost its holder money. "Yet it is executed, and well executed, and usually by some of the principal gentlemen of the county." In France the office of counselor likewise exacted a cost of its holders, yet respectable and capable individuals vied for the distinction it conferred.

Nor did the members of the convention have to look across the ocean for examples of patriotic service untied to profit. They merely had to look across the room. "Have we not seen the great and most important of our offices, that of general of our armies, executed for eight years together without the smallest salary, by a patriot whom I will not now offend by any other praise?" If such was true amid the fatigues and distresses of war, would not the country be able to find men willing to give service during peace? "I have a better opinion of our country. I think we shall never be without a sufficient number of wise and good men to undertake and execute well and faithfully the office in question."

Perhaps Franklin misread from his own past into the future of his audience. Their very presence, combined with their youth, indicated they were not like him, who had delayed entering politics until he had made his fortune. Nor were any but a few as well off as Washington, who could afford to serve his country for eight years without compensation. These men might not place profit above honor, but few of them could ignore profit entirely.

Madison recorded the reaction to Franklin's speech: "The motion was seconded by Colonel Hamilton with the view, he said, of merely bringing so respectable a proposition before the committee, and which was besides enforced by arguments that had a certain degree of weight. No debate ensued, and the proposition was postponed for the consideration of the members. It was treated with great respect, but rather for the author of it than from any apparent conviction of its expediency or practicality."

~ **Another** Franklin proposal received equally short shrift. A month into the convention the body had made frustratingly little progress. Franklin noted that the delegates had searched history for guidance and looked to the governments of other countries. "How has it happened, sir, that we have not hitherto once thought of humbly applying to the Father of Lights to illuminate our understandings?" At the onset of the troubles with Britain, the Continental Congress, meeting in this very room, had daily requested divine help in finding its way. "Our prayers were heard, sir, and they were graciously answered. All of us who were engaged in the struggle must have observed the frequent instances of a superintending Providence in our favour." Without Heaven's help the delegates would not be where they were, attempting what they were attempting. "Have we now forgotten that powerful Friend? Or do we imagine we no longer need its assistance?" Franklin remarked that he had lived a long time. "And the longer I live the more convincing proofs I see of this truth, *that God governs in the affairs of men*. And if a sparrow cannot fall to the ground without his notice, is it probable that an empire can rise without his aid?" The sacred texts declared that "except the Lord build the house, they labour in vain that build it." Franklin said, "I firmly believe this." Without heavenly aid, the delegates would build no better than the builders of Babel, divided by petty, partial interests. "Our projects will be confounded, and we ourselves shall become a reproach and a bye-word down to future ages." Humanity might well despair of establishing government by reason, and leave it to war and conquest. Accordingly, Franklin moved to start each session with a prayer and to secure the services of one or more of the clergy of Philadelphia for the purpose.

This statement was as open as Franklin ever got in public about his religious beliefs. (And it was only partially public, the delegates having pledged themselves to confidentiality.) The delegates probably did not appreciate the unusual candor in Franklin's remarks; in any case they ignored them. His motion received a second, but Hamilton and others worried that, however laudable the practice of prayer might be, to commence it at this late date would convey a sense of desperation. Franklin responded that the past omission of a duty did not justify continued omission and that the public was just as likely to respond positively as negatively to word that their delegates were seeking God's blessing on their labors.

His argument failed. After Hugh Williamson of North Carolina pointed out that the convention lacked funds to pay a chaplain, Edmund Randolph offered an amendment to Franklin's motion. Randolph suggested hiring a preacher to give a sermon on Independence Day, less than a week off, and thereafter to open the sessions with a prayer.

Franklin accepted the amendment, but the delegates put off discussion by recessing for the day, and the proposition died. Franklin remarked with some wonder, at the bottom of the written copy of his speech, "The convention, except three or four persons, thought prayers unnecessary!"

~ Most delegates had more earthly matters in mind. The nature of the executive vexed the convention for weeks. At one extreme stood Alexander Hamilton, the former protégé of Washington—ambitious, arrogant, intolerant of those less gifted than he. A certain mystery surrounded his West Indian birth; John Adams, ever uncharitable, called him the "bastard brat of a Scotch pedlar." He was small and lithe, with delicate features that made him look even younger than his thirty-two years. Yet the fire that burned inside him made him seem, to Jefferson at least (after Hamilton aimed his flames Jefferson's way), "an host within himself." Even on best behavior, as at the convention, he put people off. William Pierce, while granting that Hamilton was "deservedly celebrated for his talents," added, "His manners are tinctured with stiffness, and sometimes with a degree of vanity that is highly disagreeable."

Patriotic and courageous during the war, Hamilton nonetheless retained a decided partiality toward the British system of government. "I believe the British government form the best model the world ever produced," Hamilton told the convention. The secret of the British government was its strength, which allowed it to provide individual security. The British recognized a fundamental facet of human nature. "All communities divide themselves into the few and the many. The first are the rich and well born, the other the mass of the people. The voice of the people has been said to be the voice of God; and however generally this maxim has been quoted and believed, it is not true in fact." The people were turbulent and fickle; they rarely knew where their interests lay. "Give therefore to the first class a distinct, permanent share in the government. They will check the unsteadiness in the second, and as they cannot receive any advantage by a change, they therefore will ever maintain good government."

Hamilton's confidence in benign rule by society's betters led him to conclude that executive power ought to be vested in a single man, elected for life. "It may be said that this constitutes an elective monarchy." Let the fainthearted call it what they wished. "Pray, what is a monarchy? May not the governors of the respective states be considered in that light?" Hamilton allowed for impeachment of the executive in cases of egregious malfeasance; in this respect, he said, the executive-for-life fell short of being a monarch. But he endorsed the basic principle of monarchy, that the holder of the office ought to be irresponsible to the people.

Only then would he be free of the people's unruly passions. Earlier speakers had suggested a long term for the executive, perhaps seven years. Hamilton deemed this insufficient. "An executive is less dangerous to the liberties of the people when in office during life, than for seven years."

Franklin held just the opposite view. Not only did he rest far less faith in the British system—having, unlike Hamilton, observed its operations closely at first hand—but he had less confidence in what Hamilton (and many others) deemed the better elements in society. To place entire executive authority in one man was to court trouble. Even assuming the best of goodwill on the part of the executive, what would happen when he got sick? Physical frailty might not worry Hamilton and others in the prime of life, but, as Franklin could assure them, life lasted beyond one's prime. Eventually, of course, the executive would die; though Hamilton proposed a scheme for electing a successor, after many years under one man the government could not escape disruption.

Moreover, judgments varied from man to man, and each executive would seek to make his own mark. "A single person's measures may be good. The successor often differs in opinion of those measures, and adopts others; often is ambitious of distinguishing himself by opposing them, and offering new projects. One is peaceably disposed, another may be fond of war, &c. Hence foreign states can never have that confidence in the treaties or friendship of such a government, as in that which is conducted by a number."

The only conclusion Franklin could draw was that executive power was too potent to be entrusted to a single person. "The steady course of public measures is most probably to be expected from a number."

◆— Ultimately the convention split the difference between Hamilton and Franklin, opting for a single executive of limited term. On another issue—the one on which the entire constitutional project threatened to founder—compromise finally came as well, but with greater difficulty.

Under the Virginia plan, election to the lower house of the legislature would be according to population, with larger states—such as Virginia—having greater representation than smaller states. Because the upper house would be chosen by the lower house, this advantage to the larger states would inform the actions of the legislature as a whole. The delegates from the larger states thought this only just, not least since they were expected to pay the largest portion of the expenses of the central government.

Predictably, delegates from the smaller states objected. Under the Articles of Confederation, each state possessed equal weight within the legislature, and the small-state delegates intended to preserve this principle. Indeed, the instructions of the delegates from Delaware forbade them from countenancing any tampering with equal representation by states. Accordingly, when the delegation from New Jersey proposed an alternative to the Virginia plan—an alternative enshrining the one-state, one-vote principle—the smaller states rallied to it.

Upon the question of representation hinged the essence of the new government. If representation remained by states, then the new government would remain, to a large degree, a government of the states, along the lines of the Confederation. By contrast, if representation shifted to population, then the new government would be a government of the people. The states might retain their existence, but they would have hardly more meaning than counties in England.

This was exactly what James Madison believed they should have. "Some contend that states are sovereign," Madison declared, "when in fact they are only political societies." The states had never possessed sovereignty, which from the start of the Revolution had been vested in Congress. "The states, at present, are only great corporations, having the power of making by-laws, and these are effectual only if they are not contradictory to the general confederation. The states ought to be placed under the control of the general government—at least as much as they formerly were under the king and British Parliament."

These were fighting words, or promised to be. Gunning Bedford of Delaware demanded, "Are not the large states evidently seeking to aggrandize themselves at the expense of the small? They think no doubt that they have right on their side, but interest has blinded their eyes." Bedford accused the large states of adopting "a dictatorial air" toward the smaller, of suggesting they could make a government of their own without the small states. "If they do," Bedford warned, "the small ones will find some foreign ally of more honour and good faith, who will take them by the hand and do them justice."

Bedford's threat elicited an even sharper response from Gouverneur Morris. The larger states would not brook such secessionist talk, Morris asserted. "This country must be united. If persuasion does not unite it, the sword will." Amplifying his point, he added, "The scenes of horror attending civil commotion can not be described, and the conclusion of them will be worse than the terms of their continuance. The stronger party will then make traitors of the weaker, and the gallows and halter will finish the work of the sword."

It was just this kind of acrimony that had elicited Franklin's call for the help of the Deity; that call having failed of the convention's approval, he now interposed himself. "The diversity of opinion turns on two points," he told the delegates. "If a proportional representation takes place, the small states contend that their liberties will be in danger. If an equality of votes is to be put in its place, the large states say their money will be in danger." The time had come to compromise. "When a broad table is to be made, and the edges of the planks do not fit, the artist takes a little from both, and makes a good joint. In like manner here, both sides must part with some of their demands in order that they may join in some accommodating purpose."

He thereupon laid before the members a motion:

> That the legislatures of the several states shall choose and send an equal number of delegates, namely _____, who are to compose the second branch of the general legislature.

Franklin's motion became the basis for the grand compromise that saved the convention and made the Constitution possible. The large states would have their way with the lower house, to be called the House of Representatives, which would be selected according to population. The interests of the smaller states would be safeguarded in the upper house, called the Senate, which would be chosen by the legislatures of the states, with each state getting two—the number that filled in Franklin's blank—senators. (More than a century later, of course, the Constitution would be amended to provide for direct election of senators by voters of the states, but the principle of equal representation remained.)

～ On the eve of the final vote on the grand compromise, Franklin entertained a visitor to the city. Dr. Manasseh Cutler was a clergyman from Massachusetts, also a botanist (and later a member of Congress). "There was no curiosity in Philadelphia which I felt so anxious to see as this great man, who has been the wonder of Europe as well as the glory of America," Cutler wrote. "But a man who stood first in the literary world, and had spent so many years in the Courts of Kings, particularly in the refined Court of France, I conceived would not be of very easy access, and must certainly have much of the air of grandeur and majesty about him. Common folks must expect only to gaze at him at a distance, and answer such questions as he might please to ask." When delegate Elbridge Gerry of Massachusetts, who was on his way to Franklin's house, asked Cutler if he wished to come, Cutler said he certainly did—but, as he told a friend later, "I hesitated; my knees smote together."

What Cutler found in the Franklin garden was not in the least what he expected.

> How were my ideas changed, when I saw a short, fat, trunched old man, in a plain Quaker dress, bald pate, and short white locks, sitting without his hat under the tree, and, as Mr. Gerry introduced me, rose from his chair, took me by the hand, expressed his joy to see me, welcomed me to the city, and begged me to seat myself close to him. His voice was low, but his countenance open, frank, and pleasing. . . . I delivered him my letters. After he had read them, he took me again by the hand, and, with the usual compliments, introduced me to the other gentlemen, who were most of them members of the Convention.
>
> Here we entered into a free conversation, and spent our time most agreeably until it was dark. The tea-table was spread under the tree, and Mrs. Bache, a very gross and rather homely lady, who is the only daughter of the Doctor, and lives with him, served it out to the company. She had three of her children about her, over whom she seemed to have no kind of command, but who appeared to be excessively fond of their Grandpapa.
>
> The Doctor showed me a curiosity he had just received, and with which he was much pleased. It was a snake with two heads, preserved in a large vial. It was taken near the confluence of the Schuylkill with the Delaware, about four miles from this city. It was about ten inches long, well proportioned, the heads perfect, and united to the body about one-fourth of an inch below the extremities of the jaws. . . .
>
> The Doctor mentioned the situation of this snake, if it was traveling among the bushes, and one head should choose to go on one side of the stem of a bush and the other head should prefer the other side, and that neither of the heads would consent to come back or give way to the other. He was then going to mention

a humourous matter that had that day occurred in Convention, in consequence of his comparing the snake to America, for he seemed to forget that every thing in Convention was to be kept a profound secret; but the secrecy of Convention matters was suggested to him, which stopped him, and deprived me of the story he was going to tell.

Doubtless the story involved the dispute over representation, which was on the verge of resolution—without the snake's starving or either of the heads' being cut off. Yet the vote was not certain, and the other delegates present definitely did not want the loquacious host to make the compromise settlement any more difficult.

(Their concern also reflected their fear of the convention's president. During one early session, copies of the Virginia propositions were circulated, with the injunction that these were for the delegates' eyes only and must be guarded with strictest care. Some while later a copy was discovered on the floor of the State House and turned over to Washington. The general placed the copy in his pocket and said nothing until the end of that day's debates. Thereupon he rose from his seat and addressed the delegates in the sternest tones. "Gentlemen," he said, "I am sorry to find that some member of this body has been so neglectful of the secrets of the Convention as to drop in the State House a copy of their proceedings, which by accident was picked up and delivered to me this morning. I must entreat gentlemen to be more careful, lest our transactions get into the newspapers and disturb the public repose by premature speculations. I know not whose paper it is, but there it is." Throwing the paper down on the table, he concluded, "Let him who owns it, take it." Then he bowed, picked up his hat, and left the room— "with a dignity so severe that every person seemed alarmed," said William Pierce. Significantly, no one claimed the paper, although Pierce's heart leaped into his throat when, reaching in his pocket, he could not find his own copy. To his immense relief, it turned up later in the pocket of his other coat.)

After dark, Franklin suggested he and Cutler go inside.

The Doctor invited me into his library, which is likewise his study. It is a very large chamber, and high studded. The walls were covered with book-shelves filled with books; besides, there are four large alcoves, extending two-thirds the length of the chamber, filled in the same manner. I presume [and Cutler was in a position to know] this is the largest, and by far the best, private library in America.

He showed us a glass machine for exhibiting the circulation of the blood in the arteries and veins of the human body. The circulation is exhibited by the passing of a red fluid from a reservoir into numerous capillary tubes of glass, ramified in every direction, and then returning in similar tubes to the reservoir, which was done with great velocity, without any power to act visibly on the fluid, and had the appearance of perpetual motion.

Another great curiosity was a rolling press, for taking the copies of letters or any other writing. A sheet of paper is completely copied in less than two minutes, the copy as fair as the original, and without effacing it in the smallest degree. It is an invention of his own, and extremely useful in many situations in life.

He also showed us his long, artificial arm and hand, for taking down and putting up books on high shelves which are out of reach; and his great armed chair, with rockers, and a large fan placed over it, with which he fans himself, keeps off the flies, etc., while he sits reading, with only a small motion of his foot; and many other curiosities and inventions, all his own, but of lesser note. Over his mantel-tree, he has a prodigious number of medals, busts, and casts in wax or plaster of Paris, which are the effigies of the most noted characters in Europe.

Franklin particularly wanted to show Cutler a volume on botany, which contained the whole of Linnaeus's *Systema Vegetabilium*, with colored plates to accompany the text. The volume was so heavy that Franklin could lift it only with difficulty, but he took pleasure in Cutler's obvious appreciation of it. "It was a feast to me," Cutler said. "I wanted for three months at least to have devoted myself entirely to this one volume. But fearing I should be tedious to him, I shut up the volume, though he urged me to examine it longer."

Cutler was entranced by his octogenarian host. "I was highly delighted with the extensive knowledge he appeared to have of every subject, the brightness of his memory, and clearness and vivacity of all his mental faculties, notwithstanding his age (eighty-four) [eighty-three and a half, actually]. His manners are perfectly easy, and every thing about him seems to diffuse an unrestrained freedom and happiness. He has an incessant vein of humour, accompanied with an uncommon vivacity, which seems as natural and involuntary as his breathing."

⌐ Breathing came easier that summer for Franklin, who was used to Philadelphia's climate, than for some of the delegates from out of town. The southerners arrived dressed for the heat, but the northerners, in their woolen suits, suffered badly. The State House was comparatively cool when the sessions began at ten in the morning, but by midday the green baize on the tables where the delegates sat began to show dark spots from their sweat. The windows had to be kept closed, partly against the prying eyes and ears of outsiders but mostly against the flies that battened on the horse dung in the streets and the offal in the gutters. "A veritable torture during Philadelphia's hot season" was how a French visitor described "the innumerable flies which constantly light on the face and hands, stinging everywhere and turning everything black because of the filth they leave wherever they light." There was no escape, even at night. "Rooms must be kept closed unless one wishes to be tormented in his bed at the break of day, and this need of keeping everything shut makes the heat of the night even more unbearable and sleep more difficult. And so the heat of the day makes one long for bedtime because of weariness, and a single fly which has gained entrance to your room in spite of all precautions, drives you from bed."

Franklin survived the heat better than many delegates far younger than he, and better than he had feared. To be sure, a three-day illness in mid-July left him "so weak as to be scarce able to finish this letter," he explained to John Paul Jones in Paris. (In this same letter Franklin asked Jones to convey regards to Jefferson "and acquaint him that the Convention goes on well and that there is hope of great good to result.") But on the whole his health held up, and he attended the sessions of the convention faithfully.

Though the compromise on representation assured the success of the convention, the members still had work to do. They had to define the powers of the executive and the extent of legislative checks upon him. Should the legislature be able to impeach and remove him during his term? Franklin thought so. He considered the power of removal a guarantee both for the people and for the executive. "What was the practice before this in cases where the chief magistrate rendered himself obnoxious? Why, recourse was had to assassination, in which he was not only deprived of his life but of the opportunity of vindicating his character. It would be the best way, therefore, to provide in the constitution for the regular punishment of the executive when his misconduct should deserve it, and for his honourable acquittal when he should be unjustly accused."

Should the executive be eligible for reelection? Some members thought he must be, else he necessarily suffer the degradation of being returned to the body of the people. Franklin differed strenuously. Such an assertion was "contrary to republican principles," he said. "In free governments the rulers are the servants, and the people their superiors and sovereigns. For the former therefore to return among the latter was not to *degrade* but to *promote* them." Doubtless with that sly smile of his, he added, "It would be imposing an unreasonable burden on them to keep them always in a state of servitude and not allow them to become again one of the masters."

Who should be able to vote? Many delegates thought responsibility attached to property, and irresponsibility to its lack, and said suffrage should be restricted to freeholders. Franklin granted that the person least prone to political pressure was the one who tilled his own farm, but he would not endorse the proposed restriction. "It is of great consequence that we should not depress the virtue and public spirit of our common people, of which they displayed a great deal during the war, and which contributed principally to the favourable issue of it." Such a restriction would rightly provoke popular upset. "The sons of a substantial farmer, not being themselves freeholders, would not be pleased at being disfranchised, and there are a great many persons of that description."

What should be the requirements for candidates to the national legislature? Many delegates again wanted to see proof of owning property. Again Franklin embraced the more democratic position. Once more he voiced his dislike of everything that tended "to debase the spirit of the common people." Besides, as his own long experience of politics and politicians had taught him, the proposed restriction was no guarantee of good government. "If honesty was often the companion of wealth, and if poverty was exposed to peculiar temptation, it was not less true that the possession of property increased the desire of more property. Some of the greatest rogues I ever was acquainted with were the richest rogues." Moreover, other countries were watching America. "This constitution will be much read and attended to in Europe, and if it should betray a great partiality to the rich, it will not only hurt us in the esteem of the most liberal and enlightened men there, but discourage the common people from removing to this country."

The opinion of Europe—to which, it was fair to say, Franklin was more sensitive than anyone else at the convention—informed his opinion on a related topic. How long should immigrants be required to live in America before becoming eligible for office? Some said as much as fourteen years. Franklin thought this excessive. He was "not against a reasonable time, but should be very sorry to see any thing like illiberality inserted in the constitution." The members were writing not simply for an American audience. "The people in Europe are friendly to this country. Even in the country with which we have been lately at war, we have now and had during the war a great many friends not only among the people at large but in both Houses of Parliament. In every other country in Europe all the people are our friends." How the proposed constitution treated foreign immigrants would have much to do with whether America retained those European friends. In any case, justice dictated fair treatment of the foreign-born, for many had served valiantly during the war. The mere fact of immigrants' relocation to America should count for something. "When foreigners, after looking about for some other country in which they can obtain more happiness, give a preference to ours, it is a proof of attachment which ought to excite our confidence and affection."

~ As cooler weather approached, so did the end of the convention's work. Franklin had his way on some of the remaining issues, yielded on others. He advocated requiring not one but two witnesses to the same overt act of treason, on grounds that prosecutions for this highest crime were "generally virulent" and perjury was too easily employed against the innocent. The convention agreed. (This requirement of two witnesses would prove critical in the treason trial of Aaron Burr twenty years later.) Franklin seconded a motion calling for an executive council to assist the president. Still advocating a wider distribution of power, he said, "We seem too much to fear cabals in appointments by a number, and to have too much confidence in those of single persons." Colonial experience with bad governors should have shown the need to restrain a single executive, while his own experience as chief executive of Pennsylvania revealed the positive benefits a council could provide. "A council would not only be a check on a bad president but be a relief to a good one." The convention disagreed.

The thorniest of the final issues involved slavery. How should slaves be counted toward representation in the lower house? Naturally the delegates from the states with few slaves wanted to minimize the slave count; they pointed out that since slave owners considered slaves to be property, those same slaves should not be counted as persons. The delegates from states with many slaves objected, less on philosophical grounds than on the pragmatic one that without some allowance for slaves, their states simply would not accept the new constitution. James Wilson of Pennsylvania proposed that the new constitution adopt the expedient devised by the Confederation Congress in 1783, when the legislature allowed the states to count three-fifths of the total number of their slaves. This compromise made no one happy but none so upset as to bolt the convention, and it was accepted.

A similar makeshift disposed of the question of the slave trade. The new constitution would give Congress power to regulate commerce, but the heavily slaved states resisted infringement on the commerce in slaves. Franklin had been sharply critical of the slave trade when it was practiced by the British, and—as he would soon reveal—had come to detest the entire institution of slavery, but when the southern states made clear that the issue of the slave trade was another potential convention-breaker, he acquiesced in another compromise. For twenty years Congress could not bar the traffic in slaves; from 1808 it might do what it chose on the subject.

On September 17 the completed copy of the Constitution was ready for the members' signatures. Franklin addressed the convention for the last time. Again he spoke through James Wilson, who read his colleague's prepared remarks. "I confess that there are several parts of this constitution which I do not at present approve," Franklin said. "But I am not sure I shall never approve them, for having lived long, I have experienced many instances of being obliged by better information or fuller consideration to change opinions even on important subjects which I once thought right but found to be otherwise. It is therefore that the older I grow, the more apt I am to doubt my own judgment, and to pay more attention to the judgment of others."

Some people felt themselves possessed of all truth; so did most sects in religion. Franklin explained how the Anglican Richard Steele (upon whose writing, many years before, he had modeled his own) once penned a dedication to the Pope, in which he explained, in Franklin's paraphrase, that "the only difference between our churches in their opinions of the certainty of their doctrines is, the Church of Rome is infallible and the Church of England is never in the wrong." Franklin also quoted a Frenchwoman of his acquaintance who, in an argument with her sister, declared, "I don't know how it is, Sister, but I meet with nobody but myself that's always in the right."

As the chuckles subsided, Franklin made his point. "In these sentiments, Sir, I agree to this constitution with all its faults, if they are such; because I think a general government necessary for us, and there is no form of government but what may be a blessing to the people if well administered." He reminded once more that the strength of any government rested on the virtue of the people. "This is likely to be well administered for a course of years, and can only end in despotism, as other forms have done before it, when the people shall become so corrupted as to need despotic government, being incapable of any other."

Franklin doubted whether any convention could have done better. "When you assemble a number of men to have the advantage of their joint wisdom, you inevitably assemble with those men all their prejudices, their passions, their errors of opinion, their local interests, and their selfish views. From such an assembly can a perfect production be expected?" The wonder was how well the present assembly had done. "I think it will astonish our enemies, who are waiting with confidence to hear that our councils are confounded like those of the builders of Babel, and that our states are on the point of separation, only to meet hereafter for the purpose of cutting one another's throats. Thus I consent, sir, to this constitution, because I expect no better, and because I am not sure that it is not the best."

Franklin closed by suggesting that the confidentiality that had surrounded the proceedings ought to continue upon the members' parting. "The opinions I have had of its errors, I sacrifice to the public good. I have never whispered a syllable of them abroad. Within these walls they were born, and here they shall die." If each delegate, returning to his constituents, complained at this point or that of the new government, the total of the complaints would probably scuttle the project. On the other hand, unanimity would encourage ratification. "I hope therefore that for our own sakes as a part of the people, and for the sake of posterity, we shall act heartily and unanimously."

Achieving this unanimity required a final bit of finesse. Franklin knew full well that unanimity of delegates was not possible. Edmund Randolph was holding out, as were Elbridge Gerry and George Mason. But unanimity of the states might be attained, by polling the members within each delegation and heeding the majorities therein. Gouverneur Morris framed a formula for the signing: "Done in Convention, by the unanimous consent of the States present the 17th of September."

Franklin moved that the convention adopt this formula, and the motion carried.

～ **George Washington** signed first, followed by thirty-seven others, state by state. James Madison related the convention's close:

> Whilst the last members were signing it, Doctor Franklin, looking towards the president's chair, at the back of which a rising sun happened to be painted, observed to a few members near him, that painters had often found it difficult to distinguish in their art a rising from a setting sun. I have, said he, often and often in the course of the session, and the vicissitudes of my hopes and fears as to its issue, looked at that behind the president, without being able to tell whether it was rising or setting. But now at length I have the happiness to know that it is a rising and not a setting sun.

30

To Sleep

1787–90

∾ The next day Washington wrote Lafayette regarding
the new Constitution, "It is now a child of fortune, to be
fostered by some and buffeted by others. What will be the
general opinion on, or the reception of it, is not for me
to decide, nor shall I say any thing for or against it.
If it is good I suppose it will work its way good,
if bad it will recoil on the framers."

Washington forecast accurately. The infant Constitution received both cuffs and caresses. The cuffs came from advocates of state authority who disliked yielding power to the central government, from radical democrats who saw insufficient guarantees of the people's rights, and from assorted others who were, for one reason or another, attached to the status quo. Sam Adams had trouble getting past the first words of the preamble—"We, the People"—which he thought should have been, "We, the States." Said Adams, "As I enter the building I stumble at the threshold." Elbridge Gerry explained his refusal to sign at Philadelphia: "The constitution has few federal features, but is rather a system of national government." This was precisely what worried another New England Antifederalist (as the opponents of the Constitution came to be called): "The vast continent of America cannot be long subjected to a democracy if consolidated into one government. You might as well attempt to rule Hell by prayer." A Pennsylvanian, noting that the proposed Constitution would amplify the power of government, warned, "The natural course of power is to make the many the slaves to the few." A South Carolina Antifederalist demanded of his audience, "What have you been contending for these ten years? Liberty! What is liberty? The power of governing yourselves! If you adopt this constitution, have you the power?" To which the audience thundered, "No!" Another South Carolinian recorded the reception of the proposed charter in the back-country: "The people had a coffin painted black, which, borne in funeral procession, was solemnly buried, as an emblem of the dissolution and interment of public liberty. . . . They feel that they are the very men, who, as mere militia, half-armed and half-clothed, have fought and defeated the British regulars in sundry encounters. They think that after having disputed and gained the laurel under the banners of liberty, now, that they are likely to be robbed both of the honour and the fruits of it."

Proponents of the Constitution rallied to its defense. The most important body of argument in favor of the new government was a series of essays by Madison, Hamilton, and John Jay entitled *The Federalist*. Perhaps inevitably, the affirmative case was more complicated than the negative (the opponents simply had to shout "Liberty!"); whether from this cause or some other, the *Federalist* papers were complex and closely reasoned, and together provided a thoughtful introduction to the theory of constitutional government. The most telling installment may have been the tenth, in which Madison countered the Antifederalist argument that the federal government would be intrinsically less democratic than the state governments. In fact, just the opposite was true, Madison asserted.

"The smaller the society, the fewer probably will be the distinct parties and interests composing it; the fewer the distinct parties and interests, the more frequently will a majority be found of the same party; and the smaller number of individuals composing a majority, and the smaller the compass within which they are placed, the more easily will they concert and execute their plans of oppression." A government comprising more people would be safer. "Extend the sphere, and you take in a greater variety of parties and interests; you make it less probable that a majority of the whole will have a common motive to invade the rights of other citizens; or if such a common motive exists, it will be more difficult for all who feel it to discover their own strength, and to act in unison with each other."

℘— The morning after the convention adjourned, the Pennsylvania Assembly reclaimed its quarters in the State House. Franklin, in his dual role as Pennsylvania president and senior delegate to the Constitutional convention, expressed his "very great satisfaction" at presenting the convention's handiwork to the people of Pennsylvania for approval. He added his expectation that the Constitution would produce "happy effects to this commonwealth, as well as to every other of the United States." Further happy effects for Pennsylvania, he judged, would follow from locating the new federal government in Pennsylvania. To this end, and pursuant to the clause in the Constitution about a federal district, he recommended that Pennsylvania offer the new government one hundred square miles for such a district. (Pennsylvania agreed, but the national politics of ratification eventually resulted in the federal district's being carved out of Maryland and Virginia.) Beyond his formal recommendation, Franklin conspired in lifting the veil of secrecy surrounding the convention far enough to smuggle out his closing speech, which became a powerful argument in favor of the Constitution. Many people assumed that Franklin was the primary author of the proposed charter; his prestige added to its momentum.

It also shielded him from Antifederalist criticism. In Pennsylvania the politics of ratification was complicated by the preexisting dissension over the state constitution. Confusingly—but not illogically, given their populist predilections—most Constitutionalists in Pennsylvania politics adopted an anti-Constitutionalist position vis-à-vis the proposed national government, while most Pennsylvania anti-Constitutionalists (or Republicans) embraced the federal Constitution. Pennsylvania Antifederalists bitterly attacked the (federal) Constitution as a plot by Robert Morris and his rich friends to subvert the states and the people, the better to line their own pockets. Yet Franklin, despite his support for the Constitution, emerged largely untouched. There was good political reason for this, of course, namely, the recognition—in the words of one Antifederalist piece—that Franklin was "highly reverenced by all the people." To the extent that Franklin's federalism required explaining away by the Antifederalists, it was attributed to the "weakness and indecision attendant on old age."

The Antifederalists employed other tactics instead. When ballots were circulated for delegates to the Pennsylvania convention that would decide for or against ratification, Antifederalist Constitutionalists listed Franklin's name on their ticket, against his wishes. Antifederalists in other states turned Franklin's words against him. "Doctor Franklin's concluding speech, which you will meet with in one of the papers herewith enclosed," Madison wrote to Washington from New York, "is both mutilated and adulterated so as to change both the form and the spirit of it."

In Pennsylvania the Antifederalist efforts failed fairly quickly. The state convention met in November, and though the Antifederalists managed to stall a final vote till the following month, on December 12 forty-six members voted in favor of the Constitution, against twenty-three opposed. That afternoon a gang of celebrating sailors and shipbuilders (two groups that stood to benefit from improved commerce under the new federal government) put a boat on a wagon and hauled it through the streets of Philadelphia, shouting, "Three and twenty fathoms, foul bottom"—referring to the negative votes—and "Six and forty fathoms, safe anchorage!"

Pennsylvania's approval enhanced the Constitution's prospects but hardly guaranteed them. Ratification in February 1788 by Massachusetts (where Sam Adams, after stumbling at the threshold, picked himself up and endorsed the new charter) left the ratifiers three states shy of the nine specified for the Constitution to take effect. More troubling than the shortfall—which seemed almost certain to be made good—was the identity of two of the holdouts, New York and Virginia. If New York remained aloof, New England would be as cut off from the rest of America as it would have been during the Revolutionary War had

Burgoyne's expedition succeeded. And an American union was hard to imagine without Virginia, the home of Washington, Jefferson, and Madison, and the heart of the south.

Franklin entered the fray at a critical moment. In April he wrote a piece for the *Federal Gazette* reminding readers that even the most inspired instance of constitution-writing in all of history had come under harsh attack. When Moses descended from Mount Sinai with the Ten Commandments under his arm, had not the Israelites resisted? The Talmud told how jealous factions resented Moses and the laws he brought, saying Israel had freed itself from bondage under Pharaoh; should it now accept slavery at the hands of Moses? Franklin recognized that he was treading on treacherous, even blasphemous ground. "I beg I may not be understood to infer that our General Convention was divinely inspired when it formed the new federal Constitution, merely because that Constitution has been unreasonably and vehemently opposed." Yet, as he had said in the convention, he could not help thinking the Deity had something to do with the project. "I must own I have so much faith in the general government of the world by *Providence* that I can hardly conceive a transaction of such momentous importance to the welfare of millions now existing, and to exist in the posterity of a great nation, should be suffered to pass without being in some degree influenced, guided, and governed by that omnipotent, omnipresent, and beneficent Ruler."

Aided by Franklin's argument, Virginia's convention ratified in the early summer of 1788. Virginia's approval gave heart to New York Federalists, including the merchants of New York City, who threatened secession by their city from the state if the state failed to ratify. This tipped the balance in favor of the Constitution.

Although some final vote counting remained, on the twelfth anniversary of the Declaration of Independence, the Federalists of Philadelphia held a grand celebration. A ship conveniently called the *Rising Sun* was anchored in the Delaware; at sunrise on the Fourth of July it fired a cannon salute to the new government and the city that gave it birth. An elaborate procession began at eight o'clock, headed by the Light Horse Troop and including units representing "Independence," the "Alliance with France," and the "New Era." State and local officials marched, as did members of every conceivable guild in the city.

The place of highest honor was reserved for "His Excellency the President." Unfortunately, Franklin's stone kept him home that day, although he may have stirred to the sidewalk to see the procession turn onto Market Street just west of his house, and he almost certainly heard the music and singing. The printers' guild had put a press on a cart, and as it rolled along, those tending the press struck off and distributed the lyrics of a song written for the occasion by Philadelphia's most famous printer, President Franklin himself.

~ Ratification of the Constitution marked the end of the Revolutionary era in American history, and a most fitting climax to Franklin's public life. The previous October the Pennsylvania Assembly had reelected him again. He had intended to retire after his second term but lacked the resolve. "I must own that it is no small pleasure to me, and I suppose it will give my sister pleasure," he wrote Jane Mecom the week after his reelection, "that after such a long trial of me, I should be elected a third time by my fellow citizens, without a dissenting vote but my own. This universal and unbounded confidence of a whole people flatters my vanity much more than a peerage could do."

Yet to his relief, the Pennsylvania constitution forbade a fourth term, and as the weeks ran down to the end of October 1788, he looked forward to the retirement he had so long postponed. But because he postponed it so long, he discovered he had less to look forward to than he hoped. The excitement surrounding the Constitutional Convention had temporarily rejuvenated him. "Some tell me I look better, and they suppose the daily exercise of going and returning from the State House has done me good," he told Jane just afterward. He even thought he might make a last trip to Boston. But a bad fall on the steps of his garden that winter sprained his wrist, bruised his hip, and aggravated his stone. His afflictions kept him away from the meetings of the Executive Council and canceled all plans to travel.

The finality of this left him wistful. A Boston admirer urged him to come; Franklin replied that it would be "a very great pleasure if I could once again visit my native town, and walk over the grounds I used to frequent when a boy, and where I enjoyed many of the innocent pleasures of youth, which would be so brought to my remembrance, and where I might find some of my old acquaintance to converse with." But travel by land was too fatiguing, and travel by sea equally unappealing "to one who, although he has crossed the Atlantic eight times, and made many smaller trips, does not recollect his ever having been at sea without taking a firm resolution never to go to sea again." Anyway, the reality would fall short of the memory. "If I were arrived in Boston I should see but little of it, as I could neither bear walking nor riding in a carriage over its pebbled streets." As for acquaintances, "I should find very few indeed of my old friends living, it being now sixty-five years since I left it to settle here."

All the same, the thought of his first home would not leave him, and he would not let it go. "I enjoy the company and conversation of its inhabitants when any of them are so good as to visit me; for besides their general good sense, which I value, the Boston manner, turn of phrase, and even tone of voice and accent in pronunciation, all please and seem to refresh and revive me."

Sometimes New England simply made him laugh. In a letter to Jane Mecom he asked whether she ever saw any of their Folger relations from Nantucket. He said he himself had not of late. "They are wonderfully shy. But I admire their honest plainness of speech. About a year ago I invited two of them to dine with me. Their answer was that they would, if they could not do better. I suppose they did better, for I never saw them afterwards."

❧ Franklin's unfailing sense of humor helped him accept his afflictions. His stone was a large one, "as I find by the weight when I turn in bed." Close friends, passing acquaintances, and people he hardly knew sent him recipes for medications and instructions for treatments, but all to no avail. "I thank you much for your intimations of the virtues of hemlock," he wrote Benjamin Vaughan (who had suggested a sub-Socratic dose). "But I have tried so many things with so little effect that I am quite discouraged, and have no longer any faith in remedies for the stone."

Yet if he could not diminish the stone, at least he could try to prevent its increase. He ate less than before, largely abstained from wine and cider, and exercised with his dumbbell, which improved his circulation without requiring the kind of motion that gave him pain.

For a time innocuous palliatives alleviated the worst symptoms. "As the roughness of the stone lacerates a little the neck of the bladder," he told the Comte de Buffon, a fellow sufferer, "I find that when the urine happens to be sharp, I have much pain in making water and frequent urgencies. For relief under this circumstance I take, going to bed, the bigness of a pigeon's egg of jelly of blackberries. The receipt for making it is enclosed. While I continue to do this every night, I am generally easy the day following, making water pretty freely and with long intervals."

But Franklin's most potent medicine was his continuing curiosity and his irrepressible interest in life. "Our ancient correspondence used to have something philosophical in it," he wrote James Bowdoin, a recently retired old friend, in May 1788. "As you are now more free from public cares, and I expect to be so in a few months, why may we not resume that kind of correspondence?" Bowdoin's interest was the earth; Franklin proceeded to offer several questions for reflection. "How came the earth by its magnetism? . . . Is it likely that iron ore immediately existed when the globe was first formed; or may it not rather be supposed to be a gradual production of time?" Was the earth's magnetism related to the iron it contained? If so, had that iron ever been *non*magnetic? And if *that* was so, how had it become magnetized? "May not a magnetic power exist throughout our system, perhaps through all systems, so that if men could make a voyage in the starry regions, a compass might be of use? . . . As the poles of magnets may be changed by the presence of stronger magnets, might not, in ancient times, the near passing of some large comet, of greater magnetic power than this globe of ours, have been a means of changing its poles?" Did not the presence in cold regions of the shells and bones of animals natural to warm regions indicate that the earth's geographic poles had shifted? "Does not the apparent wrack of the surface of this globe thrown up into long ridges of mountains, with strata in various positions, make it probable that its internal mass is a fluid, but a fluid so dense as to float the heaviest of our substances?"

Some of these conjectures—about the shifting of the earth's magnetic and geographic poles, about the fluid nature of the earth's interior and its relation to surface structures—were remarkably prescient, identifying a research agenda that would keep geophysicists busy into the twenty-first century. During Franklin's day the conjectures stimulated discussion among the members of the American Philosophical Society, where this letter was read and which met in Franklin's library when he could not get out. And they showed his mind to be as active at eighty-two as it had been at forty-two.

~ And as it had been at forty-two, it was no less concerned with human welfare than with matters merely philosophical. For decades

Franklin had been troubled by shabby treatment of Indians by whites. The unfair dealings had practical implications, as when they provoked the Indians to attack frontier settlements or assist the enemies (first France, then Britain) of the people of Pennsylvania and the United States. But there was also in Franklin's thought a fundamental feeling that Indians, as members of the human race, ought to be treated better than they often were.

On his press at Passy, Franklin had printed an essay entitled "Remarks Concerning the Savages of North America," in which his first sentence made plain the intended irony of his title. "Savages we call them," he wrote, "because their manners differ from ours, which we think the perfection of civility; they think the same of theirs." The balance of the essay suggested that the Indians had the better of this argument. Franklin pointed out how admirably Indian ways suited the Indians. "Having few artificial wants, they have abundance of leisure for improvement by conversation. Our laborious manner of life compared with theirs, they esteem slavish and base; and the learning on which we value ourselves, they regard as frivolous and useless." Plato himself could not have objected to the Indian mode of political organization. "All their government is by the counsel or advice of the sages; there is no force, there are no prisons, no officers to compel obedience or inflict punishment." At council meetings the old men sat in the foremost ranks; when one of the old men rose to speak, everyone else observed a respectful silence. "How different this is from the conduct of a polite British House of Commons," Franklin noted sardonically, "where scarce a day passes without some confusion that makes the Speaker hoarse in calling *to order.*"

The Indians were exceedingly gracious to strangers, setting aside a special house in each village to accommodate visitors, and were exemplars of toleration. Franklin wrote of a missionary who told the Susquehanna the story of Adam's fall, and how it had led to great travail and necessitated Jesus' sufferings and death. "When he had finished, an Indian orator stood up to thank him," Franklin related, with a twinkle in either his own eye or the Indian's. "What you have told us, says he, is all very good. It is indeed bad to eat apples. It is better to make them all into cider." The Indian thereupon shared his people's creation story with the missionary. The missionary grew impatient, then disgusted. "What I delivered to you were sacred truths," he said. "But what you tell me is mere fable, fiction and falsehood." The Indian replied, "My brother, it seems your friends have not done you justice in your education; they have not well instructed you in the rules of common civility. You saw that we who understand and practise those rules believed all your stories. Why do you refuse to believe ours?"

As president of Pennsylvania, Franklin had occasion to apply his views to public policy. During the summer of 1786 the young Wyandot chief Scotosh visited Philadelphia. Franklin, recalling the elaborate treaty ceremonies in which he had taken part on the frontier thirty years earlier, paid Scotosh the courtesy of recapitulating some of those ceremonies at his house on Market Street. Scotosh expressed concern that white surveyors ("measurers") were encroaching on Indian country. His own people were peacefully inclined, but he could not say as much of others. "The bad people will, I fear, take occasion from the measuring to do more mischief. Perhaps the measurers will be killed. And it would give pain to me and my nation to hear such bad news."

Franklin assured the chief that Pennsylvania had no designs on his people's lands. "This state of Pennsylvania measures no land but what has been fairly purchased of the Six Nations." He explained that the land in question was under the control of Congress, then meeting in New York. He encouraged Scotosh to go to New York, and gave him money for the trip. He also sent a letter of recommendation to Foreign Secretary John Jay, explaining that Scotosh had been "always very friendly to our people" and hoping his fears could be assuaged. The young chief had expressed curiosity about France; Franklin suggested to Jay that Congress offer to send Scotosh overseas. This would benefit both Scotosh and American interests in the frontier regions. "It might be of use to our affairs in that part of the country if, after viewing the court and troops and population of France, he should return impressed with a high idea of the greatness and power of our ally."

~ Franklin's judgment that savagery and civilization were no respecters of skin color led him, in the last years of his life, to embrace a movement that was by certain measures the most radical in America. Franklin came to abolitionism via anger at Britain. The American charges that Parliament intended to enslave the colonies led some among those making the charges to examine America's own conduct in enslaving black Africans. Yet in a country where indentured servants and transported felons also provided a substantial part of the workforce, the mere existence of an institution of unfree labor was not as striking as it would seem later. Prior to his conversion, Franklin kept his slaves, George and King, as personal servants, and apparently thought little about it.

The overseas slave *trade* was another matter. It was especially barbaric, and, in its barbarity, had no real counterpart in the traffic in indentured servants or felons. Moreover, it was something British slave traders tried to force on the American colonies—even colonies that wanted no part in it. Franklin made this argument in one of his pseudonymous pieces for the London press in the early 1770s. The piece put an Englishman, an American, and a Scotsman in conversation; the Englishman called Americans hypocrites for demanding liberty for themselves while denying it to their black slaves. The American acknowledged that his countrymen were not blameless, being, as it were, receivers to the theft of Africans from their native lands. But the Americans were not entirely willing receivers, having passed laws discouraging the importation of slaves—laws the British government had disallowed as being—in the words of Franklin's American, "prejudicial, forsooth, to the interest of the African Company."

Franklin subsequently leveled sharper attacks on the slave trade. A British court ordered the freedom of a certain slave irregularly landed in England; the slave's legal costs had been covered by "some generous humane persons," in the words of Franklin, who went on, "It is to be wished that the same humanity may extend itself among numbers, if not to the procuring liberty for those that remain in our colonies, at least to obtain a law for abolishing the African commerce in slaves, and declaring the children of present slaves free after they become of age." Franklin quoted a computation that one-third of the hundred thousand persons shipped from Africa each year to America died in passage.

Can the sweetening our tea, &c. with sugar be a circumstance of such absolute necessity? Can the petty pleasure thence arising to the taste compensate for so much misery produced among our fellow creatures, and such a constant butchery of the human species by this pestilential detestable traffic in the bodies and souls of men? *Pharisaical Britain!* to pride thyself in setting free *a single slave* that happens to be landed on thy coasts, while thy merchants in all thy ports are encouraged by thy laws to continue a commerce whereby so many *hundreds of thousands* are dragged into a slavery that can scarce be said to end with their lives, since it is entailed on their posterity!

Until independence, Franklin's attacks on the slave trade doubled as attacks on Britain. He endorsed the section in Jefferson's draft of the Declaration of Independence that condemned the slave trade and Britain's refusal to allow the American colonies to restrict it—although he apparently was not surprised that the southern colonies insisted on deleting that section. Franklin acquiesced in the compromises on slavery at the Constitutional Convention, believing, as he said in his closing speech, that the bargain struck was the best that could be achieved at that time and place. If waiting twenty years was the cost of killing the American slave trade—an institution nearly ten times that old—it was worth paying.

Yet if the slave trade was evil, its evil reflected the evil of the underlying institution. By the mid-1780s Franklin was convinced slavery itself must be eradicated. To some extent his conversion to abolitionism was simply the logical consequence of his fundamentally generous view of human nature—a nature that long life and an open mind had showed him was no different in Negroes (such as those he had seen educated years before) or Indians than in whites. To an equal extent it revealed his continuing concern that unless American republicanism were founded on virtue, it would fail. As a Briton, Franklin had been able to countenance slavery as one public vice among many received from the past. As an American, he could no longer countenance it, for the new nation could not abide public vice—certainly not of the magnitude of slavery—without jeopardizing its very existence.

Philadelphia Quakers had founded the first abolitionist group— what came to be called the Society for Promoting the Abolition of Slavery and the Relief of Negroes Unlawfully Held in Bondage—in 1775, but independence and the war distracted most of those who could have made the group a force. Franklin proposed to do just that, enlisting after his return from France and accepting the society's presidency in 1787. A major stumbling block to emancipatory efforts was the question of what to do with the former slaves; Franklin advocated a carefully considered program of education. "Slavery is such an atrocious debasement of human nature," he wrote, "that its very extirpation, if not performed with solicitous care, may sometimes open a source of serious evils." Apologists of slavery pointed to former slaves who became a burden on society, and used this as an argument against emancipation. What do you expect?, Franklin answered. "The unhappy man who has long been treated as a brute animal, too frequently sinks beneath the common standard of the human species. The galling chains that bind his body do also fetter his intellectual faculties and impair the social affections of his heart." Lacking power of choice in his life, he never learned to choose; lacking responsibility, he became irresponsible. "Under such circumstances, freedom may often prove a misfortune to himself, and prejudicial to society." But this was no argument against emancipation; it was an argument for education. Society must rid itself of slavery, but it must also make provision for the entry into free society of former slaves. Franklin and the antislavery group published a plan for the education of former slaves, and he solicited public support. "To instruct, to advise, to qualify those who have been restored to freedom, for the exercise and enjoyment of civil liberty; to promote in them habits of industry, to furnish them with employment suited to their age, sex, talents, and other circumstances; and to procure their children an education calculated for their future situation in life; these are the great outlines of the annexed plan which we have adopted, and which we conceive will essentially promote the public good, and the happiness of these our hitherto much neglected fellow-creatures."

~ "Our grand machine has at length begun to work," Franklin wrote in the spring of 1789 to Charles Carroll, his colleague from the 1776 expedition to Canada. The new government, headed by Washington as president, had taken office; Carroll himself was a senator from Maryland. "If any form of government is capable of making a nation happy, ours I think bids fair now for producing that effect."

Yet happiness required virtue—as it always did for Franklin. The new Congress was contemplating a bill of rights. Franklin supported such a bill, but he worried that in the enthusiasm for popular rights, popular responsibilities might be forgotten. "After all, much depends upon the people who are to be governed. We have been guarding against an evil that old states are most liable to, *excess of power* in the rulers; but our present danger seems to be *defect of obedience* in the subjects." He offered this as a caution, not a condemnation. For himself he was willing to hope that "from the enlightened state of this age and country, we may guard effectually against that evil as well as the rest."

Happiness and virtue rested on reason. And reason advanced apace, which further encouraged Franklin. "I have long been impressed," he wrote an admirer in 1788, "with the same sentiments you so well express of the growing felicity of mankind, from the improvements in philosophy, morals, politics, and even the conveniences of common living." Present progress was rapid, and would continue far into the future. "I have sometimes almost wished it had been my destiny to be born two or three centuries hence."

The present was exciting enough. The summer of 1788 brought news of reforms in France conferring rights on non-Catholics. "The *arrêt* in favour of the *non-catholiques* gives pleasure here," Franklin wrote a Paris friend, "not only from its present advantages, but as it is a good step towards general toleration, and to the abolishing in time all party spirit among Christians, and the mischiefs that have so long attended it." As one who always deplored sectarian intolerance, Franklin was especially gratified. "Thank God, the world is growing wiser and wiser; and as by degrees men are convinced of the folly of wars for religion, for dominion, or for commerce, they will be happier and happier."

It was the following summer, of course, that produced the great changes in France. From the distance of Philadelphia the initial view was cloudy and confused. "The revolution in France is truly surprising," Franklin wrote Benjamin Vaughan. "I sincerely wish it may end in establishing a good constitution for that country. The mischiefs and troubles it suffers in the operation, however, give me great concern." Some of his concern, naturally, was for the welfare of those he had come to know in Paris. "It is now more than a year since I have heard from my dear friend Le Roy," he wrote his old chess partner in November 1789. "What can be the reason? Are you still living? Or have the mob of Paris mistaken the head of a monopolizer of knowledge for a monopolizer of corn, and paraded it about the streets upon a pole?" On the assumption that Le Roy retained his head (he did), Franklin went on to say he found the news of the violence "very afflicting." He hoped for the best, but feared for the country he cherished second only to America. "The voice of *Philosophy* I apprehend can hardly be heard among those tumults."

Yet if France survived the tumults, it—and the world—would benefit in the end. "I hope the fire of liberty, which you mention as spreading itself over Europe," he wrote an English friend, "will act upon the inestimable rights of man, as common fire does upon gold: purify without destroying them; so that a lover of liberty may find a country in any part of Christendom." To David Hartley he wrote, "The convulsions in France are attended with some disagreeable circumstances, but if by the struggle she obtains and secures for the nation its future liberty and a good constitution, a few years' enjoyment of those blessings will amply repair all the damages their acquisition may have occasioned. God grant that not only the love of liberty but a thorough knowledge of the rights of man may pervade all the nations of the Earth, so that a philosopher may set his foot anywhere on its surface and say, 'This is my country.' "

⌐ In his letter to Le Roy, Franklin explained that the new government in America gave an appearance that promised permanency. "But in this world nothing can be said to be certain, except death and taxes."

Taxes had been important in his past; death was the larger concern now. In the summer of 1789 he answered a French friend who had inquired of his health, "I can give you no good account. I have a long time been afflicted with almost constant and grievous pain, to combat which I have been obliged to have recourse to opium, which indeed has afforded me some ease from time to time, but then it has taken away my appetite and so impeded my digestion that I am become totally emaciated, and little remains of me but a skeleton covered with a skin."

His family and friends did what they could to alleviate his pain. Sally tended him with diligence and care. Her sons took dictation from their grandfather when he felt too weak to write. Polly Hewson—who had finally succumbed to Franklin's arguments that her children would have better prospects in America than in England, and had moved her family to Philadelphia—read to Franklin when the pain or medication prevented him from concentrating.

For years he had been too busy to finish his memoirs; now he was too ill. He reviewed what he had written—"which, calling past transactions to remembrance, makes it seem a little like living one's life over again," he told Abbé Morellet. And he contemplated what he might add. ("Canada—*delenda est*," he noted to himself, recalling his long struggle to win Canada for Britain.) But the sustained effort required to finish the job was beyond him.

That many were interested in his life story was evident from the queries he received. Ezra Stiles of Connecticut was one of the more forward. "As much as I know of Dr. Franklin, I have not an idea of his religious sentiments," Stiles wrote Franklin. Would he be so kind as to enlighten an old friend?

"It is the first time I have been questioned upon it," Franklin replied.

Here is my creed. I believe in one God, creator of the universe. That he governs it by his providence. That he ought to be worshipped. That the most acceptable service we render to him is doing good to his other children. That the soul of man is immortal, and will be treated with justice in another life respecting its conduct in this. These I take to be the fundamental principles of all sound religion, and I regard them as you do [Stiles shared Franklin's tolerance] in whatever sect I meet with them.

As to Jesus of Nazareth, my opinion of whom you particularly desire, I think the system of morals and his religion, as he left them to us, the best the world ever saw or is likely to see; but I apprehend it has received various corrupting changes, and I have, with most of the present Dissenters in England, some doubts as to his divinity; though it is a question I do not dogmatize upon, having never studied it, and think it needless to busy myself with it now, when I expect soon an opportunity of knowing the truth with less trouble. I see no harm, however, in its being believed, if that belief has the good consequence, as it probably has, of making his doctrines more respected and better observed, especially as I do not perceive that the Supreme takes it amiss, by distinguishing the unbelievers in his government of the world with any peculiar marks of his displeasure.

I shall only add, respecting myself, that, having experienced the goodness of that Being in conducting me prosperously through a long life, I have no doubt of its continuance in the next, though without the smallest conceit of meriting such goodness.

To this Franklin added a postscript requesting that Stiles not publish this letter, which doubtless would upset the orthodox. "I have ever let others enjoy their religious sentiments, without reflecting on them for those that appeared to me unsupportable and even absurd. All sects here, and we have a great variety, have experienced my good will in assisting them with subscriptions for building their new places of worship; and as I have never opposed any of their doctrines, I hope to go out of the world in peace with them all."

⁓ His flagging strength did not diminish his zest for political combat. He continued to seek to expand the scope of human liberty, and he resisted efforts to diminish it. Propertied groups were trying to revise the Pennsylvania constitution to grant special privileges to property; Franklin responded much as before: "Is it supposed that wisdom is the necessary concomitant of riches?" Far from claiming special privileges, property ought to accept special responsibilities. He recapitulated his earlier argument about the origins of property, and asserted, "Private property therefore is a creature of society, and is subject to the calls of that society, whenever its necessities shall require it, even to its last farthing."

He entered the fight over the college. "I am the only one of the original trustees now living, and I am just stepping into the grave myself," he declared, by way of reintroducing himself to the debate over what the young scholars should learn. As at the founding, he rejected the teaching of Latin and Greek to any but specialized scholars as an anachronism from an age that knew no other literature. Referring to the French habit of carrying hats on the arm, simply as ornaments, long after wigs displaced them from French pates, Franklin dubbed the vestigial teaching of the classics "the *chapeau bras* of modern literature."

He left the field of combat as he had entered it seven decades before—leading with his pen and his wit. In February 1790 he forwarded an antislavery petition to Congress. "Mankind are all formed by the same Almighty Being, alike objects of his care, and equally designed for the enjoyment of happiness," the petition read. At a time when the "spirit of philanthropy and genuine liberty" was abroad in America, a legislature explicitly chartered to secure the blessings of liberty to the American people could not ignore this gross denial of liberty to slaves. "These blessings ought rightfully to be administered without distinction of colour to all descriptions of people." To tolerate any less was to contradict the meaning of the Revolution. "Equal liberty was originally the portion, and is still the birthright of all men." Americans of goodwill looked to Congress for "the restoration of liberty to those unhappy men who alone in this land of freedom are degraded into perpetual bondage, and who amidst the general joy of surrounding freemen groan in servile subjection."

This petition, and the fact that it arrived over Franklin's signature, prompted Representative James Jackson of Georgia to leap to the defense of slavery. The Bible endorsed slavery, he said, as well it might, for it allowed the bringing of barbarians to the Gospel. If not slaves, who would work the fields of the south? The abolitionists should be silenced as subversive of social order.

Jackson delivered himself into Franklin's hands. Franklin wrote to the *Federal Gazette* to say that the congressman's speech "put me in mind of a similar one made about 100 years since by Sidi Mehemet Ibrahim, a member of the Divan of Algiers." For the benefit of the readers of the *Gazette*, Franklin reproduced Ibrahim's speech, which decried attempts to ban Barbary piracy and free the Christians enslaved as a result. The speech, of course, was a hoax, but, as with Franklin's other hoaxes, the bait went down before the barb was felt. Franklin took the arguments of such American apologists for African slavery as Jackson and placed them in the mouths of Muslim apologists for piracy and Christian slavery. "If we cease our cruises against the Christians, how shall we be furnished with the commodities their countries produce, and which are so necessary for us? If we forbear to make slaves of their people, who in this hot climate are to cultivate our lands?" To emancipate the Christian slaves would deprive them of continued exposure to the true Muslim faith, "sending them out of Light in Darkness." And so on, to a conclusion derisively parallel to that reached by Jackson: "Let us then hear no more of this detestable proposition, the manumission of Christian slaves."

~ Though the pen was still sharp, the hand that held it was failing. Franklin's friends and colleagues wrote what they and he knew to be their farewells. "Would to God, my dear Sir," declared Washington, "that I could congratulate you upon the removal of that excruciating pain under which you labour, and that your existence might close with as much ease to yourself as its continuance has been to our country and useful to mankind." If the united wishes of Americans, and the prayers of all friends of science and humanity, could effect a cure, then Franklin would indeed be cured. Sadly, such could not be. Yet Franklin should rest easy in mind if he could not rest easy in body.

> If to be venerated for benevolence, if to be admired for talents, if to be esteemed for patriotism, if to be beloved for philanthropy, can gratify the human mind, you must have the pleasing consolation to know that you have not lived in vain. And I flatter myself that it will not be ranked among the least grateful occurrences of your life to be assured that, so long as I retain my memory, you will be recollected with respect, veneration, and affection by your sincere friend,
>
> George Washington

In March 1790 Franklin received a visit from Jefferson. The former minister to France was on his way from Monticello to New York, to take up his new post as Washington's secretary of state. "At Philadelphia I called on the venerable and beloved Franklin," Jefferson recorded. The two shared stories of friends in France, with Jefferson supplying the latest intelligence as to how they were surviving the revolution there. "He went over all in succession, with a rapidity and animation almost too much for his strength." Jefferson expressed pleasure that Franklin had committed as much of his life story to paper as he had; the world would greatly benefit from reading it. "I cannot say much of that," replied Franklin, "but I will give you a sample of what I shall leave." Thereupon he instructed his grandson William Bache to hand Jefferson the account he had written aboard ship on the way back from London in 1775, regarding the failed negotiations with Lord Howe. Jefferson said he would gratefully read it, then return it. Franklin insisted he keep it. "Not certain of his meaning," Jefferson recounted, "I again looked into it, folded it for my pocket, and said again I would certainly return it. 'No,' said he, 'keep it.'" Not till later did Jefferson realize this was the only copy of a crucial account of the last moment when separation between Britain and the American colonies might have been averted.

Early in April, Franklin showed signs of a pulmonary infection. Whether this was related to the pleurisy he had suffered earlier in his life was (and is) unknown. His general inactivity did not help matters, nor the opium, which in its sedative influence prevented the full expansion of the lungs. He ran a fever, his breathing grew heavy, and he developed a painful cough. Yet he remained remarkably alert and good-humored.

Benjamin Rush, Franklin's greatest admirer among Philadelphians, and a physician, attended his friend during the final days. "The evening of his life was marked by the same activity of his moral and intellectual powers which distinguished its meridian," Rush noted. On April 8 Franklin dictated a letter—his last—to Jefferson, displaying his continued command of important details of the peace negotiations with Britain. As his strength ebbed further, he accepted his approaching end with characteristic—and characteristically wry—equanimity. "His conversation with his family upon the subject of his dissolution was free and cheerful. A few days before he died, he rose from his bed and begged that it might be made up so that he might die 'in a decent manner.' His daughter told him that she hoped he would recover and live many years longer. He calmly replied he hoped not. Upon being advised to change his position in bed that he might breathe easy, he said, 'A dying man can do nothing *easy*.' "

Briefly before the end his symptoms abated. Sally and some of the others allowed themselves optimism. But then the abscess that had been growing in his lung burst, and in his weakened condition he could not expel the fluid. He slipped into unconsciousness, and at eleven o'clock on the night of April 17, 1790, three months after his eighty-fourth birthday, with his grandsons Temple and Benny at his bed, he quietly died.

Epilogue

April 17, 1990

⌐ Franklin's friends could have predicted that his ingenuity
would not die with him, nor his concern for his fellow
citizens. Yet few anticipated the ingenious bequest he left
the two cities of his American life. True to his conviction
that elected officials in a republic should not be paid, he had
refused to accept his salary as president of Pennsylvania.
Some of this money he had already devoted to various
public purposes; the £2,000 that remained due him he set
aside for two special revolving funds, one for Boston,
the other for Philadelphia. Recalling the loans that had
allowed him to commence his printing career, he directed
that these funds were to be lent at 5-percent

interest "to such young married artificers under the age of twenty-five years as have served an apprenticeship in the said town and faithfully fulfilled the duties required in their indentures." The loans were to be in small amounts, no more than £60 (nor less than £15), and must be cosigned by "at least two respectable citizens" willing to vouch for the moral character of the borrowers. The term of each loan was set at ten years; as the money was repaid, it should be re-lent.

Under this scheme Franklin's bequest would be immediately useful, yet it would gain philanthropic power with passing years. By Franklin's calculation, each £1,000 fund should increase to more than £130,000 after a hundred years. He directed that £100,000 of this be spent on public works deemed most useful (in the case of Philadelphia he specifically mentioned piping in water from outside the city and improving navigation on the Schuylkill); the remainder should be returned to the revolving fund, the operation of which would continue as before, for another hundred years. At the end of the second century each fund should total more than £4 million. Franklin decreed that the Boston fund be then divided between Boston and the state of Massachusetts, with the former getting one-fourth and the latter three-fourths, and the Philadelphia fund split similarly between Philadelphia and the state of Pennsylvania.

Franklin appreciated that two centuries was a long time. "Considering the accidents to which all human affairs and projects are subject in such a length of time, I have, perhaps, too much flattered myself with a vain fancy that these dispositions, if carried into execution, will be continued without interruption and have the effects proposed." In the event, the Franklin funds did encounter various accidents, including wars, economic depressions, political wrangling over control of the funds, and an industrial revolution that significantly altered the role of apprenticeship in career advancement.

Yet at the bicentennial of his death the Boston fund amounted to $4.5 million, and that of Philadelphia, which had been less well managed, $2 million. Franklin would have been pleased—and happy at that distance to have relinquished responsibility for deciding how the money was to be spent. "Everyone and his brother is after the money," observed an official of Boston's Franklin Institute, a South End trade school founded with funds from the payout at the end of the first century. In Philadelphia, which had built a tourist industry around Franklin, initial thoughts of spending the city's share on promoting more tourism were dropped in favor of financial aid for students in the applied sciences.

Philadelphia's mayor embraced this decision as being "in the true spirit of Benjamin Franklin."

~ The spirit of Franklin was palpable in his adopted city, and undeniable across America, at the bicentennial of his death. As it happened, the University of Pennsylvania observed its 250th anniversary that same year, honored as one of the most eminent institutions of higher education in America, fulfilling Franklin's vision—and, not incidentally, having abandoned the attempt to inflict Latin and Greek on reluctant young minds. The American Philosophical Society similarly flourished, sponsoring and disseminating research by leading scholars. Libraries and fire departments were staples of city and town life throughout the land. Hospitals were equally ubiquitous. The post office delivered letters from coast to coast. Paper currency had long since ceased to provoke controversy, or even question.

Franklin's legacy in science was no less distinguished than in civic affairs. The electrical revolution he helped unleash, and for which he provided a lexicon, in time transformed the world, magnifying muscle and mind, knitting a net of information that encompassed the globe. His work in demography inspired economists and practitioners of allied social sciences. His conjectures on meteorology, geology, and oceanography, while not uniformly accurate, challenged others to correct his mistakes.

Franklin's literary legacy was equally impressive. His autobiography became a landmark of American letters, and indeed one of the great lives in the English language. Poor Richard grew only more famous after his author's death, causing most Americans to forget that any other almanackers ever existed. Franklin's bagatelles, satires, hoaxes and correspondence made him a model for commentary that always had a point but was never pedantic.

In letters, science, and commitment to the common weal, Franklin was the first—in the sense of foremost—American of his generation. Considering the length and breadth of his multiple legacies, he was probably the first American of any generation. Yet he was the first American in another sense as well. Sooner than almost anyone else, certainly sooner than anyone equally placed to act on the insight, Franklin realized that he and his fellow Americans were no longer Britons but a breed apart—a people not suited to rule by others but compelled to rule themselves. He did not initially welcome the knowledge, which contradicted his hopes for America within the British empire. But once convinced, he acted decisively on the knowledge, and did more than almost anyone else to give this new people—these Americans—a government of their own. In the Continental Congress at the start of the Revolution, in Paris during the war and the peace negotiations, at the Constitutional Convention back home in Philadelphia, he served his new country with unsurpassed energy, devotion, and skill.

At his death the millions he had touched stopped to acknowledge his preeminence and profess their gratitude. Twenty thousand Philadelphians—nearly half the city—turned out for the funeral. In the House of Representatives, James Madison offered a motion for official mourning, which passed unanimously. France took the news of Franklin's passing even harder. "He has returned to the bosom of the Divinity, the genius who freed America and shed torrents of light upon Europe," Mirabeau told the tearful National Assembly, which likewise voted to don black. Felix Vicq d'Azyr, a personal friend of Franklin's and secretary of the French Royal Society of Medicine, summarized the Atlantic gloom: "A man is dead, and two worlds are in mourning."

They mourned one who came as close as any to realizing the full potential of the human spirit. To genius he joined a passion for virtue. His genius distinguished him from others, yet it also connected him to others, for he sought knowledge not for its own sake but for humanity's. His passion for virtue reflected not hope of heaven but faith in his fellow mortals. It afforded the foundation for his greatest accomplishments, and for the glorious achievement he shared with others of his revolutionary generation.

At the precocious age of twenty-two Franklin wrote what became one of the most famous epitaphs in that lapidary genre:

> *The Body of*
> *B. Franklin,*
> *Printer;*
> *Like the Cover of an old Book,*
> *Its contents torn out,*
> *And stript of its Lettering and Gilding,*
> *Lies here, Food for Worms.*
> *But the Work shall not be wholly lost,*
> *For it will, as he believed, appear once more,*
> *In a new & more perfect Edition,*
> *Corrected and amended*
> *By the Author.*

When the time came, however, he preferred something simpler. In his will he directed that only "Benjamin and Deborah Franklin 1790" adorn the headstone he shared with his dear country Joan.

A life as full as Franklin's could not be captured in a phrase—or a volume. Yet if a few words had to suffice, a few words that summarized his legacy to the America he played such a central role in creating—and that, not incidentally, illustrated his wry, aphoristic style—they were those he uttered upon leaving the final session of the Constitutional Convention. A matron of Philadelphia demanded to know, after four months' secrecy, what he and the other delegates had produced.

"A republic," he answered, "if you can keep it."

Source Notes

The primary source for any life of Benjamin Franklin is Franklin himself: his correspondence and published writings. Several editions of Franklin's papers exist; by far the best (and a model of scholarly editing) is *The Papers of Benjamin Franklin*, published by Yale University Press, starting in 1959. The original editor was Leonard W. Labaree; the current editor is Barbara B. Oberg. The most recent volumes in this series carry Franklin's story to 1781. In the present book, citations of Franklin up to 1781 are drawn almost exclusively from this edition, and are typically cited by date alone. Other editions of Franklin papers, for the years after 1781, that have been used extensively here are by Smyth and Bigelow (see full information below). As a general rule, where the date of a document locates it unambiguously, the date alone has been given. In other cases, volume and page numbers are furnished.

Franklin's original manuscripts lie in scores of collections scattered about America and Europe. The most important of these collections are located at the American Philosophical Society in Philadelphia and at the Library of Congress in Washington. The vast majority of substantive letters by Franklin in these collections have been published in one or more of the printed editions of Franklin papers. Where such is the case, citations in the present book are to a printed version, for reasons of accessibility. In the rare exceptional cases, the archives are cited.

One of Franklin's published works that requires special mention is his justly famous *Autobiography*. Numerous editions exist; the one cited here is also edited by Leonard W. Labaree and published by Yale University Press, in 1964. It is abbreviated below as *ABF*.

For clarity and readability, most archaisms have been silently modernized. Franklin capitalized many more nouns than modern writers do; these have usually been rendered lowercase. Franklin wrote British English; where British usage and spellings persist at the start of the twenty-first century, these have generally been retained.

In the notes below, references are given only for direct quotations. The works cited include many, but by no means all, of the most important sources consulted for this book. Considerations of space preclude any effort to present a comprehensive bibliography of materials relating to Franklin's life, let alone his times. The interested reader is referred to Melvin H. Buxbaum, *Benjamin Franklin: A Reference Guide* (2 volumes: Boston, 1983–88). J. A. Leo Lemay, *Reappraising Benjamin Franklin: A Bicentennial Perspective* (Newark, Del., 1993), comprises papers by Franklin scholars; the references nicely complement those in the Buxbaum volumes.

ABBREVIATIONS

Individuals

BF: Benjamin Franklin
DF: Deborah Read Franklin
WF: William Franklin

Archives and Published Works

ABF: The Autobiography of Benjamin Franklin (New Haven, Conn., 1964).
Adams Papers: The Adams Papers, ed. L. H. Butterfield (Cambridge, Mass., 1961–   )
AHR: American Historical Review.
APS: Benjamin Franklin Collection, American Philosophical Society (Philadelphia).
Bagatelles: Franklin's Wit and Folly: The Bagatelles, ed. Richard E. Amacher (New Brunswick, N.J., 1953).
Bigelow: *The Works of Benjamin Franklin,* ed. John Bigelow (New York, 1904).
DAR: Documents of the American Revolution, 1770–1783 (Colonial Office Series), ed. K. G. Davies (Shannon, Ireland, 1972–1981).
Facsimiles: Facsimiles of Manuscripts in European Archives Relating to America, 1773–1783, ed. B. F. Stevens (London, 1889–98).
Giunta: *The Emerging Nation: A Documentary History of the Foreign Relations of the United States under the Articles of Confederation, 1780–1789,* ed. Mary A. Giunta et al. (Washington, D.C., 1996).
HSP: Historical Society of Pennsylvania (Philadelphia).
Lafayette Letters: Lafayette in the Age of the American Revolution: Selected Letters and Papers, 1776–1790, ed. Stanley J. Idzerda (Ithaca, N.Y., 1979).
LC: The Papers of Benjamin Franklin, Liberty of Congress (Washington, D.C.).
Lemay: *Benjamin Franklin: Writings,* selected and annotated by J. A. Leo Lemay (New York, 1987).
Letters of Rush: Letters of Benjamin Rush, ed. L. H. Butterfield (Princeton, N.J., 1951).
Memoirs: Memoirs of the Life and Writings of Benjamin Franklin, ed. William Temple Franklin (London, 1833).
NEQ: The New England Quarterly.

Papers of Jefferson: The Papers of Thomas Jefferson, ed. Julian P. Boyd (Princeton, N.J., 1950–).

Papers of Madison: The Papers of James Madison, ed. William T. Hutchinson and William M. E. Rachal (Charlottesville, Va., 1962–91).

Papers of Washington: The Papers of George Washington, ed. W. W. Abbot (Charlottesville, Va., 1983–).

PBF: The Papers of Benjamin Franklin, ed. Leonard W. Labaree et al. (New Haven, Conn., 1959–).

PG: Pennsylvania Gazette.

PMHB: Pennsylvania Magazine of History and Biography.

PR: Poor Richard [year]: An Almanack for the Year of Christ [year]. (All the pertinent issues can be found in PBF, under last part of the previous year.)

Records of Convention: The Records of the Federal Convention of 1787, ed. Max Farrand (New Haven, Conn., 1923).

Smyth: The Writings of Benjamin Franklin, ed. Albert Henry Smyth (New York, 1905–7).

Sparks: The Works of Benjamin Franklin, ed. Jared Sparks (Boston, 1840).

WMQ: William and Mary Quarterly (3rd. series).

Writings of Jefferson: The Writings of Thomas Jefferson, ed. Albert Ellery Bergh (Washington, D.C., 1903–4).

Writings of Madison: James Madison: Writings, ed. Jack N. Rakove (New York, 1999).

Writings of Washington: The Writings of George Washington, ed. John C. Fitzpatrick (Washington, D.C., 1931–44).

Yale: Benjamin Franklin Collection, Yale University (New Haven, Conn.).

I. BOSTON BEGINNINGS: 1706–23

10 "Coming to himself . . . this resolution": *Diary of Cotton Mather*, 2 vols. (Boston, 1911–12), 1:12, 357.

10–12 "That there is . . . imposed upon": *The Wonders of the Invisible World* (1893), reproduced in *The Witchcraft Delusion in New England*, ed. Samuel G. Drake (Roxbury, Mass., 1866), 1:55, 61, 94–95, 102–6.

12 "blame and shame": *The Diary of Samuel Sewall*, ed. M. Halsey Thomas (New York, 1973), 1:367.

12 "the first letters": Marion L. Starkey, *The Devil in Massachusetts* (Garden City, N.Y., 1969), 198.

14 "I remember well": *ABF*, 54–55.

14 "a place where": Arthur Bernon Tourtellot, *Benjamin Franklin: The Shaping of Genius: The Boston Years* (Garden City, N.Y., 1977), 105.

15 "When I was a child": *Bagatelles*, 45.

16–18 "I do not remember . . . difficulty": *ABF*, 53–54.

18 "without the least fatigue": to Barbeu-Dubourg, undated, Smyth, 5:542–45.

19 "the old feud": Walter Muir Whitehill, *Boston: A Topographical History* (Cambridge, Mass., 1959), 29.

21 "The said Apprentice": John Clyde Oswald, *A History of Printing* (New York, 1928), 355.

22–23 "still had a hankering . . . vanity": *ABF*, 58–60.

23 "Will you hear": in Thomas C. Leonard, "Recovering 'Wretched Stuff' and the Franklins' Synergy," *NEQ* 72:3 (Sept. 1999), 445–47. Although the editors of *PBF* were skeptical that this is in fact Franklin's poem, Leonard's textual and contextual reasoning is persuasive.

24 "I was extremely": *ABF,* 62.

25 "vile *Courant*": Samuel G. Drake, *The History and Antiquities of Boston* (Boston, 1856), 564.

25 "to vilify": Kenneth Silverman, *The Life and Times of Cotton Mather* (New York, 1984), 357.

26 "notorious": Tourtellot, *The Boston Years,* 258.

26 "the wicked printer": *Diary of Cotton Mather,* 2:663.

26–27 "either to commend . . . else to grieve for": *PBF,* 1:9–10.

27 "No questions": *ibid.,* 11.

27 "exquisite pleasure": *ABF,* 68.

28–29 "There is certainly . . . garnish it mightily": *PBF,* 1:11–12, 17, 19, 22, 26.

29 "The houses": Carl Seaburg, *Boston Observed* (Boston, 1971), 82.

29 "This night": *Diary of Cotton Mather,* 2:658.

29 " 'Tis thought": *PBF,* 1:27.

30 "I made bold": *ABF,* 69.

30 "Without freedom": *PBF,* 1:27, 30.

31 "Whenever I find . . . Courant": Tourtellot, *The Boston Years,* 423–25.

31 "entirely dropped": *PBF,* 1:48.

31 "Adam was never": *ibid.,* 1:52.

32–34 "I was charmed . . . scrapes": *ABF,* 63–71.

2. FRIENDS AND OTHER STRANGERS: 1723–24

36–37 "a den . . . cheap a price": Harry Emerson Wildes, *William Penn* (New York, 1974), 12, 22, 27, 119.

37–38 "large town . . . for money": Mary Maples Dunn and Richard S. Dunn, "The Founding," in *Philadelphia: A 300-Year History,* ed. Russell F. Weigley (New York, 1982), 1, 14.

40 "I recollected": *ABF,* 87–88.

42 "I was thoroughly": *ibid.,* 73.

43 "I saw": *ibid.,* 124.

44–50 "most awkward . . . pig poisoned": *ibid.,* 76–80.

51 "The reason": Dunn and Dunn, "Founding," 31.

52–53 "most affable . . . grum and sullen": *ABF,* 81–82.

54 "Stoop": to Samuel Mather, May 12, 1784, Smyth.

56–58 "He suspected . . . his promise": *ABF,* 88–92.

3. LONDON ONCE: 1724–26

61–62 "I was satisfied . . . Riddlesden": *ABF,* 93–94.

62 "a person": biographical note on William Vanhaesdonck Riddlesden, *ABF,* 296.

62 "I have lately": *ibid.,* 94.

64 "Presuming on . . . a burden": *ABF,* 99.

65 "Oh, the miserable": Thomas Burke, *The Streets of London through the Centuries* (London, 1943), 39–40.

66 "No city in the world": Daniel Defoe, *A Tour thro' London about the Year 1725, Being Letter V and Parts of Letter VI of 'A Tour thro' the Whole Island of Great Britain'* (1724–26; rpt. New York, 1969), 48.

66 "As we stumbled": Burke, *Streets of London*, 64.

67 "No person": editorial note in Defoe, *Tour thro' London*, 25.

67 "This is to give": Walter Besant, *London in the Eighteenth Century* (London, 1903), 440.

67–68 "Last Wednesday . . . not wise": *ibid.*, 238–42.

68 "The many-headed": *ibid.*, 427.

69 "spent with Ralph": *ABF*, 96.

69 "foolish intrigues": *ibid.*, 115.

70–71 "a detestable custom . . . very agreeably": *ibid.*, 100–1.

72 *A Dissertation on Liberty and Necessity, Pleasure and Pain*: *PBF*, 1:58–71.

74–76 "My printing . . . to see it": *ABF*, 96–105.

76–81 "This Gravesend . . . Thank God!": journal of voyage, *PBF*, 1:72–99.

4. AN IMPRINT OF HIS OWN: 1726–30

83–84 "expert at selling . . . do over again": *ABF*, 107.

85 "I had almost determined": to Jane Franklin, Jan. 6, 1727.

88–95 "a very civil . . . beneficial to us": *ABF*, 112–19.

95 "Articles of Belief and Acts of Religion": *PBF*, 1:101–9.

96 "Those who write": "Plan of Conduct": *ibid.*, 1:99–100.

97–98 "1. Temperance . . . Jesus and Socrates": *ABF*, 149–50.

99–100 "Something that pretended . . . by the endeavour": *ibid.*, 156.

100 "In order to secure": *ibid.*, 125–26.

101 "a paltry thing": *ibid.*, 119.

101–2 "in behalf of myself . . . lay it down": Martha Careful and Caelia Shortface [Letters], *American Weekly Mercury*, Jan. 28, 1729, *PBF*, 1:112–13.

102 "Let the fair sex . . . on hearing further": Busy Body [Letter], *American Weekly Mercury*, Feb. 4, 1729, *ibid.*, 1:114–16.

103 "a trifle": *ABF*, 120.

103–4 "now to be carried . . . will allow": *PG*, Oct. 2, 1729, *PBF*, 1:157–59.

5. POOR RICHARD: 1730–35

107–8 "I considered . . . escaped it": *ABF*, 128.

109 "He knew little": *ibid.*, 117.

111 " 'Tis generally known": Sheila L. Skemp, *William Franklin: Son of a Patriot, Servant of a King* (New York, 1990), 4.

111 "Barbara": Carl Van Doren, *Benjamin Franklin* (New York, 1938), 91.

112 "I therefore put": *ABF*, 143.

113 "civil gentlemen": *PBF*, 1:250–52.

115 "Apology for Printers": *ibid.*, 1:194–99.

118–21 "A considerable quantity . . . whole province": *PG*, various issues 1731–1734.

122 "As to the abilities . . . *Almanack*": Marion Barber Stowell, *Early American Almanacs: The Colonial Weekday Bible* (New York: 1977), xiv–7.

124 "Wit, learning, order": Bernard Capp, *English Almanacs, 1500–1800* (Ithaca, N.Y., 1979), 23.

125 "Just published for 1733": *PG*, Dec. 28, 1732, *PBF*, 1:280.

125–26 "Courteous Reader . . . R. Saunders": *PR*, 1733.

126–27 "false prediction . . . performances are dead": *The American Almanack for the Year of Christian Account*, 1734.

127 "to receive": *PR*, 1734.

128 "If falsehood": *American Almanack*, 1735.

128–31 "Whatever may be . . . April shower": *PR*, various issues 1733–42.

6. CITIZEN: 1735–40

133 *A Modest Enquiry into the Nature and Necessity of a Paper-Currency*, Apr. 3, 1729.

135 "old and lame": "A.A." to BF, Feb. 4, 1735.

137 "We will all": articles of Union Fire Company, *PBF*, 2:150–53.

137 "I question": *ABF*, 175.

138 "Though the salary": *ibid.*, 172.

138 "I saw": John Pollock, *George Whitefield and the Great Awakening* (Garden City, N.Y., 1972), 4.

138 "the awe": Josiah Smith in *The Great Awakening*, ed. Alan Heimert and Perry Miller (Indianapolis, 1967), 67–68.

139 "See!": Stuart C. Henry, *George Whitefield: Wayfaring Witness* (New York, 1957), 54.

139 "graceful and well-proportioned": *ibid.*, 27–28.

139–40 "The remembrance . . . redemption": *George Whitefield's Journals*, ed. William V. Davis (Gainesville, Fla., 1969), 29–48.

140 "the new birth": L. Tyerman, *The Life of the Rev. George Whitefield* (London, 1876), 32.

140 "I shall displease some": *ibid.*, 49–50.

141 "I preached": Henry, *George Whitefield*, 29.

141 "Mr. Whitefield's auditors": *ibid.*, 38.

141 "mad trick": *ibid.*, 49.

141 "Blessed be God": *Whitefield's Journals*, 209.

142 "His discourses": *ABF*, 147.

142 "new-light man": Merton A. Christensen, "Franklin on the Hemphill Trial: Deism Versus Presbyterian Orthodoxy," *WMQ* 10 (1953), 426.

143 "most excellent discourses": *ABF*, 167.

143 "free-thinkers": Christensen, "Franklin on the Hemphill Trial," 427.

143 "What is Christ's": *PG*, Apr. 10, 1735, *PBF*.

144 "I rather approved": *ABF*, 168.

144 "malice and envy": *Some Observations on the Proceedings against the Rev. Mr. Hemphill*, *PBF*, 2:39, 48.

144–45 "the dominion . . . impiety": *A Defense of Mr. Hemphill's Observations*, *PBF*, 2:90ff. [Note the title even though the observations in question were Franklin's, not Hemphill's.]

145 "like a boatswain": Perry Miller, *Jonathan Edwards* (Cleveland, 1959), 166.

146 "never to do": *ibid.,* 138.
146 "The God": *ibid.,* 145–46.
147 "The multitudes": *ABF,* 175.
148 "The alteration": *PG,* June 12, 1740, *PBF.*
148–50 "I had the curiosity . . . his death": *ABF,* 176–79.
150 " 'Tis true": "A Defense of Conduct," *PG,* Feb. 15, 1737/8, *PBF.*
151 "The coroner's inquest": *PG,* June 16, 1737, *PBF.*
151–52 "very false . . . him afterwards": *PG,* Feb. 15, 1737/8, *PBF.*
153 "They are in general": to Josiah and Abiah Franklin, Apr. 13, 1738.
154 "I long regretted": *ABF,* 170.
155 "brings often afresh": to Jane Franklin Mecom, Jan. 13, 1772.
156 "Thus it was": *ABF,* 170.

7. ARC OF EMPIRE: 1741–48

157 "We have had": to Josiah and Abiah Franklin, Sept. 6, 1744.
158 "half Indianized French": Howard H. Peckham, *The Colonial Wars 1689–1762* (Chicago, 1964), 30.
159 "I commended my soul": *ibid.,* 88.
160 *"Nil desperandum":* G. A. Rawlyk, *Yankees at Louisbourg* (Orono, Maine, 1967), 45.
161 "The enterprise . . . very uncertain": Joseph Kelley, *Pennsylvania: The Colonial Years,* 238–39.
161 "When I compare": notes on Assembly debates, Feb. 26–28, 1745, *PBF.*
162 "Our people": to John Franklin, probably May 1745.
163 "the most mischievous": *American Weekly Mercury,* Nov. 20, 1740.
164 "Teague's Advertisement": *PG,* Feb. 26, 1741, *PBF.*
164 "If you would keep": *PR,* 1741.
165 "From the short": to Strahan, July 4, 1744.
165 "Trust to his generosity": Strahan to Hall, Mar. 9 and June 22, 1745, *PBF,* 2:409n.
166 "In these northern": *An Account of the New Invented Pennsylvania Fire-Places, PBF,* 2:419ff.
167 "the new-invented Philadelphia Fire Places": *Boston Evening Post,* Sept. 8, 1746.
167 "That as we enjoy": *ABF* 192.
167 "Another sun": *Account, PBF,* 2:446.
168 *A Proposal for Promoting Useful Knowledge,* May 14, 1743, *PBF.*
169 "I long very much": from Colden, Oct. 1743.
170 "I cannot": to Colden, Nov. 4, 1743.
170 "I long to know": from Colden, Dec. 1744.
170 "The members": to Colden, Aug. 15, 1745.
171 "You shall know": *ibid.*
171 "I intend": to Colden, Nov. 28, 1745.
171 "Suppose two globes": to unknown recipient, copied to Colden, Oct. 16, 1746.
172 "I have not time": to Colden, Feb. 1746.
172 "My dear Friend": to unknown, June 25, 1745.
174 "The Antediluvians": *PBF,* 3:52.

175 "Of their Chloes": "I Sing My Plain Country Joan," *PBF,* 2:353–54.

176 "Sally was inoculated": memorandum, Apr. 18, 1746.

176 "Your granddaughter": to Abiah Franklin, Oct. 16, 1747.

176 "Sally grows": to Abiah Franklin, Apr. 12, 1750.

176 "I am glad": to Strahan, June 2, 1750.

176 "By an entire dependence": *Boston Weekly News-Letter,* Jan. 17, 1745.

177 "Dear Sister": to Edward and Jane Mecom [1744–45], *PBF,* 2:448.

178 "To prevent . . . our cannon": Rawlyk, *Yankees at Louisbourg,* 106–8.

178 "Wednesday last": *PG,* July 18, 1745, *PBF.*

179 "If they had a pick ax . . . *New England's* name": Rawlyk, *Yankees at Louisbourg,* 153–54.

181 "No one imagined": to Jane Mecom, June [?] 1748.

181 *Plain Truth*: *PBF,* 3:180–204.

183 "The house was pretty full": *ABF,* 183.

183 "Where a Government": *PG,* Dec. 3, 1747, *PBF.*

184 "A parcel": *PG,* Mar. 8, 1748, *PBF.*

185 "Thy project of a lottery": from Logan, Dec. 3, 1747.

185 "The Quakers": *ABF,* 189–90.

185 "the late lotteries": *PG,* Jan. 19, 1748, *PBF.*

186 "But at a dinner": *ABF,* 184.

186 "Unless we humble": Proclamation for a General Fast, Dec. 7, 1747.

186 "He it was": Logan to Penn, Nov. 24, 1749, *PBF,* 3:185n.

8. ELECTRICITY AND FAME: 1748–51

187 "This Association": Penn letters quoted in *PBF,* 3:186n.

188 "Had he not": Isaiah Thomas, *The History of Printing in America* (1810; rpt. Albany, 1874), 1:246.

189 "occasional buying": articles of agreement with David Hall, Jan. 1, 1748.

189 "Mr. Hall": to Strahan, Feb. 4, 1751.

189–90 "I am settling . . . business": to Colden, Sept. 29, 1748.

191 "Dr. Spence": *ABF,* 240–41.

191–92 "I was never": to Collinson, Mar. 28, 1747.

192 "We say *B*": to Collinson, May 25, 1747.

192 "I have observed": to Collinson, Aug. 14, 1747.

193 "I have imparted": from Collinson, Apr. 12, 1748.

193 "I am pleased": to Collinson, Oct. 18, 1748.

193–94 "what we called . . . battery": to Collinson, Apr. 29, 1749.

194 "The most interested": Joseph Priestley, *The History and Present State of Electricity, with Original Experiments* (London, 1767), 153.

194 "new and very curious . . . electrical strokes": report by William Watson to the Royal Society, Jan. 11, 1750, *PBF.*

195 "free from . . . native soil": *PG,* Aug. 24, 1749.

195–96 "The best . . . and frugally": *Proposals Relating to the Education of the Youth in Pennsylvania, PBF,* 3:397ff.

196 "Our Academy": to Jared Eliot, Sept. 12, 1751.

197 "Billy is so fond": to John Franklin, Apr. 2, 1747.

197 "My son": to Colden, June 5, 1747.

197 "It was intended": to Strahan, Oct. 19, 1748.

198–99 "Please to acquaint . . . I know not": to Collinson, Feb. 4, 1750.

199 "earthquake of the air": *Benjamin Franklin's Experiments,* ed. I. Bernard Cohen (Cambridge, Mass, 1941), 105.

199 "The flame": *ibid.,* 106.

200 "It has been fatal": to Mitchell, Apr. 29, 1749.

200 "Your very curious": from Collinson, Feb. 5, 1750.

200 "The doctrine": to Collinson, Mar. 2, 1750.

200–1 "To determine": enclosure in letter to Collinson, July 29, 1750.

202 "Silk is fitter": *PG,* Oct. 19, 1752, *PBF.*

202 "At length": Priestley, *History and Present State of Electricity,* 180–81.

203–4 "Abstracted . . . my memory": *The Speech of Miss Polly Baker, PBF,* 3:123–25.

205 "Though some others": speech by Earl of Macclesfield, Nov. 30, 1753, *PBF.*

205 "a very able": William Watson on BF's "Opinions and Conjectures," June 6, 1751, *PBF.*

205 "Every circumstance": Priestley, *History and Present State of Electricity,* 179–80.

205 "universally admired . . . esteem of our nation": Guillaume Mazéas to Stephen Hales, May 20, 1752, *PBF,* 4:315–17.

206 "The Tatler": to Eliot, Apr. 12, 1753.

9 · A TASTE OF POLITICS: 1751–54

208 "not wishing . . . any magician": to Collinson, 1752?, *PBF,* 4:393–96.

208–9 "More knowledge . . . unsolicited": *ABF,* 197.

211 "We are made": Joseph Kelley, *Pennsylvania,* 169.

211 "rabble butchers": *ibid.,* 170.

213 "from that period": *Report on the State of the Currency,* Aug. 19, 1752.

213 "very unseasonable": *PBF,* 4:496.

213–14 "The Constable": *ABF,* 173.

214 "Up Front-street . . . necessity": Order of the Mayor and Aldermen, July 7, 1752, *PBF.*

215 "Last Thursday . . . murder the rest": *PG,* Apr. 11, 1751, *PBF.*

216 "felons-convict . . . convict does not": *PG,* May 9, 1751, *PBF.*

216–17 "It is almost": Joseph J. Kelley Jr., *Life and Times in Colonial Philadelphia* (Harrisburg, Pa., 1973), 138.

217 "penitentiary . . . Spirit's keenness": Paul A. W. Wallace, *Conrad Weiser* (Philadelphia, 1945), 51–52.

218–19 "As few . . . precarious": to Collinson, May 9, 1753.

219 "The German women": to Collinson, undated 1753.

220–221 "offspring . . . reclaiming them": to Collinson, May 9, 1753.

222 "as far as a man": Harry Emerson Wildes, *The Delaware* (New York, 1940), 102.

223 "No sit down . . . it was done": William Mason Cornell, *The History of Pennsylvania* (Philadelphia, 1876), 105–6.

224 "good things": *Remarks Concerning the Savages of North America,* Lemay, 969ff.

225–26 "Brethren . . . their backs": Report on the Treaty of Carlisle, Nov. 1, 1753, *PBF*.
227 "They were near": *ABF*, 198–99.
227 "to an inconceivable": Report, Nov. 1, 1753, *PBF*.

10. JOIN OR DIE: 1754–55

230 "little known": Howard Peckham, *The Colonial Wars,* 125.
230 "He is more English": William A. Hunter, *Forts on the Pennsylvania Frontier, 1753–1758* (Harrisburg, Pa., 1960), 141.
232 "assassinated": Articles of Capitulation, July 3, 1754, *Papers of Washington*.
232 "I fortunately escaped": George Washington to John Augustine Washington, May 31, 1754, *ibid.*
232 "He would not say": *ibid.,* 1:119.
232–33 "It would be . . . by Parliament": to James Parker, Mar. 20, 1751.
234 "Friday last": *PG,* May 9, 1754, *PBF*.
235 "to be sent home": to James Alexander and Cadwallader Colden, June 8, 1754.
236–37 "a quietist . . . sort of government": Bernard Bailyn, *The Ordeal of Thomas Hutchinson* (Cambridge, Mass., 1974), 10–17.
237 "There has never": *Representation of the Present State of the Colonies,* July 9, 1754, *PBF*.
237–38 "When one": to Colden, July 14, 1754.
238 "President General": Plan of Proposed Union, July 10, 1754.
238 "We had a great deal": to Colden, July 14, 1754.
238 "How they will relish it": *ibid.*
239 "Excluding the people": to Shirley, Dec. 4, 1754.
239–40 "Such an Union . . . of the whole": to Shirley, Dec. 22, 1754.
240 "I am very weeke": from Abiah Franklin, Oct. 14, 1751.
240–41 "I received yours": to Jane Mecom, May 21, 1752.
241 "I am confident": to Mecom, undated, *PBF,* 2:448.
241–42 "I am frequently . . . I love him": to Mecom, undated, *PBF,* 3:301–4.
242 "That island": to Mecom, Sept. 14, 1752.
242 "I fear": to Mecom, Nov. 30, 1752.
243 "William is now": to Abiah Franklin, Apr. 12, 1750.
243 "I have often seen": Daniel Fisher diary, July 28, 1755, *PMHB* 17 (1893), 276.
243–44 "is thought": to Collinson, May 21, 1751.
245 "I wish": from Collinson, Sept. 27, 1752.
245–46 "Land being thus": *Observations concerning the Increase of Mankind, Peopling of Countries, &c.: PBF,* 4:227–34.
247 "Braddock is very Iroquois": Joseph Kelley, *Pennsylvania,* 322.
248 "The General told me": *ibid.*
248 "After taking": *ABF,* 223–24.
248 "These Americans": J. Bennett Nolan, *General Benjamin Franklin: The Military Career of a Philosopher* (Philadelphia, 1936), 10.
249 "the service": advertisement, Apr. 26, 1755.
249 "I cannot but honour": *PBF,* 6:22.
249 "parcel of traitors": Kelley, *Pennsylvania,* 323.

250 "What the devil": *ABF,* 228.
250 "I cannot describe": Kelley, *Pennsylvania,* 327.
251 "with about a dozen": *ibid.,* 327–28.

II. THE PEOPLE'S COLONEL: 1755–57

253 "I have succeeded": Paul Wallace, *Conrad Weiser,* 385, 395.
253 "All burned": *ibid.,* 410.
254 "most of the Indians": *ibid.,* 403.
254 "Almost all": Joseph Kelley, *Pennsylvania,* 339.
255 "The Quakers": to Collinson, Aug. 27, 1755.
255 "My dear friend": *ABF,* 212.
256 "perfectly equitable": Reply to the Governor, Aug. 5, 1755.
256 "How odious": Reply, Aug. 8, 1755.
256–57 "Vassals must *follow*": Reply, Aug. 19, 1775.
257 "We are not so absurd": Reply, Sept. 29, 1755.
257 "Our answers . . . his own face": *ABF,* 213–14.
258 "the rashest . . . in flames": to Collinson, Aug. 27, 1755.
259 "Your kind letter . . . of happiness": to Catharine Ray, Mar. 4, 1755.
259–60 "Absence rather": from Ray, June 28, 1755.
260 "You may write": to Ray, [Mar.–Apr. 1755], *PBF,* 5:535–37.
260 "I must confess . . . rather than come": to Ray, Sept. 11, 1755.
261 "free gift": *PBF,* 6:130n.
261 "The Assembly": Wallace, *Conrad Weiser,* 411.
262 "back People . . . all their lies": Morris to Penn, Nov. 28, 1755, *PBF.*
262 "Since Mr. Franklin": Nolan, *General Benjamin Franklin,* 9.
262–63 "If we cannot": to Partridge, Nov. 27, 1755.
263 "We meet": to William Parsons, Dec. 5, 1755.
263 "I am no coward": *PG,* Dec. 18, 1755, *PBF.*
264 "I was surprised": *ABF,* 231–32.
264 "The people here": Nolan, *General Benjamin Franklin,* 34.
264 "the quintessence": *ibid.,* 36.
264 "You are immediately": Commissioners to Parsons, Dec. 29, 1755.
265 "Hills like Alps . . . can invent": Thomas Lloyd to unknown, Jan. 30, 1756, *PBF,* 6:380–82.
266 "It is perhaps": *ABF,* 235.
267 "To prevent this": to Collinson, Nov. 5, 1756.
268 "So grand an appearance": *PG,* Mar. 25, 1756.
268 "which shook down": *ABF,* 238.
268 "Twenty officers . . . or malice": to Collinson, Nov. 5, 1756.
268 "abomination": Peters to Penn, Feb. 18, 1756, HSP.
268–69 "The city": Peters to Penn, Apr. 25, 1756, HSP.
269 "I much wonder": Penn to Peters, May 8, 1756, HSP.
270 "To be convinced": *Pennsylvania Journal and Weekly Advertiser,* Mar. 11, 1756.
270 "I have had": to Strahan, July 27, 1756.
270 "The militia": William Hanna, *Benjamin Franklin and Pennsylvania Politics,* 112.
271 "I had not so good": *ABF,* 240.
271 "The people": to Collinson, Nov. 5, 1756.

12. A LARGER STAGE: 1757–58

272 "Look out sharp": to Strahan, Jan. 31, 1757.

273 "Mr. Franklin's": Penn to Peters, May 14, 1757, HSP.

275 "Lady Darlington": J. H. Plumb, *The First Four Georges* (Boston, 1975), 36.

275 *"Cette diablesse": ibid.,* 37.

276 *"Robin of Bagshot* . . . choleric blockhead": Paul Langford, *A Polite and Commercial People: England 1727–1783* (Oxford, UK, 1989), 14, 23.

277 "A plain clean . . . says Poor Dick": *PR,* 1758.

278 "Snuff-coloured": D. H. Lawrence, *Studies in Classic American Literature* (1923; rpt. New York, 1964), 13–14.

278 "Were I a Roman Catholic": to DF, July 17, 1757.

279 "I had for many years": Strahan to DF, Dec. 13, 1757.

280–81 "You Americans . . . of agreement": *ABF,* 261–62.

281 "Heads of Complaint," Aug. 20, 1757.

282–83 "great pain": to DF, Nov. 22, 1757.

283 "first rate": Thomas Hutchinson, *The History of the Colony and Province of Massachusetts-Bay,* edited by Lawrence Shaw Mayo (Cambridge, Mass., 1936), 2:292.

283 "Mr. Franklin": Morris to Paris, July 4, 1757, *PBF,* 7:247n.

284 "He was a proud": *ABF,* 263.

284 "For although": WF to Elizabeth Graeme, Dec. 9, 1757.

284–85 "the privileges": WF to *The Citizen,* Sept. 16, 1757, *PBF.*

285 "by exposing": *The Citizen,* Sept. 23, 1757, *PBF,* 7:255n.

285–86 "The first thing": to Pringle, Dec. 21, 1757.

286 "From this experiment": to John Lining, June 17, 1758.

287 "My vanity": to DF, Sept. 6, 1758.

287 "The ingenuous": citation accompanying diploma, *PBF,* 8:279n.

287–88 "You may think": to DF, Jan. 21, 1758.

288 "I thank you": to DF, Nov. 22, 1757.

288 "We have four rooms": to DF, Jan. 1758.

288–89 "The hackney coaches": to DF, Feb. 19, 1758.

289 "Tell her": Strahan to Hall, June 10, 1758, *PBF,* 8:93n.

13. IMPERIALIST: 1759–60

291 "a province . . . their country": W. A. Speck, *Stability and Strife: England, 1714–1760* (Cambridge, Mass., 1977), 243–44.

291 "I am sure": John B. Owen, *The Eighteenth Century, 1714–1815* (Totowa, N.J., 1975), 84.

291 "The enemy have passed": Francis Parkman, *Montcalm and Wolfe* (Boston, 1903), 2:216.

292 "Everything proves": *ibid.,* 286.

293 *"Vive le roi!":* Howard Peckham, *The Colonial Wars,* 190.

293 "Now, God be praised": Parkman, *Montcalm and Wolfe,* 2:309.

295 "that unmannerly sect": to the *London Chronicle,* Dec. 27, 1759.

295 *The Interest of Great Britain Considered, PBF,* 9:59–100.

299–300 "She is a . . . Birmingham eyes": to DF, Sept. 6, 1758.

300 "Odd characters": to Roberts, Sept. 16, 1758.

301 "That": to Norris, Jan. 14, 1758.

302 "a most impudent": Penn to Peters, July 5, 1758, HSP.

302 "I still see": to Galloway, Apr. 7, 1759.

302–3 "that harmony . . . and assent": "Answer to Heads of Complaint," Nov. 27, 1758.

303 "disrespect": Penns to House of Representatives, Nov. 28, 1758, *PBF*.

303 "I need not": to Norris, Jan. 19, 1759.

304 "The infinite variety": WF to Graeme, Dec. 9, 1757.

305–6 "7. And the man": *PBF,* 6:122–24.

306 "We could have": to Kames, Jan. 3, 1760.

14. BRITON: 1760–62

308 "I glory": John Brooke, *King George III* (New York, 1972), 88, 390–91.

309 "My dear . . . impertinence": *ibid.,* 15.

310 "If you should . . . come to pass": J. Steven Watson, *The Reign of George III, 1760–1815* (Oxford, UK, 1960), 5–7.

310 "her want . . . going off": Stanley Ayling, *George the Third* (New York, 1972), 83–84.

311 "The conduct . . . in the grass": Watson, *Reign of George III,* 4.

311 "the man who": R. J. White, *The Age of George III* (New York, 1968), 58.

311 "I am happy": Brooke, *King George III,* 89.

311 "My Lord . . . to ruin": *ibid.,* 78.

311 "bloody and expensive": Ayling, *George III,* 65.

311 "Oh, that foolishest": *ibid.,* 90.

312–13 "deceit and circumvention . . . jockeyship": to King in Council, Feb. 2, 1759.

314 "almost rebellious": *PBF,* 9:128.

314 "not only against": Report to the Lords of the Committee of Council, June 24, 1760.

315 "Lord Mansfield": *ABF,* 265–66.

316 "A more unlucky": to the Trustees of the Loan Office, Feb. 13, 1762.

316–17 "a little work . . . universal use": to Kames, May 3, 1760.

318 "I never saw": to Kames, Oct. 21, 1761.

318 "I imagine": to Kames, May 3, 1760.

319 "whatever occurs": to Mary Stevenson, May 1, 1760.

319 "to warm": to Stevenson, Sept. 13, 1760.

319 "No one catches cold": to Stevenson, Aug. 10, 1761.

319 "Why will you": to Stevenson, May 1, 1760.

320 "The knowledge": to Stevenson, June 11, 1760.

320 "I cannot but wish": to Hume, Sept. 27, 1760.

321 "The Church": to Hume, May 10, 1762.

322 "But this opinion . . . earthquakes": to [Peter Franklin], May 7, 1760.

322 "Suppose a long canal": to Alexander Small, May 12, 1760.

323–24 "Entertainment . . . objectionable": to Pringle, May 27, 1762.

325 "Being charmed": to Beccaria, July 13, 1762.

326 "We saw all": WF to Sarah Franklin, Oct. 10, 1751.

327 "When I travelled": to Ingersoll, Dec. 11, 1762.

327 "transacted": Sheila Skemp, *William Franklin,* 40.
328 "The lady": to Mecom, Nov. 25, 1762.
329 "in opposition": to Strahan, July 23, 1762.
329 "I am now": to Kames, Aug. 17, 1762.
329 "I am very sorry": from Hume, May 10, 1762.
329 "This will be brought": Strahan to Hall, Aug. 10, 1762, *PBF.*

15. RISING IN THE WEST: 1762–64

331 "I shall probably": to Strahan, Aug. 23, 1762.
332 "Of all": to Mary Stevenson, Mar. 25, 1763.
332 "It produces": to Richard Jackson, Dec. 6, 1762.
332–33 "I arrived": to Jackson, Dec. 2, 1762.
333 "I find": to Jackson, Mar. 8, 1763.
333 "a conquest": to Caleb Whiteford, Dec. 9, 1762.
334 "glorious peace": to Philip Ludwell, Feb. 22, 1763.
334 "Throughout this continent": to Strahan, May 9, 1763.
334 "The glory . . . *were dead*": to John Whitehurst, June 27, 1763.
335 "Grumblers": to Strahan, May 9, 1763.
335 "Here in America": to John Whitehurst, June 27, 1763.
335 "many thousands": Plan for Settling Two Western Colonies, *PBF,* 5:457ff.
336 "I know not": to Jackson, Mar. 8, 1763 (with postscripts of Mar. 22 and 29).
337 "I have assured . . . iron is hot": to Jackson, Apr. 17, 1763.
338 "under the influence": Sheila Skemp, *William Franklin,* 48.
338 "I am just returned": to Strahan, Mar. 28, 1763.
339 "Notwithstanding": to Bessborough, [Oct. 1761].
340 "I am not yet": to Catharine Ray Greene, Sept. 5, 1763.
340 "I am otherwise": to Jane Mecom, Dec. 15, 1763.
340 "Now I am": to Strahan, Dec. 19, 1763.
341 "My mother": WF to Strahan, Apr. 25, 1763, *PBF,* 10:237n.
342 "I expected": to Strahan, June 28, 1763.
342 "Not an hour": from Strahan, Aug. 18, 1763.
342 "talk away": R. J. White, *The Age of George III,* 64.
342 "inexhaustible spirits . . . nothing can crush": John Brooke, *King George III,* 145.
343 "Naturally": J. Steven Watson, *The Reign of George III,* 98.
343 "That depends": Horace Bleackley, *Life of John Wilkes* (London, 1917), 69.
343 "It is certainly": White, *Age of George III,* 61.
343 "proud, pompous": Paul Langford, *A Polite and Commercial People,* 354.
343 "I do not know": Stanley Ayling, *George the Third,* 100.
343 "The King's speech": White, *Age of George III,* 66.
344 "Satan preaching . . . gentleman": Ayling, *George the Third,* 116–17.
345 "pleased to find": to Jackson, Feb. 11, 1764.
345 "I am sorry": from Strahan, Aug. 18, 1763.
345 "Surely you would not": to Strahan, Aug. 8, 1763.
346 "I fear something": from Jackson, Nov. 12, 1763.
347 "A moderate duty": to Jackson, Feb. 11, 1764.
347 "I am not much": to Jackson, Jan. 16, 1764.

348 "Why do you suffer": Joseph Kelley, *Pennsylvania*, 463.
349 "The Indians": to Jackson, June 27, 1763.
350 "I only fear": to Peter Collinson, Dec. 19, 1763.
351 *A Narrative of the Late Massacres, PBF,* 11:47–69.
353 "It would perhaps be . . . of days": to Jackson, Feb. 11, 1764.
353–54 "I chose . . . few weeks": to John Fothergill, Mar. 14, 1764.
354 "The Negroes": *Narrative of the Late Massacres, PBF,* 11:62.
355 "They appeared": to John Waring, Dec. 17, 1763.
356 "He is civil": to Collinson, Dec. 19, 1763.
356 "rank abuse": John Penn to Thomas Penn, May 5, 1764, HSP.
356 "necklace of resolves": to Strahan, Mar. 30, 1764.
357 "high presumption . . . the Crown": Resolves, Mar. 24, 1764.
357 "dirty piece": John Penn to Thomas Penn, May 5, 1764, HSP.
357 *Cool Thoughts,* Apr. 12, 1764.
358 "God has blessed": to Henry Bouquet, Aug. 16, 1764.
358 "O! fatal mistake": Kelley, *Pennsylvania*, 526.

16. STAMPS AND STATESMANSHIP: 1764–66

359 "Mr. Franklin died": Joseph Kelley, *Pennsylvania*, 526.
359 "Boers herding . . . laughing matter": to Jackson, Oct. 11, 1764.
360 "Confound": *PBF,* 11:448.
360 "most cordial": to DF, Dec. 27, 1764.
360 "Mr. Grenville . . . told him no": Edmund S. Morgan and Helen M. Morgan, *The Stamp Act Crisis: Prologue to Revolution* (New York, 1962), 89–91.
361 "It will operate": *PBF,* 12:51–60.
362 "besotted": to Joseph Galloway, Oct. 11, 1766.
362 "Will these Americans . . . emolument": Morgan and Morgan, *Stamp Act Crisis,* 93.
362 "I think it will": to Hall, Feb. 14, 1765.
363 "I hope you will": to Hall, Aug. 9, 1765.
363 "grand incendiary": Allen to Thomas Penn, Oct. 21, 1764, HSP.
363 "tomahawk": from Evans, Mar. 15, 1765.
364 "dying liberty . . . single vote": Morgan and Morgan, *Stamp Act Crisis,* 123–25.
366 "You are now . . . Thank God.": from Hughes, Sept. 8–17, 1765.
367 "In the evening": from Wharton, Oct. 13, 1765.
367 "Cousin [Josiah] Davenport": from DF, Sept. 22, 1765.
368 "I honour much": to DF, Nov. 9, 1765.
368 "I thank him": to DF, Nov. 9, 1765.
369 "It is not safe": from Hutchinson, Nov. 18, 1765.
369 "It is difficult": from Galloway, c. Nov. 20, 1765.
370 "We might as well": to Charles Thomson, July 11, 1765.
371 "If it continues": to Hughes, Aug. 9, 1765.
371 "The disturbances": to Hall, Nov. 9, 1765.
372 "I strongly recommended": to WF, Nov. 9, 1765.
372 "the violent temper": from Galloway, Jan. 13, 1766.
373 "Can it be": Morgan and Morgan, *Stamp Act Crisis,* 338.
373 "on which I have": to David Hall, Feb. 24, 1766.

373 "The moral is": to Jane Mecom, Mar. 1, 1766.

374–76 "Many, and very heavy . . . make one": testimony to House of Commons, Feb. 13, 1766.

376 "The Marquis of Rockingham": Strahan to David Hall, May 10, 1766, *PMHB* 10 (1886), 220–21.

377 "They never have": testimony to House of Commons, Feb. 13, 1766.

377 "in all cases": Morgan and Morgan, *Stamp Act Crisis,* 348.

377 "Pray Monsieur Anglais": *PBF,* 13:183–84.

17. DUTIES AND PLEASURES: 1766–67

378 "My Dear Child": to DF, Apr. 6, 1766.

379 "The Assembly": from Galloway, June 7, 1766.

379 "They are daily": from Galloway, May 23, 1766.

379 "As to the reports": to Jane Mecom, Mar. 1, 1766.

380 " 'Tis now perhaps": to Roberts, July 7, 1765.

380 "Your frequently" to Whitefield, June 19, 1764.

380 "The malice": to Samuel Rhoads, July 8, 1765.

381 "This I will never": from Hall, Jan. 27, 1767.

382 "It was set": to Hall, Apr. 14, 1767.

383 "So you see . . . well pleased": from DF, Jan. 12, 1766.

384 "I have mentioned": to WF, Sept. 27, 1766.

384 "I was again": to WF, Oct. 11, 1766.

384 "certainly well framed": *The New Regime, 1765–1767,* ed. Clarence Walworth Alvord and Clarence Edwin Carter (Springfield, Ill., 1916), 426.

384 "The Secretaries": to WF, Aug. 28, 1767.

385 "George the Third . . . ministers": Paul Langford, *A Polite and Commercial People,* 363–64.

386 "I rejoice": *The Debate on the American Revolution, 1761–1783,* ed. Max Beloff (London, 1960), 100.

386 "The confusion": to Galloway, Aug. 8, 1767.

387 "It gave me": report of debate in House of Lords, Apr. 11, 1767, *PBF.*

387 "A Friend to Both Countries": to *London Chronicle,* Apr. 9, 1767.

387 "Benevolus": to *London Chronicle,* Apr. 11, 1767.

390 "beach": to John Adams, May 18, 1787, Yale.

390 "Sally has friends": from DF, Apr. 20–25, 1767.

390 "I would not": to DF, May 23, 1767.

391 "I know very little": to DF, June 22, 1767.

391 "that Mr. B.": from WF, May [?], 1767.

392 "I received yours": to Richard Bache, Aug. 5, 1767.

393 "Though I was not": to DF, June 13, 1766.

393 "I found": to Daniel Wister, Sept. 27, 1766.

394 "Every colony": "Some Observations on North America": *PBF,* 13:346–77.

394 "well and hearty": to the Speaker et al., Aug. 22, 1766.

394 "I have stayed": to DF, Aug. 28, 1767.

394 "made him very uneasy": Margaret Stevenson to DF, Sept. 18, 1767, *PBF,* 14:242n.

394–97 "I was engaged . . . my friend's wife": to Mary Stevenson, Sept. 14, 1767.

397 "I have been": to DF, Nov. 2, 1799.

18. REASON AND RIOT: 1768–69

399 "Instead of raving": to the *Gazetteer*, Jan. 6, 1768.

399–401 "The waves . . . their senses": to the *London Chronicle*, Jan. 5–7, 1768.

402–4 "My Lord H. . . . widely different": to WF, Mar. 13, 1768.

405–6 "that no insult . . . running riot": Stanley Ayling, *George the Third*, 155–57.

406 "The scenes": to WF, Apr. 16, 1768.

406–7 "This capital": to John Ross, May 14, 1768.

407 "All respect": to Joseph Galloway, May 14, 1768.

407 "There have been": to WF, Apr. 16, 1768.

407 "'Tis thought": to Joseph Galloway, Mar. 13, 1768.

407 "I have urged": to John Ross, May 14, 1768.

408 "If this": to Galloway, July 2, 1768.

408 "It is a settled": to WF, Jan. 9, 1768.

409–10 "my fast friend . . . divine which": to WF, July 2, 1768.

411 "I have found": to Jacques Barbeu-Dubourg, July 28, 1768.

411 "I reckon": to Kames, Feb. 28, 1768.

412 "From the matches": to John Alleyne, Aug. 9, 1768.

412 "I cannot be": to Oliver Neave, *PBF*, 15:295–98.

413 "I have long been": to Evans, Feb. 20, 1768.

414 "Diir Pali": to Stevenson, July 20, 1768.

414 "Heavenly Father": *PBF*, 15:301–3.

416 "An application": to Cooper, July 11, 1769.

416 "very rash": to Bache, Aug. 13, 1768.

417 "touch of the gout": to DF, Dec. 21, 1768.

417 "He might then": from WF, Jan. 2, 1769.

417 "Every body says": from DF, Oct. 4, 1769.

418 "her constitution": from Bond, June 7, 1769.

419 "It is well known": to the *Public Advertiser*, Aug. 25, 1768.

419 "Allow me": to the *Public Advertiser*, Oct. 21, 1768.

419 "You English": *Public Advertiser*, Jan. 17, 1769, *PBF*.

420 "I am under": to Whitefield, undated, *PBF*, 16:192.

420 "I hope": to Cooper, Apr. 27, 1769.

421 "What are you doing": to Joseph Galloway, Feb. 7, 1769.

421 "It is very uncertain": to WF, Oct. 7, 1769.

19. THE RIFT WIDENS: 1770–71

423–24 "IMPORTER . . . Horrid Massacre": Hiller B. Zobel, *The Boston Massacre* (New York, 1970), 172–211.

424 "Bloody Massacre": Revere print reproduced in *The Boisterous Sea of Liberty*, ed. David Brion Davis and Steven Mintz (New York, 1998), 140.

424 "Those detestable murderers": to Samuel Cooper, June 8, 1770.
425 "The Grenvillenians": to the *Gazetteer*, Feb. 7, 1770.
426 "This party . . . to use it": to Charles Thomson, Mar. 18, 1770.
426–27 "I am assured . . . totally lost": to Galloway, Mar. 21, 1770.
428 "Being born": to "Dear Sir," Nov. 28, 1768.
428 "I am much obliged": from Galloway, June 21, 1770.
429 "our friends": from Thomas Cushing et al., July 13, 1770.
429 "entirely relying": *PBF,* 17:258.
429 "greatly confided": from Cushing, Nov. 6, 1770.
429 "I have enemies": to Despencer, July 26, 1770.
430 "In this": to Jane Mecom, Dec. 30, 1770.
430 "I do not think": to Galloway, Jan. 9, 1768.
430 "His inclinations": to Galloway, July 2, 1768.
431–33 "I was pleased . . . farther trouble": notes of interview, Jan. 16, 1771.
433–34 "I have since . . . variance with me": to Cooper, Feb. 5, 1771.
434–35 "are justly tenacious": from Cushing et al., Dec. 17, 1770.
435–36 "The doctrine . . . public ministers": to Cushing, Feb. 5, 1771.
436–37 "It is looked on . . . among us": to Cushing, June 10, 1771.
437–38 "I have read": Lee to Adams, June 10, 1771, in Richard Henry Lee, *Life of Arthur Lee* (Boston, 1829), 1:215ff.
438 "It will make": from Cooper, Aug. 25, 1771.
438 "I imagine": to Galloway, Feb. 6, 1772.
438–39 "It appeared": Jonathan Williams's journal, *PBF,* 18:114–16.
439 "Hadn't you better": to Anna Mordaunt Shipley, Aug. 13, 1771.
440 "Can the farmers": *PBF,* 18:222–23.
440 "Ireland itself": to Cushing, Jan. 13, 1772.
441 "I thought often": to Joshua Babcock, Jan. 13, 1772.
441 "I esteemed it": to Cushing, Jan. 13, 1772.
442 "They are all": to Galloway, Feb. 6, 1772.
442 "in an elegant" Henry Marchant's journal, Oct. 30–Nov. 2, 1771, APS.
442 "The good wishes": from Hume, Feb. 7, 1772.
442 "He was extremely": to WF, Jan. 30, 1772.

20. TO KICK A LITTLE: 1772–73

444 *"mon cher":* from Condorcet, Dec. 2, 1773.
445 "To you": from Beccaria, May 20, 1771.
445 "modern Prometheus": "Fortgesetzte Betrachtung der seit einiger Zeit wahrgenommenen Erderschütterungen" (1756) in *Kants Werke* (Berlin, 1968), 1:472.
445 "A place": to Royal Academy of Sciences, Nov. 16, 1772, APS.
445 *"avec une sorte":* from Barbeu-Dubourg, Dec. 29, 1773.
445 "Learned and ingenious": to WF, Aug. 19, 1772.
446 "Travelling": to Rush, July 14, 1773.
446 "of the greatest": to WF, Aug. 19, 1772.
447–49 "I fetched . . . determine this": to William Brownrigg, Nov. 7, 1773.
449 "There seems": from Cooper, Jan. 1, 1771.
449–50 "When I had been": to WF, Aug. 19, 1772.

450–51 "At length": to WF, Aug. 17, 1772.

451 "I hope": to Cushing, Nov. 4, 1772.

451 "Upon the whole": to Cushing, Dec. 2, 1772.

452 "There has lately": to Cushing, Dec. 2, 1772.

453 "There must be": Hutchinson to Whately, Jan. 20, 1769, *PBF,* 20:549–50.

453 "I have engaged": to Cushing, Dec. 2, 1772.

455 "I can now": Bache to DF, Dec. 3, 1771, *PBF,* 18:257.

455 "His behaviour": to DF, Jan. 28, 1772.

455 "I advised": to Sarah Franklin Bache, Jan. 29, 1772.

456 "In return": to DF, Feb. 2, 1773.

456 "All who have seen": to Jane Mecom, Jan. 13, 1772.

456 "He improves": to WF, Jan. 30, 1772.

456 "She is nimble-footed": to DF, Dec. 1, 1772.

457 "I still feel": to DF, Jan. 6, 1773.

457 "I cannot": to Joseph Priestley, Sept. 19, 1772.

458 "Our great security": to Cushing, Jan. 5, 1773.

459 "the sentiments": from Cushing, Mar. 24, 1773.

459 "They have had": from Cooper, June 14, 1773.

460 "I have the pleasure": to Dartmouth, Aug. 21, 1773.

460 *"for the Better": Public Advertiser,* Sept. 22, 1773, *PBF.*

461 "I was down": to WF, Oct. 6, 1773.

461 "Rules by Which": *Public Advertiser,* Sept. 11, 1773, *PBF.*

463 "I had used": to Mecom, Nov. 1, 1773.

21. THE COCKPIT: 1774–75

466 "I am glad": to Cushing, July 25, 1773.

466 "totally ignorant": to the *London Chronicle,* Dec. 25, 1773.

468–69 "The address . . . Three weeks": Preliminary hearing before the Privy Council, Jan. 11, 1774, *PBF.*

470 "bull-baiting": extract of letter, Feb. 19, 1774.

471 "unmannered railer . . . humanity": *PBF,* 21:40n.

471 "furious Philippic": *The Correspondence of Edmund Burke,* ed. George H. Guttridge (Chicago, 1960), 2:518, 524.

471–74 "the first mover . . . a successor": Alexander Wedderburn's speech before the Privy Council, Jan. 29, 1774, *PBF.*

474–75 "The Doctor": Bancroft in *Memoirs* 1:358.

475 "for the seditious": report of Privy Council committee, Jan. 29, 1774.

475 "I am very angry": to Cushing, Feb. 15, 1774.

476 "This line": to WF, Feb. 2, 1774.

476 "As things are": to Bache, Feb. 17, 1774.

476 "They may expect": to WF, Feb. 18, 1774.

477 "You and I": to Jane Mecom, Feb. 17, 1774.

477 "I am too much": to Foxcroft, Feb. 18, 1774.

477 "The admirers": to the *Public Advertiser,* Feb. 16, 1774.

478 "totally departed": *Boston Gazette,* Apr. 25, 1774, *PBF,* 21:79–83.

479 "He says": Stanley Ayling, *George the Third,* 243.

479 "We are not entering": Bernard Donoughue, *British Politics and the American Revolution* (London, 1964), 77.

479 "If they deny": Benjamin Woods Labaree, *The Boston Tea Party* (Boston, 1979), 185.

480 "hearty affirmative": *The Parliamentary History of England from the Earliest Period to 1803,* ed. T. C. Hansard (London, 1813), 17:1169.

480 "hostile invasion": Robert Middlekauff, *The Glorious Cause: The American Revolution, 1763–1789* (New York, 1982), 233.

481 "this old snake . . . mischievous enemies": Catherine Drinker Bowen, *The Most Dangerous Man in America: Scenes from the Life of Benjamin Franklin* (Boston, 1974), 241.

481 "You know": to Jan Ingenhousz, Mar. 18, 1774.

482 "Dr. Franklin": Priestley in *Memoirs,* 1:359–60.

482 "I hope": *The Letters of David Hume,* ed. J. Y. T. Greig (Oxford, UK, 1932), 2:286–88.

483 "I think": *Letters of Eminent Persons Addressed to David Hume,* ed. J. E. Burton (Bristol, 1989), 270–72.

483 "most bitter": *The Last Journals of Horace Walpole,* ed. J. Doran and A. Francis Steuart (London, 1910; rpt. New York, 1973), 1:284–85.

484 "A great empire": Hansard, *Parliamentary History of England,* 18:536.

484 "Your popularity": from WF, May 3, 1774.

484 "Such horrid": *PG,* May 4, 1774, *PBF.*

484 "I rejoice": to Cushing, Sept. 15, 1774.

485 "If you should ever": to Jonathan Williams Sr., Sept. 28, 1774.

485 "I am in": to Cushing, Oct. 6, 1774.

485 "My situation": to Joseph Galloway, Oct. 12, 1774.

486–89 "What is to be done . . . tea &c.": Franklin journal, Mar. 22, 1775.

490 "I, the underwritten": draft to Dartmouth, Mar. 16, 1775.

490 "He looked . . . national affront": Franklin journal, Mar. 22, 1775.

490 "dangerous consequences": from Thomas Walpole, Mar. 16, 1775.

22. REBEL: 1775–76

492 "Her death": from WF, Dec. 24, 1774.

493 "a valuable": to Joseph Priestley, May 16, 1775.

493 "This motion": Journal entry for Apr. 5, 1775.

494 "Yesterday evening": Broadside, May 8, 1775, *PBF.*

494 "The die": Stanley Ayling, *George the Third,* 247–48.

494 "It will surely": Robert Middlekauff, *The Glorious Cause,* 266.

495 "Will you let": *ibid.,* 271.

496 "I believe": from Jane Mecom, May 14, 1775.

497 "a tolerable speaker . . . glorious cause": James Thomas Flexner, *George Washington: The Forge of Experience* (Boston, 1965), 324–25, 332, 334, 341.

498 "A frenzy": *Papers of Jefferson,* 1:165.

499 "The youngest boy": to Jane Mecom, June 17, 1775.

499 "I have but . . . conspicuous": *Papers of Madison,* 1:149–52.

499 "a pusillanimity": Flexner, *Washington,* 1:330.

499–500 "Hath any thing . . . our cause": *Papers of Madison,* 1:158–60.

500 "a disposition": Adams to Abigail Adams, July 23, 1775, *Adams Papers.*

500 "which the youngest": to Jonathan Shipley, May 15, 1775.

500 "But, as Britain": to Humphry Marshall, May 23, 1775.

500 "She has begun": to Priestley, July 7, 1775.

500 "All Europe . . . madness": to Shipley, July 7, 1775.

501 "Mr. Strahan": to Strahan [unsent], July 5, 1775.

501 "Words and arguments": to Strahan, July 7, 1775 [quoted in letter from Strahan, Sept. 6, 1775].

501 "It has been": to Priestley, July 7, 1775.

501 "Articles of Confederation": July 21, 1775, *PBF*.

504–5 "import all . . . regularly sent": minutes of conference with Washington et al., Oct. 18–24, 1775.

505 "Here is a fine": to Bache, Oct. 19, 1775.

505 "Tell our good friend": to Priestley, Oct. 3, 1775.

507 "I have just heard": WF to Germain, Mar. 28, 1776, *DAR*.

507 "I begin": to Quincy, Apr. 15, 1776.

507 "utmost dispatch": to John Hancock, May 1, 1776.

508 "We have daily": to Hancock, May 8, 1776.

509 "an ingenious": to Bache, Sept. 30, 1774.

509 "Dr. Kearsley": from Thomas Paine, Mar. 4, 1775.

510 "I offer": Thomas Paine, *Common Sense* (New York, 1942), 21, 40.

510 "great impression": to Charles Lee, Feb. 19, 1776.

510 "that these United Colonies": *Papers of Jefferson*, 1:298.

510 "You can write": John Adams to Timothy Pickering, Aug. 8, 1822, *Adams Papers*.

510 "I am just recovering": to Washington, June 21, 1776.

511 "Will Doctor Franklin": from Jefferson, probably June 21, 1776.

511 "reduce them . . . destroy us": Carl Becker, *The Declaration of Independence* (New York, 1933), 160–71.

511 "I was sitting": *Writings of Jefferson*, 18:169–70.

512 "There must be . . . hang separately": Sparks, 1:408.

513–14 "Let the smaller . . . insurrections": BF quoted in *Adams Papers*, 2:245–46.

514 "My Worthy Friend": from Howe, June 20, 1776.

515 "Directing pardons": to Howe, July 20, 1776.

516 "I watched": *PBF*, 22:518–19.

517–18 "At Brunswick . . . and mutton": *Adams Papers*, 3:418–20.

518 "I also gave": Howe to Germain, Sept. 20, 1776, *DAR*.

519 "Dr. Franklin": *Adams Papers*, 3:422.

23. SALVATION IN PARIS: 1776–78

520 "I suppose": *Adams Papers*, 3:422.

521 "It would be": BF et al. to Arthur Lee, Dec. 12, 1775.

521 "Perhaps, however": to Don Gabriel Antonio de Bourbon, Dec. 12, 1775.

522 "On your arrival": to Silas Deane, Mar. 2, 1776.

523 "It will be proper": from John Hancock, Sept. 24, 1776.

524 "I have only": in Rush to Thomas Morris, Oct. 22, 1776, *Letters of Rush*.

525 "very magnificent": Sheila Skemp, *William Franklin*, 192.

525 "virulent enemy": *ibid.*, 212.

526 "I will not distress": from Elizabeth Franklin, Aug. 6, 1776.

526 "I have considered": to William Temple Franklin, Sept. 19, 1776.

527 "short but rough": to the Committee of Secret Correspondence, Dec. 8, 1776.

527 "almost demolished me": to Richard and Sarah Franklin Bache, May 10, 1785, Smyth.

527 "I have acquainted": to Deane, Dec. 7, 1776.

528 "The carriage . . . ever beheld": *Memoirs* 2:48.

528 "The celebrated . . . mantelpiece": Edward E. Hale and Edward E. Hale Jr., *Franklin in France* (Boston, 1888), 1:69–70; Alfred Owen Aldridge, *Franklin and his French Contemporaries* (New York, 1957), 66.

529 "Intelligent": Vergennes to Aranda, Dec. 28, 1776, *PBF* 23:113n.

530 "As other princes": to Vergennes, Jan. 5, 1777.

531 "of giving umbrage": to the Committee of Secret Correspondence, Mar. 12–Apr. 9, 1777.

531 "with which they mean": to the Committee of Secret Correspondence, Jan. 17–22, 1777.

531–32 "Their fleet . . . betrays it": to the Committee of Secret Correspondence, Mar. 12–Apr. 9, 1777.

536 "Count Pulaski": to Washington, May 29, 1777.

536 "the Baron": to Washington, Sept. 4, 1777.

536 "the Marquis": to Washington, Aug. or Sept. 1777.

536 "The bearer": to Washington, Mar. 29, 1777.

536 "Our corps": from Washington, Aug. 17, 1777.

537 "These applications": to Barbeu-Dubourg, after Oct. 2, 1777.

537 "Sir": unaddressed model letter, Apr. 2, 1777.

538–39 "The Commissioners . . . from Europe": to Vergennes and Aranda, Sept. 25, 1777.

539 "We are scarce": to the Committee on Foreign Affairs, Nov. 30, 1777.

539 "We have prevented": Washington to Lund Washington, Dec. 17, 1776, *Writings of Washington.*

540 "Not a word": Adams to Abigail Adams, Aug. 20, 1777, *Adams Papers.*

541 "In consciousness": Robert Middlekauff, *The Glorious Cause,* 372.

542 "Sir, *is* Philadelphia . . . *of war*": *PBF,* 25:234–35n.

542 "the total reduction": to Vergennes, Dec. 4, 1777.

542 "You mistake": *PBF,* 25:236n.

543 "He said": Richard Henry Lee, *Life of Arthur Lee* (Boston, 1829), 1:357.

543 "to make peace": Philip Gibbes' minutes of conversation, c. Feb. 5, 1777, *PBF.*

543 "America is ready": Gibbes' minutes of conversation, Jan. 5, 1778, *PBF.*

543 "I called on 72": Paul Wentworth to William Eden, Jan. 7, 1778, *PBF.*

544 "lively and long": Vergennes to Comte de Montmorin, Jan. 30, 1778, *Facsimiles,* vol. 21, no. 18.

24. BONHOMME RICHARD: 1778–79

546 "Let me whisper . . . wicked measures": Richard Henry Lee, *Life of Arthur Lee,* 2:124–27.

546 "It is true": to Arthur Lee [not sent], Apr. 3, 1778.

547 "That he was": *Adams Papers,* 4:69.

547–48 "On Dr. F. . . . fanatic": *ibid.,* 2:347–52.

548 "Mr. M.": *ibid.,* 2:391.

548 "The history": *Letters of Rush,* 2:1207.

549 "The life": *Adams Papers,* 4:118–19.

551 "He would grasp": Claude-Ann Lopez, *Mon Cher Papa: Franklin and the Ladies of Paris* (New Haven, Conn., 1966), 128.

551 "the magnificence": *Adams Papers,* 4:109.

551 "one of the most": *ibid.,* 4:63–64.

551 "Alas!": *ibid.,* and (for the translation) Lopez, *Mon Cher Papa,* 129.

551–52 "All the family . . . very white": *ibid.,* 134.

552 "Madame Brillon": *Adams Papers,* 4:46–47.

553 "You were kind": Lopez, *Mon Cher Papa,* 38–39.

553 "The first": to Madame Brillon": Mar. 10, 1778.

553–54 "Let us start": Lopez, *Mon Cher Papa,* 40–44.

554–55 "You renounce . . . tenderness": to Madame Brillon, July 27, 1778.

555 "Judge . . . appetites": Lopez, *Mon Cher Papa,* 47–48.

556 "You remember": to Brillon, Sept. 20, 1778.

557 "That she might not": *Adams Papers,* 4:58–59.

558 "ladies for whose": from Adams, May 14, 1779.

558–59 "She entered": *Letters of Mrs. Adams,* ed. Charles Francis Adams (Boston, 1840), 252–53.

559 "Oh, to be seventy": Lopez, *Mon Cher Papa,* 246–47.

559–61 "If Notre Dame . . . avenge ourselves!": based on *ibid.,* 259–71.

562 "He had his hair": Lee, *Life of Arthur Lee,* 1:403.

562–63 "The King . . . le Seigneur Franklin": Lopez, *Mon Cher Papa,* 179–84.

564 "When I gave": Voltaire to Abbé Gaultier, Feb. 21, 1778, in *Ouevres Complètes de Voltaire* (Paris, 1883), 50:372.

564 "my child . . . Tolerance": Alfred Aldridge, *Franklin and His French Contemporaries,* 10.

564 "There presently": *Adams Papers,* 4:80–82.

566 "When I was": Lopez, *Mon Cher Papa,* 79.

566 "My God!": *Bagatelles,* 32ff; Bigelow, 8:312ff.

569 "The Doctor . . . men's truths": *Writings of Jefferson,* 18:171–72.

570 "Come, Monsieur": *ibid.,* 170.

570 "If you Frenchmen": Lopez, *Mon Cher Papa,* 21.

570 "we do not take kings": *Writings of Jefferson,* 18:168.

25. MINISTER PLENIPOTENTIARY: 1779–81

571 "I am a king": *Writings of Jefferson,* 18:168.

572 "What have you": Robert Middlekauff, *The Glorious Cause,* 413.

572 "We have": Washington to President of Congress, Dec. 23, 1777, *Writings of Washington.*

573 "Believe me": John McAuley Palmer, *General von Steuben* (New Haven, Conn., 1937), 157.

574 "Our Great Faithful": Congress to Louis XVI, Oct. 21, 1778.

575 "the God-like": from Lafayette, Aug. 29, 1779.

575 "Dear general": Lafayette to Washington, Feb. 19, 1778, *Lafayette Letters.*

575 "zeal, military ardour": from Washington, Dec. 28, 1778.

576 "In our kingly": from Lafayette, Feb. 21, 1779.

576 "My blood": Andreas Latzko, *Lafayette* (New York, 1936), 81.
576 "If you undertake": Lafayette to Comte d'Estaing, Sept. 21, 1778, *Lafayette Letters*.
576 "I admire much": to Lafayette, Mar. 22, 1779.
578 "The Marquis": to Jones, Apr. 27, 1779.
578 "by all means": to Jones, Apr. 28, 1779.
579 "Your liberal": from Jones, May 1, 1779.
579 "No! I'll sink . . . to fight": Peter Reaveley, "The Battle," in Jean Boudriot (ed.), *John Paul Jones and the Bonhomme Richard*, trans. David H. Roberts (Annapolis, Md., 1987), 82.
580 "The scene": from Jones, Oct. 3, 1779.
580 "For some days": to Jones, Oct. 15, 1779.
580 "I must acquaint": to Jones, Feb. 19, 1780.
581 "Though an evil": to Stephen Sayre, Mar. 31, 1779.
581 "The whole": to Samuel Cooper, Apr. 22, 1779.
581 "The extravagant luxury": to Jay, Oct. 4, 1779.
581 "When I began": to Sarah Franklin Bache, June 3, 1779.
582 "Though I never": from Sarah Franklin Bache, Sept. 14, 1779.
582 "great politician": Bigelow 8:46–57.
582–83 "I take no other": to Richard Bache, June 2, 1779.
583 "Ben, if I should": to Sarah Franklin Bache, June 3, 1779.
584 "The King's ambassador": Catherine M. Prelinger, "Benjamin Franklin and the American Prisoners of War in England during the American Revolution," *WMQ* 32 (1975), 261–94.
584 "the air doth": *ibid.*
585 "This is to continue": to the Committee for Foreign Affairs, May 26, 1779.
585 "oiling the sentry's": Prelinger, "Franklin and Prisoners of War."
585 "I cannot describe": from Digges, Nov. 10, 1779.
586 "By the letters": to Sartine, Nov. 28, 1779.
586 "He that robs": to William Hodgson, Apr. 1, 1781, Smyth.
586 "a tacit cession": "Observations by Mr. Hartley," Bigelow, 8:38–39.
587 "A little time": from David Hartley, Apr. 22, 1779.
587 "But this is": to Hartley, May 4, 1779.
589 "a post in which": Carl Van Doren, *Secret History of the American Revolution* (New York, 1941), 463.
589 "Arnold's baseness": to James Searle, Nov. 30, 1780.
589 "We are naked": from Lafayette, Oct. 9, 1780.
589 "I doubt not": from Washington, Oct. 9, 1780.
590 "the unalterable resolution": to Vergennes, Feb. 13, 1781.
591 "I have, however": to Adams, Feb. 22, 1781.
591 "I have passed": to Samuel Huntington, Mar. 12, 1781.
592–93 "He has vast designs . . . admit of": Clarence L. Ver Steeg, *Robert Morris: Revolutionary Financier* (Philadelphia, 1954), 13, 38.
593 "From your intelligence": to Morris, July 26, 1781, Smyth.
594 "I am quite tired": Charles, First Marquis Cornwallis, *Correspondence,* ed. Charles Ross (London, 1859), 1:87.
594 "The moment is critical . . . Hampton Roads": Douglas Southall Freeman, *George Washington* (New York, 1952), 5:312–15.
595 "Lord Cornwallis's conduct": *ibid.,* 367.

595 "A man was killed . . . manner": Edward M. Riley, "St. George Tucker's Journal of the Siege of Yorktown, 1781," *WMQ* 5 (1948), 375–95.

595 "Our shot and shell": Freeman, *Washington,* 5:367.

595 "Our provisions": from a captured British journal in Riley, "Tucker's Journal."

596 "He might have beat": Freeman, *Washington,* 5:376.

596 "A solemn stillness": Riley, "Tucker's Journal."

596 "Welcome, Brother Debtor": *ibid.*

596 "When the King . . . Upside Down": Freeman, *Washington,* 5:388n.

26. BLESSED WORK: 1781–82

597 "My God": R. J. White, *The Age of George III* (New York, 1968), 137.

597 "to guide me": *ibid.*

598 "I wish": to Thomas Pownall, Nov. 23, 1781, Giunta.

598 "I have never": to Adams, Oct. 12, 1781, Giunta.

598 "Some writer": to Charles Dumas, Aug. 6, 1781, Bigelow.

598 "Poor as we are": to Jay, Oct. 2, 1780, Bigelow.

599 "by the absolute": Lee to James Warren, Aug. 1780, Giunta.

599 "They hate us": Adams to John Jay, Aug. 13, 1782, Giunta.

599 "He tells me": to Samuel Huntington, Aug. 9, 1780.

599 "It was evident": Jay to Livingston, Nov. 17, 1782, Giunta.

600 "We ought not": Jay to Livingston, Sept. 18, 1782, Giunta.

600 "Your enemies": from Morris, Sept. 28, 1782, Giunta.

600 "extremely sorry": to Samuel Cooper, Dec. 26, 1782, Smyth.

601 "a gentleman": Giunta, 1:341.

601 "He is a wise man": Vergennes to Montmorin, Apr. 18, 1782, Giunta.

601 "wise and honest": to Shelburne, Apr. 18, 1792, Giunta.

601 "I let him know": BF journal, Bigelow, 9:254.

601 "Yet I could": Oswald's journal, Apr. 18, 1782, Giunta.

601 "In case France": BF journal, Bigelow, 9:259.

601 "It is a sweet word": Conversation notes, Bigelow, 9:262–64.

602 "We parted": BF journal, Bigelow, 9:264.

602 "I desire": to Shelburne, Apr. 18, 1782, Giunta.

603 "On the whole": BF journal, Bigelow, 9:282.

603 "After having seen": Fox to Grenville, Apr. 30, 1782, Giunta.

604 "America does not ask": BF journal, Bigelow, 9:287–88.

604–5 "He belongs": Vergennes to Montmorin, May 11, 1782, Giunta.

605 "A, a stranger": BF journal, Bigelow, 9:295–96.

606 "I see . . . were gone": *Bagatelles,* 104–5.

606 *The Morals of Chess, ibid.,* 108–12.

608 "From him": to Deane, Mar. 2, 1776.

609–10 "as repugnant . . . to government": in Samuel Flagg Bemis, "British Secret Service and the French-American Alliance," *AHR* 29 (1924), 474–95.

610 "You are surrounded": from Juliana Ritchie, Jan. 12, 1777.

610–11 "As it is impossible": to Ritchie, Jan. 19, 1777.

611 "If the rascals": P.J.G. Cabanis, *Oeuvres* (Paris, 1825), 5:230, 248; Esmond Wright, *Franklin of Philadelphia* (Cambridge, Mass., 1986), 296.

611 "If I were not": from Burke, Aug. 15, 1781, Smyth, 8:317–19.

611 "Since the foolish": to Burke, Oct. 15, 1781, Smyth.

612 "Difficulties remain": from Burke, Feb. 28, 1782, Smyth, 8:320.

612 "the United States of America": *Political, Miscellaneous, and Philosophical Pieces*, ed. Benjamin Vaughan (London, 1779), title page and vi.

612 "Be assured": to Joseph Banks, Sept. 9, 1782, Bigelow.

612 "Supplement": Smyth, 8:437–40.

614 "The *form*": to Charles Dumas, May 3, 1782, Smyth.

614 "the most important": Fox to Thomas Grenville, May 21, 1782, Giunta.

614 "trembled for the news": Adams to Livingston, Sept. 23, 1782, Giunta.

615 "They want to treat": BF journal, Bigelow, 9:315.

615–16 "an air . . . each other": *ibid.,* 329–31.

616–17 "necessary . . . imagine": Oswald to Shelburne, July 10, 1782, Giunta.

618 "speedily concluded": Shelburne to Oswald, July 27, 1782, Giunta.

618 "This Court": Jay to Livingston, Sept. 18, 1782, Giunta.

618 "firmness and independence . . . same system": *Adams Papers,* 3:38, 82.

620 "After much": to Jonathan Shipley, June 10, 1782, Bigelow.

27. SAVANT: 1783–85

621 "Let us now": to Shipley, Mar. 17, 1783, Bigelow.

622 "Our Revolution": to Price, Aug. 16, 1784, Bigelow.

622 "the contemplation": to Edward Newenham, Oct. 2, 1783, Bigelow.

622 "My dear friend": to Strahan, Aug. 19, 1784, Bigelow.

623 "The remissness": to Morris, Dec. 25, 1783, Bigelow.

624 "You tell me": to Cooper, Dec. 26, 1783, Bigelow.

624 "the great": to Thomson, May 13, 1784, Bigelow.

624 "Is not the hope": to Vaughan, July 26, 1784, Bigelow.

625 "Meteorological Imaginations": Bigelow, 10:323–26.

626 "Universal space": to David Rittenhouse, June 25, 1784, Bigelow.

627 "In which case": to Crèvecoeur, Bigelow, 10:363–65.

627 "By this means": to George Whately, May 23, 1785, Smyth.

628 "Not less than": to Joseph Banks, Aug. 30, 1783, Bigelow.

628–29 "All Paris": to Banks, Dec. 1, 1783, Bigelow.

629 "a new epoch": to Richard Price, Aug. 16, 1784, Bigelow.

629 "It is a serious thing": to Ingenhousz, Jan. 16, 1784, Bigelow.

629 "The people were furious": Benjamin Franklin Bache diary, July 11, 1784, APS.

630 "What good": *Correspondance Littéraire, Philosophique et Critique par Grimm, Diderot, Raynal, Meister, etc.* (Paris, 1877–82), 13:349.

630 "Convincing sovereigns": to Jan Ingenhousz, Jan. 16, 1784, Smyth.

631 "In heaven": Claude-Ann Lopez, *Mon Cher Papa,* 170.

631–32 "There being": to la Sabliere de la Condamine, Mar. 19, 1784, Smyth.

632 "Touch them": Lopez, *Mon Cher Papa,* 175.

633 "The report": to William Temple Franklin, Aug. 25, 1784, Smyth.

633 "I am pestered": to Thomson, Mar. 9, 1784, Smyth.

633 *Information to Those Who Would Remove to America: Bagatelles,* 77–88.

635 "I am rather": from Vergennes, Dec. 15, 1782, Giunta.

635 "It was certainly": to Vergennes, Dec. 17, 1782, Giunta.

636 "storm of indignation": Alleyne Fitzherbert to Henry Strachey, Dec. 19, 1782, Giunta.

636 "It passed . . . consideration": Vergennes to Luzerne, Dec. 21, 1782, Giunta.

637 "that the King": Madison's notes, Mar. 12–15, 1783, Giunta.

637 "the gout and gravel": to Samuel Chase, Jan. 6, 1784, Smyth.

637 "I cannot bear": to Thomas Mifflin, June 16, 1784, Smyth.

637 "My face": to Jane Mecom, Oct. 25, 1779.

637 "Repose": to John and Mrs. Jay, May 13, 1784, Smyth.

637 "Mr. Jay": to Henry Laurens, Apr. 29, 1784, Smyth.

638 "I may then": to WF, Aug. 16, 1784, Smyth.

638 "If all": to Whately, Aug. 21, 1784, Smyth.

638 "I hope": to Morris, Mar. 7, 1783, Smyth.

638 "Mr. Jay": to Laurens, Apr. 29, 1784, Smyth.

639 "the ornament": *Writings of Jefferson,* 8:24.

639 "Justice": to Vaughan, Mar. 14, 1785, Smyth.

640 "I think it": Bigelow, 10:299–300.

641 "I went home": "To the Authors of the Journal of Paris," Smyth 9:183–89.

28. HOME: 1785–86

644 "A few": Smyth, 8:650–51.

644 "The name": to Francis Maseres, June 26, 1785, Smyth.

645 "revive that affectionate": Sheila Skemp, *William Franklin,* 269.

645 "Dear Son": to WF, Aug. 16, 1784, Smyth.

645 "Let us now": to Shipley, Mar. 17, 1783, Smyth.

645–46 "Nothing has": to WF, Aug. 16, 1784, Smyth.

646 "You are permitted": from John Jay, Mar. 8, 1785, LC.

647 "They press me": to Sally and Richard Baches, May 10, 1785, Smyth.

647 "This minister": Vergennes to Marbois, May 10, 1785, Giunta.

647 "I think": to Ferdinand Grand, Mar. 5, 1786, Smyth.

647 "When he left": James Parton, *Life and Times of Benjamin Franklin* (Boston, 1884), 2:531.

647 "who walk very easy": to Jonathan Shipley, undated, Yale.

647 "I have perused": Journal of journey from Paris to Philadelphia, Bigelow 11:191.

648 "My heart": Lopez, *Mon Cher Papa,* 299–301.

648 "I cannot . . . love me some": *ibid.,* 299–300.

649 "Had I been": from Charles de Castries, July 10, 1785, Bigelow.

649 "I feel": Lopez, *Mon Cher Papa,* 301.

649 "I went": BF journal, Bigelow, 11:194–95.

649 "I trust": to WF, Aug. 16, 1784, Smyth.

650 "my fate": Skemp, *William Franklin,* 271.

650 "The captain": BF journal, Bigelow, 11:196.

650 "We all left": from Catherine Shipley, Aug. 2, 1785, Bigalow.

651 "the thermometer": to David Le Roy, Aug. 1785, Smyth.

652 "In traveling": to Jan Ingenhousz, Aug. 28, 1785, Smyth.

652 "With the flood": BF journal, Bigelow, 11:196–97.

653 "generally agreed": Harry M. Tinkcom, "The Revolutionary City, 1765–1783," in *Philadelphia,* ed. Russell Weigley, 154.

655 "The ease": to Paine, Sept. 27, 1785, Smyth.

655 "The people": to Edward Newenham, Oct. 3, 1785, LC.

655 "Old as I am": to Williams, Feb. 16, 1786, Smyth.

655 "I apprehend": to Paine, Sept. 27, 1785, Smyth.

655 "I am now so well": to the John and Sarah Jay, Sept. 21, 1785, Smyth.

655 "The stone": to Daniel Roberdeau, Mar. 25, 1786, Smyth.

656 "I am now": to the Jays, Sept. 21, 1765, Smyth.

656 "They are": to Shipley, Feb. 24, 1786, Smyth.

657 "He ne'er cared": to Whately, May 23, 1785, Smyth.

658 "Though your reasonings": to (Paine?), July 3, 1786, Smyth.

658 "I am encouraged": Webster to Washington, Mar. 31, 1786, *Papers of Washington.*

659 "I wonder": to Grand, July 11, 1786, Smyth.

659 "I conjecture": to Thomson, Jan. 25, 1787, Smyth.

660 "The Assembly": to d'Estaing, Apr. 15, 1787, Smyth.

660 "My own estate": to Grand, Jan. 29, 1786, Smyth.

660 "I propose": to Jane Mecom, Sept. 21, 1786, Smyth.

661 "an old man's amusement": to Grand, Apr. 22, 1787, Smyth.

661 "The affairs": to Veillard, Apr. 15, 1787, Smyth.

661 "He appeared": *Letters of Rush,* 1:389–90.

662 "The accumulation": Tinkcom, "Revolutionary City," 159.

662 "It is expected": *Letters of Rush,* 1:409.

663 "The conductor": to Landriani, Oct. 14, 1787, Smyth.

663 "I lament": to Jane Mecom, Sept. 20, 1787, Smyth.

664 "This field": Carl Van Doren, *Benjamin Franklin,* 737.

664 "amuses himself": to Lafayette, Apr. 17, 1787, Smyth.

664 "He sits": Jeremy Belknap in William Parker Cutler, *Life, Journals and Correspondence of Rev. Manasseh Cutler* (Cincinnati, 1888), 2:234.

664 "I have found": to Mary Hewsom, May 6, 1786, Smyth.

29. SUNRISE AT DUSK: 1786–87

666 "Your newspapers": to William Hunter, Nov. 24, 1786, Smyth.

667 "That there should be": to Lafayette, Apr. 17, 1787, Smyth.

667 "Our public affairs": to Abbés Chalut and Arnaud, Apr. 17, 1787, Smyth.

667–68 "How inconsistent . . . the officers": Washington address, Mar. 15, 1783 (and footnote), *Writings of Washington;* Douglas Southall Freeman, *George Washington,* 5:433–35.

668 "order of hereditary": to Sarah Bache, Jan. 26, 1784, Smyth.

670 "a party of madmen . . . this mob": David P. Szatmary, *Shays' Rebellion* (Amherst, 1980), 71–81.

670–71 "most fatal . . . property": *The Boisterous Sea of Liberty,* ed. David Brion Davis and Stephen Mintz, 227.

671 "Good God!": Washington to Knox, Dec. 26, 1786, *Papers of Washington.*

672 "render the federal constitution": *Records of Convention,* 3:14.

672 "It seems probable": Madison to Edmund Pendleton, Feb. 24, 1787, *Writings of Madison.*

672 "some disorderly people": to Chevalier de Chastellux, Apr. 17, 1787, Smyth.

673 "I hope good": to Jefferson, Apr. 19, 1787, Smyth.

673 "Your presence": to Washington, Apr. 3, 1787, *Papers of Washington.*

673 "by any commercial": Catherine Drinker Bowen, *Miracle at Philadelphia* (Boston, 1966), 22.

674 "We have here": to Thomas Jordan, May 18, 1787, Smyth.

674 "If you will": *Records of Convention,* 3:85.

674–75 "The nomination": *ibid.,* 1:4.

675 "Dr. Franklin": *ibid.,* 3:91.

676 "There are": *ibid.,* 1:81–85.

677 "The motion": *ibid.,* 1:85.

677 "How has it happened": Smyth, 9:600–1.

679 "bastard brat . . . within himself": Bowen, *Miracle,* 108–9.

679 "deservedly celebrated": *Records of Convention,* 3:89.

679 "I believe": *ibid.,* 1:299–300.

680 "A single person's": *ibid.,* 1:102–3.

681 "Some contend": *ibid.,* 1:471.

681 "Are not the large": *ibid.,* 1:491–92.

681 "This country": *ibid.,* 1:530.

682 "The diversity": *ibid.,* 1:488–89.

682 "There was no curiosity": William Cutler, *Life, Journals and Correspondence of Rev. Manasseh Cutler,* 1:267–69; 2:363.

684 "Gentlemen . . . alarmed": *Records of Convention,* 3:86–87.

684–85 "The Doctor": Cutler, *Life, Journals and Correspondence of Manasseh Cutler,* 1:269–70.

686 "A veritable torture": Bowen, *Miracle,* 97.

686 "so weak": to Jones, July 22, 1787, Smyth.

686–87 "What was the practice": *Records of Convention,* 2:65.

687 "contrary to": *ibid.,* 2:120.

687 "It is of great": *ibid.,* 2:204–5.

687 "to debase": *ibid.,* 2:249.

688 "not against": *ibid.,* 2:236–37.

688 "generally virulent": *ibid.,* 2:348.

688 "We seem": *ibid.,* 2:542.

689 "I confess": *ibid.,* 2:641–43.

690 "Done in Convention": *ibid.*

691 "Whilst the last": *ibid.,* 2:648.

30. TO SLEEP: 1787–90

692 "It is now": Washington to Lafayette, Sept. 18, 1787, *Papers of Washington.*

693 "As I enter . . . fruits of it": Jackson Turner Main, *The Anti-Federalists* (New York, 1974), 122, 129, 132–34.

694 "The smaller": *The Federalist Papers,* ed. Andrew Hacker (New York, 1964), 22–23.

694 "very great satisfaction": *The Documentary History of the Ratification of the Constitution,* ed. Merrill Jensen (Madison, Wis., 1976–   ), 2:60.

695 "highly reverenced . . . old age": *Independent Gazetteer,* Oct. 5, 1787, and *Freeman's Journal,* Oct. 17, 1787; in *The Documentary History,* 2:160, 185.

695 "Doctor Franklin's": Madison to Washington, Dec. 20, 1787, *Papers of Washington.*

695 "Three and twenty": Richard Miller, "The Federal City, 1783–1800," in *Philadelphia,* ed. Russell Weigley, 164.

696 "I beg": Lemay, 1144–48.

696 "Independence . . . President": Miller, "Federal City," 164–65.

697 "I must own": to Jane Mecom, Nov. 4, 1787, Smyth.

697 "Some tell me": to Mecom, Sept. 20, 1787, Smyth.

697 "a very great pleasure": to John Lathrop, May 31, 1788, Smyth.

698 "They are wonderfully": to Mecom, Aug. 3, 1789, Smyth.

698 "as I find": to Alexander Small, Feb. 19, 1787, Bigelow.

698 "I thank you": to Vaughan, Nov. 2, 1789, Bigelow.

698 "As the roughness": to Buffon, Nov. 19, 1787, Smyth.

699 "Our ancient": to Bowdoin, May 31, 1788, Smyth.

700 "Remarks Concerning": Lemay, 969–74.

701 "The bad people": Smyth, 9:523–25.

701 "always very friendly": to John Jay, July 6, 1786, Smyth.

702 "prejudicial": to the *Public Advertiser,* Jan. 30, 1770.

702 "some generous": *PBF,* 19:187–88.

703 "Slavery is such": Lemay, 1154–55.

704 "Our grand machine": to Carroll, May 25, 1789, Smyth.

704–5 "I have long": to John Lathrop, May 31, 1788, Smyth.

705 "The *arrêt* ": to Louis Le Veillard, June 8, 1788, Smyth.

705 "The revolution": to Vaughan, Nov. 2, 1789, Smyth.

705 "It is now": to Jean-Baptiste Le Roy, Nov. 13, 1789, Smyth.

705 "I hope": to Samuel Moore, Nov. 5, 1789, Smyth.

705–6 "The convulsions": to Hartley, Dec. 4, 1789, Smyth.

706 "But in this world": to Le Roy, Nov. 13, 1789, Smyth.

706 "I can give": to Le Veillard, Sept. 5, 1789, Smyth.

706 "which, calling": to Abbé Morellet, Dec. 10, 1788, Smyth.

706 "Canada—*delenda est* ": BF notes to himself, n.d. [1790], LC.

706 "As much": from Stiles, Jan. 28, 1790, Smyth, 10:85–86.

706 "It is the first": to Stiles, Mar. 9, 1790, Smyth.

708 "Is it supposed": Smyth, 10:59.

708 "the *chapeau bras*": Smyth, 10:31.

708 "Mankind": Parton, *Franklin,* 2:609–10.

709 "put me in mind": to the *Federal Gazette,* Mar. 23, 1790, Smyth.

709 "Would to God": from Washington, Sept. 23, 1789, Smyth, 10:41–42.

710 "At Philadelphia": *Writings of Jefferson,* 1:161–62.

710 "The evening": Rush to Richard Price, Apr. 24, 1790, *Letters of Rush.*

EPILOGUE: APRIL 17, 1990

713 "to such young": Last will and testament, Smyth, 10:493ff.

713 "Everyone": *Boston Globe,* Apr. 17, 1990.

714 "in the true spirit": United Press International, Apr. 18, 1990.
715 "He has returned": Alfred Aldridge, *Franklin and His French Contemporaries*, 213.
715 "A man is dead": *ibid.,* 230.
715 "The Body": *PBF,* 1:111.
716 "Benjamin and Deborah Franklin": Smyth, 10:508.
716 "A republic": *Records of Convention,* 3:85.

Acknowledgments

∽ For their help in the various tasks required to produce this book, the author would like to thank Roger Scholl of Doubleday; Roy Goodman of the American Philosophical Society; Ellen Cohn, Jonathan Dull, Claude-Anne Lopez, and Kate Ohno of the Benjamin Franklin Collection at Yale University; Laura Beardsley of the Historical Society of Pennsylvania; J. A. Leo Lemay of the University of Delaware (for graciously making his Franklin materials available on the Internet); and James Hornfischer, my agent.

Index

HEIRS OF THE FOUNDERS
Henry Clay, John Calhoun and Daniel Webster,
the Second Generation of American Giants

In the early 1800s, Daniel Webster, Henry Clay, and John Calhoun rose to prominence in Congress when the Founding Fathers were beginning to retire to their farms. Together these heirs of the Founders took the country to war, battled one another for the presidency, and set themselves the task of finishing the work the Founders had left undone. Their rise was marked by dramatic duels, fierce debates, scandal, and political betrayal. Yet each in his own way sought to remedy the two glaring flaws in the Constitution: its refusal to specify where authority ultimately rested, with the states or the nation, and its unwillingness to address the essential incompatibility of republicanism and slavery. H. W. Brands thrillingly narrates an epic American rivalry and the little-known drama of the dangerous early years of our democracy.

U.S. History

THE GENERAL VS. THE PRESIDENT
MacArthur and Truman at the Brink of Nuclear War

At the height of the Korean War, President Truman sent shock waves around the world when he suggested that General Douglas MacArthur, the willful, fearless, and highly decorated commander of the American and UN forces, had his finger on the nuclear trigger. At a time when the Soviets, too, had the bomb, the specter of a catastrophic third World War lurked menacingly close on the horizon. A correction quickly followed, but the damage was done; two visions for America's path forward were clearly in opposition, and one man would have to make way.

U.S. History

THE MAN WHO SAVED THE UNION
Ulysses Grant in War and Peace

Ulysses Grant emerges in this masterful biography as a
genius in battle and a driven president to a divided country, who remained fearlessly on the side of right. He was
a beloved commander in the field who made the sacrifices
necessary to win the war, even in the face of criticism. He
worked valiantly to protect the rights of freed men in the
South. He allowed the American Indians to shape their own
fate even as the realities of Manifest Destiny meant the end
of their way of life. In this sweeping and majestic narrative,
bestselling author H. W. Brands now reconsiders Grant's
legacy and provides an intimate portrait of a heroic man
who saved the Union on the battlefield and consolidated
that victory as a resolute and principled political leader.

Biography/History

ALSO AVAILABLE

The Age of Gold
American Colossus
Andrew Jackson
The Heartbreak of Aaron Burr
Lone Star Nation
The Murder of Jim Fisk for the Love of Josie Mansfield
Reagan
Traitor to His Class

ANCHOR BOOKS
Available wherever books are sold.
www.anchorbooks.com